SYSTEMATIC THEOLOGY
DOCTRINE

SYSTEMATIC THEOLOGY
DOCTRINE

VOLUME II

JAMES WM. McCLENDON, JR.

ABINGDON PRESS
Nashville

DOCTRINE: SYSTEMATIC THEOLOGY, VOLUME II

Copyright © 1994 by James Wm. McClendon, Jr.

This book is printed on acid-free, recycled paper.

Library of Congress Cataloging-in-Publication Data
(Revised for vol. 2)

McClendon, James William.
  Systematic theology.

  Includes bibliographical references and indexes.
  Contents: 1. Ethics—2. Doctrine.
  1. Theology, Doctrinal. 2. Christian ethics.
I. Title.
BT75.2.M392 1986   230'.044   85-30627
ISBN 0-687-12015-2 (v. 1 : alk. paper)
ISBN 0-687-11021-1 (v. 2 : alk. paper)

00 01 02 03—10 9 8 7 6 5

MANUFACTURED IN THE UNITED STATES OF AMERICA

to my parents

James William McClendon
Mary Drake McClendon

they lived the faith I meant to write

Preface

Nineteen ninety-four. Twenty years after the event described in the Preface to *Volume I;* twenty years in which the fire of imagination, the unvanquishable flame of hope, has burned a way into the dense undergrowth of accumulated theological scholarship, burned, and been repulsed, burned, and flickered low, burned, and continued burning, until it consumed what it could of the accumulated wisdom and skill of churchly antiquity and theological modernity, leaving behind this glowing ash, this heap of scorched pages, this volume. Along the way, the first volume *(Ethics)* appeared, hot vapor from the flames, declaring how the church must live if the church was to be the church. Now the new volume addresses a question integral to the first—what must the church teach in order to live in this way? (So those who say I have "founded theology on ethics" are doubly wrong; wrong since ethics is *already* theology, wrong since this volume is *not* based on the previous one, but explores more deeply the one matter already opened there.) Consider a physiological metaphor: Christian ethics grasps the live flesh of Christian existence; Christian doctrine traces its living skeleton, the bones within that flesh that give stability and coherence to its life. Without Christian life, the doctrine is dead; without Christian doctrine, the life is formless.

I had meant to enliven these pages, as I did those of *Volume I,* with interspersed biographical chapters that would display in a sort of theological bionomy the life and faith reduced to doctrine here. It was not to be—too much had to be reported and argued through and clarified, so that the biographical chapters have come to be only sections or paragraphs on Hans Hut and Roger Williams and Georgia Harkness and others. Yet the intention is unchanged: only a doctrine that can be lived out is viable; hence the true test of these pages is their relevance to shared life in the body of Christ.

Another omission is deliberate: this volume is preceded by no 'apology' for the doctrine it displays. I offer, in Bill Placher's charming title, *Unapologetic Theology* (see Placher, 1989). What I think Placher meant by that, or in any case what I mean, is that it is the intrinsic winsomeness of Jesus' way displayed in Scripture and history, rather than some external inducement, that is alone offered here as doctrine's warrant. Jesus did not appear on earth wearing a borrowed sash proclaiming "Here is God's messenger." Rather he lived and died in a way that prepared his followers for the divine authentication in the resurrection that followed; had his life and death not possessed intrinsic appeal, even the resurrection, if it had nonetheless occurred, should not have mattered to them very much. Similarly, this volume offers critically examined Christian truth, not enclosed by philosophical or other external warrants, but as nearly as possible in its own wrappers, in the belief that its contents make their own appeal to present-day followers of Jesus Christ. If not, it is the contents, not the warrants, that are deficient. This way of proceeding is out of line with much theology since the Enlightenment. Recently, however, new ways of thought have appeared that make the present procedure seem desirable, even necessary. A third, projected volume, though it will not offer what is here abjured, will try to show more fully, as Placher and others already have, why this procedure is now best. Here, then, are the doctrines of Christian existence critically presented; their warrant lies in themselves, not (even) in some blanket prior claim to 'revelation' on their behalf. There is a revelation; yet it comes not apart from but in and through the narrative of life and faith acknowledged in *Ethics* and *Doctrine*.

Some mention (though this must not be overdone) should be made of the community of reference called 'baptist' that shapes this work. Every Christian theology is written from and for a community: the writer's community and the intended readers'. This is not only 'the inclusive community of all Christians' (a phrase whose intended 'extension' or reference necessarily displays some theological slant, itself) but some partial community, whether Catholic or Calvinist, Lutheran or Orthodox or other. My contribution is to show that one large segment of Christian believers, next in size perhaps to Roman Catholics and exceeded in age by none, is under-represented in recent theology, and to remedy that defect as best I can. Heirs of the Radical Reformation are often theologically pigeonholed as confused (though sincere) Protestants. If that is what we are, we need to end the confusion by locating our true home in Reformed or Lutheran contexts. If not, we need to know why. In either case, this present work should help locate the proper place for the heritage of Radical Reform. Yet such self-location can be isolationist and harmful. The mode of Christian faith that is the referent here, like any other mode, is finally of value only if it will make its contribution to all God's people (see Chapter Eight). The theological successors to Anabaptism wait in hope to discover that their witness is at least acknowledged in tandem with other witnesses to the one Christ. Yet they cannot expect this to happen until their own witness is theologically clear—hence this work.

Only those who have tried it know how hard it is to do such work and do it in a way that is clear enough to be understood by any intelligent and willing reader. Again and again, brevity and clarity, the need to make it plain and the need to say it soon, clash. "To the simple, all is simple," yet the matters treated here are not simple, so that accessing them is a costly task, indeed. Still another factor challenges the writing theologian: theological (and other) convictions clash with one another: the reader's convictions will not always be my own, and it is hard for anyone to read with understanding what one takes to be wrong or wrong-headed. Here I ask for courtesy, and invoke the principle of fallibility—I may be wrongly convinced, but so, my sister or brother, may you! Please try to hear me out, and when opportunity permits I will do the same for you.

An instance of such a clash is the current debate over gender terms in English—both those applied to people and those applied to God. We have discovered that the abuse of such terms creates false images of God and God's children as well—a male deity presiding over a masculine church. Yet it is simply a fact that no one has yet provided alternatives that do not create opposing false images, or do not lapse into jargon reserved to an inner circle of adepts or into unspeakable solecisms such as "S/he." What I have tried to do is write plain English that respects the oldest meanings of person-terms ("he," for example, originally meant *either* gender, as can be seen from the surviving feminine oblique cases, and "man," similarly, once did and still sometimes means everybody), while respecting changing present-day usage. In the process I have sometimes, but not always, avoided gender-terms for God, and I have often, but not always, reformed the use of personal nouns and pronouns for people. This compromise of style will not fully satisfy anyone, but it may reflect the present state of our language. What I have positively to say about God and gender is found in Chapter Seven; what I think about the respective roles of women and men in the church of God is to be found through all the chapters, not least in Chapter Eight.*

---

*Throughout the book the reader will discover paragraphs set in smaller typeface like this one. The purpose of these is to add further information or clarification to the paragraphs

Even more than *Ethics,* this *Doctrine* volume is a harvest brought in by many helpers. There were the *theological circles* that met in our Kensington home (led by Del Olsen) and in Altadena (led by Ched Myers); their members were too many to name, but included some of the loveliest thinkers I know. There were the professors who used drafts of the volume or parts of it in *experimental classes:* these include Elizabeth Barnes at Duke and Southeastern and Richmond Baptist, Miroslav Volf at Fuller, and Richard Steele at Milwaukee Theological Institute (a downtown school that caters to Black Baptists). Here I thank them and their students, and my own experimenting students as well. There were the *Overseers,* Claude Welch, David Hubbard, Elizabeth Barnes (again), and John H. Yoder, authorized by Lilly Endowment's Craig Dykstra and Jim Wind for three years to meet periodically to read my drafts, correct my errors and omissions, and, as best they could, restrain my *Schwärmerisch* excesses. How I miss their comradeship, now that the task is ended!

There were as well *individual readers* who wrote extended responses to portions furnished them and thereby set me straight time and again. Besides those mentioned in *Volume I* (many of whom served double duty), these include Colin Brown, David Burrell, Dick Carlson, John Cobb, Judith Gundry-Volf, Fisher Humphries, Rebecca Lyman, Ted Peters, Ian Pitt-Watson, Bill Pregnall, Frank Stagg, Maureen Tilley, and no doubt someone else I've culpably overlooked. Thanks to them each. Most of all, I thank my scholarly and lovely wife, Nancey, who read all, criticized all, and (best of all) encouraged all.

After the work was nearly done, in May 1993 the Lilly Endowment, encouraged by Richard Mouw, convened a Congress on Systematic Theology in America Today at Fuller Theological Seminary, its main task being to survey and discuss the draft volume. Here the major papers, by Stanley Hauerwas, Bruce Marshall, Molly Marshall, Billy Abraham, and Terry Tilley, concentrated the thought of about fifty younger theologians on the tasks addressed here. Throughout the project, I was supported by the libraries at Graduate Theological Union (especially by Oscar Burdick) and Fuller Theological Seminary, by the Church Divinity School of the Pacific and Fuller Theological Seminary, and

which precede and follow them. The reader is invited to read these reduced typeface paragraphs in the normal course of progressing through the book. Those who wish to gain an immediate sense of the book's argument may choose to pass over the reduced typeface paragraphs the first time through, and return to them later for a more detailed perspective.

for the past three years by grants from the Lilly Endowment. The fairness and generosity of Abingdon Press has amazed me. Abingdon editor Bob Ratcliff and copyeditor Steve Cox have been with me all the way, flashlights in the murk of my confusion about facts and about style. Thanks to all, and thanks to God for life and health.

Now I hand this book over to you, the reader. I am sorry to release it; there is more to be learned, more to be said, on every theme. Yet I must move on. I point out that I have written slowly, that there is much on each page, and that slow reading is in this case the best reading. In particular, I point this out to reviewers, who are at their lovely best when they take time to read what is actually written.

James Wm. McClendon, Jr.
Altadena, California
Advent, 1993

Abbreviations

Fathers. The Library of Christian Classics, vol. 1. Philadelphia: Westminster Press.)

Eusebius
  Hist. ec. Ecclesiastical History
Gregory of Nazianzus
  Theol. orat. Five Theological Orations
Gregory of Nyssa
  Cat. or. Catechetical Oration (also called Great Catechism)
Irenaeus
  Adv. haer. Against All Heresies
Origen
  De prin. On First Principles
Pliny the Younger
  Epp. Epistles. (I have quoted from Henry Bettenson, ed., *Documents of the Christian Church*. New York: Oxford, 1947)
Tertullian
  Adv. Prax. Against Praxeas
  Apol. The Apology
Trent
  The Council of Trent (I have quoted from Philip Schaff *The Creeds of Christendom*. Vol. 2. New York: Harper & Brothers, 1919)

Modern Works:

CD Karl Barth, *Church Dogmatics* 1936–69. Trans. G. W. Bromiley et al. 4 vols. Edinburgh: T. & T. Clark.

CF Friedrich Schleiermacher, *The Christian Faith*. Trans. H. R. Mackintosh and James S. Stewart. Edinburgh: T. & T. Clark, 1928 (1830)

Inst. Calvin, *Institutes of the Christian Religion*. (I have quoted from the two-volume trans. by Ford Lewis Battles, in Library of Christian Classics. Philadelphia: Westminster, 1960 [1559])

Encyclopedias:

ABD *Anchor Bible Dictionary*. Ed. D. N. Freedman. 6 vols. New York: Doubleday, 1992.

BEMCT *The Blackwell Encyclopedia of Modern Christian Thought*. Ed. Alister E. McGrath. Oxford: Blackwell, 1993.

DB *Dictionary of the Bible*. John McKenzie. New York: Macmillan, 1965.

DJG *Dictionary of Jesus and the Gospels*. Ed. J. Green et al. Downers Grove: InterVarsity, 1992.

DPL *Dictionary of Paul and His Letters*. Ed. Gerald F. Hawthorne, Ralph P. Martin, and Daniel G. Reid. Downers Grove: InterVarsity, 1993 (forthcoming).

Enc. Phil. Encyclopedia of Philosophy. Ed. Paul Edwards. 8 vols. New York: Macmillan and Free Press, 1967.

ER *Encyclopedia of Religion.* Ed. Mircea Eliade. 16 vols. New York: Macmillan, 1987.

ERE *Encyclopedia of Religion and Ethics.* Ed. James Hastings. 13 vols. Edinburgh: T. & T. Clark, 1908–.

IDB *The Interpreter's Dictionary of the Bible.* Ed. G. A. Buttrick. 4 vols. Nashville: Abingdon, 1962.

IDBS *The Interpreter's Dictionary of the Bible. Supplementary Volume.* Ed. Keith Crim. Nashville: Abingdon, 1976.

ME *Mennonite Encyclopedia.* Ed. H. S. Bender. vols. 1-4, C. J. Dyck & D. D. Martin, vol. 5. Scottdale: Herald Press, 1955–90.

NCRTW *Nineteenth Century Religious Thought in the West.* Ed. Ninian Smart et al. 3 vols. Cambridge: University Press, 1985.

NHCT *New Handbook of Christian Theology.* Ed. Donald W. Musser and Joseph L. Price. Nashville: Abingdon, 1992.

TDNT *Theological Dictionary of the New Testament.* Ed. G. Kittel & G. Friedrich. Trans. G. W. Bromiley et al. Grand Rapids: Eerdmans, 1964–76.

Double quotes (" ") are used for all quotations except for quotes within quotes (" ' ' ") and 'scare' quotes.

par.: and parallel or parallels

pass.: and throughout

Contents

Contents

PROSPECT

In good time, Flask's saying proved true. As before, the Pequod steeply leaned over towards the sperm whale's head, now, by the counterpoise of both heads, she regained her even keel; though sorely strained, you may well believe. So, when on one side you hoist in Locke's head, you go over that way; but now, on the other side, hoist in Kant's and you come back again; but in very poor plight. Thus, some minds for ever keep trimming boat. Oh, ye foolish! throw all these thunderheads overboard, and then you will float light and right.

Herman Melville, *Moby-Dick*

'Conjuring culture' through the incantatory use of biblical figures like Exodus and Promised Land requires a specifically theological, rather than a merely rhetorical or literary, figural reading. By "theological" here I mean that biblical figures are employed in synergy with a Deity who cooperates in the concrete historical realization of such figures. We have seen that in African American theological perspective, for example, Exodus becomes historical in the emancipation of slaves in the 1860s, and in the civil rights movement of the 1960s, under the historical supervision of a provident God.

Theophus Smith, *Conjuring Culture*

A true conversion (whether of Americans or Europeans) must be such as those conversions were of the first pattern, either of the Jewes or the Heathens; That rule is the golden mece wand in the hand of the angell or messenger [Rev. 21:15], beside which all others are leaden and crooked.

Roger Williams, *Christenings Make Not Christians*

What Is Doctrine?

In shaping its teaching, the church seeks to be simply the church, so that Christians may be a people who find in Christ their center, in the Spirit their communion, in God's reign their rule of life. The convictions that make such a common life possible fall into three broad, overlapping categories, those that inform Christian **living** (*moral* convictions), those that display the substance of Christian **faith** (*doctrinal* convictions), and those that open out into a Christian **vision** or worldview (*philosophical* convictions). The present volume is concerned with the second of these, those convictions that constitute Christian teaching or doctrine. It is important here that life, faith, and vision are not three realities but one: it is not as though what is done can be pried apart from what is taught or what is envisioned; rather these volumes constitute three distinct probes, three levels of inquiry, into a single 'life-faith-vision,' one whole. With this understanding, the interest of this volume can be expressed in a question: What must be taught in today's churches if they are to be what they claim to be? In brief, *what must the church teach to be the church* **now?** That question requires refinement (some might prefer "*to be authentic church now*"), yet it is not to be evaded in doctrinal theology.

Two paralyzing worries may grip anyone who takes up such a volume today. The first is a worry about bias: How can this book, or any other, utter *theological* truth—the truth about God and all that is God's— without displaying mere bias, either hidden or overt? Perhaps we, here, think this, but they, there, think otherwise, and who is to judge between us and them? If we say the revelation in our scripture refutes the claims of their scripture, will they not say the same back to us? If our history says we shall put our trust in Jesus, or in the God of Jesus, have they not other names for God, even other gods, by which they will call our history into question? Young Dietrich Bonhoeffer told his students that theology should begin in silence. Yes, but in view of this plurality of religious perspectives, a plurality that permits no easy bracketing of differences, should that silence *ever* be broken? One recalls the ancient Greek thinker Simonides, who, when his students asked "What are the gods?" hesitated so long in answering that finally they ceased to ask. Though despite Simonides this volume now stands written, might not a wise reader hesitate interminably before taking it up?

The other paralyzing worry seems just the contrary, but tends to the same outcome. Now the question is, not whether theological doctrine can be fair to the distant views of other religions and cultures, but whether it will be fair to the reader's own. Again this is a worry about bias. In one way or another each of us has acquired the religious (or irreligious) convictions we now have. Every human being comes to have some convictions, and most readers of this book doubtless cherish convictions on the very topics addressed here—last things, salvation and sin, creation and suffering, Christ and God, Israel and the churches, and all the rest. If a discussion of these happens to nurture one's convictions and resolve one's doubts, well and good. But what if the book is biased against them, undermines them? Perhaps does so in subtle ways the reader cannot foresee or avert? Theology, like major surgery, must treat matters as dear as life itself. Thus a self-protective reader may rightly wonder whether he or she really needs this operation, really needs this book.

A clever retort might be that these two worries about bias, against other cultures and religions in the wide world and against the reader's own standpoint, nicely cancel one another. For how can one fairly object that a book may lack a universal outlook when one is not willing to consider any view but one's own? Or how can one justly cling to one's own view if not yet informed about the alternative views of one's fellow believers or neighbors? Isn't such a position *itself* biased, pot calling kettle black? Yet the retort may be more clever than valid. For it seems to assume that any *particular* standpoint is necessarily unworthy, an assumption that will not stand close examination—indeed, one that defeats itself.

In any case, this volume attempts to take seriously what lies behind both sorts of objections. It takes seriously the existence of a plurality of convinced communities, not only the Christian one (or the 'baptist' one) that is this book's community of reference. It does not assume that the others are all false and this one alone true. Nor on the other hand does it assume that all are moving toward a common truth along different roads. Such assumptions are not needed at this point, for the task of the present volume is merely to be clear about Christian teaching. *Volume III* will examine some of these assumptions about others and their relation to Christian life and faith. Certainly the 'other ways' are there, and they are significant, but now we have this task. This volume properly begins in Chapter Two, and readers eager to get to the heart of the matter may wish to go to the next chapter at once. The present chapter seeks to explain (§1) how doctrinal theology is related to church teaching itself and (§2) to Bible study, and to show (§3) the relation of the present work to each of these and to its context.

This volume also recognizes that prospective readers have divergent beliefs. None of us comes to the theological task as a blank book to be inscribed by our teachers. Rather we come as formed human beings with convictions that constitute us as the people we are. And the aim here is not to remake or even directly to challenge the convictions of each reader—that is a pastoral task, not a theological one. Instead it will ask and seek to answer the question, What must the church teach if it is really to *be* the church? That is a question addressed to no single individual, but to a community; neither the author nor any single reader can provide determinate answers even if we would, and there may be a plurality of 'correct' answers in various life settings. Yet in a roundabout way and in the long run what appears here may indeed challenge the present beliefs of each of us. To hear such a challenge is a risk worth taking if the outcome, as I trust it will, "gives substance to our hopes and convinces us of realities we do not see"—the very objective realities that God, speaking in Scripture (Heb. 11:1), promises to faith. Can we begin with this trust?

§1. The Practice of Christian Doctrine

The church teaches in many modes—by the visible lives of members as well as by the preached word, by the welcome it extends (or does not extend) to human beings in all their racial, cultural, sexual variety as well as by the hymns it sings and the door-to-door witness it bears, by the presence it affords the defeated and despairing as well as by the generosity it extends to the down-and-out—and not least by the classroom instruction of members and inquirers young and old. In these ways and others the church teaches. Where in all this is the place of **doctrine?**

a. Some approaches to doctrine.—Doctrine *is* teaching (the word "doctrine" comes from Greek and Latin stems meaning just that), and

by *Christian* doctrine I will here mean *a church teaching as she must teach
if she is to be the church here and now.* (So this study is not merely
descriptive, but normative.) A church may quite properly teach many
things—that its meetinghouse is located at the corner of Sixth and
Congress streets, that Babylon was the capital city of an ancient empire,
that China is earth's most populous nation, that sanitation prevents
disease, that Rembrandt's painting is great art. Teaching such truths of
geography, history, science, and art may even be necessary scaffolding
for the church's teaching here and now. But these peripheral or ephem-
eral truths are not Christian doctrine; they do not constitute the church's
lively present existence as a church. Any and all of these 'facts' may be
overturned and cease to be useful in the church's mission: the meetinghouse may be moved; ancient historiography is notoriously subject to
revision; good science is constantly replaced by better; even artistic
judgment may change, though once formed it is the most enduring of
them all. In contrast the loss or neglect of Christian convictions—for
example, the headship of Christ in the church—will seriously impair,
even defeat, the very existence of a church.

Although not until Chapter Eight will the definitive features of authentic
Christian community ('church') be addressed, it is common sense to say in
advance that authentic Christian *teaching* is one of these features. That being the
case, is it not relevant to ask of our own teaching communities—our churches,
but also our seminaries, denominations, para-church institutions—whether they
retain the name but lack the *substance* of Christian community? "Is the church
really the church?" is a live, momentous, and inescapable issue for us.

What enterprise asks these questions, guards these treasures, explores the community's road ahead? Some may recall that theology
undertakes the critical examination of church teaching, and assign these
tasks to (doctrinal) theology. They will not be wrong, but they may
overlook the *logically prior task* of the teaching church itself. Doctrine is
not manufactured by theologians to be marketed by churches or pastors.
It is the church that must (and does!) ask questions and seek answers.
So doctrine (the church *teaching*) is the first-order task; doctrinal *theology*
is necessarily second-order. Understood as convictions shared (on convictions, see *Ethics,* One §1), doctrine constitutes communal existence. It
cannot be interrupted even for a generation without corrosive loss.
Exactly what, then, is this indispensable function called church doctrine?

This and the next section (§2) explore the church's first-order task of teaching,
while §3 provides a preliminary canvass of the second-order task, doctrinal
theology, which is the work of this volume.

i. A Catholic approach.—One idea is that doctrine consists in revealed truth imparted to the church. While these truths of revelation are said to be based upon the Bible, they are formally contained in distinct propositions (*dogmas*, doctrines) that convey the substance of divine revelation to believers. Although scholastic Protestantism (seventeenth century onward) provides examples of this approach, we will use the grand example of the Roman Catholic understanding of dogma. In any such community, imparting church dogma to the faithful is the task of the church's magisterium (from *magister*, teacher, master). This task is vested in official church leaders, ascending in the Catholic case to the Pope, who in certain defined circumstances can not only transmit old dogmas but issue new ones. More generally, the Roman Catholic Church, by way of its official teaching machinery, can condemn errors, declare the truth about Christ, sacraments, salvation, and the life to come, and in general can instruct concerning faith and morals (see Rahner, ed., 1967:199f for the primary citations). This understanding of the nature of doctrine has evolved across long centuries of experience. It is substantive and carefully crafted, making it clear why (if its main claim is correct) Catholic dogma *must* be heard and obeyed—for it is as the voice of God to the faithful. On the other hand, it is relatively inflexible, slow to adjust to changed circumstances and needs, and its long development is a shortcoming when viewed in terms of the norm of Scripture, since there seem to be in the Bible neither such an apparatus as the magisterium nor such an understanding of doctrine (or dogma) itself.

It may seem to some that Protestant Fundamentalism, heir to the earlier Protestant scholasticism, retains the chief asset of Catholic teaching (an authoritative, objectively certain magisterium) while solving its chief difficulty (just noted) by affirming the entire Bible as the authoritative, inerrant word of God—so that church doctrine is simply "the Bible, the whole Bible, and nothing but the Bible." However, this turns out not to work very well, since (1) this primary affirmation about the role of Scripture is not itself part of Scripture, but can only be another doctrine added to it; (2) nor does Scripture provide the canon of Scripture, which appeared only later; and in fact (3) historic Fundamentalism with its "five points" or the like is no more willing than Roman Catholic teaching to let the "Bible and the Bible only" speak. (For enlargement of this discussion of the Bible, Fundamentalism, and authority, see Chapter Eleven.)

There is another approach to Catholic dogma, less clearly articulated in official documents, but well represented in recent generations of Catholic theological thinking. This approach sees that divine revelation was not originally conveyed by way of propositions but "as an indistinct whole, known through a kind of global intuition." In this case, the teaching of the magisterium is indeed authoritative in its time and place, but to be so it must consult the *consensus fidelium,* the understanding of *the entire body of believers,* who embody living tradition. Thus "faith unfolds under the interior guidance of the Holy Spirit, who implants in the hearts of the faithful an instinctive sense of what is, and what is not, a valid expression of revealed truth" (Dulles, 1977:49f). The pioneers of this approach in the nineteenth century were members of the Catholic Tübingen School, notably Johann Adam Möhler (1796–1838) and Johann S. von Drey (1777–1853) (Burtchaell, NCRTW, II:111-40). Since this "organic" view rather closely parallels the theory of convictions and practices advanced in this chapter, I will not comment further on it here.

The Greek word **dogma,** which originally meant any opinion, and after that the opinion of a philosophical teacher, appears in the New Testament only in the still later sense of the weighty opinion of a magistrate or official body, having the force of law. The decree from Caesar Augustus that all the world should be taxed is in Luke 2:1 called a dogma. Correspondingly, the ordinances of the Mosaic law that were said to be abolished in Christ are called dogmas (Eph. 2:15; Col. 2:14; cf. Barth, CD I/1 §7 p. 305). Although one New Testament word for **doctrine** in the sense of what is taught is *didaskalia,* this term is used favorably only in the late pastoral epistles. On the other hand, *didachē,* **teaching,** usually meaning not merely the contained beliefs but the entire process of instructing, is common throughout the synoptic Gospels and in the Pauline and Johannine writings as well, that is, in most of the New Testament. The Revised English Bible effectively captures this verbal force of the noun *didachē* in translating Acts 2:42: "They met constantly to hear the apostles teach *(proskarterountes tē didachē tōn apostolōn)* and to share the common life *(koinōnia),* to break bread, and to pray."

ii. A Protestant approach.—While earlier Protestantism (and Fundamentalism) share the previous approach with official Catholicism, other Protestants have followed the lead of Friedrich Schleiermacher (1768–1834). This approach rejects the received Catholic and scholastic Protestant understanding of dogma (doctrine) as received truth. Schleiermacher's classic *Christian Faith* (CF) sought to place doctrine on a completely new footing. Christianity was just one (though the best) among the many religions. Religion as such was neither a kind of knowing (as Catholic and Protestant scholasticisms had assumed) nor a kind of doing (essentially a morality, as Immanuel Kant, 1724–1804, had taught), but a kind of feeling *(Gefühl)* or **awareness** (Schleiermacher, 1799, Speech 2). What distinguished religious feeling from all other, made it truly religious, was the sense of *utter dependence,* or (what Schleiermacher thought no different) the sense of a relation with God (CF §4). This awareness, in some measure possessed by all human beings, came to the fore in community (CF §6), so its conscious possession led to the formation of the various religious communities. What unites a church, then, is its shared awareness—for a Christian community, its sharing in the God-awareness Jesus himself enjoyed (CF §§7-11, 100f). In a derivative role, *doctrines* appear in a church; these are not revealed dogmas, but are "accounts of the Christian religious affections [emotions, awareness] set forth in speech" (CF §15). So doctrines express human states, not states of mind but of awareness, since awareness is the human faculty that apprehends God. Schleiermacher effectively showed that such accounts, if wedded to the primal Christian narrative of alienation and reconciliation, yielded doctrines remarkably like those Orthodox, Catholic, and Protestant churches had traditionally taught. What was new in this novel version of Protestantism was not the doctrines themselves so much as their status. In the eyes of his critics, Schleiermacher's liberal Protestantism had reduced theology, understood as doctrines about God, to anthropology, merely doctrines about human states and feelings. But to his followers, he had diminished pretentious rationalism in religion to make room for (affective) faith.

Schleiermacher went on to specify that all Christian propositions can be regarded as descriptions either of human states *or* of divine attributes *or* of the constitution of the world (a triad he made basic to the structure of the *Glaubenslehre*), and pointed out that traditionally all three forms of doctrinal expression have coexisted (CF §30). But in the "Second Letter to Dr. Lücke" he left no doubt which of the three was basic: it was descriptions of human states (Schleiermacher, 1981:70-73). Karl Barth (1886–1968), Schleiermacher's latter-day adversary, sought to correct this "Neo-Protestantism" by insisting that *essential* dogma *(das Wesen)* was identical with the word of God (which by God's action took the threefold form of preached word, written word [the Bible], and revealed word [Christ]). Essential dogma, however, could never be captured in any human utterance; it was never "the word of man" but remained always and only "the word of God." The business of church dogma, and of the *Church Dogmatics*, the title of Barth's systematic theology (CD) was simply to "tend towards" this essential dogma that was God's alone. Thus he accepted the human character of church doctrine, while maintaining (at least in his intention) the superior status of divine teaching, although the latter was not, as in "the Roman Catholic concept," readily available through the clergy, but as it were always just out of human reach (Barth, 1931:15-72; CD I/1 §7 pp. 304-15). It could be argued, however, that Barth had the worst of both sides of the argument, since he appeared to echo the presumption of traditional Catholicism (and Fundamentalist infallibility) and yet, thanks to the gap he inserted between "essential" and "church" dogma, his view remained by his own account as anthropocentric as that he rejected in Schleiermacher.

iii. The present approach.—Is progress possible here? It is worth noting first that Catholic and Protestant understandings of doctrine (dogma) display some common elements worth retaining. For both (1) there is the sense that Christian teaching is not arbitrary, not the free invention of the teacher, but is a required response to God's own **authority** in Christ Jesus. For both, God must remain God, and we obedient to God alone. Correspondingly, (2) for both there is a **reserve** concerning the capacity of even the best human teaching to express that authority adequately—Catholic dogma is not itself God's revelation; Schleiermacher's doctrines are not themselves the awareness of God but only its expression in speech. And for both (3) there is a crucial role for the Christian **community:** only the church (on whose nature, of course, they disagree) can be the setting and the agent of Christian teaching. These must be guidelines for us as well. In one regard, however, both traditional Catholicism and most Protestant versions place emphasis where the New Testament does not: With (possible) support only from the late Pastoral Epistles, they construe doctrine as discrete propositions, either transmitted from original revelation, or inferred from Christian awareness, or concretized from the threefold form of the word of God. This is an emphasis that while not wrong can easily lead to error. For it overlooks (4) an overarching feature of Christian doctrine, its character as a regular **practice** (cf. New Testament *didachē*). Since this fourth feature includes or embraces the other three, it will be the central feature of the account presented here.

   b. A practical understanding of doctrine.—The discussion of practices in *Ethics* (Six: §1) disclosed that social practices, like games, strive for some **end** beyond themselves (health for the practice of medicine, livable space for architecture), require intentional participation on the part of **practitioners,** employ determinate **means,** and proceed according to **rules.** As there, a "practice" throughout this second volume is a complex series of human actions involving definite practitioners who by these means and in accordance with these rules together seek the intended end. *Ethics* sought to widen this precise but minimal account by noting the promise and threat contained in the practices that constitute human social life: Their *promise* (here *Ethics* followed MacIntyre, 1984:175) lies in their capacity to evoke and even to require skills of participants (these are the virtues); their *threat* (overlooked by MacIntyre) lies in the prac- tices' capacity for monstrous distortion and disobedience to God's rule. (Paul refers to principalities and powers, which we may understand as practices that have become dangerous to human being.) Having this potential for good and evil, they are rightly named "powerful practices." I sought to show, for example, that each of the Ten Commandments in ancient Israel served as a rule to guide one or more of the powerful practices that constituted Israel's common life. Thus "no adultery" with all it entailed served as a guiding rule for the people's practice of family life, and "no stealing" guided their practice of property ownership or stewardship (see table, *Ethics*, p. 182). *The practice of Christian teaching can* *best be understood in these terms.* Just as "medicine" denotes not merely bottles on a pharmacy shelf but a *practice,* and "law" not merely statutes, but *another* kind of practice, our practice of doctrine is far more than the individual doctrines involved. In each case the named practice is defini-tive for and inclusive of its ingredient doctrines, laws, or medicines. There is no "thing taught" without *teaching;* no Christian doctrines apart from the **practice of doctrine.**

Treating Christian doctrine as a practice will prove itself if it ade-quately displays all the aspects of the doctrinal task—including the authority (and risk!) of doctrine, the reserve with which doctrine is rightly acknowledged, the place of rules, and the skills of the Christian community with its convictions in all this.

In this book "conviction," like "practice," is a technical term. While it has an everyday sense, here it is used more precisely to mean "a persistent belief such that if X (a person or a community) has a conviction, it will not be easily relinquished, and it cannot be relinquished without making X a significantly different person (or community) than before" (*Ethics*, p. 23; see the discussion there and in McClendon and Smith, 1994:4-13, 87-91). So convictions are not just beliefs or opinions, but are deeply self-involving. By coming to understand our convictions, we can come to know ourselves as we truly are. For our convictions show themselves not merely in our professions of belief or disbelief, but in all our attitudes and actions. Thus (in this regard like 'faith') convictions have an affective dimension, while (in contrast to mere emotion) they also have cognitive content, and (in contrast to mere habits) they entail our intentions as well as our action. The etymology of the word "conviction" conveys another insight as well: Convictions arise on the basis of argument and persuasion and thus engage the will of the one convinced. ("A man convinced against his will," goes the old saw, "is of the same opinion still.") Finally, we should note that, because growing up is a process and because self-deceit is a human possibility, we are not always (and may never easily be) aware of our actual convictions. Learning 'who I am' will take anyone time and effort. All the more is all this true of communities with their complex identities. In these terms, the present volume seeks to enable churches to discover the convictions that inform their practices, and to facilitate their testing them for fidelity and truth.

i. Participants and means.—The Christian gospel summons all to be students in the school of Christ (*mathētai*, learners, disciples). In the broad sense in which the church is itself a teacher, each member is a teacher as well. By the division of labors and gifts (1 Corinthians 12–14) a smaller number are formally designated teachers. But inasmuch as the *practice* of teaching requires learners, it engages teachers and taught alike, so that discipleship (i.e., student status) is a definitive mark of the Christian (cf. *Ethics*, p. 28). This identifies the **participants** in the practice of Christian doctrine. Participation is by invitation and is intentional— no captive church, and no mere collection of the curious, will count. As in any practice, some entering standards are involved for this instruction: not every onlooker is ready to learn or teach. This helps explain why the means also include the qualification and preparation of the participants, both teachers and learners, and this in turn involves skills in biblical and historical studies (§2 below), skills of language (at least one's native language), and spiritual sensitivity and openness. In Chapter Three it will come out that these qualifications for participants imply a *converted* company of followers. Jesus demanded serious life-changing commitment of those who would follow him.

The **means** employed in the practice of doctrine include explicit doctrines, and much (perhaps too much) has been made of this fact in the literature. We must grant the cognitive, referential role of convictions about creation, atonement, Christ, and church, for example, yet such doctrines are not the only or even the chief means of doctrinal teaching, which far more often employs narrative and parable, paradigmatic example, searching question ("who, then, was a neighbor to him?"), and striking precept ("sell all you have and give to the poor") in doing its work.

This puts the contribution of the Pastoral Epistles in proper perspective. First Timothy's readers are warned against "some who have gone astray into a wilderness of words" (1:6). In contrast, "sound teaching conforms with the gospel" (1:10f). Instruction begins with prayer, in conformity with custom (chap. 2). The chief instructors *(episkopoi, diakonoi)* must meet tests of public conduct and competence in the faith (chap. 3). False teachers insist on extravagant asceticism in sex and food, purvey myths not truth, and neglect the true disciplines—devotion to Scripture and prayer, exemplary conduct—that "Timothy" is advised to maintain (chap. 4). Specific advice concerning local problems (5:1–6:2) precedes the conclusion, a ringing commendation of the pattern of life offered by Jesus Christ, whose appearance, in God's own good time, will consummate the rule of God (6:3-21). First Timothy provides a mixture of common sense, tradition, and gospel conviction. Thus it offers a glimpse of the early Christian mission proceeding with its teaching task, and it is in this context that "healthful doctrine" *(hugiainousa didaskalia)*, good teaching that excludes false, is urged (1:10, etc.). Second Timothy adds to this line of thought two memorable themes: (1) wholesome teaching must focus upon Paul's gospel of Jesus Christ "risen from the dead, born of David's line" (2:8). Thus it is anchored both in present reality (the risen Christ) and in its past—and future—link to Israel (David's line as bearer of the promise); (2) such teaching has its unfailing resource in inspired Scripture, "teaching the truth and refuting error" (3:16). The Letter to Titus (1:5-10) joins 2 Timothy (2:2) in emphasizing a third theme: (3) healthy teaching requires provision for *future* teachers qualified in character and skill to pass the treasure on. From these books alone one cannot derive a full picture of the scope and power of primitive Christian teaching, but they illustrate an important feature of it next to be considered: the role of rules.

ii. Rules and ends.—Practices are activities according to **rules:** Not everyone who throws a ball is playing baseball; not all who utter belief-claims are Christian teachers. When we explain a practice to someone (for example, "The pitcher is the one out there who . . .") we are, consciously or not, invoking the rules of that practice. While Christian teaching sometimes employs doctrines as discrete means, more often the most important doctrines (e.g., the centrality of Christ) are not cited but *presupposed and exemplified*. This consideration led historian of theology George Lindbeck to propose that all Christian doctrines were as such *grammatical* rules governing Christian discourse. He used "grammatical" in a Wittgensteinian sense to refer, not to the rules of natural languages such as English or Dutch ("plural subjects take plural verbs"), but to the analogous rules of doctrine that show what can and cannot be meaningfully declared in Christian teaching (1984:chap. 4; cf. Holmer, 1978). This understanding of doctrine as 'grammatical' rules might seem to cut Christian doctrine off from reality claims: While for Lindbeck "We believe in one God" excluded talk of many gods (or of no God) from Christian discourse, it was not so clear that it referred to extra-linguistic (or even extra-Christian) reality (1984:80). But there is a less extreme way to read Lindbeck: On this view he is not denying that Christian doctrines refer to God above and the world outside, but is (strongly) urging that what Christians have to say about God and world cannot be meaningfully separated from the network of rules and meanings that constitute Christian teaching (cf. B. Marshall in Marshall, ed., 1990); what they teach cannot be plucked out of that network and judged apart from it any more than one could pluck out the eye of a living animal and test its vision apart from its organic membership in the animal. However we read Lindbeck, that is what needs to be said about Christian teaching as a whole: it makes sense in terms of its rules and not apart from them. It follows that Christian doctrine or teaching is not *merely* its rules any more than any other practice is merely (or even 'essentially') a set of rules. In Christian teaching as in other practices to know the rules is necessary, but to play the game is something more. The practice of Christian teaching involves qualified participants and suitable *means* (*including didaskalia*, sound teachings); it involves rules (of which Lindbeck gives a valuable account), and it involves an end or goal beyond itself. If these pages can add any corrective to previous Protestant and Catholic accounts of doctrine, it is the insistence that none of these elements can rightly be omitted. So individual doctrines function on occasion as means, but constantly as rules, in the practice of Christian doctrine.

The present account is close to that of Lindbeck, and to the Catholic Tübingen School (cited above), and to Stanley Hauerwas (see e.g. 1991), but it should be contrasted with two other views: (1) for *Marxist* understandings doctrine is epiphenomenal: material conditions determine life, and all thinking is suspect, a smokescreen. For (2) *dualist* understandings (recurrent in Christian history) doctrine is one kind of thing and life or action is another. For dualists, the problem is how thought can "flow" into action; for Marxists the problem is how to expose doctrine as the impostor it is. But for (3) a *practical* account, neither problem prevails, since doctrines that express convictions actually *constitute* community life. The main problem then becomes discovering the real doctrines, the real convictions.

Jesus came preaching the gospel of God's coming reign; into that reign he summoned followers, who enrolled as students in his school, his open air, learn-by-doing, movable, life-changing dialogue. It was surely exhilarating, yet the school of Christ was not an end in itself. Followers were summoned to a transforming discipleship, a fellowship of studies, not with a view to a rustic life-style, but for training as witnesses, messengers, apostles, and teachers under the direction of a Master whose 'good news' for the world was evidently bad news for the principalities and powers of his day. It was this purposeful program—clearer in his mind than in theirs—that required their costly apprenticeship to the radical Teacher.

Now it may seem odd to recall this story of the life-changing Master near the beginning of an academic study of Christian doctrine. Yet the placement is deliberate. For the summons to follow and the invitation to membership in the school of Christ is, by virtue of his resurrection, a live option today. As the identity of the disciples was a central element in the original story, it is likewise central (along with the identity of the resurrected Lord) in understanding the practice of Christian doctrine now. To some it may seem a demeaning step to characterize the study of theology in this way. Surely, they will say, undertaking the critical study of Christian doctrine is grander, more academic, more *scholarly*, than mere enlistment as the students of this strange and demanding master? Nevertheless, enlistment and scholarship are integral parts of one whole. Blind Bartimaeus given sight (Mark 10:46-52) is the paradigmatic Christian scholar. The selfhood-in-community that the Christian scholar can seek is continuous with the quest of the beggar or harlot, the prodigal or plodder (and with the watchful Simeon—Luke 2:25-35) who turn to Christ Jesus in hope of gaining their *sight*. This is a humbling admission. Perhaps in engaging the study of Christian doctrine one had hoped for a place of honor. It is not promised. Nevertheless, practitioners are granted a promise. It is not made to any one of us alone, but to the whole company of sharers in the task. This company is promised that finally "all of us come to the unity of the faith and of the knowledge of the Son of God, to maturity, to the measure of the full stature of Christ" (Eph. 4:13 NRSV).

Here we encounter the **end** of our practice. Its realization is corporate, not solitary—in an image, Ephesians treats redeemed humanity as one embodied self, one new Adam. The maturity it promises is not perfect Herculean development for each, but a unity inherent in *the doctrine* we teach and learn, a unity that permits the stronger to help the weaker, and whose excellence is weighed on no smaller a scale than the full story of the Christ. This means humanity on a new model, a corporate humanity in Jesus Christ.

What is said here does not abolish the distinction between the first-order task of teaching Christian doctrine and the second-order, or theological, task of critically monitoring, examining, and revising that teaching. We must describe these analytically as two tasks, yet ultimately there is only one, inasmuch as each aids the other in the one body (cf. 1 Corinthians 12). Nor is there any intention here of denying the lively possibility that a non-Christian may engage in the theological task alongside or in contest with believers. There are strangers dwelling within the land of faith and examining its constitution, just as once there were strangers within the gates of Israel, and these deserve special honor for their distinctive atheist or Buddhist or Muslim or Judaic or other contributions to Christian self-understanding, although this must not be allowed to obscure their lack of the crucial element of trust in Jesus that identifies regular participants. We may recall that theology as a human undertaking is not a device for separating but for bringing together those of the household of faith and other households: it is the *loggia* beneath which members of many households can walk to and fro as they engage in humane dialogue, and *without which there can be no such dialogue on equal terms* (*Ethics*, pp. 36, 40). It is here, and not in detached 'religious studies,' that genuinely open dialogue can occur.

iii. A caution.—Practices are arenas of human excellence. They are as well foci of demonic and destructive energy. They can nurture our best, but they necessarily risk our worst. I do not have in mind here such as Hymenaeus, Alexander, and Philetus, mentioned in the Pastoral Epistles, who by "spurning conscience made shipwreck of their faith" and were "wide of *the* faith" in their doctrines (1 Tim. 1:19f; 2 Tim. 2:17f). Certainly their counterparts exist at present and now as then are infectious troublemakers best avoided. I am thinking rather of the capacity possessed by teaching enterprises of the strictest biblical and experiential orthodoxy, impeccably evangelical, decorated with the fruits of long learning and much selfless devotion—a capacity to grind down upon those within their care and alienate or crush or shrivel them. This is not just the generic tendency of an institution to bureaucratize and institutionalize its personnel (that is another risk), but is the capacity of the practice of Christian teaching specifically to do in the name of truth what it warns against as a mark of error. Not every such mismove can be blocked in advance; it is enough for present purposes that we recognize the risk our work must incur, and that we remember even more that it need not turn out this way. There is no good reason to believe that the intense teaching community that gathered around Jesus in his career ever as such turned into mutually destructive ways. The Teacher forbade vengeance, and not only against unfriendly opponents (Luke 9:51-56); it was said of him as of Isaiah's Servant that he would not snuff out a smoldering wick (Isa. 42:2; Matt. 12:20). Perhaps this means not even a smoldering student of Christian doctrine! Is his not the single style that can subdue the raging nations—or the raging partisans of doctrine?

§2. Doctrine, Scripture, and Narrative Community

a. Teaching and Bible reading as practices.—In the previous section there emerged the picture of a disciple church engaged in its doctrinal or teaching task. So far, little has been said about Scripture, yet the Bible has ever been indispensable in the Christian church's teaching. Though other factors have always appeared alongside the Bible, demanding proper recognition, we must consider now the central role of Scripture both in the church doctrinal enterprise and in doctrinal theology, to be discussed next (§3).

In the broadest sense, the church teaches by what it is and by what it does. All its practices interact with its teaching. When other practices are faithful and whole, teaching is obedient and pure; when they are corrupt, teaching is corrupt as well. Plainly, different practices yield different elements of the teaching. The economic practices of the church, for example, help to constitute its teaching about creation and its use; its practice of prayer shapes its teaching about the One to whom and through whom and in whom prayer is offered, the all-merciful God; its practice of evangelism (or its neglect) positively or negatively shapes its teaching about salvation; its practice of hospitality to strangers shapes its teaching about the Christian mission. Yet there is an argument against founding doctrine upon any one of these practices, or any combination of them—or, as with Liberation Theologies, building it primarily upon the church's practice *(praxis)* vis-à-vis the wider society: Since each powerful practice is subject to distortion, even to demonic abuse (see *Ethics*, Six), doctrine based directly upon it is likewise liable to abuse. Thus the wise church, in the formation of its teaching, looks to practices that resist perversion. Here some have turned to the church's worship, persistent over the centuries, to provide a constant marker upon which church teaching can build.

Three of the six chapters of Calvin's original *Institutes* were built around the Apostles' Creed, the Our Father, and the two sacraments—elements of common worship well suited to catechesis. More recently, Geoffrey Wainwright has built a volume of theology upon the practice of worship in many churches, with special reference to baptism and eucharist (Wainwright, 1980). This is significant because Lord's supper and baptism—the overwhelming water, the supernatural food and drink—retain throughout Christian history a stubborn (if abused) integrity as enduring prophetic signs, let the winds of doctrine blow as they will.

Yet an even more objective and stable footing for the practice of Christian doctrine (and as we will see, no rival to this other) is the study of Scripture. A practice in its own right, Bible study continues in the church as one practice among many, yet the Bible's objective content and character—its matter comprising the story of the people of God, its historical role as the textbook of that people, its voice as the voice of God to them—uniquely fit it to be the doctrinal manual of the teaching church. How to read the Bible must occupy us next, but first we may review the ground so far gained: Within a disciple church, a learning church, teaching is not confined to the classroom, vital though it be. Willy-nilly, all that the church does instructs; in particular all its regular practices constitute its teaching. Evidently the Bible must have a place in all these practices. This is already the case, even when (at one extreme) the Bible remains a cold icon, relegated to symbolic significance, or when (at the other) it is made a graven idol, a "paper pope," receiving the more homage the more it is misread. In happier cases, the Bible truly functions as a congregational textbook, source of sermons, classroom handbook, devotional guide, practical norm. Such diversity in Bible use and misuse underlines the point made above: every practice is vulnerable to perversion. This one practice, however, contains its own corrective; the mistaken extremes border the path to be explored now.

Scholars point out many approaches to interpretation over the long Christian centuries. Different tacks have been taken, different emphases made, and course corrections have from time to time seemed necessary. An indispensable feature of Bible reading in our day is the use of historical-critical exegesis. This method is taught in every Bible school and seminary, and is the uniform presupposition of conservatives and liberals alike—though they argue about particular issues such as dates, authors, and references. It might be thought, as a result, that everyone is now a much better Bible reader than anyone ever was in the past, and that we can all look back with pity, even consternation, upon the grim times before the white light of historical-critical exegesis began to shine. Scientific truth is triumphing at long last. That impression, however, is mistaken on at least two counts.

First, a word about the "many hermeneutical methods" of the past. It is true that a variety of interpretive practices can be found in the history of Christian exegesis (Grant and Tracy, 1984). One learns of typology and allegory, of moral sense and anagogical sense, of criticism and trope. There have been exegetical battles (Alexandria versus Antioch) and exegetical borrowings (from Jews, from classical rhetoric, from Arabian philosophy, from Renaissance scholarship). But if one makes allowance for occasional excesses and extremes, the main course of Christian Bible reading has held true over the centuries to the **plain sense** of Scripture— its stories were read as (in the main) real stories about real people; its history, real history; its declarations about God and God's creatures as saying what they meant and meaning what they said. The Bible was not a code or cipher to be cracked; it was not a book of secrets; it was realistic; it spoke plain (Frei, 1986; D. Tracy in Marshall, ed., 1990). This was (in Latin) the *sensus literalis*, the literal sense of Scripture. Yet plainness did not imply triviality, for as well as (or better, within) the plain sense there was what we might today call the *point* of that plain sense. And this point was often spoken of as another sense, sometimes (but not always or even consistently) called the **spiritual sense** of the text. (Alternatively, we might call this the doctrinal sense, or even the *theological sense*—J. Barr, 1989.) Spiritual sense meant, not an abandonment or discarding of the plain sense, but its appropriation into the whole story of divine and human relations; it meant the way the plain words bore upon readers' lives in relation to all that God had done and would do in their regard. For example, Augustine in the Confessions (Book xiii) considers the text "Let there be light" (Gen. 1:3). Taking the literal sense of these words as a given, Augustine then says: "I do not think it *out of harmony with the sense* if we take this to mean the *spiritual creation. . . .*" (emphasis added). He believes that already the life of the physical universe was decreed in Genesis 1:1f. To this life, God sent not only literal light (1:3 read literally), but more to the point, creation was (by God's grace) created in such a way ("let there be light") that it would contemplate the source of its true light, its Maker, and adhere to that source, and this, Augustine concludes, is the spiritual sense of the verse.

Here we come to a third feature of the Christian reading of Scripture, namely, the **means** by which readers passed from the never discarded literal sense to the earnestly sought spiritual sense. Between the two, binding them together, exegetes found (or if we are more skeptical, they interposed) several devices. Confusingly, these were called "senses" as well; hence we have such terms as allegorical sense, typological sense, and many others. The thing to keep in mind is that these many "senses" were not for the most part independently valued, but were seen as bridges between the literal sense and what is here called the spiritual sense, or more suitably, the *point*, of a passage of Scripture.

In literary terminology, these intermediate devices are "tropes," not mere decoration, but aids to getting the point. Thus if we read Genesis 1:3 as Augustine reads it, "light" flickers back and forth between its literal meaning, the brightness that comes from a candle or from the sun, and a tropic sense, in which it is the illumination that comes to life when that life finds its relation to God. Prominent among the tropes are "types" and "antitypes." Here at least we can be sure that later interpreters were not merely projecting their own ideas into biblical texts, for the typological or figural method appears in the Bible itself, as the prophets sought to understand and appropriate the stories they had received, and as the writers of the New Testament found gospel truth foreshadowed in the Old. Thus Hosea (2:15-23) prophesies a new exodus: he finds the pattern of the original exodus (escape from bondage, new hope, a covenant, delivery from fear of enemies, plentiful land, 'my people,' and 'my God') and declares that (in a greater sense) these are the elements of God's new intention for his currently unfaithful people. And Paul finds Adam to be an example beforehand (*typos*, type) of Christ (Rom. 5:14). As in Hosea's text, the earlier example, great though it may be, is overshadowed by the latter. Christ fulfilled the divine pattern; he was the "image of God," while the original Adam had failed at that task. Typology thus stands as the chief trope by which plain sense and final point are linked; to us this may seem strained, or trivial, or mere decoration; for the biblical writers it was not merely a way to read Scripture, but was *the* way. As Leonhard Goppelt puts it in *Theological Dictionary of the New Testament*, "This way of relating OT phenomena to the present situation is the central and distinctive NT way of understanding Scripture . . . it is the decisive interpretation of Jesus, the Gospel, and the Church" (TDNT, VIII:255f).

Since this is a recommendation, we had better add that such tropic, figural, or typological reading must never be allowed to *replace* the plain sense. For example, it is current fashion to say that both religion and theology are properly expressed in metaphors and models, and some even say that there can be no (successful) nonmetaphoric religious utterance. This insistence is reinforced for many when ideologies such as feminism turn out to depend heavily upon metaphorical readings (McFague, 1982, 1987). Yet considerable caution is advisable here, for metaphor is a notoriously controversial topic in literary studies and philosophy as well as theology. There are many theories of metaphor (see e.g. M. Beardsley, "Metaphor," *Enc. Phil.* V:284-89), and none has so far met all the difficulties raised against it; far less has any provided reason to neglect the plain sense of Scripture. In any theological generation, literary theories that discard this plain sense are suspect. For balanced views of metaphor and theology or religion, see (besides Beardsley) Janet Soskice (1985, and Soskice in Abraham and Holtzer, eds., 1987), William Alston (1989), and Colin Gunton (1989).

If Scripture reading is a practice, it must proceed according to rules, and it appears that seeking the plain sense is such a rule. Are there others? Hans Frei has suggested two, or perhaps three, that apply primarily to biblical *narrative* (1986:68f): **(1)** The first is **christological:**

What Scripture ascribes to Jesus must not be denied by the reading of [other] Scripture. **(2)** The second bears upon the **unity of the Bible:** "No Christian reading may deny either the unity of Old and New Testaments or the congruence . . . of that unity with the ascriptive literalism" asserted in (1). **(3)** The third rule is simply **a license to proceed:** readings not in contradiction with (1) and (2) are permitted in the church. Evidently (3) permits, though it does not require, historical-critical exegesis.

If a reader sees the point of these rules, she or he may be ready to go on to an understanding clarified for me by Edgar McKnight: There seem to be two classes of rules that guide Christian reading strategies. There are "upper-level" rules, and (to be brief) these are coherent with the deep and widely shared **convictions** of the reading community, which in this case is a disciple church going about its Bible-reading practice. It will be evident that Hans Frei's rules (1) and (2) are of this upper-level sort: they spring from the church's conviction (1) that the one whom it knows and (in part) knows through the Scriptures is that very Jesus Christ of whom Scripture plainly speaks, and (2) its conviction that the promises to Abraham, to Israel, and to David are extended through Jesus Christ to the Gentiles, and so to all people who receive the good news. In brief, these rules go to the Christocentricity and universality of the gospel. There are as well lower-level rules; these are reading guides ('general hermeneutics'?) based on such matters as **vocabulary, grammar, and historical-critical reading,** rules widely shared among Christians and non-Christians alike. I have called these "rules"; it must be emphasized that neither upper-level nor lower-level are rules like "no loitering in the hallways," or "be home by midnight at latest." Rather they are practice-constitutive rules: one who flouts them is to be thought of not as naughty or nasty, but simply as disengaged from the practice in question, here the church's ongoing practice of Bible study (see further Fish, 1980; McKnight, 1985, 1988).

That this is so, that the church knows how to read the Bible doctrinally and that reading it thus is one of her regular practices, offers some relief, but provokes also a certain worry. Consider first the relief. The Bible is the church's book. It does not appear in the church as an invader from another planet—inexplicable, alien, perhaps as impenetrable as an ancient script without a key (for such a despairing view, see Kermode, 1979). Rather we come to faith with the whole Bible already at hand, just as Jesus had Hebrew Scripture. **The Bible is a book whose explanation centers in the one upon whom it centers—Jesus, and the God whose gospel Jesus preached** ("the gospel of God," Mark 1:14). If we have come to that center, we read the Bible aright when we read it according to the rule of the church's practice.

We may repeat here what is said above (§1b.ii) about the "lively possibility" of non-Christians engaging in the church's practice. Both for what they have to learn from and what they have to give believers, the "stranger within the gate" is to be welcomed as a guest in the circle of Christian Scripture reading (cf. 1 Cor. 14:22ff).

It is ironic that the worry has the same source as the relief. Yet these very facts have been differently represented. In modern times the Bible seemed to stand in no more necessary connection with the church than that of custom or arbitrary theological stance. Thus there arose not only the legitimate ongoing question about the exact boundaries of Scripture (the question of *canon*—see Chapter Eleven), but an ahistorical and illegitimate question: How can we possibly know whether to read, and if so by what light, what rule, to read, the Bible? Recognizing (correctly) that every reading, every translation, of the Bible is necessarily an *interpretation*, modernity in its yearning for foundational (and yet nontheological!) truth was embarrassed by the Bible and its Christian reading. Perhaps the current term *hermeneutical circle* registered this embarrassment. The term allows what is obtained from reading to be inseparable from the reader's stance. Modernity then inferred that there is a *logical*, and quite likely vicious, circularity involved in all scripture reading, though the vice can be diminished if we periodically disown our Book, disclaim our intimate connection with it, and attempt to read it as though it were indeed something from an alien world. But apart from the historical detour to be reported next, the alienation was a false one (cf. Gutiérrez, 1973; Segundo, 1979).

We may if we choose speak of the "hermeneutical circle" belonging to the letters exchanged between a pair of lovers. But the "circularity" of their intentions, vocabulary, and mutual (speech) action need not be either arbitrary, puzzling, or inappropriate. Their correspondence is not addressed to *detached* readers. So is it with Bible, faithful church, and the practice of doctrine that embraces Bible reading. They belong together.

This subsection began by reporting an impression doubly mistaken. We are mistaken if we think the church has no agreed and coherent way to read the Bible. The church has always had that. But we are also mistaken if we suppose that modern historical-critical exegesis has faithfully (indeed, most faithfully!) recovered this way. There has in fact been a detour. In the modern period (1700–?), students of Scripture often made its plain sense immaterial, its spiritual sense (or point) unavailable, and the biblical and traditional bridge between the two, the figural or typological reading, irrelevant. This is the time that Hans Frei identified in *The Eclipse of Biblical Narrative* (1974). A quarter century after that book's appearance some post-eclipse light may be seen: No longer do conservative and liberal scholars necessarily read biblical narrative chiefly (or only) to get at the "real" history to be detected behind the narrative—history which in their symbiotic quarrels was either more or less like the interposed biblical material, but which in either case was all that mattered to them. Narrative is now seen by some to do what no other text can. There is a new awareness of the point of figural reading, not only of the Bible (Lampe and Woollcombe, 1957) but of the entire literature influenced by the Bible, from Dante to Updike (on "figural reading" [n.b., not "figurative"] see Auerbach, 1953; cf. Wood, 1988). This reading sees the past figurally present, and sees the future in terms of that present and past so joined. And Christian doctrine is in position once more—if it will—to employ such readings as it opens Scripture afresh.

How will such a reading work? That question has been addressed in *Ethics* (Twelve). To summarize the results here, if we think of the Bible as a single, great story, united by characters, setting, and plot (to be sure, that single story is a bundle of stories, and non-narrative material punctuates the text as well, but here we simplify), we may describe the church's Bible-reading task as the **identification** of its **characters** (major and minor), the **discovery** of its **plot** (and its subplots), and the **exploration** of its **setting** (through its many scenes). Undertaking this complex task brings us, centrally, to the question about the identity of Jesus Christ and (through that) to the identities of God and God's people the Jews, and of Christians, and of the rest who people Scripture's pages. It brings us to the plot-line of salvation and the creation of this people. It brings us to the kingdom or rule of God as the overarching setting into which we enter if we enter this story. The task of reading in this way coheres closely, though not in a one-to-one correspondence, with the three Parts of the present volume. In fact, it coheres with the doctrinal task of the teaching church.

Character, setting, and plot or incident constitute narrative—at least biblical narrative. That leaves out, however, two vital but sometimes unspoken participants in the text—the **narrator** and the **hearers.** The biblical narrator, the ultimate giver of the Scriptures of the Old and New Testaments, is God. Occasionally this is explicit, as in the voice that speaks from heaven at Jesus' baptism (Mark 1:11 par.), or the voice from the Mount at the Exodus (Exod. 19:3ff), or the voice of many of the psalms. Explicit or not, Scripture is the tale God tells; it is God speaking; it is the word of God, not in part, not here and there, and not "within" or merely "in," but "as" Scripture. As theology this may offend some, but I mean it in the first place as literary truth: We can make *full sense* of biblical narrative only when we see its implied narrator not as the human author (who, to be sure, is fully involved at his or her own level), but as the very God of whom Scripture speaks. As Brian Wicker puts it, "The claim to be able to tell such a story amounts to the claim to be in the position of God" (Wicker, 1975:101, and esp. chap. 2 on "God" and "Yahweh").

And who are the hearers, the readers? It was said above that the church reads the Bible according to the upper-level rule of its shared convictions. It was said also that the advantage of Scripture for doctrinal practice is that the practice of Bible study, though not foolproof, is less subject to corruption, because the Bible, like the great prophetic signs, is objectively *there*, a given. How do these two claims cohere? How can the Bible remain an objective norm if it is only to be read, indeed, *can* only be read through *(someone's)* convinced eyes? For many this worry remains. The response cannot rely merely upon the intersubjectivity of community study, important though that is, for what if the community's common convictions betray the word of Scripture? Yet an adequate answer is available to anyone who has taken part in reading the Bible in the church. Whenever it speaks, its story not only supports and conserves, but challenges, corrects, and sometimes flatly defeats the tales we tell ourselves about ourselves. God's Spirit who breathed upon the writers of Scripture breathes also on us, *sometimes harshly.* The consequence is that our stubborn wills are turned, our blind eyes opened, our arhythmic hearts set beating in tempo. This is not always immediate and is never without ugly exceptions; but it happens often enough to confirm our faith in the Author of the Book.

b. Narrative community as the home of doctrine.—Now to the other "paralyzing worry" mentioned at the beginning of this chapter, the fear that Christian truth cannot be true because it is the particular truth of a particular community among many. Relativism is a pervasive (if not always paralyzing) background concern in our time, and here it comes forward, for we are to speak about a particular sort of community—the Christian church. Christians certainly have little need to be defensive about the Bible; its antiquity, breadth, and power speak for themselves. But we have just seen that in doctrinal work biblical interpretation is the practice of a community of readers. We are considering the primary case, a local community of readers who meet and work together, readers who face the interpretive task from a shared context of witness in a particular place. This does not rule out the value and significance of great national gatherings and ecumenical councils, or the value of expert exegetes, but none of these can replace concrete common reading by an assembly of disciples. Yet this primary case raises the worry mentioned at the outset.

To what sort of community is Scripture thus committed? We are further reminded that *Ethics* (One) staked out a view of church distinctively 'baptist' (a term defined there). Is not such a commitment a sectarian heightening of our problem?

   i. The ecumenical-catholic role of the community.—There has been considerable discussion in the century now ending about the "essence of Christianity," the problem of identifying what is irreducibly and normatively Christian. In the year 1900 influential Protestant scholar Adolf Harnack published a book about that essence (English title, *What Is Christianity?*), presenting the view that "God the Father and the infinite value of the human soul" was the heart of Jesus' gospel histori-cally discovered, so that Christianity in all its history was the religion that remained loyal to that gospel and to its appointed messenger, Jesus himself (Harnack, 1900:56; see Troeltsch, 1977:124-79; Welch, 1972–85 II:146-50). Meanwhile the Roman Catholic Church maintained through-out this century its own institutional claim that the "one, holy, catholic, and apostolic church" is the church juridically governed by the See of Rome (texts in Rahner, ed., 1967:chap. 8), although this claim and the Latin teaching *extra ecclesiam nulla salus*, "outside the church no salva-tion," that accompanied it were modified by the language and spirit of Vatican II (see *Lumen gentium* 15; *Unitatis Redintegratio* 4; texts in Abbott, ed., 1966). Before Vatican II, Reformed theologian Karl Barth held with equivalent dogmatic rigor that the true church was the Evangelical church, so that the Roman Catholic Church was not the true church and the Neo-Protestant (i.e., liberal, Schleiermacherian) church was not the true church (CD I/2 §23.2). In later parts of *Church Dogmatics* he no longer focused upon the church *(Kirche)*, but spoke instead of Christian community *(Gemeinde)*, once again in softer ways (e.g., CD IV/3/2 §72). Yet even in softening their claims, both sides revealed an abiding differ-ence in their approaches to Christian community: for Catholics, authen-tic Christianity was defined institutionally—it was the church ruled by the Roman See; for Protestants, it was defined functionally as the church that taught truly (Harnack), or that rightly located authority in the word of God (Barth).

   There is still another approach to the essence of Christianity. This communitarian approach finds that essence in no hierarchical body or single theological tradition, but in the faithful church, where "church" *(ekklēsia, koinōnia)* means first of all congregation, local assembly of disciples (McClendon and Yoder, 1990). This is the sort of assembly or church that has been referred to in the preceding subsections (a and b) as the community of practice, the assembly whose working textbook is the Bible. What these varieties of understanding reveal is that the *essence* of Christianity (or *real* or *authentic* Christianity) is itself "an essentially contested concept," one that by its very nature cannot be agreed on by all sides. "The essentially contested concept is, typically, a term which occurs again and again in the history of the discussion of a subject and yet is the subject of a chronic series of disputes." Examples of essentially contested concepts are those such as science, art, religion, justice, democracy. About these, there are always debates, but the fact of debate is in these cases a positive asset, enabling participants to see what is at issue in the concept itself. It is out of the resultant debates that progress is made toward realizing the goal represented by the concept (Sykes, 1984:251; cf. Gallie, 1964). *Real* Christianity seems to be just such a concept, and this means that while I will uphold a particular notion of real Christian teaching and of the sort of community that can sustain it, both my readers and I must be alert to the inherent contest, ready to hear the other side of the argument.

Yet how can anyone be content with a partial view, a "side," in the discussion of Christian teaching? Indeed, how be content with Christian teaching itself? Why not Jewish teaching as well or instead, or "religious" teaching of any and every sort, or "humane" teaching, whether or not religious? These are fair questions, and must be addressed. For the present, however, I will meet only the first of them (and later in this volume the question of Jewish-Christian relations). Why not "universal Christian," then, rather than merely *one* Christian viewpoint? But I have just given the reason: There *is* no universal agreement, but only competing claims to universality, one of which is our own.

Any claim of this sort may take one of two alternative forms. One is the comfortable view that the content, the matter of church teaching is within wide limits a matter of indifference: many historic forms are adequate; ours is one of them, but it is not important that it be shared by others or by all. This was the view of church *structure* taken by Luther, and has been a view of Christian *doctrine* taken by many Anglicans. Perhaps its most consistent advocate, though, is Caspar Schwenkfeld, leader of the sixteenth-century "Spiritualist" movement. In his great typology of medieval Christianity, Ernst Troeltsch denoted this sort "mystical" (Troeltsch, 1911). If despite its attractiveness we reject this option, it is because we find that both doctrine and structure—both the practice of teaching and the community that practices it—are constituted by rules internal to the practice itself, so that true structure (which Catholics have rightly emphasized) and pure teaching (which Protestants have rightly emphasized) are alike inseparable elements of the constitutive *practices* of Christian community. Thus the other option: The pattern and structure of church life are not entirely 'adiaphora,' matters indifferent. Although this pattern does not decree (for all time) whether deacons are to be ordained, or how churches are to organize for mission, or whether or not bread turns into something else in the Lord's supper, it does nonetheless give backbone to ordinary, authentic, catholic Christian existence—an existence in which such issues as these will certainly arise and be settled, though their one-time settlement will not absolve future Christian generations from confronting them afresh in relation to the practices (teaching, Bible study, evangelism, charity, and the like) that identify the church.

This communitarian view does not simply dismiss the claims of other Christian movements than our own to be truly evangelical, truly catholic, truly faithful—qualities that we would wish for ourselves *and* for them. (It does not arbitrarily *include* the others, either.) As noted above, this 'practical' view is contestable and when properly understood will inevitably be contested. The business of the present volume is to make clear this view of authentic Christianity. It can be rejected or (as I would hope) accepted. One of the tests of its authenticity is whether it can be proposed in a spirit of love that will win friends, not enemies, for the good news it seeks to represent.

ii. The baptist vision as hermeneutical key to church and Bible.—How the church interprets the Bible is strongly linked to the way the church interprets itself. How is its own story connected, how *must* it be connected, with the great story found in Scripture? There is strong agreement on this question among Christians. The same ancient creed that speaks of belief in "the Holy Ghost, the Lord and Giver of Life, who proceedeth from the Father [and the Son] . . . who spake by the Prophets" goes on immediately to confess belief in "one Holy Catholic and Apostolic Church" (Schaff, 1877 II:59). This confession is (with minute variations) the common property of the great Catholic and Protestant communions East and West. Christians believe that God the Spirit who "spoke by the prophets," that is, inspired the Scriptures, **continues** to constitute the inner life of the church through the ages, so that Bible and church compose one story, one reality. There is a strong link between **the plain sense of Scripture** and the church's self-understanding as a **continuation** of the biblical story.

On the other hand, when we come to acknowledge the **point** of Scripture via its **application** in the present age, this apparent agreement among Christians comes apart. *How* does the story of Jesus come to bear upon the life of the world? Is the role of the church, as the great Catholic theologies would have it, to be the channel through whose sacraments, seven in number, the grace of Christ flows to a waiting world? Is the church rather, as a pure Lutheran theology would insist, to proclaim justification by faith alone? Or is it rather, as Anglican theologies declare, somehow both of these, both Catholic and Protestant, sacramental *and* evangelical? Or is its task neither, but as a modern Quaker might testify, is rather to be the agent of the work of God in the world, doing the good that follows upon the way of Christ? We may have our preferred answer or combination of answers, but we can hardly deny that when Christians set out to *apply* the biblical story, their apparent unity splinters. We might associate this splintering with the quest for the spiritual sense of Scripture, *what we have here called the point* of the text. Is the spiritual point of the biblical narrative inward, a matter of the soul's attitude to God? Is it outward, a matter of institutional reception of grace? Is it ethical, a matter of good works in the world? Is it (in a special sense) religious, a matter of hearts strangely warmed? However we answer, we are not likely to carry with us all who read Scripture and claim to follow Christ. Once more we meet Stephen Sykes' "essentially contested" concept of the essence of Christianity.

A number of viewpoints concerning the present application of Scripture's narrative have persisted. It must suffice here to show our own reasoned answer. This is found in the interpretive link between the plain sense of Scripture and its spiritual sense. This is a historic link, inasmuch as it has been employed through all the ages of biblical interpretation. It is also historic in the sense of being the Bible's own linking device, the Bible's tropic way of holding its great story together. We may call this way *figural* or *typological*. I have called it "the prophetic vision," because it is much used by the prophets. Especially in postbiblical application, I call it **"the baptist vision"** after the sixteenth-century Christian radicals. Neither Catholic nor Protestant, spurned by both sides, they called themselves simply "brothers and sisters," or *Täufer*, "baptists" (*Ethics,* One). The baptist vision is the way the Bible is read by those who (1) accept the plain sense of Scripture as its dominant sense and recognize their continuity with the story it tells, and who (2) acknowledge that finding the point of that story leads them to its application, and who also (3) see past and present and future linked by a "this is that" and "then is now" vision, a trope of mystical identity binding the story now to the story then, and the story then and now to God's future yet to come.

How do Catholic and Protestant understandings bind the continuation (Christian identification with the biblical past) to the application (the church in the world today)? It appears that a Catholic answer is a theory of apostolic succession hierarchically maintained (a chain of episcopal consecrations?), while a Protestant answer is inward and spiritually maintained: or as Schleiermacher put it, "Protestantism . . . makes the individual's relation to the church depend-ent on his relation to Christ, while [Catholicism] contrariwise makes the indi-vidual's relation to Christ dependent on his relation to the Church" (CF §24). The baptist vision has no need to disavow either of these modes of relating Christ and church (or both—each seems to require something like the other). But neither of them can do the work demanded of it here, for (to consider first the idea of succession) if it is true that the True Church is successor to the apostles, it is equally true that all those it calls heretical and false are successors as well, while (to consider the idea of spiritual authenticity as the rule) this individual way of thinking dissolves the very objectivity it proposes to establish. "I am my own church," said Henry David Thoreau, providing a *reductio ad absurdum* of the Protestant scheme. (It has been pointed out that Schleiermacher, having made the distinction, himself takes the Catholic way!)

It must be understood that the baptist vision allows a variety of Bible readings, a variety of applications, depending on time and place and, of course, on the individuality of the readers of Scripture in each time and place. Yet the thesis of this volume is that the unity that arises by use of the vision is nevertheless sufficient to define an authentic style of com-munal Christian life, so that participants in such a community can know what the church must teach to be the church. Whether that thesis is correct remains to be seen; it is my task, and that of my readers, to find out. At this stage we may already see that this reading strategy incurs no obligation to reject everything others, employing other reading strategies, discover or believe. This is not a sectarian way, declaring all others wrong in order to be alone right. It is rather an ecumenical way, confessing the fullness of its style of Christian existence and offering it to all in the hope that in the conversation that ensues it will be adopted by all. That it has not yet been so adopted is tragically true—tragic in the persecution, suffering, and exclusion that, as *Martyrs Mirror* and other writings testify, have stalked the baptist way throughout its history. That it may nonetheless be adopted by all is only to affirm in another way Hans Frei's rules listed above: the gospel centers in Christ; the gospel is for all; the gospel opens into a world of freedom.

§3. Doctrinal Theology: A Practice and Its Context

a. Theology as a secondary practice.—In the previous sections (§§1-2) Christian doctrine was presented as a practice intertwined, in every authentic Christian community, with Bible reading. The two practices are interdependent. Without a community that lives to enact it, the Bible cannot convey its full message, while a Christian community without the Bible risks disintegration and chaos. *Now we can identify the practice proper to this volume, namely* **doctrinal theology.** This is secondary to church practice inasmuch as from a Christian point of view it need not exist, cannot Christianly exist, save in service to the other. It presupposes the church practice, investigates it, seeks to assist it. Being a consultant and helper, it may not substitute itself for or guarantee the primary practice.

To put the point linguistically, the surface grammar of doctrinal theology may take various shapes: first-person confessions, historical descriptions of church teaching, axioms or theses derived from an organizing principle, biblical exegeses, rhetorical ukases. Yet its deep structure is that of a grammar of persuasion seeking assent: It says, "This is what your present convictions appear (on such and such evidence) to be; this is what (for such and such reasons) they appear to mean. Would it be better, then (for considerations here presented) to transform these present convictions *thus?*" In such a servant's question, such a "thus?" all theology's first-person confessions, all its axioms and principles, all its arguments find their reason for being. To the theologian, theology's conclusions may seem self-evident; nevertheless, the theologian remains "Abraham's servant," remains in a figure the emissary of Genesis 24, sent by the Master to find a Rebecca, the servant's only task a faithful appeal to the bride of Christ, who when all is said and done must make her own response to this summons.

On the other hand, the teaching church stands in urgent and unending need of this theological service. There is a drive to truth and truthfulness in Christian convictions that cannot otherwise be satisfied. Apollos accepting instruction from Priscilla and Aquila, Origen teaching prospective teachers in the catechetical school of Alexandria, Augustine gathering like-minded seekers in a house outside Milan, Aquinas confronting the received *Sentences* of Peter Lombard with new thought modes received from antiquity by way of Muslims and Jews, Swiss Brethren gathered at Schleitheim to seek Christian unity amidst radical change, Calvin in Geneva lecturing to reforming scholars from across a continent, the Enlightenment universities' still-Christian academics facing the secular challenge of modernity, schools and colleges of a Christian world mission putting faith in new contexts on five continents—none of these could assume the limits of a single teaching congregation or a like-minded ecclesial body (far less a mythic 'undivided church') as the setting of their work, yet all undertook theological tasks that placed the churches in their debt.

What explains the Christian drive to truth and truthfulness that not only shapes doctrine in the church but also generates this wider practice? Nicholas Lash suggests it is a permanent, and altogether appropriate, Christian fear of (ideological) self-deceit. Christian teaching cannot reduce itself simply to parroting Scripture, or simply replicate itself as tradition, or simply propagandize its claims, for its practice is nourished by a healthy fear of self-serving beliefs, ignorant claims, or comfortable falsehoods. To consent to God as GOD is to risk the exposure of our own idolatries; it is to unmask religious as well as anti-religious illusions. "Faith in God, and God *alone*, is inherently iconoclastic" (Lash, 1986:10f). Doctrinal *theology* is the necessary response to this holy fear.

What sort of thing is this new practice to which the theological beginner is introduced, this old practice whose history he or she must begin to learn, this wide practice whose varieties and far limits spill over every horizon of definition ever proposed? In an important sense, it merges into the primary church practice it supports. Its near goal remains the same—declaring what the church must teach to *be* (here and now) the church. Its central reliance upon Scripture remains the same. Some though not all of its practitioners are the same: the professor may be a pastor; church leaders may be working theologians as well. Yet at least three things distinguish the two practices. First, theology enjoys a social leisure rarely available to those having the care of churches—a leisure that may be abused but may be well used. Second, its practitioners are far more diverse: an assorted netful of fellow scholars, often from other churches, other lands, other theological traditions, other times, join one's congenial fellows here. Third, this other task is carried on in working interaction with other disciplines, not only the subdisciplines of theology and its related studies, but history and psychology and sociology, philosophy and physics and cosmology, politics and art, law and literature. As the playing field is enlarged the players seem harder to distinguish from the spectators. Everything seems open to challenge, everything at risk. The central drive to the truth as it is in Christ Jesus, the drive fully to explore salvation in Jesus' name, to learn better the old, old story Scripture tells, to find the way of faith in hard times, requires also this twilight skirmish!

But in theology as in first-order church teaching, darkness does give way to light. The rich treasures of theology do disclose their secrets and their uses, and the skills and resources of the practice become as familiar as an old glove. Then temptation may come from a different quarter: can one not transfer all this skill and lore back into pulpit and Sunday school classroom? It is a beginner's temptation, and mistaken because it overlooks the resilient twoness of the practices: the wise teacher of literature does not confuse his lecture with a short story; the wise theologian does not offer her research paper as a sermon. Yet in less obtrusive ways all the skills of this secondary practice are indeed finally subsumed by the primary task: the truth as it is in Christ Jesus, all the truth, is for all the people of God.

b. Theology's historical setting.—Theology in each era faces tasks distinct from those faced by its predecessors and successors. The present time illustrates the point: our present context displays such pervasive change that it is difficult to find widely persuasive styles of argument or ways of thought. Ideas that seize one theologian and his or her readers seem irrelevant to another. Why is this so? Every schoolchild is familiar with the concept of changing thought-worlds—the change from antiquity to the Middle Ages, for example, or from the Middle Ages to modernity. There is considerable evidence that we are in fact now passing through another such shift (Murphy and McClendon, 1989).

A corollary is that to the extent the Christian theologians of the last two or three hundred years really belonged to their own times—were able to carry on rational arguments with scholars in other fields, able to make a good case for Christian faith *in that period*—to that extent they, too, displayed 'modern' features. Here misunderstanding is liable to arise, since many religious speakers use the term "modern" in quite a different way, to refer to Roman Catholic or Protestant Modernisms. In the present sense, however, extremely conservative theologians may be just as 'modern' as their nonconservative opponents. Immanuel Kant was in this sense modern in theology, but so was the biblical infallibilist Ernst Hengstenberg; Harry Emerson Fosdick was in this sense a modern theologian, but so was William Jennings Bryan.

Perhaps this preliminary discussion can be summed up with some generalizations. Post-medieval (i.e. modern) theology recognized the changed conditions of Christian thought. It abandoned the notion of language, including religious language, as somehow *participating* in its subject matter, and instead debated whether it was (at one pole) simply *representation*, or (at the other) *expressed the selfhood of the speaker*. Such theology gave up the claim to base truth upon authorities (either scientific authorities such as Aristotle, or ecclesiastical authorities such as Church Fathers), and instead discussed the adequacy or inadequacy of the assumed "*foundations* of human knowledge" in reason or experience. And it abandoned the medieval *cosmology* in which right and wrong, and degrees of reality itself, occupied ordered places. Instead, modern theologians located morality and reality alike in *human beings*—in a word, modernity was deliberately anthropocentric.

There was one *apparent* exception to the second of these generalizations: modern Christians were still attached to the Bible their predecessors used. But this could no longer appear, as it must have to a medieval thinker, as simply one important authority among many. Instead, foundationalist modernity had to assign the Bible an absolutely unsurpassable status. This could be done in two ways. One was by attaching it so tightly to God that it could be faulted only at the cost of faulting God also—hence modern theories of revelation, infallibility, inerrancy, and the like arose. The other was by attaching Scripture equally tightly to human experience, the metaphysical center around which modernity sought to arrange everything. On this view, prophetic books recorded the prophets' own experience, and thus spoke reliably and truly. Each of these moves produced severe difficulties for theology that are only now being reexamined.

In the main, the twentieth century remained as true to modern thought-modes as had the two previous ones. Thus for 'liberal' theologian Paul Tillich (1886–1965), the central doctrinal principle, "new being in Christ," was so successful because it was implicitly anthropocentric, *human:* the new being was *our* new being. Or for major Catholic theologian Karl Rahner (1904–84), a foundationalist theory of knowledge took shape in his concept of transcendental experience—for Rahner the experience of every human being discloses a quest for (and thus implies the existence of) God. Or (for the best modern example of all) Karl Barth (1886–1968) was consistently modern in his theory of revelation, an 'unshakable foundation' that undergirded doctrine from beginning to end.

However, "in the main" is not altogether, and in this most recent period in theological history, the modern paradigm began to crack. In the cracks, something new began to appear, ways of thought that were neither premodern nor (in the sense just indicated) modern, but crucially different from each. It is the task of the present three volumes to show how Christian practice and teaching stand in these new circumstances. *Ethics* offered such an account of Christian living in its three spheres, organic, social, anastatic. *Volume III* will investigate more fully the broad paradigm shift just sketched. In this volume we will address not the context but the inner reality of Christian teaching, its content and force. All three volumes venture the judgment that some large cultural-philosophical obstacles that have impeded Christian thinking for two hundred years or so are now dissolving or dissolved: Christian theology is in a new way free to be itself—and meet new hazards on its road.

c. Theology's political character.—Recent discussion has emphasized anew that the gospel always appears in a particular setting; that setting gives it shape as a pitcher shapes its contents. To call this context *political* acknowledges not only its geographical and cultural but also its dynamic structural character. Authentic Christian doctrine always senses this context, whether we see an Augustine contemplating the collapse of the Roman Empire, or Luther, Calvin, and the Radicals with their differing views of the Reformation era in Europe, or more recent examples. I intend to deal with the (North) American context, and America is no exception. The Atlantic crossing produced sea changes deep and broad that revealed themselves in the churches in the new land. Spanish and French efforts to make Native Americans Catholic, Puritan attempts to hammer out a polity in state and church that would produce a Protestant Christian America, the life-changing effects of the Second Awakening early in the nineteenth century, the severing of church ties between North and South prior to the Civil War, massive immigration that reshaped the social and religious map, peacemaking and militarism in the context of wars fought every quarter-century of United States history—all this demanded doctrinal response if the church was yet to *be* the church.

Thus it is more surprising that after these developments, American Christian theology is still so often bottled under European license, so often repeats arguments shaped by the state-church theological systems, Catholic and Lutheran and Reformed, that Europe spawned. Even today, when the demands of context are everywhere heard (e.g., in Robert Schreiter's *Constructing Local Theologies*, 1985) this demand seems most often referred to the (surely desirable) independence of Third World theological work, while in the United States theological issues set in Germany still dominate debate, or alternatively, imported Third World themes under the heading Liberation Theology do so. Why is this so? Why is context important in Peru and Zaire, but not in Chicago or Houston, in Malaysia and Tonga, but not in Atlanta or Los Angeles, Dallas or Des Moines?

More broadly, what *is* the American context, and how must it affect theology? (For what follows, see McClendon, BEMCT: 524-31; cf. S. Mead, 1963, 1975:chap. 4.) Although historians differ on interpretation, three enduring elements are widely acknowledged: the spaciousness of the American continent, a rich, sparsely inhabited wilderness when the first lasting English settlement appeared; the slow, inexorable appearance of liberty (especially religious liberty) with its attendant pluralism in forms unknown in the European past; and the sweet, even cloying context of success—economic, political, cultural, and institutional—as the new settlers and their churches flourished. *Spaciousness* meant the challenge of geographical discovery and the accompanying sense that God had more light, more truth, yet to break forth from Scripture (thus John Robinson's Leyden farewell to the American Pilgrims). *Liberty* (to be sharply distinguished from mere tolerance) grew partly from this very spaciousness: A 'sect' persecuted in one place had only to move to be free in fact; yet by the 1830s all the American states had disestablished their churches, and de facto freedom became enshrined in law as well. *Success* meant that the gospel had to be discovered all over again; in America the gospel was neither an anodyne for oppressed masses nor a prop for oligarchy, but the truth for people making it on their own, people who nonetheless yearned for nature's God or sought Jesus' friendship. Exceptions to success were the victims of colonization and of black slavery and the experience of the South in the Civil War and the whole nation in the Depression; each of these with its aftermath had consequences for theology.

i. The reign of God in American space.—As a single example, we may consider the relation of the gospel to the American context in space. Sidney Mead believed the spaciousness Americans enjoyed nourished their liberty. Those unhappy with religious arrangements in one colony could simply move to another; those constricted by property rights could go west (S. Mead, 1963:chap. 1). To continue Mead's story, black and white sharecroppers in mid–twentieth-century Louisiana could win economic freedom by taking factory jobs in Richmond, California, or Detroit, Michigan. Yet in each case those freedoms bumped into limits: Early Quakers were unwelcome outside Pennsylvania; nineteenth-century Mormons were unwelcome everywhere. Pioneers to the West found hostile Native Americans already there; when twentieth-century factories moved to Third World countries, their migrant United States workers were once again stranded.

Spaciousness also shaped the mind of contented, affluent, and successful Americans. Why should the favored status God had granted America not be converted into American hegemony elsewhere? Especially if it so clearly benefited the recipients? Had not America a Manifest Destiny—to annex Texas, to defeat rival claims to Oregon and California, to rule the entire continent, even to dominate the world in the name of democracy, liberty, success? Of course there was irony in these secular missions: How could domination enhance others' home rule? Why need such a spacious nation corral its own Original inhabitants? But ironic or not, the beliefs flourished. They came to full fruit when the United States after World War II became in effect successor to the old British Empire. Now the peace of the whole world seemed to depend upon Pax Americana, as once it had depended upon Pax Romana or Pax Britannica. That regular wars were required in order to maintain each of these versions of 'peace' did not strike their sponsors as insufferable irony. After all, there were the terrible alternatives—the barbarians without, or dreaded Russia! (W. Mead, 1987:1-31)

Empires, however, are expensive. The British were exhausted by the cost of two World Wars. The American economy in its turn fell behind during the long twilight struggle of the Cold War with the upstart Soviets. More severe still was the moral expense of dominating others— a lesson as old as ancient Rome. As American *dominium* faltered, there was a new perception that its cost was self-destructive (P. Kennedy,

1989). It is not our task here to provide a strategy for this declining giant, or a Christian response to the power of government in general (yet see *Ethics*, Eight). Yet at least we must see America's real if fading power as the current political context of Christian doctrine, along with success and liberty.

This construal of the context of doctrine is in purposeful contrast to those ideologies (e.g., Marxism, liberalism, feminism, the political right) that place some political, economic, or social proposal prior to the gospel. Typically, they propose singular cures for what they think ails the world. The present analysis acknowledges such contextual ills without on their basis alone defining a remedial program. Here I differ from libertarian (Michael Novak), ethnic-racial (James Cone), and gender-based (Mary Daly) theologies or ideologies as well. Preoccupied with *context*, these risk overlooking the *content* of Christian teaching, failing to see that an authentic practice of Christian doctrine grows from the gospel, not from ideological assumptions however insightful. Their position is unstable, wavering between pure ideology and authentic Christian theology.

To clarify the doctrinal task in light of the American drive to empire, we may reflect upon the ministry of Martin Luther King, Jr. (1929–68). In previous writings I have argued that King's life is not merely inspirational or illustrative (as, blemishes and all, it surely is) but theologically substantive in its own right; here was a twentieth-century 'Church Father,' a theologian towering above the theologians (McClendon, 1971*a*, 1971*b*; 1990:chaps. 3, 4; King, ed. J. M. Washington, 1986, Introduction). Now I wish to recall King's interaction with one moment in America's righteous empire, namely the Indochinese War.

Between 1955, when he led the Montgomery Improvement Association boycott of segregated public transport, and 1968, when he was assassinated while supporting a strike of black garbage men in Memphis, Tennessee, King was the acknowledged leader of the civil rights movement that sought racial justice and "integration" in American society. While these events were unfolding, American troops, a high proportion of them black, were sent to "defend the United States" in faraway Vietnam. Against the advice of other civil rights leaders, King spoke out against this U.S. war policy in 1967, in Atlanta and Los Angeles, then memorably to members of Clergy and Laity Concerned who were meeting in Riverside Church, New York City. Before the war was over, many Americans demonstrated against it, though few so early as King. What is noteworthy is not his avowal of peace in a time of war, an act that requires considerable courage in itself, but the fact that his protest grew directly from his role as a public and practical teacher of Christian doctrine.

Toward the beginning of his Riverside Church address, King in homiletic fashion named seven reasons why he must protest the war: (1) it stole energy from the civil rights struggle; (2) it sent disadvantaged blacks "to guarantee liberties in Southeast Asia" that they were denied at home; (3) meaningful social change came not through violence but through nonviolent action; (4) the struggle here in America was not just for Negro rights, but "to save the soul of America" from its own poisonous propensities; (5) King regarded his Nobel Peace Prize as a commission to work for brotherhood everywhere, and (6) by his Christian ministry to proclaim the gospel to all since Christ died for all; and (7) King was a child of a heavenly Father who cared for the suffering and helpless everywhere. These are correlative with (1) **the doctrine of last things** (here in Chapter Two); (2) **the doctrine of creation** (Chapter Four); (3) **the doctrine of divine action** in creation and atonement (Chapters Four and Five); (4) **the doctrine of salvation** (of the whole human being, Chapter Three); (5) **the doctrine of Holy Spirit and mission** (Chapter Ten); (6) **the doctrine of Christian ministry** (Chapter Eight); (7) **the doctrine of God** (Chapter Seven). In King's life and teaching, these were not two lists, but one (King, 1986:231-34).

For the rule or kingdom of God, King liked the name "the beloved community." The goal was "an integrated society wherein brotherhood would be an actuality in every aspect of social life." Some have argued that this "dream" owed much to Walter Rauschenbusch, whose works King had studied in seminary (Smith and Zepp, 1974:120). For Rauschenbusch the kingdom of God had been a this-worldly social and spiritual order toward which all Christian effort must aim. He correctly understood it as both future and present, realized and to be realized. As such the kingdom provided a corrective to other-worldly theologies. Stanley Hauerwas, writing about Rauschenbusch, has pointed out both the strength and the weakness of this understanding of the kingdom: It correctly sees Jesus as central to the kingdom (the centrality of Jesus was an emphasis King drew from his black Baptist church). But it includes no adequate account of the disciplined community, the church, that must be the kingdom's forerunner and sign. For as Hauerwas says, "When 'ethics' is understood primarily as a call for justice against the status quo, we overlook those presuppositions that are necessary to sustain such an endeavor" (1988:157; see further Hauerwas, 1985:chap. 6). It is worthwhile to ask in retrospect whether King in his desire to realize the beloved community in America's time and space omitted this essential element: Did the beloved community remain unrealized exactly because it sought only to be a disembodied church (or a church whose only body was the movement or the nation)? The issue remains with us.

At least this question shows how vital it is to set alongside the discussion of the kingdom or rule of God (see Part I, below) the exploration of the true place of Jesus (Part II) and of the church (Part III).

King's protest, with that of others, had its effect. Yet my present point is a different one. Martin Luther King worked within the political context of a perishable American Empire. The rationale for the Indochinese War, in its various stages (so far as it had any point other than protecting the tenure of successive American Presidents—see Ellsberg, 1972) was protection of that Empire. By challenging the war, King not only reaffirmed the ancient but often neglected Christian message of nonviolent direct action. He also pointed to a deep collision between Christian doctrine broadly construed and current American doctrine. Against the putative right of America to control Southeast Asia, he set the absolute right of God to be God. Against American Empire, the beloved community. Thereby King displayed Christian doctrine in context.

ii. A summary: theology in America.—Surprisingly, there have been few sustained attempts to capture the character of Christian theology in America. Yet this should be in Schreiter's sense a "local" theology (Schreiter, 1985), one whose common features define the Christian task in a region over an extended time. Sydney Ahlstrom's definitive anthology (1967) ventured no summary characterization of American theology. H. Richard Niebuhr found the distinctive (Protestant) American theme to be the kingdom of God, which he traced through three successive stages, Puritan, revivalist, and Social Gospel, yet he found the movement of the kingdom suppressed in his own day (1937:chap. 5). Herbert Richardson's sadly neglected title essay in his collection, *Toward an American Theology* (1967), turned from theology to religion in America, arguing that in America, Christianity focused not upon redemption from sin, but upon the sanctification of creation. Yet in making his point, Richardson drew not only upon the Puritans and Emerson, but upon undomesticated Eastern Orthodox thinking. Many, to be sure, have debated whether Christianity in this country was actually cognitive (Bloom, 1992), chiefly ethical (de Tocqueville, 1835), or merely emotional—once again an Old World triad better exemplified by Hegel, Kant, and Schleiermacher. None of these options fully captures the distinctive flavor of American theological thought.

My own historical judgment, which I will mention but not defend here, is influenced by H. Richard Niebuhr and by Perry Miller, the latter in his posthumous, incomplete *Life of the Mind in America* (1965). This work shows how thoroughly intellectual life in America was formed by the nineteenth-century evangelical revivals. A key case in point is the thought of the revivals' genius leader, Charles Grandison Finney (1792–1875). Miller shows that far from being emotional, as critics of the revivals assumed, Finney's was a mind informed by a distinct theory of the self ("consciousness"), presented in a rhetoric shaped by his legal training. It was this intellect that Finney and his followers brought creatively to bear on the actualities of American life.

> The heart of Finney's theology was his hatred for any form of the Protestant notion that Christian obedience is in any way "imputed" to believers, that without it and before it they are enslaved in the toils of inability. He was determined to put upon the unconverted the burden of responsibility, and brooked no opposition from metaphysicians. . . . The message of Finney was wholly American.
>
> (Miller, 1965:32)

Of course Finney is not alone either as a revivalist or as a shaper of American theology. My present interest lies in the necessity Miller (no flaming Christian believer) found, of placing Finney's thought in its context, the revivals. For that necessity leads us to a more general judgment: Every significant theology entails some such context of practice. At least, American religion is not mere doctrine—or mere morals or mere affect—but is a matter of **practices,** of thought socially active so as to embrace all three. These practices include not only evangelical *revivals,* but Puritan *preaching,* frontier *missions,* Catholic *liturgies,* Social Gospel *lobbying,* Evangelical *soul winning,* nonviolent *direct action,* and many more. Theology in America, from Jonathan Edwards to Martin Luther King, has therefore been a practice about practices, a secondary practice that sought to discover, to interpret, and (provisionally) to revise the primary practices of the Christian communities it served. It has been truest when it recognized and gave weight to, even as it sought to correct, these practices. Yet that thesis must stand here as mere hypothesis, since my business now is not (historically) to describe American theology, or all theology, but (theologically) to practice it. What I hope to do is show, throughout this book, how theology so understood can proceed.

   d. Theology's confessional place.—Every theology has a community of reference, acknowledged or not. It follows that theologians stand in continuity with those who have shared their own communities of reference. Most acknowledge that Christians depend upon works and workers in other times and in our own whose communities of reference are Christian. Less acknowledged is the continuity with a smaller number who share a more immediate community of reference. In my case, this means especially theologians oriented to baptist communities. Here I will look back almost a century to four American theologians whose work is part (though *only* part) of my confessional context. Others do well to provide other lists; in providing them we avoid phony claims to include everything and everybody.

Walter Rauschenbusch (1861–1918), son of German immigrant parents, began his first pastorate (at Second German Baptist Church, Manhattan) guided by the individualism of his own conversion and education, but the crushing experience of urban life led him to the Social Gospel: The church must preach not only individual conversion but the transformation of economics and politics also (Handy, ed., 1966). Rauschenbusch melded the themes of organic human solidarity and the human plight with insights drawn from the Bible, reform politics (Henry George), and sociology (Richard Ely) into a rich polyphony. Jesus came preaching righteousness and summoning all to a new way of life, but an oppressive ecclesial Christianity had forgotten Jesus. Now, however, a new light was dawning: it was time for institutions, not just individuals, to be converted and *enter the kingdom*—a new version of an old American theme (H. Niebuhr, 1937:chap. 4).

An annual Baptist Congress provided him a forum for these fresh views, as did books such as *Christianity and the Social Crisis* (1907). Rauschenbusch returned to Rochester and became Professor of Church History there and one of the best-known seminary professors in America. But his German connections brought him persecution when in 1914 war broke out. His prophetic criticism was now interpreted as disloyalty to his own America. In these circumstances (and in failing health) he was invited by Yale to give public *theology* lectures that became a classic of baptist doctrinal theology. By July of the following year (1918) he was untimely dead.

Three features distinguish *A Theology for the Social Gospel* (1917). Most evident, it is a lively book because it combats concrete evil. Sadly, such evil persists; many of Rauschenbusch's pages might have been written yesterday. Second, the book treats doctrinal themes central to Christian living: the kingdom of God, sin, salvation, Jesus Christ, the Bible, church, sacraments. As a historian, Rauschenbusch believed that the greatest Reformation leaders were not those who remained attached to traditional religion, but the Anabaptists, "radical Protestants" who focused upon "believers' direct experience of God, their disciplined ethical life, and their striving to be a church filled with the Holy Spirit, uncontaminated by alliances with the state and committed to a religious transformation of social life" (Minus, 1988:153). Third, and in terms of present discussion perhaps most enduring, Rauschenbusch the historian shows his readers how to put doctrine into its historical context. Where Augustus Hopkins Strong, in his massive *Systematic Theology* (1907), treated each received (Calvinist) doctrine as an *immediate* deliverance of Scripture, Rauschenbusch disclosed not only the biblical root but the historical setting of each. This gave him a lever to criticize unhealthy accretions to Christian faith; it also provided a rationale for reinterpretation in face of the "social crisis" of industrial America. Rauschenbusch has been criticized for diminishing some Christian themes: the eschatological cast of Jesus' ministry, the resurrection and deity of Christ, the sacramental character of the church, the equality of women (the last in Fishburn, 1981). Although some of these perceptions are legitimate, others, such as the claim he neglected the power and extent of sin, are simply mistaken (Rauschenbusch, 1917:chaps. 4–9).

Edgar Young Mullins (1860–1928) was Walter Rauschenbusch's contemporary, yet their life stories display striking divergences. Mullins grew up in Civil War–scarred Mississippi and East Texas. A child of poverty, he advanced with Horatio Alger swiftness and pluck. After conversion as a young man, seminary studies, and pastorates in Kentucky, Maryland, and Massachusetts, he came in 1899, in the midst of doctrinal crisis, to the presidency of Southern Baptist Theological Seminary in Louisville. From that strategic post he towered over Baptist life in the South for a quarter-century: It happened that in 1923 Mullins was at once President of Southern Seminary, the Southern Baptist Convention, and the Baptist World Alliance, an organization he had helped found.

Perhaps because he came early to denominational leadership with its demand for even-handed balance, Mullins did not follow the Social Gospel lead of his Baltimore years. Three polarizing controversies enmeshed him: (1) the Landmark controversy over Baptist roots and polity, (2) the Calvinist-Arminian struggle over human freedom, and (3) the Fundamentalist-Modernist battle (F. Humphreys in George and Dockery, eds., 1990). The first of these turned on a question of historical scholarship versus popular dogma: Were Baptists descended in a straight line from John the Baptist and the Apostles? Mullins believed not, but for the most part said little to the contrary (Ellis, 1985:chap. 3), even omitting treatment of the church from his doctrinal textbook (Mullins, 1917). The controversy over strict Calvinism displayed the inadequacy of European thought-schemes for American Christians, a people sorely in need of a theory adequate to their practice. Here at his best, Mullins struck the right chord, yet did so without clearly rejecting either the received Princeton Orthodoxy of his mentor James P. Boyce, or the individualism of the times. Opposed to the Fundamentalist scheme, yet by disposition no Modernist, Mullins gradually gave ground to his right-wing opponents, and in time even contributed a (moderate) essay to the classic series *The Fundamentals* (1910–1915). In his final book, *Christianity at the Cross Roads* (1924), he aggressively defended supernaturalism against naturalism and (theological) modernism. In each of these postures his life foreshadowed later events in Southern Baptist history (see Ammerman, 1990).

Allowing for these ironic circumstances, E. Y. Mullins still ranks (with Walter Rauschenbusch) high among baptist theologians in America. His doctrinal manual, *The Christian Religion in Its Doctrinal Expression* (1917), reveals its point of view in its title. Consciously indebted to Schleiermacher, Mullins believed he could extract from religious experience a necessary expression of the doctrines of classical Christianity: sin, election, atonement, salvation, the deity of Christ. In another work, *The Axioms of Religion* (1908), Mullins explored the competence of the individual human soul (under God, he was careful to add) in religion. From "soul competency" there followed axioms to guide every sphere of life, theological, religious, ecclesiastical, moral, religio-civic, social. For example, the ecclesiastical axiom, "All believers have a right to equal privileges in the church" yielded up Baptist polity, and to Mullins' satisfaction refuted Roman Catholics (1908:chap. 8).

For Mullins as for Rauschenbusch, the sixteenth-century baptists were pioneers; their rejection of infant baptism epitomized all that the Reformation had sought to achieve; they "were the idealists who alone stood for all that the great movement signified" (1917:258f, cf. 48, 107). Such convictions, though historically frail, were informed by the best scholarship of his day, and were head and shoulders above customary Protestant and Catholic understandings of the Radical Reformation.

Different again is my teacher **Walter Thomas Conner** (1877–1952), whose biographer, Stewart Newman, called him "not a liberal, but a liberator" (S. Newman, 1964:99-100). Where Rauschenbusch, with his patrician Germanic past, and Mullins, with his rags-to-riches American success story, typify elegance, Conner represents the simplicity of poverty. His career never deserted these beginnings. Educated at Texas' Baylor College, married and with children, Conner went north to Rochester Seminary, where he studied under Strong and Rauschenbusch. Their elegance and his plainness met and bonded. Conner wrote his thesis at Rauschenbusch's direction before returning to teach at Southwestern Baptist Theological Seminary. He settled in Fort Worth in 1910, and remained there for the rest of his life, save for a graduate year in Louisville. In doctoral work under Mullins, Conner wrote a thesis on William James, "Pragmatism and Theology" (J. Garrett in George and Dockery, eds., 1990). With his family Conner endured the Depression (1929–1939) in the employment of an institution hardly able or willing to support him, yet he stuck it out.

'Systematic theology' for many Baptist, Holiness, Mennonite, Pentecostal, and Restorationist writers was only a compendium of Scripture, but Conner's work, like Mullins' and Rauschenbusch's, differed from these. Theology had its own genre, required its own organizing principle (for Conner, "the revelation of God in Christ"), and honored its own history and practice. Like a longhorn steer, his theology had two prongs. One was *salvation*. Theological knowledge was linked to religious experience. This was not the generalized religion of humanity, but the intense, morally compelling, event-centered and eventful issue of a present Christ engaging particular human beings—in one memorable case the experience of a pioneer lad (Conner himself) who was converted at "an old-time, hoorah Methodist meeting." While theology could generalize such life-changing experience, it must not marginalize it, even for those whom society had marginalized. The other prong was *election*, God's prior choice of each, fulfilled in the work of the cross. Thus the two central chapters, "The Redemptive Work of Christ" and "Becoming a Christian," in Conner's final systematic volume, *The Gospel of Redemption* (1945), brought together God's initiative in salvation, and the disciple's appropriation of the gift, understood as "transaction," but also as process and consummation. The figural correlation of the two, the narratives of Christ's achievement and the sinner's release, was Conner's version of the baptist vision. Sophisticated as any New Divinity man, subtle as any Jesuit moralist, Conner nonetheless adhered in speech and writing to a plain style that remained close to his frontier origins. On occasion he offered a laconic defense of this simplicity: "Muddy water is no sign the spring is deep." Thus doctrinal theology was given force by his disdain for obfuscation and his skill with plain words. These were bequests to his students.

The final theologian to be mentioned here is **Georgia Harkness** (1891–1974), a Methodist woman theologian who represents the *liberal evangelicalism* that was part of my own early context. Born in Harkness, New York, she was graduated from (nearby) Cornell, taught school, and then earned a series of religion-related degrees at Boston University (Ph.D., 1923). She was still not considered eligible to teach future (male) pastors, but found acceptance teaching religious education or philosophy at Elmira College, briefly at Mount Holyoke College and at (Methodist) Garrett Biblical Institute, and then after some dark years of physical and mental suffering (roughly coinciding with World War II) she came to Pacific School of Religion (1950), which would eventually be part of the Graduate Theological Union, Berkeley. There, still not appointed as a systematician, she taught "practical theology" until her retirement in 1961. While in Evanston, Harkness had begun to share her home with Verna Miller, a musician, and they remained together until Harkness' death in Claremont, California, in 1974 (Bowden, 1977; Sicherman and Green, 1980; Keller, 1992).

Even had Georgia Harkness' theological emphases not made her inclusion appropriate here, we would do well to recognize her, in an age of changing gender roles, as America's (perhaps the world's) first woman professor of theology—at least I know of no earlier. Barely admitted to the ranks, she was not embittered: "I can honestly say I have had more encouragement than opposition," she told a reporter. "Naturally it was a bit difficult getting started. But once I was established, I had every opportunity for real service I could wish for. . . . I don't believe I've ever spoken up in a committee or other meeting in this country when I was not listened to for what I had to say, regardless of being a woman" (Frakes, 1952:1091). Attending the constitutive meeting of the World Council of Churches (Amsterdam, 1948), she listened while Karl Barth expressed firm views about the role of women, and then stood to debate with him—a memorable moment for those in attendance. Perhaps, though, her distinction was contingent chiefly upon the kind of human being Harkness was—one who did the hard work that won respect, and who then without any apparent self-regard took her place alongside her fellow theologians.

Doctrinally, Harkness was a traditionalist, but the tradition she shared was Wesleyan, with its emphases upon perfection, holy living, discipline, forgiveness, and grace. She displayed a gift for exposition: her book on John Calvin's life and ethics remains a standby for students. In her understanding of the church she came closest to baptist emphases, insisting upon the discipleship of all members and the strictly ancillary role of clergy. Her own churchly ministry was known for its prophetic emphases upon peace and social justice. For example, her work on last things (*Our Christian Hope*, 1964) explores the belief in progress, history and myth, the biblical concept of the kingdom of God, the question of individual life after death in light of Christ, and (the central content of eschatology) "Jesus Christ—the hope of the world." In the chapter that follows this one, I shall address the last things, I hope with some of Harkness' simplicity, dignity, and competence.

Other American theologians, representing other elements in the baptist spectrum, might fill out this account. Douglas Clyde Macintosh (1877–1948), a Canadian Baptist, taught at Yale. He set out to write a doctrinal theology informed by his baptist piety, but in method rigorously parallel to the natural sciences (*Theology as an Empirical Science*, 1919; Welch, 1972–85 II:228). Macintosh is interesting for his pacifist convictions (which kept him from gaining United States citizenship), while his experiential method was remarkable. J. C. Wenger (1910–), who taught in Goshen College and Biblical Seminary beginning in 1938, produced a brief *Introduction to Theology* (1954) that follows a standard Protestant arrangement but inserts insights from his heritage. A little later, and in a higher key, Gordon Kaufman (1925–), a professor at Harvard Divinity School, has written two systematic theologies (1968, 1993), relating modern liberal assumptions to his Mennonite bearings. Dale Moody (1915–92) at Southern Baptist Theological Seminary in Louisville published *The Word of Truth* (1981). Its subtitle, "A summary of Christian doctrine based on biblical revelation," reflects its exegetical focus and its strong relation to European Neo-orthodoxy (Barth, Brunner). Millard J. Erickson (1932–), longtime dean and professor of theology at Bethel Theological Seminary (Baptist General Conference, formerly Swedish Baptist), produced a conservative three-volume systematic theology (reissued as one volume, 1990) remarkable for its comprehensiveness. In traditional fashion, Erickson treats philosophical prolegomena, then God and creation, humanity, sin, Christ, the Spirit, salvation, church, and last things, providing a wealth of biblical and historical information. Guy P. Duffield (1909–) and Nathaniel M. Van Cleave (1907–), professors at the Foursquare Bible College (L.I.F.E.) in Los Angeles, published a joint volume, *Foundations of Pentecostal Theology* (1983), the best systematic work from a classic Pentecostal perspective. Although no black theologian yet displaces Martin Luther King, Jr. (above, c), special notice is due J. Deotis Roberts (1927–), whose doctrinal writings include *Liberation and Reconciliation: A Black Theology* (1971) and *A Black Political Theology* (1974). Significantly, this baptist version of black theology challenges James Cone, emphasizing reconciliation alongside liberation (see Wilmore and Cone, 1979:612-14). James Leo Garrett (1925–), a Southern Baptist theologian, issued the first volume of *Systematic Theology: Biblical, Historical, and Evangelical* (1990) remarkable for its careful annotation, references, and indices. I have commented fully elsewhere on the valuable work of Thomas Finger, a Mennonite by choice (Finger, 1985–89; McClendon, 1991b). C. Norman Kraus (1924–), a Mennonite who served as a missionary teacher in Japan and India, published two doctrinal volumes, *Jesus Christ Our Lord* (1990) and *God our Savior* (1991), written "from a disciple's perspective." These are noteworthy for the central place given Jesus Christ and for the care with which Kraus has responded to the context, not of American but of Asian readers.

* * * * *

This chapter has presented Christian doctrinal theology as a *practice* supportive of and thus necessarily related to the practice of teaching (i.e., the practice of doctrine) in Christian churches. Supplementing what appears in *Volume I* (One), it explores the present historical, political, and confessional context of doctrinal theology. The focus here, which is recent yet not merely current, American yet not isolationist, and contemporary yet not blind to tradition, should not be interpreted as disdain for still other current work or disregard for the wider Christian (and non-Christian) context, for I have presented, especially on my confessional context, only what is less known. Other recent and standard works, such as Hendrikus Berkhof's *Two Hundred Years of Theology* (1989), the *New Handbook of Christian Theology* (NHCT), Stanley Grenz and Roger Olson's *Twentieth Century Theology* (1992), and the usual one-volume and multi-volume dictionaries and encyclopedias of theology provide further help. Now we must turn from con*text* to con*tent*.

PART I

THE RULE
OF GOD

The kingship of God is a paradox, but an historical one: . . . it is the most visible appearance of that kingdom-dialectic . . . of an asking divinity and an answer-refusing, but nevertheless an answer-attempting humanity, the dialogue whose demand is an **eschaton.**

Martin Buber, *Kingship of God*

The will of the world is always a will to death, a will to suicide. We must not accept this suicide, and we must so act that it cannot take place. So we must know what is the actual form of the world's will to suicide in order that we may oppose it, in order that we may know how, and in what direction, we ought to direct our efforts. The world is neither capable of preserving itself, nor is it capable of finding remedies for its spiritual situation (which controls the rest). It carries the weight of sin, it is the realm of Satan which leads it towards separation from God, and consequently towards death. That is all that it is able to do. Thus it is not for us to construct the City of God, to build up an 'order of God' within this world, without taking any notice of its suicidal tendencies. Our concern should be to place ourselves at the very point where this suicidal desire is most active, in the actual form it adopts, and to see how God's will of preservation can act in this given situation.

Jacques Ellul, *The Presence of the Kingdom*

The God movement is not doughnuts and coffee, but justice and peace and joyfulness in the Holy Spirit.

Romans 14:17 CPV

Introduction

Christian doctrine—and Christian theology in its doctrinal mode—begins and ends with the confession, *Iesous Kyrios*, Jesus is Lord. But that confession by itself is a nonesuch, a word in an unknown tongue; uninterpreted it says nothing to us. To see its force we must see this ancient confession tightly woven into a broad tapestry of other Christian convictions. Who *is* this Jesus? That question will be explored in Part II, "The Identity of Jesus Christ." How can anyone rightly *confess* that "Jesus is Lord"? To answer will be the work of Part III, "The Fellowship of the Spirit." But now, first in the order of learning, properly proleptic, we must determine the sense and scope of *"Lord."* What is this concept of "ruler" or "sovereign" *(kyrios)* that rings so strangely in the ears of lovers of freedom and believers in equality? How can free men and women ever say *"kyrie,"* "O, Lord," to anyone or anything? To find out, we must investigate the kingdom (the dominion or realm—Hebrew, *malkuth,* Greek, *basileia)*, that is, the **Rule of God.** In this investigation, any reader who wishes to do so may certainly postpone the question whether there be such a Rule, or indeed, such a God. Our first task here is not to justify these central Christian convictions but only to make their content clear to ourselves and others. Thus there is no presumption upon the reader's good faith; apologetics and evangelism have their proper place, but our task now is the exposition, the full *display*, of Christian doctrine.

The kingdom has too seldom been a key category in Christian theologies. Though it is explicit throughout Scripture, from the creation theology of Genesis to the New Testament's concluding Apocalypse, theology long neglected this central element in Jesus' own message. Perhaps in medieval thought this was because the kingdom was taken to be only another name for the church universal or Catholic, or in the Protestant Reformation because Paul's writings were made the test of all theology and Paul says less about the kingdom, or because God's rule was associated with eschatology and eschatology was marginalized. Or more recently, the concept offended because it spoke of authority and was rightly or wrongly associated with dominant male social roles (kingdoms are ruled by *kings*). Yet gender is not a part of the true biblical concept, and the familiar term, though insufficient, is sometimes appropriate both to relay the Hebrew heritage (see below) and to contrast this King who is a shepherd, a servant, and a suffering lamb with all earthly kingships. Paul did after all use the term as one his readers would find familiar (see e.g. 1 Cor. 15:24, 50; Gal. 5:21). And as we will see, there is a sharp difference between "church" and "the rule of God." Yet it was not until Albrecht Ritschl (1822–89), stimulated by Immanuel Kant and Friedrich Schleiermacher, had made it one of the two foci of the "ellipse" of Christian thought (Ritschl's other focus was redemption through Christ—see Ritschl, 1888:§2) that the rule of God again appeared theologically significant. Yet Ritschl's *Reich Gottes* sometimes seemed only the distillation of the best of European culture, too seldom the judgment of God upon that culture. Still, he gave a lead to American theologian Walter Rauschenbusch (1861–1918), who used "the righteousness of the kingdom" as a key category in constructing his radical Social Gospel critique of Western society (Rauschenbusch, 1917, 1968). Soon, however, the decline of the Social Gospel in mid-twentieth-century America meant that once again the rule of God was theologically neglected. It was finally the biblical scholars, working in the wake of Johannes Weiss (1863–1914), Alfred Loisy (1857–1940), and finally Albert Schweitzer (1875–1965), who forced everyone to recognize that eschatology, and God's rule with it, deserve prime theological attention. Despite much past indifference, it is time for this dominion to have dominion in doctrine.

Therefore Part I of *Doctrine* is focused on the *basileia tou theou*, the rule of God. As just suggested, what this rule amounts to has been a matter of dispute among Christians. Is the rule the prophets promised the same one that Jesus announced (Mark 1:15)? Or is Jesus' proclamation an essentially new revelation? Is the rule here and now present, or is it still to come? Is it with the King James Version and one set of scholars "within you" (Luke 17:21), that is, within each human heart, God's personal presence? Or is it with the Revised English Bible and another set of scholars "among you," implying a new set of divinely ordered social relations? When in obedience to Jesus we set our minds on God's rule "before everything else" (Matt. 6:33), are we to set about remaking the world in righteousness, or are we to answer the summons to a journey inward? Present or future, interior or communal, secular or religious— we must choose, and if we answer "All the above," that must be a coherent reply and not just an evasion.

The approach I will make, to be more fully explained in Chapter Two, sees the concept of God's rule in prophetic and apostolic thought as an instance (indeed, the primary instance) of 'picture thinking,' thinking that is governed by a depiction of the end toward which everything tends. Human beings have different ways of construing the world, different grasps of how in general it works. Those who construe it in relation to God—the God of Moses, of Isaiah, of Jesus of Nazareth—must do so by thinking as Moses and Isaiah and Jesus think, and that is in such images or pictures. This sort of picture is not exactly a mathematical formula, not an inner sense or feeling; it is not exactly a blueprint, or a statistical prediction, or a philosophical premise. It is both like and unlike each of these (as they are like and unlike one another). Prophets render the biblical pictures or images in prophetic words, but the words must *evoke* as much as they *represent*; the pictures must come to life, must take shape, but can do so only as believers receive and retain and are themselves remade by these pictures.

The biblical vision of God's rule is such a picture; more precisely, it is an 'end-picture,' where end means both aim and limit of life. The end is where we end up; it is also the present intention or purpose that steers our course. Thus God's rule is unfailingly future-regarding: we live for the day when, beyond all depicting, the reality it depicts is complete. It is as well self-involving and community-involving: born in a prophet's mind, this rule comes into its own as it is shared so that it guides life for a community. If we are Christian, we aim toward the day when the vision comes true "on earth as in heaven" (Matt. 6:10). Here is a dominion boundless in extent: nothing in creation, and ultimately not even evil itself, is beyond its reach. Here is a **rule of life** immediate in its claim upon us: 'inner' in the sense of going to the heart of each disciple, 'social' in the sense of involving each with others in an ordered way of life together, and indissolubly both these at once. Here, first of all, is a reign that reshapes time itself: by it, life is now, at once, immediately confronted with a claim that is non-negotiable in the sense that in the end God will irrefutably be—God.

What, then, is this rule? The answer is as old as the existence of Israel. While there are instructive parallels and comparisons in the records of other ancient peoples, the idea of God's royal rule, a dominion marked by true justice, burst indelibly upon the world in the beginnings of Israel's history. Among the old tales gathered up in the book of Judges is the story of Gideon, who, after his divinely guided military success, was invited to be king over the Israelites. But Gideon answered, "I will not rule over you, and my son will not rule over you; the LORD will rule over you" (Judg. 8:22f NRSV). Gideon would remain a judge *(shophet)*, a charismatic leader only, because to do otherwise would seditiously interpose an earthly ruler between God and the people. According to Exodus (19f) the people had entered at Sinai into a pact or covenant with a new king, but this was no earthly monarch; it was none other than the One whom Moses had met at the bush aflame. JHWH would be the king *(melekh)* of a dominion *(malkuth*, Exod. 19:6) whose laws came not from the Egyptian and Babylonian monarchs but from this one God. Therefore its law was holy, and its sovereignty was a standing reminder of God's sole kingship. When earthly kingship did eventually appear in Israel, first in Saul and then David, it was perceived as a concessive departure from that true sovereignty, God's own. The Davidic covenant, when it took effect, was valid by being subsumed to the Sinai Covenant (Levenson, 1985); that is, the kingship of David is subordinate to the prior arrangement by which God alone is ruler and the people are responsible directly to God—so David in crucial passages is called "prince," not king (2 Sam. 7:8). Yet to concede even princely rule to an earthly David was to generate what Buber calls this "historic paradox"; it produced a tension that could be resolved only in the *eschaton:* there God's kingship would be restored at last (1967:64).

So this 'end-picture' of God's rule was clear even from early times: God was to be immediately with his people (Buber understands JHWH to mean "the Accompanying God"—cf. Buber, 1946:39-55; 1967:99); he would be the sole ruler, his rule extending, according to Deborah's Song, even to the stars above (Judg. 5:20). Far from diminishing human freedom, this dominion always stood over against oppression by earthly rulers, its sway setting against injustice true justice, against unloveliness, pure love. Later prophets redrew this picture, extended it, expanded it: for example, God's reign already secretly governed all peoples and would finally be known to all (Isaiah 40–66); the basic covenant would be succeeded by an everlasting covenant in which God's law would be internalized by each Israelite (Jer. 31:31-39; 33:38f); the frustration of this-worldly hopes intensified apocalyptic expectation (Daniel 7–12).

By Jesus' day expectation of the coming rule was intense, as the ministry of John the Baptizer, the Dead Sea scrolls, and the record of Jesus' own brief popular ministry make clear. What Jesus himself had to add to kingdom expectation was threefold: (1) Its **coming** was no longer indefinitely future, but was "at hand" (Mark 1:15 par.), so that it could be "entered"; (2) the **character** of the expected realm was to be a new order of interactive love—God's love to people, and people's love one to another, even to enemies (Matt. 5:1-12, 43-48), as exemplified by Jesus himself; (3) the **cost** of the kingdom, in view of its character and of human defiance, was a cross, to be borne first by Jesus and then by all who were his.

Outlining these themes suggests that the rule of God end-picture is one that can lead us to the whole of Christian doctrine. That rule has a politics of its own (Yoder, 1972) implying a **community** that will be its sign and foretaste, namely Christ's people and church. So Part III must constitute an ecclesiology within the (far-reaching) bounds of the realm. That the rule comes with Jesus, its royal man and eschatological Ruler (Mark 1:15; Matt. 25:31ff) requires that Part II shall be an investigation of his divine and human **identity,** that is, a Christology. What sort of rule is it, we must ask, that reaches its climax only in the execution of its Ruler? And what sort of God will be a Ruler like that? And since it stood first in Jesus' own mission, Part I, first of all, must be the doctrine of **the rule of God itself.** In the first of its three chapters (Chapter Two) the point of view, the eschatology from which kingdom thinking can proceed, will appear. Chapter Three, "The New in Christ," will investigate the Christian doctrine of salvation, showing how in this realm God's Christ remakes us, each and all. Chapter Four will explore the boundless extent of God's rule in time and space expressed in the doctrine of creation: explore how nature and culture must answer their Maker's purposes.

CHAPTER TWO

Beginning of the End: Eschatology

The old parlor stereopticon set two pictures before the viewer, who would then see the depth dimension in otherwise flat photographs. Authentic Christian faith is prophetic faith; it sees the present in correct perspective only when it construes the present by means of the prefiguring past (God's past) while at the same time construing it by means of the prophetic future (God's future). "This is that" declares the present relevance of what God has previously done, while "then is now" does not abolish the future but declares the present relevance of what God will assuredly do (*Ethics*, One). Moreover, these two, typical past and prophetic future, are not alternative visions between which to choose; they are and must remain *one* vision, one faith, one hope. Theology's business is to say how this is so. When theology focuses upon the lasting significance of the ultimate divine future it becomes *eschatology*, the understanding of last things.

To introduce this theme among the doctrines Christians are to believe and teach is to open the door to risk. There is a whiff of the radical here. Last things! To speak of the prophetic is to speak of unsettling visions, revolutionary ideas. It is to contemplate nations in disarray, families divided, the earth shaking, the very stars careening off course (cf. Mark 13:24-27). To insist that Christian faith is eschatological faith is to trouble the sleep of the smug powers *(exousiai)* that appear to control the present and also the sleep of the captive theologies that support them. For

Christians to believe and teach in contradiction to these self-assured authorities is necessarily dangerous.

Yet audacity cannot substitute for honesty, and I will have to concede (§1) that because of the many uses to which 'last things' have been put in Christian history, this is a highly **problematic** locus of Christian teaching. Then (§2) I will present the biblical approach to last things as characteristically representative or **pictorial,** with some main instances of this picture-thinking. Finally (§3), the chapter will ask how this biblical pictorial presentation is **systematically** to be understood, seeking an answer that coheres with the lived experience of the people of early Christian faith as well as later peoples in Christian history. These accounts will direct us to the central narrative of Jesus Christ as the organizing key—and thus point the way for us to move on, in the second Part of this volume, to explore more fully Christ's lordly, suffering, risen presence. This reading of eschatology must not explain away the unsettling pictures that express the Christian hope; it must not minimize them; it needs instead to show how they must be taken (and therefore what the church must teach) if the church is indeed to express *Christian* hope.

§1. Eschatology as a Doctrinal Problem

a. Four eschatological episodes.—It may be helpful to recall our task as that was defined in Chapter One. We ask what the church must teach to be the church. If the faithful church can remain silent about last things, we must say so; if eschatological teaching permits variants and options, we must acknowledge that. If on the other hand there are 'last' truths so central to the church's obedience to Jesus Christ that the church cannot be the church save by confessing and teaching them, we must acknowledge that it is so, however unpopular or awkward these truths may be. To illustrate, I recall here some episodes in the long history of Christian faith in which eschatological teaching has come to the fore.

The first of these episodes is discovered in one of the earliest New Testament writings, 1 Thessalonians. It appears that this church Paul had founded had adopted his teaching about the imminent disclosure of the Lord (*tēn parousian tou kuriou,* 1 Thess. 4:15). Meantime, members of the church had died, the anticipated disclosure had not occurred, and members were lapsing into helpless pagan grief at the loss of their newfound brothers and sisters. Paul's remedy was to offer the church a cameo scene from the awaited end (1 Thess. 4:16ff): the Lord descending "with a shout," the dead in Christ rising first, then ("we") others joining to meet him "in the air," so that all would be with the Lord. For the speculative eschatologist many questions punctuate this paragraph: when, how, in what sequence will these things occur? And for the cool comparative religionist others still: what is the ancient Near Eastern source of these ideas? What myths are displayed? What patterns recur? But the Apostle's express purpose here is neither speculative nor culture-historical: his task is to provide comfort for troubled disciples by telling them the truth. Members' grief at the loss of their friends was intense exactly because love had reshaped their lives since Christ came among them. The depth of that love is the measure of their loss. Paul's response is to assure them that their love is not canceled even by death: the dead in Christ shall rise *first* (1 Thess. 4:16). In this episode, then (and in its repetition at many a Christian graveside since), the apostolic eschatology is **pastoral** and **compensatory.**

Come to a second episode. Now the Christian movement, after some centuries in Europe, has come upon shabby, albeit prosperous, times. Its very success has brought hordes of half-Christians into the church, and many faithful men and women have retreated to hermitage and monastery in order to hold fast the faith once delivered to the saints. Hierarchy has soured Christian brother and sisterhood, and worldly ambition has corrupted old Christian establishments. It is the twelfth century. A monk is gifted with prophetic vision. Finding his monastic order corrupt beyond recovery, he withdraws to establish a new community near the Italian village of Fiore. He writes his visions—three overlapping ages or states *(status)* of God's grace, an age of the Father, age of the Son, age of the Spirit. The third age, herald of the final end, has begun. In it, all God's people will be monastics, faithfulness will flourish, while human establishments, hierarchy, the papacy itself will die away. The visions of Joachim of Fiore (c. 1135–1202) and the "figures" or pictures with which he illustrated them were never precise, never without inner contradictions. But they exerted a powerful impulse in their century and beyond—on monastic orders, on a great council of the Western Church (Fourth Lateran), on the later Franciscans and ultimately on the sixteenth-century radicals—motivating them to purify, reform, rediscover Christian faith in the West (McGinn, 1979:97-148). In this episode, eschatology was **visionary** and **reconstructive,** pointing the way to later reform.

A third episode brings us to North America. By the middle of the nineteenth century, evangelical Christianity, mainly Methodist, Presbyterian, and Baptist, had not only spread widely in the populace, thanks to repeated revivals and tireless home missions, but had given shape to the dominant cultural establishment as well. Colleges and schools, art and literature, science and politics were in the main governed at mid-century by those who professed to be Christians or who at least shared common Christian ideals. Even the Civil War, one of history's bloodiest, was fought, lost, and won mainly by Christian warriors. In any case, a foreign mission enterprise came to flourish, slavery was abolished, woman's lot began slowly to improve. In what today seems too easy a way, the Bible presided over all this, often being regarded as a simple book of truths, recording the past, guiding the present, disclosing the future. Then came a great change. Darwinism in science, a flood of immigrants formed by a different ethos, higher criticism in literature—all seemed to threaten the heartland of American biblical belief. Christians responded in two ways (Marsden, 1980:48-55). One was *adaptation* to the new: modern science and modern social thought were God's new gifts; the developing kingdom of God was identified with this new nineteenth-century enlightenment. This response, which came to be called **liberal,** had roots in early American eschatology. From Jonathan Edwards on, it had taught that Christ's final return would come only *after* a millennium (hence it was called "*post*millennial") of continuing progress within history itself. The other way was *resistance* to the new: it challenged Darwin, questioned the 'foreign' ideology and religion of the new immigrants, rejected the presuppositions of the higher criticism. This second response, in its demand for a distinctive Christian culture, had Edwardsean roots as well, but it opted for a *pre*millennial eschatology. Christ would come in fulfillment of biblical prophecy not at the climax of a thousand years of Christian faithfulness, but suddenly, in judgment upon an apostate and largely unbelieving world. Eventually this response would call itself **Fundamentalist,** and it would reach a significant peak in the twentieth century, generating its own schools, colleges, churches, and social action groups, and dominating large Christian denominations—at one time, Presbyterians, at another, Baptists and Pentecostals.

Our interest now is in the way eschatology figured on both sides of this American conflict. Despite what has been said, it is misleading to think of the great division as merely between two sorts of millennialists, 'post' and 'pre.' For in line with their theories about the Bible, the liberals lost interest in an actual thousand-year period of history, and on the other side, some Fundamentalists continued to be literal *post*millennialists. Nor was a future millennium the linchpin of premillennial eschatology, which was focused instead on a prophetic plan of the ages based more on Daniel 9:24-27 and its 70 "weeks of years," than upon the relatively obscure 1,000 years of Revelation 20:4ff. The point to note is that the controversy between (mainly premillennial) Fundamentalists and their (post or nonmillennial) modernist opponents was in effect a controversy about the Christian attitude to society. Was it to be as liberals believed an attitude of accommodation, or as premillennialists believed, of resistance? This was an enduring question: the opposing sides (albeit with somewhat changed names and agenda) survived and are still with us, and in the previous volume I have taken a stand on some of their issues (*Ethics*, Eight, "The Politics of Forgiveness") disagreeing with both sides sufficiently to have brought their crossfire upon myself. Here it is enough to see that for both sides eschatological views have functioned **in the present:** for the liberals, to ratify their optimistic outlook upon this present age; for their millennial opponents, to express a contempt of the world that they believe is itself biblical, though sociologists might label it world-denying. In this American episode, eschatology is clearly **ethics.**

A fourth episode will complete the sample. About one hundred years ago, German scholar Johannes Weiss made an important breakthrough: the kingdom of God in the New Testament did not refer to the growth of human culture (as the standard liberal view had taught), but as Weiss showed, was a thoroughly eschatological concept: Jesus and his first followers were "fanatics" who expected the imminent end of the age. Albert Schweitzer adopted this reading, which with variants has since become a commonplace of New Testament scholarship. Others might hesitate, but German theology set out in its responsible if ponderous way to incorporate this new datum. For the early Karl Barth eschatology had to do not with the traditional end of the world but with the relation of eternity (God's realm) to time: eschatology (i.e. revelation) impinged uniformly on every moment of worldly time, and "future" could be synonymous with "related to this eternal quality," namely, to the reality of God (Barth, 1921 on Rom. 8:18-25; CD I/1, pp. 530f). Moltmann, recognizing the Kantian style of the early Barth, has dubbed this approach "transcendental eschatology." A related transcendental eschatology that centered more on man *(anthropos)* than God was Rudolf Bultmann's: to live eschatologically is to live authentically in the present, thereby resisting the reign of death that will in any case overtake us each (Bultmann in Bartsch, ed., 1961). Barth's theology challenged a complacent European Christian liberalism with a God who spoke only from beyond and spoke only in Jesus Christ, while Bultmann sought to lead theology into the then current existentialist mode. Another transcendental eschatology was Karl Rahner's: if we understand this present world as the milieu of transcendental spirit, then we have grasped all that *can* be known about last things. For Rahner, the New Testament's eschatology is not revealed information about the future, but projections based on the available present (Rahner, 1978:chap. 9). So the transcendental theology seemed to have met the demand of scholarship without upsetting too much the complacent worldview of Christians in modern society. But in the following theological generation, Jürgen Moltmann took another tack, one that seemed less Kantian and less conservative. In 1964 he published (in Germany) the disturbing *Theology of Hope*, whose last chapter, "Exodus Church," took fresh bearings on the crucified and risen Christ and argued that the Christian church must break out of its socially fixed roles in society in order to become the bearer, catalyst, and servant of a new and liberated society being created worldwide. Christianity was on the side of **change** (Moltmann, 1967:chap. 5).

This last episode seems to differ from the first three, being only a wrangle of theologians rather than a story of apostles, or mystical prophets, or plain Christians struggling to cope with God's future. Yet there is a curious twist at its end. The theologians of hope (Wolfhart Pannenberg as well as Moltmann) were read by Latin American Liberation theologians, who at about the same time (third quarter of the twentieth century) were formulating theologies to do justice to the changing American hemisphere. For these Latin Americans, theology was to be based upon *praxis*, that is, upon a reconception of the church's way of acting in society. The Christian church was no longer to be, as it had been for centuries, the instrument of Hispanic power and privilege in the New World. Such new thinking appeared in both Catholic and non-Catholic churches, and new life stirred in basic communities— Christian gatherings for Bible study, prayer, and self-liberation outside regular ecclesiastical grooves. Moltmann's "Exodus church" spoke to this ferment. His eschatology, wrote Liberationist Gustavo Gutiérrez, "helps us overcome the association between faith and fear of the future which Moltmann rightly considers characteristic of many Christians" (Gutiérrez, 1973:218). And to close the loop, in North America Europe-oriented thinkers such as James Cone, Harvey Cox, and Rosemary Ruether found counsel and comfort in these Latin developments. Moltmann's emphases had dealt with the future, yet rarely with the end of history, and were in this way reminiscent of earlier American postmillennialists. "The world is not yet finished," was his theme (Moltmann, 1967:338). So this episode again shows how eschatology impinges on present history, this time in the form of **liberating self-understanding.**

b. Is eschatology doctrinal?—Now the first consequence of analyzing these episodes (and others that could easily be added) may be to disqualify eschatology as a part of Christian doctrine. If the doctrine of last things is only a screen—and a shifting screen—for pastoral comfort or church reform or social theory or the release of political energies, what right has it (any more than the statistics about church membership gathered by social scientists) to be called church teaching or doctrine? Especially if its futuristic content seems to be so wildly variable, so accessible to current ideology? Here we reach the first problem of Christian eschatology: has it any firm content at all? If so, what is it? Must it be relegated to the realm of myth, stories that are told and repeated to reflect a tribal ethos, rather than God-given truth by which Christians can live, whatever winds may blow?

The objection should not be overstated. The mere appearance of conflict between rival theories does not nullify the existence of a true doctrine. For one thing, that some individual or group may have gotten the matter wrong does not preclude others getting it right. For another, the truth may consist in complementary polar pairs, one aspect being appropriate for one human episode, the other for another. Such is the case with grace, which is God's gift, and faith, here understood as human response. Wise ministry knows when to emphasize the one and when the other; grace and faith are polar but not contradictory. Similarly, fundamentalist detachment from culture and modernist attachment to culture and the corresponding eschatological themes may reflect polar truths (cf. Marsden, 1980). Yet without some doctrinal guidelines, how are we to know whether this is the case? A longstanding interpretation of Christian eschatology says that it is concerned with **what lasts** and with **what comes last** (Althaus, 1948:29); to this we may add its concern with the relation of these two, and thus with the course of **history under the eyes of God.** These are the things about which we wish to know: about the last things in the sense of what abides, of what will remain when all else is done, and of what constitutes the path into that lasting future. To be clear about them, our first priority must be a firm grasp of biblical, and for Christians especially New Testament, teaching.

§2. Pictures of the Kingdom Coming

a. The character of 'picture-thinking'.—Much of New Testament teaching about last things is expressed in word pictures, words that specify and present future scenes; hence it may be helpful carefully to consider what picture-thinking is. Among the masters of twentieth-century thought a special place belongs to the philosopher Ludwig Wittgenstein (1889–1951). Wittgenstein believed that in his day philosophy, and with it the forms of thought in the Western world, had reached a stifling dead end. Although science had acquired great authority, it seemed to offer no opening for religion, or even for common morality. Wittgenstein believed that the accepted forms of thought and reasoning that yielded such results were profound misunderstandings. Moreover, he deeply internalized these problems of thought, and they caused him immense personal suffering. He sought to work his way out of this suffering by writing out his own thoughts; after his death his writings were gradually published by his disciple G. E. M. Anscombe and others. The resultant books disclose a mind finding its way to new ways of thinking, not only thinking in (and about) words, but also in (and about) pictures (see e.g., Wittgenstein, 1953; also Malcolm, 1984; Bartley, 1985; Monk, 1990).

Part of Wittgenstein's effort involved the reconsideration of some well-known psychological puzzles. In one of these, a line drawing represents the head of a duck. But is it a duck? Seen another way, it can instead be the head of a rabbit. What had been the duck's bill becomes the ears of a rabbit facing in the other direction; each line has a new function. This and other phenomena led Wittgenstein to clarify what it could mean to say we see something "as" a duck—or "as" a rabbit. He also investigated the role of pictures— mental pictures, in this case—associated with religious belief, such as the belief in life after death, or in the last judgment (Wittgenstein, 1967). Wittgenstein himself was of Jewish ancestry, was deeply at- tracted to Christianity, but outwardly ad- hered to no church. Yet unlike the professed atheists and skeptics of his day (one thinks of Bertrand Russell), he did not ridicule religious beliefs and the pictures in which they were entertained, or relegate  them (as did the positivists) to the category of mere emotion. By persisting in investigating what were to him profoundly puzzling phenomena such as es- chatological beliefs he attained a degree of clarity about them that can be highly instructive.

It would be more persuasive to repeat here the thought-exercises by which Wittgenstein reached his understanding of the various sorts of thinking, everyday and religious, for which he used the term "picture," but I can provide only a brief summary of some of his results. (1) 'Seeing-as' (seeing a line drawing as a rabbit, for example) is not identical with ordinary seeing (for example, seeing a drawing on an artist's pad), but it has some features in common with the other as well. In certain circumstances, *every* seeing is a 'seeing-as' (Wittgenstein, 1953:Part II, xi). (2) The futuristic pictures that characterize religious belief, such as life after death and the last judgment, are not objects of belief on the basis of ordinary sorts of evidence; and they are *not* the result of better or worse reasoning based on such ordinary evidence, either. (3) On the other hand, they are not *un*reasonable beliefs. What distinguishes those who believe in the last judgment from those who do not is not different chains of reasoning, but radically different **pictures** of how in general the world goes. (Though Wittgenstein chose not to use the words, we might say this is a difference in their respective worldviews or *convictions*.) (4) For the believer in the last judgment, "Whenever he does anything [, that picture] is before his mind"; Wittgenstein said that such a picture, once it is grasped, is *"enough to make me change my whole life"* (1967:53, 57, emphasis added).

It seems that in these reflections about everyday perceiving and about religious belief Wittgenstein correctly saw at least part of the way these diverse seeings function: interpretation in these cases is 'context-dependent.' Our task is to follow up the thought that those who *do* have "before their minds" the last judgment (and other pictures of the end) necessarily find these pictures *life-changing*. (Incidentally, conclusions such as [2] and [3] above have led some to protest that they imply fideism or blind faith, but that does not seem to me to be either true, or what Wittgenstein intended.) So to the four results just listed, I now add two that I think cohere with them: (5) What distinguishes one person's 'seeing-as' from another's is, to speak broadly, the connections that each makes between the picture itself and something more: in the duck-rabbit case, one connects it with one's knowledge of what ducks (rabbits) look like; in the case of the last judgment, one may relate it to other pictures of the end, and also to the present. *It is making these connections* (or failing to make them) that distinguishes biblical faith in the last judgment from mere fantasies that have no recognizable life consequences. (6) The required connections need not be temporal or spatial or causal ones. In order to believe in the last judgment, we need not be able to fit it into a chronology of other last (or penultimate) beliefs; in order to believe in a real heaven or hell we need not be prepared to supply its spatial coordinates with respect to earth, sun, or stars. In another vein, in order to believe in heaven, we need not believe we deserve it. What sort of connections, then, do we supply?

b. Some concrete end-pictures.—To answer, it will be best to put some flesh on these bony philosophical points, and for the sake of continuity, to begin with the picture of the last judgment as it appears in the New Testament—not to make it chief or central, but lest it be overlooked in the end!

i. The last judgment.—It was the strong conviction of the apocalyptic prophets that God who had acted so decisively to set Israel's history in motion would act again to bring that history to closure, and with it, the history of all the world. This action would finally judge Israel (and the world); it would also consummate God's salvific purpose first displayed in the Exodus. Thus the poem that concludes Malachi warns of a coming day that "like a furnace" will burn the proud and their works, leaving "neither root nor branch" (4:1). But those who fear "the name," that is, stand in awe of the very being or character of JHWH, will on that same day "break loose like calves released from the stall": for them the fire's heat will be that of the "sun of righteousness" (v. 2) as the new day dawns. The New Testament writings treat this prophetic day of judgment as a given (see 1 John 4:17; Heb. 9:27; Jude 6). Yet we have seen that such pictures have connections. In the New Testament everything is brought into connection with Jesus Christ and his coming, so that the picture of judgment now has a new center.

An example of such a connection is the judgment scene of Matthew 25:31-46. In many ways this picture repeats the themes of Malachi: a judgment day, set now in a royal court, issuing in a separation of the blessed from the cursed that becomes the final destiny of each. Of great interest, though, are the differences: there is the humanized identity of the judge, there is the image of the shepherd dividing his own flock, there is the new standard or test of judgment, there is the element of surprise for both the "sheep" and the "goats." If we understood Malachi to say that indeed there will be a final righting of earth's wrongs, a *last* judgment, then the further task of Matthew must be to show how that applies to hearers of the good news in Jesus. What is the new insight into the true nature of God's judgment?

John Donahue, in his valuable book on Jesus' parables, holds with T. W. Manson that the 'life setting' of the sheep and goats parable was the early Christian mission. As disciples went preaching the gospel, they would meet varied receptions. Yet they were to know that as the nations received or rejected "the least of these" missionaries (Matt. 25:40), they thereby received or rejected Christ and were accordingly judged. Donahue argues against a traditional "universalist" reading that finds here only the impartial hand of a God who judges not by creeds or names (not even the name of Jesus) but merely on the basis of acts of simple kindness: visiting the sick, feeding the hungry, receiving the stranger. The trouble with this simplistic reading is that it has no place for Jesus and his apostles; they are made irrelevant to the story. Donahue's own interpretation is equally free, he says, from "sectarian" narrowness; for him the real work of the parable is to teach that "justice is constituted by acts of lovingkindness and mercy to those in need"; the deeds of the nations disclose their justice or lack of it (1988:109-25). Notice, though, that for both Donahue and his opponents the parable is only about what constitutes true justice now and is not in any special way about the end of the world. Both readings rightly emphasize *what lasts* (the deeds of lovingkindness), but both wrongly neglect *what comes last*—God's own judgment. Yet eschatology is about both, and about the course of history that leads from the one to the other. Even the best modern interpretation, if it overlooks what comes last, significantly changes the parable. Is it possible to restore these final elements to Matthew's picture, and with them, Jesus the royal Judge as well?

Consider again the question, What is to be measured in God's judgment, according to this 'last-things' picture? Deeds of generosity, care, the meeting of human needs, we may answer. This is reassuring, because most of us do some of these things some of the time. But in the parable, it is only such deeds directed toward "the least of these my brethren" that count. So it is not the care we expend upon friends and family, or even our kindness to the 'deserving poor.' Such acts are not condemned here. They have their place. But in this picture, *at the end* they are not pivotal. Further, "the righteous" are startled to discover that they have performed any deeds of such critical value. "Lord, when?" they ask. But how could they not know? And it is the same with those "on the left hand"; they, too, are unaware of having neglected the King. How, we may ask, can "the nations" be so unaware of what matters so much? Is not the answer that the 'least' who were helped by these acts (or harmed by this neglect) are *in the eyes of the nations* not even the least—they are beneath the threshold of awareness and have simply gone unnoticed (Farmer, 1938:164ff)? And that is the very reason that they provide test cases. How the "sheep" and "goats" behaved when they could not think it counted—that is what counts, for that is what has disclosed their true character. What they have been and are is reflected in "their uncalculating love, their 'aimless' faithfulness" or its absence; that is what exhibits their destiny (*Ethics*, p. 59).

Consider next, Who is this final judge? We have spoken as if it were "God," and that is in a general way correct. But in the parable it is a king (acting as a shepherd) who judges, and we are told at the outset who this royal, shepherding judge is. He is "the Son of Man . . . in his glory and all the angels with him" (Matt. 25:31). At this stage of Matthew's Gospel, the term *huios tou anthropou* ("Child of Humanity," "Truly Human One") has become a technical term for the returning Lord Jesus. So it is Jesus—now crucified, risen, returning—who is the Judge. The deeds that unconsciously display true character matter finally because, even standing alone, they reflect the *relation between those who are under judgment and that One.* (Which, we can note in passing, is remarkably like the teaching about salvation by faith in him, or "in his name," that is normative in the Epistles and Acts.) Thus the grand answer to the question about judgment is indeed an answer about what comes last. He who comes last is the judge, both because his own character is the measure of human conduct, and because the kingdom or rule of God is his own rule or kingdom. He himself is the King or Judge. It is this royal judge over all the nations who is both the first and the last (cf. Rev. 1:8).

Consider third the question, What does he do at the end, this Ruler or Judge who is the Truly Human One who is the crucified, risen, returning Jesus? The answer is the *action* of the King. In ancient times monarchs were by their office supreme judge in their realms; our law 'courts' are direct successors of these royal courts. The picture here is a motion picture; it displays a King who is not history's bystander, but who sits as judge, whose judgment is not a rubber stamp of our judgments, but has an element of unavoidable surprise. It is he who judges, and not anyone else, not the "nations," not even the "least." In this final act of the play, he is the decisive Actor, disposing of all the others' actions. Only that last act can fully show the relevance of John Donahue's contextual reading: the parable is indeed a parable of a Christian mission whose aim is to bear the "name" (that is, the character) of the Christ to all nations. Judgment, as pictured here, is eschatological because it brings climactically to light that quiet history that is God's true history, and with it all other history. In this judgment the character that will be vindicated is that which *will* recognize, in Jesus the Judge, a right standard by which to be judged. We will be able to ask only this: "When, if ever, have our self-disclosing deeds revealed such character in us?"

These are the connections that this picture brings with it; the connections we must see if we see it as the *last* judgment. There are questions it does *not* answer, must not be used to answer: How are "nations" related to individual men and women under judgment? What of the judgment of those who die untouched by the message of Jesus, and those who die possessed of distorted versions of that message? What is eternal punishment, and what is eternal life (Matt. 25:46)? These are understandable questions because they acknowledge that pictures need connections. But they are mistaken if they are put as demands to *this* picture—much as if we asked where the Prodigal Son's mother was in that story, or asked where Joseph the father appears in a sculptor's *pieta.* It is this picture, this scene, that speaks; we must hear its own message; it must show us its own connections. There will be time enough for other pictures and their links.

Other judgment scenes appear in Scripture. Second Peter (2:6-9) suggests that acts of God within Hebrew history—the destruction of Sodom and Gomorrah and the rescue of "righteous Lot"—provide models for the coming day of judgment (2 Pet. 3:7, 10). Revelation (20:4, 11-15) offers sweeping, apocalyptic judgment scenes that climax with "death and Hades" themselves being thrown into "the lake of fire" (Rev. 20:14) that consumes everything—presumably indicating the abolition of every rival to the "new heaven and new earth" of chapter 21. Bible dictionaries list these and other scenes in both testaments. If we ask how in general they are to be approached, the late John McKenzie has offered two helpful guidelines: the first is that the crucial element in our being judged is our *present* confrontation with Jesus Christ (cf. John 5, as well as Matthew 25). As McKenzie says, for each of us *the* day of judgment is the day on which we make "a permanent decision to accept Jesus Christ or to reject him." Or as I have put it, "The church on the day of judgment is the church *now*." Thus judgment's inevitable surprise can be also a present surprise, the surprise of salvation here and now. The other guideline on which McKenzie rightly insists is that nevertheless, judgment is not only now, but at the end. Discount as we may the "imagery" of Scripture's scenes, this final picture remains. Even if we prefer to reduce it to the severe abstraction of a Mondrian painting in which all visual detail is erased as irrelevant, it nevertheless pictures a judgment that ends history in God's verdict and justice, not our own. (Otherwise, the evil that God opposes remains as eternal as God.) (DB, 468f)

ii. Jesus Christ returning.—Since the picture of judgment has been sketched at length, others may be treated more briefly in the confidence that the reader will see how to continue. Directly connected with the last judgment is the picture of Christ who comes finally. This picture is necessarily a composite one in the mind of the New Testament reader; it grows from a varied series of expressions (not only *parousia*, evident presence, but also *apokalupsis*, unveiling, *epiphaneia*, disclosure, and simply *erchomenos*, coming) used of Jesus, of the kingdom, and of the last day. The recovery of this picture in its biblical form is complicated further by the Gospel narratives, for in key passages, Jesus' future "coming" seems sometimes to mean his risen self-disclosure at the first Easter or even in his transfiguration (see, e.g., Mark 8:38); yet the same terms could be used to express the last coming. And there is a further problem: in main strands of New Testament teaching such as Paul's, the risen Jesus is understood to be not absent but present (cf. Gal. 2:20; John 14:18; etc.)—so how can he *return*? (Here it is helpful to learn that several of the key terms for this 'return' mean not "arrival" but "disclosure," and one of them, *parousia*, could be a technical term for the *official* visit of a ruler within his own realm.) This complexity is well reflected in the Johannine literature, where Jesus' appearance is not only "on the last day" (John 6:39), but also in the gift of the Spirit, in the eucharistic meal, at the death of believers, and in history's crashing crises. Perhaps due to deliberate Johannine ambiguity, we cannot always be sure which of these is meant in a particular passage (see, e.g., John 8:20, 9:39, 12:15ff, 14:3ff, 15:26, 21:13, 21:22f).

Traditional Christian teaching has merged these many 'comings' and assigned them all to history's end, but in doing so it may have drained the composite picture of its depth even while it intensified the distance between the first and later New Testament readers. If there is only one 'coming,' and that at history's end, then the early Christians' anticipations were necessarily mistaken. We need a way of reading Scripture that does not force the picture of his coming into our own preconceived frames, but allows its visual depth to address us in our own contexts, just as the many 'comings' of which they spoke addressed early Christians in theirs. In appropriating this depth, two points to emphasize will be (1) the futurity of his coming ("he *will* come," say the messengers of Acts 1:11): Christ has more to do yet; the end is not yet (Matt. 24:6); and (2) the continuity of the one returning with the one they already know. It is "this same Jesus" (Acts 1:11 KJV) who will come in all his comings— in our Lord's day worship, in history's course as yet unfinished, at our last end, and at *the* last end, it is ever *Jesus* Christ who comes.

iii. Resurrection.—Christ is the judge; it is Christ who comes; all the more does the biblical resurrection-picture center on this Christ. Here is a minor hitch in this volume's method; something must be said here about the resurrection of believers, while in fact this end-picture took shape only in connection with the resurrection of Jesus, to be discussed in Chapter Six (but see also *Ethics*, Part III). So we must note all the more carefully here that the biblical picture of the resurrection of believers was developed and fixed in the chemistry of new-found faith in Christ. If he arose, they believed, we, too, shall rise. Here the great picture is that provided in 1 Corinthians 15. Paul's opponents at Corinth denied all futurity to Christian faith, not because as skeptics they believed too little, but because as fanatics they believed too much. Thus Paul must write to them, with heavy irony, "No doubt you already have all you could desire; you have come into your fortune already! . . . you have come into your kingdom" (1 Cor. 4:8). In this context, Paul's strong emphasis is necessarily upon the futurity of resurrection, a futurity he displays with a painter's skill. "What is sown as a perishable thing is raised imperishable. Sown in humiliation, it is raised in glory; sown in weakness, it is raised in power" (1 Cor. 15:42f). Thus the figure of planting and harvest becomes a model for a future common life for believers, a life beyond death itself. Christ is alive; thus we shall be with Christ. "O Death, where is your victory? O Death, where is your sting?" Paul asks (1 Cor. 15:55; cf. Hos. 13:14).

Here the Apostle touches on a feature of this picture that we may well note: it is by means of our (perishable) bodies that we have to do with (likewise perishable) nature. The rocks we climb over or pile up, the living creatures upon which we feed, the other creatures we know and by whom we are known—all these are accessible to us, and we to them, exactly in our own organic, embodied selfhood (cf. *Ethics*, Three). When at last we receive imperishable bodies, then the picture that is conveyed is life in a new, imperishable natural order ("new heavens and new earth" in Revelation 21) whose features are to be known to us by way of the no longer perishable embodied selfhood that is to be ours in the resurrection.

Most of the Old Testament, however, is actually silent about any individual future beyond the surd fact of death. The Hebraic sense of corporate solidarity discouraged what was fluttering through contemporary Hellenism, the images of immortal individual souls. Thus the New Testament picture of the believer's resurrection is almost a new biblical departure (Isa. 26:19, 53:10-12, and Ezek. 37:1-14 may be exceptions). In line with this reticence, but driven by the new fact of the risen Christ, Paul with other New Testament authors anticipates a *corporate* resurrection of believers: *"we* shall rise." So strong is this "we" that sometimes the resurrection picture becomes one of a general resurrection of *all* people—the just and the unjust as well—though that leads back again to the picture of a separating judgment to follow. This suggests another set of pictures, those of death, of heaven, and of hell.

iv. Death, hell, and heaven.—The striking thing about the biblical understanding of death, when it is compared with other understandings held by ancient peoples, is its remarkably restrained, empirical, and matter-of-fact quality. While Egyptian culture evoked elaborate tales of underworld journeys by the dead and prepared extravagant pyramid tombs to ready dead monarchs for an afterlife, the Old Testament writers, with few exceptions, understood death in a thoroughly biological, factual way—it is life's end. That did not mean that they liked it; death, and especially death at the hand of an enemy, is treated as a terrible loss, and many times God is implored to save the Psalmist's 'soul,' that is, life *(nephesh)* from death. The most that could be hoped for was a ripe old age ended by a quick and merciful death, a dignified departure from this life. Yet by the time of Jesus, a change, coherent with other changes in Hebraic eschatological thinking, had taken place: now there was talk of life *after* death, and in particular the Jewish community nearest to Jesus, the Pharisees, accepted this new teaching. This hope did not change the fact that death was the enemy, so that Jesus in the Garden of Gethsemane would still face his own death with apprehension and agony—and yet with acceptance: "not my will, but yours" (Matt. 26:39). Ultimately the death of Christ became the crux of Christian under-standing; how could God allow not only death but this shameful death to destroy his unique Son? Yet out of that question, guided by reflections already present in Second Isaiah and elsewhere in Scripture, grew the interpretation of Jesus' death that shapes the Gospels themselves—his death was substitutionary, atoning, a sacrifice for others, a way of redeeming the kingdom itself (Chapter Five). Paul, in one of his para-doxes, made of death at once the "last enemy" and the path to final union with Christ: "For to me life is Christ, and death is gain" (Phil. 1:21). Thus Jesus, accepting for himself the terrors of death on behalf of his followers, succeeded in transforming for them this brute fact—we *shall* die—into another, something strange and new.

While the biblical view is matter-of-fact, it certainly treats death with the utmost seriousness. There is in Scripture no denial of death: what-ever the doctrine of resurrection meant, it did not mean that death was already abolished, or its fangs drawn. Death is real, and it matters ultimately. If there is any other "last thing" that can overcome it, it can do so only by acknowledging and accepting this last reality for what it is.

Thus there can be no surprise in seeing that the picture of death as one's end had a strong symbolic as well as a matter-of-fact value. In the beginning there was the punishment God dealt Adam and Eve for their prototypical disobedience: "Dust you are, to dust you will return" (Gen. 3:19b). Not only would they with all living things some day die, but now their death had a sad new meaning; it must be construed as punishment. The Apostle Paul took that story to mean that human death in general was to be so construed—each human being, by becoming a sinner, comes under the "reign" of death (Rom. 5:12-17). And here a second symbolic function appears: death itself is assigned a bigger-than-human role; it is viewed as an alien power arrayed against humanity, the "last enemy" of 1 Corinthians (15:26). But to see death as an alien power is also, for Paul, to see it as subject to the triumphant reversal Christ achieved on his cross, one of the enemies he there "disarmed" (Col. 2:15).

So the picture of death that remains for Christian faith is at once deadly serious and profoundly awe-inspiring: believers cannot be flip-pant about human death; it remains one of their pictures of the end; yet they cannot take it as their only picture, cannot take it as God's *last* 'last word': The disintegration of embodied existence that is threat and grim fact and punishment and loss becomes as well the terminal or transfer station where believers await another picture, another word from their risen Lord.

First, though, we must examine a related picture, that of a *hell* of punishment and destruction, that has possibly retained more power than all the rest in the modern imagination, while it has also been put to more abuse and misuse, not only by outsiders, but also by incautious Christians. Once again we have a picture with multiple renderings. The Old Testament spoke sometimes of *Sheol* (which became *Hades* in Greek) as if it were a place, but in fact it was there a poetic synonym for death—the 'place' that was no place, the realm of nonbeing, from which there was no return. God might rescue one's soul from death or Sheol, but this simply meant that though one was as good as dead due to deadly enemies or illness, God might still effect a rescue (cf. Ps. 23:4). In the New Testament there appears *Gehenna*, which had indeed in the first instance been a place, a valley near Jerusalem, darkly associated with pagan worship involving human sacrifice—the passing of children through fire (cf. Jeremiah, chaps. 7, 19). In line with literature beyond the canon such as 1 Enoch, *Gehenna* in the Gospels becomes the place of future punishment, a place of unquenchable fire, a pit where the wicked are destroyed body and soul. In Matthew it is said to be "prepared for the devil and his angels" (25:41 NRSV). Even so, the *Gehenna* image rarely appears in the New Testament outside the synoptic Gospels. Instead the threat of future punishment or warning of life's utter failure is represented by judgment (John), or by wrath, or death, or having no share in the kingdom (Paul). John McKenzie (DB, 300) suggests a reason for this shift: the first Christian missionaries did not find this Semitic picture well suited to the Gentile context of their mission, though the canonical Gospels remained faithful to the very language of Jesus. If we superimpose these several New Testament images upon one another, we have the sense of a future category (not always a 'place') of destruction, nonentity, failure, retribution, and utter loss—the denial of all that life strives for and by God's grace can be. Its fires (though not the refuse that fuels the fires) are depicted as unquenchable; its character is darkness, the absence of life and love and—most desperately—the absence of God.

One cannot pass by this one picture of last things without noting its remarkable power in Western Christendom: Those who know little else of the Christian message are nevertheless fascinated by the biblical image of hell (contrariwise, the old Germanic word chosen as equivalent to *Gehenna* can mean a place of hiding or concealment, and actually a *safe* place). In response, we can note, first, that if hell is indeed a truly ultimate picture then it is also (by our "then is now" hermeneutic) a *present* ultimate, not only present in anticipation but present in experience. Remember that the metaphors Scripture uses to describe a last-things hell are all drawn from the present experience of writer and reader: fire out of control, darkness and cruelty, suffering and the abyss—these are fearful exactly because they beset actual life in Bible times and beset it still today. Hell is a reality long before death comes; it is a 'living death' here and now. The second note is that most if not all the warnings about this present and future terror are addressed, not to nameless and distant pagans, but to God's own people, to the followers of Moses and of Jesus. "For we *know* who it is that said, 'Justice is mine: I will repay;' and again, 'The Lord will judge *his people*'" (Heb. 10:29f, emphasized).

We must also recall that this fascination with hell in modern times has produced its own powerful reaction. In the nineteenth century a controversy raged over the legitimacy of the doctrine of hell (O. Chadwick, 1975:104ff). Three possibilities appeared: (1) hell means **annihilation,** the simple cessation of being (which is punishment enough to those who love life); (2) hell is finite, and in retrospect will have seemed a sort of **purgatory** so that finally all are redeemed; and (3) hell is **endless** and without escape. Even from the last there were various saving exceptions: those dying in infancy are not liable to punishment; those who have never heard the gospel cannot be liable to the penalty of its rejection; there are other paths to salvation. Thus by the twentieth century most Christian churches had either abandoned or softened the punishment doctrine, and outstanding theologians of many schools turned to the old *apokatastasis* theory of Origen of Alexandria, the final redemption of all (*De prin.* xxi, xxxiv; cf. 1 Cor. 15:23-26). Once the flexibility and variety of biblical teaching become clear, two issues remain for Christians confronting the picture of hell: one is the question of the ethics of punishment in its relation to forgiveness and redemption (cf. *Ethics*, pp. 223f, 237f, 312); the other is the enormous moral power of the picture of hell—a picture of human impudence finally checked, demonic rebellion finally overmatched by divine holiness. My question, then, is not whether hell has a place among the end-pictures (assuredly it does), but how to assess that place rightly, how to understand hell itself; and the secret (as I will suggest in §3 below) is the ordering of the end-pictures so that it is finally Christ who dominates our understanding and employment of them each.

Earth, Karl Barth once said in explaining the phrase "Maker of heaven and earth" in the Apostles' Creed, is the creation that is conceivable to human beings; **heaven** is the creation that is inconceivable to us (1949:9). By that standard, I now face not a difficult but an impossible task—to tell about the inconceivable! Yet the central difficulty is also the key to what must be said—that it is God's heaven not ours. What must once have been the awareness of a youthful Near Eastern people, that God's abode was in the inaccessible skies above, became in time the expression of a more profound theological truth. "Heaven" was then the realm of God's perfect reign, the model for earthly aspiration: "your will be done, on earth as in heaven" (Matt. 6:10). Thus to express confidence in a future with God, the Apostle could speak of a coming heavenly habitation, in contrast with this present life which is only "the earthly frame." For "what is seen is transient, what is unseen is eternal" (2 Cor. 4:18–5:2).

Yet heaven is for Paul not only a "dwelling" (*oikos*), but also a "household" (*oikia*, an extended family), and a "commonwealth" (*politeuma*) to which Paul the exile might come home; heaven was his native country (2 Cor. 4:18b–5:4; Phil. 3:20). In this regard, the biblical heaven is utterly unlike the biblical hell—hell is alienating and lonely, while heaven is a shared estate; its inhabitants have to do one with another as well as with the mysterious, sentient angels and with their chief citizen and Lord, the Son of man and his heavenly Father.

To see heaven through eyes focused upon Jesus Christ is to meet another, related theme as well: heaven has a history, a story. In Ulrich Simon's intratextual summary, Jesus is engaged in combat not only with earthly but with 'heavenly' or spiritual beings (Mark 1:12f; Luke 10:17-20), the rebellious demons who infest human beings and oppose Jesus' coming kingship—a sovereignty whose rights they nevertheless recognize (Mark 1:24). So the triumph in Jesus' warfare is a "cosmic" victory that culminates at the cross (Col. 2:15). There these enemies and their prince (John 16:11?) are judged and defeated though not yet destroyed. Rather, the war between heaven and its enemies now enters a terminal stage (Eph. 6:11ff) that will end in the utter rout of the demons (U. Simon, 1958:chaps. 5f). If such a mythic retelling of Scripture's story strains the imagination of modern readers, it may nonetheless serve to remind us of modernity's own demonic forces (cf. *Ethics*, chap. 6), and to that extent help us to see that heaven is in the end our last hope as well.

It is noteworthy, on the other hand, that New Testament talk of the heavenly future makes nothing of many of the strongest ties in earthly life. When Jesus is challenged by Sadducees to answer a trick question about marriage after the resurrection, he simply denies its relevance to the coming aeon. God, he says, is "God of the living," a solution that not only rejects Sadducean skepticism about an afterlife, but also confutes their preoccupation with the orderly laws of inheritance and property ownership (Myers, 1988:314-17). The message of heaven in Jesus' preaching is the formation of a new *politeia*, a new earthly order of society already displacing the old. In it, family ties cannot be the *last* word, for God is forming a new, heavenly family for the age to come (Mark 12:18-27 par.). For the New Testament, heaven is corporate and communal: whether departed saints are "present with the Lord" (2 Cor. 5:8) or have "fallen asleep" (1 Cor. 15:6) for the interim before the resurrection of the saints—or whether, as many of the Radical Reformation believed (G. Williams, 1962, s.v. "psychopannychism"; see also Yoder, 1968:109ff), they are "asleep in Christ" (1 Cor. 15:18), an expression that seems to combine the other two—in any case the picture of heaven will be altogether fulfilled only in that rising with Christ in which together we share with him a corporate, communal divine life, a heavenly "life everlasting."

In Chapter Nine I will try to show that heaven's best gift, the presence of the risen Lord Jesus, is enjoyed already when as disciples we engage in the "word and worship, work and witness" of the church. Here we may note that among these, *worship* is uniquely lifted up in Scripture as the earthly analog of heaven. Already in the Old Testament this connection appears in the story of Jacob's dream (Gen. 28:10-22); it appears again at the temple dedication, when Solomon "spread forth his hands toward heaven" and prayed to a God whom "heaven and the highest heaven cannot contain" (1 Kings 8:22f). If heaven cannot, neither can our forms of worship. But in the book of Revelation, chapters 4 and 5, John "in the Spirit" finds himself before heaven's throne and witnesses heaven's own worship. There earth's best, true story—of a Lion who conquers by taking the form of a Lamb slain—is celebrated anew. If there is a cosmic correspondence between the worship in heaven and that in the congregation of God on earth, then the everlasting element in earthly worship must be its telling and retelling of the story of that Lamb.

v. The rule of God and other pictures.—There are still other pictures of the future in Scripture: new heavens and a new earth, the stormy clouds of heaven, the thief who comes by night, a recurrent, naked human figure, a great dragon, an earthquake, a certain thousand years, the keys of the kingdom, a trumpet sounding (cf. Minear, 1946). These shade over into a still richer biblical picture gallery too full to be reckoned here. One picture, however, is so central and inclusive that I have made it the heading over this Part of the present volume: the *rule* (or kingdom) of Jesus Messiah. Since this has been sketched above, it is mentioned again here only lest it be overlooked. In fact, none must be overlooked. The episodes related above (§1a) show how in varying contexts Christian need has arisen for different pictures, but their role is established not only by contextual need but also by their place in

Scripture and in the mind of Christ (cf. Phil. 2:5-11). The task now is to say how we are to come to terms with all these pictures and how they may be brought to bear upon doctrine.

§3. The Christian Doctrine of Last Things

a. Resolving the problem of eschatology.—We now have in hand nearly all the elements necessary to resolve the difficult problem of Christian knowledge of last things. The previous section has shown us the difficulty of bringing the mixed eschatological themes and pictures of the New Testament into a coherent account adequate to the demands of Christian teaching. Although many theorists, some of them quite ingenious, have shown that these themes can be assembled in various chronological schemes, no one scheme has won general assent. Are we left, then, with the practical result that while Christians have these vivid pictures, much as we might have a book of illustrations but with no text to tell us if a picture is a 'duck' or a 'rabbit,' there are no instructions for using our pictures, either? Have we no eschatological *doctrine* as such? That would be to lose all the ground gained: eschatology would be, not our first doctrine, but no Christian doctrine at all. Further progress, however, depends upon greater clarity about how the early Christians themselves understood their pictures. It has become a commonplace of theology that their teaching rested upon a mistake, though there is disagreement as to who was mistaken: Was it first-century Judaism that mistakenly thought in apocalyptic terms and was corrected by a Jesus who (although he used eschatological language) intended his message only in nonfuturistic terms (thus the "realized eschatology" of C. H. Dodd, 1935)? Or was it some of the earliest followers of Jesus (A.D. 30–50) who were the apocalyptic fanatics, so that they had to be corrected by a subsequent Christian generation who smoothed over these strange traditions in the process of composing the documents we know as the New Testament (thus Käsemann, 1969:82-137)? Or did the mistake lie with the entire New Testament corpus and especially with Paul, who expected a return of Christ so soon that there was little use in attending to everyday life on earth—a mistake that had to be corrected by early Catholicism when it recognized the true state of affairs (Werner, 1941)? Or (though this option often fails to appear in New Testament scholars' books) is the mistake our own for supposing the early Christians and perhaps also Jesus mistaken? (Trocmé, 1973:chap. 15; Travis, 1980:chap. 5; refs. in Yoder, 1972:109ff). But how could they not be?

In *Last Things First*, black theologian Gayraud Wilmore offers a helpful insight. In the course of investigating the eschatology of black churches, Wilmore came across John Mbiti's study of African concepts of time (1969). Believing with many others that despite their suppression, many of these concepts had persisted among American blacks, Wilmore inferred that the "otherworldliness" of American black churches was in fact a much more complex phenomenon than is often perceived. Black American Christians have blurred hope of liberation and hope of heaven together, yet both hopes matter. Quoting the typical spiritual, "All God's Chillun," Wilmore acknowledges that on its surface, like Mbiti's black Africans, the spiritual expresses a near expectation of another world that seems material to its core:

> I got a robe, you got a robe,
> All God's chillun got a robe,
> When I get to Heav'm, goin' put on my robe,
> Goin' to shout all over God's Heav'm.

Yet to Wilmore the spiritual speaks not only of a material heaven of fine clothing but also of an earthly world of human rights and human needs that cry out for fulfillment; the spiritual is at once a celebration of the hereafter and a present claim upon the here and now—if heaven is not Apartheid country, singers will be free to shout all over it; should they not therefore now be free *all over* earth as well? Where human needs are met in heaven's ways, God's will is being done. For Wilmore, "an eschatological people" is "one in whom the hope of the Kingdom to come provides the motivating power for living . . . [and] dominates and regulates the self-understanding and behavior." If the people of the New Testament were in this sense an eschatological people, may not **a foreshortened sense of time** have positively aided them as it did American blacks and (pace *Mbiti*) as it may have aided new African Christians in their grasp of the last things? (Wilmore, 1982:67; see further chaps. 5f) To employ a pictorial term to speak of time, the Africans Mbiti studied necessarily viewed future events from such a foreshortened perspective. For them, the time between what is near and the last things is *compressed* in order to give due weight to those last events. Without such foreshortening, what comes last might be perspectively projected into the far future and thus into insignificance—and that indeed seems to have been the consequence of some Western thinking about last things (cf. Bultmann in Bartsch, ed., 1961:5).

Now we can assemble our material and make our own approach to the doctrine of last things. One feature that has previously appeared is the diversity of past eschatological thought. The resurrections, kingdoms, millennia, visions, dreams, fulfillments, the ethnic and racial and individual varieties of that teaching display a phantasmagoria of futures, a plenitude of possibilities beyond our scope even to catalog here. Even if we could prune away subsequent outgrowth of Christian teaching and limit ourselves to the witness of Scripture alone, there would remain a plethora of futures, and no simple reduction of these has offered itself. Or perhaps we should say that where such an ordering has seemed possible to one interpreter, even to a pious, spiritual, and learned interpreter, others of equal devotion and scholarship have appeared to contradict the first—and we are back to the phantasmagoria of historical variants.

The present work's approach has discerned in Scripture certain dominant images or *pictures* of last things, pictures whose power and persistence give an order, albeit a pictorial not a chronological order, to biblical eschatology. With these pictures—of the kingdom, resurrection, death, judgment, hell, heaven, and Christ's comings—thinkers in every Christian age have consoled the flock of God, deepened their meditative insight into God's ways, guided their own lives, and formed the minds of their followers. But how are we to understand the pictures? To leap ahead, I believe the correct answer will require us to understand them *literally*, a term I take to mean simply that they must be received *as* the true pictures that they are, and as the *sort* of picture that they are. More concretely, "literally" means not as myths (at least not as that word is widely understood), not as a code to be deciphered, not as fragments of a puzzle to be assembled by clever modern fingers, and not as grotesque caricatures of themselves, but as the pictures, the true, glinting, dancing, awesome, God-given visions that, collected, constitute promise and warning to God's people. It may be that we are dissatisfied with such pictures: we may complain that they do not answer our legitimate doctrinal questions. We may (with premillennial chartmakers) prefer to be told the role of Russia, or of present-day Israel, or of America today, in "God's plan of the ages"—that is, we may prefer to correlate history as we see it with God's penultimate history. Or we may (with some theological philosophers) like to be offered a cool, clear, aseptic account, even a 'scientific' account, that will shelve these powerful biblical pictures as an adult shelves the toys of childhood. Or we may (with Bultmannian theologians) wish for a demythologized theology that by its hermeneutic alchemy will transmute Scripture's base pictures into the gold of authentic self-awareness, leaving no mythical residue behind. And alongside these high, theoretical strategies there is a homely but also powerful temptation: we want to know the future of our friends, neighbors, and near kin—want to see beyond the veil of the future, want to be satisfied that our preferences for the future are indeed God's own. But the pictures do not really fulfill any of these wants, plain or fancy. They remain just the pictures that they are, each located at once in the then of the last day and in the now of our own last truths: judgment, hell, death, resurrection, heaven, the kingdom, and the unfailing coming of our Lord.

Yet as we look at the pictures, we are not altogether without theological help and hope. For alongside them we have now introduced two skills of thinking that may be less familiar to modern, Western Christians. One is the **foreshortened sense of future time** that has frequently characterized Christian proclamation. The other is the **prophetic (or baptist) vision,** a typological approach to present-day faithfulness. By recognizing foreshortening, we give up a *misleading* sense of the future's immediacy. By the prophetic vision, disciples learn to see the present under the form of the biblical past, so that their present 'is' that past, but to see it also under the form of the prophetic future, so that the future 'is' also coming *now*. Many have grasped this trioptic biblical vision in part; my effort here is to employ it fully and consistently. By this vision, disciples live by the faithfulness of the Christ who *was* and *is* and *is to come*, the First and the Last. Thus it is with both of these tools, the recognition of foreshortening and the grasp of the vision, that we confront the glimmering, hinting eschatological pictures—the present truth of what shall be—that are God's way of redeeming our own times. With these tools we can see why, in Wittgenstein's phrase, the pictures are "enough to make me change my whole life," enough to shape the life of an entire community.

These biblical thought modes are the raw material of Christian eschatology. By their means God's people have from time to time been renewed in hope. To the extent that theology has failed to make these modes of thought explicit, it has not faithfully represented the Christian hope in last things. In cases of such failure (and does not Christian thinking in the West today present such a case?) the teaching task becomes a double one. On the one hand, the church must faithfully present the pictures themselves, all of them, since together they express the Christian hope. On the other, it must be aware of its ministry to those so enclosed by the present age that for practical purposes they cannot look at the pictures, may even think they have no need of them! It must be ready to employ its skills (such skills as the understanding of foreshortening and the explicit use of the prophetic vision) to open blind modern eyes. For this gallery of pictures is not optional; nothing can take its place. In Western culture, at least, the first needy pupil will likely be the church itself. This self-teaching will require biblical study and the study of Christian history; some representative narratives have been introduced into this chapter. These are presented as aids to the eschatological *way* of thinking as well as clues to eschatological content.

b. Test cases: Mark 13 and Hans Hut.—To make these claims concrete, I now propose to examine a crucial New Testament passage, Mark 13, and to follow it with an important but often overlooked chapter in church history, the lifework of Hans Hut.

i. Mark 13.—In line with early catechetical practice, Mark provided toward the end of his Gospel this summary of Christian eschatological teaching. (Here I am guided by the exegesis of George R. Beasley-Murray—1986.) In chapter 13 Jesus repeats for the disciples the warning that the Jerusalem temple is going to be destroyed. Then the inner circle, Peter, James, John, and Andrew, "question him privately": when will these things occur, and what is to be the sign that they are near? (13:4) Jesus gives three replies: The first (13:5-23) warns of the suffering that disciples must endure as trustees of the Christian gospel: they will encounter misleading claims and clues, there will be persecution and death, profanation and distress. The point of these warnings is made explicit: this Way is a costly way, so be on the alert; take heed (*blepete*, 13:23). Jesus' second reply (13:24-27) speaks in apocalyptic language of the final coming. With the sun darkened and the stars falling, the Truly Human One will come in clouds and will gather the elect: triumph after tragedy. Jesus' third answer (13:28-37) then repeats in parabolic form the command to be alert. Even the trees tell you when summer is coming; every household porter knows to stay at the task of guarding the door while the master is away; so must all followers stay awake (*gregoreite).* Difficulties quickly arise if we look for the chronology these three answers imply. The disciples had asked not only for the signs, but for the *time* of these events (13:4), and Jesus has apparently given conflicting answers—suffering will come before the consummation (13:5-23), all will occur within this generation (13:30), and no one knows when (but the Father) (13:32)—replies that seem incoherent if not simply contradictory. Verse 30, at least, appears to substantiate today's consensus: Mark was mistaken.

Yet we should exercise some caution here. Was Mark telling his own Christian generation what to expect next? If so, and if Mark was composed at least a generation after Calvary and Easter (indeed, after A.D. 60), the surface sense of verse 32 (the final *parousia* to come within the generation of the first disciples) would have seemed mistaken even while it was being written—yet Mark sets it down with *no* evident discomfort. And if Mark wrote after 70, then the instruction about how

Christians are to escape the siege of Jerusalem (13:14*b*) is already obsolete: that event is already past. If on the other hand, as I believe, Mark was skillfully adopting for his narrative the standpoint of the pre-Easter disciples, then all these *depicted* events, the spread of the gospel, the suffering of the missionaries, the destruction of Jerusalem, the coming of false Messiahs, and the apocalyptic last coming of the Son of man were from the time standpoint of the first disciples future events. *By foreshortening,* these would have blended or appeared to blend into one, an appearance that Mark was at no pains to remove, since his concern was with a *trioptic awareness:* (1) what Jesus had once said and done (the 'present' of Mark's narrative), (2) how everything would end up (the long future), and (3) how both of these impinged upon the 'present' needs and tasks of the Marcan church (the 'present' of Mark's readers). For Mark the great future-present message was this: the cost of discipleship must indeed be paid, but things would be coming out right in the end, an end that both in knowledge and in fact belongs to the Son and to his Father (13:32). The grammar of time employed by Jesus' inner circle, and by Jesus himself, perhaps differed from that of Mark and Mark's Greek readers (as Mark's surely differs from that of modern Westerners). It did not matter; Mark could truthfully render afresh the picture received from Jesus, for its force finally depended not on near and more distant perspectives or upon the needed conceptual foreshortenings, but upon the ultimate truth it related. Every version of the story was shaped by its ending.

ii. Hans Hut.—The baptist movement has sometimes been uneasy about its undeniable link with assorted radical thinkers and actors in Christian history, most often with the abortive Kingdom of Muenster, Germany, in the sixteenth century. Since that well-reported episode constitutes in the judgment of most a baptist failure, we cannot in fairness totally neglect the many faithful baptist episodes that were contemporary with Muenster. Among these, the case of Hans Hut (c. 1490–1527), missionary and martyr, is highly instructive. For Hut, too, has been reproached, even by sympathetic students of Anabaptism, for "too strongly emphasizing the eschatological-chiliastic angle" (ME III:777-83; V:606f). We know less than we might like about Hut's life. Born about 1490 in South Germany, he was a bookbinder and bookseller who came into the circle that included Luther, Andreas Carlstadt, and Thomas Muentzer. The latter two opposed infant baptism, and Muentzer preached a strenuous reformation that connected him with the Peasants' War. His own connection with Muentzer made Hut suspect, a man hunted by the authorities for his presumed part in the uprising.

He disappeared into crowded Nuremberg, where he met genuine Anabaptists and was converted; he was baptized by Hans Denck—on
Pentecost, 1526. He took this baptism as the sign of his authority to
preach, and to warn of an impending judgment. In mills, villages, and
towns of South Germany and Upper Austria he preached "the gospel of
all creatures": as in nature the beasts serve man (and necessarily suffer),
so human beings are meant for costly service to God. Christ's Great
Commission (Mark 16:15f) had sent Hans Hut to preach this gospel and
to baptize, and baptize he did, perhaps more than any other of the
Anabaptist evangelists.

A part of Hut's preaching was his "seven judgments" *(sieben Urteile)*
of biblical prophecy: these were divine decisions concerning the covenant (and baptism), the body of Christ (and Lord's supper), the end of
the world, the future and its judgment, the resurrection of the dead, the
kingdom of God, and the last punishment of hell. Much of Hut's elaborated eschatology, applying apocalyptic biblical passages to sixteenth-
century current events (such as the Peasants' War and the menace of the
Turks), remained a secret for his inner circle only. What he openly taught
was that all his converts must together keep God's commandments and
practice brotherly and sisterly love. Anabaptist historians Gottfried
Seebass and Werner O. Packull strongly emphasize Hans Hut's distinctive social concern: "the kingdom of God derives its life from and
through the hearts of people" (Seebass in Goertz, ed., 1982:70; see further
Packull, 1977:chaps. 3–5).

So Hut typically preached on last things in a way that disclosed his
overriding passion for social justice and equality—first, justice within
the fellowship; finally, justice in all creation. It is a connection (eschatology with ethics) that not all evangelists since Hut have remembered. Our
question is whether the tools now at hand make it possible for us to
understand this missioner who by modern standards was an eschatological fanatic and yet an authentic apostle and true martyr for Christ.
The "excessive" features that are said to have characterized his preaching—identifying sixteenth-century events with biblical passages, fore-
seeing an early end of the age, regarding the judgments of God as the
very key to the interpretation of Scripture (Packull, 1977:80-87)—are in
fact just what we might have expected of one who shared the baptist
vision, who sensed that he was living at the end of *his* times (as indeed
he was!), and who (perhaps) partook of that same foreshortened sense
of time that has so often shaped Christian eschatological thinking.
Certainly Hut's application of apocalyptic pictures to current events is
a paradigm case of the baptist vision ("then is now") applied in a time
of crisis. His employment of judgment themes as keys to biblical under-

standing foreshadows the scholarly rediscovery, three centuries later, that Scripture is eschatological throughout. And the foreshortening of time, if it was an element (Hut almost, if not quite, predicted the end of the age for the year 1528), illustrates a habit of mind that might well be appreciated by sixteenth- to nineteenth-century Africans enduring American slavery: his was a mind that saw the end of his times and the end of all time in immediate juxtaposition.

Hans Hut's own end was marked by martyrdom. He had taught his followers that when the threatened invasion by the Turks came, they should not resist it, but should separate themselves from the *Obrigkeit* or present power structure and its violence. This separation was so strict that it even brought Hut into conflict with the more flexible baptist teacher, Balthasar Hubmaier. Little wonder, then, that in Lutheran Augsburg Hut was suspected of anarchy and revolution. Seized there, and accused under torture of earlier associations with Muentzer as well as of prophecies that challenged the 'new world order' of the sixteenth century, he may have attempted escape by setting afire the straw in his prison cell. If so, the ruse failed. The smoke overcame Hut in his chains, and he presently perished. Nevertheless, his corpse was brought before the Augsburg court, where it was 'tried,' and the sentence of burning was executed upon that lifeless body. Hut remains a martyr for those who recognize not only in his evangelistic passion but also in his eschatological devotion to social justice a kindred spirit.

c. History centered in Jesus Christ.—Eschatology is about what lasts; it is also about what comes last, and about the history that leads from the one to the other. The presence of God in history is not evenly distributed (like a coat of paint on a wall) but appears precisely in connection with the pattern of salvific events, from the exodus to the last coming, that have as their focal center Jesus of Nazareth, his cross, and his resurrection. All other history gains its significance from its relation to those great historic signs. In the first coming of Christ, a new age was inaugurated, but the old age and its evil have lingered on, defeated but menacing, so that our present is still a time between the times, in which there is a necessary struggle between the two realms until the consummation in Christ's last coming (cf. Cullmann, 1950). To this view of history it may be objected that it trivializes too much—that which has gone on apart from Israel, Jesus, and the new people of God—and that it is regrettably ethnocentric and partial. So theorists have advanced other understandings such as the following: (1) Christianity is but one religious way among many that lead to God; (2) the development of Western or secular culture, even apart from Christian faith, is the fulfillment of all that God intends in Christ; (3) "Christ" is the name Christians give to progress in history, but there are many other names equally authentic. These defective rival views, some of them quite current, open issues that cannot be resolved in this chapter: Already addressed is the topic of "Christ and culture" (*Ethics*, Part II); something will be said in Chapters Four and Eight about God's election of Israel, of Jesus Christ, and of believers in Christ not as favoritism but as opportunity for suffering service; Chapters Six, Seven, and Eleven will argue against marginalizing Christ in Christian understanding; and Chapter Ten (and *Volume III*) will address the question of other religions in relation to the salvation the gospel promises. Here it is appropriate only to ask if there is a Christian understanding of history that can give due weight to Jesus Christ's claim upon disciples' lives without falling into the old ethnocentric arrogance that has sometimes accompanied this claim. I will be trying in what follows to avoid the mistakes of the traditional Christian claim while recognizing its truth: that Christ is the center of history.

Perhaps the temptation to Christian triumphalism (even the paper triumphalism of some Christian scholarship) rises in part from the conviction, authentic in itself, that in the end Jesus' kind of rule will conquer all its foes. If in the end, why not now? And if now, what likelier scenario than one in which 'Christian' scholarship dominates, or 'Christian' politics and warmaking rules, or 'Christian' economic policies win out over their rivals, or (likeliest temptation of all) one in which 'Christian' churchmanship masters the world and its lesser peoples. It seems to me that even the insightful Moltmann came dangerously close to such triumphalism when he announced, toward the end of his *Theology of Hope*, that the goal of the Christian mission must be not only salvation of the soul, but also "the realization of the eschatological *hope of justice*, the *humanizing* of man, the *socializing* of humanity, *peace* for all creation" (1967:329). Whether or not it is what Moltmann meant, it is all too easy a step from acknowledging that Christians are concerned with all the earth to the false inference that the Christian mission is by hook or by crook to achieve this ideal state of affairs. Perhaps we can take a leaf here from the life of plain Hans Hut, whose vision of Christ's overwhelming triumph in the last day was second to none, but who when he instructed his converts gave them the task, not of conquering the world with the world's weapons, but of obeying the commandments and practicing love one to another while they awaited God's own time. How much waiting is appropriate, though, and how much is unChrist-like quietism?

Can there be a Christian attitude that takes history seriously but maintains a servantlike modesty concerning its own role? We may consult here Revelation, chapter 5. The figure seated on heaven's throne holds a scroll "written within and on the back," but "sealed with seven seals" (5:1). If we reckon, with many, that the sealed scroll symbolizes the secret of human destiny, and thus of history's outcome and meaning, we may identify with the seer's distress because "no one in heaven or on earth or under the earth" can open the scroll and read that destiny. But an elder's voice consoles the seer: stop weeping; the Lion of the tribe of Judah has conquered and can open the scroll. Then the Lion appears— in the form of a Lamb "standing as though it had been slain." Where-upon heaven's worshipers, joined by all creation, sing a magnificent hymn of praise: "Worthy is the Lamb" (5:8-14). If we identify the Lamb as the crucified but risen Lord Jesus, the scene makes evident what the scroll itself must say: Exactly by the Way of that man of sorrows, earth shall be redeemed and history's last scene be the song of the triumph of that Lamb.

In a classic sermon delivered at Sjövik, Sweden, in 1988, John Howard Yoder interpreted this Revelation passage as announcing "the politics of the Lamb" (Pipkin, ed., 1989:69-76; cf. Yoder, 1988). The tears shed by John of Patmos (v. 4) are the tears of all of us as we contemplate earth's sorrows and recognize its evil—its persecutions, disease, death, its inhumanity, endless suffering, terrible slaughters. Why does God not end it all? Why does the story go on? In brief, why history? The Revela-tion's answer comes at the very end of the scene:

> You are worthy to receive the scroll and break its seals, for you were slain and by your blood you bought for God people of every tribe and language, nation and race. You have made them a royal house of priests for our God, and they shall reign on earth. (Rev. 5:9f)

In a word, what history is about is the formation of a new race of human beings, a race made of all races, a people made of all peoples. Inasmuch as Jesus is crucified and risen, the making of that new community on earth, one governed by "the politics of the Lamb," is human history's last task. This people is meant under its Lord to rule the world! But it is not to rule it as Caesars and presidents have attempted to rule (and have supposed that they were ruling)—by fire and sword, by rockets and bombs, by the power of death. That is mere triumphalism. The Lamb who creates this people provides for them a new kind of politics. Sometimes this kind works by indirect means, as when in the Nether-lands or Great Britain or the United States "free churches have helped to create free societies." At other times, it works more directly, as when a Mohandas Gandhi ("an unimmersed follower of the Jesus of the Gospels") or a Martin Luther King, Jr., shows once more that suffering for a righteous cause can overturn principalities and powers. To be sure, this politics can fail as well, and sometimes in the short run it does fail. Yet in the heavenly hymn the final outcome is certain, for there the Lamb has already passed his power to his people. According to Revelation 5:9f, the sacrificial work of the earthly Jesus has already formed this "royal" people; we exist; the new politics has begun. As Yoder puts it, "On the average and in the long run, truthtelling and the love of enemy are the effective ways to create and defend culture," that is, to give viable shape to the world, even in the present age. Relief work goes farther than war to enable a people to survive; the Red Cross outlasts the Nazi swastika cross. Further, the "new nation" of the Lamb is a *priestly* people: not a realm with priests, but a realm *of* priests, a realm in which all are priests (cf. Exod. 19:6). Being so constituted, it is uniquely situated not only to enter holy places, priestlike on behalf of humanity, but also to reach out in the name of the Lamb to near and distant neighbors wherever its priest-citizens may go. It is not irrelevant that this new people is "a cultural rainbow," a people composed of all peoples, all classes and colors and kinds, all genders, all languages, all racial stocks. History's earlier business, Yoder says, was the formation of the many peoples in all their splendid variety. This variegation was God's first work: "He created from one stock the whole human race to occupy the whole earth, decreeing how long each nation should flourish and what its boundaries should be" (Acts 17:26, Yoder's trans.). But God's new creation is by way of the politics of the Lamb. In it, without denying the variegation, the many parts are being brought into one whole. This whole is the rule of God. "The divine activity of overcoming boundaries is what the New Song is about." This is why history goes on; God's purpose in Christ is still being achieved, and being achieved by the very method by which Jesus lived and died—not by human conquest, but by the radical politics of the cross.

To all this, Yoder adds one important, clarifying theme. The setting of the Sjövik sermon was a Baptist-sponsored peace conference. There it could be made clear that this royal people's rule could be distinguished from that of the Caesars and the presidents of this world exactly because love of enemies was its theme. There it could be acknowledged that while a priestly people must sacrifice, they are strictly forbidden (by Commandments One and Two of the Decalogue) to sacrifice to strange gods: "If we follow the Great High Priest who shed not the blood of bulls and goats but gave his life for his enemies, how could we sacrifice our enemies for the sins of their politicians, or even threaten to do so?" That would be forbidden worship, idolatry. At Sjövik, too, it could be confessed that the "rainbow people" has a historic mission, which is "to interweave all the histories . . . to form one people to serve God," while "war only denies this divine vision for the globe" (Yoder in Pipkin, ed., 1989:73-75). Thus, in the last, best sense of the word "history," war and its violence turn out to be *anti*-historical.

John of Patmos (and probably John Yoder as well) could assume that his readers would readily identify the eschatological Lamb of Revelation 5 with the one John the Baptist called the Lamb of God (John 1:29). Yet I had better press that claim here: Christian eschatology is primary for faith and doctrine first of all because Jesus himself was and remains an eschatological figure. As indicated above, the historical research, the so-called Quest of the Historical Jesus of the nineteenth and early twentieth centuries, was not so fruitless as some have thought. In fact it issued in what Albert Schweitzer called "thoroughgoing eschatology," a fully eschatological interpretation of the historical Jesus. This was a result too severe for the comfortable times in which it appeared, and later scholarship has rightly revised its details. Yet the ground fact remains: Jesus was indeed a prophet who announced a new rule coming. "Behind the eschatological drive of early Christianity stands one unwavering figure of vast authority, carrying these eschatological convictions into life, even for followers not disposed to believe them or able to comprehend them." This figure was Jesus of Nazareth. He "lived and breathed eschatology; he *was* the eschaton; it was recognizing this, in the power of the resurrection, that made Christians Christians" (McClendon in Steuer and McClendon, eds., 1981:192f; cf. 1 Cor. 15:1-11). What John of Patmos recognized (and the historical Questers strained to grasp) was that by that resurrection Jesus of Nazareth not only was but is God's historic Lamb, so that after Easter, history becomes by right his history, the harvest of the cross his ongoing story. His continuing, risen life is the matrix that holds eschatological doctrine together and requires that we place it at the very doorway of doctrine: his story goes on till time's end. Jesus in biblical faith has not withdrawn to a timeless, Platonic eternity, leaving time as the realm where we must work things out on our own. He not only came, but is here and continues to come, and it is he, this same One, who is finally to come, he the First and the Last—he the center of the quiet history that links the two.

In consequence, disciples, too, are "an eschatological people." Their lives may sometimes be vivid and full of drama; or disciples' lives may attract no public gaze. Neither the one nor the other determines their significance. That is determined by their continuing relation to this one who is the very Ground of Adventure and Source of Transformation. It is he who draws the ages together. It is for this reason that the Colossian letter speaks of "this mystery, which is Christ in all of you, the hope of glory" (1:27). So we must expand our account (and the next chapter will try to do so) to speak more plainly about the way the story of each of us is drawn into and participates in the one story of "the new that comes in Christ."

Here we have set out the character and content of a Christian doctrine of last things. It begins with the existence of characteristic images (I have called them the "pictures" or "end-pictures") that depict these finalities for the people of God: hell and heaven, death, resurrection and judgment, the rule of God and Christ's coming. To interpret these requires a *literacy* or skill (Lindbeck, 1984) that takes into account the pictures' unique pictorial quality and their crucial role for faith. In this sense (but in no other) they are literal pictures: they are to be read not at discounted current value, and again not as timeless myths or secret codes or wooden facts, or by yet other misreadings (Frei, 1974, pass.). Such literacy requires some awareness of the foreshortening that has shaped the biblical (and other) depictions of the future; it requires also a steady sense of the prophetic or baptist vision that sees how the pictures of "then" shape the believers' "now." It requires awareness that the link holding all the pictures together is the narrative history of Jesus: he is the eschatological Truly Human One, the Son of man, whose first coming inaugurated these last days now in process, whose repeated comings shape the quiet history that leads us "all the way" to the very end (Matt. 28:20), and whose own last return will be judgment and salvation. Thus the Christian doctrine of last things exists as part and parcel of the doctrine of Christ Jesus; its necessary pictures take doctrinal form exactly within the frame provided by his crucified, risen, ongoing history. To express this in 'apocalyptic' form, we may with the Apocalypse (and with my advisor Nancey Murphy) say that the picture of the Lamb standing as one that has been slain—the picture of the crucified and risen one—is the master picture by which we can learn to see all the rest.

It may be felt, though, that something is still missing from our present account. Should there not be more discussion of personal survival and personal immortality, or perhaps of individual resurrection, or a doctrine of last rewards and final punishments? Should there not be something to clarify 'the intermediate state of souls,' to answer in sharp detail these questions that since the Middle Ages (and earlier) have preoccupied Christian thought so often? Perhaps in a longer book there should be. But our task has been to ask not what the church has sometimes taught or might also teach, but what the church *must* teach. This eschatological search has led to Jesus Christ as center, and our lives as significant just as they center in him. It is noteworthy that primitive Christians were not known to ask whether in the resurrection they would see again this or that beloved family member or friend, but like Paul seemed content to know that "Christ will be honored in my body, whether by life or by death" (Phil. 1:20). The same habit of mind seems to control early Christian employment of the end-pictures of hell and of heaven. As we have seen, *Gehenna* appears in the words of Jesus more than in those of the apostles. Yet Jesus' use of this term was not to encourage speculation about further human exercises in eternity, but to warn about misconduct by God's own people now: "Except you repent. . . ." And so it was with heaven: for his people it was a picture of consolation for the present burdens of discipleship. It is in this spirit that the church's present teaching must sharpen its focus on the present journey. Hell is now; but so is heaven, and "all the way to heaven is heaven" (Dorothy Day, quoted above in *Ethics*, Ten). Yet we must focus the present not by excluding what comes last, but by teaching these pictures of the end in such a way that they inform our journey everlastingly.

For present purposes, eschatology must inform our understanding of the chapters that follow in this Part: Salvation and sin (Chapter Three) must be seen in the light of the last end coming; creation or 'first things' (Chapter Four) must be understood as the alpha that corresponds to the divine omega, the beginning that can be fitly ended by our pictured end. So it must be in the later Parts: the Jesus identified in Part II can be no other than the suffering, triumphant Lamb revealed here, while the fellowship of the Spirit sought in Part III must be an end-time fellowship, already partaking of the heavenly supper of the Lamb, already dipped in eschatological waters.

CHAPTER THREE

The New in Christ: Salvation and Sin

The new that comes in Christ—life redeemed, healed, transformed—is a primary element in Christian teaching. It was the focus of a famous definition of Christianity by Schleiermacher, who found "everything . . . related to the redemption accomplished by Jesus of Nazareth" (CF §11). It sounds also at that place in the Nicene Creed that confesses *"For us and for our salvation he came down from heaven."* And perhaps a like conviction guided the editors of successive editions of the Methodist Hymnal to begin with "O For a Thousand Tongues to Sing," a placement that goes back to John Wesley in 1780:

> He breaks the power of canceled sin,
> He sets the prisoner free;
> His blood can make the foulest clean;
> His blood availed for me.

East and West, North and South, this gift from God in Christ shapes Christian faith.

Yet this apparent unanimity dissolves on closer look. For many earnest, Bible-believing Christians, "salvation" refers to a distinct new beginning in the life of each genuine Christian believer. They find its beginning and continuance (and heavenly culmination) matters of

103

fact—past, present, and future fact. This experiential understanding has been shared by evangelical Christians across the centuries. Yet many sincere followers of Christ are differently formed. With biblical backing, they hope to be saved at last, but do not presume to know how they stand now, or they see their salvation as settled not in their own life stories but once for all at Calvary. Thus words such as "saved," "redeemed," "reborn" are used by two sorts of Christian speakers with different meanings, as if in two languages with only a few common vocables. These differences are reflected in the literature of theology as well. Some books on "salvation" treat the Christian's journey now, while others deal with the prior atoning work of Christ, each written as if the other sort did not exist. So far from finding a place of agreement, we seem to have found a vast unexplored rift.

In such circumstances, it seems best to turn back to the earliest beginnings witnessed in the Old Testament and the New to ask about the origin of this doctrine or doctrines, hoping for a true view of the matter. Accordingly, this chapter will ask **(§1) Exactly what is meant in New Testament and later Christian use by such terms as "salvation"?** Who are the redeemed, and what are the New Testament terms of their redemption? **(§2) What is the proper Christian understanding of sin?** What counts as sin, and are our lives possessed by a sinful world, or is there freedom in Christ to follow another way? **(§3) How does each follower's Christian development (call it one's pilgrimage, or faith journey, or 'spirituality') correlate with the corporate life of the Christian community, the faith of the church?** Since my own approach is from the conversionist side (cf. McClendon, 1994), I must be especially alert to challenges this side has met in recent theology: (1) There is widespread dissatisfaction with the elaborate *ordo salutis* (sequence of steps in salvation) defined by seventeenth-century Scholastic Protestantism. (2) The excesses that accompanied nineteenth-century revivalism offend many. (3) The Social Gospel and Liberation Theology aimed at redemption of the social order, not the individual believer. (4) Karl Barth replaced experience-centered theology with a doctrine of salvation already achieved in advance, objectively, in Jesus Christ (but see Barth's later thoughts, CD IV/2-3, §§66, 71). (5) For some, 'salvation,' along with all inner-directed aspects of Christian experience, missed the point of common life in the body of Christ with its morality and its visible signs of baptism, Lord's supper, and the proclaimed word (cf. H. Berkhof, 1986:428). While all this deserves attention, in §3 below I will pay special attention to challenges (1) and (5) by showing how the journey that begins in the new in Christ connects with instruction, with baptism, with the Lord's supper, and with communal discernment of progress in

Christian lives, while I will address (3) the social dimension of sin and redemption in §2.

Far from neglecting the objective, saving work of Jesus Christ (4), this volume will devote a full chapter to it (Chapter Five). And as to the early Barthian concern lest a theology that begins with human experience can never escape it to speak of God, its proper theme, the present chapter is concerned neither with self-contained human experience nor with a remote God *in se*, but is concerned with God-with-us, the Savior God, and ourselves only as we come to ourselves *in relation to* that God. I leave the correction of revivalistic excess (2) to those better informed than I of its problems and possibilities.

§1. Salvation as Revolution

The key to understanding salvation aright is already implied in the location of this chapter under the reign or rule of God. This rule is an eschatological concept; we have seen the coming rule pointing us beyond history and its limits to glimpse God breaking into human life with a new order, a fulfillment, that transforms everyday life. Chapter Two provided conceptual tools for thinking in these ultimate terms: Scripture presents the last things in God-given, true *pictures* such as God's reign, heaven, hell, judgment, and the last coming of Christ. Insofar as these end-time pictures seem imminent, immediately coming upon us, we may detect the regular Scripture device of *foreshortening*, whereby the middle ground of a picture is compressed to give a clear sense of its far horizon. Lest even then the pictures remain far away, still another Scripture device, prophetic vision (in our use, *baptist vision*) declares that then is now, the church on the Last Day the church today, so that we can read our own 'today' correctly only in terms of this ultimate yet impending horizon. It cannot be too strongly insisted, here at the beginning of our discussion, that salvation is indeed such an eschatological or kingdom concept. If salvation is the reality of belonging to Christ (1 Cor. 15:23), it looks even beyond his kingship, as he delivers up the rule to God the Father (v. 24*a*). Only if we read it as such a last reality, a rule-of-God reality, can we place salvation properly in experience and in doctrine.

a. The original revolution.—Whatever confusion there may be among Christians about redemption today, it must be small compared to that which accompanied the birth of the Christian movement in the first century. Even at the first, as the early accounts reveal, there was no simple consensus about the event and its import. (Attempts to dovetail these early reports continue to frustrate modern historians.) Yet we can be sure of the upshot: the disciples' recognition that Jesus' story that had engaged them was not ended by his death. For him and for them, there was a new beginning. Strangely but surely a new era had begun.

From this point of view, their previous days of discipleship had all to be rethought. Had they not crucially misunderstood the Master? Were not the reign-of-God expectations that seemed to fail after all valid? Had they not seen, in his renewed risen presence, the day star rising, the sun of true justice ascendant? Were not their own lives incandescent by that awesome radiance? Outwardly, to be sure, everything was as before. Still the temple sacrifices were offered. The modest agricultural harvest season approached as in other years. Oppression continued. Traders bought and sold, babies were born, the old sickened and died. Yet the new the disciples knew burned within them, its pressure building until it was ready to explode conventional structures, making apostles of disciples, making their fellowship the church of God. The difficulty lay in giving adequate expression to the new that was theirs in Christ. He was Lord—but of no bounded realm: he was risen—but in no ordinary waking from a sleep. Tragedy had in fact struck; he had died, yet he was alive, and they, too, were alive—his life had overcome death and their lives were thereby redeemed. The problem that lay unresolved was one of definition, communication, expression.

How is the truly extraordinary ever to be named? To the extent that it is new, old terms are false, while new ones convey too little. The apostolic response to this situation was twofold, or better, had an inside and an outside. Outwardly, the new reality must be lived in the world. As later one would put it, "One and all they kept up their daily atten-dance at the temple, and, breaking bread in their homes, they shared their meals with unaffected joy. . . . They met constantly to hear the apostles teach and to share the common life, to break bread, and to pray" (Acts 2:46, 42). In such a seedbed a new society sprouted upon the compost of the old. The common life in Christ was by nature adventure, daily discovered, daily risked. Yet the outward adventure could not be fulfilled apart from its inner reality: Disciples must find words, a vocabu-lary and syntax, in which to proclaim the revolution.

Meeting that need, the first Christians found a language, mainly in the Scriptures, that could address the newness. When they employed it, its meanings necessarily changed to fit the originality of their situation. Thus the language of Jewish law (*justify*) and holy rite (*sanctify*), of medical healing and military rescue (*heal* and *save*), of kinship and its ties (*adopt, wed*), of life processes (*born* and *reborn*), of commercial exchange (*redeem* and *reconcile*)—these and more were adopted, adapted, pressed into service to declare the dynamic of those who shared the new reality created by the Risen One.

The technical literary term for these creative namings of the new that came in Christ Jesus is **catachresis.** This is the deliberate (as opposed to accidental or mistaken) use of language drawn from one sphere in order to indicate something in another sphere that eludes existing speech. Languages display several such devices for generating terms where none existed: simple *coinage* (as "bleen" might name a color somewhere between blue and green), *synecdoche* or *metonymy* (as when a residential address, say Number 10 Downing Street, comes to designate a particular political official), *displacement* (as when the "stoop" of a hawk describes a diner's approach to his steak supper). Where linguistic gaps appear and are filled in one or another of these ways, the result is 'misuse' only by the standard of prior use in an earlier setting. It may in fact constitute creative employment of the terms in new senses. Such was the apostolic catachretical practice (cf. Soskice, 1985:chap. 4).

Since catachresis is one of the features of *metaphor,* it may be thought that the apostolic speech should simply be labeled metaphorical. I have two concerns that resist this. (1) The first is the caution, already expressed in Chapter One, about indiscriminate use of this deeply disputed concept. What metaphor is, and what counts (on one or another theory) as metaphorical utterance, is far too uncertain to become central in any brief account of apostolic discourse (see p. 37 above). The other concern (2) grows from the recognition that (on one attractive theory of metaphor) one might be claiming too much—not every fresh application of a term is metaphorical, even if some are. I want therefore to make a less bold (but I hope less controversial) claim about the discourse of the New Testament: it frequently employs *catachresis.* The value of this perception should come out as we proceed, and if it is wrong, its wrongness should arise from actual cases, not debatable theories.

My account here of the apostolic revolution is brief and incomplete. I will tell only of changes in the meanings of words (semantic changes), not exploring equally telling changes in the structure, style, and syntax of utterance and in the story that shaped apostolic living and speaking (narrative changes) (cf. A. Wilder, 1971; G. Kennedy, 1984; G. Caird, 1980). Because much of this volume deals with the Christian narrative pattern, only a hint or two about the latter shifts can be provided here. For an accessible example of syntactic shift, consider the remarkable advice and example of the Epistle of James, in many ways so traditional. "Always *speak* and act," James advises, "as men [and women] who are to be judged under a law which makes them free" (2:12). And then "a word with all who say, 'Today or the next day we will go off to such and

such a town and spend a year there trading and making money.' . . .
What is your life after all? . . . *What you ought to say is*, 'If it be the Lord's
will, we shall . . .'" (4:13-15, emphasized). Here the new in Christ requires not new vocabulary but new grammar—doctrine revising syntax.
For a single example of narrative shift one thinks of the parables,
narratives nearly all, that shed their distinctive light upon the new in
Christ. For example, Jesus is the teller of a ghost story that (in Luke's
version, 11:24-26) reveals the calamity of a life purified of its old controls
yet not filled with the new that the gospel brings.

   One of the most serious ways the Christian mission could *go wrong* in
proclaiming its good news would be to cut itself off from this Israelite
and Jewish root, dissociating itself from the synagogue and from the
Hebrew Scriptures. Yet separation from the synagogue was widespread
even in the second century and was accelerated by the Constantinian
state church gambit of the fourth. Rejecting the Jewish Scriptures was
exemplified by Marcion of Rome (second century), whose shortened
Bible, consistent with his quasi-Gnostic views (Jonas, 1963:chap. 6*b*),
excluded the Old Testament.

   It is of first importance to retain the chief source of the new language that
marked Christian beginnings, namely, Jewish sacred writings, and chiefly those
that became our Old Testament, for in that source lies the link to God's past
salvific dealings with Israel. Here we meet afresh the **prophetic vision** that finds
in texts from the past a mirror by which to construe the holy present action of
the Savior God. *Redemption* had been God's extrication of Israel from Egyptian
oppression; now it became also God's release of Jew and Gentile as well from
sin. *New birth* as conversion to the true religion was a common expression in the
Rabbinic writings as well as in Hellenism (Rengstorf, TDNT I:664; Bultmann,
1951, I:142f, 167, 278); now in John's Gospel it became the radical fresh start of a
member of the Jewish Council who would become Jesus' disciple (3:1-3). *Entering* the Promised Land was denied to Moses—he was permitted to "see" that
country but not to "cross over" into it (Deuteronomy 34). Now both "seeing"
the rule of God arrive (Mark 9:1) and "entering" that rule (or its "life," see Mark
9:43, 45, 47) stood for the new reality to which Jesus called his followers. In each
of these examples as in many others, the New Testament employed existing
language but reshaped it to make intelligible the new that had come in Jesus
Messiah, whose own heritage and hope were funded from that same treasury.

   b. A continuing revolution.—The new began in apostolic times, but
plainly the old did not end. The world of Caesar persisted long after the
way of Christ had come; it persists even today. Jesus' revolutionary
challenge to the old order was in one sense once for all. He lived such a
life and died such a death and received such a divine acclamation—the
resurrection from the dead—as to engage and change world history
itself. (Of that engagement and change, more in Chapter Five.) Yet in
another sense, the persistence of the old order, represented in the four

Gospels by a decadent religious establishment (scribes, Pharisees, high priests), by a domineering politico-economic order (the Herods, Pilate, the soldiery, the Temple economic system), and by a sleepy, unreliable band of would-be followers (the pre-Easter disciples, including Judas)— meant that every Christian generation would need the good news of the rule of God, need converting, need to be turned, enlisted, **saved.** There will be ample acknowledgment here of the corporate character of the new in Christ and of the finished work (*tetelestai*, John 19:30) that stands behind every Christian's journey into faith. Yet that acknowledgment must not diminish the reality of the calling, election, repentance, conversion, faith, union with Christ, entry upon the way, of each follower.

It is our business now to say what the new in Christ must mean to each today. It will be convenient to present this under three headings: (1) descriptions of the new that cluster around forgiveness, faith, and (more generally) the establishing of **right relations** among believers and Christ; (2) descriptions concerned with the **presence** of Christ to (or in) believers, sometimes called union with Christ; (3) descriptions focused on the **way of life** that follows Jesus in discipleship. My hypothesis is that these are several perspectives upon, several aspects of, **one** new reality in Christ. Something, but not too much, may be made of the correspondence between these three descriptions and the three strands, *organic* (cf. presence), *social* (cf. right relations), and *anastatic* (cf. the new way of life) that structure Christian ethics (see *Volume I*). Not too much, since (as we will see) some apostolic indicators of the new in Christ straddle these categories or fall outside them. More promise lies in the hypothesis linking these three with three main types of Western Christianity: Protestant (stressing salvation as right relations?), Catholic (stressing the vision of God and divine presence?), and baptist (stressing the new way?). Yet here as well it would be wrong to ignore places at which the fit is poor and the categories overlap.

i. Right relations uniting Christ (or God) and Christians.—This aspect of apostolic witness to the new, if the most accessible, may in the end seem most problematic of our three. A cluster of catachretical terms (including justification, faith, forgiveness, reconciliation, and adoption) became in the Protestant Reformation synonymous with the new emphasis upon the priesthood of the believer, direct, unmediated access to God, and the dynamism of the Christian life that made the Protestant Reformation a driving force in European (and colonial American) history. These themes declared that every human being is a sinner, that this alienation from God could be canceled *on the basis of* Christ's redemptive work "for me" (to use a favorite expression of Martin Luther), *through* faith that simply trusted Christ, *with the result* being a restoration to God's favor that was (from the sinner's point of view) pure undeserved grace, but that was (on the God's-eye view) purchased at the expense of Christ's sacrificial death. This implied Christ's achievement on behalf of each sinner (or each *elect* sinner), and a corresponding transaction in the interior life of each one who was brought to salvation. Such accounts hold center place in evangelical church life to the present.

Two comments about this plan of salvation: It focused powerfully on a 'direct' encounter between each believer and Christ (or God-in-Christ), unmediated by church, priest, or sacrament. In this way it did recover some of the immediacy of the new in Christ of primitive Easter faith and challenged the prevalent merit-based religiosity of late-medieval Christianity. Perhaps its **essence** is captured in a phrase Protestant historian Adolf Harnack employed in another context: "God and the soul; the soul and its God" (Harnack's summary of Jesus' kingdom teaching—1900:56). By this route Protestantism tended to an inwardness, inviting intense introspection ("where am *I* in the journey of faith?") that was supported by a popular literature (from *Pilgrim's Progress* to *In His Steps*) and shaped by confessions such as the Book of Concord, Dort, Westminster, and by theologians such as Philipp Melanchthon, Francis Turretin, and Charles Hodge. The second comment regards the breadth and power nonetheless displayed by the **permutations** of this plan. Puritan thought, for example, by crossing Luther's original insight with medieval thought-modes and further biblical insights, produced variants of an elaborate doctrine of *preparation* for conversion. Puritanism provoked as well a struggle between *antinomians* and *legalists* over the place of "good works" (i.e., an orderly Christian life) in an authentic work of grace. In later Wesleyan thought, for another example, salvation was dissected into discrete stages, prominent among them an ultimate entire or sinless holiness. This view spread widely in still other parts of the baptist movement. In revivalism from Charles Finney to Billy Graham, for a third example, the crisis of conversion was distilled into "decisions for Christ," especially at public rallies, with a corresponding diminution of all that might inhibit or scale down that act of free choice.

The strengths and weaknesses of this plan of salvation must first be evaluated by their fidelity to the very New Testament descriptions it invokes. At first look, **faith** *(pistis)* and the corresponding verbal **trusting** *(pisteuein)* appear to be exceptions to the rule of catachretical formation, for they were already terms of adherence in (pagan) religious use by the time our New Testament was written (Bultmann, TDNT VI:179-82). Yet closer inspection brings a surprise: The Septuagint translators of Hebrew Scripture had used just these words to represent a Hebrew verb-form (*he-emin,* the *hiphil* of *amen*) that had previously undergone the very displacement here being traced.

The development of "faith" terms in Hebrew is instructive. The simple *(qal)* stem is "used of the mother, nurse, or attendant of a child . . . the *ni[phal* or reflexive form] in Is 60.4 [denotes] the child . . . 'carried' at the mother's side"

(A. Weiser, TDNT VI:183). To summarize, Hebrew sacred writings took a term that in the first instance conveyed "reliable (female) nursing care," transferred its reference from the nurse to the child who was nursed and so dependent on that care, and subsequently intensified the word so that it named the trust relation between God and the faithful Jew. That intensified *amen* became in the Greek Septuagint *pistis*, "faith," and *pisteuein*, "trusting," and these were among the devices Paul and other apostolic authors used to describe the new in Christ—making of them competitive parallels to the pagan language of faith. So far from "faith" and "trust" being exceptions, then, they exemplify the rule. Only the coincidence of a parallel development in Greek religion obscures this.

The Hebrew and Christian concept of "faith" thus displays three distinct features: Its deep root is found in the *qal* stem of the verb *amen* with its word picture of nurse and child, the trustworthy and the trustful. When in Hebrew Scripture this root is intensified, it becomes a key word for the divine-human relation, representing God's faithfulness and answering human trust and fidelity (e.g., Deut. 7:9; Ps. 78:37). At this stage it is indelibly joined to the *narrative* of that relationship, epitomized in Genesis 15:6f: "Abram put his faith in the LORD, who reckoned it to him as righteousness, and said 'I am the LORD who brought you out from Ur of the Chaldees. . . .'" When at a third stage "faith" signifies divine-human relations in the New Testament, it (catachretically) acquires a *fresh* narrative link: "believing on" Jesus as Lord entails each believer's acceptance of the story-formed good news about Jesus and entails a "personal relation to Christ" as well (Bultmann, TDNT VI:211). Thus "faith" was ready and waiting for Luther, who found "right relations" central to the new that came in Christ. A fresh treatment, different again, is found in H. Richard Niebuhr's *Faith on Earth* (1989).

The related terms **just, justify, justification,** are most controverted, making it difficult for students to treat them in their own Hebrew (*tsadeq* and other stems) and Greek (*dikaios, dikaiein, dikaiosunē*) contexts, independent of the role they have played in Protestant-Catholic debates. The *justice* or *righteousness* of God (the proper English term is part of the dispute) lies at the root of the concept: In an ancient time that made no distinction among the executive, legislative, and judicial functions of rulers, a king was lawgiver and judge as well. Early Israel differed from other nations by playing down earthly rulers: JHWH was Monarch, so Israel could have no earthly monarch (1 Samuel 8), and in consistency no earthly legislature or chief judge either. God was properly Monarch, Lawgiver, Judge in Israel, and finally in all the earth (Gen. 15:6). In this way of thinking, it was fitting that terms such as "acquit" and "condemn" (*naqah* and *rasha*), the task of earthly kings and judges, should be applied to God's acquittal and condemnation (e.g., in Job 10:2, 14). The earth awaited JHWH's justice, and Israel, as keeper of the law given at

Sinai, proleptically enjoyed that justice already: It consisted not in the 'rights' of modern jurisprudence, but in *keeping or restoring right relations*, 'rightwising' between each and his or her neighbor, and (preeminently) rightwising relations between each and God. Thus Jesus' reading of the law found its ultimate principle embedded in the commandment to love God and with it to love neighbors (Mark 12:31 par.). (*Volume I* sketches a modern theory of legal justice that likewise turns on the idea of restoring right relations in community—*Ethics*, pp. 223f.)

Thus Paul and others adopted the understanding of divine-human relations these themes embodied and adapted them to represent the new that came in Christ. In this case, the Christians *adopted* legal terminology (which expressed the aim of biblical justice, viz., *right relations* among God and creatures) and *adapted* it to express the radical, eschatological inbreaking of the new, the end of the ages, that disciples were coming to know in the risen Christ. So the elements of (1) justice or law (from the root terms), (2) relations set right (implicit in Hebraic law, and confirmed by the link with "faith"), and (3) the new era in Christ (the narrative link to the Jesus story) were internal to the catachretically new terms "righteousness of God," "justify," "justification," and "justified." Yet a temptation arose even in the earliest times to focus exclusively on one or another of these three elements, neglecting the rest. These distortions persist.

Perhaps the earliest distortion of justification language is attacked by the Epistle of James. It combats a corrupt idea of "justification by faith" that separates *dikaiosunē* from (2), the right human relations James saw were essential (but that he, to the confusion of some, dubbed "good works"). For James, rooted in Jewish wisdom lore, justification, faith, and right relations with God and neighbor are an inseparable monad: The lack of any one of them is the lack of all (James 2:14-26). The next distortion was encountered by Paul. He met an objection to his doctrine (Why not "persist in sin so that there may be all the more grace"?—Rom. 6:1) that perversely disregarded (3) the radical inbreaking of the new in Christ in its historic and social aspects, and corrected it (Rom. 6:2ff).

If some modern votaries of Paul (or of James) have avoided these ancient pitfalls, others have once more divided the indivisible, either by extrapolating the aspect of justification as court acquittal into a fictitious righteousness enjoyed by sinners unchanged still, or by focusing upon the inner dynamic of justification to the neglect of its communal and social dimensions, or by exalting God's victory in Christ while leaving unaddressed its demand for I-thou confrontation between each sinner and God the Judge. It is important to correct each of these where it occurs, but to pursue this task here ranges too far.

Exploration of other terms in this cluster is left to readers: Besides faith and justification, right-relation terms for the new in Christ include at least **forgiveness, reconciliation, adoption** as **children of God, brothers**

and sisters of Jesus, **friendship** with God or Christ. Each of these arose from some biblical context where it displayed an earlier sense; each shifted its sense in the Old Testament or the New or both as it was selected to bear (partial) witness to the new thing God did in Christ. Noteworthy, too, are terms that do *not* appear here: "penance" and "repentance." As Hendrikus Berkhof notes, Scripture has no word for our psychological concept of "repentance"; *metanoein* is not properly repentance but conversion—it means actively turning one's life about (Berkhof, 1986:434ff). Anything less may be barren regret.

   ii. The presence of Christ.—Before Protestantism, other New Testament ways of illuminating the new in Christ had clustered in Christian teaching. Foremost were such expressions as being "in Christ" and "Christ living or being in [me or] you-all." There were also "seeing" (God, or Christ) and transformation (variants of *morphē*), "new birth," and receiving a new spirit or Spirit. Over the centuries elements of this cluster, along with the related idea of the ("real") presence of Christ in the Lord's supper, were woven into a characteristic Catholic plan of salvation. Entrance into this plan differed, depending on whether 'baptized' infants or adult adherents were in view, so it is simplest to note what was central to both: membership in a church viewed not merely as a social or legal entity but as the mystical body of all the redeemed. This body is bonded to Christ as head to members, or (in another way of speaking) the body *is* his own; the church is "another Christ." Membership is through baptism and is maintained by the other 'sacraments' and by the active virtues of the faithful. Finally the corporate body will become the community of heaven itself. These general features embrace a wide range of participants, from the least faithful baptized Catholic adherent (and beyond that a still wider range, including those "anonymous Christians" who enjoy only a "baptism of desire," that is, who would if rightly informed seek the church's baptism) at one extreme, to the most ardent contemplative mystic at the other—and even beyond that, those whose excessive sense of union with God incurs pastoral reproof (Trent, *De sacr. gen.*, IV; Rahner, ed., 1967:chap. 10; *Mystici Corporis*, Papal Encyclicals, IV:47-54).

   The Catholic plan displayed two great strengths, its awed sense of the presence of Christ and union with God through Christ, and its communitarian reach to all real and prospective fellow believers (cf. 1 John 3:14). The first made salvation authentically religious; the second made it ethical as well. Taken together, they suggest that *unity*—with God and also with one another—might suffice as a motto for salvation in its Catholic mode. At the same time, the Catholic plan was liable to severe deformation, if for instance sacraments became a mechanistic means to the desired unity, or if Catholicity became sectarian in its claim to sole ownership of Christ and grace (cf. McClendon and Yoder, 1990). Another Catholic difficulty grew from an emphasis upon free will that, viewed psychologically, made the faithful ever free to commit ruinous mortal sin. Psychologically, this might lead in one direction to (Jansenist) moral rigorism, or in another to (Jesuit) laxity, even unbelief. With assurance of salvation dogmatically forbidden (Trent, *De just.,* ix), scrupulosity was always a temptation: A classic Catholic fear was of dying with mortal sin unconfessed and thus unforgiven. Protestant critics were quick to note each of these, all the while neglecting their own plan's flaws.

As before, though, the best appraisal comes from the terms of the cluster from which the plan had grown. Consider the expressions **in Christ** and **Christ in us** (or **in you**) **all,** found especially in the principal writings of Paul (e.g. Phil. 3:9, Gal. 2:19f, 1 Cor. 1:30), but also in other Epistles and in John (15:4; cf. 14:10f). These terms cannot properly be understood as part of the relational cluster. Their point is not merely that Christ is "in relation to" followers and they to him, though that is true. Rather, they denote something else that had to be said however language might falter in the attempt. Is such union with Christ mysticism? Perhaps the best way to respond to this question is to distinguish, with writers on the topic, between a mysticism of union and one of absorption—the faithful "in Christ" are not absorbed or dissolved (Underhill, 1961). Even the "man in Christ" of Paul's (third-person) autobiographical account in 2 Corinthians 12, who heard secrets that human lips may not repeat, continued to confess personal weakness (his "thorn in the flesh," sent to deflate him). Hence that intense union was not absorption and did not evaporate Paul the human being; rather it left him with ironic detachment from the power of God operative in his life: "when I am weak, then I am strong" (v. 10). Note once again that the "in" (Greek *en*) of the phrase "in Christ," has undergone a change: It has passed from denoting physical location to declaring—in quasi-physical, or better, ontological, realism—the presence of Christ with those for whom the new has come. This newness is individual and particular (Paul describes himself as *a* human being in Christ [*anthropon,* singular]); it is also communitarian (in Colossians, the open secret of the gospel is "Christ in you-all [*Christos en humin*], the hope of glory"—1:27). Here Scripture may foreshadow the later Orthodox and Catholic belief in communion of saints in earth and heaven.

If the Old Testament root is less apparent in the "in Christ" expressions, we find it vividly in the next terms, **sanctify, sanctification,** and **holy ones** (rarely in the singular, "saint"): *hagiazein, hagiasmos, hagioi.* In understanding the original of these concepts, the work of Rudolf Otto has been criticized but not bettered (Otto, 1923:1-41 et pass.). He showed that in widespread 'primitive' human experience, including that reflected in some of the earliest levels of Hebrew Scripture, the concept "holy" (Hebrew *qadosh*) is not the modern ethical idea, but reflects the awe and terror or dread human beings feel in the presence of the uncanny, the awe-some, the numinous (derived from *numen*, "deity"). The holy is that which in mysterious grandeur *(mysterium tremendum)* awakens such a response. In Hebrew thought this is no other than JHWH, the Holy One of Israel. Secondarily, that which is in contact with the Deity is by contagion holy, and setting someone or something apart for such contact (as the implements of the altar or the sacrificial animals devoted to it) makes these people or things holy, not in a modern moral but in an earlier holistic sense. Thus God is said to have sanctified the seventh day, since in it creation was *complete* (Gen. 2:3). The note of completeness connects us with a further sense of *qadosh:* the Holy One is the Complete One, whole in himself, needing no other, rather extending his holiness to things or people who come near him, so that they are included in that wholeness by the divine action (Lev. 10:3; Exod. 29:43; Ezek. 20:41—cf. Otto Procksch, TDNT, I:91). Of course, as Rudolf Otto points out, where God is conceived as moral, morality is integral to God's completeness and extends to his holy ones or "saints" as well, but in Hebrew Scripture the numinous force is never left behind (cf. Isa. 6:3). It carries over into the New as well: When Simon sees the net-splitting catch of fish Jesus miraculously provides, he falls to his knees and prays, "Leave me, sinner that I am" (Luke 5:8). His sense of sin is based not on moral fault, but on awareness of the profane in the terrible presence of the numinous (cf. Otto, 1923:Appendix xii).

Thus in the New Testament holiness characterizes God's Spirit and his Child, Jesus, and hence those who by contact with these become holy ones. The verbs that represent entry into this state of holiness in the New Testament Epistles typically convey action at a point of time with results that abide (perfect tense verbs), or punctiliar action simply (aorists). This rather technical point arises since in later ecclesial use, "sanctification" was represented as a process of gradual acquisition of holiness or moral purity, growth in grace, in contrast to justification, which is immediate. But this is not at all the way the New Testament writers use "sanctify" and its cognates; for them, these refer to the state, not process, of holiness. This fact may be missed even by careful Bible readers since English does not lend itself to precise replication of Greek tenses, and since holiness or sanctification is called the *fruit* of the passage from sin to God (e.g., Rom. 6:22), as if it came last. But the fruit in these passages is not fruit eventually, but fruit now—the entire argument of Romans 6 turns upon there being present fruitage. Finally, it needs to be noted that if holiness is God's gift, it is a gift of radiating power. As Otto Procksch proposes translating *hagiasmos*, "The term 'sanctifying' fits it better than sanctification" (TDNT, I:113). One recalls that in a later stage of Christian history, beautifully explored by Peter Brown, holy men and women were regarded not as mere beneficiaries but as benefactors in the community—they transmit the holiness they have from God to others (Brown, 1982). So is it with the *hagiasmoi*, the contagiously 'sanctifying' ones of the New Testament (cf. 1 Thess. 4:7-9, 1 Pet. 1:2). Thus here also the New Testament bears out my wider point: The holiness terms provide an alternate window upon the new in Christ; they point, not to chronological steps in an *ordo salutis*, but to another way of speaking the unspeakable gift of God in Christ. Their special flavor is catachretically developed from earlier (in fact, extremely old) secular or religious language about the profane versus the holy, once again to describe the new status in Christ.

Christian **perfection** (in the New Testament, *teleios*), strongly present in the Catholic tradition and brought to fresh awareness in the Anabaptists and in John Wesley, is regrettably of less use as a term for the new in Christ, perhaps because, as Hendrikus Berkhof notes, today it connotes the self-made individual, even the smug one. (More on "perfection" will appear in §3.) However, correlative terms, based on the model of **form,** are available and equally powerful. Berkhof has described their New Testament role so succinctly that I quote him:

> In Paul we find a group of words . . . *morphe, morphousthai, metamorphousthai, symmorphizesthai, symmorphia, symmorphos.* Being in the form of God, Christ assumed the form of a slave (Phil. 2:5-11), in order that he may now be formed in believers (Gal. 4:19), so that they may become like him in his death now and later be made like him in his resurrection (Phil. 3:10f, 21). For God's purpose for them is that they be made like *(symmorphos),* conformed to, the image of his Son (Rom. 8:29). For the important thing is that we, who now bear the likeness of the first Adam, shall bear the likeness of the last Adam (1 Cor. 15:49). See especially 2 Cor. 3:12-18, a central passage in this connection, with its climactic ending in the last two verses; it is clear that we become involved in a recreative narrative so that our nature, too, will possess the freedom and the glory of the pneumatic Christ. . . . Paul links the goal with the way leading to it: conformity with the exalted Christ can come about only through conformity to the way of the suffering Christ, by participating in it by faith. See Phil. 2:1-7; 3:10, and further Rom. 6:1-14; 15:1ff; 2 Cor. 4:7-11; 6:4-10; Eph. 5:2. (Berkhof, 1986:431)

To this brief summary we need only add that linguistic change was once more at work here: For example, the idea of form in Philippians 2 draws upon the concept of Adam being made in the image of God—Adam who failed the challenge of that image, and Jesus who fulfills it (see Chapter Six §3b.i). Then that Christ-image is used still again of those who are "in" him, so that for them "image of God" becomes also a term for the new in Christ.

iii. The new way of Jesus.—Although the two preceding clusters of salvific understanding, crudely labeled Protestant and Catholic, may seem between them to cover the territory, a third cluster is present to the apostolic mind. This is the most venerable of the three, explicit already in the Old Testament where the contrast of two ways (cf. Psalm 1) is a standard theme of wisdom, of the prophets, and of the law. Indeed, the original sense of *Torah*, "law," is "direction"—the path to follow. This original cluster is the one most prominent in the New Testament, being the theme of all four Gospels as Jesus calls hearers to "come, follow me," and it is only gradually overtaken in post-apostolic Christianity by the other two. While one cannot doubt that later emphases met perceived needs in the churches, it would be a mistake for us to neglect our beginning point. It may seem presumptuous to connect this beginning with the baptist movement, since in much modern history, this cluster of salvation concepts has been overshadowed even for baptist disciples by Catholic and Protestant thought. Yet this earliest way stood starkly forth in the sixteenth-century Radical Reformation.

Four quotations offer clues to Radical thought: First, a phrase from the Schleitheim meeting of early Anabaptists (1527), already quoted in *Volume I*, "to walk in the resurrection" as epitome of the new life in Christ (*Ethics*, pp. 269-72). Second, a quotation from Balthasar Hubmaier, Anabaptist leader who was martyred in Vienna in 1528: "Mere faith alone is not sufficient for salvation. . . . Yea, I confess on the strength of this article that mere faith does not deserve to be called faith, for a true faith can never exist without deeds of love" (Hubmaier, 1989:526f). To be sure, Hubmaier was writing in a (hopeless) attempt to avoid martyrdom at Catholic hands, but he did not on that account bear false witness. Third, Jacob Kautz (1500–?), sometime Lutheran preacher in Worms, who in 1527 posted seven new theses on the *Prederkirche* door, among them: "Jesus Christ of Nazareth has not suffered for us in any way unless we stand in his footsteps, walk the way he blazed before us, and follow the command of the Father, everyone in his measure" (W. Klaassen, ed., 1981a:2.10). Fourth, Dirk Philips (1504–1568), Dutch Anabaptist leader just preceding Menno, wrote: "But this is the beginning and the end of the teaching of Jesus Christ (as said above), that we sincerely repent, believe the gospel, are baptized upon our faith in the name of the holy Trinity, that is, in the name of the Father, and of the Son, and of the Holy Spirit, and are diligent by the grace of God to observe all that Christ has commanded us (Mt. 28:20)" (W. Klaassen, ed., 1981a:2.10). For Philips, repentance, faith, baptism, and obedience are alike and *together* the true path to salvation.

Seen through the lens of the Protestant plan, this third way adds something that is true, but not a part of justification by faith alone, while through a Catholic lens it needlessly lifts up a definite beginning or conversion. These perceptions are evidently powerful ones, because in course of time the baptist movement seemed to cede "salvation" to one or the other of these standpoints. Thus if we look at the later baptist confessional documents gathered in Lumpkin (1969) and Loewen (1985) what strikes the eye is apparently a straight Reformed soteriology. But the confessions may mislead us here; baptists have never been primarily a creedal people. What seems to have happened was that the cluster marking entry upon the way of Jesus was not discarded, but (doctrinally) displaced, so that in the English confessions, "walking in the resurrection" is reflected, not in the article on salvation, but in that on the central importance of believers baptism. Or, in the Southern Baptist Faith and Message (1925), the way is displaced into *confessional* (!) articles on religious liberty, peace and war, education, social service, cooperation, evangelism and missions, stewardship, and the kingdom of God (Lumpkin, 1969:396-98). What caused this displacement? Partly, the persuasive polemic of other Christian standpoints. Partly, though, it was the lack of adequate theological work reflecting the baptist community of reference, the failure to discover, interpret, and transform its insight: God's gift of salvation beginning in intentional, sign-marked entry upon Jesus' way, continuing in obedient discipleship with costly suffering, leading the redeemed all the way home.

Sinner, O sinner, come home.

And come home, not at death merely, but by taking this way *here* and *now*.

The strength of this plan of salvation lay in the tight bond it created between divine grace and a total human response. Christian conduct did not follow (by some kind of inference or induction) as a consequence of salvation: it *was itself* salvation. The salvific gift of God and its human answer in following Jesus were two sides of one reality. The plan's weakness so far has been its vulnerability to invasion from other standpoints that could allow it no space. Again and again, this way has been lost to sight, again and again recovered. In the last half of the twentieth century, one may see this recovery in such new forms of salvific community as the house churches of Communist China, American 1960s movements typified by Reba Place, Sojourners, and Bartimaeus, by Latin

American basic communities, and perhaps even by John MacArthur's "Lordship" teaching. Whether these survive, or others like them appear, depends partly upon work in Christian doctrine that seeks to discover, understand, and transform their primary insight into Christian life and conviction.

The chief test of this mode of salvation doctrine, though, must again be the cluster of New Testament terms that formed its basis. Of first interest here is **the way** *(hē hodos)*: the community was "those of the way," according to Acts, even before they were called Christians (Acts 9:2, etc.; 11:26); Paul shows the Corinthians that love is a "better *way*" (1 Cor. 12:31) and characteristically spoke, as did other New Testament writers, of the Christian's "walk" *(peripatein,* Rom. 6:4; 1 Cor. 7:17; Gal. 5:16; 1 John 1:7; etc.; *anastrophē,* Heb. 13:7; James 3:13; 1 Pet. 1:15, etc.; cf. Gal. 1:13; Eph. 4:22; 1 Tim. 4:12; and see R. Banks, 1987). In John, Jesus is himself "the way" that leads to the Father (14:5-7). To understand the force of this, we must again recall the Old Testament, where "way" *(derek)* meant simply road or street, but had come also to mean characteristic life pattern: the habit of the eagle or of the serpent, the conduct of a human being, the way of a man with a maid, while *halak,* "walk," provided a word for law derived from the Mosaic law given at Sinai *(halakah)*. This permitted setting two ways in contrast: God's way and man's. One is ever good and right, the other may be or become evil, and salvation lay in turning from it (Pss. 16:11, 23:3; Jer. 32:39, 42:3; Mic. 4:2). Thus a substantial catachretical move had already been made. "Way" in the Old Testament had become the path of salvation, and therefore was linked to the redemptive narrative: God led Israel out of slavery and into a new way of life in the land of promise.

This might seem, then, a term where no further catachresis was appropriate. Yet the consummate literary skill of Mark produced a new transformation: At first reading, *hē hodos,* the road, may seem only an awkward geographic linking of diverse tales about Jesus. Yet recent Marcan scholars find this is not so: The road is (catachretically) the Messianic life-style itself (thus Athol Gill, 1989); it is the redemptive journey, whether Jesus' own trail or that of the disciples who must follow in his steps toward Golgotha (Joel Green, 1991). Clue to this double shift in the sense of "the road" (the shift from a route through the countryside to a way of life; the shift from Old Testament promise of life with God to New Testament fulfillment in Jesus) is found in Mark's introductory quotations from "the prophet Isaiah" (actually a collage of Septuagint quotations): "I am sending my herald ahead of you; he will prepare your way." As Ched Myers shows, this quotation is like a puzzle at the Gospel's doorway: Who is the herald, what is the way? (Myers, 1988:124-

26). The answer begins to come out in Mark 8 and 9 (where "road" references reappear as well); it finally breaks clear only as disciples with the resurrection message are sent back to Galilee (16:7f)—to start the journey in earnest? Taking the road *(hodos)* requires entry *(eishodos, eiserchomai)*, and this recalls a different term, entering the kingdom or **rule of God,** a term so central that it is discussed above, in the Introduction to Part I.

Among the key terms in this cluster, **liberation** is of special interest because of its employment by Liberation Theology (see Gutiérrez, 1973:36f). Its New Testament use reveals unexpected complexity. The words usually translated "release," "redeem," and "redemption" *(luein, lutrein, lutrōsis, apolutrōsis,* etc.) were technical terms in the Hellenistic world for the termination of an enslavement. In the same vocabulary were *agoradzein* and *exagoradzein,* to purchase (a slave) from the market. These were the terms used in the Greek Old Testament to translate *gaal* and *padah,* themselves terms of the Semitic slave trade.

But in Hebrew the same words were applied to the legal 'redemption' of a criminal achieved by paying a price to the victim, and again in the Jewish sacrificial system to the 'redemption' of worshipers from such blemishes as ritual uncleanness. In these cases they implied the act of one who redeemed, and so lent themselves to theological use: God 'redeemed' *(gaal,* e.g., Exod. 15:13) Israel from Egypt; the Psalmist asked to be redeemed and delivered *(gaal* and *padah)* from his enemies (69:18); Job expected a vindicator *(goel,* 19:25) of his integrity. Since these terms sometimes suggested means of redemption (cf. *kopher),* they contributed to New Testament atonement theology, and some will reappear in Chapter Five.

Yet these are no more prominent in the New Testament than several other 'freedom' terms: *eleutherein* and its cognates (the verb translated "set free," the noun, "free man or woman"); *politeia* (translated "citizenship" in Acts 22:28); *parrhēsia,* translated "confidence" or "boldness" (as of Paul's 'liberty' while a prisoner in Rome, Acts 28:31). From these as from the preceding group we may learn that (1) God through the gospel liberates men and women from sin and hindrance, (2) this liberation is not into a random or aleatory state, but into a new polity, that of the rule of God, and (3) its citizens are accordingly bold or confident when confronting the old order with that very gospel.

The way is closely related to the one who takes it, the **disciple** *(mathētēs).* Like the other terms in this cluster, the figure of the disciple (singular and collective) is strongly narrative-tied: Disciples are *called;* they are *taught;* they are required to *follow;* they are *tested;* their testing in the Gospels is their undoing and yet becomes the occasion of their *redemption.* The development of these terms and of the many others in this cluster, such as conversion *(metanoia)*, "baptism" used as a meta-phor, and passage from death to life, is once again left to the reader.

iv. Uniting the clusters: the doctrinal task.—Each of these three clusters of salvation doctrine could be enlarged by adding biblical and historical substance, and other historic clusters might be found by casting our net more widely. The task for us, though, is to relate these three neighbor clusters to one another and to today. It is worth noting, even before we begin, that all together they do not exhaust the field. Some of our terms hover between two clusters: Is *adoption* a term of relation or of (mystical) union? Is *passing from death to life* to be grouped with salvation as journey or salvation as transformed identity? Further, there are terms that fall under none of the above and (thereby) escape soteriological attention: *people of God*, for example, is a synonym for the new in Christ in its New Testament occurrences, and there are dozens more.

If we follow the consensus noted at chapter's beginning and no longer try to relate these terms in a consecutive scheme ('called' before 'justi-fied' before 'born anew' before 'sanctified,' etc.), we may recognize that they are in fact synonyms—varied ways of pointing to the same reality, windows upon one new life, one journey all must take, one new friend-ship with the risen Christ. They are alternate sets of windows shedding varied light upon that new being that Jesus' followers find; many facets of one precious stone; many gateways into understanding salvation. This is as true of (the word) *salvation (sōtēria)* as of any other; it, too, is catachretically developed—from words that meant ordinary rescue or healing (W. Foerster and G. Fohrer, TDNT VII:965-1024). "Salvation" has no proper claim to preside over all the other words for the new, and does not do so here.

Yet different Christian traditions have seized one or another of these terms or clusters of terms, have constructed doctrines of the new in Christ mainly upon them, and have either overlooked the remainder, or sought to fit them in as best they could. As far as it goes, this is not a bad thing. But it raises the question, how we are to proceed if we seek the whole Christian witness. Perhaps the best answer is that we must learn to hear those witnesses whose regular clusters are other than our own for what they have to say in their own right. This cannot mean merely that major Christian groups or theologians come to agree about how to use these terms (as exemplified by Küng, 1981). It must mean the task of appreciating the concrete action of the new in Christ within living Christian communities. Although such a wide historical survey is be-yond our scope, we can at least seek to make clear how our own

understanding works. For this volume, that means presenting the ordered Christian life as *following* Jesus Christ (§3). Before that, though, we
must consider sin in the light of the new in Christ (§2). To this point, we
have only begun to see the new in Christ.

§2. Sin in the Light of Salvation

Throughout the preceding section ran a theme that must shape all
Christian doctrine—**the rule** or kingly reign **of God** which Jesus proclaimed. Good news: God's rule here and now overtakes human existence! So salvation cannot be understood as a human accomplishment
or as a reward for such accomplishment; rather the new relations, new
being, new way Jesus brought are gift or grace, "the grace of the Lord
Jesus Christ" (cf. 2 Cor. 13:14). This gracious royal theme remains
primary in Christian teaching about sin. Not even the knowledge of sin
is our very own contribution to salvific understanding; sin is not a
(negative) human achievement to be painted with Faustian pride. Rather
authentic knowledge of my sin, clear awareness that I am a sinner, comes
only when and as I am saved from it. Only when the strong light of grace
penetrates our lives do we see clearly the long shadow cast by past sin,
only then, the crannies of corporate or societal corruption; only then, the
menace of a future outside the coming rule of God.

Accepting this approach may seem mistaken to Christians aware that
not only outside Hebrew Scripture but within as well, the ancient world
displayed its own sense of sin. Taboo and dread of impropriety in face
of the gods or God run through the tapestry of human cultures and
religions. The Hebrew Scriptures have some distinctive words for human fault vis-à-vis God: *pesha*, rebellion against the Lord God; *avon*,
being in the wrong or being wrong in oneself, usually "iniquity"; *chethah*,
most often translated "sin," but also as an everyday "missing one's path
(or aim)." (One can correlate these three with the clusters of concepts of
the new in Christ distinguished in the preceding section.) These closely
related Hebrew stems were all translated in the Septuagint by *hamartia*,
and this in turn became the usual New Testament word our versions
render "sin." Moreover, there are typical sin-stories already in the Old
Testament: Adam and Eve in Genesis 3, murderous Cain in 4, corrupt
Sodom in 18 and 19, Joseph's brothers (and Potiphar's wife) in the
patriarchal saga of 37–50, and corresponding tales throughout the biblical narrative.

Yet we approach all these narratives with Christian eyes, or at least with gospel-influenced reading strategies. So read, they are indeed types of the disobedience, human perversity, and false aims that were to oppose Jesus when he appeared. It is noteworthy that without that gospel-shaped master story, these other narratives are differently focused; for example, post-70 Judaism never made of sin the key problem that it became in Christian thought. Judaism developed no doctrine of 'original' or inherited sin. For the rabbis, the *yetzer hara* or evil impulse was a partial explanation of human fault, but neither it nor actual sin loomed as large in this certainly highly moral religion as for Jesus' followers. (Nevertheless, Judaism displays two features valuable for us: emphasis on sin as breaking the covenant, and sin's remedy in atonement, as on the Day of Atonement—W. H. Bennett, ERE XI:556-60.) Thus our first task here is to see how sin is framed by the new that comes in Christ. This understanding can then be contrasted with the development and failure of the 'original sin' doctrine, followed by restatement of the Christian teaching.

a. Jesus Christ as the measure of sin.—Every Christian doctrine seems to require every other for its clear presentation. We must anticipate Chapter Five on the (atoning) lifework of Jesus of Nazareth in order to find our own doctrinal footing here. In that chapter, Jesus' life course, as we may glean it from critical reading of the Epistles and Gospels, will stand forth as a life of **full faithfulness**—faithfulness to his cause, faithfulness to God whom he knew as Father. The covenant with Israel, whose renewal had been promised by the prophets (e.g., Jeremiah 33), was reclaimed by Jesus son of Mary and Joseph. That covenant, to be vital, required an authenticator, one who by taking God's way within the existing social order affirmed God's faithfulness toward Israel and opened the way toward God for followers drawn from all nations. The way he took required of him (1) a visionary commitment to God's goal for the race, (2) full solidarity with the brother-and-sisterhood that would share his way and thus potential solidarity with all people everywhere, and (3) the social daring of one who would be not an everyday king but Lord of a new divine-human realm, the rule of God. All these (in traditional parlance, his 'offices' as *prophet, priest,* and *king*) were displayed in the narrative Jesus lived out. By it, he proved himself true *anthropos,* authentic *homo,* progenitor of a human strain that fulfilled (rather than once again deflecting) the promise to Adam ("Earthling") and to Eve ("Life")—the promise that in their human family God's own image would appear (cf. Gen. 3:15).

This human being, Jesus in his authentic, undiminished humanity (Jesus as the human answer to God), declares in his action—in words and work, in life and death, in historic particularity and once for all—the true anthropology promised in creation. By this faithfulness he unveils sin: Sin is whatever falls short of, whatever denies, whatever misses the way of faithfulness to God's rule embodied in Jesus Christ (cf. John 3:19, etc.). No Swiss cheese figure, this one, but human wholeness in mind and manner, flesh, blood, and spirit.

This biblical testimony contradicts those modern theologians who treated sin as creaturely limitation, a necessary feature of our created sensuous nature (Schleiermacher, CF §§5, 79, 80) or will (Ritschl, 1888:III, 380), or as a corollary of finite being (Tillich, 1951–63, II:chap. 1), or as a paradoxically inevitable yet not necessary circumstance growing from "man's involvement in nature and his transcendence over it" (R. Niebuhr, 1941–43, I:181). These readings of the human condition (and they can be matched with older and Catholic sources) have the unhappy consequence of diminishing the possibilities of the new that comes in Christ. In the name of a doctrine of creation some have thus drained the good news of actual goodness. Consequently, they also make it more difficult to interpret the true humanity of Jesus Christ. If sin is simply human nature, what sort of nature is his? The language of Scripture, and that of orthodoxy elsewhere, converge against this view of sin's inevitability: There Jesus is the Truly Human One (*huios tou anthropou*), he is the *verus homo*, and so our own selfhood, as far as it remains sinful, falls short not merely of divinity but of genuine humanity as well. If sinners, we fall short of true humanity; if he is truly human, sin is not essential or proper to human nature. He in his faithfulness exhibits the design of humanity as it is meant to be. (To err may be human, but to sin is not.) As sinners, we are indeed Swiss cheese folk, pocked with holes from heel to head. The emptiness of our sins gapes until it is closed with graceful human goodness. More broadly, a sinful human society is seen in gospel light as frothy lava, without the granite pressure of the Rock that is Christ (cf. Rom. 14:23*b*). Even so construed, sin remains problematic, a puzzling vacancy or disorder in a God-created world, but the problems are not solved by the theory of 'original' sin.

From this evangelical, that is, gospel-focused standpoint, one can make good sense of the special concerns of the New Testament writers: of John, who makes clear that there are degrees of sin (John 19:11), of Paul, who takes *sarx*, literally "flesh," as the image of the sinful self in strife with itself being redeemed, of the several Epistle writers who spell out concrete sin-lists (e.g., Eph. 2:1-3; 4:19-31), as well as the designation "sinner" (occasional in Psalms and wisdom books). This last is especially interesting inasmuch as the Gospels challenge the received use of the term "sinner": those whom society recognizes as sinners are often especially close to Jesus, yet by the Gospels' report the term had not gone dead for Jesus, who makes his own (catachretical) use of it.

b. The rise and fall of 'original sin.'—'Original sin,' the view that the pervasive presence of sin in the human species is caused by the first sin of the first human pair, is not the teaching of Scripture. It rests upon historic but mistaken readings. It is nevertheless appropriate to ask whether this doctrine should be included in Christian teaching (as is, for distinguished example, the doctrine of the Trinity), for not all that is Christianly true is explicit in the Bible. Certainly 'original sin' played a central role in Christian doctrine in the West. We may usefully note at least three moments in this history.

The first involved the early fifth-century controversy between Augustine (344–430), Catholic bishop of Hippo, and Pelagius (c. 355–c. 425), a British monk sojourning in Mediterranean lands. As it began, the controversy seemed to be one about the content of salvation and the nature of the Christian life. Pelagius had labored in mission territory, and his emphases preserved the primitive Christian theme of the resolute intention required of each convert, who could and must turn to a new path of life. Augustine represented a new direction of Christian salvation teaching: As pastor of a settled Christian community, he had won favor by emphasizing the inwardness of Christian conversion and the slow, lifelong progress that was entailed by Christian existence. Baptized Christians were victims rescued by Christ the Good Samaritan but destined now to spend the remainder of this earthly life as weak convalescents in a sheltering inn (the church) (*Serm.* 131.6; cf. P. Brown, 1969:365). The differing emphases of these two might have been resolved but for two factors: the Augustinians, fresh from their triumph over and persecution of the Donatists, were determined to crush this new opposition by any means including Imperial force; meanwhile Augustine produced a series of controversial writings (411–20) that solidified a new doctrine of inherited sinfulness. It attributed total inability to all the children of Adam "in whom all sinned" (*in quo omnes peccaverunt*), as Augustine read Romans 5:12 in his Vulgate Latin Bible (*De pecc. orig.* II, 35). As a consequence of their participation in Adam's original act, all had sinned, so that at birth all were already guilty, all were depraved, and all deserved eternal punishment. Pelagius stoutly denied these theses.

The words *eph hō* in Romans 5:12, as is now generally agreed by scholarly translations, mean "inasmuch as" or "because," or "on condition that" (cf. Moulton and Milligan, 1949:234a); grammatically they look forward to the following words, *pantes hēmarton*, "all sinned," not backward to Adam's sin. Even without this understanding of *eph hō*, the passage on which Augustine leaned was open to a better interpretation: Paul is here employing biblical typology. Adam is the *typos*, type, of the Coming One, but like all types he falls short of the coming fulfillment; worse still, in this case Adam's sin heralded the reign of death that prevailed until Christ, since (in course of time) "all sinned"— though not all so flagrantly as had Adam (v. 14). As recipients of Christ's salvation gift, then, we acknowledge Adam as our *typos* as well; his condemnation models the reign of death we incur save for the justification we receive in Christ. The relation of believers to Adam is not said here to be one of sin inherited; it is rather the relation of a model *(typos)* of failure to those whose lives are governed not by it but by the "one man, Jesus Christ" who by his grace has become *our* type (v. 17). Verse 19 is to be read in this light. It introduces no new claim, but sums up the preceding parallels in an epigram: 'Sin in Adam, salvation in Christ.' Neither in this final epigram nor in the preceding paragraph is causation Paul's theme.

Western Christianity was divided in its response to the debate: in a series of synods the Catholic church decided now for Pelagius, now for Augustine, so that by the late Middle Ages official teaching was more or less Augustinian (subscribing to 'original sin' and endorsing infant baptism as the remedy) while parish practice was more or less Pelagian (encouraging a piety of exculpatory works).

The issue was therefore ripe for discussion in the second historic moment, that of Lutheran and Reformed Protestantism in the sixteenth century. Consider the stance of John Calvin (1509–64), the Genevan Reformer, for whom Augustine's doctrines of sin and grace were paramount. Calvin's view is concisely presented in the *Institutes* (2, 1). Adam's sin (Eve is neglected) "enkindled God's fearful vengeance against the whole of mankind" (2, 4). The estrangement thus opened between God and Adam, with its entailed guilt and curse, "flowed hither and yon . . . to all his offspring" (2, 5). Children are therefore cursed in the womb. Calvin finds this patently reasonable: When the Lord entrusted the gifts of human nature as intended to Adam, but Adam lost them, he "lost them not only for himself but for us all" (2, 6). Thus, either by divine ordinance or natural inheritance (Calvin wavers between these) human infants arrive corrupt and guilty prior to their own sinful acts—which of course spring from this corruption (2, 8). If Augustine's deepest motive had been protection of his profound sense of the inwardness of sin, Calvin's was not unlike it: he wanted a doctrine that would "strip us of all confidence in our own ability" (2, 2) so that we look not to ourselves but to Christ for salvation. Thus, so far from seeing sin in salvific light, Calvin and his heirs saw salvation only through the lens of universal sin.

Before a third, twentieth-century moment unfolded, the work of Christian exegetes, Old Testament and New, made clear that the older reading of crucial 'original sin' passages was impossible. Careful historians of doctrine such as F. R. Tennant (1908) and N. P. Williams (1927), both Anglicans, wrote exposing the logical and theological inconsistencies of the church doctrine in light of Scripture and tradition. Tennant argued forcefully against the doctrine of inherited sin, and (less successfully) proposed an "evolutionary" account of sin and evil. Williams reviewed the late rise and subsequent decline of the doctrine in Western church teaching, and argued that 'original sin' could not be a universal Christian doctrine. Against this background Reinhold Niebuhr (1892–1971), American theological ethicist, attempted a mid-century recovery of the traditional teaching (1941–43, I). Consciously both post-Darwinian and post-Freudian, Niebuhr attempted no literal history of the human plight. The fall was frankly a myth. It was conceded to be, indeed flaunted, as "absurd." How *can* we be responsible for that which we have not chosen? Despite its absurdity, for him the myth was true to the psychological and moral facts of human nature as neither Pelagian nor semi-Pelagian views could be. For the fact is that sin abounds; the fact is that "man sins inevitably, yet without escaping responsibility for his sin" (p. 251); the fact is that "man cannot love himself inordinately without pretending that it is not his, but a universal interest which he is supporting" (p. 253); the fact is that the "fury with which oligarchs, dictators, priest-kings, ancient and modern . . . turn upon their critics and foes is clearly the fury of an uneasy conscience" (p. 256). Thus the "myth" was truer to the facts than any proposed rational account, and from it Reinhold Niebuhr drew a subtle, nuanced, and often insightful account of "sinful human nature." The question to be asked is whether the "myth" had outlived its usefulness, and whether a 'demythologized' account of the human condition might not now better serve theology.

For the difficulties with the received concept of original sin are many: Its implied doctrine of the injustice of God (already noted by Pelagius), its sponsorship of infant baptism and with it whole populations Christian in name but pagan in fact (a fault exposed by Calvin's contemporaries, the Anabaptists), its failure in faithfulness to the biblical understanding of salvation and sin (a failure detailed prior to Reinhold Niebuhr's mythic exegesis). Still this persistent doctrine had its value: It emphasized the primacy of grace; it acknowledged the pervasiveness and (particularly) the inwardness of sin; it exposed the shallow depth of rival views of human nature. (As Anselm of Canterbury, a medieval adherent of the church doctrine, had answered Boso when the latter proposed easy remedies for the human plight: *Nondum considerasti quantum ponderis sit peccatum,* "You have not yet considered how heavy is the weight of sin!"—*Cur deus homo* 1:21.) If a less vulnerable view displays these virtues as well, perhaps 'original sin' can be abandoned without loss.

So it is worth asking whether a fourth moment in this history has not been for some time gathering. One might refer to the pre-Augustinian rules of faith, which omit inherited sin, or begin with the Anabaptists of the sixteenth century. The very variety of the Radicals' teaching on this topic suggests change in the making. Conrad Grebel (c. 1498–1526), the valiant young humanist of the Swiss Brethren, picked up the typological note in Genesis 3: "We hold that all children who have not attained the knowledge to discern between good and evil and [so] have not eaten of the tree of knowledge are surely saved through the suffering of Christ, the new Adam, unless it can be proved to us that Christ did not die for children" ("Letter to Muentzer," in Harder, ed., 1985:290). For Grebel, the relation of living folk to the biblical narrative is figural (recall the baptist vision), not genetic. Hans Schlaffer, writing in about 1527, demands that he be shown from Scripture that original sin condemns children (Klaassen, ed., 1981a:172). Peter Riedeman acknowledged inherited sin but limited it to inclination, while guilt was for actual sin only (one thinks of the rabbinic *yetzer hara*) (ibid., 180f). It was not so much in their theorizing, however, as in their practice of believer's baptism that Anabaptists challenged the traditional doctrine: If New Testament baptism is precisely for converted believers, it cannot be meant by God as a remedy for infant guilt—thus, God being good, there can be no such guilt. The baptist baptismal practice made a theory of infant guilt appear inconsistent.

Horace Bushnell, while retaining the term "original sin," had already in 1858 argued that sin and depravity were socially, not genetically, transmitted—a real turning point in doctrinal development (Bushnell, ed. Smith, 1965:220-60). Then, early in the twentieth century, Walter Rauschenbusch considered the doctrine of sin first among those that must be restated in light of an awakened Christian social conscience. This restatement would not minimize sin in Christian teaching (a widespread misreading of the Social Gospel), but would show how sin against the kingdom of God was rooted in the social order itself. Following Bushnell, Rauschenbusch did not hesitate to retain the term "original sin" to describe this corporate sinfulness everywhere present and persisting through long ages. He commended the traditional doctrine for its practical recognition that others' sin can cause our own, not merely by the force of evil example, but by creating depraved social conditions. Under these, cruelty, or misuse of sex, or lynchings or blood feuds, or gluttonous acquisition of wealth, or oppression and economic strangulation fester. Righteousness is discouraged. Often enough such conditions are the consequence of the sin of more recent foreparents than Adam; transmitted from generation to generation, these conditions grow or wither as functions of each new generation. As enemies and rivals of the kingdom of God, such social growths constitute a collective "kingdom of evil" constituted by super-personal forces of evil—not demons and devils, but highly organized social structures perverted to the service of dynastic and class interests (Rauschenbusch, 1917: chaps. 4–9).

Here, then, are the makings of a fresh doctrine of social sin and its entailed evils. It is a doctrine that denies we can be guilty of others' sins; nevertheless we can suffer their consequences. It frees us to employ psychology and sociology to analyze the human social condition while recognizing that these sciences are not untainted by those very conditions. It leaves myths of origins (such as Freud's Oedipal scene—Freud, 1913) to those who can make scientific use of them, while it listens for the word of God to disclose the pervasiveness and power of the "kingdom of evil" in practices and institutions. It has no need to 'redeem' infants from sins they have not committed, but it will not be thwarted when it finds children drinking from poisoned social wells, for it proclaims a gospel that purges both the poisoned wells and the victims who drink. In all these ways it challenges the traditional doctrine. It cannot answer the baffling question, Whence this evil in a world God creates? but neither can the traditional church doctrine answer it (on the 'mystery' of evil, see Chapter Four §2c).

c. Restating the doctrine of sin.—The doctrine of sin has too often been construed as the pall of gloom Christians cast over any life they touch; one recalls humorist Garrison Keillor's jest that the Catholic parish in his fictional Minnesota town is named Our Lady of Perpetual Responsibility. Or one recalls the old gibe that Puritans opposed the medieval sport of bear baiting, not because it gave pain to the bear, but because it gave pleasure to the spectators. On the other hand, efforts to lighten the supposed gloom have often fallen short of the truth of sin in Christian experience: Reductive and trivializing accounts fail, as Anselm warned, to consider how heavy sin's weight is. How can we steer between these shoals? Here the effort has been to relate the Christian account to the good news in such a way that it is seen as the occasion for tears in an otherwise happy story.

> In his anger is distress,
> in his favour there is life.
> Tears may linger at nightfall,
> but rejoicing comes in the morning.
> (Ps. 30:5)

We cannot say a good word for sin if we count its cost to Jesus the faithful One. Yet we have to reckon that if his own life-story, marred by the sin of others, was finally not tragedy but (in the classical sense) comedy; when that narrative of happy ending impacts our own, our tear-stained, sin-marred tragedies are turned into comedy as well. By his grace, there is laughter in the morning.

From the point of view of believers in 'original sin,' conversionist and baptist views have sometimes seemed moralistic or simplistic or both, while the retort has been that 'original sin' theorists were morally Manichaean or dualist, making little or no room for actual salvation in this present life. Rather than perpetuate the polemic, we need to provide a conversionist account sufficiently complex to do justice to the reality of sin's disobedience, perversity, and misdirection, while acknowledging still more the reality of God's redemptive love and power to overturn it (Saiving Goldstein, 1960). The charge of 'moralism' trained on some forms of this doctrine implies that they subordinate the gospel to the precepts of mere morality. And indeed faith or religion or obedience to God must not be reduced to a morality determined on some alien basis. But what if it is the other way around? In *Volume I* the key to Christian ethics was found, not in a separate philosophical principle of morality, Kantian or utilitarian or other, but in God's creative, sustaining, and renewing action. God, not self-subsistent morality, is the source of Christian ethics. Consequently, a doctrine of sin may be profoundly ethical exactly on gospel ground. So we turn again to that volume's distinction of three strands, *organic* (having to do with embodied existence), *communal* (concerning relations with others), and *anastatic* (about God's resurrection action) (*Ethics,* Two §3). Here, however, the reverse treatment will be appropriate: our order will be (i) anastatic, (ii) communal, and (iii) organic.

i. Sin as refusal.—God is making all things new. In Jesus Christ there is a *kainē ktisis*, a new *world* (2 Cor. 5:17 NEB). Disciples are introduced to that world; entering, they must construe all things by its light. They anticipate its ultimate full disclosure (admittedly, with much groaning—Rom. 8:22). Sin is thereby revealed to be whatever opposes entry into this new world, whatever blinds or distorts the *anastatic* vision of all things new, whatever misses the way to its earthly fulfillment. The fundamental sin (or, to use an old word in a very different way now, the original sin against the new in Christ), the sin that engulfs, swallows up the sinner if committed, is the vacant refusal of Jesus' offered way.

This is the point, as I see it, of such passages as John 3 (see v. 19: "already judged because he has not put his trust in God's only Son") and in its light 1 John

3 (v. *6a:* "No one who dwells in him sins any more"): The Gospel passage warns of the danger of not turning, the Epistle celebrates the good news of that turn to faith in Christ that is the hearer's fundamental option, his or her choice between death and life, after which *persistence* in sin *(hamartanei,* present of continuous action) is clear enough evidence that one has "neither seen him nor known him" (1 John 3:*6b*). Here, too, is the clue to the proper exegesis of Romans 3:21ff: speaking of "all who have faith in Christ," Paul declares of them that *they all* have sinned, thereby they are *as such* excluded from the divine glory, but (praise God!) all are justified. Here the scope of "all" is the Jewish and Gentile members of the Roman Christian congregation. Paul is providing not a worldview but an applied doctrine of salvation by grace: Jewish Rome-dwellers, heirs of God's Sinai covenant, needed that grace—and that turn—just as Roman Gentiles did. Ephesians 2 presents a similar picture of Gentiles and Jews in complicity in sin but united by grace alone (Yoder, 1972:chap. 11; M. Barth, 1974, s.v. Ephesians 2). For correction of the misleading interpretation of Romans as a theory of 'original' and inherited sin, see the preceding section (§2b) above.

Two corollaries follow: (1) Our doctrine gives no reason to impute mortal (or in *either* sense 'original') sin to members of the human race who have not received Jesus' graceful invitation, his "gospel of the kingdom" (Mark 1:14f par.). One cannot reject what one has not been offered! Those who have not even heard the gospel cannot truly have rejected it. The diatribe of Romans 1:18-23 has been used by some to assign this sin of refusal indiscriminately to all human beings, all of whom, it is reasoned, find God "visible to the eye of reason, in the things he has made," that is, the creation. If, however, it is true that Paul's diatribe assigns some fault to faulty 'natural theologians,' we must not extrapolate this fault to make them (or everyone!) guilty of the great sin now under discussion, for refusal is not just theological error (deplorable, of course, in theological eyes), but is *refusal of the proffered good news itself.*

It is in this connection, too, that Jesus' words about "slander against the Holy Spirit" (Mark 3:28-30 par.), the "sin unto death" of the First Epistle of John (5:16f), and (perhaps) the "falling away" warned against in Hebrews (6:4-6 and 10:26-31) are to be understood: from different directions and with varied pastoral concerns these writers approach a common theme: there is a sin of sins, so designated simply because it persistently and finally refuses the good of goods. Beyond it, nothing offers hope. It is difficult, though, to invoke this warning without stirring up morbid fear in neurotic believers that they have (willfully or even inadvertently!) committed this sin. The old pastoral counsel, that concern about having committed unforgivable sin is sure evidence that one has not committed it, is sound and worth repeating. Here, though, a warning must indeed be issued to Christian witnesses. The gospel puts recipients of our witness for Christ at great risk even as it offers them great gain. Yet we ourselves are at equal risk if we fail faithfully to render the witness. And we should be comforted to reckon that refusal of our *flawed* witness by someone may be, after all, a good mark for both of us—for us, because we have not finally misled at least this one; for the other, because refusal of our flawed image of Christ may be a sign that God's Spirit is indeed leading her or him toward the true Christ.

A second corollary (2) concerns the kind of sin that, perhaps not in name, but surely in fact, does count as refusal. We remember the Gospel warning:

> Not everyone who says to me, "Lord, Lord" will enter the kingdom of Heaven, but only those who do the will of my heavenly Father. When the day comes, many will say to me, "Lord, Lord, did we not prophesy in your name, and in your name perform many miracles?" Then I will tell them plainly, "I never knew you. Out of my sight; your deeds are evil." (Matt. 7:21)

One of the virtues of some Latin American Liberation Theology is to recall that Jesus' concern is with the whole of life, so that rejecting his role as liberator is refusing Jesus himself. This refusal may take two forms: One is to substitute our own (well meant) social programs for *his* liberation; the other is to spiritualize Jesus right out of this present world, denying his relevance to politics and to history (cf. Galilea, 1981:97-109).

While the Roman Catholic doctrine of 'mortal sin' was misleading in its older forms, its recent recasting as a doctrine of a 'fundamental option,' proposed by contemporary Catholic theologians, is consonant with the present approach (J. Fuchs, 1963–67:2, 4; 1966; cf. *Ethics,* pp. 55, 293).

ii. Sin as rupture.—Human beings are made for company with one another, and together made for fellowship with God. Thus Part II of *Ethics,* "The Sphere of the Communal," focused on the social dimension of Christian life with its practices and communities. Disciples are called not into a solitary following, but into a *body,* the church. Rupture in Christian community is thus sin against the intended coming rule of God, just as ruptures in the general social fabric (estranged and severed family ties, village quarrels, broken cities, balkanized countries, nations at one another's borders, throats, and goods) are symptoms of social disease. The analysis of social ethics in Part II of the previous volume depended upon the concept of *practices,* cooperative means-and-ends human activities that at their best attain high goals but at their worst are subject to severe, even monstrous perversion. The human social life that is formed by such practices requires interconnections best described as narrative continuity and coherence. In other words, practices imply stories, and making sense of social life requires eliciting the stories it embodies. Yet it came out there that practices go wrong; they are (in the Apostle's term) "principalities and powers" whose narratives take an ugly turn, inimical to creation's welfare. Hence the master story that will redeem human life must be one that engages not only our individual but these collective stories, changing them and restoring the distorted or refractory practices. Such a master story is the history of God's way with Israel, in Jesus, and through the church. For example the Ten Commandments (Exod. 20:1-17 par.) were directions shaping existing social practices, and again today, where these practices exist, the Ten Words offer redemptive guidance (*Ethics*, Six, §§1-2), as does the teaching of Jesus condensed in the Sermon on the Mount (Matthew 5–7 par.).

From this new, 'fourth' perspective, social sin must be exposed as a narrative misdirection that defeats common sociality. It ruptures practices that but for it bear reconciling fruit in human life. A dynamic view of social existence—its practices having an end, its stories a point or goal—requires a moving rather than fixed understanding of social sin. In a nineteenth-century poet's phrase,

> Time makes ancient good uncouth.

We saw above (§1b.i) that justification is God's judicial setting-right of peoples and individuals estranged from one another and God. In this light social sin is *un*justice, rupture that hinders God's restorative right-wising activity in Jesus Christ (cf. Rom. 14:23 NRSV).

The death penalty in law, as a single example among many, was at one stage of social existence an ameliorative limit set upon the rule of revenge. Yet when the story of human social life moves ahead, what had been a check upon revenge becomes its fierce fagot, inflaming passions it had earlier quenched. Christians rupture the narrative of human redemption when they invoke this judicial killing or stand by (so many Sauls with the stone throwers' coats at their feet) while others carry it out. In the light of the cross, killing as punishment commits the evil it condemns, and (like murder) cuts short the gospel's opportunity to remake its victims' lives (cf. *Ethics*, Eleven).

iii. Sin as reversion.—Just as there is a narrative of God's restorative life-out-of-death way with our human race, and just as there are narratives of social life including the sociality of the kingdom or rule of God (significantly displayed in Israel and the church), so is there a 'narrative' of *organic* growth in human and other species, an ecological story of life in our biosphere. This life is the basis of the fuller life of the realm of God. As such, it is valuable in its own right (*Ethics*, Part I, "The Sphere of the Organic"). Rather than treat this sphere as a realm of "natural law" (drawing a metaphor, *law*, from the social sphere and applying it, it seems to me *un*naturally, to the natural) or a realm of "rights" (repeating the same mistake), *Ethics* provides an analysis of the drives, needs, and capacities that mark organic life, and in these terms analyzes our organic moral existence. The argument is that while embodied existence—the only sort we have any experience of—brings with it needed elementary guidelines for morality, these are insufficient even within their own organic sphere. This is because what seem to be 'natural' or 'ecological' issues so often involve our social nature, the sphere of human practices and worldly powers, and as well our engagement with the new that comes in Jesus Christ risen from the dead. Nevertheless, Christians sense a minimal morality that rises from our instincts or *drives*, our *needs* or limits, and our psycho-physical *capacities*. There is no room to repeat here all that is said in *Ethics* about embodied existence, about shame, blame, and guilt, and about conscience and its education, yet the popular misconceptions that discussion refutes will, if not refuted, distort our doctrine of sin as well.

What can now be added is that analogous to the narrative *refusal* of grace and the narrative *rupture* of our solidarity with one another in Christ (sin in the other two spheres), narrative *reversion* sinfully rejects the good proper to organic life and growth. We appear in nature, part of its living system. To despise this setting, to attempt in unearthly fashion to live as if in some superior position we held title to 'our own' bodies (rather than by creation *are* our bodies), or to stultify the growth processes by which we pass from infantile animal to mature human existence—all this is sin for us. In infancy we are given drives that satisfy life needs, and (a limited, but increasing) capacity to meet those needs. The human infant left to itself dies; the growing child in time learns to survive. Gradually the screams, resentments, and aggressions appropriate to infancy are outgrown. Yet infantile reversions occur; aggressive drives meeting no check destroy our bonds with nature and with one another. The developmental narrative is reversed. Where such reversion is not illness it is culpable sin against life and God its giver (*Ethics*, p. 225). In infancy we are given moral capacities proper to infancy—the smile of delight, the cry of pain. With growth comes expansion of those capacities. In conversion to Christ, we are offered new life in the body, a new power of consent to God and whatever is God's. If from that cordial consent we fall back to the private loyalties of clan, tribe, or class, we sin not only against the new social practice of the rule of God, but also against the basic moral gift of life in its organic setting. Thus the plunder of nature, the scorn of our "fragile island home" is organic sin (Santmire, 1985).

Here we must address, however briefly, the much misunderstood topic of sexual sin. To be "in Christ" is to have the full range of embodied existence, mortal, sexual, self-aware existence, sanctified by God. The Bible knows nothing of those gnosticizing versions of the 'original sin' doctrine that made embodied existence as such sinful, with sex its flagrant example. Sin comes only when we fail to bring these rich life-gifts with us into the realm of the new that comes in Christ. Then shame, blame, and guilt will dominate life in the body. In such cases, the full diapason of created and redeemed existence in all its strands is offended, and not the organic alone.

There is more to say about the Christian understanding of sin, more about the human nature that it mars and the divine purpose it aims to thwart. But we must be careful, in saying it, to respect the limits God has set upon sin (cf. 2 Thessalonians 2): We must not identify human being with sinful being; we must not erect the doctrine of sin into a barrier to goodness not even Christ can overcome; we must not be so serious about sin that we fail to be more serious still about grace. With these limits firmly in place, we can move on to consider (§3) the Christian salvation journey as a whole.

§3. Following Jesus: The Christian Journey

a. Guideposts for the journey.—Is it beginner Christians who are in best position to understand the newness of salvation? Theirs is the vivid discovery of new relations to enjoy, a new selfhood that is their own, a new path to follow. This same new light illuminates their failures, showing sin in its loneliness and gloom and disorder, and the road not taken as a way of death. Yet all of this becomes far more clear as Christian community builds and the journey proceeds. Followers find that the new relations, new selfhood, and new path are a full life adventure. So our present task is to show how the elements of salvation connect over time and space. This could not be accomplished merely by stringing together the several apostolic terms for the new in Christ—justification, sanctification, and the like. A doctrine of salvation must continue to attend to (and will likely employ) many of these terms as well as the syntactic shifts and novel narratives that signal the new in Christ, but it must relate all these to the full reality to which each bears partial witness.

We saw that the apostolic generation discovered the new in Christ when they found their own lives transformed. Where Jesus was known to be alive from the dead, everything was changed. End time was beginning, even if there was more to come. There was now a new world to experience, a new life together. This newness in the risen Christ Jesus and its availability to all people everywhere was the content of the apostolic message. Christian doctrine sprang from these beginnings (Käsemann, 1969:chap. 4), and we sketched three historic forms of it, each related to a cluster of seminal terms in the Apostolic Writings. In all three versions the gospel was not merely formative but *transformative*. As we explore the community and continuity that define the new in Christ for us, it is vital to maintain this transformative understanding throughout. Rosemary Haughton was right: the forms of ongoing community (its structures of common life, its rules of admission and maintenance, its sacraments or salvific signs) must be birth canals of transformation as well as matrices of formation (Haughton, 1980; with what follows, cf. McClendon, 1994).

Sixteenth-century Lutherans signaled their rediscovery of this transformation with the brave new phrase "justification by grace through faith alone." Later, Lutheran doctrine hardened into formulas that evoked fresh appeals for renewal by Lutheran Pietists and revivalists. For sixteenth-century baptists, too, there was a discovery of newness, signaled by their return to conversion-baptism and the path of discipleship it marked. And again the newness hardened: For some the fresh way congealed into predestinarian quietism that opposed mission and evangelism. For others baptism itself froze into a cut-and-dried formula for salvation; in this version immersion was a legal down payment to purchase the promised spiritual gifts. So a historical pattern appears: First, transformation evokes a new language and calls forth new practices to prepare the ground for transformation and to conserve it when it occurs. But with the passage of time the patterns of language and practice no longer signify and may even inhibit transformation, as when conversion becomes a mere rite of passage ("joining the church"), or the second blessing turns into a *pro forma* tradition, or speaking in tongues becomes a ritual practice. To acknowledge that forms can thus be diverted need not provoke cynicism or indifference. In biblical perspective body and spirit, inner life and outer form, sign and what is signified do indeed belong together. What does arise is that the task of defining the normative Christian journey cannot neglect the search for forms of community that will nurture both formation and transformation. One cannot ask about spirituality without also asking about the social and structural shape of the church (See *Ethics*, Part II, and Chapter Eight below).

It seems natural, if spiritual life is in question, to turn to the vast literature of 'spirituality' in search of guidelines for the relation of individual salvation to the common life in the body of Christ. And indeed treasures lie buried here. For example, there is John Bunyan's *Pilgrim's Progress* (1678–84) with its tattered pilgrim's journey from the City of Destruction to the very gates of heaven, a work especially helpful if we read its Part Two as well as its Part One. Yet attempts to summarize the entire literature of spirituality are frustrating, for these writings draw from near limitless reservoirs of teaching about the inner life, based on widely diverse structures of Christian (and non-Christian) existence—from ancient Desert Fathers to baroque coenobites, from Christ-of-culture complacency to Christ-against-culture defensiveness, from infant-baptizers to conversion-baptizers to non-baptizers, from high Christology to no Christology. Though there are exceptions, much of this literature is dissociated from church with its common life in Scripture, its signs and worship, its paths of service and its corporate growth. We need inner-Christian guidelines that are linked to Christian doctrine, to the doctrinal or teaching practice of the worshiping, witnessing, servant community with its Scripture.

The guideline, or rather the series of guideposts I propose is an obvious one. A sequence of significant communal practices in the church marks the progress of the pilgrim on the Christian journey. Thus the church's *catechesis* (not to be confused with *catachresis!*), its primary *teaching* or preaching or instruction, is distinctly related to the journeyer's first stage of **preparation.** Second, the great initiatory sign of *baptism* in the church is specially related, at least in Scripture, to the disciple's **conversion** (Greek *metanoia*). Conversion is the aim of preparation and the onset of discipleship or following Jesus. Third, the repeated evangelical sign of *eucharist* or Lord's supper as a church practice guides the faithful **following** Jesus along the way to the cross. And fourth, the (less recognized, but vital) practice of *communal discernment* both acknowledges and directs the (also less recognized) progress I will dub Christian **soaring** (cf. Isa. 40:31). By this I intend that finding of the higher way some connect with special vocation, some with what Wesleyans called perfect love or entire sanctification, some with perfection in the Christian life. 'Soaring' will require further explanation, which is forthcoming, but here we may note what the four marked elements have in common: Each is a discernible stage in many Christian lives, and each can be correlated with an element of the churches' **practice**—instructing, baptizing, communing, discerning. Christian life is calibrated by these from the very beginning. At the same time the course of each Christian life displays limitless variation in detail and remains necessarily an adventure for each.

b. A pattern of Christian spirituality.—Since the arrangement to be shown here is not obviously that of any single Christian community of reference, it may seem unsatisfactory. Like the Catholic pattern, it sees a strong link between salvific signs ('sacraments') and eventful stages in Christian pilgrimage, but it replaces infant baptism with catechesis. Like the Protestant pattern, it emphasizes inwardness, but it assigns a greater role to communal discernment and generally to communal practice than most latter-day Protestants have done. It is arguably at greatest remove from the Lutheran pattern, yet shares its eucharistic emphasis. I think the arrangement is nearest the baptist pattern of Christian life, yet not all baptists will accept what some of them have assuredly lifted high, the fourth (pentecostal?) stage in the disciple's journey. Like all theological work, this arrangement is a proposal, yet it is not an arbitrary one; for it both recognizes and hopes to transform the existing convictions of the community.

i. Preparation.—Although the term "preparation" is little used in today's Christian discourse, it preoccupied some of America's earliest Christians. Early Puritanism was an English version of the Protestant Reformation, and its leaders enjoyed a lively faith at first hand. This was the faith that they sought to transmit to their heirs in the New World. The work of grace was God's doing, not their own. Yet grace was self-involving, and Puritan preaching tried to chart and promote the inner and outer growth that would ready congregants for the sovereign conversion event. Total depravity, the consequence of original sin, was presupposed, and this created a problem: How could sinners *prepare* for something that as sinners each was held to reject—the grace of God? In New England's Boston a 1662 synod crafted an answer. Since infant children of the converted were baptized "under the covenant" (by then a doctrinal staple of Reformed theology), they already had "the being of faith" in them. Had not Calvin implied as much? To be sure, these children were not *fully* converted, but they were not without covenanted faith, either. Hence conversion must be not a single turning (such as the Puritan founders had experienced), but a long, slow *process* of preparation for full conversion (and lawful admission to congregational membership and the Lord's table). How much of the work of preparation was divine and how much human was fiercely debated, but all agreed the process was necessary (Pettit, 1989:chap. 1).

By effectively identifying preparation with conversion, these seventeenth-century Puritans made conversion itself a process. This was compounded in New England churches by the retention of infant baptism (save by a few dissidents such as Roger Williams and Harvard President Henry Dunster), for it encouraged belief in preparation as the enlargement of a baptismal "being of faith." So when in the next century's revivals and Great Awakening (1740s) leaders such as Jonathan Edwards again identified genuine conversions, "truly gracious religious affections" in Edwards' term, preparation was crowded out by the far more interesting business of discerning genuine conversions amid the revival excitement (Schuldiner, 1991:chap. 5; Edwards, 1746). In the Second Awakening (1801–), Charles Grandison Finney's "new measures" revivalism diminished the preparation process still further. Finney (1792–1875) had practiced law; he was a highly intelligent man and a practical one who believed he need look no farther into a prospective convert's past than the moment of evangelism itself. The evangelist must convince men and women of sin and demand of them faith, a demand that in frontier America was met often enough to confirm Finney's diagnosis (Finney, 1835; P. Miller, 1965:bk. 1, chap. 1).

Meantime Horace Bushnell (1802–76) ministered to a Hartford, Connecticut, congregation that found revivals unsuitable. In response, Bushnell modified earlier Congregationalist preaching into a developed theory of *Christian nurture*. He advised "that the child is to grow up a Christian, and never know himself as being otherwise" in a social setting providing for lifelong conversion ("Christian Nurture," in Bushnell, 1965:379). This teaching did not reject conversion (which Bushnell himself vividly experienced as an adult) out of hand, but it played it down in favor of a theory of "religious education" that was to inform the growing Sunday school movement in American Christianity. Here the earlier preparation-to-conversion sequence often seemed lost to sight.

More briefly we may note parallel Roman Catholic developments. In the nineteenth century, Catholic parishes opened Sunday schools and operated weekday schools, and in the twentieth century the Confraternity of Christian Doctrine (CCD) enlisted lay people and nuns to teach students not enrolled in Catholic schools. The standard manual for decades was the Baltimore Catechism ("Why did God make you? God made me to know Him, to love Him, and to serve Him in this world and to be happy with Him forever in the next."). This formation aimed, not at conversion, but at indoctrinating those deemed already within the fold. Less familiar today is the history of Catholic revivals, better known as "parish missions," in America. Preachers such as Isaac Hecker sought to revive immigrant Catholics and evangelize non-Catholics. In seeking the conversion of the latter, they led many a stray Catholic to faith as well. A successor to these efforts was the revised Catholic baptismal rite for the initiation of adults published upon the initiative of Vatican II. It directed adult candidates into a process of biblical, historical, and liturgical instruction and discipline, combined with prayer, for an extended period of time, the intended outcome being *converted* participants, and the climax being baptism (in this case, believers baptism) of the candidates (*Baltimore Catechism*, 1930:7; Dolan, 1978; *Rites*, 1976).

We may now be in position to make better use of this heritage than were Puritans constrained by a doctrine of inherited sin, or revivalists and catechists working among a scattered populace, or liberal religious educators reacting against both. The battle over how much of the work of preparation is human, how much divine, need not detain us if we find candidates who want to do what Christ invites them to do: "Come, follow me." By the baptist vision, Gospels as well as Epistles offer us the model of Jesus, and later of the apostolic missionaries, laboring long to ready women and men for the newness that God was sending among them in Christ. If today's preparation once again anticipates that newness, if it proceeds believing that by way of formation God is at work and will act to transform nascent disciples into faithful Christians, it will bear its fruit in due season. "The ground produces a crop by itself, first the blade, then the ear, then full grain in the ear," says Mark's Jesus (4:28). But this faith puts a heavy burden upon the *teaching church*. For if preparation means readiness for a transformed life journey with Christ, readiness for conversion, for a disciple life, for whatever more God offers, then the formation required is far more radical than American Christianity, resting at ease in a spacious, successful, and free land, has so far conceived.

ii. Conversion.—It is clear from the evidence of biographies and the literature of psychology that conversion or turning is a recurrent natural event for our species. We grow, we change, and growth and change compressed constitute turns, sometimes sharp ones. Conversion as such is neither supernatural nor novel. The question is whether turning *to Christ*, entering *the rule of God*, belongs merely to that natural order. That it has a natural context seems clear, just as Christian teaching is among the ordinary sorts of teaching, and Christian witness is one sort of ordinary witness. What makes each distinctive is not its visible mechanism but its objective, not the outward means but the end. It is to this end, the new way of Jesus, the new relation with God the Father and thus with all creation, the new selfhood born of the Spirit, that Christian conversion turns, and thereby becomes the turn of turns. It is not our 'religious experience,' be it intense or diffuse, but the God who is its source, the Spirit who is its companion, the Christ who is its goal that makes this turnabout extraordinary.

William James, writing from a psychological standpoint, suggests that in conversion a disunited self is unified (James, 1902:chaps. 8–10). That is doubtless so of many a conversion. But it is not a reliable index of conversion to Jesus Christ, a conversion which may set "a man against his father, a daughter against her mother" (Matt. 10:35), and so introduce antitheses between ego and internalized parental and social values. After conversion the convert to Christ may be not easier but harder to live with (see Acts 9:29), and may find it harder to live with himself or herself as well. This is not to deny that there is an interior aspect of evangelical conversion; it is only to warn that interiority must truthfully reflect actuality—which may bring peace with God and a share of the world's enmity. Moreover, the intensity, vividness, and disruption entailed by a particular conversion will likely vary in proportion to the environment in which it takes place.

Perhaps it was paradoxes such as these, as well as their historical circumstances, that caused some to deny the necessity of conversion on the Christian journey, or—what comes to the same thing—led them to treat the entire journey as 'conversion' without distinction. But if all is conversion (or all is preparation, or cross-bearing, or 'soaring') the Christian story ceases to be a story; it cannot be told, for nothing ever happens. It may be that only in retrospect can we see that along a road with many forks, there was for us a fork that was fundamental, one that has "made all the difference." Or in prospect we may see that ahead of us lies a watershed to be crossed, either over a jagged, rocky col or beyond a near-level plain. In either case, reaching the other side is the point. To that crossing, however perceived, however negotiated, corresponds a difficult or serene, tumultuous or 'natural' *conversion*—in every case a passage from death to life (Romans 6).

Here we have need of the conversion sign, **baptism,** which with other such 'remembering signs' will be the subject of a later chapter. Now baptism appears in its role as a marker. We want to remember this fork in the road, want to recall this watershed, sharp or gradual, in the Godward journey. Baptism, in the simplicity of its bath and burial and birth to new life in Christ, is the marker. We cannot say of those whose conversion is deprived of this marker that they may not continue on to the end of the road. All of us travel the road by grace if at all. The sign must not be confused with the thing signified, and there may be exculpatory circumstances to excuse such deprival in a given case. But my own judgment is that if baptism is overlooked the loss is real (see further Chapter Nine and *Ethics*, Nine). The teaching church must do what it can to bring sign and event together in the journey of each.

iii. Following.—The revivalist tradition in America seemed to treat conversion as the end of the affair. The Christian convert was saved; that settled the matter. This was reinforced in some circles by a motto ("Once saved, always saved") that perverted the Reformed doctrines of election and perseverance from which it sprang and distorted the map of the journey ahead for those taking it. In biblical light the concept of assurance informs anxious pilgrims that God does not lead them upon their journey in vain. As an account of the divine purposefulness this theme is best treated in connection with God's electing love (Chapter Four §3). Assurance is meant to bring the full power of saving grace to bear upon the full length of the disciples' trail, and to promise footsore and faltering hikers that the climb is not *too* hard and that there is relief ahead (see 1 Cor. 10:13).

It is in this light that we encounter the Lord's supper. In this remembering sign, the Christian company, stragglers as well as pioneers, are gathered, the fit and the footsore shoulder to shoulder, to receive as ration the sign of God's faithfulness in the body of Christ. Here the blood of sacrifice is poured to designate afresh the bloodline of the redeemed. And here disciples, restored by that pledge, renew their own pledge to their Master and to one another. The last supper led Jesus and his laggard followers down a street that ended at the cross. But "there's a cross for everyone . . ."! From the Lord's supper a street now leads straight to the costly, countercultural way of Christian discipleship (see *Ethics*, Eight, as well as Chapter Nine within).

Are there any of this blood-bought band, then, who fall and fail along the way? What of 'converts' who do not persevere? Are they saved or, finally, lost? On this question followers of the way have read the testimony of Scripture in different ways. My own reading says that continuing on the trail is a *defining* mark of true disciples, and that if some are misjudged (or misjudge themselves) at the outset, the heat and dust of the journey will find them out. So only the saved persevere, and all the saved persevere. Laggards must hear this double message: You must persevere, and by God's grace, you will. Can such wandering followers be distinguished from traitors in the company, "tainted disbelievers" (Titus 1:15)? This question brings us to the task of communal discernment, to which we turn next.

iv. 'Soaring.'—Discernment has been supposed and implied throughout this entire account of the Christian journey. As the teaching church prepares her candidates, as the evangelizing church baptizes them, as the disciple church gathers at the Lord's table, informal and formal discernment has been at work, distinguishing those ready for the next leg of the Christian journey, identifying converts, admitting disciples to her shared tasks and to the memorial table of her Lord. Now something more must be said about discernment and about still another phase of the journey.

In the New Testament we meet the practice of *communal discernment*. With nominations, prayer, and the casting of lots a successor apostle is chosen (Acts 1:15-26). The Jerusalem church faces a question of tactics in the mission to the Gentiles, and after discussion sends a community letter (Acts 15). The Matthean community is given guidance for dealing with a brother or sister who does wrong; congregational discernment is required (Matt. 18:15-20). What became of this shared discernment in the post-apostolic age and after? The answer seems to be that the practice continued, but at least in the West came more and more to deal with notorious sin in the church—immoral living, defection under persecution, or the like. At first these offenses were considered by the entire congregation, which heard the case and handed down judgment. In time (and in step with the developing Western doctrine of sin) the common task devolved upon bishops or presbyters alone, and the medieval sacrament of penance took shape: priests alone heard confession, assigned acts of penance, and granted God's forgiveness.

What seems wrong about this development or devolution is not that Christians judged fellow members—that practice stood on solid New Testament ground such as Matthew 18—but that the focus of discernment narrowed to cases of failure. To be sure, there were two exceptions to the negative focus on sin. As the idea of a separate Christian 'ministry' developed, communal discernment in a positive vein was called into play to select officeholders. In a controversy in fourth-century Milan over the election of a new bishop, the quarreling congregation heard the voice of Ambrose, a public official still in preparation for baptism, and chose him bishop by acclamation. The choice was not altogether happy (Ambrose was a furious adversary to Jews as well as pagans), but the story portrays the common responsibility still being exercised at that time. Men were sought (by this time women had been disqualified) who were worthy to preside at the sacred rites, to preach the gospel, to exercise charity and further discernment. At its best, communal discernment sought the Spirit's leadership.

The other exception was the discernment of holy men and women (here women were not disqualified). The standard was set by martyrs, witnesses who had given their lives for the faith. In time, holiness of life was detected in living saints as well, and the holy ones were sought out by ordinary Christians who hoped to draw upon their wisdom and sanctity (P. Brown, 1982). While the cult of saints verged upon idolatry, it correctly perceived one part of Christian discernment—the lifting up of specially luminous Christian lives as models and examples for all. The present work has continued this theme (*Ethics*, Four, Seven, Ten; cf. McClendon, 1990; see also W. James, 1902).

Anabaptist Christians restored the task of discernment to the community, no longer leaving it to ordained clergy. Still they retained its medieval focus upon rooting out sin—the practice of the ban. In consequence baptist congregations found it difficult to exercise discipline without invoking exclusion. Whatever the virtues of the ban, it conveyed a message of exclusive rather than inclusive sociality. However, these baptists also restored the entire community to the New Testament role of saints in common, including the sainthood of suffering martyrdom (*Martyrs Mirror*, 1660).

Wherever discernment was preoccupied with fault, it gave less attention to model discipleship. Yet from time to time movements arose to suggest that though preparation and conversion and persevering discipleship were necessary, there was something more to be discerned, a further gift of the Spirit, a call to press on to perfection, a depth in the new in Christ that was not only possible in the present earthly life but indeed was God's intended destiny for every disciple. As noted, in Wesleyan teaching this 'more' was "perfect love"; in nineteenth-century holiness doctrine it was "entire sanctification" or "the second blessing." And in twentieth-century Pentecostal life, it was the new Pentecost, the fresh outpouring of the Spirit in which (ideally) all were touched by the renewal signs of tongues and miracles. Yet even Christian communities that made no allowance in theory for a further stage in Christian faith often hinted at it. They acknowledged special or extraordinary 'saints.' Or they spoke of those with unusual insight as 'mystics.' Or they acknowledged difference by urging ordination on some as if office in the church were provided for an honors class. Ordination may rightly be included here if we see it as partial recognition of distinctive *vocations* in the kingdom of God.

Is it possible, then, to summarize what these varied teachings and practices have in common—the conviction that beyond conversion and loyal following in Jesus' way there is a 'higher Christian life' (to use the Keswick Movement's term), a 'second blessing' (in holiness teaching)? Is it possible to grant this *and* to insist with John Wesley that the heights are not for some disciples but for all, that they wait up the trail every Christian sooner or later must climb? At least we must not discount this possibility, must not rule out in advance such attainment for each or for all. If we do accept this, we must accept soaring as an adventurous stage, in principle less predictable than any other aspect of the Christian life. Hence the 'sign' to which it best relates is the practice of communal discernment. Discernment not preoccupied with sin and fault and exclusion may find a better task in the church, the task of recognizing vocations, acknowledging and encouraging gifts, and helping the gifted to see their role within the rule of God. To be sure, such discernment is required throughout the Christian journey—in enlisting genuine seekers for the path of preparation, in discriminating real conversions, in discovering the shared way of the cross at a given time and place in kingdom life. Yet because of the great variety of unique blessings and distinctive attainments, communal discernment meets its highest demand at this stage.

> Those who look to the LORD
>   will win new strength,
> they will soar as on eagles' wings;
> they will run and not feel faint,
> march on and not grow weary. (Isa. 40:31)

* * * * *

It may be helpful to review the ground covered in the three parts of this chapter. In the first, the profound novelty of the Christian way was singled out. The 'now' of Christian eschatological existence means revolution for individuals and communities, and this revolutionary character of the new in Christ was highlighted by examining the New Testament vocabulary that signals it. Three clusters of newness terms (correlated with Protestant, Catholic, and baptist types of Christian community) were discriminated—clusters signaling new relations with the Lord, those indicating a transformed selfhood, and those pointing to a new path of life. Taking the last as our own starting place provided one way to attend to the other two. On this approach, sin was seen as failure to follow Jesus, and 'original' or inherited sin was rejected as a doctrinal experiment that had been found wanting. It must be replaced with the concept of social sin, which passes from generation to generation, but requires each generation to answer to Christ not for its ancestors' but for its own fault. Finally, a pattern of Christian existence, the journey, drew these ideas together and linked them to stages signaled by distinctive practices in the church: instruction to *preparation*, baptism to *conversion*, the eucharist or Lord's supper to *discipleship*, and communal discernment to *soaring*. Much has been left unsaid. What of the arena, the creation with its suffering, that is the setting of this journey? Who is the Lord Jesus who leads the way, and who is the Holy One whose Son he is? What is the community in whose company the journey is taken, and what Spirit sends it forth? There is much ground to cover, but this chapter has taken a step on the way. Skipping this step may mean getting all the rest wrong.

CHAPTER FOUR

Creation and Suffering

The Bible begins in Genesis 1 with the creation of heaven and earth. It ends in Revelation 21 and 22 with the disclosure of a new heaven and a new earth to replace the old. Between these limits the entire biblical drama unfolds. Thus inscribed, creation seems firmly fixed among Christian convictions: God is the initiator and God the end of all creation. Creeds, hymns, and long generations of theologians, from Origen of Alexandria in the third century to Augustus Hopkins Strong early in the twentieth, have placed this doctrine first, before any other material element of Christian belief. Yet the current generation of Christians has not found creation easy to believe or teach. Stated as a claim about earth's history the doctrine of creation collides (or seems to collide) with geology and cosmology and biology—a collision that has found its way into school rooms, school board sessions, and high courts in America. As a valuation placed upon present existence, creation collides with the painful facts of human deformity of mind and body and with animal and human suffering in all forms. As a supposed mandate for human dominion over nature and of human beings over one another on the basis of rank, race, or gender, creation has offended lovers of nature and lovers of liberty and equality—it collides, or seems to collide, with social tranquillity and natural ecology. Yet Christians who favor liberty, revere nature, respect science, and trust in the goodness of God have not quickly found alternative statements that separate the true doctrine from these distorted readings, and newer interpretations have gained little favor even in Christian circles. In reaction to this confusion, some recent theologies have played down the biblical pictures of creation and limited themselves to austere philosophical statement, or have even passed over the doctrine in silence (thus Hans Küng, 1976).

So we must ask, has the church still a teaching duty here? I will argue that it has, that the creation witness of Genesis, Revelation, and much else in Scripture is indispensable to church teaching that centers upon faith in Jesus Christ and the God we know in Christ. If God is not God of all, God is not God at all.

On this topic if anywhere we want clarity of thought and statement, and I will seek to speak plainly, sacrificing technical precision where necessary. There will be a special difficulty in this plain speech, inasmuch as the doctrine of first things, like the doctrine of last things, reaches beyond our everyday experience and strains our powers of language. Both eschatology and 'protology,' the last things and the first, extend beyond human knowledge as such. This is the point of the Eternal in his speech to suffering Job:

> Where were you when I laid the earth's foundations?
> . . . .
> Have you comprehended the vast expanse of the world?
> Tell me all this, if you know.
> Which is the way to the home of light,
> and where does darkness dwell?
> Can you then take each to its appointed boundary
> and escort it on its homeward path? (Job 38:4*a*, 18-20)

We have seen that in treating last things, the Bible invokes picture language (Chapter Two). This is true of first things also. These first pictures function both as previews of the world that is to be (an instance of 'then is now') and as links relating the made world to God who is before all worlds.

Is the doctrine of creation a presupposition of the new that comes in Christ, so that we have come to it too late here? Many doctrinal theologians have taken this view, for example, the Swedish theologian Gustaf Wingren (see, e.g., 1960, 1961, 1979). Salvation, so regarded, may be mainly restorative of what creation provided, or would have provided had not the fall into sin intervened. On the other hand, a powerful twentieth-century theological tradition (e.g., Wright, 1962) suggests the contrary: The new in Christ was God's original provision, and creation was but a step along the way. The new in Christ would have come even had sin not intervened. While there is merit as well as difficulty in each of these views, the present work takes a different, third approach: The ultimate end of creation and redemption alike is the fulfillment of God's great kingdom rule. This rule, when it shall be achieved, will mean God's glory fully shared, imparted to all, incorporating all (see Chapter Ten). Then creation (the doctrine of divine origination and conservation) and salvation (the liberation of a people suited to that coming glory) and last things (the doctrine of the consummation itself) are partner doctrines in the exposition of the all-embracing rule of God. In a figure, creation and salvation are not parent and child; neither has birthed the other. Rather they are sisters, mutually interacting and supporting each other along with a third sibling, eschatology. And all this is in fulfillment of the rule of God, which (at least in the structure of this book) is the mother doctrine that bears them all.

If widespread confusion about creation prevails, much more than a chapter may be required to free this doctrine from the biblical, philosophical, scientific, and political perplexities with which it has been laden. That such liberating work is pursued today by many is a matter for gratitude, and we are beneficiaries of such projects as the late-twentieth-century discussions involving theology and science (see, e.g., Peters, ed., 1989) and those involving revisionary biblical studies of creation (see, e.g., B. Anderson, ed., 1984). Yet it will not be possible in this chapter even to survey these labors, to say nothing of still other studies of creation in light of art history, comparative religion, philosophy, and more. I propose only to examine in the best light available the biblical 'pictures' of creation now available to the church, to relate these to the ongoing creative work of God (and of God's creatures!), and to explore the partnership between creation, salvation, and last things just proposed. These related tasks are addressed (though not in neat correspondence) in the three sections of the chapter: **(§1) creation as God's gift and blessing; (§2) creation as part of the story of God's travail and ours;** and **(§3) creation as promise,** the last involving God's persistent providence and signlike miracles as signals of God's intentions for creation.

§1. Creation as Gift and Blessing

a. The Christian doctrine in eclipse.—A good beginning place is the heavenly vision in chapter 4 of the Apocalypse of John. As the scene opens, there is One upon a throne in a setting of sublime splendor, footed by a sea as of glass or ice, while about the throne or under it appear elders, spirits, and living creatures. Day and night these sing:

> Holy, holy, holy is God
> the sovereign Lord of all,
> who was, and is, and is to come! (Rev. 4:8*b*)

In echo of the living creatures' praise, the elders, twenty-four in number, present their own crowns before the throne and cry

> You are worthy, O Lord our God, to receive glory
> and honour and power, because you created all things;
> by your will they were created and have their being. (v. 11)

Here, then, is a primitive Christian celebration of the creation. As its first readers would know all too well, Revelation sprang from the midst of a suffering church (see e.g. 1:9). While the heavenly elders sang creation's praise, earthly elders suffered exile, imprisonment, and martyrdom.

This passage from Revelation is chosen because it so plainly represents the defiant, active faith that shaped the understanding of God in Israel and early Christianity. This faith grew, not from cosmogonic speculation either scientific or mythological, but from the cry of trust that would not acknowledge any God but God. Moreover, the passage displays features that the Christian doctrine cannot surrender. (1) **God is the origin and source of all else.** God is Alpha. The fourfold symbolism of the heavenly scene—spirits, elders, animal creatures, sea—is the heavenly counterpart of all that is on earth and beyond. Here creation is not merely human dependence, for its scope is the very cosmos, made, daily renewed, and governed by one Lord. (2) Because **creation is** perceived as **God's ongoing blessing,** as intrinsically good, the feeling-tone expressed in its praise is not helpless dependence, but irrepressible joy: "Day and night unceasingly [the creatures] *sing*" (4:8). This echoes the delight of Psalm 104 and its Old Testament heritage. (3) The **creative divine rule is** nevertheless **under constant attack.** Though declared in heaven, it is challenged by worldly powers and worldly understandings. In the preceding centuries Jewish thought had held firm to monotheistic doctrines of creation and providence when threatened by Persian dualism (E. P. Sanders, 1992:247-51). A century later than our passage, Irenaeus of Lyons had to combat a Gnostic heresy that had given up belief in divine creation. The Apocalypse of John, like these before and after it, stands firm in this persistent creation faith. (4) **God's rule is** both displayed and **enhanced by the creation.** The spirits, elders, animals, even the glassy sea enlarge the sphere of the love of God their Maker. (5) **Creation has a terminus or goal,** and that goal lies in God. God is Omega, the end of all, "who was, and is, and is to come" (4:8*b*).

Together these five constitute Christian doctrine; to abandon them would be to give up elements vital to Christian existence. Yet each of the five encounters challenges from within today's Christian community as well as from without: God as *origin* (1) is implicitly challenged by any science that proposes a self-sufficient account of the origin of nature or of human nature, and this 'scientism' is not really opposed, but is willy-nilly reinforced, by the ersatz research called creation science. 'Creation science' implies that *its own* acceptance in churches, in schools, even at law, is indispensable to belief in God as origin of all. Either sort of science, ordinary science or creation science, may tempt the Christian unwisely to place a false trust in itself. Both (2) the character of creation as itself a *blessing* and (4) the character of creation as *responsive praise* to the Creator, full of joy and delight, is diminished by creation teaching narrowly focused upon the human species. This narrowing of creation to ourselves may end in understanding 'creation' simply as a doctrine about the human experience of contingency—awareness that we and our world might not have been as we are. However certain our contingency, awareness of it misses the delight that a Christ-shaped, ecological doctrine of creation evokes. (Nor does the authentic doctrine deny that the human creature has a distinctive place among the creatures; indeed, a fully ecological doctrine can alone appreciate that place.) And finally, (3) the theme of creation as *struggle* and (5) the divine *destiny* that shall resolve that struggle—Satan banished, an end to mourning and crying and pain, the new heaven and new earth—is challenged by creation doctrines that deny to God and his Christ and the Divine Spirit a central place in that struggle. These convictions are undermined by those who recognize the struggle (thus some forms of Process Theology) while abandoning faith in the promised victory of God.

Since it is easy to make lists of desirable theological achievements (and many do that) while it is much harder to carry them out, we do well to trace to their source the mismoves just listed. Doing so will help us understand why matters have developed as they have, but will show why correcting them will be harder than deploring them.

First, we must consider the difference made to Christian thought as a whole by the enormous success, since the Middle Ages, of science and technology. Whenever in this period an intellectual issue ranged the church on one side, and *science and technology* on the other, it was the church that gave ground. This was true of astronomy (Galileo and Copernicus), biology (Darwin), and even of the industrial revolution (whose protean technology is typically faceless and impersonal). Thus while the ordinary medieval word for knowledge *(scientia)* applied to theology and philosophy as much as to any sphere of thought, in post-medieval times *science* became in the English language the name of the study of nature (including social and psychological nature, but) excluding theology. Likewise, technological *efficiency* came to be more and more regarded as the warrant for the human use of creation. The upshot has been to assign to the sciences the sovereign authority to inform us about the world's origin and destiny—and to technology to decide upon its proper use—while withdrawing that authority from Christian teaching.

Meanwhile, 'creation science,' so called, developed in order to do evidential battle with mainline science on issues such as the age of the earth and the cosmos, the evolution of the species, human origins, and the like—points at which some Christians believed Bible and mainline science conflicted (Barbour, 1971; Van Till, ed., 1990:chaps. 5–6). If (as seems highly improbable) creation science were to succeed in overturning its scientific rivals, it would still be a usurper, occupying in many Christian minds a bogus place, for it would assume under cover of science the settlement of issues that are rightly beyond the scope of (even pious) science. Moreover, if it were as it claims pure science, it would necessarily continue to change, as all science must, and the teaching it provided would soon cease to satisfy those whose Bible reading accorded with its *current* findings.

Two other themes characterize the doctrine of creation in modern times, its *human-centered* or *anthropocentric focus* and the constrictive *limit it placed upon God's ongoing relation to creation and all creatures*. As early as the Renaissance, these themes converged to change the way Christians viewed the created world. What has been called the secularization of nature paralleled the development of Newtonian science. Whereas earlier generations of natural philosophers had perceived a 'living' universe in which spirit and matter were closely intertwined not only in plants and animals but in stars, mountains, and rivers, the new scientists of the seventeenth century adopted mechanics as the model for their work. Thereby they gained some precision for their predictions, but measurably lost a sense of the awesome living mystery of nature (Griffin, 1988:Intro.). Some Protestant theologians from the Reformation onward (though not all), siding with mechanism, relegated nature to the realm of the secular, thereby reinforcing the new natural philosophy (see Gregory, 1992). Ironically, it was 'secular' nature that still prevailed in the work of twentieth-century theologian Rudolf Bultmann: Nature is an object, entirely governed by its relentless cause-and-effect laws. The religious value of creation is strictly limited, since the authentic dependence and freedom that human beings can feel must face not nature, but God only. "The Christian faith in creation affirms that man is not at home in the world . . ." (Bultmann, 1958:15, 61; 1960:213). While the architects of this anthropocentric doctrine of creation believed they were protecting faith from alien elements, the unhappy outcome was the banishing of God from nature (Santmire, 1985:chaps. 7–9).

It is these themes, then, *the dominance of science* in the world of thought, the effective *absence of God* from nature, and the *man-centered shape* of the surviving residue of the doctrine of creation, that account for the difficulties the doctrine faces in our own day. They are real difficulties, not just arbitrary barriers. Most of us in the technological West, Christian or not, tacitly endorse the first and second themes, and Christian theoreticians from Schleiermacher down to and including Karl Barth have been vacuumed into the third (cf. Santmire, 1985:146-55). We may well fail to overcome such powerful tendencies in our time. But we must try.

b. Restoring biblical creation teaching.—If the church's creation theology recovers the authentic elements of Scripture teaching (God as creation's Alpha, creation itself as ongoing blessing and struggle and praise, and God as creation's Omega), it will surely question the powerful themes of modern thought that have set the authentic elements aside. Perhaps a fresh look at these themes will suggest how the received doctrine can be transformed.

i. Scripture, myth, and science.—By now it is recognized in almost every church that the early chapters of Genesis did not fall as so many golden pages from heaven, but were from the beginning closely connected with the wider cosmological thought of the ancient Near East. The discovery by archaeologists in the last 150 years of the remnants of prebiblical cities with their still-legible tablets and inscriptions gave written and pictorial glimpses of civilizations older than any previously known. (A selection of the relevant written documents is gathered under the title *Ancient Near Eastern Texts* [3rd. ed., 1969] edited by James Pritchard, while the pictorial record is available in Othmar Keel's *Symbolism of the Biblical World* [1985].) Of special interest are the clay tablets discovered in the Mesopotamian basin, for these include creation stories, older than Abraham, that find striking parallels in the creation passages of Genesis, the Psalms, and Isaiah (see Gunkel in B. Anderson, ed., 1984:25-52). These primitive creation stories display many parallels to Genesis. For example, both include the separation of the chaotic primeval waters by a vault or firmament, providing space for dry land. More striking on a second look, however, are the differences (von Rad, 1972). In *Enuma elish* earth results from a ribald battle between a chief male god (Marduk) and a female god, Tiamat, who represents the hostile sea. She is slain and her halved carcass becomes the vault over earth and its land. In these mythological terms ancient Mesopotamians sought to comprehend the recurring floods, storms, and dry seasons whose management made agriculture possible (Kirk, 1970:chap. 3). So the myth served a scientific and technological purpose. Moreover, in the Babylonian version of the myth, Marduk founded Babylon, thus justifying its hieratic role as a world empire. By these, as well as by their myths of the underworld, ancient peoples answered their urgent questions and shaped a life together.

Besides scientific and political functions, the ancient myths served a religious one. Marduk was chief god of Babylon. Speculation says the Hebrews who worshiped Yahweh substituted his name for that of Marduk, thus generating a Yahweh myth that served similar scientific, political, and religious functions in Canaan. This might be true, but the creation accounts we find in Genesis 1–3 are written to repudiate the mythic account of the world, whether in Mesopotamian or Canaanite form. In Genesis there is no primal battle save God's commanding repudiation of chaos (though the struggle theme appears elsewhere in the Old Testament). In Genesis the earth is made, not of pre-existent god-stuff, but simply by the command of God, giving rise to the later understanding of creation *ex nihilo* (out of nothing). Sun and moon are deprived in Genesis of their sacral names lest they be worshiped; the planets and stars are reduced in rank to harmless creatures, and even their creation is relegated to a gently ironic literary aside: "he also made the stars" (1:16b). Earth is not a slain goddess—she is fruitful, but her beneficence depends upon God's creative acts. The human creature, male and female, is "in God's image," so no lesser deity than God has claim to human allegiance. It is God who has blessed people and assigned them a stewardship responsible directly to God. The politics of creation in Genesis is universalistic, telling the story of all people everywhere and showing by its genealogies that all are at least distant cousins. The biblical creation story makes no chauvinistic claim for an empire centered in Jerusalem, but reaches its terminus in Genesis 12 in the call of a desert wanderer to be the father of a multitude so that in that faithful wanderer, Abraham, *all people* may receive a blessing (cf. von Rad, 1972).

It is a long distance from ancient 'scientific' myth to modern science, which has along its way itself been shaped by the biblical creation doctrine, so that Christianity today need not repudiate science as Genesis repudiated ancient myth. Indeed, science may offer materials for a restatement of the Genesis story. Before this can happen, however, it is necessary to be clear about what is factual and contemporary in current science, and what is a mere holdover from the scientific mistakes of the seventeenth and eighteenth centuries. As noted above, Newtonian science, backed by Kantian metaphysics, found no role for God in the ongoing world, so that the religious counterpart was a stark deism. (Isaac Newton himself believed God set the world in motion and at rare intervals adjusted it; for Immanuel Kant, God was only an implicate of practical reason.) This scientific heritage made modern science methodologically atheistic, though individual scientists were sometimes (perhaps inconsistently) devout believers. In the twentieth century, however, mathematical physics overturned the Newtonian model: The physics of mass and force was only a limited case of an encompassing physics of fields of interactive energy, while quantum mechanics soon supplanted field theory. This suggested a world-picture more congenial to theology than that of Kant and Newton (Polkinghorne, 1991:chap. 7). Unfortunately, much popular science (and the weekday thought of many a working scientist) is still governed by the old mechanistic and deistic assumptions of the seventeenth century.

It is here that science-minded Christians may find attractive the ancient parallel—Genesis correcting Babylon's mythology. We need not indict popular science as mythological (yet see Toulmin, 1970) in order to explore the parallel: The biblical writers responded critically to the (mythic) 'popular science' of their day; shall we respond less critically to the (still mechanistic) popular science of our own? Biblical writers accepted some of the language, some of the plot, and some of the themes of their ancient context. But they rejected other language, other plot elements, other themes found in that same material. This critical response was made in order that the Scriptures might confess and proclaim God the Creator in terms its first readers could comprehend, terms by which they might shape their lives and reshape their world.

Until this critical task is accomplished, Christians who are also scientists will sometimes find themselves engaging in doublethink; their construal of the facts before them being shaped on one side by their technical training and their received scientific paradigms, on the other by Christian convictions that inadequately address their dilemma. Such cognitive dissonance is uncomfortable exactly because deep in the Christian consciousness God is still God, the God of truth. The appropriate relation between Christian doctrine and the sciences has been expressed by several thinkers as *consonance* (e.g., McMullin in Peacocke, ed., 1981:39-52). Admittedly, there is no guarantee that the critical response discussed here will unfailingly produce consonance between the actual deliverances of the natural sciences at any particular time and the content of Christian teaching. Nor is that in itself cause for alarm. Consonance is an ideal to be sought but not a law to be obeyed unless the obeyer possess an infallible intellectual apparatus as well as unimpeachable elements to be reconciled (cf. Wolterstorff, 1984). Failing these, if one senses a conflict between scientific teaching one believes to be true and Christian convictions one holds, the drive to consistency does not require abandonment of either forthwith. For one's (fallible) reasoning apparatus might sense a disparity where none exists; one's grasp of Christian teaching is of course less than perfect in this life; the science on the point at issue may simply be mistaken (cf. Robert Russell in Peters, ed., 1989). Yet the situation of conflict is an unstable one, exactly because consonance remains and should remain the ultimate goal.

ii. The presence of God in creation.—The absence of God has obsessed Christian thought during the century now ending—mockingly, perhaps, during the wars, depressions, revolutions, famines that rocked the century, poignantly in the poetry and novels that echoed the long withdrawing roar (Arnold) of departing faith, angrily in America's God-is-dead theological sally, pathetically in the rigid orthodoxies no longer adequate to the venues they sought still to control. Sensitive Christian thinkers, aware of the felt absence of the present God, sought by a variety of stratagems to minister to flocks stranded on this Dover Beach: the absence was really a presence in disguise, they said, or it was a testing of the faith of the faithful, or it was the judgment of God upon a malignant world. Yet after King Canute's theological command, faith's tide still ebbed (cf. Steuer and McClendon, eds., 1981:Intro.).

In *Volume I* a different course was laid. There "presence" was identified as a typical Christian virtue, and the black church in America—sons and daughters of Africa who discovered Christ in their own communities of suffering and praise—was singled out as an exemplary embodiment of the virtue of presence (*Ethics*, Three). The destination sought on that course was an awakening in Christian readers' consciousness of what 'presence' might mean, not mere physical proximity, certainly not showy stage presence, but a being-there with and for the other in sacrificial love. From that beginning can there grow a sense of the presence of God? Such a procedure might move, not from religious experience to theology, but from theology grounded in Christian practice to the renewal of that practice.

Down these lines, a second step may now be possible, moving from the Christian practice of prayer to the doctrine that undergirds that practice (cf. Thiemann, 1985). For if there is any Christian practice that presumes the divine presence, it is prayer. What I wish to show is that Christian prayer presumes God's actual presence (indeed, Christ's presence) not only in the praying, but also in the created cosmos in which prayer occurs. While the word "prayer" has a flexible range of meaning—from Tibetan prayer wheels to mystical disconnection from body and sense—its everyday use is simply petition, and this coincides with its ordinary Christian use as well. Christians pray; their prayers presume a present Hearer with power (if not always the will) to grant that petition. Pray-er and prayer and Hearer, in the happy case, are present to and for one another in the world.

Here is a single example, the prayer Jesus taught, following Matthew's version (6:9-13). If the Our Father (Catholic), and the Lord's Prayer (Protestant) are adequate names for this prayer, so is a baptist name that shows who must pray it: the *Disciples' Prayer*. On one analysis (Guelich, 1982) the prayer contains six petitions, three for God, three for the disciples ("us"). Each of the six engages creation. The first three petitions (the hallowing of the name, the coming of the rule, the doing of the will of the Father) are framed round with the inclusive components of creation, "earth" and "heaven" (6:10*c*, cf. Gen. 1:1). These petitions exemplify one great condition for answered prayer, namely that we pray as God wills that we pray. Not only does Jesus as God's own Son (cf. Matt. 17:5) teach this prayer; the petitions declare the divine creative purpose: a creation at peace *(shalom)* with its Creator, a creation that fulfills the divine rule (cf. Revelation 4), a creation that blesses God who is its blessing (Psalm 104). "On earth as in heaven" (6:10*b*) implies that this threefold petition is not only the Disciples' Prayer, not only Jesus' purpose: It is the prayer of Mother Earth herself in the purpose of God the Father (cf. Gen. 1:11ff). The second three petitions are uniquely for disciples (there is no evidence that Jesus himself prayed this prayer). They presuppose sin, and sin as rupture between human beings ("our debtors") and between us and God ("our debts"), and they presuppose the risk of the earthly journey ("lead us not into . . .") and the tension of the last days, with the threat that lies at creation's chaotic margins ("the evil one," or simply "evil"). Yet the petitions ask for created and creative wholeness in such a time—for a network of forgiveness binding up the wounded world (cf. *Ethics,* Eight), for a lacing together of souls and bodies sustained by shared (eucharistic and ordinary?) bread, for a providential leadership guiding a pilgrim church through its earthly journey ("save us from the time of trial" in the version of the Consultation on Common Texts).

In sum, the Disciples' Prayer presumes a hearer God deeply involved with the organic and inorganic world, a holy God who blesses the created order with his own presence, a nurturing God who cares about the baking of bread, a healing God who mends the ruptures of social fabric for our good, a guiding God who leads Christians through the narrow passages of time that precede the end. To acknowledge the listening presence of such a God is to acknowledge God's prior presence in creation to feed and heal and guide and bless.

iii. Humanity as creaturehood.—Those who expect here to find a 'doctrine of man' or 'theological anthropology' in classic modern style are making an understandable but unfortunate mistake. The practice in some theologies of introducing such a 'doctrine' among Christian doctrines is justified neither on biblical nor on historical grounds. The early Christians who confessed faith in God's reign, Christ's redemption, and the Spirit's fellowship (or later, in the triune God) did not set alongside these an article of faith in *anthropos* or *homo*—in human nature as such. No book of the Bible is devoted to the classical and modern task of devising a philosophical or theoretical anthropology. To be sure, the psalmist asks "What is a frail mortal?" but does so only while exclaiming at "your heavens, the work of your fingers" as well as "all sheep and oxen, all the wild beasts, the birds in the air, the fish in the sea, and everything that moves along ocean paths" (Ps. 8:3-8). Granted, the "frail mortal" is assigned in the psalm a high place. Only the gods, that is, the angelic host, rank higher, and all the rest of nature is beneath this mortal's feet (8:5f). Yet the psalm makes it clear that mortal stewardship is not determined by partitioning human nature off from the rest of nature. Nor do the Genesis references to God's image and likeness indicate such partition (1:26-30; cf. 2:7).

Much of the territory of 'Christian anthropology' has already been covered in *Ethics*. There human nature in its natural setting (Part One) and its social setting (Part Two) forms the context of discussions of human sexual and social conduct, while human transformation is treated in Part Three.

The remaining task, though, is still challenging enough. It is to point toward a Christian ecology, a view of creation that can replace the old human rulership and mastery views that have shown themselves so disposed to corrupt. Christians are nowadays accused of sponsoring rapacious attitudes to nature, and are blamed for everything from smog to nuclear warfare. While this neglects the roles of science and technology in the matter, there is regrettably some Christian fault as well (Watts, 1970; White, 1967; Ferré, 1988). Anthropocentric doctrines of creation are visibly at fault. Can there be instead an ecological doctrine of creation with conduct to match? For years, H. Paul Santmire, a Lutheran pastor, has been breaking ground for such a doctrine. In *The Travail of Nature* (1985) he argues that there have been two streams within mainline Christian theology, one *world-transcending*, even *world-denying* (or, as Santmire unfortunately names it, "spiritual") in its thrust; the other world and nature *affirming*, and rightly named *ecological*.

Tradition certainly displays the world-transcending motif, whose earliest exemplar is the distinguished Origen of Alexandria (c. 185–254), a theologian Santmire perceives in the context of "alienation from nature in an age of anxiety." Origen's view must nonetheless be sharply distinguished from that of his Gnostic contemporaries, who denied God's Creatorhood and viewed this world as alien. Rather for Origen the world is God's gracious act "to stop the fall of the rational spirits toward ultimate nonbeing." Yet this world lies at the bottom of the ladder or chain of being, and human souls are destined to rise above it again to a purer realm (Santmire 1985:44-53). Santmire traces this "spiritual" motif from Origen down to the present, embracing the early Augustine and Aquinas, Bonaventure and Dante, the magisterial Reformers Luther and Calvin (though the latter two only in part), and more recently Teilhard de Chardin (!) and Karl Barth. For all these, the world-transcending motif predominates.

The ecological motif has been prominent all along, a point often missed by Christianity's critics. The first example Santmire recalls is Irenaeus of Lyons (c. 130–200), who wrote more than half a century before Origen (Santmire, 1985:35-44). Against the Gnostics with their "metaphor of ascent" from an evil earth, Irenaeus affirmed the value of creation's history. One God is the Creator; there is no other, no mediating demiurge. The cosmos, created good, is on a long journey to its final perfection. Though human beings sinned and fell, the cosmos has not fallen, yet it will be renewed in the end times, along with the final salvation of human beings, through Christ. Those times will be the fulfillment both of the promises of Scripture to God's children and of the promise implicit in creation itself, for "the whole creation shall, according to God's will, obtain a vast increase, that it may bring forth fruits such [as] Isaiah declares [30:25f]" (Irenaeus, *Adv. haer.* V, xxiv, 2). Hence the root metaphor of Irenaeus' creation doctrine, Santmire argues, is "migration to a good land." Irenaeus' strongly end-oriented theology culminates not in escape from creation but in its ultimate full blessing.

> In Irenaeus' vision the whole creation is full of goodness, harmony, beauty, and life at all times, all continually pouring forth from the hands of God. God is not some distant ruler, far removed in the heavens, sending out his commands through intermediaries. Rather God is one who contains all things, works richly in them, gives them their individual places within the whole, and thus bestows harmony on all things. The human creature likewise is at home in the creation, not a stranger and pilgrim in an alien world.
> (Santmire, 1985:43f)

Others throughout Christian history have followed this ecological motif. These include the later Augustine, Francis of Assisi with his embrace of nature, and elements in (though not the full thought of) Luther and Calvin, Karl Barth, and Teilhard de Chardin.

It is noteworthy that in his work Santmire passes over the Radical Reformers and their heirs in complete silence. His silence cannot be repaired in this volume, yet (a word to the wise?) there are rich possibilities for a doctrine of nature in communities that found in the staff not the sword, in the plow horse not the cavalry horse, elements of the good life on earth.

If, as Paul Santmire claims, the witness of Christian history to an ecological doctrine of creation is ambiguous, is there no resolution? What about the Bible? Santmire believes that our biblical reading strategies have been so strongly influenced by the world-transcending motif that the Bible *as we must read it* bears only ambiguous testimony on this topic. For example, he accepts the critical view of John's Gospel that posits an earlier "proto-gospel" within the text, and he interprets the canonical Gospel from that proto-gospel's standpoint. This yields a

Fourth Gospel heavily oriented toward escapist thinking about the created world. "John recognizes the new creation only in the form of reborn disciples" (1985:211-13). Though plainly "fecundity" and "migration to a good land" shape other biblical books, it is only a new hermeneutic, he believes, that can provide an ecological reading of the Bible as a whole. In a concluding chapter, Santmire goes some distance toward providing such a new reading strategy (1985:chap. 10). My own confidence is that an ecological reading of the biblical creation-pictures will ultimately prevail. Yet this outcome depends in part on systematic work that can deal with issues still to be assessed in this chapter: the creativity and travail of creation itself (including the human creature), and the role of last things in interpreting the "things that do appear," the present created world.

When in this frame we seek the fitting human response to (original and ongoing) creation, guided by the magnificent scene depicted in Revelation 4, we find deeply affective awe rising from the immeasurable gap that separates Creator and creature. An expression of this same awe is found in Abraham's face-to-face appeal to the Lord JHWH on behalf of his wayward nephew Lot: "I who am nothing but dust and ashes . . ." (Gen. 18:27). Abraham's awareness, in Rudolf Otto's analysis, is not primarily *conceptual*; it is creature-feeling or *creatureliness (Geschöpf-lichkeit)*, a sense of the numinous rising from its strong contrast to our creaturehood. The elders doff their crowns and lay them down before the throne of the One (Rev. 4:10). At some distance from this, and closer to rational reflection, is the response of finitude encompassed by God the beginning and God the end (Rev. 1:8). I see myself afloat in a very small boat on a very large ocean; thus one may sense the divine origination and terminus of all. Otto's term for this Schleiermacherian sense of dependence is *createdness (Geschaffenheit)*. From it there arises a thoroughly rational consciousness of God as first and final cause (1923:9f, 20f). My preceding paragraphs have addressed the need for both creatureliness and createdness. There is need as well for a third sort of response—*the creature's own creativity*. In the quest for an ecological doctrine of creation, this is ground to be further explored (see §2b).

What we have already seen gives us some reason to question the modern dominance of a 'mythology' based upon a world without God, the corresponding perception that God is absent from the world, and the misplaced focus upon the human creature to the neglect of all others (cf. *Ethics*, Three). If those powerful challenges can themselves be challenged, we may yet depict creation in authentic Christian terms, a creation whose Alpha and Omega is God, and one whose blessing and struggle and presence with God were never totally lost to believers' sight.

§2. Creation as Travail

So far we have some idea what the church might teach about creation, yet we have found obstacles to the success of that teaching mission—notably, widespread passive acceptance of an outmoded science, the modern assumption of God's real absence from the world, and the arrogant modern Christian focus upon the human creature. The task now is to seek out features of Christian teaching, creation's **travail** (this Section) and creation's **promise** (§3), that can press beyond these obstacles. An adequate church doctrine today should have neither the anthropological focus of recent Christian thought, nor the cosmological focus of Christian antiquity. Can it instead display a *communitarian* embrace of "all creatures great and small" in their relation to God and one another? Can it see God and creation in ecological interaction?

The Hebrew verb *bara'*, translated "create," never appears in Scripture with any subject other than God. God is uniquely the Creator of "earth's farthest bounds" (Isa. 49:28), of all that is. This verb appears in Genesis 1:1, and from that entire chapter hasty readers have inferred that creation was instantaneous, once for all, and without analogy. If this were true, we could not even say what "create" meant, for nothing whatever would be like it. Happily, here and elsewhere the distinctive verb is used alongside synonyms that describe not only instantaneous origination but a process with many stages, an instance being the pictorial six (or seven) days of creation. *Bara'* itself is used of the creation of the great sea beasts (Gen. 1:21) and of human beings (Gen. 1:27)—perhaps singled out because the popular mythology had assigned each of them an independent origin. *Bara'* is also used, however, of the blowing wind (Amos 4:13), of the recurrent life cycle of "living creatures great and small" (Ps. 104:25b, 30), and of the coming divine glory of the last things (Isa. 4:5). These are all said to be the Creator's work, and so is God's creation *(bara')* of the smith who forges deadly weapons and the "destroyer" (presumably the army) that employs such weapons (Isa. 54:16). We must soon talk about the smith and the destroyer as well, but the present point is that creation, even in its originative sense, is not limited to the *world's* beginning; creation is the ongoing originative activity of God within the world as well. In this regard some have spoken of "continuous creation," and others of ongoing preservation or conservation of the world. So creation is not only origination "out of nothing" (a view explicit in Scripture only in apocryphal 2 Macc. 7:28), but also the sustaining or renovating of already created material. In that sense, our world (and we) were created again this morning, even this instant (cf. Col. 1:16f). How, then, does creation teaching consist with the cause-effect world of everyday, in which we ourselves grow grapes, build roads, make babies—and endure the passing away of all these things as well? Is God the creator, if we *and* nature create? Is God the *destroyer* as well?

a. Pictures of creation.—Alongside the Bible's distinctive "create" word (Hebrew *bara'*, Greek *ktidzein*) synonyms appear that do correspond to human creative activity. George Hendry urges that five major "models of creation" be taken into account: molding, struggle, design-and-execution, expression, and generation (1980:chap. 8). Borrowing Hendry's categories, I will supplement them as seems necessary.

i. Molding.—Out of existing material God forms or shapes the creature. This is said of all creation in Isaiah ("by myself I *stretched out* the heavens, alone I *fashioned* the earth," 44:24); it is implied of the human creation ("in our image," Gen. 1:26, which von Rad, 1972b, tells us is meant in pictorial literality); it is stated, again pictorially, in the second Genesis creation account ("from the dust of the ground," Gen. 2:7; "took one of the man's ribs," 2:21f), where the raw materials employed tell us something about creation's continuities—of human beings with Earth, of woman with man. Most striking as a picture of creation is the image of the potter and the clay. This image is employed in Scripture in at least two ways. One (Isa. 45:9; Job 33:6; Rom. 9:19ff) forms an argument about the creature's *standing* in a fictional debate with the Creator about good and evil. This will be discussed later. The other (Jer. 18:1-11) has a different theme: What the potter can achieve depends in part on the clay at hand: Clay may be too soft to stand, or too stiff to work, or its substance ill-suited to the hardening furnace's fire. Or it may be just right. A good potter makes what she can of the clay, perhaps modifying its texture to improve results. Here we meet afresh an idea from the previous section: Alongside the Creator's own creativity is the creative potential (or the want of it) displayed in the creature. A line in Adelaide Pollard's gospel song, "Mold me and make me / After thy will, / While I am waiting / Yielded and still" expresses the surrender that is surely one moment of authentic creaturehood. Yet Jeremiah's message from the potter's house suggests a bigger role for the clay:

> You are the potter, I am the clay;
> Make me the chalice Of a new day.
> Here all my power, Talent and skill;
> Fire them for action, Creative Will.

For our action, too, both our yielding and our overcoming, is creation. What we have yet to explore is the sense in which not only angelic or human creatures, but also animals, plants, and inorganic nature, including finally the smallest quanta of energy, constitute creation's web, each segment created yet creative, each in its part fashioning the cosmic whole.

ii. Struggle.—We saw that the ancient Near East envisioned a world made by a titanic creation battle between gods, land rising above chaotic water, light dispelling ancient night. Since these conflict myths exalted pagan deities, the authors of Genesis subordinated them to purer themes. Yet other biblical writers employed the myths, at least as expressive poetic pictures: The primeval monster, Leviathan, or Rahab, or the Dragon, or the Sea (Isa. 27:1; 51:9b-10; Pss. 74:13f; 89:9-11) is defeated by mighty JHWH—but not utterly erased. Perhaps this theme appears again in the character of the Genesis tempter serpent (Gen. 3:1-15) and the ongoing enmity between God and the Satan or Adversary (Job 1:6–2:7), continues in the Gospels (e.g., Mark 1:13; 3:23, 26; Luke 10:18), and climaxes in the final punishment of the Devil (Rev. 20:10). This dramatic element in biblical theology is relevant as we examine creation's travail. More accessible to many, though, is the idea that creation is intrinsically costly. It has its price. There is no scientific or artistic or political creation, no new state, no work of high art, no product of hard thought but takes its toll upon the artisan. In this vein, does God, too, find creation and suffering inseparable?

Here we recall a figure encountered in Chapter Two: Hans Hut. As we saw there, Hut after his conversion traveled across South Germany and Austria, preaching and baptizing. His message was "the gospel of all creatures": All suffer; that first premise could be accepted without demurrer by the men and women Hut addressed. Yet the "all" is not merely human beings, but all creatures, indeed all creation. Hut pointed to examples ready to hand in medieval Europe—the horses and cattle, sheep, pigs, and fowl of daily farm life. All these worked and died in human service. As they fulfilled what Hut and his hearers took to be their purpose, so did the Christ fulfill his purpose by suffering and dying on the cross. Likewise, believers, upon hearing this gospel, would see that their calling was to suffer in Christ's cause, patiently and humbly fulfilling their roles as they awaited the imminent end (Hut, 1526–27:392-94; Armour, 1966:chaps. 2–3). It is interesting that the gospel of all creatures as preached by Hut (along with Thomas Muentzer and perhaps others) put to Christian service a fact, animal suffering, that would be scandalous in the nineteenth century, when evolutionary doctrine unfolded a still larger panorama of the suffering inseparable from life itself—of nature red in tooth and claw. Again in the late twentieth century this same fact became another sort of scandal as moral philosophers argued against human inhumanity to beasts (Midgley, 1978). Our present interest is to see that the gospel of all creatures (the name probably came from Mark 16:15, through a misreading of the Vulgate Latin) declined merely to link suffering and guilt, suffering and punishment. *But related suffering, instead, to ongoing creation: to exist is to suffer.* Yet suffering, while not defined as punishment, nevertheless might have a point; it might be related, not to past misconduct, but to creation's purpose and future glory.

iii. Design and execution.—A maker has a plan; a builder follows a pattern. The tabernacle and its ark were built, according to Exodus, by Bezalel, a man specially chosen by JHWH and filled with the spirit of God so that he was skillful in many crafts (Exod. 31:1-5). The sacred tent and box were built to "a design shown to you on the mountain" (Exod. 25:40), that is, as part of the divine instructions for the covenant people. As it was with God's appointed meeting place on earth, so was it with earth and heaven and all their furnishings: If Bezalel was a skilled builder, God was a builder of surpassing skill. That is, God could create after a pattern, and did so. Such thoughts gave rise in Greek antiquity to the "design argument": we can see nature's design; must it not have a Designer? In biblical thought, however, the insight was followed rather by awe and wonder:

> You it was who fashioned my inward parts;
> you knitted me together in my mother's womb.
> I praise you, for you fill me with awe;
> wonderful you are, and wonderful your works. (Ps. 139:13f)

iv. Expression.—To speak of artisan and artist leads on to creation seen as the expression of its creator's skill, inner vision, and artistic aim or goal. JHWH is himself "enfolded in a robe of light" according to Psalm 104. Thus the grandeur of things expresses concretely what the metaphor of God's garment suggests. The vision of the psalmist ranges over a light-filled world, the sky a translucent fabric tent overhead, earth's floating foundation-beams beneath, and between them wind, clouds, fire, mountains and streams, floods and springs, these last calling to mind God's rainbow promise to Noah and his family. At the springs, animals quench their thirst; for cattle there is grass; for people, vegetation; grain, wine, and oil appear in abundance. Even Leviathan splashes by, now only a playful monster to be admired (104:1-26).

> All of them look to you in hope
> to give them their food when it is due.

What you give them they gather up;
when you open your hand, they eat their fill of good things.
When you hide your face, they are dismayed.
When you take away their spirit, they die
and return to the dust from which they came.
When you send forth your spirit, they are created
And you give new life to the earth.
May the glory of the LORD stand for ever,
and may the LORD rejoice in his works! (Ps. 104:27-31)

The psalm's lyricism means to match earth's own, since "the world is charged with the grandeur of God" (Hopkins).

Among the human arts the gossamer art of the word ranks highest of all. Its quintessential expression is God's spoken *word*. Although the word is the means of immediate creation in Genesis 1 ("and God said . . ."), it is sometimes itself God's creature, spoken to convey God's purpose: "it will not return to me empty without accomplishing my purpose and succeeding in the task for which I sent it" (Isa. 55:11). Scripture is God's word, that is, God's artistry, and in John's Prologue, "word" is the eternal Word, ever with God, the light that is the source of all light (1:1-5). Here, though, we have passed beyond creation; the eternal Word is no creature but (by ancient Christian confession) very God.

Hendry notes that some ancient Christians, borrowing from Plato, considered creation not merely God's expression but an *emanation* from God. Yet most judged this excessive and mistaken: it made creation a necessity, an impersonal process that was nevertheless part of the personal God (Hendry, 1980:158-60).

v. Generation.—We saw that "descent from the gods" is a familiar model of creation, recurring in many cultures. It is the more remarkable, then, that Scripture was quite restrained concerning God's originative fatherhood: God was not a *biological* father. "LORD, you are our Father; we are the clay, you the potter, and all of us are your handiwork" (Isa. 64:8)—and if handiwork, then not the issue of a divine begetting. The bull calf was a fit object for sacrifice, not idolatry, in Israel. Thus already in the Old Testament as in the New, God is in metaphor an *adoptive* Father: (Jer. 3:19). Jesus in the Gospels calls God "Father" (and himself "Son") in a unique sense: "no one knows the Father but the Son . . ." (Matt. 11:27). Note that in that passage the "Father" is also "Lord of heaven and earth"; the (unique) Father of Jesus is none other than Israel's (adoptive) Father, and when ancient church councils wrestled with the meaning of such passages, they decided that "the concept of generation is applicable only to the relationship between God the Father and the

Son: only the Son is begotten of the Father, all others are created or made" (Hendry, 1980:150).

The infrequent biblical references to God as creative Mother are, when they appear, less restrained. The psalmist is "calm and quiet like a weaned child clinging to its mother" (131:2)—and that mother, in the psalm's figure, is JHWH. In Psalm 22, God is the midwife who delivered the psalmist at birth (22:9), and perhaps, in a change of figure, the very womb *(racham)* that bore him was God's. That is explicitly the case in Deuteronomy: "You were unmindful of the Rock that bore you; you forgot the God who gave you birth" (32:18 NRSV). In a similar figure Moses asks God about his responsibility to his countrymen: "*Am I* their mother? *Have I* brought them into the world, and am called on to carry them in *my* arms, like a *nurse* with a baby?" (Num. 11:12*a*) The implication is that it was JHWH, not Moses, who "brought them into the world" and is therefore responsible for ungrateful Israel. Yet God's creative mothering is not confined to human offspring:

> Has the rain a father,
>> or who has begotten [*holid*] the drops of dew?
> From whose womb [*beten*] did the ice come forth,
>> and who has given birth [*yelado*] to the hoarfrost of
>> heaven? (Job 38:28f NRSV)

Phyllis Trible notes that the poem "uses the root *yld* for both the begetting of the father and the birthing of the mother." Since the point is to emphasize human inability and divine transcendence, "No human images, not even parental ones, can encompass the divine creativity." Nevertheless, the verb *(chayal)* used of God's giving birth in Deuteronomy 32:18 is otherwise used only of a woman in labor pains. There God is such a woman, bearing Israel in divine travail (Trible, 1978:67f, 62-70). In a like passage in Isaiah, God speaks to the exiles in Babylon, describing both originative and renewed creation (Isa. 42:5-25). The theme is the costly pain of this creative labor, pain both for God and for God's people:

> Long have I restrained myself,
>> I kept silence and held myself in check;
> now I groan like a woman in labor,
>> panting and gasping.
> I shall lay waste mountain and hill
>> and shrivel up all their herbage.
> I shall change rivers into desert wastes
>> and dry up every pool. (Isa. 42:14f)

Here we meet converging themes, the travail of birth for both mother and child, for God and for nature including human nature. These must occupy us next.

b. Synergy: God and nature.—If we turn from these biblical vistas to our doctrinal task today we find a growing awareness that our species is continuous with nature. We are part and parcel of the universe, and live in symbiosis with other living things and in mutual dependence upon the earth. Science fiction may picture our descendants abandoning a failed earth to occupy some other, hypothetical planet, but such fantasy cannot overturn reality: Dust we are; our selves, like earth our floating home in space, are composed of ancient star dust. Jürgen Moltmann points out that this (late-modern) awareness has guided some European thinkers away from the old materialist focus upon *work* as the sole medium of human relation to nature (earth as an object to be manipulated in the interest of work) into a new double focus: Alongside the economic category of work is the understanding of earth as the *home place*, entitled to all the care of home (Moltmann, 1991:45f; cf. Bloch, 1986). Yet the new awareness of earth as home is only a fragment of a wider Christian vision.

i. Recent science and synergy.—The old deterministic clockwork model of nature, inherited from the Enlightenment, is no longer adequate. Rather than a nature forever running automatically in iron conformity to its own causal laws, the science of cosmology draws upon data from astronomy and high-energy particle physics to reconstruct a cosmos of dynamic, open emergence. Cosmologists posit a big bang, their playful name for a hypothetical initial event at time zero ($t = 0$). All the parts of the cosmos were much closer together at first and still recede from one another as from an initial explosion (thus astronomer Edwin Hubble at Caltech in the 1920s). Initially so close and so hot, the predecessors of the cosmos' present components at near-infinitesimal early time ($t = 10^{-43}$ seconds) interacted to form the basic physical forces of nature. With these forces there would simultaneously have arisen the laws and constants that continue to characterize them (W. Stoeger in Russell, et al., eds., 1988; Gore, 1983). While this does not tell us where or how God's continuous creation was involved, its very complexity presents an attractive new scenario for God's action. Whether that action focused upon aleatory features, or upon systemic causality, or both, is not a question scientific cosmology can answer, but its current content is friendly to the proposal that God's method in ongoing creation was interactive from the first amid interactive primitive particles, long before there were living cells or animals to form cooperative intentions.

That the interaction had a directed outcome—for example the lives of pur-pose-guided migratory birds, animals adapting as well as adapted to climates, or human beings capable of perceiving all this—is a further inference that is supported by the so-called fine-tuning phenomena: When the basic proportions of the cosmos such as the ratios of the primary forces to one another fell into place, their inter-relations were such that life would eventually be possible in the universe—gravity not too strong or too weak, for example (Barrow and Tipler, 1988; R. Russell in Peters, ed., 1989:196-99; N. Murphy in Russell, et al., eds., 1993). Once again, some have employed this fine-tuning for a new argu-ment from design, but that is not the present point, which is only that by the data *interaction* characterized nature from its (infinitesimal) beginning.

A second illustration of interaction comes from biology. Under-standing the history of life on earth now depends upon some version of evolutionary theory formed in the wake of Charles Darwin's discover-ies. From the first some biblically oriented theologians welcomed Dar-win's work, arguing that evolution was God's method in creation (Welch, 1972–85:II, chap. 6). Yet the dominance of evolutionary biology brought with it the recognition—anathema to the old deterministic science—that the biological "processes of the world as a whole are not unfolded as predetermined sequences of events, like the development of a mammalian embryo from the ovum." Rather, "The chief charac-teristic of progressive evolution is its open-endedness" (Arthur Pea-cocke in Peters, ed., 1989:37; cf. Polkinghorne, 1989). In other words, investigating an ocean floor or jungle or forest or desert, one cannot even in principle predict what variations will take form in its ecological web, what new forms will emerge, and how these will creatively alter the symbiotic system they help constitute so as to enable still new emer-gents—new creative possibilities.

For a third illustration, we may turn to physical anthropology, and to the appearance of "man the promising primate," to quote the title of Peter Wilson's book (1980). As I noted in the previous volume, the "promising primate" of Wilson's title was first of all primitive woman, who accepted her ongoing relation *both* to her offspring *and* to her mate and by the implied promise of that double bond created the primitive family, thus bringing to birth not only her offspring, but the extended family, tribes, peoples, and culture itself (*Ethics*, pp. 93f). If to this anthropological premise we add the facts of primitive religion or wor-ship as established by anthropology and archaeology, there emerges an elemental account of a human nature and culture with new creative possibilities indebted to the first human promisers as well as to God's promises. Created co-creators are a grander creation than robots.

One somber note must be added: the higher into this complex sphere of consciousness and self-consciousness that nature rises, the more evident are the struggle, suffering, and evil that accompany all its creativity. Culture, that is, cooperative human society, finds itself opposing "the selfishness of the genes" that work strictly for their own survival; the emergence of thought entails a struggle in itself (a point painfully evident to at least one theological writer); the rise of consciousness more generally means a new access to pain. We will see that God the Creator is not remote from these developments, and is supremely the passionate (rather than impassible) God. The freedom of human co-creators is in part freedom to struggle (Philip Hefner in Peters, ed., 1989:219-23) and to suffer, to be a Jacob at the ford of the Jabbok, wrestling *with* God the Creator.

It may trouble some that references to *God's* creative action are coolly interspersed here with references to natural and human creativity. Without biblical faith there will doubtless be too little motive to speak of both human and divine creation, and my point here is not to legitimate such faith, but only to investigate the path it must take. Still, some may object that it is meaningless to speak of God's action in the world, since the world (they say) is fully explained by its own exclusive causal laws. There is more to be said about that, but it cannot be included here. In any case there are two senses in which believers must speak of God's action in the world. The first sense is analogous to human action: We intend to act and (barring unexpected obstacles) we regularly carry out our intentions. Must it be different for God? If it is objected that we act via our bodies, while God has none, the reply is that the immediate analogy is: we to our bodies as God to nature. I intend to swing my leg in a place-kick; I set the ball in place, get ready, and—kick. The forces of electromagnetism, gravity, et cetera, and all the laws that describe them, are in my own leg and so at my beck. Are the same forces denied, there or elsewhere, to God their Creator and Master? (cf. Plantinga, 1967; McClendon, 1969; Peacocke, 1979:131-46; Alston in Hebblethwaite and Henderson, eds., 1990; and per contra Polkinghorne, 1989:chap. 2) Only a determinism that would deny human agency and turn us into robots can consistently deny divine agency on deterministic grounds, and the price of such consistency is a repudiation of the very human initiative that made modern culture and science possible. The other sense in which God acts is indeed beyond human analogy—God is Alpha and Omega, God creates, sustains, terminates. In this sense God is (in an adjusted sense) the 'cause' behind all our causes; God's "let be" (Gen. 1:3) is the awesome source of every natural source, and so of the world of action in its entirety.

ii. God and nature in travail.—The doctrine of creation appears alongside the other central Christian teachings in Paul's Letter to the Romans, where it takes a surprising form:

> . . . but we must share his sufferings if we are also to share his glory. For I reckon that the sufferings we now endure bear no comparison with the glory, as yet unrevealed, which is in store for us. The created universe is waiting with eager expectation for God's sons

to be revealed. It was made subject to frustration, not of its own
choice but by the will of him who subjected it, yet with the hope that
the universe itself is to be freed from the shackles of mortality and
is to enter upon the glorious liberty of the children of God. Up to
the present, as we know, the whole created universe in all its parts
groans as if in the pangs of childbirth. What is more, we also, to
whom the Spirit is given as the firstfruits of the harvest to come, are
groaning inwardly while we look forward eagerly to our adoption,
our liberation from mortality. It was with this hope that we were
saved. Now to see something is no longer to hope: why hope for
what is already seen? But if we hope for something we do not yet
see, then we look forward to it eagerly and with patience.

(Rom. 8:17b-25)

Here we are provided a lens upon the doctrine of creation as it appeared
in the first century. Paul does not begin with the idea of a perfect creation
later marred (as does much subsequent theology, Catholic and Protestant); his starting point is present Christian suffering. Paul and his
readers had to share the *excruciating* way of the cross. Yet this sharing
was the way to a glorious future which far outweighed in importance
all it cost. This standpoint made possible a significant enlargement
(Rom. 8:19-22). Creation itself is burdened with such suffering "in all its
parts" (8:22). This is not meaningless suffering, any more than the shared
cross is: Creation's suffering (here Paul reflects Isaiah 42:14ff) is the labor
of a woman giving birth; God's labor pains (thus Isaiah) are those of
creation (thus Paul), and the two, God's and the world's, are mediated,
brought together, by the labor pains of the Christian fellowship, who in
company with their Master suffered and were sustained by God who is
Spirit: "through our inarticulate groans the Spirit himself is pleading for
us, and God . . . knows what the Spirit means" (8:26f). Paul crowns this
explanation with a summary that reiterates our present theme: "in
everything, as we know, [God] co-operates [*sunergei*, 'synergizes'] for
good with those who love God and are called according to his purpose" (8:28).

Romans 8 opens for us three topics, God's travail (implied), creation's travail
(explicit), and the future of creation with God. The first will be addressed here,
the second, in following Subsection iii, and the coming glory in Section §3 of this
chapter as well as in Chapters Two and Ten.

We saw that the primordial myth of a struggle between good and evil,
a god of order and light versus deities of chaos and night, was suppressed but not totally eliminated in the Bible's accounts of creation. Jon
Levenson, interpreting these biblical pictures of creation-as-conflict,

does not dispute the underlying theme of the present three chapters—the rule, or in Levenson's term the mastery, of God. Yet he warns that the motif can be stated in so absolute a manner as to miss the standpoint of Scripture (Levenson, 1988:chaps. 1–4). God as creation's master had restrained, but not destroyed, the chaotic primordial waters. Then in the flood "all the springs of the great deep [the waters beneath] burst out, the windows of the heavens were opened, and rain [the waters above] fell . . ." (Gen. 7:11f). In the flood, chaos returned, though Noah and the life in his care were spared by God. So with God's permission, chaos *could* return. Only the covenant with Noah (Gen. 9:8-17) guaranteed the waters would not invade again. In the Psalmist's version of events,

> You fixed a boundary which they were not to pass;
> they were never to cover the earth again. (Ps. 104:9)

A more unsettling case, Levenson argues, comes from those passages such as Psalm 74, Isaiah 51, and Isaiah 54, where the post-creation survival of chaos is said to threaten God's elect people. In the perception of Psalm 74, chaos has indeed returned, threatening God's ancient victory; where, then, is God? (Levenson, 1988:17-20; cf. Ps. 74:9-21) Levenson's exposition, however, does not address the reality-status of primeval chaos. Did chaos timelessly pre-exist creation, as the *Enuma elish* taught? Is chaos actually within God himself, an element of God's own nature, as some speculative theologians have theorized? Or is 'chaos' with its threatening waters but a poetic substitute for the intrinsic difficulty God and creation encounter in the struggle entailed in attaining their goal? The first option is ruled out by the divine origination of all that is: "through him all things came to be" (John 1:3). The second was strongly rejected by the early Christians in the conflict with Gnosticism: "God is light, and in him there is no darkness at all" (1 John 1:2; cf. James 1:17f). This leaves the third option: the divine struggle, dramatically described in Scripture, is no other than the potter's struggle to shape workable clay into a work of art; it is a struggle that encounters the 'evil' of hard work and variety in material, but not the evil of cosmic dualism. So the church must teach, if I have reasoned correctly here. Yet we do well to let Jon Levenson's Jewish word come last:

> Like all other faith, creation-faith carries with it enormous risk. Only as the enormity of the risk is acknowledged can the grandeur of the faith be appreciated. (Levenson, 1988:156)

In the fourth-century Arian debate, theologians made a sharp separation of God the impassible Father from his incarnate Logos or Son. This idea reappeared, after Nicaea had condemned Arianism, in the Orthodox reluctance to impute suffering to the *divine* nature of the (two-natured) Christ (see Chapter Six §2). From these beginnings sprang the teaching of divine impassibility, which as we have just seen is bound to have severe difficulties with the Bible (cf. Mozley, 1926:86-104). Today, however, there is fresh discussion of a suffering Creator (MacGregor, 1975; McWilliams, 1985; Fiddes, 1988; on Process Theology, see Chapter Seven §2).

A comprehensive view must include these elements: (1) For God to continue to be God, there must be that about God which is utterly reliable. This is God's nature or character, the qualities inherent in God's Godhood. While we must canvass these qualities in Part II of this volume, the quality assumed here is God's creative love, the love that sets out on the costly adventure of creation itself. Yet (2) to speak of adventure (and of love) implies reciprocity, God's ability to enter into loving relations with what is outside God and by doing so to bring about changed circumstances in the world. Since these changes are relational, they imply change not only for the world, but also for God. Creation is itself such an act of change, and ongoing creation is a series of such changes. God-who-has-created is other than God-who-only-might-create. Then (3) the changes involved in this world by the human adventure (and who knows what other adventures elsewhere in the cosmos) entail the risk of further suffering: to love is to suffer (Haughton, 1981), and to love recalcitrant or rebellious or sinful creatures is costly suffering indeed. Yet (4) we can be sure of the divine capacity thus to suffer creatively since, as Geddes MacGregor (1975) among others has pointed out, the very act of creation on the part of an all-sufficient God involves a divinely necessary rejection, a deliberate surrender, not of concern and active involvement, but of the solitary hoarding of free existence. Such a view of creation is strictly and historically necessary if we believe in God as the lover and giver God known in Israel's journey, the God we know in Jesus Christ. As Paul's groaning Spirit in Romans 8 suggests, not only can Christians believe in a passionate and suffering Deity; they *must* do so. Must, if they are to be truly Christian in thought as well as in life (cf. Rom. 8:29*a*).

c. Why suffering?—It is not uncommon for recent systematic theologies to discuss at this point "the problem of evil." This phrase is borrowed from the "philosophy of religion" (N. Murphy, NHCT, 355-59). Here a special literature called "theodicy" ("justifying God"!) has grown up. This is argument whose aim is to "justify the ways of God to man" (Pope); it is a modern philosophical reply to the charge that since such and such evils are perceived in the world, God has failed to be God. Some writers suppose the genre to be much older, as old as the book of Job, but I hew to the stricter definition of theodicy as a post-Enlightenment enterprise. On this view its originators are an Irish Anglican archbishop, William King (1650–1729), and the German philosopher Gottfried Wilhelm Leibniz (1646–1716). At least the theodicy that shows up in some theologies of creation is modern, not only in its time of origin, but in its underlying assumptions. I hope briefly to show here that this enterprise is ill-conceived, and then to indicate an alternative as a Christian approach to suffering in creation.

Present-day theodicists follow in the steps of their Enlightenment models. An example is the work of philosopher of religion John Hick (1922–). For Hick there is "a contradiction or apparent contradiction between the reality of evil on the one hand, and religious belief in the goodness and power of God or of the Ultimate on the other." Theodicy's method is to resolve this contradiction, either by adjusting its judgment about God's goodness and power, or by grading and classifying evils, or both. For example, Leibniz viewed God as "an infallible calculating machine" creating the best of all possible universes (this one), while the aesthetic conception of evil construes it as a necessary element in a greater good. Yet this 'Augustinian' view, Hick says, cannot adequately account for the origin or destiny of evil. Thus he himself adopts an 'Irenaean' theodicy that includes some of the previous elements but modifies the scheme by positing a gradual growth of human conscience and sensibilities to explain the origin and destiny both of evil and of the moral cosmos (Hick, 1978; cf. Hick, *Enc. Phil.* III:136-38). Certainly there is some merit in these careful maneuvers (Mathis, 1985:78-93). Their great difficulty seems to be that they rescue God at the expense of making the evils Christians confront and those they commit somehow tolerable, or even to be expected. Yet if they were tolerable, would God's redemption of the world really be necessary? More than that, would God's own suffering—centrally, in the cross of Christ—really be in vain, since the world is nice enough as it is?

My judgment is that modern theodicy occupies a false standpoint, one from which a true assessment of the situation is not possible. Here I cannot fully expose this illusory standpoint (awaiting *Volume III*), yet I can at least suggest the kind of internal difficulty the work of modern theodicists from Archbishop King to the present faces. First, in order for anyone to say anything on any subject whatsoever, *some* standpoint must be taken up, and furthermore, for us to take the speaker seriously, that standpoint must be consistently maintained. (For a homely example, an automobile owner goes to a paint-shop friend and asks for a low-cost paint job. Subsequently, he complains to others that his new finish is of inferior quality. Is he now speaking as an unbiased expert on paint jobs, or as a friend who feels betrayed? From first to last, what standpoint has he occupied? Without knowing, what sense can we make of the case?) Now theodicists say they see the world as defective in certain respects. It displays evils. On the other hand, they say, its evils are understandable, or for the best, or only what we might have expected. They are not totally disappointed, and they tell us to believe in its 'painter,' the Deity! But what or whom do they believe in? Are they consistent in their stance? Are theodicists God's friends complaining that their Friend has let them down? Or are they detached observers of friendship, themselves perhaps friendless (or Friendless?) who nonetheless advise believers to keep on believing? It is not clear. And lack of clarity vitiates their advice. Where do they stand?

Terrence Tilley has expanded questions like these into a book (Tilley, 1991). He distinguishes between "theodicies" and "defenses." Theodicies are arguments put forward by academic philosophers who wish to abjure *all* standpoints, but who nevertheless want to make judgments about God, the world, and evil from their (impossible, mid-air) position. Nonetheless, they tend to accept the world as suitable enough (ignoring truly troubling human evils) while they offer a bland Enlightenment God as its sponsor. Defenses, on the other hand, "seek to show that an attack against the religious believers' claims . . . does not affect, and should not affect, the quality of assent religious believers give to their beliefs" (Tilley, 1991:130). More generally, we might say that such defenses as Diogenes Allen's *Traces of God* (1981) are accounts of God and creation meant to show that unbelief has misunderstood God—and therefore misunderstood the world. They speak in faith and thus do not pretend to occupy a standpoint from which one could *judge* God (the literal meaning of "theodicy"). The academy's assumption of its own pure neutrality on what it sometimes calls "the God question," if correct, means that theodicists and their debate opponents necessarily start from a *counter-creation assumption*. They assume that there exists at least one place in the world (their academy) where God can be shelved, a place that neither owns nor is owned by God. From such a place, they assume, it is fitting to discuss "God's existence" as people in Los Angeles might detachedly discuss the existence of the New Guinea bumblebee (cf. McClendon and Smith, 1994:chap. 3). Such an assumption stultifies the debate.

Does skepticism about theodicy damage the case for a doctrine of creation? If we shelve theodicy (rather than God), in what mode can we discuss the suffering creation? A first move might be to look again at the book of Job. There a different but equally negative view of 'theodicy' (represented by Job's 'friends') appears.

The structure of Job consists of a prose beginning and ending (1:1–3:1; 42:7-16) with a middle that poetically explores the plight of the protagonist. (One hypothesis about the making of the book is that the beginning and end are a traditional Middle Eastern wisdom tale that shows how, in spite of the worst, things work out for a good man, Job, who suffers; into that limited traditional tale, the biblical poet and editor has sandwiched the reflective speeches that make up the body of our book.) To read less than the whole composition is to read something other, something less, than biblical Job (admittedly, many prefer less). Job is without fault, yet he suffers. He is without sin, but he suffers more than anyone. Though the remote source of his suffering is God's Adversary, and finally God (1:6-12; 2:1-6), its immediate causes are common occasions of much real human suffering, a fact that gives the tale its poignancy. Loss of his livestock, destruction of his home and his children, wasting disease, the defection of a spouse, and (from the poetic center of the book) the eloquent but flawed *theological practice* of his friends—these cause Job overwhelming pain. It is important to see that this lifelike situation is deliberately and transparently fictional. While many Jewish exegetes have seen this, Christians dare not over-look it, for by Christian account, "All alike have sinned." Jew and Gentile, insiders and outsiders to God's history, all fall short of God's glory (Rom. 3:23). So the book of Job raises what is *for it* only a fictional question, What if an utterly faithful man were to suffer outrageously? but it can give no adequate answer, for the fact it envisions had not occurred in reality. (Thus Tilley is probably correct to find Job imponderable when viewed by itself—1991:106-10.)

In Jesus of Nazareth, the dilemma Job raises turns into dread fact. The book of Job turns out to have been proleptic—a tale of terror come true. Jesus is Job, not in the sense of being an ancient patriarch deprived of flocks and family, but in living the life of full faithfulness that the text imputes to Job himself. All Christian attempts to cope with suffering creation must begin with the real Job—with Christ crucified—and there-fore with the hope of grace great enough to call out of actual (and sometimes unbearable) suffering the "glory, as yet unrevealed, which is in store for us" (Rom. 8:18). The limit of proleptic Job is its inability, apart from true history, to evoke this grace. Therefore those who read the textually problematic verse, Job 19:25, with the Revised English Bible, "But I know that my vindicator lives / and that he will rise last to speak in court" must see it as referring not only to the final speeches of the Almighty (Job 38–41), but as a prophetic reference within the canon to the true story that was to come.

Christians may tentatively divide the severe evils they and all creation suffer into three categories. *The first* is suffering from evil that appears to them *senseless and inexplicable*. The book of Job points to that kind of suffering when in the prologue it reveals the agreement to test Job. His suffering had a point that Job could not know, as in many a real-life case we can find no point to the evil we endure. I believe this to be the most terrible suffering. We cannot easily bear the hand of God that inexplica-bly meets us as the hand of an enemy or adversary; we find it hard to praise the Creator who strangely sustains the nuclear weapon–smith and the destroying army—nor should we expect to find otherwise. Warlords starving a nation to death, ethnocide in Auschwitz and Cambodia, infanticide willfully cruel—Job's outraged protest speaks for suffering humanity when it confronts such senseless suffering. Where *is* God, anyway? Faithful Jesus in Luke advises any prospective sufferer when he tells his disciples in Gethsemane, "Pray that you may be spared the test," but he himself, though he prayed that prayer (Luke 22:40b-42) was not spared the test. Facing senseless, unavoidable suffering, the disciple's only hope is to act responsively. To do this, however, one must bring that suffering under one of two other categories.

In this light, the *second category* is sometimes painfully welcome: suffering as *punishment*. It is easier to suffer when I deserve it than when I do not. Here the pastor Christian must avoid perils on either side: One is met in Job's friends (and Jesus' enemies) who blame Job in whose story there is no fault (and Jesus in whose history there is none). On the other side, though, is the perilous urge to deny a sufferer's authentic admission: "This has come on me as deserved punishment." A generation of seminarians trained to detect (or anyway suspect) neurotic guilt needs the conviction that there is real guilt—and real punishment—as well: "All alike have sinned" describes congregants (and their pastors) well enough to warn us against psychologizing all real guilt away, and from Cain, to Ananias and Sapphira (Acts 5:1-6), to the last judgment, real punishment may ensue. That some suffering is punishment is a step toward release for moderns mesmerized by what they take to be a morally empty cosmos.

Happily, there is a true gospel to replace the false. Some suffering, the *third category*, is *redemptive*. There is pain that makes well in the life of the body, and this is so in the life of the spirit as well. In redemptive suffering creation touches and is touched by the history of salvation. How suffering is redemptive in the paradigm case of Jesus of Nazareth is the topic of the chapter to follow, and how the people of God are involved with him in that suffering and thus in that very redemption is treated there and in Part III (as it is in *Ethics* Eight). The question not answered in the present chapter is whether the first two categories, senseless suffering and punitive suffering, can themselves be redeemed by the third, so that redemption can be the last word of a suffering God to suffering creation. Yet one such question can be discussed here. Creation itself looks forward to a fulfillment that is its goal and vindication. This Section has raised questions about human creation and destiny, about God's creative action on and in the world, and about the relation of redemption to creation, and at last we are in position to address these topics (§3).

Christ not only discloses the shape of creation; he is the actual creative agent of the Godhead: the Redeemer is the Creator (cf. John 1:1; Heb. 1:2; Col. 1:16f). This theme is already present in the later portions of Isaiah as well. Yet it can better be pursued here when the doctrine of God's triunity is presented (Chapter Seven).

§3. Creation as Promise

Now that we realize the vast size of the known cosmos (a multiple of 15 billion light-years) and now that we may contemplate the aeons-long timespan of earthly (to say nothing of other?) life forms, with their amazing fecundity and development, what shall we say is the *point* of it all? *Why* creation? Why *this* creation? Why is it thus and not otherwise? And what is the destiny of all this energy and matter and life, including of course our own human life? If we reject atheism (which spurns the question) and deism (whose God leaves creation strictly on its own) how shall we answer? To begin, let us return to the vision in the Apocalypse of John (Revelation 4) with which we began. This will remind us afresh of the pictorial nature of our 'protological' and eschatological knowledge; it will remind us as well of the vector of biblical thought toward creation's destiny. Revelation's scene ended with creation praising God the sovereign Lord, who "created *all* things" (4:11)—an audacious message to Asian Christians suffering beneath the Roman Imperium. Yet the vision is not ended; there is a second scene. The One on heaven's throne holds a scroll written and sealed, and an angel asks who is worthy *(axios)* to take it, break the seals, and open the scroll. The first answer is that no one in heaven or on earth can do this. But an elder (the term evokes the leadership of synagogue or church) comforts the seer: The "Lion of the tribe of Judah, the shoot . . . from David's stock" has won the right to open the scroll (Rev. 5:1-5). Next appears "a Lamb with the marks of sacrifice." The Lion is identified as no other than this Lamb. Whereupon all creation joyfully *sings* "Worthy is the Lamb," and "Praise and honor" to God and to the Lamb (Rev. 5:6-14). If we suppose with Ted Grimsrud (1987) that the scroll reveals the point of creation with all its suffering (but see Charles, 1920 I:137f), we do so partly because this is something suffering Asia Minor saints would gladly know. The pictorial symbolism of Revelation 5 implies that creation's goal will be found in history, and concretely in the story of Israel and Jesus. It implies that the wanted answer is found not apart from but exactly in connection with the paradigmatic suffering of the "Lamb slain." It announces that thanks to that Lamb, creation will find its way to the "praise and honor, glory and might" of its one Ruler (5:13).

To make this announcement is to suggest the inadequacy of other ways of determining creation's destiny. The Apocalypse's suffering readers would not learn the contents of the scroll by sniffing Anatolian blossoms, or find sufficient wisdom in running brooks or the starry heavens—far less by heeding earthly Caesar's imperious demands. The point of creation is known through Israel's story and known most clearly in its climax at the cross.

This is not to deny God's presence in all things (including all suffering), nor the congruence of all things with the message of this secret scroll. It does not rule out the immediate awareness of God's presence in nature wherever that presence is felt. Such awareness, what George F. Stout called the fundamentally valid insight of animism (cited in H. Farmer, 1963:22), has been less accessible in some times than others, less accessible to Mondrian than to Rembrandt, less accessible to classicist than to romantic poets:

> And I have felt
> A presence that disturbs me with the joy
> Of elevated thoughts; a sense sublime,
> Of something far more deeply interfused,
> Whose dwelling is the light of setting suns,
> And the round ocean and the living air. . . .
> (William Wordsworth, "Tintern Abbey")

Others have felt no such thing, yet it does not matter, for by the heavenly scene of Revelation 5, the scroll's writing comes clear in the human story itself exactly where it intersects heaven's story. What is vouchsafed to Rembrandt and to Wordsworth is only *lagniappe,* a lovely extra thrown into creation's bargain without further charge.

Some may object to giving such weight to the heavenly vision—may unwisely wish even to exclude heaven with its promise from theology. Unwisely, for the truth about created existence involves creation's doubleness: it is "heaven *and* earth," not earth or the physical cosmos alone, that God has created.

Jürgen Moltmann has given a useful account of heaven's troubled passage through modern theology. For early modern Christians, confronted for the first time with a physical universe located in infinite three-dimensional space, it was expedient to shift the concept of heaven to (future) time—it was not a place, but only the end state of the Christian soul. For Marxian criticism, this was "pie in the sky" once more, and heaven was simply identified with God—and dismissed as God was dismissed. Yet Moltmann argues that these progressive 'solutions' of the problem modern Christian thought had set were defective even from an earthly standpoint. To be sure, we no longer have the cosmology of the ancients, with heaven above and hell beneath. Yet without the duality of the creation of "heaven and earth," heaven is no longer present to represent the created energies, potencies, and possibilities of God for all creation (Moltmann, 1991:chap. 7). In this case, though, we would no longer meaningfully pray "on earth as it is in heaven," for there would be no heaven to give that prayer sense.

Perhaps a hint for reconceiving heavenly creation lies in the mathematics of space developed in the nineteenth century—significantly, in the time *after* the philosophical Enlightenment had decided against heaven's existence. One breakthrough was the development of non-Euclidian geometries, as rigorous as Euclid's, but with changed axioms. Another was the recognition that standard plane and solid geometries were only the beginning of a series that engaged more and more dimensions. Just as three-dimensional solid geometry accepted the constructions of two-dimensional plane geometry but went beyond them, higher-dimension geometries, though they could not be directly visualized in our three-dimensional intuitive world, could be conceived, and their contents reflected new insights back upon geometry in lower dimensions. Scientific writers such as Karl Friedrich Gauss and Hermann von Helmholz and the brilliant Anglican clergyman Edwin Abbott Abbott wrote to stir the human imagination with these discoveries. Abbott's best-known work, *Flatland: A Romance of Many Dimensions*, published under the pseudonym "A Square" (Abbott, 1884), made vivid to nineteenth-century Christian readers the unstated analogy: As our world ("Spaceland") was to Flatland, so heaven was to our world. Heaven's entities could not be grasped directly, though they might see and affect us, as Spaceland's people see and affect Flatland. These developments in mathematics are accessible through Brown University mathematician Thomas Banchoff's *Beyond the Third Dimension* (1990). Banchoff, a believing Christian, is aware like Abbott of the analogical implications of his work. Heaven is not "the fourth (or fifth) dimension," but this analogy with a mathematics unavailable to Enlightenment thinkers assures us that the Christian belief in heaven is not beyond reason. Once again Jacob's dream-angels, ascending and descending (Gen. 28:16-22), remind us of the truth invoked in the Disciples' Prayer: Heaven, the unseen creation, penetrates but is not confined to our world.

a. The creation of a people.—Creation in Genesis does not end in Eden. Not only Genesis 1 and 2, with their accounts of cosmic and earthly beginnings, but the subsequent chapters (3–11) display the LORD God creatively at work. Once human creatures are onstage, creation becomes explicitly reciprocal, as creative creaturehood interacts with a Creator who displays flexibility suited to his living clay—ourselves. How does such a Creator deal with rebellion (chap. 3)? How with Cain's sin, more ruinous than Eve's and Adam's (chap. 4)? Always there is God's query, "What have you done?" (3:13; 4:10); always there are God's new arrangements in response to human blunders (3:14-19; 4:11-15); always there is the multiplication of the adolescent human stock. Out of God's (apparent) creative folly, our progenitors appear (chap. 5), and after the flood narrative there is a table representing the human authors' map of the inhabited world (chap. 10). From the people of the West (Tirus = Etruscans?), to peoples of Asia Minor to the North, to Ethiopians (Cush) and Egyptians (Mizraim) to the South, God's creative concern reaches humanity entire. Among the rest, yet unprivileged in this inclusive account, is the people in the East called Aram (Aramaeans), and among them a progenitor named Arphaxad (Gen. 10:23f). What accounts, though, for the constant enmity, conflict, linguistic diversity of the species? Our authors answer with the story of Babel, where human pride brings division, so that God must interact to multiply languages and disperse the human world into its internecine fragments. The unity that human power and human hubris cannot achieve (Gen. 10:6-10; 11:1-9) now becomes the task of the Creator—whose method is to work by means of the adventurous obedience of one Abraham, child of Arphaxad, child of Shem (thus von Rad, 1972:139-63).

i. The creation of the many peoples.—Hence no rigid demarcation separates the 'prehistory' of Genesis 1–11 from 'patriarchal history.' Both are shadowy remnants from time beyond memory; both reveal God creatively at work. In the earlier narrative, God creates culture and peoples; in the latter, God creates a people for all peoples. For from Abraham (despite obvious generation gaps) the line leads straight to Moses and Sinai, and from Moses to Matthew's Jesus. In Abram, future Abraham, God finds a response, countercultural obedience, and from it generates a "great nation" (Gen. 12:1-3). It is clear, even from this formative call, that this nation will be not a substitute for any of earth's other nations, not a master race to rule or ruin all the nations, but the very means by which the divine blessing will flow out to all.

> The LORD said to Abram, "Leave your own country, your kin, and your father's house, and go to a country that I will show you. I shall make you into a great nation; I shall bless you and make your name so great that it will be used in blessings." . . .

The promise is threefold: A great nation from Abram's seed, blessing (i.e., material prosperity and divine presence) for his life, and—here the winsome biblical twist—Abram's *being* a blessing for all the rest of humankind:

> One who blesses you I will bless; curse those who curse you; bring all families of earth to see themselves blessed in you. (Gen. 12:1-3)

Abraham is not called to found a religion, or himself to be a missionary. He is simply to occupy the land and be blessed in person and in his and Sarah's posterity (Bloom and Rosenberg, 1990:74; Westermann, 1968).

The appearance of this people for all peoples, then, need not be looked at only from the side of God's remedial or redemptive work (though we will in due course consider that); it may be seen as another stage of the original creative purpose of the Maker of heaven and earth.

In the Renaissance, awareness of social change led many to link the 'powers that be' tightly to God. Some Protestant theories found their way into confessional documents, and some of these, never revoked, anathematize "Anabaptists" as dangerous anarchists. It is helpful to remember that in the sixteenth century both sides (magisterial and baptist) presupposed a state aligned with some church (Schleitheim 1527 IV-VII [Yoder, ed., 1973]; Calvin, *Inst.* IV, 20). After the Enlightenment modified church-state relations in Europe and North America, some Reformed scholars sought to reestablish the divine right of government under a "cultural mandate" in Genesis 1:28—a mandate to dominate and subdue the social order, extended to Adam but best fulfilled by Christians (e.g., Van Til, 1959). This "Dominion" theme was adopted by some right-wing religious movements in late-twentieth-century America (Christian Reconstructionism). Basing a mandate for Christian political dominance on creation teaching in Genesis, however, is no more compelling than basing it on *de facto* European church-states. For Christ authorizes no armies, levies no taxes, indeed, exercises no authority save by the persuasion of suffering love, and a "creation mandate" apart from Christ is hardly Christian. It is high time, though, not only for Catholics and Protestants but for baptists as well to rethink the grounds of political legitimacy under the new circumstances, that is, apart from the ubiquitous church-state and state-church. For baptists, this means recognizing that human beings, as self-conscious, intentional organisms, not only eat and reproduce and die; we also plan, we build cities and make music and pray, so that if earth's biosphere is to be healthy we human beings must guide it in ways that matter. Yet as heirs of the Genesis story, we do not stop with chapter 1 or even chapter 3, but see ourselves as Abraham's heirs, by virtue of Jesus. And when we come to Jesus, we come to the politics of Jesus, which as John Yoder has shown, is not just internal instruction for disciples, but provides a way of confronting the sinful, fallen 'authorities' in a social revolution still under way. In this sense—a concern for all creation and a willingness to take Jesus' way in it—there is plenty of room for a creation theology for baptists (see further *Ethics* Six §2; also below Chapter Eleven, §4; Yoder, 1972; 1985*b*; Mouw, 1990:chap. 6).

ii. Providence and election.—I have avoided sharp distinctions between God's initial and continuing creation, and even between divine creation and responsive co-creation. So there is little reason to make a further fundamental divide between creation as preservation or conservation, on the one side, and providence on the other. Both refer to God's continuing involvement with the world, and both imply God's engaging an interactive created order. If we wish for greater precision, we can say that creation is the overarching concept that includes all these, while preservation is the concept of God's ongoing care for the world of things, and providence God's ongoing care for the world of people. Seeing this as only a stipulated distinction rather than a real difference brings out the actual interdependence of all three.

God's providence may be summed up in three memorable phrases. First, God knows and cares. This is the suggestion of the term itself: Providence *prov*ides, that is, sees beforehand; providence pro*vides*, that is, makes provision for what is foreseen. In the early, authentic teaching material called Q, Jesus declares that sparrows, a cheap food for poor Palestinians, could not fall to the ground "without your Father's knowledge" (Matt. 10:29), the implication being that the Father knows, sees, cares about the flights and falls of each of us. It cannot be too strongly emphasized that this does not insure any against falling, or disaster, or death. It does assure that neither we nor the solitary fledgling cheeping in its nest shall live or die alone. It brings us back to the doctrine of the *present* God, and does so on the authority of one who knew how it was to feel alone, knew what it was to fail and to die. Some philosophers fond of theodicy speculate that God cannot know contingent future events, finding curious comfort in the image of a future-blinded deity. This seems a sadly different view of God than that of Old Testament and New, where God's actions (and on occasion God's inaction) are never explained on such ground: Rather, God foresees and foretells the good that Cyrus will do (Isa. 44:28) and the evil that Pharaoh will do (Exod. 6:1); most tellingly, more surely than any sparrow's fall, God foresees the path Jesus takes (Acts 2:23—*prognosei*).

This introduces a second element: the providential **God rules and overrules.** Since God's rule is the comprehensive theme of these pages, we note only that a part of its means is the very action of God, in, with, and under creation's action, sketched in this chapter. More difficult, perhaps, is the concept of overruling, the thought that God in providing for creation finds it on occasion right not only to foresee but to alter the contingent outcome of the world's processes. This overruling is daunting for many a modern Christian, and even a spiritually sensitive Anglican theologian, Austin Farrer, has denied it: "[God] does not let natural forces have their heads up to the point only at which their free action would conflict with some fixed principle of higher purpose, for example the welfare and safety of mankind, nor does he, when that point is reached, substitute miracle for nature and stop physical forces from indulging in their characteristic behavior" (Farrer, 1966:88). We shall speak soon of miracle, so let it here be said that this may be only a dispute about words: The question is not whether God *can* defeat natural processes for providential purposes (God can), but whether God typically turns the course of history toward the divine goals. Farrer is so far right; God typically lets nature be nature. If a speeding auto meets an animal's—or a child's—flesh, the auto's steel and plastic are not dissolved. Time and again, God lets destruction destroy. On the other hand, we know that events, including what seem the worst events, have conspired to effect God's ultimate purposes—the creation of a people, the redemption of the race, the glory of God's coming Sabbath rest. This is the overruling that is here affirmed.

In the later chapters of Genesis, Jacob sends ten of his remaining sons to Egypt during a famine to buy grain, keeping with him only Benjamin the youngest. The brothers return to Canaan without adequate supplies, but with the news that Simeon, one of their ten, has been kept as a hostage by the overlord of Egypt, who demands that when they return for more grain they bring the youngest brother 'as proof of their honesty' (Gen. 42:1-34). Jacob is overwhelmed: "You have robbed me of my children. Joseph is lost; Simeon is lost; and now you would take Benjamin. *Everything is against me*" (Gen. 42:36). Yet the reader of Genesis knows the undisclosed truth: the 'overlord' is none other than Joseph, long ago sold into slavery, whose love for his family is still strong; Simeon is safe in Joseph's care; the apparent calamity is going to issue in survival for the family and ultimately in a safe sojourn in Egypt and the re-creation of Israel. Jacob's "everything is against me" is just the reverse of the providential truth. Moreover, the doctrine of providence enables us sometimes to see the reality of good within actual evil. A little later in the story, Joseph discloses himself to his brothers. They are terror-stricken: this man has the power—and the right—to take ultimate revenge upon them for their past treachery. But Joseph, believer in providence, banishes their distress with the paradoxical declaration: *"it was not you who sent me here, but God"* (Gen. 45:8). God rules and overrules.

Third, **God purposes and disposes.** Here appears the concept of God's *election or choice.* It is well that we meet this powerful but controversial topic only here, after taking space to display God's rule in terms of the eschaton toward which all things move, in terms of the salvation that God provides, and in terms of the interactive creation that is the mode of God's worldly action, for this preview may keep us from some familiar blunders.

That God elects or chooses is a staple of Scripture's narratives: Shem—and not Ham or Japheth; Aram—and not his brothers; Abram—and not Nahor or Haran. The choice of Jacob (and not Esau) becomes in Scripture the choice of Israel, renewed at Sinai: "out of all peoples you will become my special possession; for the whole earth is mine" (Exod. 19:5*b*). Israel's election discloses the fiat of an unhindered JHWH. The genealogies of the Gospels (Matt. 1:1-16; Luke 3:23-38) suggest a continuity between these Old Testament choices and the choice of Jesus, God's elect Son, in whom disciples, too, are elect. Once we take seriously the divine prevenience both in creation and redemption, election seems inevitably to follow.

Augustine wrestled with the apparent clash between the predestination required by divine sovereignty and the fact that within the (ostensibly elect) Catholic community many were unworthy the name. Had election failed? His solution was to distinguish an invisible church from the visible one. The former, seen only by God, was composed of the truly elect, but its membership did not correspond to that of the church visible. Augustine's predestinarian views were hardened by the battle with Pelagius: Election, as pure grace, refuted the self-achieved salvation teaching Augustine opposed. Although he was honored in medieval Christianity more in name than in substance (Aquinas, for example, sought to temper Augustine's predestination teaching), both Luther and Calvin, the leading magisterial Reformers, strongly reaffirmed Augustine in the interest of their own struggle with perceived semi-Pelagianism in sixteenth-century Catholicism. Luther inveighed against free will; Calvin made election an element of his account of how we receive the grace of Christ in Book III of the *Institutes* (3, 2, 25), though his less cautious successors elevated it to become a cardinal element of Reformed teaching. This development was aided by the anti-Arminian decrees of the Synod of Dort with its "TULIP" (total depravity, unconditional election, limited atonement, irresistible grace, and perseverance of the saints). Thence Augustinian predestination was injected, via Puritanism, into American theology's mainstream. Yet the American scene was not congenial to themes rooted in ancient theological wars. Evangelism was the urgent need, as farsighted Protestant (and later, Catholic) leaders saw. An evangelist such as Jonathan Edwards could rationally relate Augustinian divine election to human free will (Edwards, 1754), but his arguments were too subtle for most. In practice, evangelism with its appeal to free human decision ("Whosoever will") won, while election remained on many churches' books, but was little proclaimed. Facing still other doubts about the Augustinian doctrine, Karl Barth at mid–twentieth century attempted a new statement: Jesus Christ and only Jesus Christ is truly elect in his own right; but he is God's representative of humanity, so in Christ all others—the entire race—are elect as well (CD II/2, chap. 7). This Barthian view seemed to some (though not to Barth) to entail universalism, the salvation of all without exception, and thus raised anew the very problem (a churchful of unregenerate sinners) that had moved Augustine toward his earlier version of election.

The doctrine of election or predestination in Scripture viewed as a whole seems fully to warrant none of the paths ecclesiastical doctrine has so far taken. Old Testament scholars point out that the roots of predestinarian thinking lie long prior to Israel's history in the mythic religious worldview delineated by Mircea Eliade and others. For that view, mythic events are real, and can only be played out, echoed, by profane history. Such themes reappear in extra-biblical apocalyptic thought. But in biblical predestination, history matters, real events matter, and their divine cause lies in a purposive God whose creative work is not ended. Thus the covenant with Noah and company includes in its scope "all that lives on earth" (Gen. 8:20–9:17). Here was a new decision taken by God facing a new human situation. In it God is the prior, selecting agent, and 'all that lives,' the beneficiary. In subsequent covenantal calls and choices God elects Abram, chooses Sarah (and not Hagar), selects the Davidic line and the priestly line, so that anyone born in those lines is included in their covenants (see e.g., Num. 25:12f).

In the New Testament, however, something new appears. Now Christ is heir to the Old Testament promises and is chosen of God as well (Gal. 3:16; 1 Pet. 1:20; Luke 9:38). In Christ, his followers (and *not* all that lives) are elect. Biological heritage is now superseded (cf. John 1:13), replaced by a new, inclusive family whose *prospective* membership is without limit—thus the universalist tinge in Paul (e.g., Phil. 2:9-11; on biblical election, see Mendenhall, IDB II:76-82; III:869; F. F. Bruce, IDBS:258f). Via New Testament catachresis, "election" became another synonym for the new that comes in Christ (Chapter Three). Like other synonyms, it takes its place in witness to the fullness of that new creation, in which God's good takes time, and by which no living thing is a priori excluded.

Before closing the historical account we should glance at a still overlooked chapter of Christian history—the Radical Reformation. George Williams singles out election as one of five "vaguely ecumenical catholic, universalistic . . . teachings of the Radical Reformation" (1962:834). Here, however, we breathe a different atmosphere. Williams gives as instance Camillo Renato, a radicalized Franciscan friar and humanist scholar, who after being imprisoned in Bologna fled to the Swiss mountain cantons. There he labored to reform the churches. Reshaping the 'sacraments' (he preferred the term *segni*, "signs"), Camillo introduced a meal-based Lord's supper (eucharist always part of a love-feast), rejected "papal" baptism, and promoted use of the Rule of Christ (Matt. 18:15ff) in the congregations. His predestination teaching moved in a broadly inclusive direction: Christ's elect were present wherever human love shaped life; thus "predestination . . . was confirmed in humaneness" (Williams, 1962:546-49, 565-71, 842-43). Other radicals held these and still other views. Melchior Hoffmann, for example, regarded Strassburg as the elect *site* for the imminent events of world regeneration (Revelation 14); Hans Denck taught that God's election to salvation was based on God's foreknowledge, citing texts in Isaiah to prove his point (Denck, 1975:79).

Our understanding of God's electing love (Snaith, 1944:chap. 6) in Christian teaching should not shape but be shaped by the understanding of the rule of God already unfolded here. (Calvin to his credit saw this, and attempted to restrain what would nonetheless in his followers become a runaway doctrine.) We should note in this context typical internal restraints upon the Augustinian doctrine: Election is to service before it is to salvation; it is positive not negative (no 'horrible decree'); election does not cancel or negate free human response to God (Conner, 1945:chap. 2). Yet when all that is said, it remains true that election as taught laid a bogus burden upon the churches of magisterial Protestantism and upon those baptist fellowships that came under their influence. What is wanted is a doctrine that insists in regard to creation and salvation and last things as well that God remains a God of electing love, whose choices are never made to set the creation or some part of it at naught, but who always chooses in wisdom for creation's good and (what is the same thing) for God's ultimate sharing of the divine glory with the creature (cf. Mullins, 1908:chap. 6). If in that spirit we read, for example, in Ephesians: "Before the foundation of the world he chose us in Christ to be his people, to be without blemish in his sight, to be full of love; and he predestined us to be adopted as his children through Jesus Christ" (Eph. 1:4-5*a*), we may recognize such a spirit, for, as Ephesians continues, "God's secret purpose" was that "everything in heaven and earth might be brought into a unity in Christ" (1:9f). Still, the old associations of the doctrine die so hard that (in my judgment) this part of Christian teaching is of little present service. We do well to emphasize the rule of God in every effective way, while exercising great reserve with regard to this Augustinian deposit. Above all, there must be *no gap* between what we know of God in the biblical narrative that climaxes in Jesus Christ and what we say of God's inclusive, electing love.

   b. Miracles and the point of creation.—Karl Heim describes the "Thomist conception of miracles":

> Should God wish to act in sovereign fashion, He proceeds to arrest the course of the world-machine through the *miraculum suspensionis*. Then He interferes actively and inserts into what is already there an interpolation which originates directly from Himself. This being achieved, He sets the machine in motion again by the *miraculum restitutionis*. (Heim, 1953:171)

Whether or not this was Thomas Aquinas' meaning, it was a view of miracle that guided David Hume as he sought to deflate the pretentious Christian apologetic of the eighteenth century and its understanding of miracle as "breaking natural law." For Hume, "natural law" described ordinary human expectations: hot gases rise; heavy bodies fall downward. If a 'miracle' is reported, credence in the report cannot far overweigh the mental habit that expects custom to prevail in a given case; thus it is not unreasonable to reckon the report either an exaggeration or a falsehood (Hume, 1777*b* Sect. x). Hume did not (as is often wrongly claimed) 'disprove' miracles, but he sapped their apologetic force even while fixing the "Thomist" view of miracle in cultured minds.

   The biblical understanding of miracle does not depend upon the modern concept of natural law in either its Humean or Newtonian senses. In Scripture the idea of miracle (Greek *teras*, "wonder")—or as in John's Gospel and elsewhere, "sign" *(semeion)*—does not suppose the irruption of God into a nature from which God is usually absent, but does reckon that God may act within nature (where he is already present) vividly to display the divine intention for nature. This view concedes that such signs have little or no apologetic value—they speak "from faith to faith"—from the faithfulness of God to the eyes and ears of human faith. On the other hand, they do not in general presuppose that we believe either in immutable 'natural law' (whatever current science may make of such a term) or in its 'suspension.' Miracles, in short, are signs, divine actions within creation in which the presence of God shines forth in power for (creative, and especially) redemptive ends (cf. John 20:30f).

Such a brief account will hardly satisfy the philosophers of religion, who must wait for clarification in *Volume III*. Yet our present task is important in its own right. It is to distinguish the sorts of signs that do appear in biblical and Christian history, so that we may see their place in creation and redemption. There are in my view three classes of such signs.

The historic signs are pillars of the divine program for earth, way-marks set, like the cairn at Jordan's crossing, to show that God in his creative-redemptive journey passed this way. Here the paradigm, the sign of signs, is the *resurrection of Jesus Christ from the dead*, a historic event dividing the ages, the fundament of living Christian faith (see *Ethics*, Nine, and Chapter Six within). In the resurrection, God owns his presence in all the history that reached its crest in Jesus of Nazareth; in the resurrection, our share in that history is affirmed as well; in it, the vector of creation toward its holy destiny is imprinted. Around this central sign, lesser signs gather—the empty tomb, the appearances to the disciples throughout the first Eastertide. Judgment may vary as to the authenticity and value of any one of these subsidiary signs, but if we see them as tributary to the Jonah-sign itself, the resurrection, we are free to estimate the contribution each makes without challenging the roof beam, Christ's resurrection from the dead, beneath which all reside.

Other great historic signs include *creation* itself, perhaps the electing *call of Abraham*, certainly *the Exodus event*, including the deliverance of Israel from Egypt and the covenant at Sinai, each with its own subsidiary signs (the plagues in Egypt, the Reed Sea crossing, the wonders in the desert, and the entry into the land of Promise); the *birth of prophecy* in Israel associated with Elijah and Elisha attended by signs of God's presence, power, and prophetic purpose; and the *captivity and return of Israel*, marked by prophetic fulfillment and still further prophecy. In the New Testament, we might follow the Gospels in listing the *mission of Jesus*, from its baptismal beginning to the removal of his body from cross to tomb, associating with it the remarkable circumstances of his birth, the healings and nature-signs that accompanied his ministry, and the numinous events attending the crucifixion (raising of Lazarus, for example). Finally, we may list the creation of the new community, the church, by the gift of the Spirit at *Pentecost*, as the historic sign next after Jesus' resurrection, since it declared God's purpose to share the risen Christ with all humanity. Here subsidiary signs are the tongues of fire and the tongues of the nations (Acts 2), and still other subsidiary signs are recorded in the Acts of the Apostles. Notable among these is the conversion of Paul.

No argument is made here for the exact identity or precise number of the great historic signs of Scripture. However the list takes shape (is the conquest recorded in Judges a great historic sign? is the establishment of the Davidic monarchy?), a remarkable feature is the scrupulous economy of the miracles it embraced. Outside these few monumental events just listed—creation, exodus, prophecy, exile and return, the Christ event entire, the birth of the church, each with its comet's tail of subsidiary signs—there is a scarcity of wonders in the religion of the Bible. This stands in sharp contrast to its neighbor cults. It is as if the whole of creation in its integrity and handsome growth were so valued that God, like the master mariner of a beautifully trimmed ship, would touch the helm as little as need be to keep the intended course. Note, too, that the great historic signs cannot be located by the test of 'breaking' natural law (cf. Pannenberg, 1968:98). The resurrection of Christ clearly transcends the regularities we otherwise know. So does the Reed Sea crossing. Israel's exile and return, however, seem on their face typical of many forced population movements in the ancient Near East. And many have seen prophecy as part of the wider phenomenon of ecstatic religion.

Second, among the subsidiary signs that cluster around each historic sign, some are deliberately repetitive. Let us call these recurrent subsidiary signs **the remembering signs**—signs of the divine presence and purpose that directly correspond to and recall the aim and force of one or more great historic signs. Thus Scripture lists God's gift of *the Sabbath* as the remembering sign of creation and also as the remembering sign of the Exodus. The Sabbath looks forward, as well, to the great final Sabbath, God's waiting rest (Hebrews 3:7–4:11). *Prophetic preaching*—especially prophetic preaching based on an exact Scripture text—recalls and renews prophecy, and with it all the historic signs that Scripture proclaims. *Conversion-baptism* is the remembering sign of Christ's life, death, and resurrection, and of the Pentecostal birth of Christian community as well. *The Lord's supper* remembers the death and resurrection of Jesus, and also the Exodus, inasmuch as its origin lies in the Passover rite. More will be said of the remembering signs in the chapter (Nine) reserved for them.

Finally, a third class, **providential signs,** may be distinguished. Of course all the signs are providential. These are distinctive in being addressed especially to the needs of individual groups and followers of the way. "This will be a *sign for you,*" the angel says to the shepherds (Luke 2:12). So the swaddling clothes and manger were not themselves great historic signs, nor was there any command to repeat them (a fact that may disappoint crèche-makers). In Luke's birth story, these items were distinctive providential markers to guide the shepherds. There are many other such signs in the biblical stories and in church tradition. Here also we can locate, so far as they are authentic, the wonders attached to the lives of remarkable Christians (their healing influence, for example). Here, too, belong providences that have spared and directed the lives of humble believers in every age: their conversion and their special calling, prayer and its answers, circumstances that converge to lead disciples into and along their way within the way.

In the signs, God's people are pointed to creation's point; in them, God's salvific purpose is disclosed; in them the last end of all things appears. Taken together, the historic and remembering and providential signs do this work. There is no requirement that these three classes of sign be sharply distinguished from one another, or that all distinguish them alike. The classes overlap. Viewed as guidance to him and to the Damascus church, Paul's baptism is a providential sign; viewed with others' baptisms as subsidiary to Pentecost and Easter and Calvary, it is a remembering sign; viewed with his Damascus road conversion, it is part of a great historic sign, the opening of the Christian mission to Europe. So its *sign*ificance can be *assign*ed in more than one context, and yet these (and every context of God's signs) have in common their relation to the central creative and redemptive biblical story itself.

* * * * *

At the end of this chapter and of Part I, "The Rule of God," a brief reprise is in order. It was inevitable, with bountiful, multifarious, suffering *creation* as its topic, that this chapter should be diffuse. Its task was made harder by the three-hundred-year-old tendency to assign the full understanding of nature to natural science alone, to dissociate God from the world (the absence-of-God theme), and to focus creation thought only upon the human creature. These tendencies could not be defeated in this space, and they continue, powerful even though unspoken, in readers' minds and in today's churches. Yet they have been resisted here in three ways. The first was to expose them by recalling the broad biblical view they themselves displaced—God as creation's Alpha and Omega, creation itself as God's blessed work, struggling, suffering, ongoing. Romans 8 and Revelation 4–5 were key passages for us. The second move was to unfold more fully the concept of creation as work in progress, and to relate God's suffering and ours to that ongoing divine labor. This entailed rejection of the impassive and impassible God and the 'nice' world of theodicy. Third, creation was examined as an arena of promise whose destiny lies in its relation to what lasts and what comes last (Chapter Two) and to the new that comes in Christ (Chapter Three). At this point we might have but did not explore the concept of creation "in Christ," postponing that until Chapter Seven, when we shall be exploring more fully the relation of Jesus Christ to God. Here our understanding of signs, guided by the Fourth Gospel but extended to refer to all creation's history, displays the point of creation in a way natural science (and a philosophy that banishes God from the world) cannot. This chapter's version of Christian creation teaching, for the reasons indicated, is incomplete and some may find it unpersuasive. It will have done its work, though, if it points a way ahead for Christian theology—work to be done by many hands rather than work completed already. Perhaps what is said here may free some for that work. In any case, the chapter has sought to celebrate creation as it is.

PART II

THE IDENTITY OF JESUS CHRIST

That Jesus Christ is very God is shown in His way into the far country in which He the Lord became a servant. For in the majesty of the true God it happened that the eternal Son of the eternal Father became obedient by offering and humbling Himself to be the brother of man, to take His place with the transgressor, to judge him by judging Himself and dying in his place. But God the Father raised Him from the dead, and in so doing recognised and gave effect to His death and passion as a satisfaction made for us, as our conversion to God, and therefore as our redemption from death to life.

Karl Barth, *Church Dogmatics*

All of this language of imitation and participation, all the pious and pastoral meditation on the believer's cross, takes on a new dimension if we take the measure of the social character of Jesus' cross. The believer's cross is no longer any and every kind of suffering, sickness, or tension, the bearing of which is demanded. The believer's cross must be, like his Lord's, the price of his social nonconformity. It is . . . the end of a path freely chosen after counting the cost. It is . . . the social reality of representing in an unwilling world the Order to come.

John Howard Yoder, *The Politics of Jesus*

Who and what he was, did, and underwent are all inseparable from the fact that he is. (The reverse is obviously equally true: That he is brings with it the manifestation of who he is and what he did. The affirmation some theologians make of the importance of Jesus' historical factuality, coupled with their denial of any significant content given with this factuality, seems to be completely artificial. A human fact, significantly apprehended, cannot be separated in this way, except in the most artificial philosophical dogmas.) Once again, if in the resurrection he was most clearly manifest as Jesus of Nazareth the Savior, then it was here also that the accounts could say that he lives.

Hans W. Frei, *The Identity of Jesus Christ*

Introduction

Exactly who or what is the God we are meant to trust, serve, and worship? It appears that Christians cannot answer this question, cannot bear true witness to God's identity, without reference to Jesus Christ. That is, the identity of God as Christians know it is tied to the identity of Jesus Christ risen from the dead. To say how this is so is a task of Christian doctrine, perhaps its central task. Certainly, doctrine must approach these two identities together. This will involve the identity of the Spirit of God as well. This dual—really treble—identity is the topic of the three chapters that follow. There is no theological novelty in treating God with Christ. The formula of Matthew instructs baptism "in the name of the Father and the Son and the Holy Spirit" (28:19). The old Roman baptismal confession, preserved in the so-called Apostles' Creed, expanded this. Baptismal faith (the faith that identifies believers) is not only "in Jesus Christ his Son" but also "in God the Father Almighty" and "in the Holy Spirit." By the fifth century this complexity in Christian worship and obedience had issued in the doctrine of the Trinity (Chalcedon, 451), and most Christians (not all) followed that ancient lead. Though we will test the traditional results, our approach, like the early churches', will be from the side of God's historic action witnessed in the New Testament—the achievement, and the centrality for faith, of Jesus Christ himself.

Whether Jesus' identity is to be examined before or after exploring his life's achievement (whether the correct order is 'work before person' or vice versa) is a question that has exercised theologians, but it cannot well arise in the present approach, for all three of these chapters are concerned with the identity of Christ, and all are concerned with his earthly (and ongoing) work. The relation between 'work' and 'person,' between Jesus Christ as the locus of God's action and the

193

character and being of the God who so acts, is necessarily reflexive. On the one hand, the Gospels focus upon his action in history (the work), but on the other, the implicit readers of the Gospel story of that work are those to whom the risen Christ is present in person. We know the risen Christ, we meet him today (thus Chapter Six), yet we learn from the New Testament that the One we meet is the very Jesus of whom it speaks. If we share the baptist vision ("this is that") we read the stories of him then to shed fresh light upon our encounter with him now and to anticipate our fateful final meeting ("then is now"). Each implies the other.

All three of the chapters that follow attempt also to relate our present doctrine to the preceding Christian debates and decisions. These discussions have been continuous from apostolic times to the present. In Chapter Five we will meet major types of atonement teaching. In Chapter Six we will review major paradigm shifts concerning the person of Christ over the centuries. These variations, some of them profound, make it difficult to present this historical material clearly yet briefly. At least it can be shown that *certain persistent questions* have been present to Christian thinkers throughout all the changes. It will be helpful to note these questions here at the outset. The **first** grows from the extraordinary place assigned to Jesus in Christian faith. It seems presumptuous— "blasphemous," some of his contemporaries said—to intersect the identity of this one man with the identity of God. How can this be? In moral terms, **what right has Jesus Christ to absolute Lordship**—the Lordship that Scripture assigns to God alone? Without a satisfactory answer, faithfulness to Christ is either necessarily fanatical or necessarily limited. So all Christologies that invite faith must somehow answer this question.

Second, can there be an answer to the first question that does not directly and immediately offend the high teaching of God's oneness that emerged in Israel's long story—the teaching we call monotheism? God alone is GOD, and God is one. God is sole and unique. "Hear, Israel: the LORD is our God, the LORD our one God; and you must love the LORD your God with all your heart and with all your soul and with all your strength" (Deut. 6:4f). This *Shema* of Israel's faith is her gift to the world, and multitudes receive that gift thanks to the name of Jesus, for they are Christians. How can any of the recipients of this great gift of God's oneness, this delivery from "gods many and lords many" into the purity and beauty and truth of one only God—how can these heirs of monotheism also embrace the Lordship of Jesus? **How can monotheists** (concretely, how can Jews) **tell the Jesus story** as their own? (The monotheistic conviction of Islam expands the problem.) That question has been present for Christology from the beginning, since like Jesus the first witnesses were themselves Jews and as Jews were inheritors of the doctrine of the one God.

Finally, **third,** wherever Christology appears it has faced the question of the uniqueness of Jesus' *human* life and its relation to the lives of others. If we grant, as recent Christian teaching has granted with a near-unanimity unequaled since the days of his earthly career, the full humanity of Jesus of Nazareth, what does that imply about the spiritual possibilities of human life in general? Does it follow that his kind of life can be ours also? That what he did, his followers can do (cf. John 14:12)—that and more! An answer may take one of two divergent paths. It can hold that in contrast to all others who share a human nature, Jesus' unique relation to God issued in a life that was both unsurpassable and unapproachable. That seems to express well the reverence Christians feel for the earthly life of their Lord. Or contrariwise, an answer can hold that exactly because of his unique relation to God he entered upon a road (as a pioneer, *archēgos*, Heb. 2:10) that each of us must travel as well. And that seems to express well the appeal to discipleship in the Gospels: "Come, follow me." But which is it to be? In brief, **how Christ-like,** how like the Master, **are disciples' lives to be?** Though less explicitly than the first two, this question as well has underlain the historical Christologies.

Independently, George Lindbeck has discovered "three regulative principles" at work in the formulation of the ancient christological creeds: (1) the *monotheistic principle:* The God of Abraham is the one, only God; (2) the principle of *historical specificity:* "the stories of Jesus refer to a genuine human being who was born, lived, and died . . ."; (3) the principle of *christological maximalism:* "every possible importance is to be ascribed to Jesus that is not inconsistent with the first [two] rules" (Lindbeck, 1984:94). The big difference is that Lindbeck neglects my third question, as all too often it has been overlooked in practice.

As the third question shows, the relation between the identity of God and that of Jesus Christ brings with it a further identity-question—who are Jesus' disciples? Who is to be counted as Christian? There is a danger of presumption, a risk of self-righteousness, even in addressing this question, and we must be self-critical if as Christians we raise it. Yet *Ethics* showed that the Gospels not only identify Jesus and his first disciples; their very structure invites each hearer to accept the good news and thereby to take up a disciple role in step with those in the original story. This is an invitation to enter a strange new world in which our own identities will be tinged with a new character (*Ethics*, p. 339). This aspect of the identity-question was reopened already in Chapter Three of this volume.

It may encourage some to note, here at the outset, that the concept of identity is by no means a univocal one, and this Part will invite its further clarification. To begin, identity simply means the continuity of any entity—"That is the identical, the very same mountain lion we saw in this canyon yesterday—the one we named 'Pussy.'" The effort to establish such identity often brings us, however, to a second sense of identity, namely likeness of features or attributes: "This is the identical scent we noticed when we were last here." This sense of sameness or identity is not the 'numerical' identity claimed in the two alleged sightings of Pussy the mountain lion, but is an identity of *quality*. Connecting these two, however, is a third sort of identity, narrative identity, which binds together persistent 'numerical' identity with continuing—or changing—qualities displayed by a character in a story. At book's end, Huckleberry Finn is the numerically same, yet qualitatively somewhat different, Huck the reader met on page one of the narrative. It is this third sense of identity, narrative-based identity, that should prove its worth in the pages that follow.

CHAPTER FIVE

The Saving Cross:
Atonement

One way to investigate the identity of Jesus Christ concentrates on external facts about him that survive the most searching historical scrutiny. We are no more limited to these facts than we are limited to the records in the county or parish of our birth when we assert our own identities. Nevertheless, such data have their use. Based on public documents, Jewish, Roman, and Christian, today's historians know that Jesus was a Palestinian Jew who lived in the early Roman Imperial period. He was born about 7 or 6 B.C. and was quietly brought up in a pious home without wealth or privilege. He became by baptism an adherent of John the Baptizer, and began a teaching and healing program of his own around A.D. 27 or early 28. Less than three years later, in Jerusalem at Passover, the hostility of the national political and religious leaders reached a climax. He ate a farewell meal with an inner circle, and was in short order arrested, examined, and condemned by collusion between Jewish and Roman authorities (Pontius Pilate then being Roman Procurator). Jesus was executed as a criminal enemy of the Senate and People of Rome by crucifixion. This was on the morning of Friday, April 7, A.D. 30. He died that day, aged about thirty-six. These facts have a high degree of historical certainty (Meier, 1991:406-9).

Matching these certainties, though, is uncertainty about exactly what happened earlier in Jesus' life, and in what order it happened, an uncertainty reflected by the bare bones of the previous paragraph. This being so, it is all the more striking that we are so well informed regarding his death. This concrete factuality is acknowledged in the Apostles' Creed, which says Jesus was "crucified under Pontius Pilate," that is, by Pilate's (Roman) authority and thus at a fixed time in history. Of course, Christian knowledge of his actual life is not so limited, for we have the four Gospels in the church. A drive to truthfulness within Christianity has subjected these writings as well to relentless historical scrutiny, and no responsible Christian teacher reads them altogether apart from that scrutiny. My intention is to give the historical inquiry full weight, limited only by my competence as an outsider to its intricacies, while continuing to treat the New Testament as the Spirit's witness to the churches (see Chapters One and Eleven for clarification of this approach). A noteworthy fact is that the oldest narrative strand of the Gospels converges with the testimony of scientific history to focus upon Jesus' last days on earth. In a catchphrase of New Testament criticism, the Gospels are "passion narratives with extended 'introductions'" (Kähler, 1896:80 n. 11; cf. Kee, 1977:30). So whether we know about Jesus by historical research or by truth-oriented Gospel reading in church, we are led to the story of his death as the linchpin of understanding. Clearly, though, the Gospels were not assembled as so much data for modern historians' computer searches. The purpose of these writings was to identify Jesus Christ, not as a minor Palestinian figure of the age of Tiberius, but as the Savior of the world. The Gospels aimed to present further insight concerning a present Friend rather than the profile of a stranger. Like all the authentic early Christian writings, they assume Christ risen, yet their focus is upon the cross. A similar focus is found in the rest of the New Testament. Paul, for example, tells the church at Corinth that "while I was with you I would not claim to know anything but Jesus Christ—Christ nailed to the cross" (1 Cor. 2:2). Other examples may be found in the non-Pauline epistles, for example, Hebrews 2:14: "so that by dying he might break the power of him who had death at his command, that is, the devil"; or 1 Peter 1:19: "You were set free by Christ's precious blood, blood like that of a lamb without mark or blemish." The resurrection and the cross constitute the New Testament *kērygma*, its essential proclamation.

Yet there was from the first a difficulty in this focus: Early preaching had to face the fact of the cross not as an asset for proclamation, but as an obstacle to gaining a hearing for the Christian message. The founder, Jesus, had died what ancient peoples considered a contemptible death as a criminal. The cross appeared as a shame to be explained, and its interpretation as ransom or sacrifice for sin or the like therefore remained paradoxical, even after the triumph of the crucified had become widely evident. Our first move will be to trace the doctrine of atonement that developed, later than the New Testament, in ongoing attempts to overcome this difficulty. The prior question then was not that of the modern believer who asks, "By what means does the cross effect my salvation?" but was rather, "*Since* Christ is God's own Savior, why the cross?" Starting there, I will examine **(§1) the historic church teaching on atonement.** Then I will seek fresh bearings in **(§2) the Scripture teaching of atonement.** Finally, I will present **(§3) the saving achievement of Jesus Christ in present light.** All of this will of necessity be only in summary form—the lifework of God's living Word, topic of Christian reflection for two millennia, compressed in a few pages!

§1. Atonement in Christian Thought

A remark on vocabulary is in order here: When the Bible first appeared in our language, English was young, and many of today's words either did not exist or had meanings since lost to sight. Both things are true of the English word "atonement." It was coined in the sixteenth century, made from "at" plus the existing "onement," which meant "joining into one," or *reconciling.* Thus "at-onement" was about unification—neighbor with neighbor, or God with us. Later, the word came to refer to the means or agent of reconciliation, and still later to a compensation or price paid to effect reconciliation. Thus Christ's at-one-ment can properly mean either the reconciliation Christ achieved, or the means or cost by which he achieved it, or both; using the word does not commit us to all that it has (sometimes) meant.

a. Greek Christian thought.—The history of Christian atonement teaching was changed for the better by the appearance at mid–twentieth century of a little book of lectures delivered at the University of Uppsala by a Swedish professor, Gustaf Aulén, not long before the rise of Hitler and the beginning of World War II. Arguing that atonement doctrine was not merely a struggle between the "Latin" or satisfaction view epitomized by Anselm around A.D. 1100 and the "humanistic" or moral view of modern theologies, Aulén called attention to the first thousand years of church history, dominated, he said, by a "classic" type, the *Christus-victor* atonement teaching (Aulén, 1931). (It is not true, though, that the patristic teaching had been entirely overlooked before Aulén: For example, early-twentieth-century American theologian William Adams Brown as well as others had singled out this "Greek" view for attention—ERE V:642.) The human plight that salvation had addressed, on this ancient view, could be described in several ways: One of them, addressed by Aulén, was colorfully expressed as being enslaved by the devil. Another common description, related to the first, was (not guilt, but) *corruption.* Human nature was infected by sin, and as such was prey to death and the powers of darkness. Into this dark human arena Christ

had entered, God enfleshed, and had redeemed human nature by sharing it; he had rescued it from death and evil, had vivified, even deified,
the flesh he had assumed. He had overcome Satan.

By recalling this early and partly forgotten chapter in the history of
doctrine, Aulén's lectures renewed interest in the contemporary doctrine. In America his new emphasis upon Christ as *victor* was in due
course picked up by certain Mennonite theologians, including John
Howard Yoder (unpublished but influential lectures), J. Denny Weaver
(1984), John Driver (1986), Thomas Finger (1985–89 I:346-48), and Norman Kraus (1992). These found in *Christus-victor* an alternative especially suited to baptist doctrine, and we must see in what sense this may
be so. First, though, we must collect some exemplars of the ancient
teaching itself, not to provide a 'theory' (or a 'metaphor') by which we
should guide our own atonement thinking, but first to see the depth,
variety, and richness of the ancient attempts to say why the cross was
not a discredit to Christian claims.

The brief letter of an anonymous disciple, addressed **To Diognetus**,
belongs to the earliest Christian apologetic literature. Its introduction
promises answers to three questions: why believe in the one God; how
explain the remarkable affection Christians bear toward one another;
and how justify the Johnny-come-lately novelty of a religion that nevertheless claims ultimate truth about human life and destiny. Implicitly, it
addresses the pagan challenge to the worthiness of Christian belief. Not
incidentally, *To Diognetus* provides a remarkable portrait of Christianity
as lived around the year A.D. 129:

> Although they live in Greek and barbarian cities alike, as each
> man's lot has been cast, and follow the customs of the country in
> clothing and food and other matters of daily living, at the same time
> they give proof of the remarkable and admittedly extraordinary
> constitution of their own commonwealth. They live in their own
> countries, but only as aliens. They have a share in everything as
> citizens, and endure everything as foreigners. Every foreign land is
> their fatherland, and yet for them every fatherland is a foreign land.
> They marry, like everyone else, and they beget children, but they
> do not cast out their offspring. They share their board with each
> other, but not their marriage bed. It is true that they are "in the
> flesh," but they do not live "according to the flesh."
>
> (*To Diognetus* 5:4-8)

Here the unstated topic is corruption and confusion, the state of pagan
existence. Though Christians live in the midst of such general corruption, they are destined for (and have begun to enjoy) incorruptibility

(6:8). Only the intention of the one, merciful God can account for this phenomenon. God's secret plan was communicated to his unique Child *(monō tō paidi)* even before creation (8:9), but God strategically withheld the plan while the race was being led farther astray by its own impulsive sins. When at last human nature seemed lost beyond hope, the plan was put into effect: God "took up the burden of our sins," gave his own Son to be a ransom for us—"O sweetest exchange"—and justified sinners, the righteous one for the many. No wonder believers have lives so joyful and loving; no wonder they can bear one another's burdens; God by his gift has made them "gods" to their neighbors (9:2-6).

Two or three generations later (c. 185), **Irenaeus,** an Easterner come West to Lyon as missionary, elaborated this Greek theology of history in his *Five Books Against Heresies,* a defense against Gnosticism. As a counterpoint to its polemic purpose, *Against Heresies* declares afresh that God has a progressive plan for creation, unfolded in Hebrew and then in Christian Scripture. At first, the way of righteousness and love was extended to Abraham, not by way of law and compulsion, but in order that Abraham might be a friend of God. Later, the law was given, but its tenure expired with John the Baptizer. Servitude to the law was fully ended in the Lord Jesus Christ, who renewed the original Abrahamic covenant by enlisting followers to be his friends and the friends of God (*Adv. haer.* IV.xiii.iv; IV.ii). Here appears Irenaeus' well-known doctrine of recapitulation: by entering human life and progressively perfecting all its stages (infancy, childhood, maturity, death itself) in line with God's original creative intent, Christ liberated humanity from corruption in each stage (II.xxii.iv). This he did in two senses: Recapitulation imparts "immortal life to our corruptible humanity" (an almost physical implanting of deathless life in human soil), and by Christ's moral obedience the race recovers the standing it had lost in Adam's plunge into sin. Christ "was made what we are, that he might make us completely what he is" (Franks, 1962:22-25, citing *Adv. haer.* V, Pref.). Next, Irenaeus explains the servitude from which Jesus Christ redeems sinners; namely, slavery to the devil. Here the ransom idea is put forward. Though God could have liberated humanity by *force majeure,* it befitted Christ as God to act reasonably, and so "reasonably redeeming us with his blood [he] gave himself as a ransom," buying back his own possessions rather than destroying created nature by use of violent means (V.i.i; Franks, 1962:27-29). The idea was that Satan, by successfully tempting human beings, had acquired a claim to them; they were his prisoners awaiting redemption. Christ is offered to the devil as a payment of that ransom; the exchange was duly made at the cross; but in the resurrection God reclaimed his Son, so that both his risen Son and redeemed sinners are God's.

This early atonement theology becomes more intelligible to us in light of its social context. It sprang from a pre-Constantinian church in which Christians were a distinguishable minority, persecuted, disadvantaged, conscious of the oppressive powers of darkness identified with the state and with the wider society. Two of those powers, the Jewish state and the Roman Empire, had collaborated to secure the execution of the Lord of glory. But what appeared to be a loss to the kingdom of God was instead gain, for God had raised Jesus from the dead, and the cross, that emblem of shame, had dramatically become the sign of God's power to turn evil into good. Here the defeat of Satan by the entire life mission of Jesus of Nazareth bespoke early Christian political and social awareness. As Jesus had recapitulated all of human life, Christians were set free to follow Christ's way at every stage of their own lives. Now, said Irenaeus, Satan was "bound with the same chains with which he had bound man"; that is, Christ's obedience to God's way of life had, in a nice reversal, overturned Satan's disobedience to that way; the freedom from sin's corruption fixed a limit that the environing society for all its military and social power could not transgress (*Adv. haer.* V.xxi).

So Christ's victory over the powers heralds the triumph of a community that is socially relevant even when outwardly diminutive and despised. Yet see what soon happened. With the Constantinian shift, the formerly persecuted Christians rose to become the established religious power East and West. No longer was the church poor and persecuted. Now the ransom imagery took on a new coloring: The 'good' power could easily be construed in continuity with the Christian Emperor and his orthodox church; the 'evil' power thus became anything that opposed imperial church and 'Christian' Empire in their holy union—anything, whether it was palace intrigue, or barbarian nations on Rome's borders, or Christian 'heretics' within or outside the Empire. Thus we must amend Denny Weaver's judgment (1990), that in the post-Constantinian period the ransom theory no longer possessed a social component. Rather the social component had changed; now the Empire presented itself not as the Christians' enemy but as the very kingdom of God. Is it surprising that with this another change took place? In a Cappadocian version of the ransom theme (fourth century), God had won the battle against tricky evil by trickery; he had *deceived* the devil by placing Jesus as bait on the cross. The devil swallowed the bait and was captured (Gregory of Nyssa, *Cat. or.* xxiv). Here is a story whose political import has taken a new direction. Such divine deception could too easily serve as the legitimation of imperial power maintaining its 'righteous' empire by hook or by crook—a vice common enough in that era to have given us the adjective "Byzantine" as a label for devious knavery as a path to power. A theology of atonement that began by reflecting the politics of Jesus had slipped into the service of the standing order.

At this point we may assess the strengths and weaknesses of this "first thousand years" of atonement teaching. With Aulén, we can say that Greek theology did see the work of Christ squarely in line with God's own work in history. (This will appear more clearly when we compare with it later versions.) Another strength is the seriousness with which the Greek teaching viewed the conflict between God-in-Christ and devilish evil, and the assurance of God's final triumph. These features may explain the revival of this 'classic' understanding in the 1930s and 1940s, when the relentless rise of totalitarian politics chilled many. In whose hands, finally, did earth's destiny rest? *Christus-victor* teaching with its third-day resurrection of God's power offered an answer. As to weaknesses, it was all too easy at mid–twentieth century (as easy as in Byzantine days) to confuse God's final triumph with the maintenance of military Christendom, losing sight of the nonviolent way of the cross. At its worst, a further weakness, the Greek atonement theology slipped into mythical, Manichaean dualism in which ultimate good eternally confronted ultimate evil, with the outcome forever in doubt.

b. The Latin West.—A new context, that of the missionary Christianity that sought to evangelize northern Europe, brought with it new developments in atonement teaching. The new outlook crested in the work of **Anselm** (1033–1109), a careful and profound Catholic theologian. Anselm's study of atonement was presented in a little book *(Cur Deus homo?)* that has shaped Western religious thought on this topic as perhaps no other outside Scripture. Aulén set out to exclude its influence in the name of his "classic" doctrine, but perhaps we can be more generous.

Anselm intended to establish two theses, to each of which he devoted a Book of *Cur Deus homo?* (the title is best translated simply "Why a God-man?"). The first thesis is the helpless human plight. In early Greek theology, evil was shared corruption; penetrating from beyond human life, it was an enemy that could be personified in the devil. In Anselm's doctrine, on the other hand, the human plight arises from the status of each sinner. The devil remains an entity to be reckoned in the total scheme of things, but the main problem is the guilt of each of us. Since this sinful status is so general and so unavoidable, perhaps it represents a complaisant (Constantinian) acceptance of the world order as it is. On the other hand, Anselm's doctrine questioned the ever-growing sacra-

mental and penitential system of medieval Christianity as a remedy for
that interior fault. Although the practice of penance taught that there
must be "satisfaction" for sin, it had not contemplated how heavy a
weight sin really was ("*Nondum considerasti quanti ponderis sit peccatum,*"
I, 20f).

Anselm's second thesis sets forth the divine remedy for this plight.
None can satisfy the "debt" of sin but God, yet none should satisfy it but
those who have incurred it, that is, ourselves *(homo)*. To Anselm, as to
many a twentieth-century analyst, the human condition presented itself
as self-evident to any thinker: Our guilt cannot be self-healed. He
thought he saw a necessary remedy that could be seen quite apart from
our scriptural and churchly knowledge of Christ *(remoto Christo,* Pref.).
The solution, logically compelling even apart from what is in fact known
of Christ, is that there be a God-man, the *Deus-homo* *(homo,* like old
English "man," meant the species; *vir* alone meant the male). As man the
God-man, though himself without sin, *ought* to make satisfaction, and
as God he *can* do so. In Anselm's view, Chalcedonian Christology (see
Chapter Six below) exactly matches this understanding (II, 6f). Since *Cur
Deus homo?* is written in dialogue form, Boso, Anselm's respondent, next
demands to know how the death of the God-man counts as atonement
for all this human sin. The death cannot be punishment, for Anselm has
contrasted satisfaction and punishment *(satisfactio aut poena,* I, 15). Rather,
the solution turns on the *worth* of the God-man; a life of such incompa-
rable greatness, yielded up *(datur)* to God in obedience, is a far greater
good than all human sin is an evil; thus the gift of that one life outweighs
all sin (II, 14f).

Anselm proposed replacing earlier atonement teaching such as we
saw in Irenaeus. He found these earlier accounts—of the obedience of
one (Christ) restoring what was lost through the disobedience of one
(Adam), of the conquest upon a tree of the devil who tempted at a
tree—to be only beautiful pictures; they were mental constructs, fictions,
not facts. They were seemly conveniences *(convenientias)* pleasing to
believers, but lacking the solid necessity that could convince "unbeliev-
ers" of the truth of the gospel (I, 3f). Yet after Anselm provides his own
account of the God-man who has both the responsibility to remedy the
human plight and the right to do so (so that satisfaction would necessarily follow upon the giving of the God-man's life), he will still speak of
the fittingness *(convenientias)* of this story (II, 19). Why does he claim that
his own "convenient" account is rational as others are not? His argument
comes down to two assertions that are now less than self-evident: (1)
that God's honor *requires* satisfaction for human sin; and (2) that the
God-man's life, "yielded up" to death, *constitutes* just such satisfaction.

To interpret these associations, scholars have explored Anselm's thought-world. Italian-born, he had risen to become Abbot of a Benedictine abbey in Normandy, was well known to the Norman conquerors of England, and was summoned by them (in 1093) to become Archbishop of Canterbury. The broad matrix of Anselm's thought was **legal**—there was the jurisprudential character of Latin theology from Tertullian onward, the lingering imperial law in the former provinces, the canon law expressed in the church's penitential practice and in the governance of his abbey at Bec, the Germanic customary law with its *Wergild* or compensatory payment made to avert retribution by another. All these were woven into the fabric of Europe's medieval society as Anselm knew it. Certainly the feudal system held that the seriousness of a crime stood in proportion to the rank of the offended victim. Yet attempts to equate the *satisfaction* God must exact with one or another element in that social fabric—with feudal honor, or with the *Wergild* that averted revenge, or with the penalty assigned a penitent upon confession, or with any other single element—have found no consensus. Colin Gunton has the matter right: Satisfaction for Anselm is a metaphor (Gunton, 1989:84-96), perhaps catachretically developed from one or another of these elements, but in any case fully intelligible only within the context of the thought of Anselm himself (similarly McIntyre, 1954:3.2).

A shallow reading might see Anselm's God as little more than a feudal duke defending his honor in medieval society, even at considerable cost to the duke's own family. Such a reading could appeal to the eleventh-century European society depicted in the Song of Roland. Historically, Roland was a commander who died defending a pass in the Pyrenees to protect Charlemagne's retreating army. In the immensely popular Song, Roland accepts his fate out of fierce pride laced with scorn of Ganelon, who has betrayed him, and out of loyalty to the remote and helpless emperor. (This outlook, and the Song itself, are unforgettably captured in Henry Adams' *Mont St. Michel and Chartres* [in Adams, 1906:354-70] and again in Erich Auerbach's *Mimesis* [1953:chap. 5].) Yet to read the Song of Roland is to see that Anselm's construal of God, of the world, and of human life rose far above this medieval setting to insights more profound. For Anselm, God's concern is not with his own honor, for that cannot be diminished by anything outside God. Rather, God is concerned with the "universal order and beauty" of the universe, his creature (I, 15). The real question Anselm addresses is simply this: Is the universe just? Pre-Christian Greek thought had asked that, and had held that it was, since Zeus secured that each god and mortal ultimately got exactly what each had coming. The law of the universe, then, was the law of retribution. Anselm is aware of that ancient conception, but he claims that for God there is a higher satisfaction, a way of righting the universe "than which there can be no greater." That higher satisfaction, God's righteousness, is fulfilled in the obedience of the Son. His obedience is the proximate cause of his own death, but its deepest consequence is the enfleshing—and thus the 'satisfaction,' that is, completion—of God's own justice. Anselm says no less than this, but says it in the 'conveniences' of the language at hand, a language filled with the overtones of life on the frontier of Christian Europe (cf. Gunton, 1989:chap. 4).

Perhaps Anselm's thesis can be sharpened by contrasting it with a like mode of atonement thought some centuries later, when the magisterial Reformers, locked in a struggle with a still-unreformed Roman church, sought to show that the full adequacy of Christ's redemption obviated the Catholic system of indulgences and penances. Replacing these ecclesiastical penalties, a *penal* view of atonement came to forceful expression in the teaching of **John Calvin.** He followed Anselm's teaching that Christ rendered God favorable "by the whole course of his obedience" (*Inst.* II, 16, 5), but departed from him by abandoning Anselm's either-or distinction between satisfaction and punishment:

> No—it was expedient at the same time for him to undergo the severity of God's vengeance, to appease his wrath and satisfy his just judgment. For this reason, he must also grapple hand to hand with the armies of hell and the dread of everlasting death. . . . He suffered the death that God in his wrath had inflicted upon the wicked! . . . "My God, my God, why hast thou forsaken me?" [Ps. 22:1; Matt. 27:46] (*Inst.* II, 16, 10f)

Here, then, is a deliberate mixing of the 'Greek' and 'Latin' images of atonement. An even richer mixture (as Aulén concedes) is found in **Martin Luther:** the shame of the cross, Christ as fishhook to catch the devil, Christ accepting God's wrath upon himself in our place—all are tumbled together by Luther in a rich broth of conviction (Luther, ed. Kerr, 1966:52-57). In Luther we see the sort of use of these diverse traditional teachings that I will defend in the final Section (§3).

For the **Anabaptists** a different set of concerns prevailed. Their hearers were little drawn to the Old Church teaching, yet they were deeply offended by a Protestant version implying that, since Christ had done it all, Christians need do nothing. A pamphlet some attribute to Michael Sattler, titled "On the Satisfaction of Christ," expressed this widely shared Anabaptist view: Christ's work was to be shared by true disciples. Did not Paul say that "I fill out in my body what was lacking in the afflictions of Christ" (Col. 1:24)?

And where would the dear prophets and apostles be left, yea, also Christ Himself, who prophesied for so many years of the great suffering of the friends of God in this time, if the members of Christ would not need to suffer just like the head?

(Sattler in Yoder, ed., 1973:112)

It was penal doctrine, though, that flourished in most of northern Europe, finding its way in 1553 into Cranmer's (42) Articles of Religion, in 1618–19 into Holland's Reformed Synod of Dort, and in 1647 to Westminster in England (Articles of Religion II, Canons of Dort II; Westminster Shorter Catechism 27). There it was taught that Christ, though fully innocent, died as punishment for the sins of the world (or more exactly, of the elect). God inflicted upon Christ, through evil human hands, the infinite evil that was man's due. Thus God could be at once merciful and just: with the debt to justice paid, the divine mercy could flow free.

What is remarkable is that the features of penal teaching that most offend present-day moral sense—a God who *must* extract punishment, a substitution of innocence for guilt, a payoff for ill desert exact to the last quantum—were the very ones that made the theory attractive to the moral Puritans who were its most ardent teachers. Robert Paul claims that none before had assembled those elements—and just those—into such a story as the penal doctrine tells. The word "payment" (in the first place a commercial, not a juridical term) already appears, to be sure, in Irenaeus and in Anselm. But focusing exclusively upon penalty was a new, seventeenth-century venture. Why just then? Once more there was a new social context. In that century English folk on both sides of the Atlantic were hammering out the legal rights that were to constitute Anglo-American constitutional democracy. In a series of brilliant moves, English lawyers fought for a justice of fairness to the poor as well as to the powerful. New case law forbade arbitrary detention, the refusal of bail, Star Chamber proceedings, and like abuses of power. There was, for example, the right of bail, by which a friend or relative might stand as *surety* for another so that he or she need not rot away for life. Was Christ not by analogy humanity's surety? Tellingly, the chief architects of the penal theory of atonement, John Owen and Thomas Goodwin, were not only academic theologians but public figures who shared these justice concerns. Thus when they spoke of God's justice in the cross, their model was a newly reformed English justice that by analogy would permit Christ to stand in sinners' place to guarantee that even God's power would not be abused. Seen in that context, the penal view of atonement has its own dignity (Paul, 1960:117-31). Yet when in later centuries the law became more humane, the story Owen and Goodwin told of Jesus' saving work would seem inhumane in the same way that 'progressive' seventeenth-century justice, with its now archaic procedures and penalties, appears inhumane by today's standards. Thus, as with the Greek and Anselmic forms of atonement teaching, it appears again that a story told in one time and place distorts the work of Christ when *dogmatically* repeated in a very different time and place.

Other variants on the legally rooted Anselmic teaching appeared, and one of them, the so-called *governmental* view first expounded by **Hugo Grotius** (or De Groot, 1583–1645), a Dutch legal theorist, was felt by many to have the merits of the satisfaction heritage without its defects. God is now not a judge but (closer to Anselm) the Governor of the world, whose task it is to maintain goodness in face of sin's rebellion. A governor need not inflict every penalty legitimated by law, and so it is with God's governing. Earthly governors sometimes choose to make a penal example of flagrant offenders, thereby justifying the pardon of others without such a relaxation of the law as to encourage further disorder. The moving thing is that God as Governor chose to make a penal example not of earth's worst offenders but of his own Son; thereby he disclosed his great love, freed himself to pardon all who would repent, and maintained universal order. Although this approach had many of the liabilities of strict penal atonement, it was in at least two respects different: it posited not quantitative but 'exemplary' retribution, and the death of Christ was not for each sinner retrospective (atoning for past sin) but, like modern views to be surveyed next, prospective; it concerned itself, not with what believers *had* done, but with what they *would* do (Grotius, 1614). Thus it is a mixed case—a fact which in time would diminish its prestige.

Now to an overview of the legal or Latin type of atonement doctrine: To its credit, first, is the gravity with which this type views sin. God cannot overlook sin's sinfulness. Further, it hails the achievement of Christ as a great historic fact—God's monumental sign to humankind. Third, it provides a rationale for substitution, for "Christ in our place," and makes effective use of the altar-language of propitiation and sacrifice—a harder task for the earlier, Greek view. On the other hand, the legal type in all its variants displays some common weaknesses. It drives a wedge of separation right into the Godhead, separating the roles of the Father and the Son in redemption. God demands justice; Christ pleads for mercy. That is a parody of the best of the Latin theologians, but it is a recognizable parody, and one that could not fairly be addressed to the author of *To Diognetus*, or to Irenaeus or Gregory of Nyssa. And finally, doctrine of this type sometimes projects its archaic *setting* into the present—a scandalous example being the penal view, which dignifies seventeenth-century standards of criminal justice, including barbaric capital punishment.

c. The modern West.—The previous examples of atonement teaching differed from one another in reach or thrust. The *Christus-victor* type saw Christ's achievement aimed at evil (or at its personified head, the devil).

Thus it can be characterized as an *evilward* (or *devilward*) type. The point of Christ's saving work is to defeat the devil. In contrast, Anselm and the form of the doctrine that followed him, not least the penal teaching, showed Christ's achievement aimed back toward God and the satisfaction of God's honor or justice, so it is a *Godward* type of atonement teaching. Of course, such categorizing does not fully describe the view of any of the great theologians. Each reckoned the impact of atonement on other targets as well, so that each type had not only a 'Godward' and 'evilward,' but also a 'manward' vector. Yet the distinction is useful if it helps focus the main concern of the atonement teaching we are next to consider, which falls under this third or *'manward'* type.

This being so, it is natural to ask whether teaching had not long since appeared that saw Christ's principal work as the changing of human nature. In fact, it had. **Abelard** (d. 1142), a brilliant younger contemporary of Anselm and a Parisian monk, had argued against both the 'ransom' and the 'satisfaction' views of atonement:

> How cruel and unjust it appears, that anyone should demand the blood of the innocent as any kind of ransom, or be in any way delighted with the death of the innocent, let alone that God should find the death of His Son so acceptable, that through it He should be reconciled to the world!
> (Abelard, *Commentary on Romans*, quoted by Franks, 1962:145)

Admittedly, Abelard here distorts Anselm's (and Irenaeus') outlook, but as history showed, the distortion was not farfetched. Abelard's own view is that it was love—the love Christ kindled in those whose nature he shared—that was the sole cause of redemption. Christ's perseverance in love to us ("even unto death") evokes a like love in those who experienced it, and thus his merits pass to them, so that they can appropriately be forgiven. "Her sins, which are many, are forgiven; for she loved much" (Luke 7:47 KJV), albeit a misleading translation, epitomizes Abelard's view (Franks, 1962:142-49). Though he was a distinguished medieval theologian, Abelard's view of atonement remained subordinate until it reappeared in the Radical Reformer Faustus Socinus, and most powerfully in the nineteenth century, when Schleiermacher and Albrecht Ritschl on the continent, McLeod Campbell in Scotland, and Horace Bushnell in America would repeat and expand it. Like Abelard's, the reach of all these accounts was to change ourselves—they saw the reconciling work of Christ aimed not at the devil (or at faceless ranks of structured evil), still less at God, but chiefly at Christ's human sisters and brothers. Perhaps the epitome of this work is found in a landmark book by Anglican theologian Robert Campbell Moberly

(1845–1903), whose very title, *Atonement and Personality* (1917), shows the new emphasis.

Our best access to this type, however, both for what it says and for what it omits, is in the work of American Congregationalist theologian **Horace Bushnell** (1802–76). An influential Hartford, Connecticut, pastor, Bushnell was troubled by the theological dogmatism that seemed to him unresponsive to the religious need of his congregation and the spiritual truth he himself knew inwardly. In middle age he had experienced a deeper gospel conversion that provided new insight. In its light he delivered public lectures (at Yale, Harvard, and Andover) that offered an American theological vision, Calvinist in its roots, that rivaled the successful Unitarians in the appeal to religious experience, and yet was distinct from them. Some of these lectures became a book, *God in Christ* (1849), dealing with three related topics: incarnation, Trinity, and the work of Christ. Nearly two decades later, he reworked the last of these in *The Vicarious Sacrifice* (1866). Here Bushnell most clearly took up the modern view. Christ did not die to pay a debt owed by humanity to God, or to suffer the punishment due a fallen race. Far less did he die as a ransom to the devil. The atoning work could be summed up in two words—vicarious sacrifice—to be explained next.

In America Jonathan Edwards had been credited, on the basis of a few remarks, with the "Governmental" view of atonement generally traced to Hugo Grotius. Whatever its source, this "Edwardean" view, as it was called in New England, was widely received among the dominant Congregationalists of Bushnell's day. For example Caleb Burge's representative *Essay on the Scripture Doctrine of the Atonement* had made a special point, as had the penal view, of the salvific merit of Jesus' pains, while Jesus' obedience, in contrast, played no part in the atonement. The reaction of the Unitarians, led by William Ellery Channing (1780–1842), was vigorous: That the death of Christ could produce a change in God was a pernicious idea. God required no substitute to make satisfaction for sin. Moreover, Channing argued, the Calvinist (i.e., 'Edwardean' or governmental) scheme made no provision for the development of Christian character. Were sinners to be saved by Christ from hell but not from their sins? Bushnell had to reckon with these debates (citations from H. Shelton Smith in Bushnell, 1965:19f).

In an age accustomed by Reformed doctrine to think in terms of divine justice, penal rectitude, and the redemptive value of pain, Bushnell's task was to make use of the traditional substitutionary language without reinforcing such thought-patterns. He found a foothold in Scripture: Matthew 8:17 quotes Isaiah in order to describe Jesus, who "took our illnesses from us and carried away our diseases." In reality Jesus had appeared not as a prophet or priest or king but as a healer; in the King James version, Jesus "bare our sicknesses." This bearing paralleled the bearing of our sins. Jesus did not contract the diseases, nor did he endure God's punishment for the sins; he bore them vicariously in the sense that he "took them on his feeling, had his heart burdened by the sense of them." He suffered the impact of others' sickness and others' sin in his work of taking them away. By his sympathy and friendship, and in his chosen role as the people's Healer, Jesus expressed the identifying love that ultimately entailed the loss of his life. By "vicarious," Bushnell meant something less than his Calvinist and something more than his Unitarian contemporaries. God had not sent Christ as humanity's sub-stitute to accept the punishment incurred by sin. Against that view Bushnell mounted all the now familiar arguments: It was immoral; it failed to reflect either God's nature or our own best moral sentiments. Yet "vicarious" claimed more than an evangelistic Unitarian such as Channing would allow—Christ was more than a helper of others, did more than influence them or endure the evils that the innocent as well as the guilty suffer in life. These things were true enough, but they fell short of the gospel. In fact, "vicarious" and "sacrifice," the two words of Bushnell's thesis, had to be understood together, though at the outset his account of sacrifice was less forceful than that he would ultimately adopt. To sacrifice, he first said, was to "burn upon an altar" in some other's place; it was to "make loss" for another, that is, to engage for the other in some costly and self-abandoning enterprise. Such an engage-ment was Christ's task; its motive was love; and love "is a principle essentially vicarious in its own nature, identifying [its] subject with others, so as to suffer their adversities and pains, and [take] on itself the burden of their evils." Thus he brings his followers' lives into line with this divine life. Restored by Christ to God (the at-onement), they are drawn into this sympathetic love; now they, too, enter redemptively into the work of at-onement. Redemption, aimed at each human being, brings "all souls redeemed" into the vicarious work of sacrifice along with the Healer himself (*The Vicarious Sacrifice* in Bushnell, 1965:280-87). Had Bushnell known it, he was close to the old Anabaptist theme of three centuries before.

In *The Vicarious Sacrifice*, Bushnell's understanding of atonement displayed the distinctive modern feature—its psychological character. Where Irenaeus and even Anselm had seen Christ's work on a world canvas, defeating structural or demonic evil, or satisfying God for sin's destruction of the beauty and order of the universe, and where for the Anabaptists bloody martyrdom always hovered as near as the menacing alliance of state and church, Bushnell for his part interiorized and individualized. Christ's work is formed by his sympathy for human-kind. This is God's own sympathy or love; in Bushnell's term, it is "the

moral power of God" (1965:297). Forgiveness creates partners in the
attitude of love for others, so the forgiven themselves become vicarious
sacrificers in spirit. To be sure, this interiority has outward consequences, deadly ones for Christ, but the locus of interpretation is within.
In contrast to earlier 'objective' accounts, we may rightly call this type
'subjective.' The strengths and weaknesses of this approach are part and
parcel of the doctrine as presented. On the one hand, each disciple has
a role in the work of atonement. The forgiven sinner's response to Jesus
Christ is not only gratitude and awe as in Irenaeus and Anselm, but also
the will to take up Christ's work. To be forgiven is to become a forgiver.
This is the great positive strength of Bushnell's teaching. Yet from this
position he can offer no clear explanation of how the costly work of
Christ authorizes or accomplishes our forgiveness—a lack of which
Bushnell himself was deeply conscious. To put the matter differently,
there is here no clear account of the fact of redemption prior to response
on the part of its recipient. (This weakness would lead some twentieth-
century theologians such as Karl Barth to revert to earlier forms of
atonement—cf. CD IV/1 §59.) Again, this subjective type fails to explain
the central role of Christ's cross, leaving it a mystery why it was necessary that Christ should suffer not sympathy but death—and death at the
hands of the state. Here even more than in Anselm, the actual shape of
Christ's death seems incidental to his mission rather than essential to it.
Yet it was exactly the role of the cross in Christianity that church teaching
had set out, many centuries earlier, to explain.

In fairness to Bushnell, though, more must be said. Some infer that
experiences in later life showed him how costly forgiveness can be for
those who are sinned against, so that by analogy he could see more
clearly how costly forgiveness must be for a holy and loving God.
However reached, the insight led him to revise Parts III and IV of *The
Vicarious Sacrifice* in a new book, *Forgiveness and Law* (1874). Bushnell
thought the revised account, since it incorporated both elements, should
be called "subjective-objective" (Bushnell, 1965:276). Yet the added 'objective' element did not take him far from the earlier psychological
analogy between God's nature and our own. Just as forgiveness, even
when granted by those with a will to forgive, is inwardly expensive, so
is there inward cost for a forgiving God. Bushnell's interpretation of
forgiveness as costly interior work by the self has already been explored
in *Ethics* (pp. 225-27). Here we can raise a further question: How can it
be the work of Christ that achieves God's forgiveness, if God by nature
is eternally one who forgives, eternally works to forgive? Can God have
waited until Jesus' day to be a forgiving God? Bushnell's answer was
that what God in eternity does, making atonement via costly forgive-

ness, Christ in his mission repeats and represents and by representation makes effectual (1965:306-9, 337). Yet this answer displays once more the strength and the weakness of the position. It is strong, as it brings the work of Christ once more into line with the work and nature of God the Father. It is weak, as it leaves uncertainty about the primary, objective value of Christ's own incarnate life—the life whose story in scant outline was our starting point.

§2. The Biblical Teaching of Atonement

When we bring together the main types of Christian atonement teaching, a jarring lack of fit appears: These forms of doctrine seem simply irreconcilable. 'Theories,' some have called the varied forms of atonement teaching, and have intended exactly this point: these are not merely perspectives on the work of Christ, seen now from this angle, now from that, but are in the strict scientific sense rivals, so that in choosing one all the others must be rejected. I have not spoken of the several teachings as theories, and while the element of conflict among them is evident, it is not clear that the great theologians uniformly meant their accounts as theories, if by a theory we mean an overview adequate to organize the entirety of Christian teaching on a topic. Yet that is just what a theory is. In the plain speech of Walter T. Conner, a theory is "a string long enough to tie up all the facts." Such sweeping theoretical work was often not the intention, far less the achievement, of traditional atonement teaching. So we must think further about how to regard the diversity and the mutual disagreement. If we can do this better in light of a fresh look at the biblical material that stands behind it all, that is our next task.

It seems clear that the several atonement accounts *cannot* simply be mixed together and baked in a single loaf. For one thing, each possesses a main ingredient. Now, Christ's work *cannot* be mainly devilward *and* mainly Godward, though of course the doctrine might include some of each. Yet as theories the main direction of thrust is a *defining* aspect of each. Nor can there be any gainsaying that Anselm, for example, explicitly denied that Christ's cross was a ransom (or bait) to the devil, while Abelard, and successors such as Bushnell, explicitly denied that Christ made satisfaction to God for others' sins. "Combination" does not explain how such disagreements can be resolved. Nor can we overlook the fact that the proponents of these teachings were making serious claims to truth; they did not mean to put forward fancies or fantasies.

a. The situation of the New Testament writers.—Recall again the new reality that gave rise to the New Testament writings: Christ is risen!

Disciples found themselves living in the presence of the living Jesus Christ. In the proper place, I will join those who insist the resurrection is no less than a fact, an extraordinary fact, of history. That and more. Here it is enough merely to note that the first disciples indeed took it to be such. It was the central conviction by which the first witnesses to the resurrection now lived: Jesus is presently alive, and he is God's Christ. We have seen in Chapter Three that this conviction defined not only their Lord's new status but also their own. It was "the new that came in Christ." Their lives were now shaped by a new set of *relations;* they were transformed by a new *being;* they found themselves traveling a new *way.* All this was theirs, and theirs to share; they were apostles, messengers, sent with glad tidings: "The promise has been kept; a new age has come!"

To proclaim the new, though, meant one had to explain it. What had occurred to make this state of affairs possible? The answer already at hand was, "Christ is risen." The *Christus praesens,* Christ being present, both enabled and explained the new life together. Still, to say he was "risen" meant nothing unless they said first that he had died, and there was the catch. The Master they hailed was a condemned criminal who had suffered an execution reserved for notorious outlaws. How was the shame of that death to be coupled with tidings of salvation? Their first answer lies at the very root of New Testament atonement teaching. Yet no contemporary record of it survives. Nevertheless, the answer is vital, for out of those events—the cross and resurrection and the apostolic proclamation—grew the New Testament writings themselves.

We noted the uncertainty of many events in the life of Jesus, and similar uncertainty extends to the time of the post-Easter Christian beginnings. There is certainty, however, about one general feature of this intertestamental time: the Jewish literature produced then is preoccupied with *last things.* In troubled times, the apocalypse had become a standard literary form. (Surviving examples of this Jewish and Christian material are gathered in English translation in two volumes edited by James H. Charlesworth [1983–85], and some of it appears in the New Testament in the Apocalypse of John and in Mark 13 and its parallels.) Half a century ago, C. H. Dodd took this eschatological focus as the key to the earliest Christian proclamation, arguing in *The Apostolic Preaching and Its Developments* (1936) that the primitive Christian *kērygma* (proclamation) could be discovered in the preaching reported in Acts and by Paul (e.g., Acts 2:14-39; 3:13-26; 10:36-43; 1 Cor. 15:1-7; Rom. 1:1-4; 8:34): (1) Jesus is the one promised by the Scriptures; (2) by his mighty works, death for our sins, and resurrection as our intercessor he has inaugurated the anticipated new age; (3) God's Spirit is now offered to all peoples, who must therefore repent, be baptized, and expect the consummation of the age.

Our concern is with the earliest message, but our question is still more pointed: How did the apostolic preaching interpret Christ's saving work? More recently, Dale C. Allison, Jr., reconsidering Dodd's thesis, has provided substantive help (Allison, 1985). The time-scheme of many Jewish and Christian apocalypses includes a period of trouble or tribulation before the time of triumph. Thus Jesus' suffering and death was the tribulation, and his resurrection was the onset of the final triumph. *The eschatological view of that death and resurrection is the early view we seek. The death of Jesus marked the end of an age; the resurrection began one.* As Allison summarizes:

> Why did the first Christians associate the end of Jesus with motifs otherwise connected with the end of the age? The closest parallels to the phenomenon in question occur in Jewish texts for which past occurrences and present experiences belong to the eschatological time of trouble. The explanation of such texts is this: events of history were thought sufficiently close to eschatological expectations so as to encourage some Jews to believe that certain of those expectations had come and were coming to pass. Something similar happened in the early church. Jesus had proclaimed that the kingdom of God was at hand, that eschatological suffering and resurrection were near. Hence, when he suffered and died and subsequently appeared alive to his followers, they concluded that the eschatological drama had opened, that the final tribulation had begun with the suffering and death of the Messiah, that the general resurrection had begun with his resurrection. In brief, the eschatological expectations of the pre-Easter period were drawn upon in the attempt to understand the crucifixion and Jesus' conquest of death. (Allison, 1985:170)

I believe Dodd and Allison offer a credible first answer to our question. Yet the teaching of Jesus and that of the early church reflect a background broader than apocalyptic. The preaching of the cross was shaped for hearers in a Hellenistic world; it sprang from reflection upon Jewish Scripture; and we must see the difference both these facts made to Christian understanding. So far, we have noted one telling fact: The explanation of the cross (and of the resurrection) was nothing apart from the concrete account of the cross (as tribulation) and of the resurrection (as eschatological dawn). These events were signs, they themselves were explanatory; they might evoke but did not depend upon some underlying philosophy of history or theory about God's heavenly actions. Some may think this obvious, but as we will see, it is crucial.

b. Metaphors—the Old Testament in the New.—The New Testament is so saturated with the Old that it can hardly be read, much less understood, without the other. Yet the New Testament understanding of the Savior and the cross is truly novel; there is no single Old Testament motif that fully prepares us for it. Perhaps the nearest approach lay in two concepts, on the one hand that of a coming Messiah-King (or an apocalyptic Son of man), and on the other that of a Suffering Servant of JHWH. Yet these remained separate in Old Testament Scripture and came together first in the person of Jesus as understood in earliest Christianity. Indeed, this suggests a more general truth—there was no 'expectation' of Christ in Scripture that could have enabled even the keenest Hebrew reader concretely to foretell Jesus' ministry, his suffering, his death and resurrection. Continuity exists, but it is apparent only in light of the events themselves. (The same must be said, of course, of the continuity of Sinai with Abraham, or the continuity of the synagogue with the temple.) We saw that in C. H. Dodd's recovery of the earliest Christian proclamation, its first element identified Jesus as the one promised by Scripture. This theme persisted in the earliest (surviving) Christian documents—the Letters of the New Testament. *These Letters drew their metaphors of Christ's work mainly from the Hebrew and Greek Old Testament.*

Here again a brief reminder of the role of metaphor in Scripture is in order. Metaphors are not the furniture of some fairyland of unreal or pretended existence; metaphor is not an alternative to true utterance, or a way of avoiding the (literal) truth, but a native device for speaking the truth in as plain and helpful a way as may be. *Metaphors* may be contrasted with *similes,* which are tropes that merely offer a comparison: "The package fell *like a stone.*" They may be contrasted with *symbols,* which (at least in my use in this volume) are only convenient but arbitrary indicators: $ symbolizes the dollar. And they may be contrasted with *signs,* which (again in my use here, and I believe in common use) are indicators exactly because they are a part of what is indicated: thus when *clouds* are a sign of rain it is because they can bring rain. Janet Soskice, in her useful work earlier noted, defines metaphor as "a form of language *use* [emphasis added; she might well have said, a form of *utterance*] with a unity of subject-matter and which yet draws upon two (or more) sets of associations, and does so, characteristically, by involving the consideration of a model or models" (Soskice, 1985:49). This rough-hewn but helpful sentence reminds us, as Soskice does at greater length (1985:103-17), of Ian Ramsey's exploration of "qualified models" in religious utterance. Here it is enough to offer a single example of metaphor: When Duke Senior in *As You Like It* consoles his fellow forest exiles, he speaks of

... books in the running brooks,
        Sermons in stones, and good in everything. (act 2 scene 1)
Is this mere fancy? Had the Duke better have spoken of sermons in books, and

stones in running brooks? If we see that he did not misspeak, it may be because we think that "drawing upon two (or more) sets of associations" and employing "a model or models" can tell more about life in the Forest of Arden or elsewhere than such an amendment ever can. As we examine the New Testament metaphors and models of atonement, then, we are in search of truth spoken best (or, as we shall see, spoken next best) in just this way. As in Chapter Three, we will find that metaphors are often created by *catachresis* (shifts of meaning in terms).

i. Metaphors of law: justice and judgment, punishment and substitution.—It is small wonder that in telling of Jesus' cross the early missionaries turned to law and its borderlands; they were themselves engaged in activity perilously beyond the law's limits. The Apostle Paul's laconic report sets the tone: "Five times the Jews have given me the thirty-nine strokes; three times I have been beaten with rods; once I was stoned . . ." (2 Cor. 11:24f). Yet his marginal status had been foreshadowed in Hebrew Scripture. As the exilic Prophet Isaiah sang of the Servant,

> He was arrested and sentenced and taken away,
> and who gave a thought to his fate—
> how he was cut off from the world of the living,
> stricken to death for my people's transgression? (Isa. 53:8)

The cross was punishment, whatever else it was—capital punishment meted out to flagrant violators of Roman rule. Of course, punishment may reflect injustice rather than justice, and that is the fate of the Servant. John McKenzie in the Anchor Bible begins Isaiah 53:8 thus: "By a perverted judgment he was taken away" (1968:130f). At least, Christians knew this was true in Jesus' case; he had not deserved his fate but had been condemned in a hasty, unfair trial. If he was born "under the law," it was "to buy freedom for those who were under the law" (Gal. 4:4f)—a freedom Jesus won, said Paul, only by enduring the law's full weight. Hence the words of Isaiah 53 reverberate through the Epistles when the cross of Christ is mentioned (with Isa. 53:1-11 LXX cf. e.g. Heb. 5:8; 9:28; Rom. 4:25; 5:18f; Phil. 2:9-11; 1 Cor. 15:3; 2 Cor. 5:21; Gal. 4:27; 1 Pet. 2:22-25). As McKenzie says, "The prophet clearly sees an innocent Israelite who rescues his fellow Israelites from suffering by bearing their suffering himself" (1968:134). We need not resolve all difficulties of interpretation (to whom or to what did Isaiah refer in the first place?) to know that the New Testament writers applied his description to Christ crucified. Isaiah's account of unjust punishment, substitutionary suffering (for unjust punishment endured *in place of* another is not as rare as some think), and innocent victimization spoke to them of Jesus—the connection was a prime instance of what this book calls the prophetic vision. Though there is no straight path from the Epistles to the penal atonement doctrines of the sixteenth and seventeenth centuries, there is something more valuable: Corrupt justice interprets the deep meaning of the cross. In Soskice's words just quoted, the Apostle draws upon two (or more) sets of associations and does so by involving the consideration of a model or models. In this case, the associations are (1) Jesus' death and (2) (corrupt) justice; the latter is a model that interprets the former.

I mention only two more of the New Testament's legal metaphors. Paul in Galatians 3:13*a* says "Christ bought us freedom from the curse of the law by coming under the curse for our sake." This addressed the *shame* evoked by the primitive missionary message: Crucifixion meant not only the shame of the hanged (to say nothing of the shame of the hangman!) that capital punishment imposes even now, but a still further demeaning shame as well, because the cross was reserved to those beyond the pale of ancient society—rebels, traitors (J. Green, "Death of Jesus" DJG:148). The Apostle acknowledges that, citing Deuteronomy 21:22-23: "Cursed is everyone who is hanged on a gibbet" (Gal. 3:13*b*). Hanging was accepted as a punishment in Deuteronomy, but only with the warning that such punishment *pollutes* (not only the hanged one, but the very) *"land which the LORD your God is giving you."* Paul's point, then, is this: Law, whether Roman law or Jewish law, sets up its insiders and its outsiders, its taboos and its exclusions. Now Galatian Christians were in danger of stumbling back into just such taboos—of which touching a dead human body was one, not to mention touching a crucified human body. But Christ, being crucified, actually became such an unclean, untouchable one, since he died on a cross meant for barbarian criminals. Thereby he broke the barrier of such insider-outsider exclusion, redeeming those who loved him from the power of all "curse" laws. It is not that God cursed Christ and had him crucified. Rather it is that Christ, by taking his place as one accursed (hanged or crucified) broke through that "curse" rule: Disciples certainly could not count Christ "accursed." Having taken his beloved body down from the cross, how were they to reckon him, or anyone else in that same humbling fix, unclean or "accursed"? They were freed from the law, the old Jewish law or the current Roman social law, by his submission to it. By law or custom, the shame of the cross polluted Judea, where Jesus was executed. More generally it polluted the Roman Empire, where such executions were still common. The cross was the law's curse, the land's curse. When law and land had turned upon Jesus, treating him as one polluted, then land and law had cursed—themselves. God in a paradox had turned the tables; the attempt to make Christ accursed by shamefully executing him had extended hope of salvation to all—even the perpetrators of the curse themselves.

Reversal is involved in still another legal metaphor: "It follows that there is now no condemnation [katakrima] for those who are united with Christ Jesus" (Rom. 8:1). Arndt and Gingrich point out that *katakrima* is probably not "condemnation" but its sequel—the punishment itself. To explain why there is no punishment for those in Christ, Paul goes on, ". . . by sending his own Son in the likeness of our sinful nature and to deal with sin, he has passed judgement *(katekrinen)* against sin within that very nature" (v. 3). Here is full metaphor; two sets of associations merge. At Calvary not Pilate but God is Judge; not Jesus' sins, but ours are judged; but punishment issues from God's judgment neither for Jesus nor for us, for in this case God's judgment is acquittal and life in the Spirit.

Like sermons in stones and books in the running brooks, the bizarre jurisprudence of Jesus' criminal process speaks to the Apostle of another process in which in Christ we receive (not mere justice, but) life by acquittal! Other legal metaphors invite analogous exegeses—tasks necessarily left to the reader.

Surprisingly, one anticipated element does *not* appear in the New Testament. With reason some have designated God's righteousness the central theme of Paul's great doctrinal epistle, Romans. It is, in Anders Nygren's words, "the fundamental concept of the Epistle" (1952:9). Thus we might expect at least one of the Apostle's involved arguments to invoke the satisfaction of God's justice by Jesus' death. This simply does not appear. Where "justice" *(dikaiosunē)* and Christ's death converge in the text, they always do so via some other metaphor of that death. For example, in Romans 5:9 Paul tells his readers "we have now been justified *[dikaiōthentes]*," and then he refers to the cross. But his actual words are, "justified by Christ's sacrificial death" (in Greek, *en tō haimati*—an explicit sacrificial term). There is no New Testament example of a courtroom metaphor in which God is the righteous judge, Christ the defendant, and the cross a penalty paid. At the least, this brings out the creative novelty of the Latin atonement teaching!

ii. Metaphors of military victory.—In Chapter Four we saw that an ancient creation-myth, older than the Bible, telling how the gods had fought to establish supremacy among themselves, served as a primitive explanation of creation. Although this myth was supplanted by the author of Genesis 1, it appears in the poetry of Isaiah, Job, and the Psalms. In Pauline teaching, the ancient theme reappears. The alien gods are the "principalities and powers" that have long threatened the rule of God on earth, only here their defeat is linked not to original creation or Hebrew Exodus, but to the cross. In Galatians Paul writes to a congregation tempted to return to a religion ringed round with the ritual restrictions that the Apostle had by God's grace escaped. In order to persuade these "foolish Galatians" of their folly, he writes that "we" (the human race?) had long been subjected to enslavement by these "elemental spirits of the universe" *(ta stoicheia tou kosmou)*, but now God had sent the Son to "buy freedom" for the enslaved, and thus there was no sense in remaining enslaved any longer (Gal. 4:3f). They are gods, these *stoicheia*, but properly speaking not gods at all for those who in Christ know the true God and are filled with God's Spirit (vv. 5-9).

The struggle even then for an appropriate terminology for these "elemental spirits" foreshadows the difficulty present-day readers may have in dealing with this way of thinking. What are we to make of 'gods,' demons, devils, 'elemental spirits,' and the like? (cf. *Ethics*, Six §1b) Yet as John Driver, writing from long missionary experience outside the Enlightenment West, says:

> They were taken seriously in the New Testament era when they were understood as invisible, spiritual forces which enslave and oppress people in a bondage from which they are unable to break free themselves. These forces were understood to lie behind many of the religious, social, and political institutions. In fact, the earliest confession of faith—Jesus is Lord—was also a denial of the loyalty claims of all other powers. (1986:71)

In the Galatians passage just cited, Paul does not directly refer to the cross. A parallel passage in Ephesians does so, however: "for he annulled the [power called] law with its rules and regulations, so as to create out of the two [Jew and non-Jew] a single new humanity in himself, thereby making peace. This was his purpose, to reconcile the two in a single body to God *through the cross*, by which he killed the enmity" (Eph. 2:15f). It is more common, though, to associate the victory metaphor not with the cross alone but with Jesus' incarnation in its entirety (as in Galatians 4), or with the *resurrection*, as in Ephesians 1: "His mighty strength was seen at work *when he raised Christ from the dead*, and enthroned him at his right hand in the heavenly realms, far above all government and authority, all power and dominion" (vv. 19*b*-21*a*). The note of military triumph is especially vivid in the Colossian Letter, which pictures the celebratory parade granted successful generals after a great victory: "[At the cross] he disarmed the cosmic powers and authorities and made a public spectacle of them, leading them as captives in his triumphal procession" (Col. 2:15).

Finally, we may note that these metaphors are applied not only to the work of God in creation, and to the work of Christ in the days of his flesh, and to the final consummation (e.g., Revelation 19), but also to the continuing battle disciples must wage against the "superhuman forces of evil" (*ta pneumatika tēs ponērias*, Eph. 6:12). Though their defenses are always nonviolent—integrity, the gospel of peace, faith, salvation—with them disciples can "quench all the burning arrows of the evil one," their only offensive weapon "the word of God" with prayer (vv. 14-17).

iii. Metaphors of kinship and redemption.—In the Old Testament the strongest social unit is the family. Since descent was patrilineal, the family was designated *beth ab*, the house of the father, and its scope was wide indeed—not only the father and husband, but "his wife or wives and concubines, his children, slaves or retainers, clients or resident aliens, widowed or expelled daughters, and unmarried adult sons or

daughters" (DB, p. 273). In some contrast to today's evanescent family, the Hebrew family exerted an inescapable moral claim upon all its members. The sin and guilt of one was the sin and guilt of all. Early Hebrew religion had required the patriarch daily to make sacrifice for all his family (echoed in Job 1:5). Thus when the amphictyony or confederation extended kinship to the several tribes, first under Saul the Benjaminite and then under mighty Judah's David, this was not only a political achievement but a widening of the claim of family duty. The sense of participation passed to a widening circle, the tribe, the nation, and ultimately all Israel, considered not only as an ethnic clan but as a community of faith with an enduring history (Deut. 26:5f par.).

Such moral solidarity explains the function of the kinsman-redeemer or *goel*. Primitive family members, in the event of injury to any of their kin, had been expected to pursue the offender and exact justice, perhaps by the rule "life for life, eye for eye . . . wound for wound" (Exod. 21:24f). If its function was to deter aggressors by the fear of such vengeance, this remedy may have been worse than the danger it addressed. This is implied by the law's provision of Cities of Refuge (Num. 35:11). In these, inadvertent killers (and presumably others less innocent) could find sanctuary until a proper trial could be arranged. With the growth of solidarity in Israel (the Sixth Commandment forbade murder of any Israelite) the *goel* survived now as one who had the right to redeem (*ga-al*) ancestral property put up for sale. In a time of national despair, Jeremiah redeemed property for his own family at Anathoth, by this act expressing God's steadfast promise to redeem *Israel* from its time of troubles (Jer. 32:6ff; cf. Ruth 4). It is in light of this history that we are to understand the poetic name of *goel* given to JHWH—some thirty-five times in the Old Testament, and particularly in exilic Isaiah (DB, p. 70). Thus Proverbs 23:10f:

> Do not move an ancient boundary stone
> or encroach on the land of the fatherless:
> they have a powerful Guardian *(goel)*
> who will take up their cause against you.

and also Isaiah 41:14:

> Have no fear, Jacob you worm and Israel you maggot,
> It is I who help you, declares the LORD;
> your redeemer *(goel)* is the Holy One of Israel.

Goel is one vivid stem for "redeemer" and "redemption" in Hebrew. The other, more general term *(padha)* refers to the buying back (and sometimes merely the buying) of persons or other living beings. The broadest principle of the law of sacrifice was that all firstborn creatures belonged to God, yet firstborn human beings might be redeemed by the paying of a fixed sum of money (Num. 18:15-16). Alternatively, the tribe of Levi were said to be substitutes for the firstborn of each tribe—in place of others, all Levites were to assist Aaron's sons in the priestly office (Num. 3:11, 46-51). These two concepts of redemption merged for New Testament writers seeking to account for the death of Jesus. (Here, as in the Septuagint, the Greek terms are *lutron, lutroō,* and *apolutrōsis.*) The latter terms in both languages were also used of the manumission of slaves. Where in standard English translations we find "ransom," "redeem," and "redemption," such thought stands behind it (Dentan, IDB IV:21f). Consider "In Christ our release is secured and our sins forgiven through the shedding of his blood" (Eph. 1:7). In this passage Christ is the Liberator; he achieves our liberation by being our *goel;* and beyond that, our kinsman-redeemer himself becomes the sacrifice! In this mix of metaphors, the buying back is drawn up into a range of images that transcends the capacity of any one of them to speak the full truth.

Kinship metaphors for atonement are not limited to the formal transaction of 'redemption.' For there are as well other rich New Testament images of family: adoption into God's family, Christ as the Brother of the entire family of brothers and sisters in God, and behind all, the patient figure of the waiting Father. These, because of the solidarity of family that stands in their Hebraic background, shed apostolic light upon the mysterious cross.

iv. Metaphors of sacrifice.—When we come to sacrifice we enter a conceptual world remote from modern Western thought. The previous spheres, legal, military, and familial (the latter including family slaves), are greatly changed in modern life, yet in some form they remain within our experience. Sacrifice, however, only suggests "pagan sacrifice," perhaps with grotesque rites and superstitious aims. Or it suggests Old Testament practices superseded in both Christianity and Judaism. The term does survive in a secular sense, as in the sacrifice of brave soldiers for their country, but here its meaning has become simply expenditure of life or goods in a cause. In this last sense, the great 'sacrifices' of modern history have been its total wars with their mass attacks on civilians and the relentless massacres of entire populations (genocide). These concepts are remote indeed from the biblical notion.

The biblical practices, already old though not yet discontinued in Jesus' day, were themselves developed from still earlier human rituals already obsolete by the time biblical history begins. These earlier practices can at best be hypothetically reconstructed by historical examination of Scripture, combined with study of the archaeological remains of prehistoric Near Eastern peoples compared with anthropological study of survivors such as Original Americans and Aboriginal Australians. Amid vast excitement, it was discovered about one hundred years ago that there were striking similarities among the ritual practices of these scattered peoples and the ancestors of the Hebrews (James et al., ERE XI:1-39).

Several organizing ideas of sacrifice have been proposed. Sacrifice is said to be essentially a gift (bribe?) to shape the gods' behavior, or a thanksgiving gift for favor granted, or it is piacular (to expunge sins), or atoning (restoring good relations between deity and worshipers), or purifying. Old Testament sacrifices could be found that fit each of these and other subcategories (peace offerings, wave offerings, whole burnt offerings, cereal offerings, blood offerings, scapegoat offerings, the Passover feast, and yet more). If our goal is to clarify the notion of sacrifice behind the New Testament metaphors of the work of Christ, we need not settle the issues that divide the theorists. In so rich a field of study, each view has some merit. Certainly prebiblical sacrifice involved *participation*, often in the form of a feast: in consuming the sacrifice the deity was consumed and thereby appropriated (Hubert and Mauss, 1898:chap. 2). From such a rude beginning (perhaps paralleled by early Australian and early American patterns of totem and taboo), biblical sacrifice developed into a sacred ritual feast (W. Robertson Smith, 1889:lect. 6). Now it was no longer overtly the god who was consumed, for JHWH was spirit and life. Yet the idea lingered—"the life (or spirit) is in the blood"—and blood, the life force of animate bodies, remained the central medium of participation in the sacrificial feast.

By the time of our biblical texts, though, the blood is perceived as too holy, too spirit-laden, to be consumed by worshipers—it is reserved, poured out to God upon the ground or the altar, or sublimated in sacrificial fire. Though in the next section I will acknowledge the contrary view of René Girard, I take **participation** (the persistent goal of worship, cf. Chapter Nine, §1) to be at the very heart of sacrifice (for a broad overview, G. Anderson, ABD V:870-86).

In the Old Testament period the chief sacrifice was the *Passover feast*, which had acquired strong *historical* associations with the Exodus and the journey of the liberated people to the Promised Land. (By the prophetic vision, in the New Testament the Passover lamb, the "Lamb of God," is Jesus, while the mediator of that vision is Isaiah 53, where the Servant is "like a sheep led to the slaughter," one "who had given himself a sacrifice for sin"—Isa. 53:7, 10.)

The Exodus 12 record of Passover institution displays many of the features on which Christianity was to draw. The setting was the final *plague* the LORD brought upon Egypt, the death of all the firstborn, a plague from which Israel must be protected (chap. 11). The event changes the *calendar:* Nissan is now to be the first of the months. The feast is observed *family by family,* not governed by sacrificial priests or performed by individuals. The sacrificial animal must be *without blemish,* a male yearling sheep or goat, *slaughtered* between dusk and dark. Some of the *blood* must be smeared on the doorposts as a sign: "when I see the blood, I shall pass over you." It must be roasted whole (entrails, head, shins, and all), and eaten with unleavened bread and bitter herbs. The preceding days are days without leaven in the household. And all this because *"on this day I brought you out of Egypt"* (Exod. 12:1-20; Childs, 1974:chap. 8).

In early Christianity the Passover became the context for two intimately related elements—the Lord's supper and the cross. In 1 Corinthians we can see them together in Paul's apostolic teaching. The background is debate within the congregation about eating sacrificial meals. Some said that since idols were unreal, liberated Christians might attend the pagan feasts and gorge on the consecrated meat just as they pleased. Others strenuously objected. Paul, granting some points to each side (idols were to be sure unreal, but the congress with idolatry remained real enough for those who partook), in this case emphasized discipline rather than liberty, and drew a set of parallels that show how strong in his own mind were both the links and the antitheses connecting (1) current pagan sacrifice, (2) Jewish temple sacrifice, (3) the Exodus, (4) the Lord's supper, and (5) the (sacrificial) death of Christ. Paul's apostolic freedom of action had not been mere willfulness on his part; if one would follow his example one would exercise tender regard for every prospective convert: "so that in one way or another I may save some. All this I do for the sake of the gospel, to have a share in its blessings" (9:22f). Yet not even Christian ritual can of itself constitute such sharing. Recalling the Exodus and the warnings it contained against crude sacramental magic (10:1-13), Paul teaches that neither freedom (in the abstract) nor rules (for rules' sake) are to be the guide for Christians. The point is *having a share,* and for Paul the antithesis is between having a share with the idols, their food, their demonry, over against having a share with the Lord, the Lord's table, and conduct befitting the Lord's community (10:14-22). The measure of rites of sharing is the end they serve, so disciples may "eat or drink, or do anything else, provided it is all done to the glory of God" (10:31). Shortly, Paul returns to his deepest theme: "on the night of his arrest the Lord Jesus took bread, and after giving thanks to God broke it" (11:23-26). Here 'sacrifice' in one sense (the ritual meal) designates, describes, defines 'sacrifice' in another (the Lord's saving death). (The 'scare quotes' remind us that in both cases the meaning of sacrifice is stretched, metaphorical.) Just as the Passover meal takes its historic meaning from the last plague and the Exodus, here the Corinthians can understand their own rite only in light of its link with "the night of his arrest." Given that passion time, plainly, his "body . . . is for you"; given that event, his blood like blood splashed on doorposts and lintel is the sign, the seal, of "the new covenant" (on the Lord's supper, see further Chapter Nine).

Much has been made of the translation (and meaning) of a cluster of sacrifice-words in the Greek Bible and in the New Testament, *hilaskomai* and its cognates. In classical Greek, these words referred to sacrificial human action designed to placate a god. The same words reappear in the New Testament, for example in Romans 3:25 (*hilastērion*), and in 1 John 2:2 and 4:10, where Jesus is the *hilasmos* for our sins. A fundamental difference is that in the New Testament (and already in the Septuagint) God is the subject, not the object, of the action. Nowadays, English "propitiate" usually stands for the older, pagan act of placating God, and "expiate" bears the meaning of sin-removal or sin-covering that is addressed (not to God, but) to sinners. This use, we might note, is somewhat arbitrary, as in their history these English words have sometimes exchanged meanings. In today's terms, are the New Testament *hilaskomai*, and so on, passages saying that Christ *propitiates* God, or are they saying that in Christ God *expiates* human sin? The matter is debated, but most recent judgment favors the latter view (Büchsel, TDNT III:300-318; Cousar, 1990:62-66; J. Gundry Volf "Expiation, etc." in DPL). In any case, these, like the other sacrificial expressions of the New Testament, remain metaphors, and it is a mistake to force them into modern doctrinal molds.

In no ordinary sense of the words was Jesus put to death as a religious sacrifice: priests did not slaughter him; accepted biblical ritual did not require but rather forbade anything of the sort. No sacral words were spoken at his slaying; no altar smoke curled skyward to please the nostrils of a primitive god. Yet when the metaphoric way of speaking invokes sacrifice, then the associations of Passover, of Exodus, of the Last Supper, and of the death of Jesus are brought together so as to illuminate the last of these.

Elsewhere in the Epistles, sacrificial metaphors recur. The most extended instance is the book of Hebrews, which recalls not Exodus but the national sacrificial system epitomized in Leviticus. Once again there is a contrast: For Hebrews' author, Christ is God's Son; he is also God's high priest, not in the Aaronic order, but in that of a shadowy patriarchal figure, Melchizedek (Heb. 4:14; 5:1-10; Ps. 110:4). As the Aaronic priest enters the sanctuary beyond the curtain, so Jesus, in "the power of a life that cannot be destroyed" (7:16) "appeared once for all [*hapax*] at the climax of history [*sunteleia tōn aiōnōn*] to abolish sin by the sacrifice of himself" (9:26). In the freedom of metaphoric utterance, priest and offering were one. At one stroke this sacrifice abolishes "once for all" the previously prescribed Hebrew sacrificial system and by a single offering (*prosphora*) brings to maturity those whom it consecrates—those who must therefore now take up the way of suffering their pioneer has opened (2:10; 10:14; 11:32ff). The Letter to Hebrews is a mine upon which many atonement-doctrine claims have been staked. There Jesus experiences death for all mankind (*huper*, 2:9); he makes expiation for the sins of the people (*hilaskesthai*, 2:17); he makes believers his partners (*metochoi*, 3:14); he establishes a new covenant (*diathēkē*, chaps. 8–9); enduring the cross, he ignores its disgrace (12:2). Yet the dominant metaphor throughout is sacrifice.

c. Beyond metaphor—the gospel narratives.—The several sorts of doctrine, East and West, medieval and modern, that proponents call "theories of atonement" can each appeal to metaphorical strands within the New Testament. No 'theory' lacks its metaphor or cluster of metaphors in the Epistles; moreover, there are underutilized metaphors, such as the family with its solid ties, that might be expanded into still other 'theories' alongside the metaphors of titanic warfare, of law, and of sacrifice. Yet before we resign ourselves to a hopeless intrabiblical war of metaphors, we must ask if development into contending theories is the proper function of these texts. Did Paul, for example, when he invoked the "righteousness of God," intend to plant what must grow into the satisfaction discourse of Anselm's *Cur deus homo?* Was the intent of the Johannine Epistles, with their use of the old "mercy-seat" stem from the Greek Bible, *hilasmos,* a deliberate first step toward the post-Reformation penal or governmental accounts of atonement? If we answer No, it must be because we see a different role for these metaphors, one at odds with their extrusion into 'theories of atonement.' And we urgently require this other role (their place in the gospel narrative), since it is not possible to line up even one set of New Testament writers behind any one 'theory' without embarrassing anomalies. This other role becomes most evident in cases where the Epistles scramble or mix the metaphors.

i. Mixed metaphors.—Consider the Colossian Epistle, written late enough that if 'theories' were to be the shape of the future, one might already have been in the making here. The unnamed opponent is early Gnosticism, which 'solved' the shame of the cross by separating the divine Son from the earthly Jesus prior to death: If Christ was the savior, he could not have died on a cross; what was crucified was only a human shell whose divine occupant had earlier come and gone (cf. Irenaeus, *Adv. haer.* III.xi.iii). Colossians will have no part of this strategy. It insists upon the incarnate, flesh-and-blood facticity of the death of Jesus, and it makes its own defense against the shame of the cross. Here (1:13-22) appear the "thrones, sovereignties, authorities, and powers" that in Paul's earlier writings are the enemies of God's rule. The cross defeats them, but victory does not begin with the cross: God had originally made all these "invisible orders," and had made them "in him," that is, in the Son, who is therefore rightfully their ruler: "For in him God in all his fullness chose to dwell, and through him to reconcile all things to himself, making peace through the shedding of his blood on the cross—

all things, whether on earth or in heaven" (Col. 1:19f). We might suppose this "peace" to be that of a military conqueror who by defeating all enemies takes his unchallenged place, supreme in this world; clearly, in that case, the cross was the chaos-battle, and its outcome was victory. The *Christus-victor* motif would then seem firmly in place. Yet to read the passage in this way is sadly to misread it, turning the 'triumph' of the Son into an ordinary imperial victory—one that by all the evidence never occurred! The Christians are still suffering; the Crucified One is still despised by the world. If Colossians is to make good its triumph claim, it must show that the Son's is a different *kind* of peacemaking than Caesar's (cf. Matt. 5:9f, *eirēnopoioi*, peacemakers who endure persecution). Consequently a rash of metaphors of the cross break forth in this text. The cross is rescue and release—here are metaphors of family-redemption (1:13). The cross is reconciliation (*apokatēllaxen*, 1:21) a term that simply means to change or make change—for example to settle a commercial account. The shameful "death in his body of flesh and blood" (no metaphor, but grisly fact) 'reconciles' by bringing disciples into God's presence. The word used for presence (*parastēsai*, 1:22) is frequently a legal term, as when a court requires one in custody to be *presented* for judgment. At this judgment, though, believers are presented "without blame or blemish" (1:22)—a sacrificial image. In short, we have in Colossians a rich mix of metaphors, and if by this time some of them had flattened into ordinary use, still others had pushed up to express the gospel without regard to any 'theory': conquest passing into slave-redemption, into the reconciliation of things separate, into sacrifice, each without cost to the overall intention of the author to show the story of the cross beyond every metaphor, human shame turned into God's grace.

Other cases of metaphor-mixing (e.g., Col. 2:14f; Rom. 3:24f) show that Colossians 1 is not unique. Each raises once more the question: do not metaphors of Christ's work imply *some* narrative or meta-narrative, some overall view in which each may find its metaphorical place? Indeed they do, but the great story to which all contribute is no other than **the gospel story itself.**

ii. The gospel in the Gospels.—The first Christians had a gospel story but no Gospels. Often it is said that the deaths of some of the Apostles produced the realization that Christians needed the original story written, leading to the production of written Gospels. This 'memoir' view has some merit, but a stronger motive than reminiscence shaped the new genre. In the previous volume, the Gospels were characterized as identity documents. They identify the risen Christ with Jesus, their principal character. By offering a 'definite description' of Jesus, each Gospel functions (in speech-act terms) to **identify** him. Secondarily (but not incidentally), the Gospels also identify "the disciples," a wayward band of followers who collectively and one by one are transformed in the course of the narrative. A striking feature of the Gospels is that just as they tie the identity of Jesus (the one in their story) to the identity of the risen Christ (the one known in their readers' experience), they also invite contemporary readers to identify themselves with the wayward but transformed disciples of the story. The Gospels rhetorically invite readers to *become* participating disciples. They do this by telling the story (the plot) that discloses the chief characters in a setting (the coming reign); thus they provide the essential elements—character, plot, setting—of authentic narrative (*Ethics*, Twelve).

Now we can more clearly see how the Gospels were good news. They address directly the chief hindrance to participation faced by Jew and pagan alike—namely, the cross. As noted at the outset of this chapter, the crucifixion of Jesus is the Gospels' main event: they are "passion narratives with extended 'introductions.'" Yet the "extended introductions" can on no account be set aside: The Gospels make sense of the cross exactly by setting it within their own longer story. And all this— Jesus the chief character, the cross as plot—is placed in a setting that C. H. Dodd long ago identified as itself inescapable, the coming rule (*basileia*) of God. This evangel-narrative is the story that grounds the metaphors of the death of Christ. Slave-release and (crooked) justice, cosmic triumph and ultimate sacrifice, all find their home in the story told by Matthew, Mark, Luke, and John. The Gospel story itself (and not the later 'theory' stories of Irenaeus and Anselm and the rest) is what finally secures the Christian gospel: Jesus lived his life and died his death in such a way as to make his present claim upon non-Christian and Christian as well—neither shame nor scandal, but unqualified Good News.

Luke's Gospel, with Acts the "longest and most complex narrative in the New Testament," is a prime example of this turning of the tables via the cross. Robert Tannehill's literary analysis of Luke-Acts shows how its unified plot discloses God turning failure into success in the Gospel of Luke, only to see that success tempered by the sometimes limited achievement of the apostolic mission in the book of Acts (Tannehill, 1986–90 I:1f). Interpreting Luke's Gospel, Tannehill works mainly with the narrative roles, that is, the characters and their parts, showing how Luke weaves these, with plot and setting, into a rhetoric of narrative persuasion. In the Prologue (Luke 1:1-4), Luke the author promises readers that by presenting the events "in order" *(kathexēs)* he will enable them to know *(epignōs)* the facts they have learned (1:4). Tannehill understands this "assurance" to be not mere confirmation of the facts or mere correction of the chronology of Jesus' life, but reassurance in face of the "strong countercurrent" in the Jesus story (Tannehill, 1986–90 I:12)—Jesus' loss of popular esteem, his official rejection by Jewry, his crucifixion by Rome, his fixed status as an accursed victim. Luke reassures readers by setting the countercurrent within the long purpose *(boulē)* of God (Luke 7:30; Acts 2:23; 4:28; 5:38f; 13:36; 20:27). This purpose unifies the narrative, and explains the reason for such passages in Luke as the birth narrative, the announcement of eschatological mission at Nazareth, the passion sayings, and the historical reorientation of the disciples who walked toward Emmaus. These events are necessary *(dei,* cf. Luke 13:33 with Acts 9:16), not in the sense of fixed fate, but in the sense of what God's narrative purpose requires. In this frame, the opening birth stories set expectations for what is to follow: at last, God's saving purpose will be seen to embrace Jews and Gentiles. Next, Jesus accepts his mission, and goes about releasing sins and healing sicknesses. He is open to outsiders, ministering to the oppressed and excluded. But then comes a "tragic turn": Jerusalem rejects its messianic king. Yet God integrates this rejection into the divine purpose, overruling human purposes. The disciples can understand none of this, but at Passover and Easter, a crucial change occurs. The Gospel ends on a note of hope. A strength of Luke's account is that in Acts the story continues (as is only implied in the other Gospels), and there it becomes clear that the way of the cross is not left behind, but must reappear in the ongoing Christian mission (Tannehill, 1986–90 I:8f; 2f).

We saw at the outset of this chapter (§1) that the true story of Jesus was seen by the Gospel writers and the critical historians alike to come to sharpest focus in his trial and death. For the earliest Christians, exalting in Christ's resurrection, this focus was at once problematic and unavoidable. Over the centuries later Christians contributed "theories" (but were they that?) to reconcile the fact and its shame, or to "explain" the cross. The New Testament writers had not done that, but had employed lively metaphors that linked Jesus' death to Old Testament themes. Yet metaphors are nothing without the narratives in which they come to life. The written Gospel was the New Testament's ultimate contribution to Christian understanding. Our business now is to see how that constitutive *narrative* worked and works, relating both metaphors and "theories" to itself.

§3. How Jesus Saves

It may be helpful here to take our bearings afresh. In this Part II of *Doctrine*, the focus is upon the identity of Jesus Christ. Who is it whom the church confesses to be Savior and Lord? At this chapter's beginning we recalled the secure historical facts of Jesus' existence. These are neatly focused by the creed's "crucified under Pontius Pilate," or, with an important difference, by the Apostle's tradition: "died for our sins, in accordance with the scriptures . . . raised to life on the third day" (1 Cor. 15:3f). Paul's report of what had been handed on to him shows this dishonorable death inescapable for the apostolic mission, and already in New Testament times Christian thought sought its rationale, while later tradition eventually provided more and more elaborate (and mutually conflicting) stories having the same goal. A fundamental role of all these narratives was to answer the question, Who is Jesus Christ? They answered by saying in effect, "Jesus is the one who by his tribulation inaugurated the new age" (the earliest preaching), or "the one who on such and such terms endured this passion" (the Gospels), or "who facing such and such enemies (or obstacles, or needs), met them by the cross" (the historic atonement-types). These assorted identification strategies have at least one thing in common—all have a narrative shape. To identify Jesus and account for his cross, they narrate. Sometimes, as in the Gospels and Acts, the narrative form is explicit; sometimes, as in the Letters, it is implicit, and setting, characters, and plot are visibly variegated in all these texts.

a. Atonement theories as **midrashim.**—It follows that the church's identification of Jesus is the story of Jesus. To the question, Why the cross? the right story, rightly told, is the right answer. The next chapter will show this right story effectively answering the underlying questions that have shaped christological doctrine. Yet "the right story" seems to beg the question. Granting the necessity for narrative (a case argued in *Ethics*, Twelve), which is the 'right' story? From many Gospels, ancient Christianity selected four, not one. And when we recover the narrative shape of the later 'theories' of atonement, we find conflicting narratives. *Which* story is adequate? The full answer will take us beyond this chapter, and indeed, on to *Volume III.* Yet a beginning can be made here.

We may begin by taking a leaf from Jewish interpretive practice. Commentary on the Hebrew Bible was important from the beginning of Rabbinic Judaism, and had attained a high degree of precision by 500 C.E. It fell into two classes, legal clarification of Scripture *(Halakhah)* and narrative exposition *(Aggadah).* To the latter class belonged rules for exegesis, verse-by-verse comments on texts, and rabbinic sermons. In time all this was collected into volumes arranged according to the books of the Hebrew Bible, and these were eventually translated into the vernacular (S. Hurwitz, ERE VIII:624-28). An instance is *Genesis Rabbah,* a multivolume commentary on Genesis, which took final form by 400 of the Common Era (Neusner, ed., 1985).

Two features of this practice are of present interest. First, the rabbis exercised what would today seem extreme freedom in interpretation.

They never rejected the text of what they held to be inspired Scripture, but they never seemed constricted by it. Interpretation was set alongside contrary interpretation without apparent discomfort. Most often, *midrash,* as these interpretations are named, enlarged the biblical story. For a single example, the comment on Genesis 22:1 provides an argument between Isaac and Ishmael, his older half-brother. Each claims to be more beloved than the other, and young Isaac boasts that he is willing to sacrifice one of his own limbs. Whereupon, "the Holy One, blessed be he," interjects a comment: "If I should tell you to offer yourself up to me, you would not refuse" (Neusner, ed., 1985:270). Thus a narrative with at best minimal footing in the text enlarges the great narrative of the 'binding of Isaac.'

The second feature is equally interesting. Rabbinic *midrash* was especially concerned to indicate contemporary relevance. An example, again from *Genesis Rabbah:* By the fifth century, Rome remained a powerful presence in the East, and this had become (as Jews saw it) a "Christian" presence. So the story of Israel in Genesis—of Abraham and Sarah in Egypt and Canaan, of Ishmael and Isaac, of Jacob and Esau, of Joseph and his brothers—is retold in the *midrashim* with an eye on this threatening Roman Christian power—a power that claimed to be "true Israel"! In response, the rabbis' narratives contrasted the privileged and unprivileged heirs in Genesis, noting how Isaac not Ishmael, Jacob not Esau, in turn inherited the promise. Rome was Esau, or Rome was Ishmael, they implied. Thus the commentary acknowledged the kinship of Israel and Christian Rome, while resisting the Roman claim to be true Israel (Neusner, 1987:chap. 8).

It would be a mistake to make too much of this parallel. I am not claiming that Christian theologians of atonement consciously adopted Jewish exegetical methods, or that they conceived their work, as did the Tannaim and Amoraim, as word-by-word illumination of the biblical text. Those are real differences. Nevertheless, there is a striking parallel here, for the chief atonement doctrines of Christian history exhibit implicit or explicit narrative forms. Irenaeus and Gregory with their conflict and ransom plots, Anselm and Calvin with their tales of a quest for divine "satisfaction," Abelard and Moberly and Bushnell with their psychologizing analyses of a costly inner journey—all posit atonement **narratives.** Further, the Christian thinkers, like the rabbis, exercised powerful theological imagination in (re)forming their narratives to make the message clear. Again like the rabbis, they formed their stories against particular historical settings. *Diognetus* and Irenaeus (not unlike the authors of *Genesis Rabbah*) worked in awareness of powerful Rome. Anselm defended a divine honor greater than the feudal honor of the

Song of Roland. Bushnell told of a healing Jesus who might evoke the repressed sympathy (and heal the overt alienation) of hustling, bustling America. Each found light in the pages of the New Testament, informed by the Old, for his own time and place in the churches' long journey.

In Chapter Eight we will have reason to compare the parallel paths of church and synagogue once more. Here the comparison provides perspective on the contribution of Christian tradition to atonement doctrine.

Of what use now are these varied, free readings of the Jesus story? Or, as some would ask, which is to be ours? Is not the answer this: *None are ours, since the setting has changed—and all are ours for the light they shed on the one story of Jesus and God*. What we gain from all is not only a sense of the care their makers shared, but the responsibility they accepted toward their own generation under God. Each of the great Christian *midrashim*, as we may name these 'theories' from the past, has its special thrust or force, worthy a place in today's doctrine. From the ancient *Christus-victor midrash* we gain the theme of cosmic conflict fought out on earthly terms as many a witness endured demonic evil and held fast to Christ, who (once for all) has overcome. From the medieval (and later) satisfaction *midrashim* comes awe at the divine righteousness working in Jesus and at work still. In the modern subjective *midrashim* (with their Anabaptist antecedents) we recognize the self-involving character of the cross.

> Renouncing all, they choose the cross,
> And claiming it, count all as loss,
> E'en home and child and wife.
> Forsaking gain, forgetting pain,
> They enter into life.
> (Jörg Wagner, 1527, *Ausbund*, 1564,
> trans. David Augsburger, 1962)

Yet none of these narratives was meant to replace, but only to illuminate, the story Scripture tells.

My intuition is that the church will return to the theme of sacrifice, historically very little explored. The New Testament's sacrificial metaphors have so far reappeared only in subordinate roles. Bushnell called his great work *The Vicarious Sacrifice*, but his account owed little to the ancient rites. Anglican theology centered the work of Christ in the incarnation not the cross, while its sacrificial focus was related chiefly to eucharistic doctrine (Franks, 1962:448-55; cf. Hicks, 1930).

The appearance late in the twentieth century of the work of René Girard, a French-American student of culture and a Christian, illustrates this recurrence. For Girard, the principal role of culture is to resolve the endemic human drive to violence, so prominent in the twentieth century. His works address its cause and remedy (e.g., Girard, 1977). He *equates* sacrifice with violence, and sees sacrificial ritual as only a routinizing (and to that degree a limiting) of the destructive drive in human nature. Its paradigm is scapegoat rituals. Here violence is (partly) curbed; the violence against the scapegoat substitutes for the murder of our actual rivals. Though such formal rituals are now abandoned, societies still create inner cohesion by finding a target against which to vent their hostile drives. Jews have frequently endured this victimization (Girard, 1986). Jesus was crucified, according to Girard, as a scapegoat. Yet Jesus, whose life and teaching utterly opposed violence, brought an end to violence for all who would follow him. His death signals the end of the kingdom of violence and is thus ironically a sacrifice to end all sacrifice. Unfortunately, Girard believes, historical Christianity has largely missed this central point, returning to sacrificial ritual (the mass) and to sacrificial politics ('Christian' civilizations founded on violence) just as if Jesus' divine message had never been delivered. So Girard's theological message (in this regard closely paralleling that of this book) is a summons to radical recovery of the original gospel (Girard, 1987). It would be pretentious to offer here a minuscule appraisal of Girard's overall enterprise, of which his interpretation of the cross forms a small though crucial part. Clearly he assesses sacrifice, and sacrificial death, very seriously, only to reject the aspect of sacrifice as fellowship with deity and to construe it as part of the human race's original sin of violence against substitute victims, whether animal or human. Further interpretation of Girard is left as work others may undertake (cf. Theophus Smith and Mark Wallace, 1994:Intro.).

b. Jesus' saving work—and ours.—Christian atonement teaching comes in narrative form. It is, to quote the gospel song, "the old, old story / Of Jesus and His love." It came out at chapter's beginning that the *unquestionable* facts about Jesus are far too sparse to explain what the cross involved, much less to show how in connection with it God and humanity are made one. Yet what of the (challengeable, yet true) story Christians know? In asking this question, we return to the chapter's beginning with its original question, "Since Christ is God's own Savior, why the cross?" still confronting us.

i. Binding the strong man.—From time to time in this work we have returned to some form of the constitutive narrative of Christian faith; now we do so again. The story can only partly be told until its full harvest is gathered into the barns. Yet it remains at the center of all that Christians do and teach and dream. It is from the first a story of electing love—God in love chose Abraham, and from that choice the people Israel sprang. Israel was not chosen for its ethnic or cultural superiority ("How odd of God / To choose the Jews"—Dorothy Parker), nor to hoard the divine blessing, but in order that through it the blessing might be extended to all. This is witnessed in Exodus by the roles of Jethro (i.e., Hobab) and Melchizedek. Jethro in the narrative is Moses' father-in-law, but remarkably, he is also said to be a priest, and a priest who acknowledges that JHWH is "the greatest of all gods, because he has delivered the people from the Egyptians" (Exod. 18:11). This has caused debate about the existence of a Yahweh-cult prior to that of Israel. However that debate is resolved, the striking thing is that the present text of the Pentateuch allows the priest of *Midian,* a hated enemy, to be God's own worshiper. As R. F. Johnson says, "It remains a startling reminder of the comprehensiveness of OT religion that [Moses,] the initial and perhaps foremost proponent of Yahweh . . . should have been sheltered, married, employed, and counseled within the precincts of a priest of Midian" (IDB II:896f). A similar argument rises from the better-known case of Melchizedek—see Genesis 14 and Psalm 110 and its parallels.

From Israel's point of view, the prior question, though, was how to get free from alien sovereignties—an explicit need, whether with William F. Albright (1957:254ff) and John Bright (1953:17-22) we see Israel's national origins focused on the Exodus, or with Norman Gottwald (1979) we locate them in the book of Judges. The divine provision, in either case, was that the nation's fundamental law would not be set by the arbitrary will of an Israelite king, but would rest upon a two-sided covenant: God's part to be Israel's true ruler and lawgiver; Israel's, to keep that law and thus become a "nation of priests" (not, banally, a nation *with* priests). Israel is to be a go-between nation, God's missionary to all the earth.

> I have carried you on eagles' wings and brought you here to me. If only you will now listen to me and keep my covenant, then out of all peoples you will become my special possession; for the whole earth is mine. You will be to me a kingdom of priests, my holy nation. (Exod. 19:4-6)

In time, to be sure, Israel and Judah had their kings, their chariots, their conquests. Yet the 'original' arrangement—God's covenant-love *(chesed)* and God's law *(torah)*—was never utterly lost to sight; it restrained the arrogance of power and invited return to the **rule of God** so nearly lost.

This tug-of-war between Israel's divine commission and her wayward obedience is well known to us because of a unique institution—*biblical prophecy.* Though continuous with other ecstatics, the prophets—source of at least fifteen Old Testament books—bore a distinctive message, "the word of the LORD," and played a decisive part in our story. Their message, simply put, was **God speaking:** God who demanded *tsedeqah* and *mishpat,* righteousness and just action; God who protested on behalf of the victims of oppression; God who held rulers to account; God who summoned Israel to a future, ideal community. This forward look defined the popular idea of prophecy, though apart from the rest of the message its futurity is misleading, since prophets primarily addressed the here and now (Blenkinsopp, 1983; cf. P. Hanson, 1975).

A third element, **priesthood and sacrifice,** was present from the beginning and loomed large in Israel's public life; it provided part of the setting of Jesus' career, and as we have seen furnished New Testament writers with metaphors of his work. Unlike the **rule of God** and **prophecy,** however, it remains in the background of our story, passing off the stage for Judaism in the year 70, and later returning to Christianity only in a misconceived dehistorizing of Christian practice via the medieval "sacrifice of the mass."

God's rule and the rule of human systems, God's word and human words—these were still wrestling, Jacob with his angel, when Jesus of Nazareth appeared. Each of the Gospels is careful to link that appearance with the rule of God, prophecy, priesthood, and promise. But Jesus' venture concentrated on the promised rule (Mark 1:15 par.). This is not merely old but new; God makes a new beginning in Jesus' proclamation. A new world is coming; trust the good news!

Joshua had fought a war of conquest in claiming the land for JHWH. Jesus fought a war of myths. At least that is the way Amos Wilder (1982) and after him Ched Myers (1988) characterize the nonviolent warfare Jesus waged to establish once more on Joshua's own territory, Canaan's land, the new rule of God. From *Jordan,* where this second Joshua passed through the waters en route to conquest, to *Jericho,* whose wall of disbelief collapsed when blind Bartimaeus, authentic disciple, gained sight by faith, to *Jerusalem,* where the first Joshua never marched, the Prince of peace made his triumphant way. God's rule required justice of a sort beyond the rule of law (Myers, 1988:chap. 14); God's reign promised sins sent away and human hurts healed; God's word pierced the injustices of military power (Rome) and religious power (Jerusalem); God's Servant and Son challenged the iniquity of dominating family structure and of ethnic pride; God's Wisdom and Power exorcised the demons that rage within hurt human souls; God's Messiah (but that was a secret) drew men and women into a new fellowship (the disciple church), ordained a new social order (love of enemies), evoked a new hope (the coming of the Truly Human One and the Age to Come). Joshua, the new Joshua, was marching on.

Of course it did not work. The enemies plotted; the disciples doubted; the women were afraid. The invitation to be part of the collective Truly Human One, when extended to all disciples at Caesarea Philippi, enclosed an invitation for them to share the cross. Jesus saw it coming and warned them; compulsively, they asked instead about the Age to Come. Had they had their way, there would have been no cross; had he had his, there would have been thirteen. They declined the honor. One betrayed him; one denied him; all fled (Mark 14:50). He was executed with some other enemies of the powers that be—he alone on a cross where all were to have borne witness. Christ was in their place—by the baptist vision, it was our place. He was buried then, one for all. God was dead.

The sequel both denied and affirmed what had gone before. It denied it: In the resurrection God raised Jesus Christ, that same one, up from the dead, alive with God forevermore. (That reversal occupies the following chapter.) The enemies did not prevail as they intended. The disciples, doubting, returned to follow him. The sequel also affirmed what had gone before: The resurrection was God's sign of self-identification with Jesus who had taken the nonviolent way of the cross. It was God's way, God's *only* way. Our story reveals the continuity of the church that came after with the story of Jesus' earthly career. After their fashion, and in their way, these following disciples then took up the cross; tradition says some died by it; faith declares that all the faithful lived by it. The chief obstacle to their faith, the cross, became the chief content of their faith. God's rule, by the way of the cross, prevailed.

ii. Conclusions.—It remains to test the conclusions reached earlier. The thrust of three historical types of atonement teaching was respectively toward satanic evil, toward God, and toward human nature itself. Clearly, the constitutive story displays the first, devilward vector. It is a constant vector, as old as the divine creative struggle recorded in the Psalms, and climaxing in Jesus' earthly encounter with the representatives of oppressive government, social conformity, and mendacious religion. He met them all with prophetic righteousness; he opposed them; they crucified him. That his defeat was paradoxically the total victory of God's way concludes the constitutive story in triumph. Yet it does this without the weakness of the *(midrashic) Christus-victor* teaching with its fateful link to military Christendom and its abjuration of nonviolence.

The second thrust, toward God, may seem more difficult. In what way does the Jesus story 'satisfy' God? Yet surely that is just what it does if (and only if) it is God's own story—if, as argued above, we cannot exclude God from the action, but must see the Jesus story as exactly what God would do, exactly what God was satisfied to do, on earth. "The universal order and beauty of the universe" (Anselm) is not primarily the order of the stars in their courses or of the *lex talionis* fashioned by human culture. It is the beauty of human community shaped by forgiving, redeeming love—the beauty Jesus lived and died to create. God's satisfaction is no medieval myth; it is God's own action on the scale of

Jesus of Nazareth. The divine artist completes creation's work by enacting redemption's beauty. Thus the constitutive story overcomes the great flaw of the legal *midrash* upon atonement: in the constitutive story, what Jesus does in our place is not merely what God requires but what God does, what God suffers (cf. Chapter Four §2).

The third thrust, toward our own human nature, is evident in the constitutive story, too: Jesus acts to change human life, and he does change it. But finally, it is only his full faithfulness enacted in the cross that changes disciples from observers to participants—from men and women who admire Jesus to women and men who follow him. Thus the constitutive story has the objectivity, the given quality of God's prior action, that Bushnell, for one, knew was needed. So the great story has all the positive elements the *midrashim* from Irenaeus and Anselm and Bushnell have helped us to see, but has them without their special liabilities—without the mythic improbability of a satanic hostage-taker, without the flawed image of a petulant or willful God, without the distorted picture of disciples who can save themselves ("Lord, we are able") by their discipleship—elements that are defects in the *midrashim* taken in themselves.

We have now well begun our theological quest for the identity of Jesus Christ. Seeking to identify him by his work, we find that work involving the personhood of the worker, and the next chapter will pursue that involvement. Yet each inquiry presupposes the other, and we will not reach a time or place where the following quest ceases to point back to the present one.

Jesus the Risen Christ

It is no accident that this chapter stands at the center of the middle volume of this theological work. The title chosen for the young Bonhoeffer's Christology lectures, *Christ the Center*, is a good one for any theology that would be authentically Christian. In approaching such a center one rightly pauses, either to confess the inadequacy of all speech or writing, or to exclaim with Scripture at "the breadth and length and height and depth of Christ's love," praying to know it, even though it is "beyond knowledge" (Eph. 3:18f). Yet alongside this awed gratitude is another impulse, equally Christian, that summons us to think clearly, even critically, about Christ's proper place, to discover in the order of thinking whether the order of devotion is rightly placed, whether in meeting Jesus as the risen Lord we indeed meet true man and true God, so that Jesus Christ can rightly be the center of Christian theology.

In pursuing that task we will draw upon the preceding chapter, where the identity of Jesus was approached by investigating his life's achievement. This approach had the advantage of beginning where the New Testament crests: with the gospel story. Yet when the identity narratives we call Gospels were first circulated, the task of interpreting them gave rise to further questions, and these to still others, until the first great post–New Testament theological debate, the ancient christological controversy, had taken shape. It continued for centuries, and gave lasting (some said permanent) shape to Christian thought. For baptist Christians, to be sure, these controversies and conciliar 'decisions' of the second, third, fourth, fifth, and later centuries do not have the authority that they exercise in creedal communities such as the Catholic and Orthodox. Yet all of us are the heirs of these discussions and must take them into account in our thinking, albeit with an attentive eye toward those counted losers as well as toward the winners (for truth is not always, or even usually, allied with the kind of power that wins fierce ecclesiastical and political wars).

Yet it will be of little use to review these old schemes of thought unless they are seen to address live issues. Therefore this chapter first asks (§1) about **the identity of the One who confronts the church today** (in its worship, in its kingdom work, in its evangelical witness, and in its biblical word), singling out the resurrection of Jesus Christ from the dead as the key to identifying that One. Then (§2) some of the **historic models by which Christians have sought to interpret Jesus** are taken up and tested for inner coherence, and further tested by asking whether they address the underlying christological questions all face. Finally (§3) **another model, that of narrative identity,** is presented and tested by the same standards. Here discipleship to the Risen One is found to serve as a correlative clue to his identity and to our own.

§1. Who Is Jesus Christ Now?

The identity that Christian teaching must clarify for itself is not first of all that of a teacher who lived and died in long ago Palestine. Christians are not a people of antiquarian taste, roaming the relics of lost civilizations, looking for some 'light from the past' that might illuminate their weary minds, and (as it just happens) seizing upon a certain radical rabbi as most interesting of all. We do not begin, then, by asking whether such and such a one was the true God come to earth, or even asking, *Was* this one truly human, flesh of our flesh? Our question is not past but present: *Is the Risen One who confronts us here and now, today, in the common life of the church—is* this one true God, true man, one risen Jesus Christ? For it is this present Christ with whom we must come to terms; it is in him that we must seek our answers. As Bonhoeffer put it in the little book already referred to, "The understanding of the Presence opens up the way for the understanding of the Person" (1978:43).

It has recently become the custom to distinguish Christologies "from below" and those "from above." As Norman Kraus explains, the former begin "with the account of a concrete historical person"; the latter begin with "an ontological picture such as was developed in the third and fourth century creeds" (Kraus, 1990:36). Neither of these seems honest as a method, however, for each purports to begin in ignorance of what it surely knows, that is, the rest of the story. And both seem wrong insofar as they neglect the actual beginning point for any Christian community: the church now confronts a present Christ. This may be beginning "from below" in a sense; like all good theology it tries to discover present doctrine. Yet the one who is present, the present Christ, is not in the grave, but is the risen Lord. So perhaps this is Christology "from above," though not from the ancient creeds. Yet perhaps it is better to concede that it is neither one?

a. *The present Christ.*—To speak in this way of Jesus Christ in the midst is to invite two sorts of challenge. "The present Christ" may be misunderstood as being only a claim made about the spiritual experience of individual or gathered Christian believers. Or it may be contrary to what Christians think they know about life in this age, simply incredible. Since the latter challenge is on its face more serious, it is here addressed first. Addressing it will put us in position to correct the former, anthropocentric misunderstanding of Christian convictions.

The fact (and the mode) of Christ's present presence is a matter of the highest importance for theology. Others have addressed this under the headings of a sacramental real presence, or of a Christ-mysticism, and their witness must be weighed. But there is a preliminary demurrer: does not the narrative of the ascension (Luke 24:50f; Acts 1:1-9) actually teach an absent rather than a present Christ? Yet the answer must be No. For the role of the ascension is exactly to prepare the way for the full gift of God's Holy Spirit to the disciple community. The Spirit's coming is throughout the New Testament the inward divine means by which the Christian community, and thus the individual disciple as well, are provided access to the present Christ. Here a paradigmatic instance is Stephen's vision in his martyrdom. He sees "the glory of God, and Jesus standing at God's right hand," that is, in the place of God's own majesty. Where, then, a trinitarian may ask, is the Spirit? But the text has already answered: "Stephen, filled with the Holy Spirit, and gazing intently up to heaven, saw . . ." (Acts 7:55-59). By the Spirit's filling, Stephen sees that the Christ present to him is the exalted Christ.

If the Spirit is God at work within, how, concretely, does God work to realize Christ's presence today? The New Testament points to at least four related practices: the Risen One present to his church in common *worship*, present in kingdom *work* and disciple *witness* to friend and stranger, and present in hearing the biblical *word* itself. Let us test these, beginning with worship. Reserving further analysis until Chapter Nine, it is enough here to say that in common worship disciples meet their Lord. This is the case whether it be laborer Christians under the claim of hot gospel preaching and heartfelt gospel music, or the earnest prayer meeting of concerned Christian women confronting the daunting challenge of overseas missions, or the weekly (and more frequent!) breaking of bread by Swiss Brethren and their successors, or the quiet awe of the Society of Friends gathered to await the inner light. In each case this worship, along with the possibly better-known liturgies of Protestant and Catholic churches, has been the very substance of *meeting*. "For where two or three meet together in my name, I am there" (Matt. 18:20). Thus *meeting room* or *meetingplace* (rather than the often used "sanctuary") is the fitting name for these diverse places of worship.

That Christ is present in the disciples' *witness* and in kingdom *work* as well is the firm promise of Scripture (Matt. 28:19f: "I will be with you always"; cf. Matt. 25:40 KJV: "unto . . . the least of these"). Christians have often sensed that when they followed in the Master's steps of service and when by word and deed they told his story, they did not work and witness alone. In their faithful witness and work for Christ they found Christ himself fully present; their action was truly his. Especially has this been the awareness of those who risked reputation, injury, and life itself for the cause of the homeless, the hurt, the helpless. One luminous instance among many, striking in its reversal of more familiar motifs, is the story in *Martyrs Mirror* of Dirk Willems, the baptist who in 1569 fled his persecutors across the winter's ice. When his lone pursuer broke through the ice, Dirk turned back to save the other from certain death. Thus Dirk was caught, and tried, and burned to death for his 'Anabaptism.' But as he suffered he cried out "over seventy times" to "My Lord, my God," and the like (*Martyrs Mirror*, 1660:741f; cf. McClendon, 1991b). If we judge that his Lord was indeed present to him at the stake outside the Asperen town wall that day, we can associate his story with unnumbered others, reaching back to Stephen the first Christian martyr (Acts 7:54-60), that link Christ's presence and this costly passion.

Characteristic of worship, work, and witness alike is a pervasive mode of Christ's presence: the read and studied *word* of Scripture. John Baillie speaks somewhere of realizing the Presence "through the pages of a book," the Bible. The "old, old story" that the book tells is supremely this story; in it, we meet Jesus, and are reminded of Cleopas and another disciple who, en route to a village named Emmaus, met a stranger who showed them in "the whole of Scripture" the things concerning the Messiah (Luke 24:27). The Emmaus road is traveled again even when the one who opens the Book for us is painfully poor or distressingly inept or personally unappealing. The story of Jesus, told in faith in the congregation as "the simplest sermon" (Bonhoeffer), *is* Christ present; it is the word, the Word, of the living God. In the practice, again Christ is there. It is told that Bonhoeffer startled more than one of his Finkenwalde students by saying, as they sat down together to review the sermon manuscript the student had produced, "Now let's see what God is saying to us in your sermon" (cf. Fant, 1975). This understanding of Christ's presence was neither mechanical nor magical; it did, however, mean that God's faithfulness was unfailing: "my word . . . will not return to me empty" (Isa. 55:11). If the broader principles of this present book are correct, the Bible, interpreted according to the "this is that" baptist vision, serves as norm and guide for worship, work, and witness as well; these are means of Christ's presence exactly when and as they function as the true-to-type repetitions of the word of God that itself presents the Risen Christ (cf. *Ethics,* One, pp. 31-35).

b. An excursus on knowing.—Does "knowing the Risen Christ" even make sense, though? Such 'knowing' (if that is what it is) seems significantly different from knowing Thom, or Nancey, or Ereina, or Juan. Yet if knowing Christ is so utterly different, might even to call it "knowing" be more bold than true? While a fuller discussion of the theory of knowledge must await *Volume III*, it may be helpful here to point out a few features of knowing (and of the word "know") that will affect our answer. It will come out then that the verb "know" in English is used in several distinguishable ways, depending on whether that which is known is fact, or skill—or knowing another who knows *us*. Consider some differences between these sorts of knowing. First, to know *someone* (Thom, or Ereina) is in important ways unlike knowing *that* (Thom has a haircut, or Zimbabwe's capital is Harare), and these again are unlike knowing *how* (to tie a square knot). For a first difference, I can 'know that' at second hand—if you knew such and such was the case, and you told me, it is fair, usually, to say that now I, too, know that such and such was the case. But I cannot *know Thom* in this secondhand way. If you know him, and you tell me you do, it does not follow that now I know him—though perhaps I now know something more about him. Second, then, if I am to know him at all, Thom and I must get acquainted. If we follow plain English usage here, anyone who is to know Thom must somehow or other manage to meet Thom. To illustrate this, the writer of a biography may know a great deal *about* Franklin D. Roosevelt, including many things that Franklin's wife, Eleanor, never knew. Yet it is still perfectly intelligible to ask the highly informed biographer, "Did you ever know him yourself?" So knowing FDR is not merely the sum of (even vast) knowledge *about* him. Admittedly, there are exceptional cases where the indispensable meeting and exchange with another take unusual, even bizarre, form: You are blind, and get to know your secretary by his voice alone. Or you and I are in adjacent prison cells and we 'meet' only by code rappings on the stone wall that separates us. Yet significantly, we may actually get to know one another (and not just about one another) in that way. Hence (a third point about English usage—for other languages make similar points in their own ways) we can claim to know another only when the other can properly claim to know us also. Thus I don't say I know Meryl (a film star), because though indeed we were once introduced, and even chatted a bit, I think "She wouldn't remember *me*." And this is not mere modesty on my part; it is strict adherence to the reciprocal grammar of the word "know" when used of knowing persons. For in our language, "knowing another" is necessarily reciprocal, and in this way is beyond mere "knowing that" or "knowing how," though it incorporates aspects of these two: I will not claim to "know her" if I know *nothing about* her; not claim to "know him" if I cannot say how I came to do so.

Now apply all this to a contemporary disciple's knowing her Lord: First, knowing the Risen One, because it falls in the class of acquaintance with other persons, is not a mere knowing *about* Jesus of Nazareth; second, the requisite meeting, though here as in other cases absolutely indispensable, is evidently of the exceptional sort, recalling the equally odd resurrection narratives; third, the ways of knowing—worship, work, witness, word—are indeed ways only if in each one genuine *reciprocal* relations between ourselves and the Risen One are established. Thus true hearers of the word will not only hear but also obey (James 1:22) if what they encounter is indeed that living Word. And Christian *worship* that knows its holy Object cannot be carried on by mere spectators or observers, however keen. Instead, in the remembering signs and in the dynamics of prayer and in all their worship, disciples engage One who meets them there. Again, authentic kingdom *work* cannot be mere moral self-investment, however selfless ("Though I give my body to be burned"—1 Cor. 13:3 KJV), for it is truly undertaken only in company with One who works in, and with, and through our own working. And again *witness* for Christ, if it be a way of knowing him, cannot be some kind of propaganda. If it is witness, it is an engagement with others in which the stranger encounters Christ in the witness and the witness finds Christ in the stranger. In all these forms, our claim, to know Christ, will be grammatically appropriate—a plain claim that plainly can be tested—if and only if a reciprocal relation between him and us is thus established, and if and only if in that reciprocity Christ is ever the initiator, ever the primary partner, while our confessing to know him is hedged with suitable eschatological reserve. Paul incorporates these both, God's prevenience and our eschatological reserve, when he writes "now I know in part; but then shall I know even as also I am [already] known" (1 Cor. 13:12 KJV). The Risen One knows us in our work and worship as well as through word and witness; thus in part, but truly, we know him also. To put the matter in motto form, knowing is a social, not a solitary, accomplishment.

Correspondingly, biblical concepts of work and worship, word and witness, are also social and not merely individual aspects of Christian life. The characteristic biblical words here are "fellowship" *(koinonia)*, and "congregation" *(ekklēsia)*. "*Christian fellowship*" means that Christian community is in every instance community of which the Lord Jesus is a member; he witnesses exactly when and as the community truly witnesses, he prays (in his mediatorial humanity, 1 Tim. 2:5) when and what the community prays; he shows hospitality when the church becomes a refuge and a sanctuary; he strengthens, counsels, rejoices in new life delivered, celebrates at weddings, weeps at funerals, befriends, chastises, gives to the needy, loves his own, sends upon mission—all this as and when and where the fellowship called church does each and all of these things (cf. Bonhoeffer, 1978:58f). The Colossian Letter says that God's secret purpose is expressed in this motto: "Christ in you, the hope of glory" (1:27). What modern English translations leave concealed, however, is that here as so often in Pauline writings this "you" *(humin)* is plural; the body of Christ is not I but we, not me but us. *Christian* fellowship means that the congregation is never alone: "For where two or three meet together in my name, I am there among them" (Matt. 18:20).

c. The resurrection as key to Christ's identity.—So Jesus Christ is alive: Otherwise we cannot know him. Our personal acquaintance, this strange corporate friendship, does not by itself tell us what happened on the first Lord's day, but it does make the question of what happened then a live issue for the teaching church. Let us inquire about this.

i. The appearances.—Christ's presence today gives perspective to our reading of the resurrection 'absences' (as we may name the stories of the empty tomb) as well as the appearances to disciples (for one summary of these, see 1 Cor. 15:5-8). Some suppose that knowledge of the resurrection was easy for the first generation but has now become more difficult. Is it not the other way around, though? We have the vantage point of long experience; we have "so great a cloud of witnesses"; we can distinguish the modes of his presence because they have been affirmed and clarified in the ongoing "lively experiment" (Roger Williams) of many Christian generations. Søren Kierkegaard addressed this paradoxical fact under the heading of "contemporaneity" (1844; 1850). The first disciples lacked our apparent advantages; still it is their Jesus with whom we are contemporary. Yet, if the church of the future needs our witness, we need the primitive witness even more, for, puzzling as the early appearances clearly were, their witness in Scripture still provides a typical pattern by which to structure our own awareness of the Present One.

Certain recurrent features of this witness show us what we may anticipate. First and foremost, the appearances (including here the 'absences' with them) give evidence that in having to do with Jesus after Easter, the disciples were having to do *with God* as well. This is brought out in the texts by their numinous character, and by the awe, even bewilderment, of the witnesses: they were dumbfounded, astonished, speechless with awe, we are told over and over again. These testimonies are of transcendent importance because it is only as we are assured that the Risen One is bearer of true Divinity that our worship is protected from idolatry: "You must have no other god besides me" (Exod. 20:3). 'Risen presence' apart from God would be mere necromancy, mere superstition; risen presence is *Divine* presence or it is nothing to faith.

Second, the appearances conveyed a message about *the future.* They prefigured the gift of the Spirit to disciples; they gave direction for mission; they indicated that the coming reign, far from having been defeated in the Master's crucifixion, was now to be the disciples' concern because it remained God's own concern (see, e.g., Acts 1:1-11; John 20:21-23). Rather than retreat and defeat, they were summoned to service in a new order, subjects now of a risen Lord. To see the present Christ in this scriptural frame is to see our own kingdom work and witness, our daily prayer, and our Bible hours being conformed to the vector of God's coming rule as well.

Third, the appearances signaled that the future with Christ would conform to what the disciples had known of him before. In short, despite some difficulties in recognition, the followers collectively made sure that the One who was alive was the very one they had known, *Jesus of Nazareth,* that man. This awareness is especially prominent in the 'absence' episodes where it is another (an angel?) who displays the empty grave. "See, here is where your master lay." Most of all, this note of continuity tells us that our *own knowledge of his presence requires for its very intelligibility the resurrection of Jesus Christ, that one, from death.* If he is present, death for him is ended.

For the resurrection itself was neither the appearances to them nor the Presence we find with us; nor was it the descent of the Spirit; nor again was it the formation of the church. Rather the resurrection was and is that prior event that has made each of these, the appearances, the giving of the Spirit, the Christian movement itself, and our own witness today possible. The resurrection is the *principium*, the basis, from which these follow as consequences, indeed as results. Therefore it is only by a logical fallacy ('affirming the consequent') that the various appearances, or the empty tomb, or even today's living testimony in the church, are made into proofs of the resurrection (per contra Pannenberg, 1968:chap. 3). They do, however, coherently point to it, for they are what we might expect to find if the resurrection itself is true.

But in the Gospels the disciples were initially baffled, for they had not expected a contemporary resurrection at all. When Jesus had there predicted his resurrection they could have understood him to mean only that he would rise *at the last day* (J. A. T. Robinson, IDB IV:45), for in their time this was a standard Jewish expectation. To their utter surprise, what was to have happened at the end came instead in the midst of time. They could hardly take it in. But when they did, everything was changed. Some have supposed that the resurrection is a mere hypothesis, suited perhaps to the worldview of a bygone era that believed in wonders and miracles; no longer credible today. We will consider the "myth versus history" school of thought in the next section; here I can point out that the passing of an age has not canceled the demand that we offer a reasonable account of the fact that Christian believers then and now encounter a living Christ. If our theory about what can happen in history denies the very possibility of resurrection as explanation of this central fact, then perhaps as Richard R. Niebuhr has suggested we need to give up, not the resurrection, but our present theory of history (1957). For the doctrine of the resurrection of Jesus Christ from death is not the mere residue of an outworn worldview.

Nor does the apostolic testimony permit us to construe Jesus' resurrection as *the mere resuscitation of a dead body*, in a class with the restoring to life of a drowned swimmer or the reviving of an electrocuted lineman. Such a resuscitation (and is this not what other raisings in Old Testament and New amounted to?) cannot even account for such features of the appearance accounts as the ability of the Risen One to pass through closed doors and to appear and disappear at will. Far less can it do justice to the new *status* that the New Testament assigns to the risen Lord Christ. We recognize this status in his granting power to his community to forgive sin—for it is in resurrection light that Christians must read Matthew 18:18-20 (the "Rule of Christ" to the Anabaptists), as well as John 20:19-23 (the breathing of the forgiving Spirit into the Apostles).

ii. The resurrection itself.—The concept of a new status brings us very close to the New Testament's own understanding of Jesus' arising from the dead. If we focus on the human story of Jesus we see a man vividly conscious of God's electing choice of Israel and of his own destiny with regard to that election: Somehow it will be fulfilled in him and in the followers he will choose in turn. So, beginning with his baptism at the hands of John, Jesus took the way of commitment to the rule of God, commitment to God's choice, the life that it demanded, and the cost that it exacted. Confronted by opponents, threatened by authorities, abandoned by friends, he held fast to his Father's way—and died faithful to it. Now what? Beyond the suffering that reached its depths in his state-sponsored execution, there was death itself. Death in Hebrew thought was understood not as utter annihilation, but rather as descent into a shadowy realm of loss (cf. Chapter Two). Clearly the body was destroyed, and clearly there could be no human hope that disregarded the integrity of life in the body. Dead in body, Jesus of Nazareth was utterly and hopelessly—dead. No 'immortality' offered comfort to his story.

Yet where God is concerned even death's finality is not final. And the Jesus story is also the story of God's utter involvement. God acted; God raised Jesus Christ from the dead "on the third day," that is, after the intervening Sabbath of rest. What did, what could, that "raising" be? I have tried to say what the New Testament writers did *not* mean by the event they called the "resurrection," or the "awaking" from sleep, of Jesus of Nazareth. What *did* they mean? I answer that *this was an act of God in time, reversing history's judgment as represented by the authorities, by the opponents, even by the hapless friends of Jesus. All these read history's judgment to be: death to this one. The resurrection opposed that judgment by entering God's own judgment: life, Life to this same one. God reversed all human judgment by identifying the life of Jesus of Nazareth afresh with God's own life, so that from that time, and in accordance with an eternal purpose of God, the history of this man, Jesus of Nazareth, was to be counted identical with God's inner history, in such a way that in the knowing of Jesus Christ God could be truly known.*

How can God 're-identify' a human life? In answer we might pause to ask wherein human identity consists in any case? Life encounters unending change. People even 'change their identities.' They do this by changing their addresses and their documents, their facial hair, their occupations—even their mates and their ostensible sex. Moreover, they sometimes change inwardly as well: amnesiacs forget who they are; some deranged people behave as two or more 'persons' in one body. Further, society exercises the power to make 'nonpersons' out of those it considers to be deformed, or monstrous, or politically obnoxious, banishing or destroying them, and willy-nilly society often simply forgets the weak and the helpless. In the face of all this power and our own frailty, our selfhood seems a fragile thing, a frail chip afloat in the rapids of natural and social destiny. But if we believe in God, we believe in one who has the absolute right (as Creator) to identify each one of us, and in that divine-human relation alone we find our identities secure. "Who am I?" is finally unanswerable save in relation to God our origin and God our destiny.

As Jonathan Edwards perceived (1758:397-400), the God who has the authority to identify us each, and who knows us and cares about us with an unceasing full consent or love, has by the power of that undiminishable love the authority to identify us afresh as his own children. Indeed (as we saw in Chapter Two) it is a part of our hope that in Christ we too shall be newly identified by God after our death as his own children. But two things make the re-identification of Jesus unique: First, his comes in the midst of time, while the rest of us await a general resurrection (cf. Chapter Two, §2). And second, Jesus is not identified merely as one of God's children (itself a glorious destiny) but is re-identified, resurrected, as *the unique sharer of God's own identity: for us, by this resurrection, the whole story of Jesus is God's own story.* In the resurrection of Jesus Christ from death, the life of God is made Jesus' life, and Jesus' story (including as its suffering depth his actual death on the cross) is assumed forever into the life of God (who thus assumes death also into his life—the death of God), so that his entire story is now designated as eternally God's own.

This is the proleptic teaching of John's Gospel in its entirety. Writing of Jesus who lived in Palestine, John tells what he knew to be true of the risen Christ. It is also the teaching of Paul in Romans. Christ Jesus was "proclaimed Son of God by an act of power that raised him from the dead" (Rom. 1:4, *ex anastaseos nekrōn*). Someone might justly argue that the status Paul ascribes with the words "Son of God" is less than the full identification of Jesus with God, and that point has been long debated in Christian theology. What cannot be denied in this passage, however, is that God in the resurrection designated, granted, decreed (*horisthentos*, an aorist participle) a new and supreme status to Jesus Christ, so that all Christian grace and mission, indeed the very gospel Paul preaches, depends upon that one eventful grant.

To the objection that this teaching reserves full Sonship to Jesus Christ *only* after the resurrection (and that such postponement smacks of a perverse adoptionism) we must first reply that there are some things in God so deep, so fully Godlike, so true to God's own nature, that there was never a time that they were not true of God. One of these deep things is God's unalterable intention to redeem the world by identifying Jesus' life with God's own life. This was true before all worlds; it was true in the birth depicted by Matthew and Luke; it was still true at the time of Jesus' cry of dereliction on the cross. Thus when at Jesus' baptism the divine voice said "my beloved Son" (Matt. 3:17 par.) it declared as an effective present destiny what was already and eternally God's purpose. The term "adoptionism" is nowadays used in criticizing Christologies that seem to imply "God had to wait around" for someone like Jesus to appear so God could "adopt" the lucky winner as his Son. In that sense, neither Paul nor the present writer is to be reckoned adoptionist: Jesus' Sonship is unique, and it was what God intended for him even "before the foundation of the world" (Eph. 1:4). Spanish adoptianism (note different spelling) is still another program with still another purpose—see encyclopedias of theology.

The resurrection is therefore the actual vindication of Jesus as the Christ; it is as well the formal vindication of God as the Lord of history, and it is the prospective vindication of the world through faith in the crucified and resurrected One (*Ethics*, Nine). Christ's resurrection in the midst of time is an eschatological event, declaring God's ultimate purpose for creation itself, and thus affording to faith a window on the end of the story. To the resurrection itself, the empty tomb and the other appearances are witnesses, as is the birth of primitive Christianity, as is the presence of Jesus Christ to his people today.

There remain for this 'narrative' understanding of the resurrection questions about the significance of the empty tomb and about the nature of Jesus' resurrection body. Could not God have identified the story of Jesus of Nazareth as God's own while allowing the body of the earthly Jesus peacefully to return to mold and soil—dust to dust? If this is conceivable, as I believe it is, it was possible. So the better question is whether it would have been more fitting for God in his act of identification simply to abandon the tomb with its now redundant contents or whether, as Christians confess to be the actual case, to empty it (thus providing a further, secondary sign that would witness to the primary event). I am content to reckon that what did happen was that the tomb was emptied exactly *because*, as the angelic messenger said, "He is not here, but is risen" (Luke 24:6 KJV). Is that not indeed more fitting? As to Jesus' resurrection body, that is best related to what has already been said about bodily resurrection (Chapter Two §2): Our bodies constitute the very possibility of our engagement with one another in this world or any other. Likewise the furnishing of a "spiritual body" (1 Cor. 15:44) to the risen Lord was suited to the Easter encounters, since precisely that body would engage the disciples, establishing his new risen identity and its continuity with the Jesus they had known, as they began to discover their new world—the spiritual age that was beginning. We may think of both the empty tomb and the accessible but spiritual body of the Risen One as instances of what seventeenth-century theologians (and others before them) used to call the "condescension" or "accommodation" of God—meaning not divine snobbery, but God's glad choice of ways and means fitted to human capacities and language and forms of thought.

In the resurrection God guarantees that the One the church now knows and worships and strives to obey is no ghostly projection of our wishes, but is the resurrected Christ—the very Jesus who lived and drew followers and gave his testimony in the death on the cross. This may be the point, or a part of the point, of the writer to Hebrews who exclaims (13:8) "Jesus Christ the same yesterday, and today, and forever." *The resurrection*, in other words, *is the link between the earthly Jesus and ourselves;* without it, we might at best revere a memory or idolize a phantom. Since it has taken place, faith in Christ is anchored in history, exactly in the history of God's own Israel. Yet, as was pointed out at chapter's beginning, this biblical standpoint raised problems for Christians in antiquity and again in modern times that more than any other cried out for solution and consequently preoccupied Christian minds for centuries. To these persistent problems we now turn.

§2. Rival Christological Models

There can be no pretense of reporting in this chapter, even of summarizing, the many christological proposals Christians have adopted. A visit to the library will reveal that volumes, not mere chapters, would be required for the task. However, it is possible to show how this doctrine has taken form under a few dominant types or models (McIntyre, 1966). These models have developed organically, one growing out of another over the Christian centuries. By indicating some of the main models, in only a few pages we can glimpse the development of this thought as a whole. This will be particularly helpful as preparation for Section §3, where I will indicate still another model that I believe can most helpfully guide present understanding in the teaching church.

As we turn to these models, it will be useful to think again of our three underlying questions (Introduction to Part II), remembering that together these point to connections between Christian doctrine on the one hand and Christian morality and worship on the other. Question three goes especially to the level of Christian morality: *How Christ-like must disciples' lives be?* Question two addresses Christian worship with its implied doctrinal claims: *How can monotheists tell the Jesus story?* But question one addresses both of these—doctrine as it designates the place of Christ in prayer and proclamation, and morality as it declares the authority that can and does determine the shape of Christian lives: *What right has Jesus to be absolute Lord?* We need to keep these bearings before us if we are to see how the great models have addressed their common tasks.

a. The Logos model.—The early formulations of Jesus' identity were worked out in the context of the missionary expansion of the Christian movement in the Roman Empire. This involved the missionaries and their converts in two sorts of reflection. One was about appropriate Christian behavior. What kind of family man or woman, what sort of citizen, what sort of participant in the wider society was a Christian to be? What right had Caesar's state to the new Christian's allegiance? Did the rites of initiation and renewal (baptism and Lord's supper) bring about changed lives of themselves, as pagan mystery rites claimed to do? Was Christianity a way of life for the present or only a prophylactic for an afterlife? Finally, Greek or Roman inquirers would hear that "Jesus Christ" was their redeemer, but *who or what was Christ?* If only that last one could be answered properly, perhaps answers to all the preceding questions would fall into place. The other sort of question had to do with missionary strategy itself: How could the gospel of Jesus make its claim, make sense, in a world that was perfectly willing to assume one high God, but that remained open to wild permutations of religion and morality even while it yearned for a salvation that would offer deliverance from this fleshly life and from mortality itself?

In these missionary circumstances, although the primitive Christologies reflected in some New Testament writings (e.g. the Epistle of James) had survived here and there, they came to seem inadequate as the gospel spread, and were eventually attacked by some Christians as "Ebionitic"—a word of obscure origin that may have first referred to poor, pious Jewish Christians in Palestine. Caught in history's backwater after the destruction of the Jerusalem temple in the year 70, these so-called Ebionites would have clung to Jesus as the prophet and Messiah who would soon come again. Ebionites were scorned by fourth-century sophisticates such as Eusebius (*Hist. ec.* xxvii), but we must note that they had in them the root of the matter: a firm grip on the human Jesus; a firm belief in his resurrection and return. Perhaps their fault was simply not to have moved with the Christian majority in changing times; regrettably we know too little of them (cf. G. Schille, ABD I:935-39).

Better known were the Gnostics. A rich vapor of ideas, teaching, and speculation spread across the Empire from the first through the third centuries. Crystallized as a movement that attached itself to many religions including Christianity, Gnosticism taught salvation by way of secret knowledge *(gnosis)* available only to insiders, knowledge that offered escape from this evil world of matter. Theirs was no Ebionite Messiah of flesh and blood; Jesus had only seemed (*dokein*, hence the pejorative label, "docetic") to be a man of flesh, only seemed to die; his actual mission had been to impart the secret *gnosis* of salvation, for flesh could play no role in salvation (cf. K. Rudolph, ABD II:1033-40). Today explicit docetism is defunct in Christian theology. But Gnostic modes of thought reappear in modern existentialism (Jonas, 1963:chap. 13), in Karl Jung's psychology, and wherever among Christian believers mind-matter dualism holds center stage. Thus unreflective docetism still haunts Christian teaching about Christ as it did in the early centuries. In quite different ways, both Ebionites and Gnostics were able to give a decisive answer to our question three ("We *are* indeed becoming Christ-like," they might have said), but their failure to provide satisfying answers to questions one and two limited their effectiveness in the long run.

Though these old patterns of Christian thought now seem dead ends, at least they served to arouse the early thinkers who produced the Logos Christologies. The Logos model was the first widespread post–New Testament model, for it was employed by many of the best minds of the second and third centuries. Apologists such as Justin Martyr (fl. 150) and Irenaeus (fl. 180) in the West, and teachers such as Clement (150–215) and Origen (185–254), both of Alexandria, developed this model so forcefully that it remains a distinctive, albeit inadequate, voice in Western theology even today. The root metaphor, though apparently biblical (Hebrew *dabar;* LXX *logos,* a term which reappears in the prologue of the Fourth Gospel—see Chapter Seven §1), is in their use of it much more closely related to pagan philosophical thought. On this view, God, the high God, is remote and unapproachable. Yet God's *logos* (reason, idea, word, story) is everywhere, being, as these philosophers taught, the logical glue that cements together the known universe. Unsurprisingly, Christian apologists ("contextualists," they might be called today) saw in logos the very vehicle needed to explain the Jewish Messiah to pagans. Christ was the Logos incarnate—not actually the high God, yet truly divine, and as accessible to the wise by reason as to the simple by faith. Logos Christology enjoyed popular success, but its critics saw in it a deep flaw: The gap it opened between the (inaccessible) superordinate God and the accessible (but not fully divine) Christ. John's Gospel (1:1-3) may seem in today's versions to resolve any doubt here: "the Word was God." But in Greek these words can be read to say merely that the word is divine or *a* god *(theos),* not *the* God *(ho theos).* In retrospect, the value of the Logos Christology lay not in its aptness for later times but in its liberating role when it first appeared: Despite the subordinate place it assigned to Christ, it answered the question of Christ's rightful authority (question one) better than Ebionites had, while it overcame the dualism of the Gnostics by affirming the identity of the (spiritual) Logos and the (human) Jesus. In this way it eventually contributed to the formulation of trinitarianism, as well (for an accessible manual on this early period generally, see Norris, 1980).

b. The two-natures model.—The Logos model also formed the intellectual background for the teaching of Arius, a presbyter in ancient Alexandria, known in history as archheretic since he was on the losing side at Nicaea (325). In the spirit of the earlier Logos model, Arius seemed to say that the Logos or Son was in important respects *un*like the Father *(heteroousios)*. The Word was created out of nothing—a step backward from Origen's conception (Grillmeier, 1975:230). From this, Arius' opponents inferred that "there was when he was not." Certainly Arius' opponent Athanasius, also a presbyter or teacher (and later bishop) of the Alexandrian church, replied that the Logos or Word was *of one substance (homoousios)* with the Father. Although some scholars have long argued that the driving motive of Arius' teaching was the preservation of rationality in theology at any cost, others (Gregg and Groh, 1981) have maintained that Arius' real interest was to hold up Christ as the ideal type or goal of human progress. In that case the deep issue for Arius was question three: He wanted to offer teaching that could promote spiritual growth in a century when early Christian fervor was evaporating. In any case, like many of his opponents he held that Christ had no human soul (the Logos took its place), and thus (seen in retrospect) the human nature of Christ was as incomplete for Arius as the divine.

In the year 325, the Roman Emperor Constantine, first imperial convert to Christianity, summoned the bishops of his new church to a council at Nicaea, near the Eastern capital, Constantinople, to resolve the crisis created by the spreading Alexandrian quarrel. One might wish that the pastors of antiquity had met upon their own motion and considered means of keeping the church authentically Christian in face of its adoption to be the Empire's official religion. Instead, the surface issue at Nicaea was technical and metaphysical: One must acknowledge one supreme God; that was taken to be God the Father. How, then, could Christ's place be other than (an Arian) second place? In answer, Nicaea produced a model creed that supported Athanasius (and condemned Arius) by confessing the eternity and identity of substance *(homoousios)* of the Son with the Father: The Son was "God of God, Light from Light, very God from very God, begotten, not made." It also confessed that the Son "was made human" *(enanthropesanta)*, though without defining the resulting human nature. The strength of the Nicene decision was that it attributed full deity to the living, risen Christ. Hence, the very substance of God could be encountered in Christian practice and worship. Thus, question one had a firm answer: Jesus' right to Lordship was grounded in his substantial nature. But what of question two? From a historian's point of view, Nicaea is important because this answer led to the two-natures model: Christ had both a divine and a human nature. Its weakness in its own time and place was the inadequacy of this response to the main concern of question two: how was this high claim about Christ to be related to the very human Jesus story related in the Gospels? Besides that (and perhaps Arius' own chief concern), there was the question what difference all this could make to Christian conduct and character (question three)? Finally, the council failed in its political purpose. It did not make peace between the churches. The losers' views were anathematized; Arius himself was banished, and in the long run with him much of 'barbarian' Christianity north and west of the Roman Empire. Meanwhile in the following century a clamor of theological voices would ring the changes on all the issues Nicaea had not settled.

Noteworthy among these subsequent voices were the 'Cappadocian Fathers,' Basil of Caesarea, Gregory of Nazianzus, and Gregory of Nyssa; these invented new distinctions and offered new clarifications of the recently established Nicene orthodoxy. The Cappadocians insisted on the full human nature of Christ, and proposed that the permeation of Jesus' human nature with the divine was merely potential from the time of his conception and birth, and complete only after the ascension—a hint toward progressive incarnation. Thus these Caesarean pastors sought (far more than Alexandrians such as Cyril) to keep hold of the real life story of Jesus amid the winds of theological speculation (cf. Jenson, 1982).

Another noteworthy variant on the two-natures model after Nicaea was that of Apollinaris of Laodicea (d. 390), who held that Christ's body and soul were human, his mind or spirit *(nous)* divine. Since Apollinaris assumed that human nature was tripartite, his Jesus was thus defective in humanity (as indeed that of both sides at Nicaea may have been). For better or worse, Apollinaris made this defective view explicit, though his intention was merely to emphasize Christ's divinity more clearly. In opposition to him, the Antiochenes, Theodore of Mopsuestia (d. 429) and his pupil, the influential Nestorius (d. 451?), insisted on the full human-ity and full deity of the one Christ. Jesus possessed a complete human consciousness and will, and (as Nicaea had said) was fully divine as well. But Nestorians made a contrary mistake: they failed, according to their opponents, to stress the union of the two natures in one person. Nesto-rius held, for example, that Mary should not be called *theotokos*, "Mother of God"; that seemed grotesque. Rather, Mary was mother of the human Jesus. To his adversaries (whose motives were mixed) Nestorius seemed to teach a Jesus who like an actor plays two roles (or wears two hats), divine and human, in a single play; roles (or as they said, *prosōpa*, faces) united by a shared will. It is noteworthy that the discovery in modern times of Nestorius' own book, the *Bazaar of Heracleides*, has at least tempered many of these ancient criticisms: Nestorius' two-natures Christology was not self-evidently better or worse than his adversaries'; it was different.

What Cyril of Alexandria and his followers neglected to recognize was what kind of human nature Nestorius was talking about. Because (a la Irenaeus) of the perfect obedience Jesus offered up to God, he was the first person since Adam and Eve to be truly human; that is, only he in all of history's sad misadventure had willed as God willed, loved as God loved, and hence lived in accordance with the divine image in which humanity was created. For this reason Jesus' humanity was the mirror image of the indwelling Logos with which it was united. In the technical terminology of their argument, this yielded not a hypostatic but a prosopic union (Chesnut, 1978).

The great opponent of Nestorius was Cyril of Alexandria (d. 444), whose political prestige protected his own rather dubious solution of the problem of the 'hypostatic' or substantial union of divine and human. Cyril, as the heir of Athanasius and Apollinaris, insisted that Christ had strictly speaking only one nature, the divine; after the eternal divine Word joined humanity to himself in the womb of Mary, the resultant human being was *anhypostatic* or 'impersonal': Since by Cyril's day, Christology was complicated by disputes about exactly what constituted human "nature" *(phusis)*, Cyril would say that Christ was human, but not *a* human being. It was better, he thought, to say that Christ was a *divine* person who had taken on flesh. While formally Cyril asserted Christ's humanity, he steered perilously close to abandonment of the two-natures model itself. Cyril's disciple Eutyches (c. 378–c. 452) took the fateful additional step: Though human nature remained in the earthly Christ, it remained only as a drop of water in a bucketful. This was indeed near the old docetism, and Leo I of Rome wrote a letter to the East correcting Eutyches' blunder, though whether the ever more Latin Westerners really understood the Greek Easterners (and vice versa) at this stage seems doubtful.

These varied currents converged at the Council of Chalcedon (451). There on one side were those who above all sought to hold to one coherent nature or will in Christ—to hold to the unity of his incarnate personhood. These were called "monophysites." They sympathized with Apollinaris and Cyril, and were condemned at Chalcedon, though they represented a large part of Eastern Christianity. At the other extreme were those who saw the importance of confessing Jesus Christ

both fully human and fully divine, but who found themselves incapable
of giving a clear account of the link between the two. The leader of these,
Nestorius, had already been excluded at the Council of Ephesus two
decades earlier. Between these Cyrillians and Nestorians were the allies
Rome and Constantinople—as it turned out, the future voice of the
Catholic West and the Orthodox East. These powerful partners made
terminological concessions intended to carry the remaining participants
with them as well. The resultant "Definition" of the Council of Chalcedon (451) declared Christ perfect in manhood, perfect in Godhood,
consubstantial *(homoousios)* both with the Father and with us, born of
Mary (who is thus called *theotokos*), so that the two natures, divine and
human, continue after the union, "unconfusedly, unalterably, undivid-
edly, inseparably" in one "hypostasis" or self-identical person (Norris,
1980:155-59; Grillmeier, 1975:Sec. 3). This settlement, with its four famous adverbs, prevailed (though not without dissent) in the West at
least until the nineteenth century, and the Definition remains the principal document of Western creedal orthodoxy. Yet as already indicated,
Chalcedon drove away the Nestorian and Monophysite East, large and
enduring Christian communions that affirm Nicaea but cannot accept
Chalcedon.

How well, though, did Chalcedon with its two-natures model address
the *underlying* christological questions? Positively, it affirmed a transcendent ground for the Lordship of Christ (our question one), his full
deity, yet despite formal affirmations of his human nature, the Christ
thus affirmed seems remote indeed from the humble Savior of the four
Gospels—a remoteness borne out in Byzantine art with its *Christos
Pantokrator*, a Christ fit to rule empires, but hardly recalling the way of
the cross. Chalcedon's concern with rational coherence (question two)
is genuine enough, but it must nevertheless be asked whether the severe
paradoxes of the Chalcedonian Definition did not violate even ancient
rationality (McIntyre, 1966:chap. 4). Finally, the Definition seemed indifferent to the concern of Monophysites (and that of Nestorians) for the
Jesus story as a viable model of conduct for disciples—touching our
question three. In this regard, the churches and particularly the early
monastic movement were sometimes more Christian than the theology
represented by the creeds.

The two-natures model raised still other problems it could not solve.
One was this: Did Christ acquire his human nature directly from God in
a fresh creative act, or indirectly, through inheritance from his mother?
Attempting to answer, sixteenth-century baptist leader Menno Simons
concluded that since (as the natural science of Menno's day taught) the
female parent contributed nothing to the genetic heritage of her off-

spring, Christ must have acquired his human nature directly from God, merely passing through Mary as through a tube. By Catholic and Protestant traditions, this impugned Jesus' full humanity, and thus provided one more charge to level against Anabaptists in general—a charge repeated in textbooks even today! An early target of this hostility, Joan Bocher of Kent was burned in 1550 at Smithfield outside London for repeating this teaching of Menno's.

Meanwhile other baptists followed Pilgram Marpeck (d. 1556): Also accepting the two-natures model, Marpeck taught that only through his humanity could the Savior be approached by believers, so that Jesus' full humanity, far from being diminished, was the very key to salvation.

On the other hand, if Jesus inherited human nature from Mary, should he not have inherited what was considered the universal human blight of original sin as well? This question led, in the nineteenth century, to the promulgation by Pope Pius IX of the dogma of the "immaculate," that is, sin-free, conception of Mary in the womb of her mother, the legendary "St. Anne." Immaculate conception was a teaching that fit both the two-natures model and also nineteenth-century cultic devotion addressed to Mary. Perhaps rather than either defend or too harshly condemn either of these vagaries (Menno's and Pius IX's) we can attribute them to the limitations of the two-natures model, whether its adherents were Anabaptists, Catholics, or Protestants.

c. The historical model.—It was not only its own paradoxes that finally choked out the two-natures model, but the new modes of thought that began to flower in the eighteenth century and bore their ripe fruit in the nineteenth. The new model was to be historical; it would find its difficulty not in accounting for Christ's humanity but in acknowledging his divinity. Thus it would find itself unable to answer underlying question one, at least as that question had previously been understood. The historical model seemed to place not pope or Bible, but historical research, in the seat of authority. But was historical research fit for such lordship? This difficulty was schematically anticipated by Gotthold Ephraim Lessing (1729–81), who perceived a "wide, ugly ditch" between the "accidental truths of history" and the "necessary truths of reason"— a ditch Lessing said no one would ever jump over. His warning became a motto, symbolically marking the chief puzzle the historical model would face throughout its career.

i. Eschatology and the historical Jesus.—Immanuel Kant (1724–1804) proposed *Sapere aude,* "think for yourself"—that is, exercise critical judgment—as the motto of Enlightenment. Indeed, the optimism of the eighteenth century was never higher than in its confidence that if thinkers had the courage to throw off the ecclesiastical (and governmental) shackles that had bound them, history would at last yield real knowledge. Nowhere was this confidence higher, or more exhilarating, than in the question about who Jesus really was. Lessing, just quoted, also published the "Wolfenbüttel Fragments," portions of a long manuscript work by Hermann Samuel Reimarus (1694–1768), a deistic Hamburg professor. By taking up a 'rationalist' (i.e., miracle-denying) historical stance toward the entire Bible, Reimarus initiated a train of thought that would remake European thinking about Jesus. Reimarus saw that Jesus' preaching had turned upon the call to repent and the announcement of God's kingdom. So, he concluded, Jesus did not aim to found a religion or establish a church. Jesus instead meant to bring in an earthly kingdom that would deliver the Jewish people from oppression. The Gospel account of the passion and resurrection is unhistorical. Rather, when Jesus was destroyed by the authorities, the disciples chose to pretend he had arisen from the dead, while staking their own hopes on an imminent divine intervention, a "second" coming, to overcome the actual tragic ending of the Jesus story. So on Reimarus' view eschatology was the chief thing in early Christianity—along with profound dishonesty and massive self-deception!

Although Albert Schweitzer (1875–1965) in his great survey, *The Quest of the Historical Jesus*, goes on for several hundred pages to detail the work of the questers who followed Reimarus, he believed that after him "the whole movement of theology, down to Johannes Weiss was retrograde," made no progress, since none of the successors till Weiss (followed by Schweitzer) recovered the eschatological character of Jesus' mission (Schweitzer, 1906:13-23). The task of the quest was to face up to this realistic historical reading of the Gospels and nevertheless to rescue from their pages a Christ worthy of worship (a task not made easier by the latent anti-Semitism of most of the questers—see Chapter Eight §2). While Schweitzer canvassed historians, the greatest theological names were Schleiermacher and Hegel. For Friedrich Schleiermacher, religion was a kind of feeling or awareness (*Gefühl*), and the human Jesus' awareness or God-consciousness was perfect in its kind. This perfect awareness constituted a "veritable existence of God in him"—and in that sense constituted Jesus' identity—while the conveyance of his own intense awareness of God to the disciples was Jesus' redeeming activity, his salvific work (CF §§94-101). Clearly the new historical model of Christology was here at work.

Georg W. F. Hegel, Schleiermacher's contemporary in Berlin, was a professed Lutheran who saw his philosophy as elevating and clarifying true Christian teaching. History for Hegel consisted in successive civilizations, each advancing past its predecessor, all together embodying the progressive self-realization of the Absolute Idea (which religion poetically called "God"). Christianity was the "absolute religion" because only it expressed the overriding *idea*, which was the union of humanity and divinity (1821). This idealistic abstraction of Christian teaching may seem a long way from the concrete question, "Who is Jesus Christ?"; nevertheless, the theological and philosophical impact of these two rivals stimulated a growing avalanche of research and speculation. Thanks to Schleiermacher and Hegel, the new, historical (and psychological) model began to take firm shape. Remote from the thought-forms of two-natures Christology, it centered upon two enduring tensions—one between *history and eschatology*, the other between *history and myth*. We must now attend to the first of these tensions.

As Schweitzer could see in retrospect, for much of the nineteenth century the eschatological theme that Reimarus had emphasized was suppressed or dismissed. David Friedrich Strauss, to be sure, recognized the authenticity of the eschatological passages in the Gospels, but for him these were overshadowed by the role of myth. Meanwhile the followers of Albrecht Ritschl, led by their great historian Adolf von Harnack (1851–1930), struggled to interpret Jesus as essentially a teacher of timeless religious truth, dismissing Jesus' proclamation of an imminent return as merely due to the worldview of late Jewish antiquity (Ritschl, 1888; Harnack, 1900). Harnack was stoutly opposed by the French Roman Catholic Modernist, Alfred Loisy (1857–1940), who independently stood closer to Schweitzer and Weiss (see Loisy, 1902). Weiss, in a sixty-seven-page essay (1892) achieved a complete victory, by the standards of German historical science, for the view that Jesus' intended kingdom was to have been nothing but a future kingdom, apocalyptic not gradual, even though this showed Jesus to have been mistaken, so that his strange 'kingdom' was utterly without spiritual value to late-nineteenth-century Europeans. Albert Schweitzer, for example, believed that Weiss had brought the quest for the Jesus of *history* within sight of its goal, but Schweitzer's own concluding chapter, "Results," found such a historical Jesus of no religious value: the historical Jesus "passes by our time and returns to His own" (1906:399). Eschatology, we might say, had swallowed up history.

ii. Myth and the historical Jesus.—Consider now the other tension within the historical model that has drawn lasting attention: the place of myth. David Friedrich Strauss (1806–74), a tutor in theology at Tübingen, thought he could solve the christological problem by locating a myth-making tendency within the Gospels. The myths that Strauss identified (such as the transfiguration and the feeding of the 5,000) would serve as clues to the Hegelian "idea" that Jesus' life represented. This idea, as the "myths" confirmed, was the concept of Absolute Spirit expressing itself through the entire history of the human species. Strauss' book was a sensation; translated into English (by 'George Eliot' the novelist), it was often reprinted and everywhere discussed. Though the eschatological school with its unyielding historicist picture of Jesus was in its time to triumph, the myth theorists would remain a powerful solvent at work within that historical model, for the idea of myth seemed at a stroke to relieve the Gospel accounts of their most difficult historical feature (since by definition miracles were not historical events), while at the same time it attributed a positive 'religious' value to these stories. What by Strauss' lights could not be true of Jesus (e.g., that he rose from the dead!) was in an adjusted sense true instead of the entire course of human history. It was not Jesus but "humanity" that dies, rises, and ascends to heaven as it displays an emerging communal "higher spiritual life"—and that is the real substance of the Christ myth (Strauss, 1846:#149).

What is the proper place of myth in Christian theology? Already as the New Testament period drew to a close, the mythic impulse of old Greece came washing in upon the young Christian movement. As early as the later New Testament books, it became necessary to resist that influence. "Have nothing to do with godless and silly myths," wrote the author of one later epistle (1 Tim. 1:4; see also 2 Tim. 4:4; Titus 1:14; 2 Pet. 1:16). Of course the word "myth" is used today in myriad ways, many of them innocuous (Kirk, 1970). I believe, however, that when two particular senses of "myth" are combined, the result is a powerful and perverse tendency in present-day theology. For one writer, "myth" may be used to mean a story of the gods (or of God). If this stood alone, it would appear that the entire Bible is (as a matter of definition) "mythic," and if that is all that is claimed, no harm is done. On the other hand, "myth" sometimes means a story of events outside our time and space, in "another world," *in illo tempore,* and thus nonhistorical, a use that is typical of what Mircea Eliade calls "archaic" religions (1949:chap. 1). If the Bible is in this second sense a mythical book, it cannot be a historical one. Or rather, to the extent that its contents are mythical, they are not historical. Again, this is a harmless claim if it merely notes that some biblical stories seem to have no earthly referent. But when the two senses are combined and **in combination** applied to the central biblical narrative, then the Bible, to the extent that its account of Jesus is mythical, can speak of God only at the cost of being unable to speak of history. Thus it will be unable to make any sense of God's historical involvement with

Jesus of Nazareth. If incarnation is *in this double sense* a myth, the historical model is helplessly unable to answer underlying question one, "What right has Jesus to be absolute Lord?" because such an understanding of the historical Jesus is necessarily mythical—and thus outside history itself. In sum, the mythic Jesus, if divine, is not historical (and therefore *not* incarnate), while Jesus, if historical, is not mythical and in these terms not divine. Case closed.

One would have thought such difficulties sufficient to turn the masters of the historical model away from myth altogether. Yet in our own century one influential German theologian and his followers, and an entire school of English Christologists as well, each working with versions of the historical model, have employed myth as a central concept. Rudolf Bultmann (1884–1976) made *Entmythologisierung* (usually translated "demythologizing") a central task of Christian exegesis. His program, still deeply embedded in post-Hegelian idealism, combined enormous skepticism about the actual Jesus of history with intense antisupernaturalism. The stated goal of his program was to escape the hardening of dynamic gospel insights into objectified factual claims, for these necessarily miss the point of the biblical myths. Their point was to stress the transformation of human existence by faith here and now. Yet Bultmann did not thereby escape all of the difficulties that beset the predecessors who like him employed the historical model.

In a world of thought rather more accessible to English readers than Bultmann's are the British scholars who produced *The Myth of God Incarnate* (Hick, ed., 1977). The common theme of this collection is suggested by its title: the incarnation is a myth, appropriate to the sanctuary, perhaps, but unacceptable in the historian's study. The wedge these authors drove between incarnation and history seemed to make simple the answer to our question two (How can monotheists tell the Jesus story of the Gospels?): as historians, they simply cannot. Yet this consequence is not certain, partly because the essayists in this volume never say clearly what they mean by myth. A positive use of their contribution in other terms will nevertheless be attempted later in this chapter (§3b.i).

iii. Assessment of the historical model.—Though it was most novel and most discussed, the historical model was not the only one afloat after the Enlightenment engulfed European thought. The two-natures model was continued, especially among Catholics and conservative Protestants, and was accepted by many baptists as well (e.g., Wenger, 1954:193-200). Variants such as the kenotic Christology (Thomasius, Dorner, Forsyth; see Welch, ed., 1965) made concessions to the historical model without abandoning the two-natures. The early Karl Barth (CD I/1) advanced a revelation model (cf. McIntyre, 1966:chap. 6), but shifted to a narrative model in his later work. Yet in modern times it is finally the historical model, accepted by theologians as diverse as the cranky Reimarus (before 1778) and the intensely orthodox Lutheran Wolfhart Pannenberg (1968), that has so far prevailed, and responsible Christian theology today must make some disposition of it. Because of the sort of historicism on which it depends (Frei, 1974, 1975), it is in fact now desirable to find a successor to the historical model, though its philosophical difficulties, highlighted by Frei, will not be explored at length here. As we have seen, even on its own terms the historical model had severe deficiencies. Unable to cope with Jesus' divinity, it produced no satisfactory answer to underlying question one (the question about Jesus' rightful authority), and even in its much imitated mythic variants it provided no answer to underlying question two (about telling the story of God incarnate). These two defaults might have been enough to bankrupt this model had it not also provided a highly successful way of answering underlying question three (How Christ-like are disciples' lives to be?).

To see this one success, let us follow twentieth-century Scottish theologian Donald Baillie, who produced his own *psychological* variant of the historical model. In his valuable book *God Was in Christ* (1948), Baillie called one chapter "The Harvest of Liberal Theology." Part of that harvest, he said, was the end of docetism. As long as the two-natures model persisted, people still paid lip service to the human Jesus, but they had not really accepted the consequences of their confession. Did it mean humanity as the nineteenth century had come to perceive humanity, or only humanity as it was viewed by antiquity? In answer, liberal theology (Schleiermacher and Hegel) and the historical model brought a new appreciation of the human Jesus, so that it seemed to students they were as near as yesterday to the one who walked and taught in Galilee and Judaea. For them this entailed the full humanity of Jesus' personal existence—a human body, a human mind, a human self. These in turn entailed the humanity of his psychic makeup. (In today's terms, he would have had a score on a Stanford-Binet scale, and a personality that could be categorized by a Myers-Briggs test.) His knowledge was limited. The insights he displayed were fully human insights; his emotions were human emotions; his moral life developed as do human moral lives; his temptations were real temptations; his faith was human faith; the miracles or signs he worked were done through that human faith, and he said the disciples would do even more than he (Cairns, 1928). The Jesus this yields is in modern eyes truly and fully human. Though the historical model left much to be desired, we do well to celebrate these real gains that it brought in its train: It brought the confession of Christ's humanity into its own day.

No one should underestimate the achievements of those who labored through eighteen centuries to produce the results so swiftly skimmed in this section. Yet neither honor nor diminishment was the goal of the preceding paragraphs. What was wanted was an account of the extensive *changes* that changing contexts evoked. We may revere some or deplore others, but together they teach us this: if we would answer for our day such questions as they answered for theirs, we must be open to revising the *models* (not the biblical data, but the current scaffolds from which we work) that have served Christian thought. Here the oldest models are not scorned; nor are recent models self-evidently superior; of every proposed model we must ask how it serves the task of Christian thought *in its own generation*. Is a helpful new model now at hand?

§3. Toward a Narrative Christology

A serious task therefore awaits us in this chapter. How are *we* to answer the questions that have lain beneath christological reflection through the long centuries? That we shall answer them is a matter of great urgency. It may underline the urgency to restate these questions in the form of demands upon the teaching church: (1) A teaching church must teach the Lordship of Christ. On that Lordship hangs the whole of Christian moral life understood as the realm in which Jesus Christ has first claim and supreme claim upon disciples' lives. (2) A teaching church must teach the unity of God. On that unity hangs the Christian doctrine of creation, the acknowledgment of one world made good, and made for the good, by one God; on it hangs as well the unity of Christians with God's Israel, with the heritage of the prophets, and still more. Only a searching sense of the oneness of God can drive out of the Christian church the bazaar of anthropocentric pieties peddling their many lords, many gods (cf. 1 Cor. 8:5). (3) A teaching church must teach the authenticity of life in Christ. This is the disciples' life, imperfect insofar as each life has room for growth, but perfect in its Spirit-given fidelity to Jesus' kingdom and cause. On this possibility of authentic spiritual life depend the significance of the voluntary church, the meaningfulness of the doctrine of eternal life, the viability of the way of the cross as the disciples' true way, and more as well. Every Christian generation must respond to these demands.

a. Today's many Christologies.—The place of Jesus in Christian faith is a question that has fascinated the centuries, and as the twenty-first century looms, the interest in and the variety of approaches to this topic have increased not diminished. No selection of these, even at chapter's length, can do justice to all the options provided. It may be helpful to mention here three that have influenced my own thinking even where I have followed a different path. *Karl Barth* (1886–1968), original even in his reaction against his own teachers, early on produced what has been called a revelation model for Christology (McIntyre, 1966:chap. 6). In this model, Christ's unique role was to constitute God's self-disclosure. This was Barth's way of circumventing the troublesome skepticism that came with the historical model: It mattered little for the early Barth what historical research discovered about the Jesus of history, for in Jesus, God had spoken his own Word; Scripture witnessed to it; theology's task was simply to hear that living Word, nothing more (Barth, CD I/1). Then, in the final part-volumes of *Church Dogmatics,* Barth adopted a narrative model to talk about the identity of the reconciling God. Thus under the heading of "The obedience of the Son of God" Barth speaks of "the way of the Son of God into the far country" (IV/1 §59), while in the next part-volume he writes of "the homecoming of the Son of Man" (IV/2 §64). Such language is certainly analogical (some would say mythical), but it shifted the focus of twentieth-century Christology, pressing it beyond the historical model.

One of Barth's American students, *Paul van Buren* (1924–), became intensely interested in the question of the theological relation of Christianity to present-day Judaism; his corresponding Christology, developed in a series of works over twenty years' time, has proposed a bold revision of the place of Christ: Jesus is the Christ of the Gentiles, but not the Messiah of the Jews. Judaism has always had its own access to God the Father; it is in no need of a *revealer* of God (here van Buren employs the early Barth's revelation model), but that is precisely the need of the non-Jew (van Buren, 1980, 1983, 1988). Positively, van Buren's work deepens Christian faith's particularistic historical root without subscribing to the 'historical' model as such. Even if in its stark negations van Buren's understanding does not prevail in Christian thought, it certainly challenges it to relate Christology afresh to the longer, Jewish story from which it springs (see further Chapter Eight §2).

John B. Cobb, Jr. (1925–) brought Christian theology including Christology into intense dialogue with the profound Buddhist thinking of Asia (Cobb, 1975, 1982). Earlier, he had developed (and then left aside) a broad vision, inspired by J. G. Herder and Karl Jaspers, in which Jesus is the bearer of a new sort of human nature. Every great advance in human civilization has been characterized by a new type of human existence: the emotive humanity typical of primitive man, the new rational humanity that marked the millennium preceding Christ's appearance, the aesthetic creativity of the Homeric (or mythical) age, human life viewed from an ethical center in Hebrew prophetic existence, and finally the "spiritual" existence typical of Jesus and some of his great followers such as the Apostle Paul (Cobb, 1967). Here Cobb's work, which may be classed as a psychological variant upon the historical model of Christology, reflected one important advance within that model: human nature is not (as ancient Christian theologians had assumed) a fixed item. If human nature is capable of radical variation in different historical stages, Jesus could be truly human yet truly different from others, human yet profoundly ahead of us, so that faith must first ask, not whether Jesus is like most of us, but whether we in his grace can become like him. Broadly stated, Cobb's contribution has been to widen the scope of contemporary christological discussion.

Some readers will know that these three are but a spoonful from the cream of recent theological work in this area; many other theologians, Tillich, Rahner, Thornton, Schillebeeckx, Boff, Altizer, Pannenberg, Moltmann, Macquarrie, Dunn—this chapter, and indeed this volume, could be filled with their productions, even in highly compressed accounts. Yet the three may serve to illustrate my point: Christology today is not just a matter of preserving past orthodoxies, for neither the two-natures model nor its most recent successor, the historical model, is adequate to specify the identity or display the centrality of Jesus Christ. That remains a creative theological task in this (and every) generation.

b. A narrative model for Christology?—It might please some if today's christological task were merely the combining of positive features from approaches of the past and present. Yet it is already clear why that plan will not work: Though we can learn from each era, the models on which earlier approaches were formed now appear partly incoherent. And the integrity of each project so depends upon its model that it cannot successfully be grafted into another. We are instructed by our ancestors in faith; we learn from their attempts, especially if we see each set against the historical context in which it appeared and the dominant model in which it was cast, but since our thought is not at home in those molds, we cannot take any, even the most famous such as Nicaea or Chalcedon, at face value without archaizing ourselves. All deserve respect; none can take the place of Scripture—or of hard work now. Such theological attempts as those just noted by Barth, van Buren, Cobb, and others should rather make us bold to answer in our own terms the urgent questions about Christ.

i. The story that counts.—So we begin with a narrative passage that is perhaps the oldest christological reflection in the New Testament itself, Philippians 2:5-11. If, as most scholars believe, Paul here quotes an early Christian hymn, these words had their origin in the generation immediately following Jesus' resurrection, that is, around A.D. 30 to 60. One's eye is caught by the 'high' Christology of this hymn: "that at the name of Jesus every knee should bow—in heaven, on earth, and in the depths—and every tongue acclaim, 'Jesus Christ is Lord,' to the glory of God the Father" (Phil. 2:10f). The end of Christ's ministry—total Lordship; its sign—every knee bending in obeisance, every voice sharing the primitive Christian confession, "Jesus Christ is Lord." So this passage shows that from the beginning our first question was at hand: What right had Jesus of Nazareth to such universal obedience? At least such a high vision of Jesus' role helps us to understand the appearance and long dominance of one interpretation of the hymn: that it speaks of a *heavenly* being who emptied himself (2:7), the pre-incarnate Christ, existing "in the form of God" (2:6); it is this heavenly being who laid aside his trappings to take up a human existence. On this view, this is an 'incarnation hymn,' parallel in meaning to the prologue of the Fourth Gospel. So say many interpreters.

But is this the original meaning of the passage? It is at least worth noting that while the first great Christian exegete, Origen, appears in the Latin text of Rufinus to say that he supports this reading, Rufinus allows Origen also to note that "some say" the self-emptying was the emptying of the soul of Jesus *after* it was enfleshed (*De prin.* IV.i.32). Perhaps Rufinus was protecting Origen's by-then-questioned 'orthodoxy'; thus a critical reader cannot help wondering whether Origen himself was not among the "some" who held to a historical, human 'self-emptying.' For Friedrich Loofs has canvassed the patristic evidence more generally, and concludes that the view that later became orthodox was not the reading of the earliest fathers (Loofs, 1927–28). For example, Cyprian, writing still later than Origen, in a paragraph he heads "That There Is Given to Us an Example of Living in Christ," offers this Philippians passage as a parallel, not to John 1:1-14, but to John 13:14f, the pericope in which at life's end Jesus humbles himself by washing the disciples' feet (*Treat.* XII.iii.39).

By the third century, Cyprian's was certainly becoming a minority reading of the Philippian hymn, but it has come into its own again in recent exegesis (citations in McClendon, 1991c). A further reason for this contemporary judgment besides the early church evidence just mentioned is the evident parallel with Philippians 3:4-11, where Paul recounts his own experience of laying aside, not heavenly glory, but earthly privilege in order to follow Jesus' way. Paul says he was entitled to self-confidence, being after all of the right people, a good tribe, the right school of thought, and being possessed of impeccable zeal. He had abandoned all this (the actual language is stronger) in order to come to Christ and be "conformed to his death." Verbal echoes between this chapter 3 passage and the chapter 2 hymn suggest that the Apostle *wanted* his readers to see a parallel: Paul's story, in this regard exactly like that of Jesus, was a standard to be imitated.

Is it possible to see the Godlike image attributed to Jesus (*morphē*, v. 6) *not* as the characteristic of his heavenly pre-existence (for which, after all, "God*like*ness" seems far too weak, far too 'Arian') but of his human circumstances as he set out to make his career? Paul the proud Pharisee, Jesus the gifted young leader? Then we would read of Jesus' refusal to grasp equality with God not as a Miltonian tale of a heavenly God who refused to rebel, but as a reference to the human Jesus' earthly temptations—which the Gospels condense into a single story that unfolds at much greater length (cf. Luke 4:1-13 with the realistic tests Jesus faces throughout Luke). If we read Paul this way, he refers here to a Jesus who might have been made a king (cf. Matt. 4:8-10 par.; John 6:14f), but who instead identified himself and his cause with servants and serfs, outcasts and victims, to a degree that led the authorities to arrange his death—an outcome that is just the cost of obeying God in this world (Luke 4:8). On this reading, the argument Paul makes in both chapters, in 2 and again in 3, concerns the character of discipleship, and in each he founds his argument on examples his converts would have to accept as persuasive models: (1) first the earthly career of Jesus their exemplary Master, and then (2) his own example. Hence the dominant feature of 2:5-11 has never been a heavenly-descent myth, for it is not a passage about the pre-incarnate acts of God, but one that juxtaposes Messiah Jesus' earthly vicissitudes with the vast claim of his Lordship—on earth, but also in heaven and over the nether world.

If this reading is adopted, though, how is the expression "being in the form of God" (Phil. 2:6) to be understood? If we draw upon the two-natures model we will see this as one more evidence of what the New Testament surely teaches elsewhere, the eternal deity of God the Word (Heb. 1:1-3; John 1:1-14). That reading, however, allows Paul to add nothing here by way of example to his appeal to the Philippians; instead it creates further problems (Phil. 2:7) about how deity can "empty" itself—problems that were the nemesis of nineteenth-century kenotic

Christology (Welch, ed., 1965). If, though, we believe that Paul's hymn sums up the Jesus story primitive Christians already knew, the story the four Evangelists were soon to expound, then the early Christian reading is appropriate. In this case we must understand that "the image of God" in Scripture is not a designated state but a task set, not an ontic level enjoyed but an ideal to be realized (cf. TeSelle, 1975:16-31). That achievement was the goal that had earlier been set for Adam and his partner—a goal our first ancestors failed to reach because of grasping pride or greed. It was Jesus' goal also, and he did attain it—by refusing the greedy grasp of the prize. Rather, he was "minded" (Phil. 2:5) to take the servant way. That, says Paul, is why God gave him the name that is above every name. Since he took that way, at last every knee will bow to him in order to glorify God (Phil. 2:9-11).

Readers limited to the English text may find this argument less than persuasive, since not only the Tyndale tradition (King James Version, etc.) but most other translators have followed the traditional exegesis that is here challenged, and their translations reflect it. An important exception is the *New Jerusalem Bible*. As a supplement, I offer here still another (rough) translation of Philippians 2:5-11: Here (in the style of King James' translators) I have italicized the words that show exegetical assumptions.

[5]Take to heart among yourselves your being in Christ Jesus: [6]who, mirroring God *on earth*, turned back the temptation to rival God [7]and poured out his life, taking a servant role. Bearing the likeness of *Adam's* race, sharing the human lot, [8]he brought his life low, obedient to death (death by a cross). [9]So God raised him up, and gave him the name outreaching all names: [10]that in the name of Jesus every knee should bend—in heaven, on earth, in the depths—[11]and every tongue together say, "Jesus, Christ, Lord," to the glory of the Father God.

Elsewhere, I have noted that even if this translation's assumptions are correct, the passage has *evoked* still another, heavenly story (McClendon, 1991b). Is it this way, or the other way around? Indeed, must we decide? Or do both readings legitimately speak to today's Christian community?

The story shared by all the Gospels is the one that provided the climax of the previous chapter, the story of one of us who found his own mission in the teaching of the prophets and immediately in the message of John the Baptizer. He accepted baptism as his rite of commitment to that mission: to be the royal Son precisely by being the Suffering Servant (Mark 1:11 par.). Through the days that followed, and not only in the desert, he faced and faced down the temptation to abandon poor, suffering, defeated Israel (Yoder, 1972, pp. 94-150). Instead, he proclaimed to its people a kingdom-at-hand characterized by an alternative, indeed a countercultural, life-style, one whose keynotes were *expectancy* (he was an eschatological *prophet*), *openness* (practicing a *priest*like penetration of the barriers that divide us from God and one another), and *creativity* (thus disclosing himself a numinous *king*-in-waiting). He prayed passionately; he taught others to pray. He summoned followers, men and women to be bearers with him of the reign he saw already coming—summoned them all to be, in his code-language, the "Truly Human One." His proclamation came not only in puzzling yet liberating words (his parables) but also in significant signs (the healings and feastings). Then, provocatively, he entered Jerusalem, thereby challenging the powers in charge, and doing so in ways that displayed once again the character of his coming rule. Challenged by opponents, abandoned by friends, condemned by authorities, he remained faithful to his mission to the death—a death that was (in more than one sense) for others, a death that completed his unfaltering obedience to God his Father, a death that was a judgment entered and executed.

Now it is noteworthy that the Jesus story summarized this way (and to this point, one may note, the summary largely parallels Mark's Gospel supplemented by Q, though stopping short of Mark's textually irregular ending) is one that antiseptic modern historians (who have so strongly influenced the theology of the historical model) might concede to be substantially true. Yet as it stands, the story cries out for further explanation. Whence this stunning authority to come, to summon, to announce, even to die? What meaning had this life? And what about that curious Gospel ending? If we consult the rest of the New Testament, we find two further, broad explanatory features, one being the accounts (in Matthew and Luke) of a wonderful beginning of Jesus' life, the other the account throughout the New Testament (though less clearly in Mark) of an astounding unending ending: Jesus awakened from the dead! These two, the birth accounts and the record of Jesus' resurrection, require further theological scrutiny, though they cannot be treated either together or alike.

ii. The miraculous conception.—According to Matthew and Luke, Jesus' wonderful birth, and more especially his conception in a virginal womb, sheds important light on his identity. (Much else in the New Testament [e.g., John 1:1-5] finds illumination in a heavenly pre-existence, which we will examine in Chapter Seven.) Matthew and Luke provide Jesus with genealogies, and also speak of his conception "by Spirit" (*ek pneumatos*, Matt. 1:20; cf. Luke 1:35, *Pneuma hagion epeleusetai epi se*), clearly implying a virginal conception (though not, it should be noted, a "virgin birth" or an "immaculate conception," these being terms that make two quite different claims, based on later ecclesiastical views about Mary and Mary's own mother—R. Brown, 1973, 1979). Have these testimonies concerning Jesus' virginal conception been allowed adequate theological weight in this chapter? In answer, the following may be considered.

First, these Gospel stories *do not say* or suggest that it is by virtue of this marvelous conception that Jesus was *divine*. The Holy Spirit is not presented here as a Jupiter-like father deity who impregnates a human mother. Close attention to the language of the narratives rather suggests the Spirit as the human Jesus' divine Mother, conceiving Jesus exactly when and as Mary conceives him. Humanly speaking, Mary conceives Jesus; divinely speaking, the Spirit does so. A human event is understood to have been a divine action. So these conception stories do exalt the holy or Spirit-shadowed beginning of *a holy humanity*, perhaps the beginning of a new level of humanity that will be attained in Jesus of Nazareth (Luke 1:35; cf. Cobb, 1967). *Second*, there is *no suggestion* in these accounts that this beginning apart from normal coitus is the cause or source of Jesus' *sinlessness*, for this last notion was introduced only later, when Christians had begun to think human sexuality as such sinful. On the other hand, these accounts *are a fittingly numinous introduction to* the story of a life that will display, by the time it reaches the cross, a *full faithfulness* to the Holy One of Israel. *Third*, and consequently, the virginal conception is *not a touchstone of Christian orthodoxy* or a dogma to be believed on pain of damnation (again, such thinking implies a later belief system that supplants biblical faith). The virginal conception *is instead a sign of* faith for the faithful, speaking to many (admittedly not to all) believers of what is signified by this sign, namely *the full presence of God in the full story of Jesus.*

The biblical birth accounts, understood by way of these three denials and three affirmations, should be regarded as valuable, if subsidiary, parts of the full story. Regretfully, experience shows that such an understanding is limited to the few in the modern world. Except for these few, that world hears the birth stories only to discount them as myth, or legend, or sheer fabrication, or alternatively it convulsively embraces them for what they are not—clubs with which to cow unbelief or bludgeon half-belief into full submission. One can only deplore this misuse, and hope for a rising generation better suited to receive the true value of the story Christians recall at Christmas. Meanwhile, the *central value and definite limits* of that story just stated should be clearly noted (see further R. Brown, 1979).

iii. The resurrection sign.—For the teaching church, the resurrection of Jesus Christ from among the dead to his new status and destiny (1 Cor. 15:25-28 par.) has a very different role from that of the birth and infancy narratives. Although these have their accepted place in Scripture, and though they point as signs to Jesus' extraordinary coming presence, the resurrection in sharp contrast is *itself* God's great historic act creating that new presence among us. The resurrection is the historic sign by which other great historic signs are measured (the Reed Sea crossing, the birth of prophecy, the mission of the church), and it is these great historic signs that the remembering signs (prophetic preaching, Lord's supper, baptism) and providential signs (significant events in Jesus' life, the answers to our own prayers, other blessings) must evoke and reclaim (cf. Chapter Four §3). Only in their polar positions, one set at the beginning, the other at the culmination of his earthly life, are Jesus' conception and his resurrection comparable, and even in this regard they are asymmetrical, for the lesser gains all its value exactly by its reference to this greater sign. Thus the two Gospels that do tell the story of earthly beginnings can do so only as resurrection-documents, while had there been no resurrection of Jesus from the dead, there would have been no Luke or Matthew, or any gospel at all (cf. 1 Cor. 15:14). The narrative that identifies Jesus is radically incomplete apart from the resurrection that opens that story to us: Christ is raised; therefore we too can know him; therefore the gospel is good news to us. And that resurrection, as we have seen (§1), is nothing less than God's *(re)identi-fication of the entire earthly life of Jesus of Nazareth, from conception to its last breath, with God's own immortal life.*

Here we may remind ourselves of the counterpart, in the two-natures model, to this resurrection-centered identification of Jesus. This was the Cappadocian teaching that though the incarnate one was from the outset truly human, truly divine (as Nicaea had already taught), the permeation of the human by the divine was gradual and only complete after the ascension. The humanity of the baby born to Mary was affected by the presence of God only so much as was appropriate to human babyhood, and so it was through every stage of his earthly life.

On the other hand, this narrative identification is *not* in harmony with the distinctively modern view that God's presence was a function of Jesus' *consciousness* of God. This makes considerable difference if we consider, for example, Jesus' cry of dereliction (Mark 15:34-38 par.). The historical model's Schleiermacher, basing Jesus' divinity on "His personal self-consciousness," finds the cry of dereliction an embarrassment—for how could anyone reckon with a diminution of God's full presence at the crisis of Jesus' life? (Schleiermacher, CF p. 460). On a narrative view, though, the cry in Mark's narrative and Matthew's only indicates Jesus' final relinquishing of those tempting dreams of another path to glory, less costly than death on a cross. But that sort of temptation had been faced before, and faced down, when in the Garden of Gethsemane he had sought to gain approval of some other way than the way of the cross (Mark 14:36*a* par.). So Jesus' *sense* of abandonment is indeed expressed in the cry, but the fullness of divine presence coheres with the fullness of sacrifice; the utter identification of God's life with Jesus' own in the death of Jesus means that God tastes human death at its godless worst; here two stories, human and divine, finally—converge.

As noted above, the understanding advanced here should not be read as the logical counterpart of that ancient adoptionism identified by Adolf von Harnack as one of two basic early Christologies: "Jesus was either regarded as the man whom God hath chosen, in whom the Deity or the Spirit of God dwelt, and who, after being tested, was adopted by God and invested with dominion (Adoption Christology) [Harnack here cites *Shepherd of Hermas*]; or Jesus was regarded as a heavenly spiritual being (the highest after God) who took flesh, and again returned to heaven after the completion of his work on earth (pneumatic Christology) [Harnack cites the Apostle Paul, Hebrews, and several Apostolic Fathers]" (Harnack, 1896:I, 191-93). Other historians challenged this analysis, but in any case the label "adoptionist" became merely a term of reproach in twentieth-century theology: "Adoptionists" wrongly believed (1) that God held out divine sonship as a reward to the first successful claimant, and (2) that as things turned out, Jesus won the race. It would follow that Jesus' own 'salvation' was a matter of merit, so that the merit theology that evangelical Christianity had valiantly opposed was inserted by 'adoptionists' not into the story of believers but, far worse, into the story of their Lord. Apart from Harnack, did anyone in modern times really hold this view? In any case, it must be affirmed here that there was never a time when God did not intend to raise Jesus from the dead, never a time when the whole story pointed to anything less than the ultimate exaltation of this One who was God's self-giving presence. In present terms, Harnack's mistake was to have split that one story into two, assigning its sundered parts to different patristic authors and tilting to one part. See Subsection (c) below.

iv. The story continues.—In light of the preceding, that is, *in resurrection light*, apostolic Christianity can be construed as the continuation of the Jesus story already begun. In this sense the familiar features of the apostolic beginnings, namely missionary expansion and church formation, take on new significance, since these constitute further identifying marks of the Risen One. Embedded in these, there is the practice of apostolic *baptism*. When administered *in Jesus' name* (later, the triune name; see Acts 2:38; Matt. 28:19f) baptism counted as the incorporative sign that united believers to the community of witnesses to the resurrection (Rom. 6:4). Thus the rite that identified his followers at the same time identified him (or him with Spirit and Father) as the followers' Lord. Another practice is the solemn yet celebratory *meal of remembrance* (of *anamnēsis*) whose character and significance as thanksgiving for salvation, as pledge of solidarity with the risen Lord and with one another, as foretaste of the heavenly banquet soon to come, was so intertwined at every point with the life of the risen Lord that Paul, writing before the appearance of the passion narratives in our Gospels existed, nevertheless names this ritual meal not "salvation supper" or "passion supper" (though those names might have had good claim), but simply "Lord's supper," where the Lord is the risen Lord Jesus Messiah (1 Cor. 11:20ff). Again, the identification ran both ways—to disciples and to Master. Further apostolic practice that may be recalled here is the apostolic teaching, in which *faith* is faith in Jesus Christ (see, e.g., John 14:1), *salvation* is through Christ, the *gospel* is the good news "of Christ" (see Gal. 1:7). There is as well this fact: in a missionary community perpetually on guard against idolatry, prayer is practiced not only "in the name of" (i.e., as the agent acting in the character of) the Master; prayer is also addressed directly to Jesus, one bit of primitive evidence being the preserved Aramaic phrase *maran atha* (our Lord, come—1 Cor. 16:2). Beyond this, prayer by New Testament Christians is addressed to God, or to God the Father, and in or through the Spirit (see, e.g., Acts 7:54-60), but to and through no other (cf. McClendon, 1990:Appendix). In all these practices, what designates disciples as such designates Jesus as the Risen One as well (cf. *Ethics* Twelve).

Now we come to two aspects of the apostolic witness that provide a larger element of self-interpretation—what seem to be the elements of primitive christological reflection. One of these is the Epistles' refusal to identify Jesus as ever in any sense a sinner. Like us in all other respects, in that one he differed (2 Cor. 5:21; Heb. 4:15; 7:26; 1 Pet. 1:19; 2:22; 1 John 3:5). This 'sinlessness' has already been positively interpreted (Chapter Three) as apostolic recognition of the *full faithfulness* of Jesus of Nazareth, a faithfulness that disclosed his unique intimacy with his Father.

The other apostolic contribution calls for a bit more discussion. This is the appearance in the witnessing community of certain defining *titles*, often metaphoric, by which they identified the Risen One in his earthly ministry. These titles (among the chief were Messiah or Christ, Son of man, Son of God, Savior, Word, God (!), and in a special sense, simply the Son) in most cases were phrases or terms from Hebrew Scripture catachretically applied to the One whose identity the apostolic writers wished to make vividly plain. Painstaking volumes of modern scholarship have been devoted to studies of these terms or titles (e.g. R. Fuller,

1965), some to a single term such as "Son of man" (e.g. Borsch, 1967). At some points today's teaching church must exercise special care if it is to employ these ancient titles faithfully. For example, in the previous chapter we saw that the biblical term "Truly Human One" *(huios tou anthrōpou)*, perhaps Jesus' favorite self-designation, was a collective term that he sought to apply to his followers as well as to himself. "Son of God," contrary to what a casual Bible reader might imagine, does not in general biblical use denote a divine being, but more commonly means "chosen of God" (said of angels, Job 38:7; of David, 2 Sam. 7:14; of faithful Hebrews, Deut. 14:1). "Savior" *(sōtēr)* is biblical, but also occurs in Hellenistic religious use, and was perhaps a term employed contextually in the mission to the Gentiles.

The purpose of the preceding paragraph is to list some of the titles that reflect the apostolic witness to Jesus. These are not meant to foreclose further possibilities: Jesus was for Dag Hammarskjöld a Brother; for the gospel hymn, "What a Friend We Have in Jesus," a Friend. Theologies make other proposals: for some Asian theology Jesus is a Guru, perhaps for feminist theology a Companion. Every century, too, adds its image of the living Christ who confronts it contextually. If theology would be faithful to him, the question must ever be whether the terms proposed are faithful to the apostolic witness that declares that *Jesus* is the Christ; it is *he* who rose; we can truly know no other Savior, and "Jesus Christ is the same yesterday, today, and for ever" (Heb. 13:8).

Among the apostolic names, the last three listed above (Word or *logos*, God, and Son in a unique sense) are direct witnesses to their conviction that in having to do with the Risen One whom they knew to be Jesus of Nazareth, they were having to do with the one true God. As these apostolic marks testify, Jesus' resurrection was no mere resuscitation, no shadowy survival of another great human soul; Ultimacy itself had touched their lives when they touched his, and by that Ultimacy they were saved from their sins—this was the apostolic witness. As such, it constituted a continuation of the story that found its own center in the Easter rising of the Truly Human One.

c. The resurrection and two-narrative Christology.—Yet we must now ask whether a theology committed as is the present one to the definitive role of the Jesus *story* itself can deal with the deep questions that lie beneath the historic christological quest. Is the theological recovery of that narrative in its longer setting and its broad sweep any substitute for the finely elaborated theories of the Logos or two-nature or historical or other models? A reply must begin by noting that all through the long biblical and postbiblical story whose *center* (Bonhoeffer) is Jesus of Nazareth, we have continually found ourselves engaging not one story, but two. There has been the story, beginning with Genesis, of what God has been doing to make a place for his people with himself and thus with one another. That story, with its overtures from a JHWH who walks with his creatures in the garden in the cool of the day (Gen. 3:8), from a Redeemer God who leads his people out of Egyptian slavery, from a God whose word goes forth to do what it will do and will assuredly not return empty-handed, from a holy God whose patterns of living are patterns that make for wholeness and life, not death, a God who chastises only to restore, who comes to comfort, to heal, comes with a Lover's caress—that is no new story when once again it focuses, this time upon Jesus who is "Christ the power of God and the wisdom of God" (1 Cor. 1:24). That last is one title that Paul gives to Christ *crucified*, thereby designating exactly the cross as the ultimate power (what our forebears called the "condescension") of a God who all through the story has been reaching out, reaching down, to us. We can follow P. T. Forsyth in naming this story *kenosis*, the self-giving of God (Forsyth, 1909:lec. 11).

Yet alongside that story there is another—of trembling Eve and Adam who do, though faultily, confess their sin to the God who walks in the garden, of the daughter of Levi who entrusts her babe with a Hebrew name to a little boat surely named Hope, and of a daughter of Pharaoh who withdraws from that same boat the infant she will in the Egyptian tongue name Moses; of prophets, men, and women too, who dare not, dare not speak any word but the Lord's own; of priests and people who keep the faith and rebuild the shattered wall of God's Zion when punishment time is at an end; of a Jewish lass named Miriam who has a baby she is commanded to call Joshua-Jeshua-Jesus, Savior, and who "kept all these sayings in her heart." And (as no lesser a steward than liberal theology has called us to remember afresh), the greatest of these men and women of faith was that very Jesus, who against all odds, in what must have seemed the worst of times, lived a life of full faithfulness, fulfilled his mission and was fully rewarded by his heavenly Father. To match the other, we may call this second story the *plērōsis*, the divine fulfillment in human life, God's self-fulfillment by way of human investment (Forsyth, 1909:lec. 12).

That the two stories are two, not simply one, implies not only the permanent distinction between Creator and creature, Redeemer and redeemed, but also the failure and fragmentation that have been a part of the creature's story. From Adam (and Eve) to Cain, from Samson (and Delilah) to King Ahab (and Queen Jezebel), from the Pharaohs to the Caesars, from Sodom to Corinth, from Babel to every modern Babylon, in both sexes, among all peoples, and at every level of power, the human story has displayed as well a dark side. So the two stories mark off not only the Creator from creation, but the Redeemer from the redeemed. If nevertheless the human story reaches out to the divine one, answers it, corresponds to it, that means that the spirit in the creature is moved by the Spirit that is God's own. That the human story despite its blemish and fault and ruin nevertheless again and again reaches up bespeaks not the cooperation of two divinities, but the narrative power of one God who, in making our human story, made it for "yourself, and our heart is restless until it rests in you" (Augustine, *Conf.* I, i).

Here a willing reader might nonetheless balk. Have we two stories or is there really only one? Take for example the Joseph saga in Genesis 37–50. Is this not *at once* a story of human treachery (the malicious brothers, the slave traders, Potiphar's wife, and the rest) and *at the same time* a story of divine providence (as Joseph says in forgiving his brothers, "It was not you who sent me here, but God" [Gen. 45:8]). That seems right. Would it be better, then, to speak of two *points of view* regarding the one story, as Bruce Marshall and Michael Goldberg, each in his own way, have led me to ask? Very well, let us say two points of view. Nevertheless, there is an ineluctable twoness here, and it appears once again when Jesus of Nazareth enters the story. Yet it is important now to see the differences in the two sequences of narrative, that of Joseph and that of Jesus, as well. For in the Joseph story the twoness is vivid: God is never "in" the brothers' wickedness in the way God is "in" Joseph's subsequent forgiveness of the brothers. Meanwhile, Joseph himself often leaves something to be desired: After all, he had been the insufferable brat who had provoked his brothers' hatred (Gen. 37:1-11), and still in Egypt that insufferable quality may sometimes have reappeared. When we come to Jesus, though, these blemishes in Joseph the type disappear. Evil is still present in the narrative about Jesus—there are tricky opponents, there are stupid disciples, there is inexorable Rome. And in some sense God is "in" all that evil as God had been "in" the brothers' knavery, turning it to good (cf. Acts 2:23). Yet for the place of God in Jesus' own story, *no qualifiers are needed*; the action of Jesus is God's action; what Jesus suffers, God suffers. Here the twoness of the story, however we care to name it (two stories, two points of view), converges completely, and we see a human story that God will without qualification acknowledge as his own (Rom. 1:1-4). To reply to the objection that all this talk of twoness and oneness in narrative does not correspond very well to classic two-natures-in-one-being Christology would only be to repeat what I have said earlier in the chapter: It does not. Two-natures Christology has had its day, and we need not return to it save as to a monument of what has gone before. All honor to Athanasius and Basil and Leontius, but they did not write Scripture, and it is to Scripture that we must return in fashioning our convictions.

Therefore we have these two stories, of divine self-expense and human investment, of God reaching to people even before people reach to God, of a God who gives in order to be able to receive, and a humanity that receives so that it shall be able to give. Together, they constitute the biblical story in its fullness. *And now the capstone word is this: these two stories are at last indivisibly one.* We can separate them for analysis, but we cannot divide them; there is but one story there to be told. Finally, this story becomes gospel, becomes good news, when we discover that it is our own.

This version of Christology is certainly not trouble free. Yet if we will now examine the problems it generates (though in this volume, examine them only summarily, as we have earlier examined others) we should find one happy consequence: these problems are manageable; they are of our own era, our own place in history, our own conceptuality and understanding. Another age will no doubt find another way to display these mighty claims of Christ; if this is our way, it must show that by answering for us the perennial questions of Christian teaching about Jesus Christ.

First, then, what of underlying question one? What right has *this* Jesus, the Jesus rendered in this one narrative that is two, to be Lord of us each and all? The answer like the question is inextricable from the story. Jesus, the risen Jesus upon whom the story concenters, has this right if (and only if) in this very story we are confronted, as by an unimpeachable authority, with *God's own claim* upon our lives. Challenged by official-dom in their capital city, Peter and John are forbidden to speak to anyone "in this name." But these two answer that they "cannot possibly *(ou dynametha)* give up speaking about what we have seen and heard" (Acts 4:20). In that "cannot possibly" lies all the force of their answer. They appeal, not to their own stories (though these are acknowledged), not to religious experience, or the authority of Holy Writ, or the collective rights of free Jews, but to the dynamic claim of the One who has confronted them in the resurrection. So the Waverer (Simon) and the Watcher (John) become the Rock and the Witness, claimed by a living story that rightfully commands. That there is more to be said about authority will soon be acknowledged (see Chapter Eleven). More, but not other, for I cannot find any authority greater than that which these witnesses acknowledge. Notice now, though, that something goes on here akin to what Kant saw as the categorical imperative, or Royce as loyalty to loyalty, even something akin to that allegiance so imperfectly expressed in recent appeals to biblical 'inerrancy.' This is the sense that in, with, and under this story one meets its Lord and our own. Here one meets a Present Christ.

The weakness (if it *be* a weakness) in this narrative way of speaking is that it cannot, without betraying Scripture and straying into mythol-ogy, speak of an infant Jesus in full possession of all human and divine powers. The babe rather possesses the promise of the life that God will acknowledge, finally, as God's own. The proper claim of Christ's Lord-ship here is not the sentimental "little Lord Jesus asleep in the hay," but the far more significant claim that life lived in a truly human childhood can be of absolute value when it issues in such a story as this—the story of Jesus of Nazareth. Luke's Gospel captures this well with its anticipation themes: a life of promises made and promises at great price kept.

We come to the second underlying question. How does two-narrative Christology address the problem of coherence, the problem we expressed by asking how monotheists (e.g., Jews) can tell the Jesus *story?* Here *all* the advantages seem to lie with our model. For the two-narrativist, the puzzles of substance and *hypostasis,* of *ousia* and *persona,* do not arise; they were alien puzzles when read into the Gospels; their proper place was only on a long contextual byway of the Christian intellectual journey. This underlying question certainly remains, but now its form is this: How can the ever-active God be rightly, and supremely, associated with one story among earth's many? This is the problem of particularity, and we have met it before. "How odd of God to choose the Jews" (Chapter Four). To contemplate this mystery is to think again of providence and of election. In the grip of these profundities one can justly ask, "How can Jews (or Christians) tell the *Exodus* story?" For the same particularity is at work at this and each place in Scripture. The biblical story is always two stories—God's and ours—told together. To grasp the mystery of God at work within the Exodus, or to find the answer to our own question two, Jews and Christians must learn ever to construe divine election as election to service, service to others, so that Abraham's God (and now the risen Christ) is thereby disclosed, by serving all, to be the God of all the earth (Gen. 12:3). Particularity in Christ is divine election, and election is justified only if it is the womb of servanthood.

On this account, the second underlying question leads directly into the third, expressed here in the form, "How Christ-like are disciples' lives to be?" Here, again, two-narrative Christology has a full advantage when it replies that if both these narratives, and they inseparably, are the story of God creating a redeemed people, then the third question can be answered only from the standpoint of concrete self-involvement in that story. Absolute Lordship on Christ's part (question one) entails nothing less than perfect discipleship on our part (here John Wesley stands with the witness of Scripture). This conveys a grand assurance with regard to question three: God is with us absolutely. It leaves narrative theology at a considerable remove from that complacent churchmanship or culture Christianity that accepts the traditional Christian status quo as the norm for the teaching church. The chapters still to come will explore more fully some aspects of discipleship and community, as have some chapters above and in the preceding volume. Already it has arisen that, symbolically speaking, the earthly Jesus may have anticipated not one cross on Calvary, but thirteen (Chapter Five). Discipleship meant (and means) commitment to the social radicalism of a nonconformist Christ; it required (and requires) not inner torments (*Anfechtungen*) or guilty consciences but entire reorientation to a life with Jesus that will necessarily collide again and again with the powers, with the world's No, that is, with a cross (Mark 8:34f).

Is such discipleship even possible? Possible not simply for the eccentric or fanatic, but for plain Christians plainly committed to the Master? It seemed not, in the first generation. These disciples, we know, failed to follow (Mark 14:50). But they had a pioneer in the way of obedience, one who broke a trail they could follow, made a way they could take. He broke trail for us, too (Heb. 2:10; 5:8f). But in this case, the God with whom we have to do is a Christ-like God, in contrast to those imperial gods of our fears and fantasies that have driven us in ways opposed to Jesus. Yet reflection upon such a God is a task requiring further work, and to that work we now turn. We will find that it does not divert us from the center established here.

The Identity of God

If the preceding chapters provided answers, they did so only by raising fresh questions. We now know a way to express in current terms the ancient witness of Christian faith: Faith's Lord is true man, true God, one risen Jesus Christ. A two-narrative christological model permits us to say this without falling back on alien thought-modes from the past. The story Scripture tells is the story of God. It reaches its climax in Jesus risen from the dead. Concurrently, Scripture tells a moving human story that climaxes in that same resurrection. The two narratives, divine and human, are seamlessly one narrative throughout; though they may be distinguished for analysis, they cannot be separated without harm. The story that discloses our salvation (Chapter Five) also identifies our Lord (Chapter Six). The trouble is that this narrative approach to the identity of Jesus Christ draws on information about God that has not to this point been investigated. Is God, as these chapters seem to say, a God of whom such 'true stories' can even be told? Can God properly be discovered within Scripture's story? More particularly, can God be the subject of a story about any mortal being, even if that mortal be Jesus Christ? To put the question more generally, *Who (or what if anything) is God?* Certainly earlier chapters, and *Ethics* as well, evoked similar questions about God. This was appropriate, for all parts of this Christian theology presuppose other parts where matters earlier assumed can in their turn be addressed. Yet in the preceding two chapters on Christ's achievement and identity, such questions about God were all the more urgently present, even when unspoken.

This, too, was deliberate. For I have been approaching the doctrine of God in the only way that as a Christian I can. If matters seem otherwise, perhaps that is because somewhere amid our mental furniture lies another idea of God, a 'God' whose credentials are established elsewhere. Yet that alternative strategy is exactly what the work here challenges. The God under discussion all along, the God of God's rule or kingdom (Part I), the God whose story is also a human story about Jews and Jesus and Christians (Part II), is no remote Absolute abstract in the heavens, no First Principle posited by someone's philosophy, far less is God the Nobodaddy of popular culture, or the nonexistent *theos* of post-Enlightenment atheism. Rather, "God" here is God known in the story Christians call gospel—the Jesus story in its full depth and length and height.

Consequently there is an important role, though not a foundational role, for this chapter on the doctrine of God. Though it cannot provide a different approach to God than that already made, it can clarify that approach. It can do this by precipitating what has gone before and bringing to light what might have been obscured along the way. Its primary task will be to show the dependence of the Christian doctrine of God upon the narrative we call gospel. This may keep us from a 'Marcionite' disengagement of Christian thought from its Hebrew base or a 'sectarian' disdain for the history of Christian thought. Looking backward from Jesus' day, this narrative link should also provide a safeguard by making it hard to dodge the question (the second of the underlying christological questions) concerning the relation of the God of Jesus Christ to the God of Abraham. Looking forward from Christian beginnings, it should provide assurance that what the churches thought and taught in many past intellectual contexts is relevant to what they must think and teach now. Second, while abstruse philosophical thought can never provide a foundation for Christian faith, it has sometimes served to display the inescapable place of God in that faith. For this reason we will also view some philosophical contributions to thinking about God. These have had a negative but also a positive effect upon the Christian understanding of God. These two tasks will occupy the first two sections of the chapter: (§1) **The Gospel of God**, and (§2) **Some Philosophical Lessons in Divinity.** Finally, a closing section, (§3) **The Deity of God**, will recapitulate this material in light of modern atheism, and give special attention to the question, how we must name and identify God now.

§1. The Gospel of God

Jesus began his brief but earth-changing ministry, according to Mark, by proclaiming "the gospel of God" (1:14). The wording may strike us as odd; perhaps it grated upon the ear of the other Gospel writers as well, for they avoided it; clearly it perplexed later copyists, who changed Mark's text to read "the gospel of *the kingdom* of God." For how could "God" be good news? (Or if the good news is not God, what *is* God's gospel?)

a. Its religious context.—Answering that question requires some sense of the Hellenistic religious world in which the Christian message appeared. Historian Robin Lane Fox has pictured the pagan culture Christians met. The gods (and the supreme God, understood, however, as no rival to these others) were familiar if extraordinary inhabitants of the ancient world. It is too easy for us today to imagine otherwise—to imagine that Athena and Hermes, or Jupiter and Venus, were mere verbal decoration, as they are for us. We do not, despite the etymology of "venereal," attribute venereal disease to the goddess Venus. Lane Fox's evidence shows how different the ancient reality was. The phenomena of divinity were real enough to evoke loyalty and to satisfy reasonable empirical demands as well. The gods were present and active, for good or ill. Of course one did not as an everyday occurrence *see* them, yet this was not because they were unseeable, but because they revealed themselves only as they chose. At the conclusion of what seemed a conversation with an ordinary mortal one might discover, from telltale signs such as a sudden disappearance, that one had actually been talking with a god or goddess (Lane Fox, 1987:chaps. 1–3).

This sheds light on the report in Acts (14:8-18) that at Lystra in Asia Minor, after Paul and Barnabas had achieved a remarkable healing of a man lame from birth, the Lystrans shouted ("in their native Lycaonian") that "the gods have come down to us in human form," taking the genial Barnabas for Zeus and the articulate Paul for Hermes, the divine message-bearer. As the story continues, the priest of Zeus brought oxen and garlands to the gates, and with the people prepared to make a propitiatory sacrifice to these human-looking deities. The Lystran mistake was all too likely, for it was common knowledge that the gods *did* appear, and what more natural than that this divine pair should visit a location devoted to them? Nor is the confusion unique to this passage of Acts; Paul on Malta was again reckoned a god, and Peter more than once had to show others he was not an angelic visitor (Acts 10:25f; 12:15; 28:6; Lane Fox, 1987:98-101).

The pagan gods satisfied the longings of many for religious experience. A second-century religious novel by Apuleius, the *Golden Ass*, provides evidence. Its protagonist, Lucius, has been enchanted as punishment into an ass. He petitions the great goddess Isis, who in answer reveals herself to him in a dream, giving Lucius exact instructions about what he must do in the next day's ritual in order to regain his existence. "I and I alone," she tells him, "have the power to prolong your life beyond the bounds appointed by your fate." At the ritual, the miracle occurs; the exultant cry from the crowd, Arthur Darby Nock tells us, "is as at Lourdes when the word goes forth that there is a cure." But this is only the beginning of the story. In contemplation and dreams, in ritual service to the goddess, in the faithful management of his interior life, Lucius is prepared for the "second birth," the full enlightenment that the priest of Isis teaches him to seek. On the long awaited day, washed, prayed over, and clothed in a linen garment, Lucius passes through the mysteries that it would be unlawful to report: "I visited the bounds of death; I trod Proserpina's threshold: I passed through all the elements and returned." Later, he advances (not without considerable outlay of money) through still further initiations to still higher rank, and is spiritually fulfilled. Quoting still another source, Nock highlights the I-Thou relation another convert finds in Isis: *"those who invoke thee in their trust in thee see thee"* (Nock, 1961:138-52). If paganism declined, it was not for want of personal religion.

The pagan deities also laid claim to their adherents' public conduct. Robert Wilken has shown how Roman religion distinguished between reputable religion *(religio)* and mere fanaticism *(superstitio)*. The distinction did not turn upon one versus many gods, for the Roman pantheon was well populated; it was common knowledge that each city or people had its distinctive deities. The mark of true religion was *pietas,* a term that originally meant fidelity to one's parents and more distant ancestors, but came to include loyalty to one's community and the gods who presided over it. In fact, these two were indistinguishable; neglect of public worship by any citizen undermined the city or state; loyalty to ancestors and loyalty to civic deities were one thing, not two. Thus participation in the state religion was not, like Lucius' experience, primarily an individual matter; it was undertaken by the entire civil community, the priests being merely the agents of the people for performing the rites correctly. "One did not speak of 'believing in the gods' but of 'having gods,' just as a city might 'have laws or customs'" (Wilken, 1984:58). The gods preserved the state, maintained its order and its transitions from ruler to ruler, and by their *providentia* ensured the rationality of the whole world. In support of this religious *via media*, Plutarch derided its alternative rivals, atheism (a philosophical oddity) and superstition, the mark of the latter being arbitrary, vengeful gods who dealt capriciously and willfully with mortals (Wilken, 1984:54-67).

Furthermore, ancient paganism did not lack thinkers with philosophical capacity to see beyond the plenitude of gods or to sum them up as one austere 'God' *(theos)* or as 'divinity' *(theios)*. Such theological abstraction had been achieved long since by Plato (427–347? B.C.E.) and Aristotle (384–322 B.C.E.), but probably reached its zenith in Porphyry of Tyre (died after 301 C.E.). A deeply religious student under Plotinus (and like him scornful of Christianity), Porphyry believed it valuable to gather from centers such as Delphi and Claros the very words of the gods, oracles collected over the years. Porphyry's lost work, *Philosophy from Oracles*, sought to correlate these utterances with Platonic philosophy and his own religious views. Beneath the Most High God, "the all-powerful, most Kingly and sole Father of mortals and blessed Immortals," Porphyry located lower ranks of pagan "angels"; these were the 'gods' of mythology and tradition. The end of such philosophy is deliverance, attained by self-purification and the knowledge of God which might be gleaned from these utterances (Lane Fox, 1987:191; Copleston, 1985 I:473-75).

b. The God of the gospel.—The preceding facts may give us pause. If neither philosophical acuity nor moral freight nor access to religious experience distinguished the God preached by the Christian evangelists from the God-awareness of the pagan world, in what sense was the gospel news? It may be hard now to find the answer, for much that was pagan found its way into the Constantinian religious settlement in the fourth century and shaped Christian practice and belief. For a genuine alternative, we must read the New Testament (for what follows, cf. my essay in Steuer and McClendon, eds., 1981). Yet that cannot mean, as it might have half a century ago, "discovering Jesus' (or Paul's) teaching *about* God," for we misunderstand that teaching if we detach it from the career of Jesus (thus separating his *word* from his *work*). New Testament study today demands reading the text itself, not some ideals or concepts strained from it. And as previous chapters have argued, Jesus cannot be separated from Easter and Pentecost—the resurrection of Jesus Christ from the dead and the gift of the Spirit to the disciple fellowship. The "God of Jesus Christ," then, is not merely the God of Jesus' personal awareness, nor even of word *and* work apart from what came before, came with, and came out of that word and work—not apart from the Hebraic and Jewish past, not apart from the Palestinian setting, not apart from the outcome in the early church. "The God of Jesus Christ" is rather the God known to us in this unreduced story.

We need somehow to condense this rich data without mutilating it, and I will follow an arrangement familiar to the readers of *Volume I*: the Christ movement is marked by three historic moments or spheres of force, the *organic, the corporate,* and the *anastatic.* Here, however, I reverse their order.

i. The anastatic moment.—This note sounded in this volume when the eschatological thrust of Christian teaching appeared first among the topical chapters (Chapter Two). It appeared yet again in the preceding chapter, where the resurrection of Jesus Christ from the dead was reckoned to be the keynote in the gospel's music. Now something more must be said on this theme, for it plays a major role in the New Testament. Indeed, we might say that the great gain of New Testament scholarship in the past hundred years is that we can no longer ignore this anastatic feature. That the Pauline Epistles (and the figure of Paul their author) are fraught with resurrection and eschatology, that the Gospels are resurrection-documents, written in Easter light and anticipating the end Easter signaled, that the Apocalypse is not an oddity but authentic New Testament literature—all this points toward some sufficient explanation, some potent eschatological presence behind it all, and that presence can hardly be any save Jesus himself. Albert Schweitzer was so far right: the real Jesus is the eschatological Jesus. It follows that the God of the gospel is a God who authorizes, who engages, whose end is found in the End toward which the Jesus story and indeed all things move. **God is a pioneer, a trailblazer of destiny.** This is vividly evident in the story Hebrew Scripture tells. When Moses at the burning bush demands the 'name,' that is, the definitive character of the *numen* that confronts him, he is offered a name with a cryptic meaning. For millennia, Platonizing Christians (nearer to Porphyry than to Moses) have read that name, *Ehyeh asher ehyeh,* shortened to JHWH, as "I am that I am," timeless Being. Yet the Hebrew verb is imperfect and causative, so that the Revised English Bible like others inserts a corrective marginal reading: "I will be what I will be" (Exod. 3:14). More freely, we may paraphrase the name Moses learned: "I will always be ahead of you. Find Me as you follow the journey." The justification of this translation is the narrative context of the passage—the Exodus story itself.

In consequence, God is a God of transformation as well. When in its liberal or modern period Christian theology focused upon transformation, it did so with a distinctively human center. Thus Schleiermacher, conceding the monotheistic and teleological character of Christianity (features it shared with others), went on to specify its particularity: "in it everything is related to the redemption accomplished by Jesus of Nazareth"—that is, the renewal of human nature accomplished in the Redeemer's own human nature and communicated by him to his followers (CF §11; cf. §§94, 100, 101). The alternative insight, resting on good New Testament ground, is that the transformative distinctive of Christian faith lies finally in the character of God. Christianity is a religion of transformation, the world is a world of transformation looking to the renewal of all things, exactly because the God who made the world and who redeems the creature is a God of transformation: God says "I will always be ahead of you; I will be what I will be; *that* is the 'I am' that I am." It follows from this that sin does not set the course of world history, however mightily it deflects it. In a sinless world, God would still be the God of change, still be the God of adventure, and transformation and adventure would be God's typical gifts still.

ii. The corporate moment.—More briefly because more familiar, we note two further aspects of the God of Jesus Christ. One is **the social nature of God.** Where the gods of paganism were capable of brief encounters, the God of Scripture Old and New is a covenanting God, one who promises ongoing companionship and who keeps every promise. In the wake of fresh comparative discoveries about Semitic language, Norman Snaith documented the Hebrew Bible's words for God's love. One is *ahabah*, from a general Hebrew stem for love of many sorts (sexual love, love of objects, of wisdom, etc.). This word came to be used of God's love for Israel understood as "electing love" or "unconditioned love"— that is, love which is explained by no quality whatsoever in the beloved, but springs unsought from the loving heart of the lover. The other great word is *chesed*, which Snaith translates "covenant love" (cf. Snaith, 1944:chaps. 5–6). English translators of Scripture, sharing Snaith's new linguistic knowledge, have competed to represent it best. The Revised English Bible, for one good instance, often renders *chesed* "unfailing love," as in Psalm 63:3. This is the love that stays loyal at whatever cost to self. We understand Jesus' faithfulness in taking the way of the cross to be *unfailing love* if we know the long promises of God declared in Scripture.

Our central exhibit of God's sociality is the doctrine of salvation (Chapter Three). God is a resident missionary. The news Jesus publishes is not only of future but also of present reunion. God the Savior offers present fellowship to the people of earth. This is the gospel of God. As God's *shaliach* (ambassador) Jesus reunites sinners with their Maker and with one another in the kingdom he proclaims. Jesus is in Origen's term the *autobasileia*; he himself is God's rule. Union with God, friendship with God, participation in the life of God (to recall three main aspects of salvation) all presuppose the divine sociality enacted in the Christ story itself.

iii. The organic moment.—The third moment is **God's relation to nature,** organic and inorganic—to the world, to the round globe, to the cosmos in which humankind is an integral if infinitesimal part. To the New Testament thought-world as to the Old, God is Creator. This Creator's relation to nature is not merely an account of origins; God is creatively *present* in the story the New Testament relates (cf. Chapter Four). This was implicit in the collections of miracle-stories that historians think circulated among believers before the first New Testament writings. Helmut Koester summarizes the evidence for these (1990:3.2.1). For example, Paul's missionary opponents wooed the Corinthian church by presenting "letters of recommendation" (2 Cor. 3:1) that listed the mighty achievements they had accomplished—healings, exorcisms, ecstasies, visions, prayers (cf. 2 Cor. 5:13; 12:1-9). Other evidence comes from the existing texts of the Gospels of Mark and John. Behind these, scholars detect similar commendations of Jesus—lists of the mighty works attributed to him. John 2–11 is named by scholars "the Book of Signs," beginning with the wine miracle at Cana (John 2:1-11) and culminating in the raising of Lazarus (11:1-45). All this constitutes evidence of God's character: in early Christian belief, God is "ruler of all nature."

What is remarkable, though, is that these mighty works of God are not heightened, but moderated, in the New Testament. Perhaps in a miracle-happy age the gospel could not have gotten off the ground without some such attestation. Yet in canonical Scripture one finds great restraint in reporting it. Paul, for example, declines to furnish the Corinthians with any 'letters of recommendation' on his own account. His self-distancing report of a vision (2 Cor. 12:2-4) is followed by the report of a trial (a "thorn in the flesh") from which he three times prayed the Lord to free him, only to be told, "My grace is all you need; power is most fully seen in weakness" (2 Cor. 12:8f; cf. Borsch, 1983:111-27). The 'Book of Signs' in John reports the miracle chain from Cana to Bethany (John 2–11), but laces it with another chain of signs—new birth and baptism in chapter 3, life-giving drink in chapters 4 and 5, bread from heaven in chapter 6, light and sight in chapters 8 and 9, rescue through faith from death in chapters 10 and 11—a chain like the first, yet with distinctly 'natural' signs interpreting Jesus by declaring his healing, saving mission to and through the organic world itself. Spectacular signs, real though they are, may distract and delude, yet this second chain equally declares the **ongoing, creative, earthly presence of God.** The Wisdom literature witnesses to this in still another mode, by emphasizing God's orderly control of the cosmos.

c. The Word, the Spirit, and the Father.—The New Testament provides no theoretical tracts upon 'God the Adventurer,' 'God the Companion,' 'God the Effectually Present One.' ~~Rather, these themes merge to declare God present in Jesus Christ, who is the center of the story, and to declare God present in the fellowship of the church.~~ To see this double presence is to come to the very core of the Christian doctrine of God. It is to see God in Christian perspective as unmixed Good News.

i. God in Christ.—It is worth recalling here once more the questions (Part II, Introduction) that have shaped the search for the identity of Jesus Christ. Expressed as demands, these require a teaching church to teach *(1) the Lordship of Christ, (2) the unity of God, and (3) the authenticity of the common life in Christ.* Historically, these demands became clear at various stages and were met with uneven skill by assorted Christian theorists. As we saw in the previous chapter, they evoked a variety of models: Logos, two-natures, historical, and still others. Yet behind all these lay the age of the New Testament, where these underlying questions first arose. While we must be careful not to impose later thought upon them, it is significant that the New Testament writers fulfilled all three of the classic demands: In the New Testament, the presence of God is fully and truly realized in the life, death, and resurrection of Jesus Christ, and Christ's peerless Lordship, the Spirit's presence in community, and God's Oneness are together maintained.

We may glimpse this in part through the eyes of an unfriendly witness. From the year 112 there exists a letter (*Epp.* 10.96) from Pliny the Younger, a high career diplomat serving in Bithynia, to the Emperor Trajan in Rome. Describing the new *superstitio,* Pliny wrote of some Christians he had arrested that "on an appointed day they had been accustomed to meet before daybreak, and to recite a hymn antiphonally to Christ, as to a god, and to bind themselves by an oath (*sacramentum*), not for the commission of any crime but to abstain from theft, robbery, adultery, and breach of faith, and not to deny a deposit when it was claimed." Pliny reported his compliance with current Roman practice: he had sent to their deaths those who did not recant. As for hymns "to Christ, as to a god," there is more to be said. The Prologue of the Fourth Gospel (1:1-18) is construed by some as a hymn. Could something like it have been one of the hymns that Pliny's Bithynian Christians sang before dawn?

Hymn or not, the Prologue of John's Gospel stands apart. Its key term, *logos,* is not used of Jesus in the rest of the Gospel, though "God's only Son" (1:14, *monogenous*) is echoed in John 3:16 and 3:18. Even if this latter term should not be translated "only-begotten" (as it is in the Vulgate and King James versions), it certainly bespeaks a unique *relation* between Jesus and the God he calls Father. What is that unique relation? The Prologue's definitive answer is that Jesus, that flesh-and-blood human being *(sarx)* is the pre-existent *logos* of God (1:1, 14). It is tempting, in light of the later Logos model (see Chapter Six, §2), to understand this

as a contextual description, Christians offering Hellenistic readers a
term for Jesus such as their own philosophers might use. In this case
logos would be the rational order of the universe, its intrinsic structure
(Kleinknecht and Kittel, TDNT IV:69-143). Certainly some have understood this to be the Prologue's point (Bultmann, 1971:1-18). If so, John
meant that the rational divine order of the world took human shape in
Jesus—a convenient foothold for future Constantinianism! (cf. Yoder,
1985a:chap. 6). It seems more faithful to the Prologue itself, however, to
read *logos* as does the Septuagint, in translation of Hebrew *dabar*, and to
associate it with the *speaking, the word of God* in Hebrew Scripture (Gen.
1:3; Deut. 33:9; Pss. 33:6; 68:11; Isa. 40:6-8; 55:10-11; Amos 3:8; cf. Wisd.
of Sol. 9:1-2; 18:15). Jesus is God's utterance.

There is a rich parallelism between the Prologue and Hebrew Scripture:
Compare John 1:1-5 with Genesis 1:1-5 ("In the beginning . . ."); or John 1:11 with
Hosea 1:8ff (God's own people rejecting God and disowned by God); or John
1:14 with Isaiah 7:14 ("made his home" and *Immanuel*). Raymond Brown believes
the words translated "grace and truth" (1:14) are correlative with Hebrew *chesed*
and *'emet*, "reliable or unfailing love" (R. Brown, 1986:14). Dale Moody, noting
the parallel between the *Shekinah* glory that represents God's awesome nearness
in the Aramaic Targums of Hebrew Scripture and the "glory" (*doxa*) of John 1:14,
writes: "This gospel is seen in a new light when viewed against the Aramaic
background" (IDB IV:317-19). A further parallel is *logos* as wisdom in Jewish
Wisdom literature (Proverbs, Sirach, Baruch, Wisdom of Solomon) (T. Tobin,
ABD IV:353-55).

Scholars differ about Hellenistic versus Hebrew antecedents here, but
there can be little dispute about the parallel between its Prologue and
the remainder of the Gospel. *Logos* is not repeated in the Gospel, because
the equivalent of *logos* is no single item in the Gospel but its entirety
understood as the Word that God spoke in sending Jesus Christ (Kittel,
TDNT VI:124-36). The Gospel narrative is God's spoken word, and Jesus
the living chief actor of that gospel is God's word enfleshed, he is the
word at human scale. This refers not to the lesser sign of the wonderful
birth of Jesus—a topic that does not attract this Gospel writer—but to
the sign of signs, the life, death, resurrection of *monogenēs theos* (John
1:18), the unique, the only God.

It is noteworthy, though not a linchpin of my reading of the Prologue, that
logos, a many-valued Greek word, can also mean *story* or *narrative* (Debrunner,
TDNT IV:69-72). If "story" is closest to its intended meaning here, the Gospel's
story line—the story of a Divine One who loves and lives to save, who suffers
and dies but overcomes (see e.g. John 3:16)—is no contingency for a single age
and a small planet, but expresses in this compressed way the eternal character
of God: "In the beginning was this story; the story was with God; it *was* God.
Through the story, all things were made, and without it, nothing. . . ." No

impersonal myth, this story, but the life of God enlightening the darkness of the world at this place and time—and forever (see this chapter's conclusion).

To ask whether the pre-existing divine *logos* of John's Prologue was a distinct 'hypostasis' or 'person' (technical terms of the later Christology) is to ask a confused question. John's thought-world is closer to the Old Testament than to such later concerns. (The same is true of the parallel passages in Hebrews 1:1-3 and elsewhere.) Rather we must ask if John firmly identifies the pre-existing *logos* with the one God. He does. The story that follows, the body of the Gospel, must then be God's own story throughout, although it is a fully and truly human story as well (M. M. Thompson, 1988). It is this Gospel's art to convey this wonderful truth in almost every chapter. Thus, if Pliny's hapless Christian victims were guided by John's Gospel, they did not merely sing (as Pliny supposed) "as to a god"; they sang to Christ *as to the only God*—a fact beyond Pliny's conception. For the God of the Gospel became human in Jesus, and at Gospel's end one disciple fitly exclaims, "My Lord and my God" (John 20:28).

ii. God as Holy Spirit.—We are considering the God of Jesus Christ in a heuristic or exploratory frame of three spheres, as developed in *Ethics*. Throughout anastatic, corporate, and organic (or natural) fields of force, we glimpse God in Jesus Christ as God the Adventurer, God the Companion, and God the Powerfully Present One. Only in the roughest way do these correspond to later, refined trinitarian categories. Nor does this threefold sketch sum up what the early Christians knew about God; at best it creates a workspace for investigating the spheres, in and beyond their own lives, in which God was God for them. Clearly, in Jesus their risen Lord, they knew one who acted in all these spheres or modes: The God of Jesus Christ signaled the advancing End, stood with them as a present Friend, ruled earth and cosmos as creative Power. The dynamism and breadth of this conception, matchlessly epitomized in the Prologue, is fit preparation for the Jesus story that follows.

There is as well the approach to God in Scripture by way of the Spirit-consciousness of the early Christian community. "Spirit," like "word," was a part of the Hebraic heritage, and it translated easily into the Greek and Latin thought-world as well, where missionaries could employ *pneuma* and *spiritus* to proclaim the gospel of God. In its Hebrew form, *ruach*, we sense not a substance but an event—the breathing of an animal, its very life; it is the air of life for human beings, also; without it, they die. Spirit is God's gift, and like the wind (also *ruach*), it signals the Lord's active presence. So "spirit" denotes the powerful, effectual presence of God, and hence that power by which God speaks to his servants the prophets (DB, 840-42). A typical passage is Ezekiel's call. The prophet sees a vision, and God's word commands "Stand up, O man, and let me talk with you." Whereupon "a spirit *[ruach]* came into me and *stood* me on my feet" (1:28–2:2). Here God's word is his demand, while God's *ruach* empowers Ezekiel to comply with that demand. Spirit (and other terms for God's immediate action, such as Angel, Wisdom, and Word) is sometimes personified in the Old Testament to make vivid the active presence of God in the world (cf. Robinson, 1928:Introduction).

The New Testament writers inherited these thought-modes from the Old, adapted them to express the new that had come in Christ, and adjusted them to the new context in mission. The radical new thing was that the Spirit now was the Spirit of Jesus; God's Spirit had become the Spirit of Jesus Christ. Two or more generations after Pentecost, the Gospel writers would link old and new by presenting God's Spirit (or Holy Spirit, which means the same, since holiness is God's alone) as the dynamic divine aid to Jesus during his earthly ministry, and as the Spirit of Jesus promised for the coming time of the church. The outlook is captured in Luke-Acts' account of the first martyrdom:

> Stephen, filled with the Holy Spirit, and gazing intently up to heaven, saw the glory of God, and Jesus standing at God's right hand. "Look," he said. "I see the heavens opened and the Son of Man standing at the right hand of God." At this they gave a great shout, and stopped their ears; they made a concerted rush at him, threw him out of the city, and set about stoning him. (Acts 7:55-58a)

In this numinous moment, Stephen sees the glory *(doxa)* of God and Jesus seated in the place of authority. Yet he does not see *the Spirit, for the Spirit, intimate enabler, was within him,* allowing Stephen to see the vision of Jesus in his place and to die a faithful death (7:60).

The New Testament, then, advances the understanding of Spirit it receives from the Old. The Spirit never clearly becomes as it did in later Christian writings a "distinct divine person"—terminology to be clarified in the following Section (§2). What the New Testament does do, as its central narrative demands it should, is to broaden and deepen the biblical idea of *God* so that God's true role as Trailblazer and Co-conspirator and Divine *Dynamis* is conveyed. Our present business is to secure a base line in Scripture that will guide understanding as, in the next Section (§2), we review some key contexts of subsequent Christian thought.

iii. God as Father.—The ancient world was accustomed to think of the supreme God as a father. "Father Zeus" was supposed to be the literal progenitor of the Greek gods, and hence an honorific father to mortals as well. This conformed with an ancient and recurrent human myth by which nations originated as the spawn of their deities—a primitive creation tale. The Hebrews, too, knew God as the originating father of their peoplehood, but there were two significant differences: (1) JHWH was an *adoptive* father. There was no hint here of sexual procreation. And (2) this adoption was a liberation; precisely, it was redemption from Egyptian bondage.

> I have heard the groaning of the Israelites, enslaved by the Egyptians, and I am mindful of my covenant. Therefore say to the Israelites, "I am the LORD, I shall free you from your labours in Egypt and deliver you from slavery. I shall rescue you with outstretched arm and with mighty acts of judgement. I shall adopt you as my people, and I shall be your God." (Exod. 6:5-7a)

According to Genesis, Robert Hamerton-Kelly points out, Israel in Egypt already had a claim on God's unfailing love, for Israel was descended from Abraham, Isaac, and Jacob—the *fathers* of Israel. In this regard, however, the Exodus constituted a subversive break with the authority of the past. Not only the spurious claim of father Pharaoh to rule Israel, but also the legitimate claim of the Hebrew past—the patriarchal past— was overturned by substituting for it a new authority, a new, covenanted fatherhood that looked toward the future and placed its hope there.

> If only you will now listen to me and keep my covenant, then out of all peoples you will become my special possession; for the whole earth is mine. You will be to me a kingdom of priests, my holy nation. (Exod. 19:5-6a)

In place of the rights of patriarchy, whether those of Pharaoh or those stemming from Abraham, a new 'fatherhood' is inaugurated, based upon the fidelity of JHWH but also upon the fidelity of the 'kingdom of priests,' the people themselves. Indeed, Abraham's own discovery had been finding God on the move; he had to abandon his "father's house" (Gen. 12:1) in order to encounter God in faithfulness. "So 'father' means freedom in two senses: freedom from human bondage, and the freedom for a loving relationship with God based on faith rather than fate" (Hamerton-Kelly, 1979:100).

More important, "Father" was Jesus' chosen word for God. In this choice, not inevitable in the Judaism of his day, Jesus appropriated both these elements of the Exodus account: (1) Jesus' Father was the *liberator* from bondage. This included religious bondage, political bondage, social and cultural bondage, and the bondage of one's own sin. (2) Jesus'

Father was the familiar divine *friend* awaiting the cry of the human heart. Gospel writers attribute "Father" to Jesus, speaking either to or about God, as many as 170 times, while Paul, following Jesus' lead, uniformly opens and closes his letters with reference to "God the Father"—a practice scholars believe reflects the earliest patterns of Christian worship as well (Kasper, 1984:140-44).

But in the second and later centuries, something else happened. The "Father" Jesus knew as intimate and as liberator was assimilated in Christian speech to father Zeus, the maintenance God of things-as-they-are. This assimilation became particularly tempting after the Constantinian settlement, when the Roman emperor became officially (and perhaps not insincerely) Christian. Now the one Empire was thought to be sustained by the one God, who in keeping with the old myth was the supreme Monarch. Even as the doctrine of the Trinity developed, this monotheism was maintained, securing the ultimate rightness of the *status quo ante*. If in these circumstances Christians prayed to "Our Father in heaven," it was perhaps uncertain whether theirs was the radically subversive prayer of Abraham, of Moses, and of Jesus, or the smug, patriarchal prayer of the powers that be (cf. Peterson, 1951; Schindler, ed., 1978; Moltmann, 1981:chap. 6).

*   *   *   *   *

This section has not summed up the New Testament doctrine of God—a task best left to biblical encyclopedias. Our task was different. It was to show the Christian good news as good news about God. This did not mean that pagans were offered some (or some more) 'religious experiences,' or that benighted ancients who lacked a morality were offered one, courtesy of the Christians. Of course, when the gospel appears, experience changes. Of course morality changes—yet the news is greater, more radical, than 'experience' or 'morality' can indicate. Was it then a new *philosophy* of God? More than that, also, as we shall see. The God Christians know is the God of Jesus Christ, that is, the God known to them as they know the risen Christ and share the fellowship called church. Neither Christ nor Spirit is confined to the pages of the New Testament. So we have searched there and beyond for the impact of Jesus Christ, and the entailed impact of God's Holy Spirit—a wider search, and one hardly begun here. The results to this point will disappoint some. Spheres of action for Jesus' God have been indicated, and names for God named, some familiar, some strange. Yet "God" has not been defined here, or God's essence described, apart from the Israel-Jesus-church story itself. There is a reason for this apparent omission, but it can best be presented (§3) after a brief philosophical review (§2).

§2. Some Philosophical Lessons in Divinity

It is appropriate at the outset to say something about the impact of philosophy on Christian doctrine. The point is sometimes made that all human conduct and thought presuppose some philosophy or other, and in the sense that our everyday convictions are fodder for the philosophers' professional ruminations, no doubt this is so, though to dignify the rough-and-ready convictions of our daily lives as 'philosophy' may be excessive. What is more clearly the case is that when human convictions, including the ones Christians believe are God-given, are disputed, philosophical weapons are regularly brought into play by one or more of the parties. This has happened in connection with many Christian doctrines—one thinks of eschatology, or of sacramental theology—but with none more frequently than the doctrine of God. "The God of the philosophers," meaning a philosophical concept of God, has thus become a set phrase in these discussions, even though, as we will see, there is no single philosophical concept of God. (Nor is one to be expected, since philosophers are as likely as the rest of us to be shaped by their own diverse convictions.) I propose here to review three episodes in the history of Christian thought, recalling the impact of philosophy upon theology in each case: (a) for its lasting influence, *the early trinitarian controversy*, (b) for its (since distorted) theological clarity in a difficult time, *the theism of Thomas Aquinas*, and (c) as an American representative of still powerful subjectivist modernity, *the transcendentalism of Ralph Waldo Emerson*. The process should heighten our awareness of the contribution of philosophy to Christian doctrine as well as its cost.

a. The trinitarian controversy.—We saw in the previous chapter that the attempt of early Christians to interpret the gospel of Jesus Christ gave rise to questions whose resolution led to still further debate. The ultimate outcome was the formation, amid controversy, of ancient Christology in its Logos and two-natures models. The same controversies had another side, bearing on the Holy Spirit, on God the Father, and on what came to be called the divine Trinity. The concerns about Christ's status and his relation to God were matched by concerns regarding the Spirit's status and relation to God, and of course the relation between Christ and the Spirit. Thus all the topics we know as trinitarian arose explicitly between the second and sixth centuries in the work of theologians

~~previously noted—Origen and Tertullian, Athanasius and Arius, Cyril~~
~~and Nestorius, the Cappadocians (Basil and the two Gregories),~~
~~Augustine, and John of Damascus.~~

i. The Logos stage: latent trinitarianism.—Near-trinitarian thought
appears in the New Testament. Second Corinthians' grand Pauline
benediction ("the grace of the Lord Jesus Christ, and the love of
God, and the fellowship of the Holy Spirit, be with you all," 2 Cor.
13:14) was written in the fifties. It seems to attribute equal dignity
to three correlative targets of Christian faith, Christ, God, and
Spirit, while "God" for Paul is regularly "God our Father" (e.g., 2
Cor. 1:2). Moreover, this triadic attribution seems to have been a
widely shared feature of early Christianity: it recurs in the Apocalypse (e.g., Rev. 1:4f) and again at the conclusion of Matthew as an
element of early Christian worship ("baptize them in the name of . . ."
Matt. 28:19f), and it seems to stand behind many other New Testament passages as well (see dictionaries of the New Testament). Yet
as we have seen, in these writings there is little or no evidence of
the theological speculation that was to come later. Thus many prefer
to speak here of the divine *Triad*, reserving the term "Trinity" for
what was still to come. Neither word appears in the New Testament
itself.

We saw in the previous chapter that Logos Christologies were
shaped to combat two rivals, Ebionism, which was content to speak of
Jesus the prophet who had risen from the dead and would come again,
and Gnosticism, a full-fledged religion in itself, which taught an elaborate chain-of-being cosmology extending from the inaccessible high
God through many spiritual intermediaries (one of which might be
called *logos*) to the poverty of earthly matter. Gnostic inclusivism made
a place for Jesus, but its 'salvation' meant escape from matter and its
evil rather than following the earthly way of the cross to the end.
Against these, Logos theologies (Justin and Irenaeus in the West, Clement and Origen in the East) waged a two-front intellectual war: Against
Ebionism, they insisted on the deity, in some sense, of the pre-existent
Logos who had taken flesh in Jesus of Nazareth, while against the
Gnostics they maintained tight links between the Logos and God (citing
John 1:1) on the one hand, and between the Logos and Jesus (John 1:14)
on the other. At the same time, there was the Holy Spirit, "most
honorable of all the beings" (Origen, *In Ioh.* 2.10.75), though the Spirit's
status would require further clarification. All this provided material for
a coming doctrine of a triune God, and Origen (fl. 250–280) provided
still another element by teaching the eternal generation of the Son, not

in a biological sense, but in the sense in which the sun in the sky continually generates its own brilliance (*De prin.* 1.2.4).

While the not yet canonized New Testament and ongoing Christian worship were two powerful factors shaping the Logos model, philosophy was another. In his late twenties Origen had been a student in the Neoplatonic school in Alexandria, whose pagan teacher, Ammonius Saccas, also taught Plotinus. Plotinus later put forward his own philosophical trinity: the one (Plato's supreme, impersonal God), the mind *(nous)*, and a third element *(psyche*, soul), which causes the world of sense experience. It is significant that Plotinus the Pagan and Origen the Christian independently developed such 'trinities' (on Plotinus' influence on Christians see D. Allen, 1985:70-81).

ii. The two-natures stage: patent trinitarianism.—The Council of Nicaea (325) set the stage for the next development. Although its creed confessed the full deity of Christ ("of one substance *[homoousios]* with the Father") it added merely "we believe *[pisteuomen]* in the Holy Spirit," without further elaboration. Clearly there was more work to be done, but there were many hands for the task. Athanasius, during one of his forced exiles (358), wrote "Letters to Serapion," which taught that "the Spirit is fully divine, consubstantial with the Father and the Son" (Kelly, 1960:257). Meanwhile Bishop Basil of Caesarea, one of the 'Cappadocian' trio, began to teach his biblically conservative flock similar views. It is interesting that according to fellow Cappadocian Gregory of Nazianzus, Basil as late as 372 still carefully avoided speaking openly of the Spirit's deity. His method was a tactful reserve. Yet by 375, Basil composed "On the Holy Spirit," which was close to the Athanasian view. Finally, it was Gregory of Nazianzus, summoned to imperial Constantinople to defend Nicene orthodoxy against the Arians, who took the final step, asserting in his "Fifth Theological Oration" the Spirit's consubstantial deity and distinct essential being (Gregory, *Theol. orat.* 5.28-33).

The positive arguments that Athanasius, Basil, and Gregory made that today might seem persuasive are chiefly four: There is Scripture, in which the Spirit's role is divine in scope and power, and where the Spirit appears "within the Triad" (Athanasius, *Ad Serap.* 1:21). There is the close relation of Spirit to Father and Son in the liturgy. Perhaps most powerful, the Spirit makes believers partakers of divinity (as the baptismal formula implies), and so the Spirit must be divine. The most original argument, though, is that of Gregory of Nazianzus, who advances a sophisticated case for theological *development:* Old Testament, New Testament, and Christian history ("among us") represent successive stages of revelation. It would have been confusing to disclose the Son's deity while in the Old Testament the Father's deity was being established, and equally unsuitable to make known the Spirit's full deity until the disciples had received the Son. Now at last, in the fourth century A.D., the time had come for the promised greater truth of the Spirit to be disclosed (Gregory, *Theol. orat.* 5.26f; cf. John 14:26). This was not modalism, since the successive stages did not erase previous ones.

Given this divine Triad, the problem was to provide a rational way to maintain the divine unity. These ancient thinkers keenly felt "tritheism" as a reproach. Harry Wolfson distinguishes the two main ways by which they met the problem: The oneness of monotheism could be a oneness of divine *rule* or a oneness of divine *substratum*. The former device was early employed in ways many judged heretical: dynamistic and modalistic 'monarchianism.' The first of these held merely that an 'energy' or *dynamis* from the one God came as the Son upon Jesus or as the Spirit upon disciples. The second device, Sabellian *modalism*, taught that the three had been chronologically successive modes of the one divine Being, each only God for a season, or rather for an earthly aeon. This was more persuasive, but had its own evident difficulties—if the present was the age of the Spirit, there was no more Father or Son. Yet the idea of monarchianism or singular divine rule could be employed in more acceptable ways: If the Father was the one Ruler, upon whom Word and Spirit were internally dependent, the singularity was maintained, only now at cost of the subordination of the two (Son and Spirit) to the supreme One. Or (Wolfson's other main way) monotheism could be maintained by way of the substratum: in this version Being *(ousia)* was common to the Godhead, while distinct *personae* (not meant in our modern sense of "persons") or *hypostaseis,* foci of being, were the property of the Father, the Word, and the Spirit respectively. And this was the solution adopted in the Council of Chalcedon (451). The three were internally and timelessly related; the Father 'ungenerate,' the Son 'generated' by the Father, the Spirit 'proceeding' from the Father. As had the earlier versions of trinity, this latest owed much to philosophy, in this case to Aristotle's *Categories* and *Metaphysics* (Book Delta). In the latter work, Aristotle had said that things may be one because they share an underlying substratum, or because they are of one genus, yet there remained for Eastern theologians the resultant difficulty of explaining the intended distinctions between Father, Son, and Spirit without re-enforcing the suspicion that, after all, Christians taught belief in three Gods (or even four, if the substratum counted separately) not one God (Wolfson, 1970:chap. 15).

Here help had appeared earlier in the West, where Tertullian (c. 160– c. 230) and later Augustine (354–430), with their Latin austerity, held to a simpler monotheism. For Tertullian, Father, Son, and Spirit were *personae (Adv. Prax. 25)*, by which he meant something like appearances rather than (modern) individual persons (even today, we retain Tertullian's ancient Latin sense of "person" when our playbill lists the *dramatis personae*, the roles in the play). Augustine explained the oneness of the triune God in a fresh way by means of a psychological analogy. As in all human perception there is the thing seen, the mental image, and the intention or will that relates these, so in God there is a corresponding relational structure; indeed, the divine *personae* are not substances (which would be tritheistic) but *relations* (Augustine, *De trin.*; citations in Kelly, 1960:271-79). Such ways of thought bound the Trinity together dynamically, and were eventually echoed in the East in the relatively late Greek concept of *perichōrēsis*—the understanding that the three *hypostaseis* penetrate one another completely. Augustine expressed his view of indivisibility in a motto, *Opera trinitatis ad extra indivisa sunt:* the action of God toward that outside God is not to be assigned to one or another 'person' alone (see Welch, 1952:s.v. "opera"). The Father creates, but creates "by the Word," while the Spirit acts as Creator Spirit. And so with all the works of God.

There is much reason to be sympathetic with the goals and achievements of ancient trinitarian thought. It took the raw material of Scripture (ahistorically understood, to be sure), correlated this with the main motifs of Christian common worship, and produced a doctrine that remained intact for centuries while the intellectual world in which it had taken shape expired, and a new world, our Middle Ages, struggled to be born. Yet certain difficulties, linked with the underlying idea of "God" in the doctrine, persisted. Was God the remote deity of Aristotle and the Neoplatonists? Or was God the God of Jesus and the prophets, dynamic, demanding, personal, immediate? Ancient trinitarian teaching could provide ad hoc answers to these questions as required, but it could do so only by keeping some elements of its own teaching temporarily out of sight. And the oneness and threeness of God were resolved in such different ways by the East and the West as to hasten the dissolution of Catholic unity (*Filioque* controversy). Clearly, more thought was demanded, and in time, more would appear.

b. The theism of Thomas Aquinas.—Although many interpreters of Christian doctrine leap from Augustine straight to Thomas Aquinas, it is important to recognize the flavor of the long interval separating these two, an interval in which Western thought shifted farther away from the Platonic models that Augustine himself had only partly left behind. The theological tools of the late thirteenth century thus came to include not only the Scriptures and the patristic *catenae*, topically arranged chains of quotations from earlier Fathers, but also philosophical texts from Neoplatonists such as Pseudo-Dionysius (fifth or early sixth century) as well as from Arabic Muslim and Sephardic Jewish philosophers, including Ibn Sina (Avicenna), Ibn Rushd (Averroës), and Moses Maimonides, to say nothing of many less well-known medieval thinkers (Burrell, 1986).

Thus a lively Aristotelian tradition came to challenge the older Christian Platonism. Thomas Aquinas (1225–74) learned from his teacher, Albert the Great, that in contemporary Paris, the case for Christian faith must be made in Aristotelian terms.

Three features of Aristotle's work were of special importance for Thomas. First, Aristotle had begun metaphysical reflection from the actuality of existing things. What was most evidently real was not eternal forms (Plato) or unformed prime matter (Pre-Socratics), but the given items of daily life—this house, that table, that individual named Socrates, this book on the table. Yet such things fell into classes, so in a secondary sense "substance" could be assigned to the species 'table' or 'man,' and it was possible, finally, to think of a class of pure substance, altogether free of matter. That would be God. Furthermore, Aristotle's was a universe in motion. Everything moved, and the causes of events were found in that motion. One thing moved another, and the First Cause, or Prime Mover, was God, the matterless substance. God, however, did not move, but was fully occupied with his thought (his or its, for Aristotle's God seems strangely impersonal). Other things were moved by their attraction to this Prime Mover. Finally, Aristotle was a subtle logician, treating logic as a necessary implement of all branches of philosophy, and withal a follower of Plato in his attention to linguistic analysis.

After several preliminary works, Thomas Aquinas made his Aristotelian case in an apologetic *Summa contra Gentiles*, and then turned to the systematic unfolding of the faith in the *Summa Theologiae* (later called *Summa Theologica*). Here the Aristotelian influence continued to show itself. After establishing its task ("the fundamental aim of holy teaching is to make God known"), Thomas set out in the three Parts of *Summa Theologiae* to treat God, the journey to God, and Christ who is the road for that journey. Meantime, he continued to write extensive commentaries on the Bible, while teaching and preaching without interruption.

All of these Aristotelian themes converged in a chief problem Thomas faced in the *Summa Theologiae*. In brief, how could the remote Prime Mover of Aristotelian philosophy be replaced by the dynamic, biblical God of Jesus Christ without inviting immediate dissent from his philosophical conversation partners, the contemporary Aristotelians? Thomas' answer was to begin with Aristotle's given realities—individual things. From them, by five "ways" or paths, one could argue to a cause behind each and all. The Thomas of the five ways has sometimes been regarded as a naive rationalist who (mistakenly) believed the existence of God (and the contents of the divine nature) could be proved to all comers from scratch, so that any reasonable thinker must logically be compelled to believe in God. If any medieval thinker held this view, however, it was not Thomas. More accurately, the *Summa Theologiae*'s five ways aimed to corroborate or precipitate for Aristotelian thinkers the inchoate Christian belief in God. The aim was to bring out not only *that* God is, but particularly *what* God is, and that by showing what God is *not*. They start from premises that are everyday (medieval Aristotelian) knowledge, but the set of mind they presuppose is one that wants to know about "God . . . as the beginning and end of all things," that is, about the Creator God of biblical faith (*ST* 1.2.Intro.).

This goal is easily overlooked when a philosopher or historian (e.g., A. M. Fairweather, editor of the Library of Christian Classics' Aquinas—1954:50) omits from his selections the crucial *introductions* and *outlines* with which Thomas Aquinas prefaced his text. The unpurged text does appear (Latin and English) in the 60-volume Blackfriars edition of the *Summa* (Aquinas, 1964–76).

These arguments for the existence of God (an existence that can be doubted, but is shown to be contextually reasonable) are of first importance for Thomas not because of rampant atheism, a phenomenon still future in the thirteenth century, but because God's *being* God (i.e., existing) and God's being *God* (i.e., having the divine essence) were, in God's case as in no other, identical. So the five ways are not only arguments for God but also pointers to that essence, at least in a negative way: By displaying God as the source of whatever else there is, the five ways signal the *difference* between God and all else (*ST* 1.2.Intro.). Thomas conceived God as altogether other than creation. For this reason, at this stage of the *Summa*'s argument, Thomas holds that we can know not what God is, but only what God is not (*secondo quomodo sit vel potius quomodo non sit*); we must by the five 'proofs' consider the ways in which God does *not* exist (*ST* 1.2.Intro.). The distinction between created and uncreated being (between the world and God) demarcates the limit of earthly attempts to express God's reality. At this point (*ST* 1.3-13), Thomas presents what appear to be a number of qualities God possesses (simplicity, perfection, goodness, limitlessness, unchangeableness, and oneness) and explains each. It seems both Catholic and Protestant scholasticisms have taken this apparent value to be full value, and have produced extended discussions of each of these as *attributa divina* (Garrigou-Lagrange, 1943; Muller, 1985:48-50), divine attributes.

While in the main not saddled with such scholastic theologians, baptists have nonetheless here and there smuggled such language into their own confessions of faith. For example, the Second London Confession of the Particular Baptists (1677, 1688), eager to display its "hearty agreement" with the Westminster Assembly and the Congregationalists (and consequently with medieval scholasticism) on these matters, declared God "immutable, immense, eternal, incomprehensible, Almighty, every way infinite, most holy, most wise, most free, most absolute . . ." (Lumpkin, 1969:236, 252). Given the general misunderstanding of the role of these terms, one suspects that neophyte Baptist ministers, if obliged to study this classic confession, could sympathize with the term "incomprehensible," in any case (McClendon, 1966*a*).

Yet if David Burrell and others are correct, these latter-day heirs of Thomas Aquinas have missed the Angelic Doctor's point, which was not to describe the Aristotelian God afresh, but to use the concept of a limiting source of all else in order to *establish the limits* of what Christians could say about the God they knew to be "the beginning and end of all things." In the Aristotelian tradition, God's being and God's essence were inseparable; God, given his essence, could not not-be; for God to be God is the same as to be, period. It followed that God's existence is a different *kind* of existence, which must be the source of all other kinds. This distinction is sufficiently radical, Burrell would have us believe, that to apprehend it requires a *conversion* on the part of the reader. For it pictures a human existence immeasurably vivid because its source is a divine existence more vivid still (Burrell, 1986:3.3.1; 2.1.1).

Timothy McDermott gives a hint of the sort of (intellectual) conversion Thomas demands. God's relation to creation, he says, is in a way like the relation of Tolstoy to the characters in *War and Peace.* The vast difference is that Tolstoy's characters cannot communicate with their author. They exist in a fictional world and cannot escape it; they cannot even envisage their real author, Leo Tolstoy: "though they exist for him, he doesn't exist for them." Yet God's 'characters,' his creatures, are given a *real* existence, one that permits them to communicate not only with one another, but with God whose name they knew. Having their existence from God gives them that privilege. That makes such real existence unique in comparison with any other—and it suggests that God's existence, as "the beginning and end of all things," since it is in this way sharable, is indescribably great (McDermott in Aquinas, 1989:xxxi)—a gospel of God, indeed!

Finally, the rich linguistic resources of Aristotelian philosophy guide Thomas as he goes on to talk of God in biblical terms. What was just discussed is categorized as analogical talk of God *(analogice dicuntur)*; to that, Thomas can add metaphorical talk *(metaphorice de Deo dicuntur)*— according to Aristotle, a philosophically less important category. Taken together, though, the two sorts of discourse enable Thomas to make the great biblical affirmations: God is not only (analogically) wise and just and good, but is (metaphorically) the active, providential God, not only knowing but loving and doing, even while remaining the 'simple' and indescribable Deity who is beyond all human powers to define or to encompass (*ST* 1.14-26). Even Thomas' ultimate step, the exposition of God's trinitarian nature (*ST* 1.27-43), retains an Aristotelian flavor, because the basis of his triune account of God is what has happened in history—the history the Bible records, from earth's creation as a dwelling place for a people, to the repeated efforts of God to establish living intercourse with all people by way of Israel, the people for all peoples, through the coming of Christ to be Israel's emissary, God's emissary, to all the earth. These are facts, and what remains for doctrine is to make clear what the facts have to do with the nature of the undefinable God whom Aristotle long ago posited. Thomas' response is that only by way of the disclosed facts can we approach God's being, and the facts demand that God's being be triune—a God who is the source, and who is the source made available, and who is the available source enabling earth's peoples' response. Father, Son, Holy Ghost—one God. That is not a truth of Aristotelian philosophy, but it is a biblical revelation expressed via Aristotelian method (cf. McDermott in Aquinas, 1989: 63-65).

c. Emerson's Transcendentalism.—The medieval synthesis of Christian doctrine persisted strongly in the modern period. It remained almost unaffected by the sixteenth-century Reformation: God for Luther and Calvin remained the God of the synthesis, and Radical Reformers, save for proto-unitarians such as Faustus Socinus and his community, added or subtracted little. Enlightenment deism filed a minority report (leading Blaise Pascal to cry in protest against the God of the philosophers), yet for the time being the center held; theism, not deism, remained the teaching of the Christian church, and even the critical philosophy of Immanuel Kant clung to the necessity of God, "the ideal of pure reason," as the guarantor of morality and religion alike. Right through the eighteenth century, explicit atheism of the sort represented by the French Baron d'Holbach remained a philosophical oddity in Christendom. In the nineteenth century, however, a change set in, to which we may assign the name "subjectivism," or more insightfully "anthropocentrism." In nineteenth-century Europe, religion, including Christian doctrine, came to be viewed as a strictly human phenomenon so that God was not the author but the artifact of the religious consciousness. While subtle and reverent thinkers saw that, strictly speaking, this starting point did not invalidate the Christian teaching (for, unless it necessarily deceived itself, what the human mind construed to be divine was in itself no less divine in consequence of the construal), its practical consequence for many was to relativize and diminish God. If Christian truth was only Christians' truth, only a way of thinking, perhaps it was still true, but perhaps not. Was theology itself only anthropology, only human nature writ large? (cf. Welch, 1972–85 I:Part I, "The Possibility of Theology"). This change of thought deserves separate attention.

The most acute illustration of theological subjectivism is doubtless the humanistic atheism of Ludwig Feuerbach (1804–72), leader of the Hegelian left, whose work became the springboard for young Karl Marx. Feuerbach understood Hegel's idealism (the real is the rational) to point directly to the grandeur and self-sufficiency of human nature. Hegel was wrong only to conceive this as a mental or spiritual *(geistlich)* rather than a material phenomenon: for Feuerbach, *Der Mensch ist was er isst*—man is what he eats. Yet this was not to demean but to exalt human nature: The 'God' humankind ignorantly worships is but its own self projected upon the skies, and Feuerbach showed that the elements of Christian theology such as the incarnation can be reinterpreted as covert acknowledgment of this secret truth (1841). A far less radical version of this subjectivist tendency may be found in Friedrich Schleiermacher, whom Karl Barth was to see as "half-inclined towards the same goal" of reducing theology to anthropology. But Barth conceded that Luther was equally vulnerable to Feuerbach's alchemical reductions! (Barth, 1972:534, 538). With Schleiermacher, however, one must proceed with far more caution. It is true that his theological method, extracting everything in religion from the human sense of utter dependence, founded Christian doctrine also on that basis (Schleiermacher, CF §§4, 29). In his case, though, one must distinguish between the way God is known and the God who is known in this way, a God who is no illusion or projection, but the ultimate cause and source of all else (CF §§36–40). Schleiermacher's strict divine determinism might more fairly expose him to the charge of unduly reducing—not divinity, but—humanity, a reduction that owed more to Augustine and Calvin than to modernity.

The American figure who best illustrates both the strength and the weakness of modern subjectivism is neither of the above, but **Ralph Waldo Emerson** (1803–82). Descended from a long line of New England Puritans, Emerson early sensed a call to ministry at a time when unitarianism, theologically rationalist and liberal but socially conservative and elitist, was reaching its American zenith. After wrestling in this context with debilitating doubt (and suffering the death of his beloved young wife), Emerson finally accepted a call to Second Church, Boston, by then a unitarian parish, only to resign his pulpit over his refusal to observe the Lord's supper as an enduring ordinance. Emerson withdrew to his nearby Concord home, where his life and thought turned inward. He began to produce first a set of journals, then public lectures and published writings that staked out new ground in American religious thought. Here Emerson's philosophical context was New England Transcendentalism, but this was not so much an influence upon him as it was himself projected upon the group (Henry David Thoreau, Orestes Augustus

Brownson, Theodore Parker, Margaret Fuller, Amos Bronson Alcott, Isaac Thomas Hecker, among distinguished members), especially during its early stages. The wider influence for all these came from European romanticism (Herder, Schleiermacher, Coleridge, Carlyle) and for Emerson from Immanuel Swedenborg, a Swedish rationalistic mystic. Ultimately, the deep source of Transcendentalism lay in Plotinus and Platonizing mysticism (S. Ahlstrom, NCRTW II:29ff).

The focus of Emerson's teaching was upon the human self and its place in nature or, as he preferred to write, Nature. Alongside Thoreau, Emerson represents a somewhat mushier chapter in Americans' long love affair with the natural environment: In the woods, he writes in *Nature*, "I become a transparent eyeball; I am nothing; I see all . . ." (Emerson, 1983:10). As the self incarnates nature it must learn to trust itself ("every heart vibrates to that iron string"), must follow the law of nature, a law that teaches us to "seek good ends" or to be "at heart just," must be attuned to the spirit that puts nature forth through us "as the life of the tree puts forth new branches and leaves through the pores of the old." This *nature-mysticism* is the heart of Emerson's message. If we ask about the place of God in this scheme of things, Emerson is inclined to give us no direct answer. Partly, this is because he has learned to be highly suspicious of dogma, inherited 'truth,' received answers. Partly, his indirection is integral to his evocative literary style, which is inseparable from its content. Yet we can fairly say that God for Emerson is the *anima mundi*, the soul of the world, expressed in physical and especially organic nature, discerned in the free intuitions of mystic spirits like his own, and fulfilled in the sensitive awareness of a romantic age.

If style and substance are inseparable in Transcendentalist theology, it may be possible to suggest the whole by reviewing a single essay, "The Over-Soul" (Emerson, 1983:383-400). Human experience summed up, Emerson begins, counts for little, because the intervals of authentic experience are so rare. "Our faith comes in moments; our vice is habitual." These authentic moments have but one source. It is "that Unity, that Over-soul, within which every man's particular being is contained." Our own souls are the organs of this Over-soul; "there is no bar or wall" that separates the two. To open oneself to its influence is to be empowered, it is to be "related to all its works . . . particular knowledges and powers." It is to have a clue to all intercourse between human beings, as well. "In all conversation between two persons, tacit reference is made, as to a third party, to a common nature shared. That third party or common nature is not social; it is impersonal; it is God." Here the term "revelation" is invoked—"an influx of the Divine mind into our mind"—to explain all authentic religious phenomena over the ages. When such revelation comes, it discloses our soul, that is to say, the one Over-soul, to ourselves. Thence comes what we call genius among men, yet "the soul that ascends to worship the great God is plain and true; has no rose-color, no fine friends, no chivalry, no adventures"; it is its own authority and wants no other. "The soul gives itself, alone, original, and pure, to the Lonely, Original, and Pure."

Here, then, is an authentic New England religiousness, democratically available, as near empty of content as the severe abstractions of a Zen master or the meditative goals of a medieval contemplative, yet quite without the external baggage of monastery or cult center. Emerson could be read and was read in every schoolhouse; his meditation could be practiced in the orchard or the dairy; it did not hope so much to rebut as to transcend the daily religion of everyday Christians. While it honored churchly intentions, it passed over churchly practice, for the most part, in silence. It was Yankee mysticism; it was transmogrified Americana; it was two hundred proof subjectivity.

What of God, the God of Jesus Christ, in this ensemble of thoughts? Clearly, the Trinity is rejected. That rejection, achieved already in the literal reading of Scripture by post-Puritan rationalists from the time of Jonathan Edwards' great opponent, Charles Chauncy (1705–87), had long since become a fixture of the New England standing order except for the radicals of the New Divinity and the rear guard of Old Calvinists. To elite New England minds, unitarian doctrine was the quintessence of Protestantism. When in 1838 Emerson delivered the Divinity School address he had no need to fight that battle afresh; Harvard Divinity School was already unitarian and would remain so for a century. The task was rather to recover what had been lost with trinitarianism, the immediacy, the dynamic presence of God. Jesus, though a miracle-worker, was for the new standing order purely and only human; the Spirit was but an influence from God. Emerson's response, and the heart of Transcendentalism, was to assign to each human being what liberalism denied to Jesus. For Emerson, Jesus was not dogmatically speaking the Son of God, but every living soul was a son of God, a locus of the Over-soul. The Spirit was assuredly not as with the trinitarians a divine hypostasis, but God who is nothing, nothing but spirit breathes within every rock, inspires all events that are authentically human, opens to every opened mind. "In how many churches, by how many prophets, tell me, is man made sensible that he is an infinite Soul; that the earth and heavens are passing into his mind; that he is drinking forever from the soul of God?" (Divinity School Address, in Emerson, 1983:84).

Emersonian subjectivism is best understood in its contrast with European subjectivism. While the Transcendentalists borrowed and bent the language of Kant and Schleiermacher, Coleridge and Wordsworth, they never delved into the hermeneutics of suspicion created by Feuerbach (V. Harvey, NCRTW I:291ff). Whereas Feuerbach's religious humanism was compelled to uncover every God-illusion, for Emerson and his friends the Over-soul was not illusion but illumination; it was reality itself come to light. On the other side of the account, however, there was a fracture between Emerson's explicitly Christian terminology ("God," "Jesus," "Spirit," "Soul," etc.) and his early and enduring rejection of the Scriptures and church tradition alike. At first his dissent was expressed in terms drawn from Swedenborg and rationalist unitarian thought; later it came by way of his own developed theory of nature and its revelatory role (S. Ahlstrom, NCRTW II:29-38). Perhaps this rejection best reflected itself in Emerson's general lack of interest in the vital moral issues that racked America in his day—slavery and its aftermath, the Civil War, women's liberation struggles, the coming battles for social justice in an industrial society—issues in which the churches, whatever side they took, were deeply involved. The Over-soul, though, was remote from all that.

Given the long decline of theistic conviction of any sort within the Unitarian Universalist movement in the century just past, the strongest echoes of Emersonian thought are to be found elsewhere. Students of American religion may think of the cluster of movements that Sydney Ahlstrom denotes **harmonial religion:** "those forms of piety and belief in which spiritual composure, physical health, and even economic well-being are understood to flow from a person's rapport with the cosmos" (Ahlstrom, 1972:1019). These would include Christian Science, New Thought, the Unity School of Christianity, and writers such as Ralph Waldo Trine (1866–1958), author of *In Tune with the Infinite,* and Norman Vincent Peale (1898–), author of *The Power of Positive Thinking,* and his successor, Robert Schuller of Crystal Cathedral. More recently, it would include California's silenced Dominican priest, Matthew Fox (1940–), and the New Age movement he typified. Yet the striking feature of Emersonian thought is its presence within the culture—and the churches of the culture—apart from any organized conveyance. In the apparent neglect of his teaching, Emerson triumphs still.

§3. The Deity of God

It begins to be clear why no 'definition of God' shapes this chapter. Certainly, such definitions appear in the literature (see dictionaries of theology), yet they mislead. Every realm of discourse has its primitive concepts—physicists speak of energy, mathematicians of equality, ecologists of nature, poets of beauty—and none are the worse for their inability to define or analyze their own primal element. If faithful utterance about God falters or fails, this does not discredit the speaker but illuminates the limitless task, and what is said here must not at last succeed where it is failure that best keeps faith with the task. Awe, not categorization, monitors theology's Godward threshold. There is a silence in heaven when the Lamb breaks the seventh seal (Rev. 8:1). To violate that silence may constitute rash disregard of the Lamb, and of heaven itself.

a. Providential atheism?—As our times unfold, atheism sounds its tonic pitch. So recently as the eighteenth century, this was not the case. Even skeptical philosophers in that century retained 'God' as part of the metaphysical furniture, though doing so mattered less as time went by. The narrator in David Hume's *Dialogues* stakes out a minimal position: God's existence is granted ("what truth so obvious, so certain?"), yet the question about what kind of God there is turns out to be equally troubling for traditional believers (Hume, 1779:4). In the following century, however, matters were different. Feuerbach in philosophy, Marx in economics, Nietzsche in literature, Comte in social science, Lenin in politics all agreed to dethrone God—to erase the puerility of any God, to discard the needless hypothesis, to break the illusion, to overcome the tyranny. This nineteenth-century assault was followed by widespread indifference. Many contemporary Europeans and Americans, finding they could no longer take God for granted, lapsed into uncertainty. It seemed God could neither be proved nor disproved. This being so, it would be pleasing if God's reality mattered less, and for a great many this came to be the case. Though some might still wonder, in their idle hours, what one *could* believe on so 'intangible' a topic, others were content not even to wonder. In the spirit of eighteenth-century philosopher Julien de La Mettrie, they found they had "no need of that hypothesis." Thus there arose a misleading simultaneity between the silent awe that waits upon the Unbounded One and the silence of confusion congealed into indifference. Even when both silences occur at once, they are neither identical nor coherent. The one is

silent as a nun, breathless with adoration (Wordsworth)

while the other inhabits lifeless space unstirred by any wind. This incoherent double silence has touched the theology of the time. On the one hand, Christian theology like Christian faith trembles before the mighty heritage of Israel, of Jesus, and of the living Spirit in communion. On the other, Christian theology is stultified by attempts to provide "the secular meaning of the gospel" (early Paul van Buren) or alternatively by attempts to secure an embalmed perpetuity for old time religion. These crosscurrents vex the theological silence (cf. Gilkey, 1969; Lash, 1988:chap. 14).

i. Nietzsche.—Friedrich Nietzsche (1844–1900) comprehends so many of modern atheism's themes that his life-and-thought (which were much of a piece) stand duty for many others. His mad intensity (Nietzsche died insane) thrusts him above yet not separate from the Western European culture he embodied. More than any single figure, he embodies that culture's turn to a post-Christian stance—its long-postponed rejection of the Constantinian synthesis. Educated a German Lutheran, Nietzsche never forgot his past. Hence his atheism was not, for example, Buddhist or positivist, but distinctly 'Christian,' even Protestant, as he bound his thought about God fast to the biblical narrative, however incorrectly he read the latter. Nietzsche knew that God and the Jesus story must swim or (as he intended) sink together. A brief quotation conveys the flavor:

> I regard Christianity as the most fatal seductive lie that has yet existed, as the great unholy lie. . . . I reject every compromise position with respect to it—I force a war against it. Petty people's morality as the measure of things: this is the most disgusting degradation culture has yet exhibited. And this kind of ideal still hanging over mankind is "God"! (Nietzsche, 1901:no. 200, p. 117)

Despite all the good reasons he knew for disbelief, Nietzsche realized that Christian faith persisted in the world; it could not be overturned by reasons alone. Therefore he provided a *genealogy* of faith to show the illusory nature of God so that we can be liberated from God: so that finally "God is dead." In one version of his genealogy (*Thus Spoke Zarathustra*, 1885) Nietzsche proposed to show the progress of the race— and of his own life story as its recapitulation—from *camel* (or ass) *to lion to child*. At the first stage, "The ass carries the burden of Christian values; then, when God has died, it carries the burden of humanistic values, which are human all too human; finally it carries only the burden of reality when no values at all are left" (Nietzsche, quoted in Neusch, 1982:116). In contrast to Jesus the camel, stands the lion who rebels (Nietzsche himself), roaring No to all absolutes. The lion's is a necessary stage in the journey, for we must reject all who claim mastery over us. Yet this rebellion is only temporary. Then comes a final stage, the child's, a stage of affirmation. "The child is innocence and forgetting, a new beginning. . . a sacred 'Yes'" (Nietzsche, 1885:27). Thus the child is the forerunner of Superman. In this mode Nietzsche believed he himself incarnated the atheistic humanity of the future.

To accept Nietzsche's self-account as revelatory both of his own li history and also that of the modern West is not to accept his evaluation of either. The journey he endured, his own mad descent into the mael-strom of godless selfhood, does mirror the West's descent. Yet is this better understood with Nietzsche as the West's conquest of an outworn faith, or as its (and his) tragic failure to realize the gift it was offered? To personalize the inquiry, was Nietzsche a victor over the gospel, or was he the willing victim of a debased gospel? As Carl Heinz Ratschow asks, "To what extent [was] Nietzsche's vitriolic attack on Christian thought and values . . . directed narrowly at the sort of exaggerated piety en-countered and fostered in his childhood home?" (NCRTW III, 64) More broadly, to what extent have the very God-concepts Christianity has transmitted from its many-valued past gestated and nursed the atheism of the present? If we can answer, we may begin to separate the silence of awe from the silence of atheism. I believe the 'death of God' thinking of Nietzsche's nineteenth century and of so many in the twentieth implores the community of faith to purify and strengthen its awareness of God. Then atheism will itself have served a providential purpose, as God turns evil into good.

ii. Christian sources of atheism.—To what extent has the doctrine taught in the churches, like the exaggerated piety Nietzsche is said to have endured, nursed viper atheism in its bosom? An answer appears in Michael J. Buckley's account of the origins of modern atheism. His central thesis is that Christian religion in the modern period (Descartes to the present) lost its way, was alienated from itself, and in that self-estrangement opened a fissure from which intellectual and cultural atheism issued (1987:358-63). To narrow it down, who were the theologi-cal culprits? Nicholas Lash points to two influential seventeenth-century figures, a Louvain Jesuit, Leonardus Lessius (1554–1623), and a Parisian Franciscan, Marin Mersenne (1588–1648), finding within Buckley's de-tailed account the evidence that implicates these two. Although both Lessius and Mersenne wrote *against* the rarefied atheism of their own day, both treated it as only a philosophical issue rather than a religious one (Lash in Marshall, ed., 1990:134-36). To quote Buckley,

> Both [Lessius and Mersenne] acted as if the rising movement were not a rejection of Jesus Christ as the supreme presence of God in human history, whose spirit continued that presence and made it abidingly evocative, but a philosophic stance toward life brought about by . . . the state of the world, the personal dissolution of the moral virtues, or the collapse of religious unity.
>
> (Buckley, 1987:33, 65-66, et pass.)

good intent (Lessius and Mersenne) pushed the
identity into second place—where it was lost to
was left to confront merely the god of Enlighten-
account is true, the surprising result is that biblical
ɔdern atheism are alike opposed to Enlightenment
lated reasons. The biblical heritage must reject a
theism that discards the story of God; modern atheism must oppose that
same theism because it maintains oppressive cultural illusions. It seems
that without their common opponent, biblical Christianity and contemporary atheism might open a direct conversation long postponed. To
begin, they might agree that the presence of the Holy One of Israel is
never to be merely posited, but is relevant only when *practiced*.

Another question is the degree to which the Christian doctrine of God as
taught in the churches and believed by their people remains at fault and needs
to be recast. Take today's vestigial grasp upon the **trinitarianism** once hammered out in ancient Christianity. How is the trinitarian doctrine of God taught
(and heard) in today's church? Most common are impersonal or personal
analogies (and in the latter case social or psychological analogies) that purport
to explain the 'threeness' of God (with what follows, cf. Humphreys, 1982). Least
promising of these are the impersonal analogies: God is like sun, its light, and
its produced warmth, or like three rings that intersect as (somehow) Father, Son,
and Spirit do. These supposed parallels in physical processes or bare symbols
illuminate nothing. No child or adult inquirer, learning them, moves far toward
the biblical story of God. Next come the personal analogies. There is long-stand-
ing theological conflict between the advocates of 'social' and 'psychological'
analogies. For the former, God is best likened to a community of three individuals, Peter, James, and John (or to be more current, Peter, Paul, and Mary). As we
saw, a version of this attracted the Cappadocian theologians of the fourth
century. The alternative, first employed by Augustine, is psychological: God is
compared, for example, to (1) the human mind, (2) its self-knowledge, and (3)
its self-love (*De trin.* XV, vi, 10). God here is less a community and more a single,
thinking being with coordinated functions. As Augustine himself showed, using
psychological analogies does not rule out social ones; each can correct the
deficiencies of the other. Yet both sorts fail the church, as do the impersonal
analogies, at a crucial point: there is little in them to send hearers back to the
narrative from which Christian knowledge of God springs. They give no hint of
Israel's history with JHWH; no clue to New Testament disciples confronting a
risen Christ; no path to a Pentecost where Israel's promise and disciples' wonder
converge upon a future present. They miss all that, distract from it, and thus
effectively deny it. Can they themselves be the root soil of popular atheism?

Competent interpreters argue (§2b) that diversion from the biblical
story was contrary to Thomas Aquinas' intent. Yet it was his successors
who generated the diverted **theism** of the following centuries (Lessius
introduced the *Summa* as a text at Louvain), a cluster of detached
philosophical propositions supposed to be self-authenticating apart

from Scripture. Whereas Thomas had moved from his elemental "five ways" directly to the triadic God of Scripture read through triune tradition's eyes, these seventeenth-century theists delayed that move in their effort to maintain a philosophically pure God-concept—thereby demoting Scripture's story. From that century on, much energy was absorbed in attempting to relate God to the emerging Newtonian world-view. In this discussion, trinitarian thought fell still farther into the background (J. Cobb, ER VI:17-26).

What of the contribution to atheism made by modern **subjectivity?** Here we find a mixed case. Feuerbach, and Marx and Freud after him, were as explicitly atheistic as their varied social contexts permitted. Yet theirs is not the only anthropocentric strand; there is Schleiermacher, and there are the Americans, Emerson and Thoreau. To claim, as Barth seemed to claim concerning Schleiermacher, that if these latter had only been consistent they too would be Feuerbachian atheists, is unfairly to dismiss their thought. Emerson rejected, not God, but established relig-ion, not the Over-soul but the spirit of conformity:

> We have contrasted the Church with the Soul. In the soul, then, let the redemption be sought. . . . The stationariness of religion; the assumption that the age of inspiration is past, that the Bible is closed; the fear of degrading the character of Jesus by representing him as a man; indicate with sufficient clearness the falsehood of our theology. It is the office of a true teacher to show us that God is, not was; that He speaketh, not spake. The true Christianity,—a faith like Christ's in the infinitude of man,—is lost.
>
> (Divinity School Address, in Emerson, 1983:88)

In that religious rejection, though, he found no path that returned to the narrative faith New England had spurned. Emerson rather turned his face farther West, to the Orient with its ancient religious philosophies, and his pilgrimage never brought him with other Wise Men, still wester-ing, to Bethlehem—or Calvary or Easter (Clebsch, 1973:chap. 4).

Summing up, atheism has provided a powerful impulse in Western religious thought, one whose impact is felt both outside and within Christian faith. The struggle was never fully joined, because the chief philosopher opponents of atheism proposed in its stead only a pale theism, a "God of the philosophers" who could not endure atheism's corrosive acid (McClendon in Steuer and McClendon, 1981:181-205). A touching if scandalous example of this impulse within the Christian (and Jewish) theological fold was the "God is dead" episode in American theology in the 1960s. More or less independently, a number of theolo-gians (notably Thomas J. J. Altizer, Paul van Buren, William Hamilton, and Richard Rubenstein) adopted Nietzsche's motto, "God is dead," as a hallmark of their own thought. Like Nietzsche, they sensed the incompatibility of a biblical God divorced from incarnate presence in the world, and yet for a variety of reasons they found that presence incredible. From that common ground, they went separate ways. As Axel Steuer and I later wrote:

> If one . . . comes to believe that [God and world] are utterly incompatible, there are five possible solutions. One can (a) reject God, as the death-of-God theologians did; that is called atheism. Or one can (b) reject contemporary culture; that may be called fundamentalism, but it is a heroic option too little investigated by academic theologians. . . . Or one can attempt to reconstruct culture, either (c) along archaic lines (T. S. Eliot) or (d) along futuristic lines (Norman O. Brown). Or one can (e) reconstruct the concept of God.
>   (1981:12; cf. Hamilton, "Death of God," NHCT)

Perhaps, however, what was needed was not so much reconstruction of a concept as recovery of a reality.

b. The uses of philosophy.—The preceding discussion showed how moderns such as Nietzsche argued for atheism by a 'genealogy' that undermined the Christian understanding of God. This was providential if it served to prick and explode God-concepts that were in fact empty, but atheism in itself understandably yielded no fresh understanding of God. This subsection will investigate an alternate possibility: Can *sympathetic* philosophies aid current theological thinking as faith seeks to reclaim its primal understanding—seeks to recover the gospel of God?

i. Process philosophy.—Alfred North Whitehead (1861–1947), the British-American thinker who fathered process philosophy, developed his systematic thought over against the growing atheism of his day. A skilled logician, Whitehead was particularly impressed by early-twentieth-century physics, and devised a metaphysics consistent with it. In addition, he made a prominent place in his system for both God and religion. Thus he seemed to many mid-century theologians, especially those at American universities where science reigned, to offer the possibility of reconciling science and religion, science and God. Certainly that would have been no small gain. Yet this initial promise of process thought had to be weighed against the highly particularized notions of 'God' and of 'religion' that Whitehead adopted as he adjusted them to the constraints of his own system.

In the Whiteheadian philosophy, the basic counters were (1) process itself (as an alternative to classical "substance"), (2) 'creativity,' a kind of generally distributed drive or energy that ceaselessly appears in all events, (3) the eternal objects (which may be compared with the timeless forms of Platonism), and (4) minuscule physical-emotional events called "occasions," which interact to constitute the process of nature. God, human selves, and material things were not among these basic counters; they were 'societies' composed of and shaped by them. God in Whitehead's scheme did have a special, dual role (though not an ultimate role): as a favorable influence upon (all) occasions, God (acting as primordial God) guided them, and as an impressionable receiver, God (acting as consequent God) retained forever in the divine memory all that occurred, giving the whole process a kind of immortality (Passmore, 1968:337-44; D. M. Emmett, *Enc. Phil.* VIII:290-96).

Whitehead's process thought might have remained little more than a footnote to twentieth-century philosophy had it not provided the impetus for Process Theology, which flourished in Chicago at mid-century. Within that school of thought, the work of John B. Cobb, Jr., is representative. Following Whitehead and Charles Hartshorne (1897–), Cobb held that God's power in the world is persuasive, not coercive: God is always good but in many cases lacks the power to effect that goodness; thus "the problem of evil" (in its academic form) is solved—the evil itself is of course still there. Cobb believed that process thought remained closer to the God of Scripture than had classical theism. For example, since God's initial aim in each of the world's "occasions" can be accepted or rejected in the freedom each occasion enjoys, God naturally accepts risk and adventure (cf. §1 above). Yet in light of this freedom, whether God will finally prevail over other elements in the cosmos must remain in doubt (Cobb, 1965; Grenz and Olson, 1992:130-44).

This is not a complete account of any of the Process doctrines of God explored by philosopher-theologians (e.g., Hartshorne, 1941, 1967; Ogden, 1966; Griffin, 1976). Many of their assertions, such as that God is perfect in goodness or love, are standard Christian teaching that requires no comment. Yet what has just been said hints at difficulties in the Process conceptual scheme that make its 'God' less attractive than one might have hoped. Some of these difficulties can be briefly noted here. Take first the Process claim to offer a new synthesis between science and religion. Two difficulties arise: The science Whitehead took as his model was early-twentieth-century physics, with its minute electro-physical events captured in fields of force. Many hoped to draw from this physics an account of all nature including human nature, so that science could ultimately be reduced to atomic physics. Accordingly, the analogy of human selfhood would not be invoked in thinking about God. Rather, 'God' (and human individuals) would each be reducible to 'societies' more akin to physical fields of force than to the Bible's JHWH. Behind this lay still another reduction: the philosophical assumption (one not bolstered by the logical complexity of later-twentieth-century science) that no distinctive sort of reasoning was to be invoked in thinking about God. For Whitehead, God's being (or rather, process) had to *exemplify* the features of the cosmos rather than cause them. God was part of the cosmos, not its transcendent author (Whitehead, 1978:34; cf. H. Smith, 1988:307f).

This leads directly to the second difficulty: God is here no longer the Creator, the First and the Last, but is merely a valuable member of the larger cosmos or 'reality,' an element alongside more primal elements such as 'occasions' and timeless forms (Burrell, 1982:130-32). If God is not transcendent, he (or it) cannot be God the Redeemer, either, for he or it is no longer in position to ensure that finally all shall be well. Nor can God be Alpha and Omega, the source as well as end of all things. This criticism springs from what was said above in Part I, The Rule of God. There eschatology and salvation and creation (*with* its suffering) were presented as triplet doctrinal siblings, all from the womb of God's providential rule.

Nevertheless, Christian doctrine has much to learn from process modes of thought. Science does offer a formidable challenge to Christian teaching today, whether as an adversary (Appleyard, 1993) or as an ally (Murphy, 1990). Again, Christian morals and doctrine have philosophical implications, and these must be determined afresh in every new context. Although our knowledge of God and Christ is not merely a doublet of scientific knowledge (since it is also related to our knowledge of other selves and to knowledge understood as a capacity or skill—see Chapter Six §1b), the presuppositions of scientific knowing are in certain ways comparable to these (H. Smith, 1988). Moreover, Process Theology helpfully emphasizes the *dynamism* of Godhood revealed in Scripture and correctly models divine activity upon *persuasion* not coercion; upon love, not force (D. Williams, 1968:130-41). To that extent it contributes to Christian doctrine. Its overriding fault is its failure to direct its adherents back to Scripture's story of God—to the LORD of the prophets and the Father of Jesus, to the risen Lord Jesus Christ, and to the Lord the Spirit, who gathers believers in pentecostal power.

ii. Philosophical analysis and tradition.—Consider next the work of Alasdair MacIntyre (1929–), a Scot transplanted to North America. Two episodes in MacIntyre's career reflect two moments in twentieth-century philosophy, first, *analysis,* and later (MacIntyre's post-Hegelian) *traditionalism.*

Soon after MacIntyre began work, still in his mid-twenties, he edited (with Antony Flew) a volume, *New Essays in Philosophical Theology* (1955), that swiftly became indispensable reading for philosophers of religion. Two features distinguished the *New Essays* from other work in its field. One was the analytic and empirical style in which its contributors worked. The other was the deliberate inclusion of both explicitly Christian (e.g., editor MacIntyre) and non-Christian (e.g., editor Flew) contributors.

Philosophical analysis, or analytic philosophy, had its modern origins among those philosophers, especially at Cambridge University early in the twentieth century, who found the received Hegelian idealism and British empiricism no longer fruitful; it was a revolutionary movement, and like so many revolutions had consequences not anticipated by its originators. The root idea of analysis was that dissection was a main task of philosophy: either what there is, the known world, could be analyzed into manageable elements, or the language that described it could, and the result in either case would be a new clarity about both words and things. Its earliest forms were the work of G. E. Moore (1873–1958), who especially examined the analysis of *concepts,* and that of Bertrand Russell (1872–1970), whose 'logical atomism' offered an atomistic program of analyzing both propositions and the external world. This latter style of analysis crescendoed in the *logical positivism* that flourished in Vienna between the World Wars and was echoed in Britain by A. J. Ayer's *Language, Truth, and Logic* (1936). Yet logical positivism proved to be a dead end; its best exponents abandoned it, and analytic philosophy either receded into 'linguistic analysis' preoccupied with Sisyphean problems of meaning and reference, or took a new turn in the work of another Austrian (and secret Christian believer), Ludwig Wittgenstein (Chapter Two §1), as well as in 'ordinary language' philosophers such as Oxford's John L. Austin (1911–60). It is only in light of these last sorts of analysis that productive philosophy of religion has issued; here it must suffice to mention the work of Christian philosopher William Alston (1921–) (see, e.g., Alston in Steuer and McClendon, 1981; Alston, 1989). Readers may see Austinian and Wittgensteinian influence in the present book as well, and may trace its origins in James M. Smith's and my *Convictions: Defusing Religious Relativism* (1994), and its outworking in forthcoming *Volume III.* On early analysis see M. Weitz (*Enc. Phil.* I:97-105).

MacIntyre's contribution to the *New Essays,* "Visions" (pp. 254-60), was a straight piece of empiricist argument. It denied all evidential value to "voices and visions" heard and seen by Christians. The essay might have been written two hundred years earlier by David Hume. Other essays in the collection treated the existence (but not the nature) of God, the "meaningfulness" (or lack of it) of religious language, miracles, death, and religious knowledge. This was a style of inquiry that did not long detain MacIntyre, however. He moved on to other standpoints and topics—Marxism, psychoanalysis, and the atheism they shared, then philosophical sociology, and next, for a long stay, ethics. Others found lasting satisfaction in British-American analytic philosophy; MacIntyre, for all his changes of conviction and intellectual interest, never did.

There was a direction in all his changes. MacIntyre drew ever nearer a principle or method that (with other post-Hegelians) he owed to the German master: *the content of philosophical thought is inseparable from its history*. This guideline, exemplified in much of MacIntyre's earlier work (1966; 1984; 1988), is explained and defended in *Three Rival Versions of Moral Enquiry* (1990), delivered as Gifford Lectures in Edinburgh. Here MacIntyre comes home to Scotland, to (Roman) Catholic Christianity, and to a philosophical method fitted to cope with the relativism that his own past work had in its varied course embodied.

MacIntyre's "rivals" in *Three Rival Versions* are the *encyclopaedists* and the *genealogists*. By the former, he meant those theorists, typified by the Edinburgh makers of the nineteenth-century *Encyclopaedia Britannica*, who sought to sum up human knowledge from a single point of view, one that they took to be completely unbiased, universal, indefeasible in principle, however much new facts might change it in detail. By the genealogists he meant those theorists (not only Nietzsche, but the French Structuralists and Deconstructionists—Michel Foucault, Jacques Derrida, Gilles Deleuze) who sought to undermine and overturn traditional Western intellectual life, including its lingering God-consciousness, by a subversive review of its contents. Against both these, MacIntyre ranged *tradition*, the standpoint he had come to occupy, which understood moral inquiry to depend upon skills garnered over generations, imparted to learners by teachers who have earned the right to teach, and who with their learners constitute a moral community. This sort of community over time, MacIntyre argued, "is a condition for genuinely rational inquiry," moral or other (1990:60). It follows, I would reckon, that such community is a necessary condition of a believer's knowledge of and knowledge about and knowing interaction with God. The community shares practices that form its life and inform its teaching.

MacIntyre's claim is that though the three 'versions' of inquiry are incompatible and indeed, incommensurable, there is nevertheless a rational way to resolve their disagreement: The winner will be that version that can encompass the other two by showing them unsustainable on their own grounds and by their own lights. *Three Rival Versions* offers such an argument against encyclopedia and genealogy.

It is not my business here to follow out the consequences of MacIntyre's argument (which already has a formal parallel in *Ethics*, Twelve), but only to show that by it, the authentic "God of the philosophers" can only be a "God of tradition." This leaves aside narrower questions (Which tradition among many?) but MacIntyre's answer, rather like mine and Smith's in the work previously noted, is to invoke the dynamic interaction between competing traditions—the contest between his "rival versions" being a grand illustration of such interaction. This is all the assistance that we can expect from philosophy in quest of the Deity, the Godhood, of God. If God be for us, MacIntyre implies, our philosophical path cannot go by way of genealogy or encyclopedia—cannot go by way of the unavailable Archimedean standpoint (cf. McClendon and Smith, 1994:chaps. 5f)—nor can it go by way of a Nietzschean revolt against all standpoints. It can only go by way of a modest learner's stance perhaps best exemplified by what the New Testament calls *mathēteuein*, the practice of discipling.

c. Trinitarian theology and narrative.—This section is not an independent treatise on trinitarianism, but only an attempt to assemble under that heading doctrinal material already displayed elsewhere in this (trinitarian) book. It may thereby provide useful connections to theological work done by others in other modes.

i. The heritage of revelation theology.—In 1934 Karl Barth named the first two chapters of his *Church Dogmatics* "The Word of God as the Criterion of Dogmatics," and "The Revelation of God" (CD I/1). Many followed in this 'revelation' path. In 1936 my own teacher, Walter Thomas Conner, named the first of his two doctrinal volumes *Revelation and God* (1936). In 1940 H. Richard Niebuhr delivered the Nathanael W. Taylor Lectures at Yale Divinity School, subsequently published as *The Meaning of Revelation* (1941). This mid-century theology failed if it meant to be either primitive (in the sense of a full return to biblical origins) or modern (in the sense of providing self-evident foundations). It did something else, though, that was indeed biblical and Christian: By recognizing the primacy of divine initiative, revelation theology found in the doctrine of God two factors or facts: One was the costliness of the divine self-giving. The other was the transformation of human life that the divine initiative required. These factors have been explored in previous chapters, the costliness of God's creative engagement in Chapter Four, the human transformation it yields in Chapter Three, and both in Chapters Five and Six. Yet a word more about each is now in order.

The final chapter of Deuteronomy is a funeral eulogy for Moses, such a prophet as Israel had not since seen, one who knew the LORD "face to face" (34:10). That indeed follows from, but it does not quite report, what Deuteronomy says. The exact words are that *the LORD knew Moses face to face.* Such was the openness of the man that God could come to know Moses in this immediate way, "as one man speaks to another" (Exod. 33:11). Our reaction may be that God knows everyone already, and it is surely true that in one sense God does know all creatures beforehand and inside out (Ps. 139:1-6). Yet "knowing," we saw before, can also be that reciprocal action which the knower only achieves as she or he is also known: it cannot be at second hand, it involves encounter, and it is necessarily mutual. In these ways knowing *someone* differs from mere knowing *about* or knowing *how* (Chapter Six §1b). This tells us that God cannot *in this sense* know us except as we know God also. There is effort for both sides in the meeting: knowing has its price, namely at-onement. Nor should we with some speak here of "the human face of God": it is better to see this way of knowing as characteristic of God, and thus to speak of the divine face of women and men when they turn toward him (cf. Exod. 34:29-35; 2 Corinthians 3). Accordingly, 'revelation' must itself be reciprocal: God, as Richard Heyduck has helped me see, gets to know any of us only at considerable cost to God—and some cost to ourselves.

H. Richard Niebuhr, one personally conscious of the cost of such knowledge, wrote of our knowledge of other selves that "we cannot know here save as we are known. We cannot be the *doers* but must first suffer knowledge of ourselves" (H. R. Niebuhr, 1941:145), and it is in light of that costly reciprocity that the younger Niebuhr interpreted the mid-century doctrine:

> Revelation means the moment in our history through which we know ourselves to be known from beginning to end, in which we are apprehended by the knower; it means the self-disclosing of that eternal knower. Revelation means the moment in which we are surprised by the knowledge of someone there in the darkness and the void of human life; it means the self-disclosure of light in our darkness. Revelation is the moment in which we find our judging selves to be judged not by ourselves or our neighbors but by one who knows the final secrets of the heart; . . . revelation means that we find ourselves to be valued rather than valuing and that all our values are transvaluated by the activity of a universal valuer. . . . When we find out that we are no longer thinking him, but that he first thought us, that is revelation. (H. R. Niebuhr, 1941:152f)

This is the Deity who gets to know Moses; this is the Father who gets to know Jesus as a parent gets to know his child; this is the God of the apostles and prophets who fills them so that they can meet God face to face. Here lies the Deity of God.

ii. The story of God.—Where a previous generation invoked 'revelation' as a catch-all concept, ours turns to narrative, a concept equally venerable—and equally vulnerable. Caution needs to be exercised here not only because of the many meanings of "narrative" and "story," but also because no one of these meanings, any more than 'revelation,' can bear the heavy weight of our theological finitude, ignorance, and want. Rather we must find ways to say in terms of story—that we are not God; even that "God is in heaven and you are on earth, so let your words be few" (Eccles. 5:2).

Nevertheless, we have this true story, and in it we have found the good that loves us, the only power we can trust, the wholeness (or holiness) that heals our broken world. This is a long story. Even its *near* roots run back four thousand years into Sumerian and Egyptian soil. Maybe the God-awareness of Abraham and of Moses was contoured by such earlier God-consciousness. We surmise; we do not know. Yet we do know that in their awe and to their need the God of this story appeared. Here I repeat the earliest summary of that story in this book:

The Christian story in its primal form tells of a God who (unlike gods of human fabrication) is the very Ground of Adventure, the Weaver of society's Web, the Holy Source of nature in its concreteness—the one and only God, who, when time began, began to be God for a world that in its orderly constitution finally came by his will and choice to include also— ourselves. We human beings, having our natural frame and basis, with our own (it seemed our own) penchant for community, and (it seemed) our own hankerings after adventure, found ourselves, before long, in trouble. Our very adventurousness led us astray; our drive to cohesion fostered monstrous imperial alternatives to the adventure and the sociality of the Way God had intended, while our continuity with nature became an excuse to despise ourselves and whatever was the cause of us. We sin. In his loving concern, God set among us, by every means infinite wisdom could propose, the foundations of a new human society; in his patience he sent messengers to recall the people of his Way to their way; in the first bright glimmers of opportunity he sent—himself, incognito, sans splendor and fanfare, the Maker amid the things made, the fundamental Web as if a single fiber, the Ground of Adventure risking everything in this adventure. His purpose—sheer love; his means—pure faith; his promise—unquenchable hope. In that love he lived a life of love; by that faith he died a faithful death; from that death he rose to fructify hope for the people of his Way, newly gathered, newly equipped. The rest of the story is still his—yet it can also be ours, yours.

This story, depending as it does upon the language of Scripture and its tradition, drives us back to trinitarian expression of the doctrine. Yet there are objections to trinitarianism. Does it not imply that God lacks wholeness or entirety or oneness, only existing (or 'subsisting') in three parts or 'persons'—does it not imply tritheism? Again, does it not force the free, dynamic language of Scripture into a mold, asking of the Bible what it will not yield, namely, the doctrine of later centuries? Finally, does not trinitarianism with its names Father, Son, Holy Spirit provide gods of gender rather than the God beyond gender, thus relegating itself to the past?

As noted above, Latin *persona* meant an actor's mask, and thus the role the mask denoted. (For Latin theologians it translated Greek *hypostasis*, "focus of being.") In time, however, Boethius (c. 475–525) defined *persona* as "an individual substance having a rational nature," and the word so defined was applied to human individuals and to the three *personae* of the Godhood as well. This had unfortunate consequences both for the understanding of human nature and for the doctrine of God. For the human self-understanding, "person" (a word we get directly from Latin) served to disembody and dematerialize the self; no longer were we bodies sharing common clay; we were 'persons with bodies'— bodies to be disposed at our will (cf. *Ethics*, Part I). For the understanding of God, this new definition of *persona* was even more corrupting: God was now *three* disembodied *personae*—"persons" in the modern sense, discrete individuals. Clearly this was tritheistic and false. In today's terms, God is neither a person nor **three** persons; the term "person" is so debased that it no longer functions usefully for the Christian community, and should be abandoned (Welch, 1952, s.v. *Persona*, Personality, "Persons"; Lash, 1988:275-80).

To each objection to a narrative-based trinitarianism, though, there are strong replies. There are indeed forms of the doctrine of Trinity that are vulnerable to the first failing. Social trinitarianism sometimes claims that "the revelation requires us to believe in God as the divine Trinity wherein each person is fully personal in the modern sense of the word" (Hodgson, 1943:155). The trouble with this formulation is that it led Professor Hodgson to treat his own theological construction, "God in three persons," as the given and known element, while relegating the oneness of God to a realm of mystery necessarily beyond our knowing (Welch, 1952:254). Surely this is just contrary to the story that the doctrine is set to conserve, a story in which one God, over against all earth's gods, is Israel's Redeemer: "Hear, Israel: The LORD is our God, the LORD our one God" (Deut. 6:4). That oneness is not fractured but *deepened* in the chapters of the story that reaches its climax at Calvary and opens to all peoples at Pentecost. (To read otherwise is to find in the New Testament not the long awaited new covenant of Jeremiah 31:31-34, but a different covenant with a different god; then Marcion would be right, and Christian belief mere novelty.)

Likewise the other two objections meet stronger replies. It should be conceded at once that the trinitarian doctrine as such does not appear in Scripture. Rather, "Trinity" was invented in order to encode and protect what does appear in Scripture, the one God who is truly Israel's Father, truly eternal Word, truly life-giving Spirit. The same response applies to those whose sincere cultural concerns protest the classic "images" of God the Father and the Son as gender-biased (Schüssler Fiorenza, 1984). Theirs is not an objection to the doctrine as such but only to its terms; they would be correct to insist that alongside the traditional terms others may be inserted: "Parent" as well as Father; "Child" as well as Son. Yet in fidelity to Scripture (where *pater* and *huios* are repeatedly part of the New Testament texts) these others must appear alongside, not instead of, the classic terms, and in honest acknowledgment that the proposed substitutes have their own defects.

In particular, functional formulas such as "Creator, Redeemer, Sanctifier" or the like fail as liturgical substitutes for "Father, Son, and Holy Spirit." Substituting functions for identifying modes (e.g., "Redeemer" in place of "Son") too easily slips the link with the biblical narrative, fails to identify God as the God of the story, and suggests that Spirit and Father are *not* the Redeemer. The replacement of divine names with functions or tasks hints at a drift toward vagueness, and meanwhile suppresses, if it does not deny, the *relation* of Creator to Redeemer to Sanctifier that the biblical terms (as for example in Matthew 28:19f) reflect (Talbert, 1992; cf. Kimel, ed., 1992).

The trinitarian doctrine, understood as an encoding of the biblical narrative of God, identifies God provided it is recognized as just that— an encoding meant to return us to its source. To say that God is Father is to recall that God is the creative source of all things, the JHWH who chose Israel, the "Father in heaven" to whom Jesus prayed. To say that God is Son or Word is to be reminded of the faithfulness of God displayed in Jesus Christ risen; it is to recall the humility of his radical earthly life, the triumphant tragedy of the cross, the wonder of Easter and Pentecost. To say that God is Spirit is to remember that Easter and Pentecost are for us a beginning, not a termination of God's new action; it is to recall the prophetic gift witnessed in Scripture and the many gifts granted the new fellowship; it is to be reminded of a link binding God above us, God within us, and God beyond us in mission. To use the language of Trinity *understood thus* is to see the answer to all three of the questions that underlie the quest for the identity of Jesus Christ. It is to see the absolute *right* of the risen Christ to be absolute Lord. It is to see how faithful Jews and other biblical monotheists *can* tell the Jesus story, since it is but a climactic episode in the long story of Immanuel, God with us. It is to locate the holiness within Spirit-gifted community, and thus to *identify* that community with the miracle of Easter and Pentecost.

From ancient times to the present, doctrinal theologians have wondered what disciples knew in knowing God to be Father, Word, and Spirit (§2a above). Is the doctrine only 'economic,' an account of the divine self-disclosure *as it appears* in the story? Or is it also 'immanent,' a (true) account of the very being of God, in whom the Word is eternally generated by the Father from whom also the Spirit eternally proceeds? (The Catholic West added that the Spirit eternally proceeds from Father *and* Son, adding *Filioque* to its creed.) This 'economic versus immanent' question can be expressed thus in our terms: Is the God we know in the story—the One who called Abraham, knew Moses, spoke through the prophets, lived and died and rose again in Jesus Christ, descends upon the church in pentecostal power, demanding our conversion—is this 'economic' God the real God, or is there some other, secret God beyond God? The answer of faith is that this is "the true God" (1 John 5:20); the 'economic' doctrine is the 'immanent' doctrine—this is the identity of God.

I do not mean here that there is nothing more to say about God. There is much more. Those who say that Christian theology has God alone as its subject matter have a point: All the preceding and following chapters (and all three volumes) share in the witness. For example, there are profound implications in trinitarian teaching for all who seek God, provided we do not misread and wrongly teach God's triunity as being about *three* of something or other. Thus Nicholas Lash helpfully reads the doctrine of the Trinity as a set of *rules correcting our natural errors* concerning God. Trinitarian doctrine, he says, is "more fundamentally a matter of ensuring correct reference than it is of attempting appropriate description" (1988:258). First, there is the mistake that identifies God with everything. The truth of *pantheism* (represented in this chapter by Emerson and company) is retained in the doctrine of God as Spirit, which maintains the presence of God in community while demanding that conversion be the hallmark of community if God is to be known there. A second natural mistake, common in our time, is to conclude, since God is no *thing*, that God is nothing. The truth of *atheism* (represented in this chapter by Nietzsche and company) is already expressed in the doctrine of God as the Creator-Father, who is no thing in the cosmos, but is other than the cosmos entire. To disregard this rule is idolatry, and it is an idolatry that atheism generates, since humanity will have its gods when there is no God. The remaining, third rule bears upon this third, natural error concerning God, the error of *particularity* (represented in this chapter by a wooden trinitarianism). God is idolatrously said to be here and not there, this and not that. It is an error repeated within Christianity, says Roman Catholic theologian Lash, by "ascribing divine status to the language and institutions which mediate the memory of Jesus" (1988:271). The corrective use of the third rule is to *link* the first (God as Gift or Spirit) with the second (God as Other or Creator). The link (God as Word) "furnishes us with the pattern or figure" by which we may correlate the other two. Without that link, Lash warns, Spirit dissolves into pantheism and Father vanishes into atheism. In the Word, though, we have a particularity that is authentic as it issues in community whose role is to be catholic or universal, including all people—our own concern in Chapter Ten below (Lash, 1988:266-72).

* * * * *

Christian teaching about God faces temptation from two directions, one from a confined Jesus-faith, a blind particularity; the other from a bland 'theism' that blends into pantheism. Between these divergent paths lies the christological center of the doctrine of God. *Integral* to that center are the Father of Jesus and the Spirit of Jesus; from that center flow the practices of Christian community that will concern us in the chapters still to come.

> Before all time began there was a Story
> Told in eternity: rend'ring God's face.
> Life of the living God, poured out as glory,
> From God's full store granting grace upon grace.
>
> Word that was manifest, tangible, sublime,
> Off'ring God's story-formed shape to a world:
> Curving space, galaxies floating in space-time,
> Kingdoms, dominions, earth's history unfurled.
>
> Infinite Deity, radiant, streaming,
> Gleaming in darkness, creating new life,
> Never the dark that could vanquish that blazing
> Brightness of God overwhelming our strife.
>
> Into the world through a human life—Jesus
> Comes to his own though his own stand aloof;
> We people blind; oh, may God yet forgive us:
> Race shelt'ring Deity under its roof!

PART III

THE FELLOWSHIP OF THE SPIRIT

Although we are all equally priests, we cannot all publicly minister and teach. We ought not do so even if we could. Paul writes accordingly in I Cor. 4[:1], "This is how one should regard us, as servants of Christ and stewards of the mysteries of God." ¶ That stewardship, however, has now been developed into so great a display of power and so terrible a tyranny that no heathen emperor or other earthly power can be compared with it, just as if laymen were not also Christians. Through this perversion the knowledge of Christian grace, faith, liberty, and of Christ himself has altogether perished, and its place has been taken by an unbearable bondage of human works and laws until we have become, as the Lamentations of Jeremiah [1] say, servants of the vilest men on earth who abuse our misfortune to serve only their base and shameless will.

Martin Luther, *The Freedom of a Christian*, 1520

I have nothing more to say on the subject of the change in my religious opinions. On the one hand I came gradually to see that the Anglican Church was formally in the wrong, on the other that the Church of Rome was formally in the right; then, that no valid reasons could be assigned for continuing in the Anglican, and again that no valid objections could be taken to joining the Roman. Then, I had nothing more to learn; what still remained for my conversion was, not further change of opinion, but to change opinion itself into the clearness and firmness of intellectual conviction.

John Henry Newman, *Apologia pro Vita Sua*

Further, dear fellow members in Christ, you should be admonished not to forget love, without which it is not possible that you be a Christian congregation. You know what love is through the testimony of Paul our fellow brother; he says: Love is patient and kind, not jealous, not puffed up, not ambitious, seeks not its own, thinks no evil, rejoices not in iniquity, rejoices in the truth, suffers everything, endures everything, believes everything, hopes everything. If you understand this text, you will find the love of God and of neighbor. . . . But if you love the neighbor, you will not scold or ban zealously, will not seek your own, will not remember evil, will not be ambitious or puffed up, but kind, righteous, generous in all gifts, humble and sympathetic with the weak and imperfect.

Michael Sattler, Letter to the Church at Horb, 1527

Introduction

For some this Part comes too late, far too late, in this study of doctrine. Its location here seems to them to suggest that one can properly talk of the new that comes in Christ, of the knowledge of God, of Jesus and his royal rule, *apart from* the fellowship of the Spirit—apart from and prior to *church*. These would protest that believers' relation to Christ is nothing apart from their relation to one another. They need to be reminded, though, that all parts (and all volumes) of the system presuppose one another. Talk of practices at the beginning of Chapter Six (common worship, kingdom work, disciple witness, biblical word) presupposed the existence and reality of the community of saints. It is in the church where Christ is present that these form knowledge of the Risen One. So this third Part is primary, not derivative. By the same principle, much concerning God's rule and the identity of Jesus Christ must be assumed without repetition in the present Part: The community of the Spirit belongs to the realm of God's rule; the church is the church of the risen and returning Jesus Christ. Without these pillars of cloud and fire before, we will gain no ground here.

It will come out that there is a variety of approaches to Christian community, and our goal must be to treat each fairly. An element in fairness is disclosing in advance where one stands. My own orientation is toward a 'gathering church' or 'local' style in ecclesiology. The doctrine of Christian community begins with (though it does not end with) the actually meeting, flesh-and-blood disciples assembly. What is said in Chapter Eight about Christian community, in Chapter Nine about the signs (ordinances, sacraments) of salvation, and in Chapter Ten about the Holy Spirit and mission will turn upon the character of church as tangible, as local, as gathering. That need not mean that the universal dimension of Christian community is overlooked. Chapter Ten will focus upon a vision of *ecstasy* and *intimacy*. Both extend in purpose to all people, drawing them into one 'syzygy' of holy unity. Chapter Nine, whose topic is Christian worship, will address afresh the question of common 'remembering signs' (baptism, Lord's supper, preaching) that are taken to be marks of any believing Christian body anywhere: These are not only local but universal signs of salvation. And Chapter Eight, first of our three, will begin with a survey of the ecumenical task that confronts the entire Christian community in a new way in our times. It will then go on to explore the Jewish basis of Christian community, asking if that basis is eroded beyond recovery, as some teach, or if the "this is that" and "then is now" vision opens the way to a reconsideration of Jewish and of Christian community. Old barriers have come down, and now we must ask of the flesh-and-blood local congregation how it echoes in its present life Jesus' prayer, "May they all be one . . . that the world may believe" (John 17:21). A baptist ecclesiology must in this sense be catholic in order to be faithfully baptist.

The 'gathering church' starting point determines other matters as well. Some teachers of doctrine have described the church in terms of its *functions* (e.g., Tillich, 1951–63 III:182-216; Erickson, 1990:1052-67). Such an approach falls short, for if we are to emphasize the human reality of church as gathering congregation (as I will do), a functional account on top of that is likely to make the church seem altogether instrumental—which is not the line I take. One may, to be sure, see the present chapters on worship and mission as functional, telling what the church does or practices. (Even gathering may be called only functional.) If they are read this way, though, the reader must avoid the conclusion that these are meant to be the *sole, defining functions*. For the church has other roles—as servant to the world, as teacher of God's people, as a catalyst of unity, and more. And these others are equally critical for the church's being really the church, though they are not given equal space here. I have chosen worship and mission both as valuable and as likely to be neglected at present: others, differently located, will see different needs and rightly emphasize other tasks. Developing one or more of these would be a good way for a reader to carry the work forward.

Another approach to churchly definition is by way of so-called *notae* or marks. One famous list of these is drawn from the Niceno-Constantinopolitan Creed (381): "[We believe] *one holy catholic* and *apostolic* church." Unfortunately, by the time this creed was drafted, Christian understanding had been narrowed in ways that left these four marks important, but far from definitive. For example, they fail to tell us that the church must center upon Jesus Christ, or that the church to be the church must be loving as well as holy. Nevertheless, use will be made of these marks in what follows, and one of them, holiness, must be addressed at once, for it is all too easy, when we begin with a gathering assembly, to overlook that this flesh-and-blood, tangible fellowship is at the same time God's holy church. In fact, this may seem presumptuous, since "holy" (*qodesh, hagios*) is a biblical word for God's Godhood: it is God who is the holy One. Thus when the Greek Orthodox priest at communion cries out "Holy things unto the holy," the fit response is "One only is holy, one only is the Lord." Nevertheless, the priest speaks well: a true congregation is composed of God's holy ones, God's saints (*hagioi*). So there is a tension in our ecclesiology between the concrete earthly reality and the divine reality; between the assembly that prays for holiness, and the Spirit-gifted church of Jesus Christ.

Still another approach locates *models* or *images* of church and seeks through them to indicate the reality that together they represent. Avery Dulles, for example, in successive chapters treats the church as society, mystical body, sacrament, herald, and servant (1974). Paul Minear lists ninety-six such images in Scripture alone! (1960) Though this is not the organizing method here, as it may too easily conform to existing presuppositions about the church, such studies are useful supplements to our work.

Another feature of Chapter Eight, specially related to the baptist approach that shapes this version of Christian doctrine, is the treatment there of the relation of Christianity to Judaism. Since World War II and the *Shoah* (Holocaust) a great deal has been written on this topic in a new voice. Still, there has been no extensive treatment of what Paul van Buren calls "the Jewish-Christian reality" from the standpoint of a local-church ecclesiology that shares the baptist vision. It will come out in Chapter Eight that this radical standpoint makes a radical difference, and that here things can be said that traditional ecclesiology made impossible.

Finally, something must be said about Christian faith as an expression of the idea of community. In the strife-torn century just ending, this has become newly important. We live in a time when nations and peoples worldwide have been torn apart from one another, and thrown into the rage of conflict, by their political, economic, and *religious* convictions. It happens that as these lines are being written civil wars are raging in the region formerly called Yugoslavia. One of the deep causes of such conflicts is political (old, festering grudges inflamed by past wars), another is economic (the resentments fanned, and those caused, by the old oligarchies as well as by the spread and recession of world Communism), but a third is religious. Long ago this region was a meeting-ground of East and West, and the rivalries of Eastern and Western

Catholicism still leave their mark upon the Orthodox and Catholic churches. Moreover, a significant Muslim population still exists in Southern Europe, left stranded by the withdrawal of the Ottoman Turks in the sixteenth century, and these Muslims are the object of hatred on the part of 'Christian' neighbors. These current wars may only be the latest Crusade! Still, there is no point in pointing the finger of blame at others in such matters until Western Christians have achieved understandings of Christian community that can issue in peace not war, in love of neighbor (and of enemy!) not destruction of neighbor. The fellowship of the Spirit is not even imaginably ours until it takes shape as a fellowship of peace and love open to the neighbor—even the enemy neighbor—as to the Lord.

The Quest for Christian Community

Since medieval times, but most evidently since the time of the Reformation, the doctrine of the church has been proclaimed by one and another with such ardor and such set views that newcomers might suppose it the most fixed of Christian doctrines. Surely, one could gather from any one of these doctrinaire accounts, all others are wrong, and it alone is right. Yet if we adopt such a dogmatic spirit, explaining all views but our own as someone else's contextual error or outworn opinion or stubborn resistance to plain truth, a great puzzle arises: How is it, despite the others' perceived stubbornness, perceptual lag, or error—how is it that their mistaken teaching has lasted so long and been embraced by so many with such goodwill and good consequences? This is the problem that Protestants face in the existence of chronically vigorous Catholicism. It is also the problem that Catholics confront, now after five hundred years of history, in vital, ongoing Protestantism. Moreover, both Protestants and Catholics, when they do not ignore it, meet the same puzzling problem in the baptist movement as it persistently reappears, century after century, in their midst. In short, the main problem that ecclesiology (the doctrine of Christian community) must address is not scarcity but an embarrassing abundance: more than anywhere, in

331

this part of Christian teaching multiple paths appear, while weighty consequences lie in wait down each path.

Whether acknowledged or not, this doctrinal division among Christians is awkward in practice. Christians are never just Christians; they are Greek Orthodox or German Baptist or Roman Catholic or Missouri Synod Lutheran or Iraqi Nestorian or French Reformed or. . . . The list extends far beyond these, and an account of the variety, even if limited to North American church bodies, would exceed the space limits of this volume (Piepkorn, 1977–79; cf. *Ethics*, One §1). Now these varied bodies drive wedges between authentic followers of Jesus, imposing divisive limits upon membership, communion, and eligibility for ministry—limits based in many cases on long-ago history or on ethnicity or gender as well as on present convictions. Yet such limits clearly fly in the face of well-known Christian teaching:

> As many of you as were baptized into Christ have clothed yourselves with Christ. There is no longer Jew or Greek [categories of ethnicity and tradition], there is no longer slave or free [economic and social power], there is no longer male and female [gender and role]; for all of you are one in Christ Jesus. (Gal. 3:27f NRSV)

Even divisions based more clearly than these on principle seem out of harmony with Jesus' high-priestly prayer: "May they all be one; as you, Father, are in me, and I in you, so also may they be in us, that the world may believe . . ." (John 17:21). In the Fourth Gospel, the unity of disciples is grounded in Christ's unity with the Father, a unity that entails, creates, ordains *community*. Such community is not well expressed either by polemical Christian doctrine or by endlessly divisive Christian practice. Rather, much of this doctrine and practice is a discredit to its sponsors. This sets our theological problem: Theology must accept its share of the discredit for these divisions and do what it can to repair the fault.

§1. The Doctrine of the Church in an Ecumenical Age

In fact, much Christian theology of the passing century proposed just such repair. A new word (or a new use of an old word) acquired twentieth-century currency. "Ecumenical," which had earlier meant "worldwide" (from Greek *oikoumenē*, "the inhabited world," see Matt. 24:14; Acts 17:31; Rev. 3:10-16), has come also to mean "tending to (worldwide) unity." It is significant that the origins of twentieth-century ecumenism lay in the continuing Christian drive to world mission: In the new mission fields staked out by baptists and mainline Protestants in the nineteenth century, as well as those entered still earlier by Jesuits, Franciscans, and other Catholic missioners, the need for greater cooperation among Christians became evident. Recognition of this need led Protestants (in the steps of an earlier initiative by Baptist missionary William Carey) to convene a World Mission Conference (Edinburgh, 1910). There *evangelism* and *unity* emerged as dual Conference goals (Rouse and Neill, 1967:355-62). From this birth (or rebirth) of ecumenism sprang movements such as The Universal Christian Council for Life and Work (Stockholm 1925; Oxford 1937), and The World Conference on Faith and Order (Lausanne 1927; Edinburgh 1937); and these movements converged in the formation of the World Council of Churches (Amsterdam 1948) (Rouse and Neill, 1967:pass.). The Council gained the support of many Protestant and Catholic bodies, such as Anglicans, Reformed, Lutherans, and, in a measure and with delicate caution, the Roman Catholic Church. It also enlisted some Orthodox and baptist bodies (Fey, ed., 1970:pass.). These developments, with their aftermath in the work of the World Council of Churches and its regional counterparts, engaged theologians to produce an ecumenical *theology* adequate to the changed situation created by the new movements. It is noteworthy that these developments occurred in a century racked by two World Wars and many lesser conflicts. The disorder of the world served as a powerful stimulus to the quest for worldwide Christian life and order. The achievements of this century of effort were significant. Where, previously, Christian bodies hardly spoke to one another except to transmit accusations, a new sense of community began to appear. The ecumenical movement, Anglican Archbishop William Temple declared already at mid–twentieth century, was "the great new fact of our time" (Mackay, 1964:7).

Yet in connection with all this change, serious flaws and hitches appeared. One, hinted above, was the sharply limited Roman Catholic participation. The ecclesial basis of the World Council of Churches seemed difficult to fit into Vatican categories: Genevan ecumenism was one thing; Roman catholicity was another. It was not easy for them to converge. Even now (1994) the Roman Catholic Church remains an interested outsider, not a "member church." Of greater relevance to this volume is the persistent nonparticipation in conciliar ecumenism by most baptist peoples. To be sure, some highly motivated baptist bodies participated from the first. In particular the Christian Church (Disciples of Christ), a denomination grandly ecumenical in intent from its beginnings, and the strongly cooperative Church of the Brethren should be singled out. Yet these and a few others are exceptions within the wider baptist movement. Most Pentecostal bodies have not only steered clear of the World Council of Churches, but have openly rejected it (Sandidge in Burgess, et al., eds., 1988:901-3), while the Southern Baptist Convention, despite its time-honored inner diversity, likewise found it could not enter national or international ecumenical bodies (W. Estep in Woolley, ed., 1971:1684f). For some fundamentalist and separatist baptists, such abstention was based on fear of entanglement with "liberal" theology, but this was not the motive for those Southern Baptists whose 1940 rejection of the initial invitation to participate in the World Council of Churches had a distinct ecclesial basis: The Southern Baptist Convention was "in no sense the Southern Baptist Church"; hence it could not become a member of a "fellowship of churches." This reasoned rejection is the more credible, as the Convention was not at that time steered by the Fundamentalists who were to ecclesiasticize it half a century later. The courteous 1940 letter of regret is worth reading in full; I quote only one sentence: "The thousands of churches to which our Convention looks for support of its missionary, benevolent and educational program, cherish their independence and would disapprove of any attempted exercise of ecclesiastical authority over them [such as the proposed membership implied]" (text in *Annual of the S.B.C.*, 1940, p. 99, cited in Barnes, 1954:285-87).

This was in fact a crucial issue. The World Council of Churches would accept as members only "Churches," while Southern Baptists collectively believed their Convention was no "Church." Although the earliest stages of twentieth-century ecumenism had been shaped by Y.M.C.A.-trained leaders such as John R. Mott, who saw the ecumenical movement as bringing about friendship and mutual aid between individual Christians of different denominations and different lands (and not incidentally, fostering international peace), these practical motives were superseded by the outlook of the mid-twentieth-century World Council generation led by the Dutch ecumenist, W. A. Visser 't Hooft. The chief architects of the World Council simply discounted radically congregational baptist ecclesiology. They had some justification for their disregard: not all baptists saw the issue alike, and in this as in all things, baptist motives were doubtless mixed. Yet Henry P. Van Dusen, writing in the ecumenically minded *Christian Century*, took the world ecumenical leadership's intransigence to task: If real Christian unity was the goal, why not make room for major congregational [and, we might add from our perspective, also for Roman Catholic] understandings of "church," as well as for the existing, valuable, but dominantly Protestant consensus? (Van Dusen, 1952:848-51)

Our accurate assessment of the problem of Christian unity depends on clarity about the doctrines of 'church' in question. How *do* Protestants, Catholics, and baptists differ ecclesially? What have they in common? And what light do these differences and commonalities shed on the quest for Christian community? A pioneer in exploring this question was Lesslie Newbigin, a Church of Scotland missionary who was elected a bishop in the newly forming Church of South India after World War II. This was a regional union body bringing together various Western missionary churches in the subcontinent. Later, while serving as a World Council of Churches Secretary, Newbigin developed his India-based insights in a book, *The Household of God* (1954). As the Scot saw it, the "Church Universal" is necessarily composed of three main types or strands, each biblical in source and inspiration, while no one of the three can alone constitute the fullness of the church. The three were Protestant, Catholic, and a third type that Newbigin named "Pentecostal," but which by his description corresponds to the baptist movement of the present book.

For Newbigin, the seed plot of *Protestant* church existence is "the congregation of the faithful." This interpretation turns upon "faith" as a Reformation keyword and upon the magisterial Protestant Reformers' teaching that when enacted in faith, word and sacrament together constitute the church. Following Luther here, Calvin had written that "wherever we see the Word of God purely preached and heard, and the sacraments administered according to Christ's institution, there, it is not to be doubted, a church of God exists" (*Inst.* IV.1.9). On this view, church is by definition not an institution but an event—a repetitive event, as Sunday by Sunday acts of preaching and of sacramental ministry constitute the church anew.

What the Protestant type lacked, Newbigin said, was an adequate sense of the continuing life of the Christian community, "one fellowship binding the generations together in Christ" (Newbigin, 1954:47). This lack was exactly met in the *Catholic* type, whose roots, as surely as the Protestant, lay in Scripture. Now, however, "church" means "the body of Christ"; Christians are "made incorporate in Christ primarily and essentially by sacramental incorporation into the life of His Church" (p. 61). Just as human family members are born into their families, so baptism, eucharist, and other sacraments incorporate members into Christ's mystical body. "Mystical," and not just spiritual body, for the church in its Catholic type is a realistic entity, subsisting in "an unbroken institutional succession from the time of the apostles" through the ages. Yet, like Protestantism, this Catholic type was incomplete, since it tended to make of church "a purely historical institution, the trustee of an absent landlord" (pp. 88f). So both types preserve a partial truth, a biblical truth, while each provides something the other lacks.

Why, then, was a third type necessary? Newbigin's answer was that it must provide an element that the other two types omit: the gift of the Spirit. What makes the *Pentecostal* type distinctive is not only that (like

Protestantism) it seemed to neglect order and structure, while at the same time (like Catholicism) it emphasized a new substantive status in its members; this third type did something more. It reckoned with "an actually experienced and received reality," a genuine new start in life for each member of the church, springing from the fresh gift of the Spirit to each (p. 95). Here again Newbigin recognized a strong biblical foundation. The experienced reality of the Spirit's presence was a given fact of biblical Christianity: Paul says "anyone who does not possess the Spirit of Christ does not belong to Christ" (Rom. 8:9*b*). For Newbigin's third type, this was not merely a formal but an actual possession—otherwise Christ is not really Lord of his church (p. 101). It follows from all this that authentic *church* appears only when the three types converge (as in the Church of South India?), but where they do converge, there appears a full three-cornered witness to Christ (p. 102).

Here an objection will occur to readers who feel that their own 'type' of church includes the very elements Newbigin assigns to some other type. It is important to see, though, that he is not trying to *describe* existing Protestant or Catholic (far less, existing Pentecostal or baptist) churches, many of which would fit his account very imperfectly. Rather, in sociological fashion, he is constructing a typology of pure elements, perhaps never found as such in the world, but useful for his constructive task. The pure types may exist, for all he can say, *only* in combination with others. His final point remains: none should be omitted in *any* existing church.

There seem to be two substantive objections to Newbigin's scheme. The first is that his description of each type, while useful, is unreasonably narrow. What we may call "event-congregationalism," the church constituted afresh whenever the word is purely preached, et cetera, is a view that would hardly occur to any Protestant in practice, where the ongoing *community that meets* is just as truly "church" as are the episodic meetings themselves. And indeed, Newbigin concedes this obvious point, however much it spoils his pure *schema* (Newbigin, 1954:chap. 2). If we are fully to take up his viewpoint, we must therefore ask similar questions about each of his three types. At the outset, I will expect each type to represent not a single feature but a polar tension; this will provide a more complete definition of the type. Second, Newbigin's *schema*, growing as it did from European conversations about church 'reunion,' and from the practical experience of forming the Church of South India, gave insufficient attention to the conditions of healthy ecumenical growth for each ecclesial type viewed in itself. The argument made it appear that none could flourish except by merging with the other types. Yet today such mergers are rare. **What I hope to furnish is an ecumenical strategy for such a post-merger season.**

Surveying Newbigin's work after nearly half a century, its gains seem to be principally two: it introduced a third 'corner' into the Protestant-Catholic debate, and it made clear that at best any of these types of church existence, standing clear of the other two, was only provisional. Both these results stand. The baptist voice must be heard (and in order to be heard by others, must learn to hear itself); likewise, each ecclesial voice is provisional, awaiting future, even eschatological, completion. The fact that we await final fulfillment at the day of the Lord should foster, not prevent, whatever can be realized now (cf. Chapter Two).

a. The Protestant type.—There is a strong local-church element in Protestantism. Newbigin was right to emphasize this, with its biblical roots. His episodic or event-focused typing of the Protestant church as a 'happening' at least indicates this local element, even when one adds the accompanying idea of an ongoing fellowship that meets to hear the word and administer the sacraments. What Newbigin did not adequately emphasize is that as a distinctive movement, Protestantism has a history. It began at a particular time in a particular place. The time was the Renaissance; the place was Europe. There have been many renaissances in European history, cultural rebirths of one sort or another, but in northern Europe the most consequential, generally called *the* Renaissance, grew from Italy in the fourteenth century and culminated in the North in the sixteenth—culminated, we might say, in the Protestant Reformation. Its hallmark was the attempt to purify culture by a return to the sources. In philosophy, this meant a fresh reading of the Greeks and Romans; in literature, it meant tapping the vital energies of the vernacular languages; in art and architecture, it meant restating the calm verities of classicism; in religion, it meant a new look at the Bible. The Renaissance criticized Medieval style as "corrupt (and modern!)" and, especially through representatives such as Erasmus, it repudiated the stylized religion of the late-medieval church in favor of what it considered original Christianity. It is a mistake, then, to think of the Renaissance as anti-religious, for it hoped to purify all contemporary life, not reject it (R. Porter in Yolton, et al., eds., 1991).

Although, with the exception of John Calvin and Oecolampadius, early Protestant leaders (Luther, Carlstadt, Melanchthon, Zwingli, Bucer, and their English counterparts) were not first-order Renaissance scholars, and though Luther had some characteristically harsh things to say about such scholarship, the Protestant movement was in part a response to the new cultural context, of which all its leaders were aware. This contextual response both gave impetus to and set limits upon Protestantism. It existed to make *that* response.

In ecclesiology, then, Protestants were not simply local-church pur-
ists, streamlining liturgy and clarifying the gospel; they were as well
people of the Renaissance, and as such were opposed to any form of
religious idolatry. This deep principle in their sense of church (and in
their sense of culture) was what Paul Tillich called *the Protestant principle*,
the resolve that nothing should be a god to them save God alone. This
produced a tentative, suspicious attitude toward all traditional ecclesial
forms, and with a grand consistency included equal (or nearly equal)
suspicion of Protestantism's own forms as well. "What makes Protestantism Protestant," Tillich wrote retrospectively, "is the fact that it
transcends its own religious and confessional character, that it cannot be
identified wholly with any of its particular historical forms" (Tillich,
1957:162).

Accordingly, there can be no neat summary account of the *contents* of Protestant ecclesiology. Questions of membership, ordination and church office, the
administration of baptism and eucharist, the 'congregational' or 'connectional'
or 'episcopal' governance of the churches and their relation to civil government
were differently decided within the two main Protestant branches, Lutheran and
Reformed, and differently inside each as well. Diversity was not inconsistent,
however, since it grew from the play of the two principles, one the emphasis
Newbigin identified as the immediacy of church as event (well exemplified
when anyone says, "Church is at eleven o'clock"); the other, the Protestant
principle that warns the community of faith against idolatrous dependence on
any earthly embodiment of Spiritual Presence—any, not to except event-congregationalism. Between these two, the 'here' and the 'nowhere,' a great tension
persists (Tillich, 1957:chaps. 11–12).

My account of Protestantism's tension is not meant to deprecate or
devalue its ecclesiology. Quite the contrary; in its ongoing adaption to
its own time and place lay its strength. That strength may be measured
by the fact that over five centuries, as the Renaissance passed into the
Enlightenment and thus into the fading modernity we know today,
Protestantism maintained contact with the culture, adapted itself in line
with its principles—and survived. That a significant Protestant movement, both Evangelical (Lutheran) and Reformed, remains in place in
post-Christian Europe and in America, as well as in the Third World
(where a chief carrier is the Anglican communion), is a tribute to its long
staying power. It is worth noting, though, that already at mid–twentieth
century, Paul Tillich, a perceptive reader of the relation between church
and culture, thought the "Protestant era" was at an end (1957:230-33).
More optimistically, Protestants may as Newbigin believed require a
leavening of "Catholic substance" (Tillich's term), and no small portion
of radical baptist faithfulness as well.

b. The Catholic type.—Newbigin, as we have seen, characterized the Catholic type of church existence as *corporate:* all that he had to say under this heading—about Jesus and the apostles, about the "people of God," about human nature's continuity with all nature, and about the role of Christian sacraments—sought to give substance to this Catholic element. "The Christian life is life in the Body of Christ, a life which involves the identification of ourselves with His death and resurrection, in faith, baptism, and the Lord's Supper" (Newbigin, 1954:75). Catholicity, Newbigin might be taken to say, means sacramental solidarity, in Christ, with the whole company of the faithful.

The difficulty with this view is that it seems far too indefinite. To what Christians of goodwill does it not apply? What is to be included as "Catholic" can only be clear to us if we see what is to be excluded, and that requires further specification. I propose now to attempt such a specification, following the concept of the *Catholicity of the Church* put forward by American Jesuit theologian Avery Dulles in all his writing, but particularly in a book of that name (Dulles, 1985). Dulles provides a wider sweep of related ideas than Newbigin, and we will find at least one of these ideas standing in tension with a simpler understanding of the Catholic type—thus once again a polar tension will appear.

Dulles treats the catholicity of the church as an outgrowth of "the catholicity of Christ"—who reconciles "to himself all things" (Col. 1:20 NRSV). His chapters treat the church in relation to nature, the church's reach to all people, and the church's long continuity through time. In his outline, Catholic catholicity is "from above" (from God and Christ) and "from below" (based in nature); it exists "in breadth" (to all people) and "in length" (through time and its tradition). Hardly any of this surprises. Drawing on the ablest Catholic writers—Newman, von Hügel, Tyrrell, Blondel, de Lubac, von Balthasar, Rahner, Congar—Dulles assembles under these four headings the long continuities of Catholic thought, persuasively displaying the coherences that typify Catholic self-understanding. The continuity with nature underlies both incarnational ("from above") and sacramental ("from below") Catholic thinking; the church's inclusive and expansive drives toward humanity show its self-understanding in breadth; finally, Catholic tradition, developing over the centuries, displays its catholicity in length (Dulles, 1985:1-105). So far, there is little that would not be affirmed by most self-styled Catholics, Orthodox, Anglican, high-church Protestant, or other.

Next, however, Dulles turns to the *sacramental and hierarchical structures* of catholicity, and some may not follow him here. To begin, there is an institutional element in all religion (von Hügel, 1923:123). In Catholicism, sacraments are constitutive in the institutional element; as such, they are neither peripheral nor merely symbolic; rather each sacrament "is a particular actualization of the Church's essence and gives an ecclesial grace specific to itself" (Dulles, 1985:114). In baptism, the church incorporates new members; in penance it pardons and reconciles errant ones to itself and thus to God; in the eucharist Christ is its real food (though not physical food), a meal that unites the church inwardly even as it unites the church with Christ and Christ with all creation (1985:114-18).

It is in the institution of hierarchy, culminating in papacy, though, that Dulles' "Catholic principle" shows its distinctive face. The episcopal college provides a reliable witness so that every generation can hear an authentic gospel. "Christ speaks and acts in and through his authorized witnesses," just as the Gospel says: "Whoever hears you, hears me" (Luke 10:16). The episcopal hierarchy, to be sure, is never the sole power in the church. Vatican Council II, without denying hierarchical power, sought to modify its sole dominance so that "pastors and faithful can engage in fruitful interchange" in a church no longer committed to rigid autocratic rule. Yet the "royal power" of hierarchy, "a body of pastors having apostolic authority," is essential to the Catholic Church, essential, Dulles says, to catholicity (1985:119-26).

> The mission of the Church is too vast to be accomplished by any single group of members. It requires the kind of unity in variety of which Möhler spoke in his analogy of the choir. In this choir Christians of every social condition and calling can find their place, provided that they allow the leaven of the gospel to permeate their activity, and do not cut themselves off from the total Catholic communion. (Dulles, 1985:126)

Not only is catholicity incomplete for Dulles without episcopacy, but episcopacy is incomplete without papacy. Interestingly, though, this American Jesuit finds it appropriate to approach Roman primacy by way of the catholicity of the *local* church. He quotes Joseph Ratzinger: "The local Churches are not administrative units of a larger apparatus but living cells, each of which contains the whole, living mystery of the one body of the Church" (Ratzinger, *Concilium* 1, p. 44, cited in Dulles, 1985:133f). Here the sense of "catholic" is "true" or "authentic"; each "living cell" is an authentic whole, a concrete style of Christian existence that bodies forth Christ's presence. Such a church, of course, is never isolationist; it necessarily reaches out to other churches. In that interaction arises the possibility, Dulles would say the necessity, of papacy. Each bishop, by representing to his diocese or local church the universal church, exercises a catholic function. Together, the communion of churches is maintained by the collegiality of the bishops. The bishop of some local church must serve as chief bishop, thus locating a *center* of unity; that service is performed by the bishop of Rome (1985:127-38).

The present point is simply to insist that papacy is part of the Catholic type of church existence, and cannot be ignored, though it necessarily creates a tension with the other pole of catholicity. Catholicity must have a center, and (as it happens) "Rome is the center, the principle of unity; Catholic is the periphery, the principle of diversity" (Dulles, 1985:146). Given Rome's centripetal force, both poles are necessary. Certainly many who call themselves Catholic reject this centripetal pole. What about the Orthodox, the Anglicans, the high-church Lutherans, and all who insist on their own catholicity, that is, their existence within "the church universal," while rejecting the Roman claim? In answer, we must remind these that each finds in its history a formal separation from Rome, prior to which it acknowledged some sort of Roman primacy (cf. George Williams in Basden and Dockery, eds., 1991:329), while in no case was the divisive issue primacy as such. Thus each of these ecclesial bodies bears in its history witness to the primacy it currently rejects. So even the rejection expresses the characteristic tension. This distinctive catholic tension corresponds to that of the other types. To embrace papacy is, as Dulles claims, a Catholic characteristic, one more honored, to turn a proverb, in the observance than in its breach, since most of the world's practicing Catholics are, for all the tension it involves, nevertheless *Roman* Catholics.

c. The baptist type.—At the end of the nineteenth century, most church historians still divided Western Christianity into "Protestant" and "Catholic" types without remainder. It was recognized that there were significant differences within each type; it was recognized, too, that Greek and Russian (or more generally, Eastern) Orthodoxy provided yet another Christian outlook not easily assimilated to Latin Catholicism. In the main, though, "Protestant and Catholic" covered the ground. Czech Brethren (the oldest) and Baptist (then the most numerous) radicals were understood, and for the most part even understood themselves, to be variations on Protestant themes. With Methodists, they were considered impure Protestants. Pentecostals had not yet arrived on the scene. Only in high scholarly circles was it realized that a separate stream of Christian existence, neither Protestant nor Catholic, had appeared (or reappeared) in the fifteenth century, a stream destined to require intense theological attention in the twentieth.

The standard understanding of the Czech Brethren (1500s), the Anabaptists (1600s), and their fellow Christians was set by sixteenth-century Protestant and

Catholic polemics, typified by the tracts and histories by Heinrich Bullinger, Zwingli's successor in Zurich, and imitated by some historians to the present. Early in the twentieth century, however, Ernst Troeltsch had opened the way for a sociologically sophisticated analysis of European ecclesiology with his recognition of "mystical," "church," and "sect" types, the latter also (and more suitably) called *Täufer* or baptists (Troeltsch, 1911 II:639f, 729f). In the United States, Franklin H. Littell submitted a dissertation to Roland Bainton at Yale that was later published as *The Anabaptist View of the Church*. In it Littell maintained that the distinctive character of sixteenth-century Anabaptism was its understanding of community: "The Anabaptists proper were those in the radical Reformation who gathered and disciplined a 'true church' *(rechte Kirche)* upon the apostolic pattern as they understood it" (Littell, 1952:xvii). Meanwhile, working as a historian at (Mennonite) Goshen College, German-trained Harold S. Bender gathered scholars to produce *The Mennonite Encyclopedia* (1955) and to found *Mennonite Quarterly Review*, enterprises that displayed the entire baptist movement as neither Catholic nor Protestant, but a distinct community, characterized by discipleship, peace, and love, originating with the sixteenth-century Swiss Brethren. John Howard Yoder and other Bender students sharpened and popularized this perception in a series of pamphlets and writings. The indefatigable research issuing from these revisions of traditional Christian church history remains indispensable; however, as early as 1960, correctives of the Bender 'revision' began to appear. It is much to the credit of the Mennonite historians that these revisions were promptly published in the pages of *Mennonite Quarterly Review* and in a supplementary fifth volume of *The Mennonite Encyclopedia* (ME). William Klassen, in the summary article there on Anabaptism, sketches the work of more sociologically oriented historians such as Walter Klaassen, James M. Stayer, Claus-Peter Clasen, Werner O. Packull, Klaus Deppermann, Hans Jürgen Goertz, and others (ME V:23-26). The common themes of these revisionist-revisionists are that Anabaptism originated in more than one place ('polygenesis' rather than 'monogenesis'), that the line between pure or pacifist and impure or nonpacifist Anabaptists is difficult to draw, and that the distinctives Bender, Littell, and John Howard Yoder had singled out were less distinct on a broader view of social history (Stayer et al., 1975).

Apparently Newbigin wrote *The Household of God* in broad ignorance of all these scholarly discoveries. His brilliant typology seems rather to have come from his intuitive sense of the need of the wider Christian community. He knew something was missing, and his description of "Pentecostals," owing more to the book of Acts than to any firsthand knowledge of twentieth-century Pentecostals or other baptists, was an innovative attempt to fill that need. "The Community of the Holy Spirit" (Newbigin's relevant chapter title) was his recognition that "neither [Protestant] orthodoxy of doctrine nor [Catholic] impeccability of succession can take the place of this." Thus "if we would answer the question 'Where is the Church?' we must ask 'Where is the Holy Spirit recognizably present with power?'" (Newbigin, 1954:94f).

From this starting point, Newbigin was able to sketch as if from its felt absence a picture of the community of the Holy Spirit that strikingly converged with the reality others discovered within the existing baptist (or believers church) stream of Christian life. (1) The gift of God's Spirit is *the starting point* of life in the body of Christ. Newbigin did not work out the close relation of this conviction to believers baptism, but he did see its connection with New Testament *koinonia*—"a common sharing in the Holy Spirit" (Newbigin, 1954:47). This looks quite like the understanding free church folk epitomize in the phrase "a regenerate church membership," where new birth, life delivered by the nurturing divine Spirit, is a necessary condition of membership. Yet not all have seen what Newbigin saw, that the Spirit in individuals may come to nothing apart from the Spirit in the community. (2) However, this gift leads directly to a problem: How distinguish the authentically spiritual from the spurious and the fanatical? To answer, a real and primary gift of the Spirit to the churches, the gift of *discernment*, must be granted. In the New Testament, Newbigin writes, it is assumed "*both* that the Holy Spirit is free and sovereign, able to work in ways that demand rethinking of our traditional categories, *and* that [the Spirit] gives to the Church the necessary gifts by which [the Spirit] may be known (*e.g., I Cor.* 12:10)" (Newbigin, 1954:106). This insight made spiritual discipline primary in the Radical Reformers, issuing among them in the ban—though the latter grew out of all proportion to the discernment that was its core. (3) From these, Newbigin derived another note, a corrective to his own Reformed tradition. In the latter, the truth of divine election had led some to concentrate upon God's secret workings by the Spirit. On the contrary, Newbigin sees the Christian third force, its life starting always with the Spirit, pointing consistently to the actual work of Christ in history, since Lord and Spirit are not to be divided. It is not the elect known only to God, but the "actual visible society which he founded, that must inform the mission and message of the church" (Newbigin, 1954:112f). Practice took priority over extruded (and abstruse) doctrine.

Here, then, we have a third type of Christian community, a third understanding of "church." It is local, Spirit-filled, mission-oriented, its discipleship always shaped by a practice of discernment. To some, it will sound simply too good to be true! And indeed, in practice the churches of the Radical Reformation and their heirs have often fallen far short of this pattern. Yet Newbigin has failed to point to the tension that can correct many of these failings. This overlooked element is the baptist vision, with its two motifs, "this is that" and "then is now." The first motif, the requirement that the church now be seen in the frame of the New Testament church, is the regular presupposition of Bible reading in these communities. It demands that the context of self-interpretation in the church of Jesus Christ be the Christian community, attested in

Scripture, that grew up from his ministry on earth. It requires that the reading method by which the first Christians once approached the Bible (a method they learned from the Bible itself) be again employed by Christians today so that their understanding of Christian community is framed, shaped, by that original bench mark of understanding. That bench mark will again and again yield the features Newbigin notes, yet these features are not fixities of canon law or tradition, but will if true be discerned independently as the living church reads afresh. Such a church is by nature provisional, subject to correction arising from further Bible reading (Yoder, 1984:chaps. 1 and 6). The other motif of the baptist vision is forward and endward: "then is now." The church on judgment day, the church that must give final answer only to Jesus the Lord, is already present—it is the church today. Thus the church sees itself not only in a frame of biblical narrative, but also in a frame of biblical expectation. It reckons that God has only begun to do what God will do. Newbigin is right to see baptist community as Holy Spirit community; counterposed to this, though, are the motifs of the baptist vision. Here, again, is evidence of the provisional nature of the present church: the church must change, for God is on the move, and the end is not yet. There is more to say about this third type, and some of it will be said in final Section §3.

* * * * *

Reviewing, we begin to see why the chapter title describes a "quest," rather than an achieved state of Christian community. Jesus prayed for his present and future followers (the Evangelist tells us), "May they all be one." That prayer was not visibly answered at the beginning, and it still is not. So in ecumenical perspective, the forms of Christian community so far achieved are at best tentative or provisional steps toward the full unity Christ commanded. At least three major styles of being 'church' have made their appearance, each expressing some degree of confidence that it is the appropriate type for all, yet the experience of the actively ecumenical century now ending makes it still more clear that no one type of Christian community is (for example) capable of simply absorbing the other two. This suggests that all three types may be provisional, and there are elements within each to confirm that judgment. *The upshot is that, in a sense not true of other doctrines of the faith, Christian ecclesiology is provisional ecclesiology; it looks toward a fulfillment not yet achieved.* To recognize this is essential to the ecumenical strategy we seek. Even so, there is one further consideration, not yet examined. The Christian movement was born in a Jewish setting, and subscribes to

Scripture that preserves God's great promises made to Israel. How the community of Christians is related to the community of Israel is thus a topic of great relevance. Is the people of God composed of Jews and Christians? Of one but not the other? Or is that no longer a relevant question in the dispensation of the Spirit? In the next Section, we will seek to answer, and will find still another reason to regard all community now under God's rule as at best provisional.

§2. The Jewish Root of Christian Community

The plan of this volume provides insufficient space for a topic of profound interest to Christian teaching today—the relation of the church to Jews and Judaism. It can at least be noted that the local-church approach made here frees us from an initial dilemma others face: Those who begin with a 'church universal' often find it difficult to allow any divine redemptive purpose outside that church. For example, some have even expanded the definition of church to include historical Israel, a move that seems at once presumptuous and historically mistaken. Yet 'universal church' universality seems to require something like it. Another historical Christian approach is to say that the church is "the new Israel," displacing the old—an outlook that appears nowhere in the New Testament.

Paul's classic discussion of the relation of Christian and Jew is found in Galatians, Romans, and (if Paul wrote it) Ephesians. In Galatians and Romans, Paul argues for the primacy of faith as the unifying power of God for Jew and non-Jew alike:

Do you suppose God is the God of the Jews alone? Is he not the God of Gentiles also? Certainly, of Gentiles also. For if the Lord is indeed one, he will justify the circumcised by their faith and the uncircumcised through their faith. Does this mean that we are using faith to undermine the law? By no means: we are upholding the law.

(Rom. 3:29-31)

This is so because faith is even more fundamental, more elementary, than the law in the relation of God to God's people. Abraham, for example, was "justified," set right with God, through his faith. "For what does scripture say? 'Abraham put his faith in God, and that faith was counted to him as righteousness'" (Rom. 4:3). And what was true of Abraham is still true: "our faith too is to be 'counted', the faith in the God who raised Jesus our Lord from the dead" (Rom. 4:24). As Paul estimates Israel in his day, however, a blindness had come over it (a circumstance not without precedent in Israel's long history): Israel has (in part) acquired a false set of priorities: Israel (and some church members in Galatia as well!) have been treating law as a substitute for faith, acting (contrary to the law itself) as if faith were not needed, whereas "it is those with faith who share the blessing with faithful Abraham. On the other hand, those who rely on obedience to the law are under a curse"—a curse from which only the cross can deliver them (Gal. 3:9-13). This leads Paul to reflect further on the providential purpose of God in allowing this confused behavior on the part of Paul's fellow Jews. Briefly mentioned in Galatians 3:14 ("The purpose of this [behavior] was that the blessing of Abraham should in Jesus Christ be extended to the Gentiles"), God's providential plan is more fully expressed when Paul writes to a Roman congregation that includes both non-Jews and Jews:

> As an apostle to the Gentiles, I make much of that ministry, yet always in the hope of stirring those of my own race to envy, and so saving some of them. For if their rejection has meant the reconciliation of the world, what will their acceptance mean? Nothing less than life from the dead! If the first loaf is holy, so is the whole batch. If the root is holy, so are the branches. But if some of the branches have been lopped off, and you, a wild olive [a non-Jew], have been grafted in among them, and have come to share the same root and sap as the olive, do not make yourself superior to the branches. If you do, remember that you do not sustain the root: the root sustains you. (Rom. 11:13b-18)

For Paul is confident that in the long run, even the "lopped off branches," as he considered currently faithless folk within Judaism, would gain or regain faith and be grafted back into the main trunk, which after all was their own (11:19-24).

> . . . once that has happened, the whole of Israel will be saved, in accordance with scripture: From Zion shall come the Deliverer; / he shall remove wickedness from Jacob . . . for the gracious gifts of God and his calling are irrevocable. (Rom. 11:26-29)

Ephesians carries this theme forward. The church (here as previously, on my reading, the church local) cannot be a congregation of strife between its Jewish and non-Jewish members, for the long purposes of God are disclosed *in the church*. And on Paul's view, that purpose is already being realized. Ephesians is probably a circular letter, addressed to a series of churches in Ephesus, Laodicea, and elsewhere in Asia

Minor. Its vision of church is therefore generic (generic and not cumulative; no one congregation is singled out, nor are all summed up as one, yet each in the circuit is addressed). Nonetheless, the image of church in the Letter is a catholic one: when church is church, it is "filled by (or is the fullness of, *plērōma*) the One who fills the entire universe"—the risen Christ (see Eph. 1:22 Greek). What then of Jew and non-Jew in such catholic congregations? The Letter's answer is that their former separation is now resolved; while previously non-Jews were excluded as such from God's covenants and promise, in this new setting they are included; the consequence is "peace to you who were far off, and peace to those [i.e., Jews] who were near; for through him we both alike have access to the Father in the one Spirit" (Eph. 2:17f). Is this a description of actual Asian congregations in which non-Jew and Jew enjoyed a shared messianic faith? Apparently it is. It was in any case their calling, to be lived out by apostolic command, however imperfectly they succeeded (Eph. 2:8-10; 4:1-6).

a. Three Christian views of Judaism.—This brings us to the stance of Christian congregations facing Jews and Judaism in our own day. On Paul's analysis, Israel in the first century was significantly missing out on the new developments: A "partial hardening" had come upon it—for non-Jews' sake! Yet that was not to be a permanent state of affairs. Once non-Jews have been admitted "in full strength," then "the whole of Israel will be saved" (Rom. 11:25f). But what would it mean for non-Jews to be admitted to the people of God "in full strength"? I propose to consider three recent Christian approaches to Jew and Christian before God prior to sketching my own (provisional) answer in Section §3.

Though it will not be one of the three views judged worth a hearing, we must remember that a widespread Christian view of Jews and Judaism both in modern times and before is that the role of Jews as God's Israel, the "people of God," had been superseded by the Christian community. To be sure, Judaism had survived, but it had survived as an Ichabod, a witness to the severity of God's judgment upon a people that rejected his Son, or as a mere fossil, interesting, perhaps, to the comparative religionist, but of no value to the continuing history of salvation promised to Abraham's seed. The latter view was expressed by Friedrich Schleiermacher, among others. He wrote that "Christianity does indeed stand in a special historical connection with Judaism; but as far as concerns its historical existence and its aim, its relations to Judaism and Heathenism are the same," since "almost everything else in the Old Testament is, for our Christian usage, but the husk or wrapping of its prophecy, and that whatever is most definitely Jewish has least value" (CF §12). Thus he discards or diminishes both the living religion and its primary Scripture.

i. Paul van Buren's understanding of Jews and Christians.—Paul van Buren (1924–) is an American Episcopalian who is perhaps still best known for testing, early in his career, the limits of the received Christian doctrine of God. During what he wryly calls "my atheistic period," van Buren wrote books and articles, notably *The Secular Meaning of the Gospel* (1963), that classed him with mid-century "Death of God" theologians (Chapter Seven §3a.ii). Sometime in the 1970s, however, there came a great turn: Paul van Buren rediscovered the resurrection, the Godhood of God—and Judaism (van Buren, 1980–). In his earliest summaries, van Buren sketched out the main lines of his approach to Judaism. Two events in the twentieth century, he believed, made a Christian reassessment inescapable: One was the genocidal camps and death squads of Hitler's Germany (1933–1945), an episode in European history known as the Holocaust: Jews estimated at six million in number perished at the hands of Nazis, many among the perpetrators being at least nominal Christians. The other event was the subsequent establishment of the modern state of Israel. For van Buren, the savage and systematic destruction of Jews was a consequence of earlier wrong attitudes on the part of Christians, attitudes that had their roots in Christian doctrinal theology. The re-establishment of a Jewish state in the historic "land of Israel," on the other hand, was a sign from God, a divine rejection of the Holocaust to be compared to the resurrection of Jesus Christ from the dead. Where Christians by their teaching and Westerners by their action or inaction had permitted or caused the Holocaust, implying divine abandonment of Jews, God in contrast had established the state of Israel as a "city of refuge," a place where Jews might be assured life, not death. Consequently, Christian theology must now ask how and to what extent its earlier relegation of Jews and Judaism to fossil status was mistaken, and indeed the great Christian denominations of Europe and America had by 1980 begun to reflect such reassessment (and confess their own complicity in the Holocaust) in their public statements (cited by van Buren in Steuer and McClendon, eds., 1981:55-66).

How, then, should the Jewish element within "the Jewish-Christian reality" be understood? Van Buren's first point is central: In a theology based on revelation (note van Buren's filial debt to Karl Barth), the primary medium of revelation is Israel's history and Scriptures (van Buren, 1980:40-44). The mistake both Jews and Christians have made is failing to take seriously the revelation value of postbiblical Jewish history. God still acts. For a prime example, Jews have rejected the church's Jesus Christ, and this (altogether appropriate) rejection is a necessary datum for a Christian theology of Israel today. By rightly rejecting the church's version of Jesus, Israel (i.e., Jews and Judaism) summons the church back to "the fear of the LORD." A proper theology of Israel will correspondingly emphasize Israel's testimony to creation and the strong link between creation and covenant; it will construe creation as a risk on God's part, including the risk of such monstrous human evil as the Holocaust; it will reckon with Israel's election as a people to inhabit a land and to become custodian of Torah—the way of life witnessed in the law (van Buren, 1983). Nonetheless, van Buren managed in his third volume, *Christ in Context* (1988), with considerable agility to produce a strongly Christ-centered account of Christian doctrine proper, focused upon Jesus Christ alive today and present to the church, and upon the church as the context in which Jesus is met in word and sacrament, in the neighbor, and (never to be forgotten) in a living Israel.

ii. Rosemary Ruether's challenge to Christology.—Rosemary Radford Ruether (1936–), a Roman Catholic expert on early Christian writings, is best known for her aggressive theological feminism (ed., 1974a, 1983). However, as early as 1974, she published a study of Christian-Jewish relations, *Faith and Fratricide* (1974b). In this less well known study, she argued that the origins of Christian anti-Semitism lay in a long conflict between Christians and Jews over the messianic idea. Though focused upon the patristic writings, and in a measure upon the New Testament as well, this book was intended as a scholar's sidelong comment upon the anti-Semitism of our own times (1982:chap. 2).

What is at once stirring and troubling about *Faith and Fratricide* is that it sees anti-Semitism not as a misplaced by-product, but as spewing from the very heart of the Christian gospel. As Ruether puts it, anti-Judaism (hardly distinguishable from anti-Semitism) is "the left hand of Christology," the negative side of the positive affirmation that Jesus is the Messiah. Since "the Jewish religious teachers rejected this claim, the church developed a polemic against the Jews and Judaism to explain how the church could claim to be the fulfillment of a Jewish religious tradition when the Jewish religious teachers themselves denied it." In other words, Christians and Jews always have had different ideas about who Messiah is to be—for Jews, Messiah's coming was a public event in world history that would establish the reign of God, while for Christians, once their first, naive expectations of Jesus were dashed, the reign of God was interiorized or projected into the indefinite future (1982:57f). (Whatever was true about first-century Jews in general, Ruether's image of early *Christian* eschatology is profoundly different from that presented in Chapter Two of the present volume.)

In brief, Ruether held that historical Christianity had been from New Testament times onward committed to a view of Jesus the Messiah as a divine invader, rather like a space alien, and to a view of Israel and

Judaism as superseded by Christianity. These were equally ancient and persistent views, and were in fact only the two sides, she said, of one Christian stance. The Holocaust was the predictable outcome of the Christian view of Christ (per contra, A. Davies, 1979).

One might have expected, given the serious nature of this charge, that Ruether would therewith announce her resignation from the Catholic Church, but this did not occur. In a short, later work (1982) written as an intellectual autobiography, she elaborated the charge of anti-Semitism against Catholicism and indiscriminately against all Christians, and proposed anew a two-step remedy: The trouble is the dogma of "fulfilled messianism." So Christians must abandon this dogma and frame their doctrine about Jesus as Messiah in terms that are "proleptic and anticipatory" rather than "final and fulfilled." Thus, like Jews, Christians will await a Messiah who is still to come, the difference between the two expectations being that Christians will expect the one returning to be Jesus, while Jews will not. Yet this difference will not matter, since the second dogmatic revision is to see Christianity "not only as proleptic, but also as paradigmatic." That is, the chief elements in the Christian story of Jesus are contextually applicable to the people to whom they first spoke, but not to other people elsewhere. The cross and resurrection are true for the early Christians and even for their Catholic successors, but not for all people everywhere—and evidently not for Jews today. "Thus we can begin to find . . . new possibilities of human solidarity" (1974b:chap. 5; cf. 1982:71-73).

Ruether is to be commended for recognizing earlier than many theologians certain undeniably 'Christian' roots of anti-Semitism and anti-Judaism. Patristic experts agree that these ugly patterns appeared in the Church Fathers alongside the misogynism that has been another target of Ruether's attack. It may be, though, that the Catholic upbringing that her autobiography skims past so lightly has played a more powerful role in her early-church scholarship than she concedes. Is it the case, as traditional Catholics supposed, that the patristic writers' views can simply be read back into the New Testament itself? Can "Christians" and "Jews" be as neatly separated in the first century as in the fourth? Were the understandings of messianism of late second-, third-, and fourth-century writers also those of the first Christians? Or had the parting of the ways that sadly but surely occurred in the second century served more as cause than as consequence of the ill will that followed on both sides? These questions will rise again in what follows.

iii. John Howard Yoder and the fall of the church.—The views of Paul van Buren and Rosemary Ruether, while they do not exhaust the field, are broadly representative of recent Protestant and Catholic rethinking of Jewish-Christian relations in that both accept fairly traditional views of Jesus and Paul, while both evince liberal guilt over the Holocaust. In these regards they seem at considerable distance from the Paul of Romans 9 through 11, who deplores the failure of some of his Jewish contemporaries to acknowledge God's good news in Jesus, but at the same time warns believers in Jesus against any smug complacency—*God has not abandoned Israel*. The Apostle Paul, we might say, is more even-handed in his warnings than van Buren and Ruether in their rather different circumstances managed to be. If we are to attain a balance like his, perhaps we have something to learn from Radical Reformation historian and theologian John Howard Yoder (1927–). Yoder, even before Ruether and van Buren, had found a new direction in first-century history. The best-known example of this work is *The Politics of Jesus* (1972), a book relating present-day ethics to Jesus' ministry and its apostolic witness. Regrettably, Yoder's parallel work on Christianity and Judaism has not yet been offered for publication. I propose here to summarize this work (using unpublished material) as an alternative both to traditional Christian arrogance toward Judaism and to the assumption, promoted by Ruether, that Jews and Christians have always been at odds. As John Yoder put it in a 1977 lecture, *tertium datur*, there is a third way.

Yoder's interest in this theme was stirred by his perception that there is a close parallel between the 'believers church' or baptist sense that Christian community stands in need of *restoration* because of its previous deformation at the hands of establishment (or Constantinian, or patriarchal) Christianity, on the one hand, and the need after the Holocaust to *recover* a somehow lost understanding of the proper relation between Christianity and Judaism. Could there be here not only a parallel, but a connection? Was this not two separate losses but one great loss? In answer, Yoder begins with Abraham, who represented for biblical writers that which others can receive from the Hebrew heritage (Matt. 3:9 par.; Luke 3:8; Gal. 3:6-29; Hebrews 11). Abraham's *faithfulness* (a better translation than "faith" or "belief") is a Hebrew heritage or gift that according to Scripture God purposes to share with all the world. This heritage always places God in contrast with the gods of the nations, whose typical gifts are communal wealth and security; thus Jews inherit not simply another ancient religion, but a unique gift for all the world. To speak concisely, what had its beginning in Abraham with its climax in Jesus was a *new definition* of God—one who ordained a servant peoplehood. Joseph in Egypt may stand as representative of this servant-hood—Joseph who found in God strength to disobey his earthly superiors and strength to pay the consequent price in suffering; Joseph whose unperceived loyalty to his pagan owners was ultimately vindicated, so that they honored his God, who then used him to save Egypt—returning good for evil. Faithfulness entails *obedience*, and the biblical heroes are those who are able to leave the security and comforts of their homelands in order to obey God: Abraham leaving Ur, Moses leaving Egypt, Jeremiah leaving Jerusalem. So God, Yoder is convinced, is not as many suppose the enforcer of existing culture, but is the One who savingly leads his people into a new culture that is somehow to benefit all. (Thus at the outset Yoder challenges those aiming at evangelism of Jews *and* those opposed to the evangelism of Jews, for they alike assume that today's Jews are outside the salvation story.)

This brings us to Yoder's rejection of the inevitability of Christian-Jewish separation. The parting of the ways might not have occurred, need not have occurred, and for a few crucial decades *did not occur*. It is essential neither to Christianity nor to Judaism. It will therefore be valuable to revisit the stage of Jewish and Christian history prior to the parting to see what might actually be recoverable in present practice. This will be doubly interesting, because revisionary Christians who ask such questions will find in ancient Judaism a commitment to just such questioning: Jews then, like baptists and others now, questioned the direction being taken by mainstream Christianity. Radical Christians today question Byzantine secular politics and ecclesiastical establishment. Perhaps they have much to learn from Jews, who raised similar objections in the fourth century and before.

The standard account of Jewish-Christian relations, Yoder goes on, says that from the first, Jews and Christians rejected one another. This standard account starts with a hypothesis of 'normative Judaism' that rejected and was rejected by Jesus. But if as Yoder argues there was no such 'normative Judaism' in his day, Jesus could not have rejected it, while research shows that in fact Jesus was much closer to later rabbinic Judaism than to later anti-Judaic Christianity.

An objection to Yoder's reading of the first century is the apparent anti-Jew-ishness of some passages in the Fourth Gospel. "The Jews" argue with Jesus (2:18), seek to kill him (5:16-18; 7:1), disbelieve and deny him (8:57; 9:18), arrest and try him (18:12ff), and demand his death of Pilate (19:7-12). On the other hand, almost as many passages in John show Jewish affirmation of Jesus: some Jews believe on Jesus (11:45; 12:11); others are serious inquirers (3:1ff); Pilate, uncorrected, identifies Jesus with Jewry (18:33; 19:14-21); and early in the Gospel Jesus says salvation is "from the Jews" (4:22). Yoder here follows the careful analysis of Urban von Wahlde (1982) to resolve the conflict between these sets of passages: in brief, the negative ones refer to "the establishment"; that is, to a leadership cadre that opposed not only Jesus but many other elements in the pluralistic Judaism of the day; the positive ones to other Jews. A near parallel, for Yoder, was the Vietnam War era in America, when many Americans spoke with bitter disdain about what "the United States" (or even "we") were doing in Southeast Asia, without meaning thereby to condemn most Americans including themselves. It is only in this sense, Yoder argues, that the author of the Fourth Gospel, traditionally a Jew, "condemns the Jews." From the other direction, apparently Jews who followed Jesus were never excluded from (or ceased to worship in) the Jerusalem Temple, which until the year 70 was the institutional center of Judaism. On another front, it was not un-Jewish to recognize a particular individual as Messiah; Rabbi Aqiva among others did so without having his Jewishness questioned. "Son of God," as a name for Messiah, was not un-Jewish, either. On this score, Yoder holds, first-century non-Jewish Christians might reasonably be understood as a distinctive but authentic part of pluralistic Israel, along with Essenes, Pharisees, Sadducees, and Zealots, while the compromise over food laws (Acts 15:20) makes it clear this participation was the understanding of Jewish Christian leaders at the time.

A parallel argument, Yoder sees, must be made concerning the alleged anti-Jewishness of the Apostle Paul. Perhaps from Luther onward, certainly from the time of Adolf von Harnack, Paul has been read as one who was "converted from Judaism" on the Damascus road, rejected Judaism in his arguments about the law, and was "the great Hellenizer" of Christianity. Yoder, following the trend of more recent New Testament scholarship, argues the contrary case: Paul is "the great Judaizer" of Gentile Christianity. Paul's Damascus road awakening was one that made a better Jew of him, one who ceased to persecute his fellow Jews as with them he followed Jesus Messiah. He continued his connection with the Temple, consistently invoked his Jewish heritage, and so far from provoking the later Jewish-Christian schism, consistently rejected it, as the later Pauline witness of Ephesians confirms. Paul regards the dawn of the messianic age in Jesus as the fulfillment, not the rejection, of Judaism; his attitude to the law is a thoroughly Jewish one; and his missionary aggressiveness was but the continuation of established first-century Jewish policy. It was a heartbreaking reality for him that not all Jews agreed—a heartbreak not unlike that of most faithful Jews in most centuries before and since—but he believed that even that sad reality was a means toward the ultimate salvation, not of all people everywhere, but *of the Jews* (Rom. 11:26).

According to Yoder, only after A.D. 135 or later was there the parting of ways that traditional historians (and Ruether) project back into the first century. After 135, with the Bar Kochba rebellion crushed, Judaism began a slow withdrawal from its outward world mission. Isaiah 66:23, which earlier Judaism might have read as promising an ingathering of Gentiles to Judaism, was now interpreted only as saluting a minimal Noachic covenant that required no mission to Gentiles. Correspondingly, there was now Jewish rejection of the increasingly Gentile Christian community—a rejection that was reciprocated, Justin Martyr (A.D. 165) being an instance. This second-century split was for Yoder the original "fall of the church" that many assign to the much later time of Constantine. It was a real fall, because when Christians cut themselves off from their Jewish root, they cut themselves off from the divine intention expressed in and through Abraham's heirs, the people called Israel.

For Yoder, the parallel between (1) baptist Christians, (2) first-century, still-Jewish Christians, and (3) other Jews then and later is even more striking when viewed not doctrinally but sociologically. In common, these communities maintained a radical social distance between themselves and the powerful dominant majority. All three built their common life not around a hierarchical liturgy, not around an earthly monarch who maintained their creed, but around the Bible. Their culture was shaped by a text. Yoder thinks this cultural style enables us to understand the so-called pacifism of Jesus better than the standard attempt to 'spiritualize' his teaching. Jesus (not without frequent reconsideration) turned away from violence; so (Zealots excepted) did most Jews of his day. Like others, he renounced the attempt to restore the Davidic monarchy, regarded the holy war as a thing of the past, and (with many Jews from Jeremiah onward) accepted another role in a Gentile world order. The books of Esther and Daniel suggest that a faithful life can be lived under pagan kings. The direction of Scripture points to a future in which Jews (and Christians) are to "have no king but JHWH." Trust in God was the theme of Isaiah, of Jeremiah, and of Jesus. In each case, this theme entails suffering for the righteous. When Christians gave up the way of suffering, substituting for it the Constantinian state-church sustained by Caesar's might, they were acting out *their parting* from a way that Jews for the most part have sustained, despite 'Christian' antagonism, until this day. Some may contest Yoder's reading, as some will the previous two readings of Christian-Jewish history; what is so far clear is that there is more than one way to read that history and that the present is a time of historical revision (cf. Dunn, 1991).

The views of van Buren, Ruether, and Yoder represent a debate in progress, not the settled results of the debate. It is important to recognize this, and to see that not everything in Christian theology is already worked out. In this spirit, in the following Subsection (b), I will present yet another view, closer to Yoder than to the others yet learning something from each, and going on beyond Yoder to ask what kind of Christian community is appropriate in light of the facts (and theories) under debate here.

b. *The anguish of the Jews.*—One need not more fully agree with van Buren, Ruether, or Yoder in order to concede one common theme: Christians and Jews are uniquely related, and neither people can rightly understand itself without the other. This seems evident for Christians, who (at a minimum) recognize that Jesus of Nazareth, Mary his mother, and all the first generation of Christians were Jewish, that the Bible of the first Christians was the Bible of Israel, and that from the beginning Christians defined themselves in Jewish terms as followers of the Jewish Messiah. Had not the Lord, speaking in Matthew 25, said "anything you did *for one of my brothers here* . . . you did for me" (Matt. 25:40)? It is perhaps less obvious that Jews from the first century onward have consistently defined their identity over against and thus in terms of the Christian movement. This became tragically clear in the long centuries in which Jews in the Mediterranean world and in the West were an intransigent minority in a 'Christian' culture. We will inspect this phenomenon next. It was equally true, however, of the rabbis at Javneh who in the aftermath of the fall of Jerusalem in 70 C.E. undertook to define (and thereby did create) rabbinic Judaism, the Judaism of Mishnah and Talmud that almost alone among the existing styles of Jewishness was suited to survive. For rabbinic Judaism defined a response, a development of the Hebrew-Jewish story alternative to the Christ of later Christian tradition, and certainly alternative to the dejudaized gentile Christianity of Catholic and later of Protestant faith.

The beginnings of Jewishness as such date not from Abraham the pioneer, or from Moses the liberator, or from David and Solomon the kings, but from Jeremiah the refugee. Judaism—people, religion, polity—begins with Jerusalem's fall to the Babylonians in 597 B.C. and its subsequent destruction in 587-86. After that, the old Hebrew race, old Israelite cultus, old Judaean politics would never return. Jeremiah (active 626–580) had predicted this outcome, and was dragged by it into exile in Egypt. He was, in Paul Johnson's phrase, "the first Jew" (1987:79). One way to understand this scattered Israel becoming Jewry is that it was only a temporary interruption, for under Nehemiah and Ezra some Jews did return from Babylon, while a few poor folk had never left Palestine. Yet numerically, the greater number of Jews after 587 would remain in diaspora; no attempt to collect them was ever successful for more than a minority of Jews for a short time. This meant that substitutes replaced all the old localized Hebraic institutions. Lifting up of hands in prayer substituted for the evening altar sacrifice (Ps. 141:2); an obedient way of life ("the law") substituted for political independence; the long-evaded kingship of the LORD substituted for the brittle Hebraic dynasties. Periodic attempts (today, social historians might call them "fundamentalist") to recover the old ways enjoyed brief but uneven success; for almost five hundred chaotic years there was a Second Temple (its doomed successor was abuilding in Jesus' day); a Hasmonean dynasty, the Maccabees, fought its way to power and lasted less than a century; the present state of Israel has endured barely half a century. For the most part, Jews not only went into 'exile'; they emigrated to new lands, Babylon, Syria, Egypt, India, Greece, Rome, and eventually beyond. There they settled, 'sought the peace of the city' that sheltered them (cf. Jer. 29:7), and became witnesses among the nations to a Deity not made with hands, a God who was not a human project, while keeping a Torah or way not conformed to the customs of host nations, some of which were 'Christian' lands.

It was this separate peoplehood—a vast experiment across time, otherwise unknown to world history—that according to most specialists gave rise to the phenomenon of anti-Semitism. The term is recent (1879) and a misnomer (since it refers not to Semites but to Jews), but it names a persistent attitude. No nation on earth was prepared for a people who would exist in but not of the existing ethos, a people who would share labor, trade, language, wealth, and common law, but would reject intermarriage, the local gods, and (by their food laws) even table fellowship. Jews were strange! As aliens, they evoked the peculiar form of hatred called (in a Hebrew image) *scapegoating*—Jews were a handy target for xenophobia, became the butt of scurrilous legends, all refutable, all believed; and often they suffered violent and unjust persecution—as recalled in story form in the books of Esther and Daniel. Being a diaspora witness turned out to be a costly enterprise, a suffering way in which faithfulness required deep and unshakable conviction (Johnson, 1987:chap. 2). Jewish history passed a kind of threshold in the second-century parting with Christians, for this prefaced the horrendous chain of events to be mentioned next, the "anguish of the Jews" suffered at Christian hands. These are events I had rather not report, for they are shameful for Christians, reflecting a history that, like the Thirty Years' War (Catholic and Protestant), the Spanish Inquisition (Catholic), and the Jonestown, Guyana, massacre (baptist), is a discredit to the Jesus movement in all its parts. Moreover, my reluctance is widely shared. Except for one highly publicized event, the German and Nazi Holocaust (1933–45), most Christians are unaware of the chain of suffering, inflicted in Christ's name, that has defined two millennia of Jewish history, and Christian theologies and church histories typically leave it out. As Edward Flannery, Catholic author of *The Anguish of the Jews*, puts it, "The pages Jews have memorized have been torn from our histories of the Christian era" (1965:xi). The full story requires a book, but I propose only to relate, however inadequately, some episodes that typify it.

i. Ambrose of Milan.—In the summer of A.D. 388, Callinicum, a town and military garrison on the Euphrates, experienced tension that erupted when the Catholic bishop incited Christian monks to set a synagogue afire. The Roman viceroy reported this outrage to the Emperor, Theodosius, who ordered the Callinicum bishop to restore the synagogue and punish the monks. Ambrose, bishop at the imperial seat in Milan, had a different view of the matter. He preached a sermon, attended by the Emperor, that at once displayed Ambrose's theory of the relation of Catholic church to Roman state, and disclosed his attitude toward these distant Jews. About the latter, Ambrose seemed to know only that they were the victims of this desecration at Christian hands. Yet their synagogue, he confidently announced, had been "a place of unbelief, a home of impiety, a refuge of insanity damned by God himself." As evidence, he cited Jeremiah 7:14-17! The sermon ended, Ambrose confronted Theodosius in the nave of the church and threatened him with excommunication unless the Emperor countermanded the order to the Callinicum bishop to make reparation. Theodosius submitted, so the mass continued. The episode tells us more about Ambrose and Theodosius, shapers of the future 'Christian' Empire, than about disorders in a distant garrison in the East. Ambrose's judgment in this case, in the words of his admirer S. L. Greenslade, was "warped to the point of bigotry" (Greenslade, ed., 1956:226-52).

ii. The Black Death.—The fourteenth century, celebrated in Barbara Tuchman's *Distant Mirror* as a time whose energy, learning—and agony—reflect our own, was a time of extraordinary difficulty for the Jews of Europe. It was an age of Gothic art, knightly honor, and a dawning Renaissance, yet also the century of the Black Death, an epidemic of bubonic plague borne along by huddled populations living in rat-infested towns amid deplorable sanitary conditions. In three years (1348–50) the plague destroyed perhaps a third of Europe's population (Tuchman, 1978:chap. 5). Crazed by fear and beset by ignorance, the populace sought a scapegoat and found—the Jews. Under torture, Jewish suspects were made to 'confess' that they had poisoned the public wells with a mixture of lizards, spiders, frogs, human hearts, and stolen sacred hosts! As a preventive measure, the entire Jewish population of one town in southern France was burned to death. Other prudent town councils throughout Europe tried their Jews even before the plague reached them. A regular pattern of accusation, trial, torture, confession, and burning developed. There were as well suicides, as Jews sought to escape the plague of 'Christians.' Seized Jewish property accrued to the torturers. Christian flagellants appeared, fanatical Catholics who roamed Germany and France "expiating their sins by stirring up attacks on the Jews." Flannery estimates that more than two hundred Jewish communities were destroyed in this scapegoat rage. Perhaps significant, the attacks were worst in German lands; "Well over 10,000 were killed in Erfurt [Luther's future birthplace], Mainz, and Breslau alone" (Flannery, 1965:109f; cf. Girard, 1986:1-11).

iii. Shoah.—Germany, though not unique, had by the dawn of the nineteenth century perhaps the longest and ugliest record of anti-Semitism in Europe. (For what follows, see Johnson, 1987:Part 6.) Nevertheless, the century seemed to promise a new era. Assimilation had almost merged many Jews into the life of the new German Empire. Germans were the best-educated, best-civilized, best-ordered of Europeans, and Jews contributed even beyond their number to German culture. Many were 'baptized' in infancy, cementing a cultural tie with a religious one. Yet just beneath this bland surface, anti-Semitism churned. And in thirteen fateful years of the next century (1933–45) Germany disrupted and extinguished not only its own Jews but nearly all European Jewry. The *Shoah* ("Desolation") or Holocaust thus became a central event of modern Jewish history (Johnson, 1987:470). In those years about six million Jews were murdered, most of the remaining three million were forced from their homes, work, families, and (in many cases) faith, and the lingering stain besmirches modern Europe on a scale matched only by Stalin's savagery against his own people and the desolation of two World Wars themselves.

These outrages are in fact tightly related. World War I best explains the German frenzy. For one thing, the war's savagery broke down German discipline, turning a law-abiding citizenry into an arena for political and ideological murder. From this arena the monomaniac Adolf Hitler emerged. Concurrently, the loss of the war demanded a scapegoat, and the Jews, still separate, a people within the people, were at hand. The evil genius of Hitler merged these afterbirths of war into one weapon: Germany would master itself and the world by uniting against the Jews. To be sure, Hitler cannot bear the blame alone: He won power legally, and secured the support of the universities, the intelligentsia, the bankers, industry, *much of the church*, the army, the *Volk*. Once in power, Hitler obtained laws (Nuremberg Decrees, 1935) that devalued Jews and incited his internal armies to attack them with random violence, culminating in the orgy of *Kristallnacht* (9-10 November, 1938). Thereupon, Hitler's lieutenants marshaled all branches of the state bureaucracy to "eliminate" Jews from Germany in the name of racial cleansing and public order.

Where earlier, war had led to anti-Semitism, now maniac anti-Semitism led to war. Most European Jews were in the East—Poland, Transylvania, Russia. A war to the East, starting with the defeat of Poland, enabled Hitler to create a vast concentration camp (the General Government zone) in Poland. Here all Jews could be transported, imprisoned, and destroyed. The first plan was to force all to work until they died: *Vernichtung durch Arbeit*, "destruction through work." The average laborer survived for five months. But this was too slow, and specific "death camps" were named where interned Jews could be gassed and burned—Auschwitz, Majdanek, Treblinka, Belzec, Chelmno, Sobibor. Meanwhile, Hitler invaded the Soviet Union, and adopted a new method: Behind every armored column followed a death battalion of the SS and Gestapo, instructed to segregate, rob, and annihilate the four million Jews living in the invaded territory. Two and a half million fled. Four German battalions reported early successes, exterminating "125,000, 45,000, 75,000, and 55,000 respectively." Thus it is only an isolated fact that one of the Commanders of unit C, responsible for 30,000 deaths in Kiev alone, was a Christian pastor, theologian, and official of the Evangelical Church of Germany. Together, 'work' camps, death camps, death battalions, and random killings (as in the battle to destroy the Warsaw ghetto) are reckoned to have destroyed 5,933,900 of Abraham's seed.

iv. Le Chambon.—What should Christians have done in face of these episodes, and particularly in face of the fully documented Holocaust that occurred within living memory? The final episode related here, while it has a grim side, may provide a partial answer. Certainly it relieves the uniform gloom of the previous three (for what follows, see Hallie, 1979). A remote and poor mountain village in southeastern France, Le Chambon sur Lignon, was mainly populated before Hitler's invasion by congregants of a French Reformed church and by a smaller, more rural congregation of Plymouth Brethren, the latter a biblically conservative baptist movement. The Protestant Temple was served by André Trocmé, a clergyman of profound social conscience who was committed to nonviolence. These circumstances—Le Chambon's remote mountain location, the staunch independence of the Protestants, who remembered their Huguenot origins, the even more radical independence of the Plymouth Brethren, and the activist nonviolence of Pastor Trocmé—converged to produce an atmosphere totally unreceptive to developments in Vichy France. The French had surrendered to Germany in June, 1940, and an anti-Semitic national government under the leadership of Marshal Henri Philippe Pétain, who emulated Hitler, controlled the unoccupied South. So when on the one hand orders came from Vichy to 'deport,' that is, send to the camps, the Jews who had taken refuge in mountainous Le Chambon, while on the other hand Trocmé proclaimed from the Temple's pulpit that the people must create a "city of refuge" where no Jew's or other victim's life was forfeit, the Chambonnais responded to the pastor's sermon, not the anti-Semitic decree. This, said Trocmé, was "lest innocent blood be shed" (cf. Deuteronomy 19). The Christians concealed their refugees, forging their papers, hiding them in the thick woods, disguising them as family members, escorting them when appropriate to the Swiss border. In all, perhaps 5,000 lives were saved, all without use of weapons or harm to anyone else, though some Chambonnais were arrested and deported to their deaths. Three convictions seem to have guided their behavior during the crisis years: the Old Testament model of an ordained refuge, Trocmé's broad interpretation of the Sixth Commandment (Exod. 20:13; cf. *Ethics,* pp. 310f), and their Sermon-on-the-Mount style of nonviolent action. To these must be added a profound sense, especially by the Plymouth Brethren, that these hunted Jews were God's chosen people. One German-Jewish refugee, approaching a Brethren farm to buy eggs, was asked if she were Jewish. Frightened, she admitted that she was, and was startled to hear the farm wife call to her husband and children, "Look, look, my family! We have in our house now *a representative of the Chosen People!"* (Hallie, 1979:182f).

v. Retrospect.—This Section began with recognition that Christian community is historically rooted in Jewish community. Those who find the New Testament authoritative cannot elude that rootage, and theologically must ask its significance for holy community now. An intervening task is to acknowledge that Jewish suffering at Christian (or perhaps 'Christian') hands has damaged if not destroyed this bond. Admittedly, the anguish of the Jews at 'Christian' hands cannot be blamed upon all Christians alike. Writhings of corporate guilt neglect the message of Ezekiel, who wrote during an earlier period of mutual reproach among God's people (see Ezekiel 18). We may if we like identify with the Chambonnais rather than with the 'Christian' commander in Hitler's death battalion. *Yet we are entitled to do so only if we agree to follow Jesus in a way that will not again lead to the anguish of the Jews.* This is finally a question of community: What kind of community will make it impossible for believers in Jesus to be at the same time enemies of his brothers and sisters according to the flesh (Matt. 25:40)? What kind of community will reject the link with the state's coercion that led so many Christians into the maelstrom of violence? What kind of Christian community can reclaim its heritage from before the time when "the parting of the ways" denied the Jewish footing of Christian community? Christians have not yet adequately answered these questions. Until we do, we have a deeper reason than that explored in Section §1 to reckon that Christian community (and, by Christian light, all Jewish community) is only provisional, awaiting recovery of Jesus' own vision.

This acknowledgment opens a perspective upon evangelism addressed to Jews. It is not the case, as liberal sentiment would have it, that the original gospel has nothing to offer Jewish people. They, too, have needs that Jesus fulfills. They like others can be blessed by the Spirit poured out on "all flesh" at Pentecost. Yet the fateful choice of second-century Christians to isolate their communities from Jewishness, the tragic Jewish participation in this parting, and (most of all) the subsequent centuries of evil poured out upon Jews by professed Christians—all this has made it unlikely that today's informed Jew can even *hear* the good news. (If, despite every obstacle, some do, they are exceptional beneficiaries of God's grace.) The recovery of a kind of community that renounces all triumphalism, all pride of place, and all anti-Jewish bias is therefore a precondition of the fulfillment of God's undying promises to Abraham's seed. Clarity about what has happened in the historical events Christians forget (or never learned) should assist in this recovery. Such historical rethinking is for the sake of truth; it should also be understood as vital for the sake of evangelism, or rather, pre-evangelism. Nor should it be supposed that this pre-evangelism is mainly an education of Jews; it must first be an education of Christians. In this education, Jews of goodwill can play a vital role: For example, how much do Christians have to learn about the messianic tradition of present-day Judaism? How much can it inform Christian messianic understanding? As J. B. Metz asks, to what extent are Christians ready "to recognize the messianic tradition of Judaism in its unsurpassed autonomy; as it were, in its enduring messianic dignity, without Christianity betraying or playing down the christological mystery it proclaims"? (Metz, 1981:23)

What remains here is to sketch the lines of a type of Christian community, however provisional, that may address these needs and at the same time respond fairly to the ecumenical demand.

§3. Christian Community in Radical Reformation

The broad requirements for Christian community have been approached many times in these volumes. Such a community must be suited to the (three-stranded) Christian life together, that is, to the future God promises and the creation God provides as well as to the social pattern displayed in the cross of Jesus. It must be a community at once redeemed and redemptive. It must center upon the present living Jesus Christ in Holy Spirit power. All this could be inferred from *Volume I* and from Parts I and II of the present volume.

Following Lesslie Newbigin, however, we are aware of Christian community in several distinctive types. Two of these, the Protestant and the Catholic, are so well known that one can assume readers' familiarity with them. A third, called free church or believers church or heirs of the Radical Reformation, and here usually baptist, is vast, but at first inspection amorphous, and in its wholeness little known. Its communal structure, like its doctrine and morals, is known only by bits and pieces, and not as the character of one ecclesial type. Some know what it means for Pentecostals to speak in tongues; others see the point of the immersion of new members; others make sense of the practice of the Rule of Christ (Matt. 18:15-18); yet others appreciate the paradoxical claim that "this [present gathering] is a *New Testament* church." My task here, following the lead of historians such as Franklin Littell, Donald Durnbaugh, and John Yoder, is to grasp not the parts but the whole, *not the tokens* (various religious bodies, other than classic Protestant and Catholic, that embody many of these features) *but the type,* and to show the way the type fulfills the demand of Christian ethics and doctrine. *Ethics,* we recall, picked out Radical Reformation features that sprang from a biblical reading strategy. It found a practice of Scripture-reading central to the practices of mission, liberty, discipleship, and community that together identify the type (*Ethics,* One, §2). (One must only be careful, in searching out these features, to recognize that types overlap: there is a family relation between Catholic, Protestant, and baptist types; to know the features of one is to know at least some of the features of the others as well.)

In any case, the present Section will not, like many a manual of ecclesiology, lay down structural rules for every Christian community, or even for all baptist communities. I hope only to show some distinguishing characteristics of this style of Christian life together. We will see three circles of Christian community (each inclusive of the next in order): First is the overarching *rule* of God; within it, the *people* (or *peoples*) of God; finally, the concrete gatherings—the (local) *churches* of God. The final step will be to apply to these 'gathering churches' some tests set by the demands of Christian existence explored in Sections §1 and §2. These moves cannot answer all the questions that arise in the quest for Christian community. I hope they will suggest work others will pursue.

A special difficulty is that in picking out the desired features of Christian community we tend to overlook its undesirable features. Theologians at mid-century sought to take account of this 'realistic' aspect of community life: Bonhoeffer in his *Communion of Saints* (1964:144-55), James Gustafson in a work on the church as a *human* community (1961), Langdon Gilkey in a book on church and world (1964), all were at pains to uncover the seamy or sinful dimension of churchly existence. In present terms *the line between church and world passes right through each church* (cf. *Ethics,* p. 17). The trick is to acknowledge and respect this fact without being buffaloed into despair at the church's flaws or tempted into cynicism about their remedies. In despair we forget the wonder of the gospel unveiled in human history, while in cynicism we lower our eyes and miss "the glory which shall be revealed in us" (Rom. 8:18 KJV).

a. The peoples of God.—God's reign or rule *(basileia)* issued in the creation of a people and peoples (Chapter Four). Here we focus again on this peoplehood. Toward the end of Paul's Letter to the Galatians some remarkable sentences appear:

> Circumcision is nothing; uncircumcision is nothing; the only thing that counts is new creation! All who take this principle *[tō kanōni]* for their guide, peace and mercy be upon them, the Israel of God.
>
> (Gal. 6:15f)

The final four words seem to disregard all that Paul has just argued (but see 5:5-6), and there is much dispute about them. On one account, by *the Israel of God* Paul referred merely to Christians who accept his 'canon' of judgment; on another reckoning, he meant descendants of Abraham, Isaac, and Jacob; and there are intermediate positions. (The phrase may have been a self-designation of Paul's opponents which he adopted—Longenecker, 1990:298f; see also Betz, 1979.) The matter is unresolved.

Whatever Paul meant in Galatians, I here adopt this phrase, "the Israel of God," for my task. I believe Paul recognized the ambiguity of "the Israel of God" in the new circumstances created by the death and resurrection of Jesus Messiah. After that world-changing event, everything could be construed anew. The historic people of God—a people in whose membership Paul treasured his own place (Gal. 1:13f)—was still in place, not superseded, not discarded. Yet there was a new plant in God's garden (cf. Rom. 9:6; 11:13-26), a growing new people of God, God's sons and daughters through Jesus the Son. The Israel of God had been enlarged, opened in a new way to outsiders, and thereby wonderfully transformed. Israel now meant not a people but at least two peoples, and the key was the new creation that had remade the world.

The strongest argument for my use is Romans 9–11, written later than Galatians. Paul like a prophet there admits he is near despair over current Jewish resistance to the gospel (it seems to him that his fellow Jews "ignore God's way of righteousness, and try to set up their own"—10:3). He has to ask if God has rejected his people. The answer, though, rings clear: "Of course not! . . . God has not rejected the people he acknowledged of old as his own" (11:1f). Instead, he reasons that God's remarkable goodness to non-Jews (who certainly did not *deserve* such grace) is a sure sign of ultimate divine faithfulness to Jews: As Johannes Munck sums up Paul's case, "The Jews are now disobedient in order that they may in turn obtain mercy, the same mercy as was shown to the Gentiles" (1967:139).

Here, then, is a first-century picture of peoples still being formed into one people. Already they are citizens of one *basileia*, the rule of God. If we call that people-in-formation *the Israel of God*, we refuse to exclude from it either Jews or non-Jews, either Samaritans or Romans, either those with a rich biblical past or those with no mentionable past. It is a people made out of peoples, a future-oriented, gift-created, plural community of destiny, whose canon or entrance standard is in every case *new creation* (Gal. 6:15).

As noted above, many would call this people of peoples a "church" (or perhaps, "the church," or "the Church") but that was not Paul's usage. For the word "church" *(ekklēsia)* had been preempted in Jewish and early Christian use to translate *qahal*, which meant not Israel but a gathering of, a concrete assembly of, the people *(am)* of Israel. And the established secular use of *ekklēsia* in Hellenistic Greek was of a political meeting, such as a city council—this very use appears within the New Testament itself (Acts 19:32-41). Accordingly, Paul does not present a primitive Jerusalem congregation running its baronial fences around a widening spread of converts—one extended 'church' operating through many branch outlets, a kind of ecclesiastical McDonald's, Incorporated. The Pauline view is rather of an earthly, here and now *new creation*, a new people, whose character is to gather in assemblies, each original, each dependent upon the present Spirit, each gathered around the risen Christ as was their Palestinian prototype (Banks, 1994). This primitive pattern may have mere historical interest for those who see it as embryonic, only to be completed in a later ecclesiasticism. For our understanding of community, though, this people-shaped beginning has typical and thus lasting value.

A people made up of peoples! Here we have a biblical way to interpret what Newbigin has shown us. His types are realized not so much in national or international 'church' structures (which manifest in every case a bureaucratic sameness) as in the variety of living peoples within God's full Israel. At the broadest sweep, there are besides Jewish people a Catholic people, a Protestant people, a baptist people, and these in their turn consist in such 'sub-peoples'—an Anglican people, a Swedish Lutheran people, a Mennonite people, for examples.

Our English word "people" comes from Greek and Latin stems that indicate the entire human stock (the root is *ple*, which appears also in English "complete"; the Hebrew stem, *am*, on the other hand, denotes kinship. Yet on the biblical view, the entire human race *is* one kinship stock, so in Scripture the two senses converge (see e.g., Isa. 42:5, where *ha am* means "all humanity").

So there is always in Christian use a broader and narrower sense of "people." At the broadest reach, God who rules the earth has only one people, *ha am*, humanity. God then creates a people (cf. Chapter Four) that is to be a people *for* all peoples, a "kingdom of priests, a holy nation" (Exod. 19:6; Gal. 3:8; 1 Pet. 2:4ff). This is the original Israel. By Jesus' new creation, peoples appear within that people; tribes, we might say, within the confederation, so that Paul can distinguish non-Jewish as well as Jewish peoples—in his image, engrafted and lopped off branches (Rom. 11:13-26) of God's Israel. Within that widening Israel of God today we can distinguish many such branches, tribes, or peoples, and these not only constitute the rich plurality of the people of God, but in their diversity (or perversity!) threaten its unity.

The role of peoplehood has engaged some more than others. Methodism as a movement came into being in the eighteenth century as a consequence of the Evangelical Revivals in Britain and America. The Wesleys sought to maintain their witness within the framework of the Church of England, but it was not to be. Surely if slowly, Methodists developed a sense of peoplehood. Concomitantly there was an institutional urge, and national ecclesial structures paralleling Anglican ones (bishops, jurisdictions, etc.) developed in America as in England. Yet early American Methodism, as Michael Cartwright has shown, was vividly conscious of being "the Methodist *people*," and today's United Methodist Church, if it has lost this sense, has lost a vital clue to the discipline and mission that justify its existence (Cartwright, 1992). Mennonites in their several institutional formats retain a wider sense of peoplehood as well, while facing within it a conflict between ethnicity (Swiss or German surnames, styles of cooking, and the like) and a more biblical sense of peoplehood (Bender, 1971; Redekop, 1989; Yoder, 1984). For Baptists, too, this self-designation has been a favorite; there is no single institutional format corresponding to the people called Baptists (cf. Basden and Dockery, eds., 1991). Regretfully, I do not know about Pentecostal and still other use of the 'people' concept.

Two theological lessons emerge: The first is that peoplehood provides a powerful incentive to unity that transcends, and sometimes conflicts with, the nation-state. In the wide world, those conscious of a peoplehood that reaches beyond national borders (one thinks of Jews, but also of Arabs and Chinese) seem better able to transcend the consuming fires of nationalism. Yet second, like the original chosen people, such peoplehoods as Baptist, Methodist, and the like are justified only if they serve as provisional means toward that one great peoplehood that embraces all, the Israel of God, the end toward which the biblical story moves (see further Chapter Ten).

b. Guidelines for a local ecclesiology.—The claim so far is that the Christian concept of community comprises three circles or spans. There is the *rule* (or kingdom) of God; within it is God's Israel, the *people* of God; within these the local *assemblies (ekklēsiai)* of the peoples. It is this third, inmost span that English versions of the New Testament designate by "church" and "churches." This does not imply that a church can be a church in isolation; no church can deny its shared subordination to God's rule, its shared membership in God's people, its common status as a church among the churches. Yet in each 'local' church (the expression is a redundancy) the wonder of community formation in Christ has occurred; whether it is a storefront Pentecostal fellowship or a timeworn ecclesial structure in place for a thousand years or more, this concretion of the Israel of God gathering around the risen Christ—for all its faults, with all its promise—is once again a church of God.

i. The church.—What constitutes authentic Christian community today? In light of what has been said here, what makes a church now God's church? The difficulties we have confronted—the challenge of ecumenism, the awareness of our overlooked Jewish basis—appear to make this a presumptuous question. Christians are not yet in possession of their promised home. In the words of the Letter to Hebrews, "Here we have no lasting city," for "we are seekers after the city which is to come" (13:14). Yet this does not signify that we must travel without a map. The rule of God requires church *members* subject to that very rule. The centrality of Jesus Christ demands church *leaders* led by Christ crucified and risen. The fellowship of the Spirit implies a *common life* whose practices suit, not this present age, but the age to come—a community at once redeemed and redemptive.

These themes (God's rule, Christ's leadership, the redemptive fellowship of the Spirit) dominate the summary portrait of Christian community in the last two chapters of Hebrews. "The kingdom we are given is unshakeable" (12:28); it is God's gift, God's achieved fact. There is no call to 'build' this rule of God, but only to "submit . . . to our spiritual Father" (12:9). The foundation of the church is not democracy but theocracy, not the rule of spiritual commoners or of spiritual aristocrats, but only the "devouring fire" from the throne of "the God of peace" (12:2, 29; 13:20). Lest the community misinterpret these awesome words, they are juxtaposed in each case with a focus upon "Jesus the pioneer" who "endured the cross" (12:2), upon "Jesus the great Shepherd" now "brought back from the dead" (13:20). He is the center of the community, its stylist and living authority, witnessed by leaders "tireless in their care for you" (13:17), who imitate his example and must answer to him and who therefore deserve loyalty. Such a community is (typical) "Mount Zion, the city of the living God, the heavenly Jerusalem" (12:22). When the earthly assembly gathers, the barriers dividing present earth and heaven disappear, and the gathered angel myriads join the earthly saints, these members of an elect people (already "enrolled in heaven"—12:23), while the presence of God the Judge presides over all. Here, too, as from beyond the divide, appear departed saints ("good men and women made perfect"); here, to seal our pilgrim participation, is Jesus in person, ministering not the blood of retaliatory justice (Abel's useless blood), but the blood of the new covenant (12:23f; Moffatt, 1924:216-19). Then Hebrews proceeds to list the redeeming practices of this gathering community: its worship, its hospitality (13:1f), its sharing of goods (13:16), its ministry to prisoners and victims (13:3), its acceptance of order and discipline (12:9-13; 13:4, 7, 17).

How is such community formation to work for us? In what sense are we to "belong to one another" (Rom. 12:5) in Christ? Is there any once-for-all answer? Recent New Testament scholarship suggests there cannot be, as no single pattern of church life appears in the New Testament itself. Rather we must here apply the long continuities of Christian teaching developed in preceding chapters: God's rule, Christ's centrality, the Spirit's koinonic presence. From the rule of God—a consent-seeking, creative, salvific rule—comes *membership* that consents to that rule. In baptist parlance, that has meant receiving the Spirit, obeying the gospel, receiving Christ, taking up discipleship. It implies a disciple church, shaped by its distinctive conversion-baptism. In the centrality of Christ—a centrality focused on his resurrection presence—comes *leadership* that says No to social control shaped by the old aeon and Yes to a fellowship shaped by that crucified and risen presence. In baptist parlance, this means leadership as ministry or servanthood not imposed from without or standing on its rights. From Spirit-gifted *community practices* comes the vector of a community that lives between the times, adapting, adjusting, transforming, interpreting so that the church can be the church even as it helps the world to see itself as world (*Ethics*, Eight, §3). Thus the church's gifts and practices seek the goal God sets it.

When in difficult circumstances Latin American Catholics earlier in this century began to meet weekly for prayer, Bible study, evangelism, and social justice, they had no intention of forming new 'churches'—they only sought to meet felt needs. Yet the outcome was the rise of the *basic Christian communities*, neither church nor parish, that so strongly interacted with Liberation Theology. "Prayer, Word, Life: these are the three elements common to every meeting" (C. Boff, 1981:54). Basic communities presented the hierarchy with a new situation calling for fresh theological reflection (L. Boff, 1981). Let us conduct our own brief reflection here. The basic communities appear to repeat the phenomenon that produced Bohemian Brethren in the fifteenth century, Anabaptists in the sixteenth (both from Catholic roots), and in successive centuries Baptists, Brethren, Restorationists, Pentecostals, and more. Do the basic communities replicate the baptist vision? Certainly its standard of membership answers Yes. Here is a people met to pray in Jesus' name, to seek his truth in Scripture, to act in his way. Basic communities also share our reading strategy—the baptist vision. Problems come with the control that the hierarchy seeks to maintain over its sacraments and priestly leadership. Whether that control will prevail is a question that time will answer. If control is maintained, the basic communities may subside into pietistic cells, may become a devotional way and no more. If control falters, if the spirit of church breaks out among basic communities, the links with Rome will be strained, perhaps past the breaking point. The outcome may depend on the type of internal leadership the basic communities develop.

ii. Church leadership.—The concept of leadership, like a knife separating joint and marrow, divides the church's worldly self-understanding from the self-knowledge given it by the Spirit of God. God's promise to Israel to be "my special possession" meant "You will be to me a kingdom of priests, my holy nation." All nations had priests—a class of sacral figures, sun-gods or holy warriors or sacred prostitutes who maintained relations with deity. Israel would not qualify herself by having these. Rather, her distinctive would be to serve as a priest-people, God's mediator nation, a people in the interest of all peoples and in that regard holy—not a nation with, but a nation of, priests (Exod. 19:5f). Jesus adopted that central theme of Israel's covenant existence and made it central for his followers. According to Mark, Jesus renounced afresh the leadership style of non-Jews: "You know that among the Gentiles the recognized rulers lord it over their subjects, and the great make their authority felt. It shall not be so with you" (Mark 10:42f). Jesus reversed the order; the leaders were to be last. "Whoever wants to be first must be the slave of all" (10:44). The remarkable thing is that Jesus accepted this as a guide for himself as well: "For the Son of Man did not come to be served but to serve, and to give his life as a ransom for many" (10:45). Did the followers understand him at this point? Evidence that in time they did so is that while the primitive church felt free to borrow leadership names from Scripture (e.g., "prophet"), from Jewish practice ("elder"), and from the wider culture (*episkopos*, "overseer"), the readily available term "priest" is never applied in the New Testament to any Christian leader except Jesus the great high priest (Heb. 4:14ff; 6:13ff), but only (in echo of Exodus 19) to the new-chosen people of God (1 Pet. 2:9). This speaks of deliverance from the world of sacral authorities into the world of the good news.

The distinction in kind between 'lay' and 'clerical' office has no clear New Testament roots. Those who find such distinctions essential to the being (or well-being, a lesser claim) of the church must trace these orders to the post-apostolic age, where gradually there grew up the following distinctions: bishops exercised authority in liturgy and discipline over the Christians in a city or diocese; where 'parishes' multiplied, elders or presbyters (the latter term later shortened into English "priest") presided over parishes at the bishop's will; deacons remained at the bishop's beck, or were advanced to become priests. These distinctions were rejected at the Reformation by some, or were maintained as matters of custom or civil law. Many advantages granted to 'clerics' (or 'clergy') were withheld from lesser Christians (see Cooke, 1976:s.v. "bishop," "presbyters," etc.). Protestants and the churches of the Radical Reformation sometimes rejected, sometimes maintained these arrangements in whole or in part.

Here, then, is a place with room for radical reformation in the church. To accomplish it, rather than once again skewering that rather shabby American professional class, 'the clergy,' the approach must be radical abolition of 'the laity.' Here 'laity' is not with the New Testament a people of God (*laos*, see iii below), but a passive, second-rank Christian class, rated below even the 'clergy.' Even this abolition (which will be harder than it sounds) should be sought not negatively but positively, by advancing a worthier idea of the status of disciples. Such a concept is already present in the distinctive Pauline concept of gifts to each (and thus to all) members. First Corinthians 12, dealing with a contest within a church over place and honor, offers lists of such gifts; among them apostleship or mission (Paul's own gift) is listed alongside "helping others" and "speaking in tongues" (the Corinthian favorite—1 Cor. 12:27-31). Leadership, ecstasy, and the humblest service are alike gifts of the one Spirit of God.

This concept bloomed in the Ephesian Letter. There, as extensive exegesis and theological reflection disclose (M. Barth, 1974, II:425-97; J. Yoder, 1987), the "fullness of Christ" (*plērōmatos tou Christou*, Eph. 4:13) refers not in a Greek way to ideal individuals, but to a 'body of Christ' composed of women and men to each of whom the Spirit had given "a particular share in the bounty of Christ" (Eph. 4:7). Illustrations of (and not exceptions to) this inclusive gifting of the church were "apostles . . . prophets . . . evangelists" whose subservient but vital task is "to equip God's people for work in his service," not as butchers, bakers, or candlestick makers, but in "the building up of the body of Christ" (Eph. 4:11f). The Pauline vision, in other words, is that the church to be the church must be not a company of privates led by ordained captains (on ordination, see Chapter Nine, §2) but a company of equals, equally gifted by God's Spirit, equally responsible for the community-building whose accomplishment is the fullness of Christ.

Here, then, is the challenge of radical reformation in ministry: not a set-apart ministry of those who work for God while others work for themselves, and not a flock of secular 'callings' (doctor, lawyer, merchant, chief) tended by a shepherd with a religious calling (priest or preacher, pope or pastor), but a *people set apart*, earning their daily bread in honest toil, to be sure, but living to become for others the bread of life. Such a gifts-to-each concept requires rethinking both discipleship and baptism. Every member is called to discipleship; baptism (we will see in the next chapter) is commissioning for this ministry; thus it occupies the place ordination must in churches that celebrate a "clergy." This does not mean there can no longer be itinerant 'apostles' or 'evangelists' or local 'bishops' or 'elders'; it does mean that these must be seen as only part of the fullness of Christ. For on this view bishops are part of the laity; on this view every Christian is a cleric. True Christian leadership is not achieved by exalting (or by denigrating) the gifts of the few, but by discovering that the Spirit has a gift for each. Every member is a minister (Eller, 1990). Yet for most this is clearly ground to be gained, not already reached.

Informed Protestants will connect the preceding paragraphs with "the priesthood of all believers." This doctrine, based on Martin Luther's fresh reading of the New Testament, held that the essence of (Roman Catholic) priesthood was already present in each baptized believer ("Pagan Servitude of the Church," text in Luther, 1961:345f). This Reformation move was contextually appropriate, but the doctrine has often later been read as mere individualism in religion, or as a mere denigration of existing church leaders. Its radical counterpart today must therefore insist on the corporate nature of believing priesthood (1 Pet. 2:9) in order to generate a fresh construal of church leadership—one not alien to Luther's intention.

iii. Toward the Israel of God.—At this stage the baptist quest for Christian community seems caught between opposed difficulties. Its concept of church seems indistinguishable on one side from any and every community, while on the other its churches seem locked into rigid ecclesiologies that find no common ground. Is there a way between these shoals? What is needed is acknowledgment that a church, understood in a New Testament sense as faithful folk in a place sharing Spirit-led practices, needs not only shared practices but the narrative *tradition* of their sharing. Further, any church needs a modest institutional home in which these practices and this narrative inhere (*Ethics*, p. 173; Tilley, 1994). Yet all these needs, we saw earlier, are met by a peoplehood that adjoins other peoplehoods in the one Israel of God. A people is not a single, local church, nor is it the basis of a church (Christ alone is that basis). Nor is a people the overarching kingdom or rule of God. Yet in obedience to that kingdom rule, and sharing a common vision and story, a people may live out God's rule by nurturing the churches that God raises up within it.

Here is a justification of Christian general bodies such as the Roman Curia or the Southern Baptist Convention. Some call these institutional structures "churches," and we may as a courtesy use the word their way. Yet general bodies are not in the present sense churches (not local congregations), nor are they the people they serve, nor (need we add?) are they the kingdom of God. Institutional general bodies are agents of peoplehood and servants of each church. At their smallest, they serve a few churches, at their grandest, perhaps millions. In any case, in a time of ongoing quest for Christian community, they meet urgent needs of churches that find in them their own grasp upon God's grand whole.

Such agencies must meet two tests: In the first place they must serve those needs (such as education, mission, common witness and service) that help the churches they serve to be faithful churches, and in particular they must provide an ecumenical open window through which the churches can reach out to one another in shared peoplehood and, beyond their own people, reach out to others in the Israel of God. What the agencies are forbidden to do is to lead the churches into (new or continuing) unfaithfulness or apostasy—that is to accept a demonic role.

Certainly a baptist ecumenism cannot be adequately expressed in such denominational (or transdenominational) agencies. This is because the true genius of Christian community lies not in them, but in the church (once again, in the biblical sense, "gathering congregation") itself. To read Romans (or Ephesians) with such an awareness of church may be difficult because existing translations embody a later image of a 'church universal.' Nevertheless, in faithfulness to the demand of Christian community, a 'this is that' reading strategy is required. (Here as so often, historical-critical exegesis and the baptist vision are allied.) At Rome, for example, first-century Jews and non-Jews met in a new fellowship. God's acceptance of all had transcended *kashruth* dietary rules, yet those who keep the rules are not chided or upstaged in Romans; rather the Roman fellowship must accommodate itself to its *kashruth* members, inasmuch as gratitude to God (for food and for salvation) is the wider meal-rule that embraces both sorts of Christians. "Those . . . who eat [non-kosher?] meat also honour the Lord, since when they eat they give thanks to God [thus consecrating their food?]; and those who abstain have the Lord in mind when abstaining, since they too give thanks to God" (Rom. 14:6).

* * * * *

If *membership* in the church is intentional, then the church becomes a live circuit for the power of the Holy Spirit. That is the power of unity that the ecumenical movement seeks to realize in the churches. If *leadership* in the church is a gift among gifts granted in the fullness of Christ, then ordination (not provided in the New Testament) and hierarchy (opposed there) are not essentials of leadership, and may concretely resist the realization of that fullness. If *the church itself* is a sign of the rule of God, the foretaste of humanity reconciled to God, then to come to church is to come "to Mount Zion, the city of the living God, the heavenly Jerusalem, to myriads of angels, to the full concourse and assembly of the firstborn who are enrolled in heaven" (Heb. 12:22f).

It is in this gathering assembly that the baptist vision must recover its first-century openness between Jew and non-Jew. The church *must* do so because this barrier 'predicts' the fate of all other barriers—of race, ethnicity, tradition, class, gender—to the unity for which the church exists. Only the church that recognizes in every Jew a brother or sister (and one who may someday hail Messiah Jesus) is a church fit for the Pentecostal commission:

> But you will receive power when the Holy Spirit comes upon you; and you will bear witness for me in Jerusalem, and throughout all Judaea and Samaria, and even in the farthest corners of the earth.
>
> (Acts 1:8)

CHAPTER NINE

The Signs of Salvation: Christian Worship

We come now to an uncomfortable part of the systematic task. Many have sensed a strong conflict in the very idea of baptist worship. On the one hand, it restores such gospel ordinances as believers baptism (conversion-baptism), ancient monuments in the heritage of Christian worship. There is as well the deep, contagious enthusiasm of baptist gatherings, whether in the austere breaking of bread by Plymouth Brethren or the splendid chaos of an evangelistic rally with its singing and earnest preaching and wrestlings with God in prayer. On the other hand, some sharers of this way feel a keen sense of loss, even unchristian envy, when they behold the long heritage of liturgy preserved among others' treasures but discarded by their forebears. These may be surprised to learn that strangely similar distress is felt by the best informed within the Protestant and Catholic heritages, whose knowledge of the past teaches them that, despite the virtues their own traditions retain, their liturgies are alienated from life (Bouyer, 1956) or trapped by historical circumstance, and who may envy baptist freedom to change. Can such change maintain the lively practices of radical reformation yet deepen the links to the whole of Christian faith? Perhaps so, provided there are strong threads connecting the doctrine of worship to all the rest of Christian teaching (cf. Wainwright, 1980). If there are, the task of this chapter seems clear, whatever its prospects of success: Worship, to be Christian practice, must be a prayer for God's rule on earth (cf. Part I), must be enacted in the presence of the risen Jesus Christ (Part II), and must be guided by God's Holy Spirit (Part III). Therefore each part of Christian doctrine should emerge more fully here. The chapter's plan, however, is proper to itself: This is **(§1)** to find **the heart of Christian worship; (§2)** to provide clearer doctrinal understanding for the distinctive **'remembering' signs of baptism, preaching, and eucharist;** and **(§3)** to discuss in light of these the appropriate **shape of Christian worship.** The task is to say here not all that can fairly be said on any of these topics, but only enough to show the theological line of direction. The rest must be worked out by specialists and (more important) by faithful Christians in their assemblies.

§1. The Character of Christian Worship

In an often quoted definition, Evelyn Underhill says that worship is "the response of the creature to the Eternal." This is a grand conception of worship that includes in its scope all creation, earthly and heavenly as well, insofar as the creation glorifies its "Origin, Sustainer, and End" (Underhill, 1937:3). It is necessary, though, to qualify this definition at once: While calling worship "response" lifts up the privilege of making answer to our Maker, it fails to suggest two definitive marks at least of biblical and Christian worship: (1) Christian worship is a two-sided practice, divine and human, never just a monologue but a dialogue throughout; and (2) authentic Christian worship is never a path to power, never a way to control God or God's gifts. Much that is called Christian worship fails these tests. 'Worship' closes in upon itself, turns into a kind of therapy that seeks to impress its 'audience.' Or alternatively, Christian worship is perverted into magic, an attempt to extract favors from God or God's lieutenants, the 'saints.' Since to define Christian worship only as "response" leaves open the door to these ways of diminishing prayer and liturgy, by itself our first definition fails; definitions must show what a thing is at least by showing us what it is not.

To make this clear, consider two defective understandings. **Affective worship** supposes its goal to be *changing the worshiper* by way of the worshiper's feelings. Services are acclaimed when they are "impressive" or "inspirational." Prayer is auto-suggestion (or other-suggestion); preaching manipulates audiences; singing arouses enthusiasm. So common worship becomes not response to God but corporate self-arousal or mutual entertainment; we sing the hymns to one another, teach and preach at one another, pray (finally) at one another! Who can deny that there is some truth in all this? Yet there is a profound moral argument against this subjective interpretation of worship: offered as the whole truth, both the theory and the worship it validates are viciously false; they constitute a self-contradiction. For true Christian prayer addresses not oneself or one's fellows but the heavenly Father and present Lord; when God's word is preached it is another voice than the preacher's for which we are to listen; the bread broken is food indeed, not psychotherapy; baptism is not in the name of the church or the minister, but in the name of the Trinity. Are they only deceits, then, these cries to God, these solemn vows, these sign-actions in God's name? If so, we require not so much truer insight into worship, but the abandonment of worship for the falsehood that it is (per contra, Don Cupitt, 1980:chap. 5). The truth in the affective theory must be retained—there is a feeling dimension in authentic worship—but its falsity must be renounced all the more firmly in an age that blithely reduces everything to psychology.

The other distorted view, **magical worship,** may not seem so tempting, but its long history suggests that it, too, appeals to something deeply embedded in human nature. The following distinction between magic and religion is assumed here: in religion, creatures submit themselves to their God to discover and pursue God's way for them; in magic, the magicians gain power over the gods (or over God!) for their own ends. Magic means manipulation; it follows prescribed rites in order to achieve supernatural control. It is all too easy for members of one style of Christian community to believe that those of another style are practicing magic (and of course in a given case they may be exactly right); it is perhaps less easy to perceive the implicit magic in our own style of worship—less easy for Catholics to see that the mass may become a manipulative ritual, less easy for Protestants to see that 'prophetic' preaching may turn into an implied demand that God shape history according to Protestant ends, *less easy for baptists to see, let us say, how an all-night prayer meeting for a critically ill child of the congregation may be magical manipulation: "If only we are faithful to pray, how can God refuse us?"* As with the subjective theory of worship, it is right to acknowledge the truth of the magical theory: there is a 'magic' in worship, an element beyond all earthly calculation. God does answer prayer: the heartfelt prayer of the faithful is "effectual," as James (5:16) assures us, and all our worship matters to God, being joined to the ceaseless worship of heaven itself (Rev. 4:8, 5:8). Yet God never surrenders the initiative to earthly magicians of any stripe; in worship, no Protestant fidelity, no Catholic conformity, no baptist fervor can capture and control the divine sovereignty. Evelyn Underhill's first word must here be our last: worship rightly construed is at heart the practice of **interactive creaturely response** to what God does and requires and promises: it is neither human manipulation nor God-magic, but is **two-sided conversation, dialogue, with the God of grace.**

a. The vector of worship.—All these concerns must guide us, but here we have found the theme: the divine initiative and its human answer constitute Christian worship. Indeed, this is the line of direction, the narrative plot, throughout all the Scriptures: God *summons* Abraham and *fulfills* Sarah; God *frees* Israel; God *anoints* David; God *punishes* but *restores* a rebellious nation; God *sends* Jesus, *accepts* his death, and *raises* him from the dead; God *pours forth* as Spirit; in the end the risen Christ *returns.* Each of these divine-action initiatives both requires and (in the happy case) enables a human response which is taken up into the divine action: Abraham (with a sometimes amused Sarah) *obeys* the call; Israel *crosses* the Reed Sea; David *rules* his people; the people, chastised, *renew* their covenant faithfulness; Jesus at Jordan and again in Gethsemane *accepts* his ministry; Spirit-filled believers *speak* in new tongues; the faithful church *expects* the coming of Christ in his kingdom at the end. In sum, **God acts and enabled people answer; in the broadest sense this elicited answer is their reasonable worship** (Rom. 12:1).

Thanks to the work of Chapter Six, we are in better position here to express the sense in which God is present in Christian worship. Such worship is required by faith in Jesus who not only once lived and died, but who rose from the dead, and having risen is fully alive. His resurrection enables his ongoing presence in and to his community. This presence is the *objective* driving force, the external engine that drives Christian worship. And alongside Easter (Luke 24) stands Pentecost (Acts 2). Facing the reality of a living Christ, disciples at Pentecost discovered a divine presence welling up within themselves as well, the presence of God who is Spirit. The Spirit became the *subjective* driving force, the internal engine of Christian worship. The first great historic sign, Easter, yields a Christ with us as a present friend; the second, Pentecost, yields disciples who can recognize that Christ. Now we can say more directly why worship is more than mere *human* response: if it is biblical in spirit, the response is Spirit-given, Spirit-led, and thus always more (though never less) than human. In this worship, we meet the present Christ; in this worship, that very meeting is the Spirit's gift. These are the twin engines that drive Christian liturgy; they are the two poles about which our theology of worship must revolve.

The terms "worship" and "liturgy" do not often appear in Scripture, yet together they express well the biblical initiative-and-response theme. In English the word "worship" first meant a quality of the owner, the great one so addressed (even today a person of quality or rank is sometimes called "your worship" or "her honor," terms implying that worship and honor are intrinsic properties of those so addressed). It was because a human individual already possessed this property that he or she could in a secondary sense be 'given' worship. Just as the verb "to honor" means to acknowledge or recognize one who by her acts or qualities intrinsically possesses it, likewise "to worship" means to give place to one who is worthy. This worth was in Old English called "weorthscipe" ("worth-ship"), hence our word "worship." To worship one is to give that one *appropriate* recognition and by doing so to set oneself in *appropriate* place with respect to him or her. Thus to worship God is to acknowledge the worth or honor that is (already, and independent of our worship) God's own, and consequently to find our own location beneath God.

"Liturgy," on the other hand, is less at home in English; the word was borrowed via Late Latin from Greek, where (if we avoid excessive etymologizing) it meant originally any public service or ceremony, and in Greek Christian times meant the Christian worship services, eucharistic and other. To speak of divine *worship* thus puts stress on the one worshiped, on God's Godhood, while *liturgy*, in contrast, stresses the worshiping congregation, the respondents, and their common action. Together, the two repeat the bipolar definition of worship proposed above.

Some writers have wished to separate "liturgical" from "nonliturgical" public worship, intending by the former to designate regularity in order and content and by the latter some lack of these, but the distinction is nugatory—everywhere worship has *some* pattern, *some* regularity as well as variety—and we will shortly find better ways to distinguish typical Catholic, Protestant, and baptist liturgies. For the worship of God-in-Christ-by-the-Spirit implies at very minimum a *pattern* of initiative and response in which we return to God some token of his gift to us:

> We give thee but thine own,
> Whate'er the gift may be. . . . (William W. How)

The shape of public worship, the shape of a biblical liturgy, will of necessity reflect this divine-initiative-human-response pattern if it is Godward, if it is Christ-centered, if it is Spirit-filled.

b. Jesus and the Spirit.—Jesus Christ is alive; he promises his presence "where two or three are gathered" in his name (Matt. 18:20). The Christ who brings us fully into the present by his presence takes the initiative: we do not produce him by some liturgical conjure or evoke his memory by some spiritual stimulus; rather we expect him as we expect a lover, a friend, an elder brother who has promised and whose promise, whose *troth,* never fails. When we come obediently together, the Risen One is there. It follows that the significance and reality of worship cannot be a function of the size of the crowd. Authentic church can be as few as two of us, with him the third. If you and I are granted an interview with our country's president or sovereign, we cannot be further honored to learn that a large crowd will be there as well. To meet with the Risen One is honor enough. Yet the meeting must be "in his name," that is, a meeting appointed to encounter our Lord and do his business, to carry out his designs not our own.

Therefore Jesus' 'real' presence is not limited to the eucharist (far less to its food and drink), but from the earliest Christian beginnings has meant a renewal of the sort of Presence that the disciples knew during the forty days (Acts 1:1-5; Underhill, 1937:152). He keeps his promise to be present as truly in a meeting for simple children's prayer "in his name" as in the solemnity of Quaker meeting or the splendor of high mass. On the other hand, if I am invited to such an encounter with him, it ill suits me to be late or absent. It is in this character of the fitting or suitable that we properly conceive Christian worship as *obligation.* It is an obligation that grows not out of church (or civil!) law, but from the very fittingness of congregating where Jesus promises to be. For such a meeting, all places are potential assembly grounds, all times potential trysts. We may with good reason prefer some certain place, be it a clearing in the forest or a cathedral, and again with good reason may seek out one another and our Lord especially on the Lord's day or the Jewish Sabbath, but where and when is not the issue now.

Why is he thus present? That is, to what *end* is Christ present? In what way is his presence determinative for our prayer and for all our liturgy? In this volume we have identified Jesus Christ with the unique narrative of his life (Chapter Five). Thus to say that he is present *in a way that matters* (cf. medieval arguments about "substantial" and "real" presence) is to say that the one of whom this story tells is present in such a way that *the story continues,* present in a way that makes no sense save for the story to this point, a way that shapes the story still to follow. Hence there can be no better 'honoring,' no better 'worshiping' of the one who meets us in Christian liturgy than recalling that story, any of its parts and especially its high moments—not only (as in triumphalist liturgies) the unexpected resurrection that is its climax, not only (as in somber Good Friday rites) the abysmal suffering of the cross, but also (as in many an evangelistic song and sermon) the kingdom-oriented life journey of the one who reached that abysmal depth and sublime height. Previous chapters have emphasized the narrative character of Christian faith; this one must insist that the same narrative remains central when we are confronted by the risen, hidden presence of faith's Lord. It is the narrative of One present who knows the cost of daily life faithful to God's rule; who knows better than we how such faithfulness faces its ultimate crisis; knows, beyond that, the outcome of faithfulness, the risen life into which we, too, are being drawn.

This holy presence cannot be reduced to our awareness or 'experience' of the presence. Jesus was there with all the disciples on a certain mountain in Galilee, and *though some were doubtful* about his presence, *all* knelt to worship him (Matt. 28:16f). His presence itself, rather than immediate awareness of it by one or another, was the guide; for such awareness was not shared by all. The promise is not, "Where two or three are gathered, you will have such and such *worship experiences*." He only promised to be at hand. If we do not sense his presence, there he is yet, hidden, perhaps ignored or overlooked or forgotten, perhaps officially banished from our worship by someone's theology. Yet there. Nor is his presence merely a hyperbolic expression for the presence of other believers: we are there, *and* he is. The congregation, to be sure, is called "Christ's body" (1 Cor. 12:27; Rom. 12:5), and in Christian thought that powerful utterance has serious work to do. But his presence cannot be limited either to the fellowship of believers or to the signs of salvation such as baptism and preaching and eucharist; these signs, and we who come to worship, are there, but his secret presence is prior to them, more than they, more than we. The Christ who is known to us in the storied fellowship, known in the signs, is present in his own right, as one of the fellowship, as a witness to our baptisms, as a listener to the preached word, as a sharer at the holy table. "Then why don't I simply see him?" Because he elects now to be present thus and not otherwise. And when in the Father's wisdom his time has come, when he shall appear not to some (as has happened) but to all, that will be the end, the *parousia*, the *apokalypsis*, the final appearance that will confirm what each present tryst anticipates.

"On the Lord's day," writes the author of the last book of the Bible, "the Spirit came upon me; and I heard behind me a loud voice, like the sound of a trumpet, which said . . ." (Rev. 1:10f). Readers, familiar with the prophetic tradition, were sure to infer a causal link: had the Spirit not come upon John the seer, that trumpet voice would not have been heard. God who sends the message enables the messenger to receive it, and God's enabling agent is God Who Is Spirit; this in sum is the teaching of Scripture (cf. Chapter Seven above). What is distinctive in the Apocalypse of John is not this regular prophetic link, but its affirmation in the context of Christian worship. Prophecy is alive in the opening of Revelation, and it flourishes on the Lord's day—the new-found worship day of the Christian community.

The Revelation of John is notoriously a book that can be read in many ways by many readers. One important reading, though, takes this Lord's day coming of the Spirit as an entering wedge: the setting of the book is the early liturgy, the primitive Christian practice of worship. Clues to this interpretation are the messages to the seven churches (chaps. 2–3), the heavenly *worship* scene that frames the dramatic revelation of events to come (chaps. 4–5), the persistent mining of Old Testament (and apocalyptic?) *doxologies, invocations, hymns,* and *prayers,* and the *dramatic structure* of the book as it drives like a great enacted liturgy through earth's vicissitudes (persecution and sorrow, death and sin) to its consummation in new heaven and new earth (cf. Shepherd, 1960). If this interpretation is correct, it will not dissolve still other readings (the theme of worship in a biblical context regularly appears in support of other themes, never just alone), yet it provides light on the role of the Spirit. Briefly summarized, this role is threefold: There is the *coming* of the Spirit upon the Seer (or "carrying him away") that enables the heavenly-earthly vision (1:10, 17:3, 21:10). There is the vast, numinous *Presence* that is God's Holy Spirit, rendered in Revelation's curious code-language as "the seven spirits of God" (3:1, 4:5, 5:1); third and perhaps most interesting at present, the Spirit *speaks* in and to the church and to those who will hear the church: "Hear what the Spirit says to the churches" (2:7, 17, 29; 3:6, 13, 22), and in 22:17:

> 'Come!' say the Spirit and the bride.
> 'Come!' let each hearer reply.
> Let the thirsty come;
>   Let whoever wishes accept the water of life as a gift.

This is the Great Invitation or summons to humanity to be filled with God's own Spirit. So the Spirit guides the seer as the seer shows the church the Spirit in the midst, a presence that issues in the invitation spoken by the Spirit through the mouth of Christ's bride, the church.

One corollary of the Spirit's empowerment and direction of the church's voice in worship is this: the church, the bride, need not fear to give voice to her truth *grandly.* It is said above that Revelation's authors—the human author and the divine one—mined the scrolls of Scripture to extract its rich language of praise and prayer. If the Spirit who inspired Scripture breathes also in Christian assemblies, are believers not authorized *by this divine author* freely to employ that high language of Zion, its language and its stage directions, in their worship as well? I believe the Revelation is fitly placed at Scripture's end as a *reprise,* guiding us back to the *sanctus* of Isaiah ("Holy, holy, holy is God the sovereign Lord of all"—Rev. 4:8; cf. Isa. 6:3), ordaining a priestly race of men and women in royal service (5:10; cf. Exod. 19:6; Isa. 61:6), extolling God's self-imparting final aim ("Victory to our God who sits on the throne, and to the Lamb" 7:10; cf. Ps. 47:9), and reminding us anew that the Spirit, the inward engine of that purpose, is God's means to that end (1:10, 17:3, 21:10). Here is language of hymn and verse worthy of memorization and declamation, the epic of a race redeemed. "Let the redeemed of the LORD say so" (Ps. 107:2 KJV) might be a motto for Revelation's inspired worship models.

Yet the Spirit's presence is not only to authorize sacred eloquence. Jesus welcomed those who brought little children seeking his blessing (Mark 10:13-16 par.), and there is a place in worship for their lisping speech as well. In the next chapter we will explore the charismatic, pentecostal gifts of speech and action and bring out their importance for any Christian gathering. Heavenly speech, common speech, children's speech, ecstatic speech—we come full circle, for the prophetic movement took its rise in Israel amid the phenomena of ecstasy; the prophetic gift was not mere ecstasy (a common human property), but the appearance among the ecstatics of some who had a word from the LORD. So this gift demanded discernment: a people qualified to know a prophet when they heard one. Today the Spirit works in worship not only to bring forth exalted and memorable ritual (God's catholic gift?), and not only to inspire prophetic witness (God's protestant gift?), but also to bring forth a people taught by the Spirit to recognize God's authentic voice, a people skilled to reenact the "old, old story" of the kingly priesthood of Christ (Yoder, 1984). Perhaps that hearing, discernment, reenactment can be well described via the baptist vision, an interpretive device that must shortly engage us here again.

c. The signs and tradition.—Earlier (Chapter Four) we met the concept of *signs*. There the focus was upon God's action in creating, and alongside that, God's further action within creation. It was argued that what the world calls miracles are best construed as God's distinctive, self-disclosing signs, acts that make God's presence and power evident for redemptive purposes. Events such as creation itself, the Exodus and Sinai, the installation of ancient Israel in Canaan land, the birth of prophecy, the judgment of Israel, its exile and a remnant's return, the birth of the Messiah, his redemptive life and death and resurrection, the Spirit's outpouring at Pentecost, the mission to the Gentiles—these were named **great historic signs;** they are crucial events in the history of redemption. Associated with them are some lesser signs. Some of these belong to the immediate penumbra of the great signs: the burning bush is connected with the Exodus; the fall of Jericho belongs to the entry into the land of promise; the miracle works of Elijah and Elisha accompany the birth of prophecy; Jesus' mighty works are hollow apart from his mission; the empty tomb points to the resurrection; speaking in tongues, to the day of Pentecost.

Remembering signs, though, are associated with the great historic signs not as their historical penumbra but as their (repeatable) *monuments*. Because the Christian rite of baptism recalls the baptism of Jesus and his death and resurrection, it functions as a remembering sign of faith in him. Our immersion recollects his death and burial; our overwhelming by the water of baptism recalls the overwhelming of suffering that he endured. If the preaching of the gospel tells the redemptive story of Jesus (with all its antecedents in Israel and all its consequences for God's kingdom), it, too, is a remembering sign; its antecedents are the great historic signs that together constitute the good news. Because the Lord's supper gives thanks for Christ's broken body and shed blood, it is the distinctive paschal remembering sign. It recalls as well Jesus' feastings with his followers, both in the days of his flesh and in his resurrection returns. God acts to make these *remembering signs* effectual, just as God originally acted in the great historic signs themselves. But while the historic signs embrace all the people (Pentecost, for example, standing for the gift of the Spirit to all disciples, then and later—see Chapter Ten following), the remembering signs are more particular: faithful preaching and believers baptism and the common supper **apply** the great gift-event, Pentecost, to particular hearers of the gospel, to particular believer candidates, to particular faith communities today. The historic signs are world-historical, once-for-all; the remembering signs connect that great narrative to this or that believer or believing community now.

Providential signs are a third class of God's sign-acts: Neither world-historical events nor remembering repetitions, these are instances of the distinctive guidance God gives to individual lives for designated kingdom tasks. Where is God leading each disciple? What tasks are set before each? *By providential signs* we are helped to see each Christian life as a journey (cf. Chapter Three). On that journey, the providential signs are vocational guides, showing the road and encouraging the traveler. Here again the distinguishing character of God-given signs is that they direct our lives to God's rule or kingdom, show us how to make Christ the center, confirm us in the fellowship of the Spirit. In this sense, authentic providential signs, in Jonathan Edwards' phrase, delineate "truly gracious religious affections." By that test Edwards was inclined to discount as of no clear value one way or the other many 'signs' such as heightened religious feeling or excitement (common in revival times), voices heard, visions seen, and the like. Since these might be signs of authenticity or might not, they are not reliable. But truly gracious religious affections,

Edwards argued, are recognized because they come from God, are "attended with the lamblike, dovelike spirit and temper of Jesus Christ," and bear fruit in authentic Christian practice (Edwards, 1746:197-461).

To sum up the discussion to this point: understood as interactive response, the human responding by God's grace to the divine, worship is a communicative practice. In a broad but true sense, all worship is prayer. This communication, carried on in the public language of Christian liturgy, is not confined to Hebrew or English or to any natural language. Instead, God has provided for it an inclusive sign-language. To communicate with God we are expected to learn that language. The signs fall into three classes: the great historic signs that created the people of God, the remembering signs set in the local assemblies of that people, and various providential signs that guide particular journeys.

This three-part analysis is not hard and fast; Jesus' baptism in Jordan must belong to the first two classes, and any believer's obedient baptism, if it becomes for another a providential sign and guide for his or her own life, belongs to both the second and the third. There may be signs that are hard to classify any way. Yet in a rough-and-ready way these three classes provide the matter, the chief material, of Christian common worship.

It will occur to many a reader that though the terminology of this chapter displays some novelty ("signs of salvation"), its concepts are familiar and traditional. Once we are reminded that certain signs—baptism, preaching, the memorial meal—have been focal for Christian worship through the centuries, is our work not done? What remains save to acknowledge that tradition has fixed upon forms for all the above, to note various departures from these forms in Christian history (both degenerate and reforming departures), and in the end to recommend one more pattern out of the past? Is not liturgics a task for historians and artists, rather than for theologians or church leaders? Is not the answer to the question, What must the church teach about worship to be the church, simply this: *let tradition speak?*

But what will tradition say? The broad catholic liturgical principle, as Evelyn Underhill tells us, has been grandly inclusive: every range of human feeling, every sense, every historical moment is sooner or later to be enclosed in the sweep of liturgy (Underhill, 1937:chap. 12). Provided only that essentials are maintained, nothing human or divine is alien to Catholic worship. Meanwhile Protestant worship has been marked by a drive to purity; here the gospel and the gospel only is to guide (Underhill, 276f). Thus sixteenth-century Protestant Reformers introduced changes aimed at eliminating much of Catholic ritual and ceremony, while Luther (in particular) restored the chorale or congregational hymn, and both Luther and Calvin exalted the preaching of the gospel, though Lutherans retained more, and Calvinists generally less, of Catholic eucharistic and baptismal practice. That seems to make a clear enough difference between these two senses of tradition and its use. However, the matter is more complicated than that. For modern liturgical research, carried on first by scholarly Roman Catholics and only later by others, discovered that the received liturgies of the great Christian traditions embody layer upon layer of encrusted *change* (see e.g. Dix, 1945; Bouyer, 1956; Jungmann, 1959; Brilioth, 1961). Accordingly, these liturgists saw their task to be penetrating backward, through the Magisterial Reformers and the Council of Trent, through medieval piety, to discover worship practices in documents such as the Gelasian Sacramentary (sixth century) and the *Apostolic Tradition* attributed to Hippolytus (c. 215) that ultimately reach back almost to the New Testament itself. This Catholic drive to purity at least matched that of the Protestants. If one discovered what was 'originally' central, and determined how subsequent accretions must be treated, was there not a basis for liturgical renewal? For example, Hippolytus shows the liturgy of the word preceding the liturgy of the table; was not that sequence, then, theologically normative? Introit and gradual and communion hymn were added later; were they not therefore optional? Withholding the cup from the laity was an ad hoc change; could it therefore be overruled? Thus Catholic liturgy grasped what had seemed a purely Protestant principle.

Meanwhile, however, Protestant churches in recent decades have sensed a poverty in their own severe principles, and some have sought to incorporate fragments of Catholic worship, perhaps ignorant of the reasons that led their own ancestors to severe simplicity. Thus "services of lessons and carols" are made to do duty as a substitute for midnight Christmas mass for many Protestants, and some Protestants shroud the climax of Holy Week in a candle-snuffing *tenebrae*. But the larger liturgical framework that makes sense of these borrowed elements remains largely unknown to them. Thus theological clarity is missing while subjective worship still seeks its private goals, though now in borrowed mummery. Nevertheless, here and there a clear gospel note shines through in Protestant churches also, expressed in sermon, song, and sacrament.

It might seem that (to speak now in the generic) these catholic and protestant motifs—the recovery of past rites, the purification of present rites—exhaust Christian options; baptists have nothing left but to choose between them, or (as with Anglicans) to try to combine the two. And indeed most historians of liturgy, peering through Catholic or Protestant eyes, have seen baptist worship in just this way—as a (poorer) cousin of their own or their rivals' worship. Only Quaker communal silent mysticism has generally escaped this liturgical brush-off. Sometimes the reality justified this view. Although sixteenth-century baptists were at first closer to Catholic models (McClendon, 1991a), later on, Protestant influence prevailed. This dependence was heightened because several main baptist groups sprang from Reformed contexts.

Nevertheless, another element has been continually present in baptist liturgies. Recognizing this element is essential both to the realization of baptist worship and to the wider ecumenical task. That overlooked element in Christian worship is the baptist vision, the hermeneutical principle ("this is that" and "then is now") by which Scripture interprets present practice. This chapter's thesis is that by this enacted principle the church at worship can know itself to be the church.

This claim coheres with what is said above about the presence of Christ in worship and the presence of the Spirit there. "*Jesus* is the Christ" may be the oldest Christian confession; it is certainly the christological focus of the baptist vision. This *is* that—the *Christ* who meets us now in worship is "that same *Jesus*" who lived and died and lives again. Then *is* now—the Messiah who will return is also present now in succor and judgment. The claim coheres as well with the role of the signs. These appear in fresh ways in baptist worship, not excluding the appearance of the providential signs in charismatic worship. "Come, Holy Spirit," the (implied even when unspoken) *this* of every Christian assembly, invokes the Pentecostal *that* and the gift of the Spirit to the church as soon as it was truly church. In authentic baptist worship, all the signs are needed and all are effectual. Without the guideposts furnished by the great historic signs, we would have no idea how to apply the baptist vision to the shaping of worship. What would stop us from taking David's dancing before the ark, insecure loincloth flapping (2 Sam. 6:12-23), as the *primary* working model for worship, or by what right would we prefer Paul's account of the Lord's supper (1 Cor. 11:23-26) to Simon Magus' liturgical lust for power and pelf (Acts 8:14-24)?

In answer, **the centrality of Christ is witnessed by the place of the great signs** of which his resurrection from the dead is chief; the remembering signs realize these divine sign-acts in our common worship; directed by these, the providential signs find in the baptist vision their checkpoint and norm. Now these related elements must be examined one by one in the following Section.

§2. The Remembering Signs

The previous Section has recalled the distinctive character of the remembering signs among all God's **signs of salvation.** They are neither the primary signs (such as the resurrection of Jesus Christ from the dead), nor the most intimate of signs (such as the answer to a disciple's heartfelt prayer), but stand between as pointers to both: they are distinctive in calling the church back to remembrance of the great story of salvation and expectation of its end. Looking backward and forward, they declare the present presence of Christ with his people. Among these, three have so commended themselves to the biblical witnesses and to the historic new people of God in the church as to deserve special comment here: baptism, marking the conversion of one who takes the way of Jesus; prophetic preaching, marking God's persistent showing and correction of that way; and the Lord's supper, recalling the climactic moment in the story (cross and resurrection) and affirming the renewal of the pledge each in baptism makes in answer to God's proclaimed word.

There may be other remembering signs: Preeminently, there is the Sabbath or Lord's Day. Roman Catholics have designated seven "sacraments" (are these remembering signs?); Hubmaier included fraternal admonition beside baptism and supper (Hubmaier, 1989:§23); Luther and Calvin subsumed baptism and supper under "proclamation" and omitted preaching as such; Brethren, some Baptists, and others include foot-washing. There is nothing to be gained here by a hard-and-fast list, since the remembering signs shade over into providential signs, and in another direction into given community practices such as hospitality and meeting for worship. Here the plan is to treat at greater length three paradigmatic remembering signs that are of prime interest to churches now and in past ages (especially the New Testament age) as well, but these neither define nor exhaust the category. They neither delimit what the church must teach to be the church, nor are they simply adiaphora. While disagreements exist, the examples chosen here make a strong definitional claim upon us.

a. Baptism.—Primitive Christian discipleship, as *Ethics* emphasized, began with a future-oriented rite. Immersion was the sign of their new orientation to the coming rule of God. The immediate root of this ceremony was the movement of John the Baptizer, with its message of *judgment near at hand* (Mark 1:2-8 par.). John required *conversion* (*metanoia*), and for those converted, baptism signaled remission of sins, God's transforming forgiveness (*eis aphesis hamartion*). Each of these three elements—(1) entrance into a community awaiting the new age dawning, (2) conversion to that newness as a condition of admission, and (3) God's putting away of the sins of each—appeared again in the baptizing performed by those gathered around Christ risen. But two further notes appeared in Christian baptism: (4) the "name" of Jesus (later, the triune name) as the identity mark of each candidate and of the new community itself ("baptized into the name," *eis ton onoma*), and (5) the gift of the Spirit of God to the community and to each member upon his or her baptism. The focus in *Ethics* was on the moral force of this primitive rite: its relation to Jesus' first, baptismal step on the road to the kingdom; its relation to each believer's own life story as each turned into God's new path; finally, the "this is that" convergence of these two, of Jesus' baptism and our own. This recapitulation of Jesus' exemplary baptism in our obedient baptism marks a convergence of narratives. The story of the baptized is of entry into a realm where the old has passed away, the new has come (*Ethics:* Nine §1c; cf. 2 Cor. 5:17 REB).

i. How baptism works.—But how does *baptism* accomplish such deep things? How can some gallons of water (and some words) make outsiders insiders, beget anew, banish sin, merge our lives with the risen One's life, transmit God's Holy Spirit? How can any rite admit, or convert, or remit, or identify, or endue? (for what follows cf. McClendon, 1966*b*) In *Ethics* the task was to oppose submoral understandings of baptism so as to link it indelibly with life in the resurrected Christ. Now the task is to lift up its liturgical setting without diminishing by a whit the moral dignity of baptism. It will not be enough to point out that it is God and not the Christian assembly, God and not the candidate, who does these things, for while in Scripture the believer, the community, Christ, and the Spirit are all depicted as active agents in baptism, Scripture also speaks of the baptismal act itself as effectual (cf. Luke 3:16, 1 Cor. 1:14ff, Acts 2:38, with 1 Pet. 3:21). Is this last not magical? Does it not retract all that *Ethics* said about baptism as a *moral* act? In answer one may argue that in Scripture it is only conscious, responsive, responsible candidates who are thus baptized (thus Reginald Fuller's authoritative New Testament survey in *Made, Not Born* [1976] makes no mention of infants). With a certain bias, one may also claim that New Testament baptism only "represents" or "symbolizes" conversion independent of baptism and prior to it. But in this latter claim we hear not the voice of Scripture but one side of a modern debate about sacraments versus "mere" symbols, a debate in which both sides employ language unknown in Scripture itself. Although interpretive language is wanted, it must begin from what we find in Scripture, rather than conceal from us what is there.

In these recent arguments, many baptists, in their understandable attempt to avoid a mechanistic concept of spiritual life, have taken the term "symbol," rather than "sacrament" or "mystery," to explain how the signs of salvation work (see e.g. the Baptists' widely circulated New Hampshire Confession, 1833, in Lumpkin, 1969:366, or the Evangelical Mennonite [EMG-EA] Articles of Faith, 1980, in Loewen, 1985:328). It is interesting, though, that earlier baptists avoided generic terms such as "symbol" and "sacrament" altogether (cf. Schleitheim, 1527, in Yoder 1973:36), or confined themselves to biblical terms such as "sign" (Second London Confession, 1677, in Lumpkin, 1969:291). In any case, there can be but small objection to the language of mystery and sacrament, provided the original sense of these terms is retained. "Mystery" was borrowed from the Hellenistic mystery religions, into which neophytes were inducted by secret ceremonies. The Christian *mysterion* was an *open* secret, its content spread far and wide by the apostolic preaching. The mystery of entering God's new dominion is no other than the mystery that in Christ God reconciles the world to himself: *Jesus* is God's open secret (Bornkamm, TDNT IV:802ff). "Sacrament" belonged to another thought-world, that of Roman civil religion. In Latin lands, a *sacramentum* was a pledge or sacred promise: and early baptism was certainly such a pledge, made to God by candidate and community alike (Rahner, 1965:415). Thus Christian baptism was an initiation rite to Hellenes and a loyalty-pledge to Romans, in their terms a *mysterion* and a *sacramentum*. Both contextualized (i.e., put baptism in a familiar local context) but otherwise left unexplained the question, How does it work? It was later developments, connected with infant 'baptism,' that gave "mystery" and "sacrament" their magical cast. Since even at the beginning they explained too little, while later, out of context, they 'explained' too much, I prefer to avoid these terms here.

What may be overlooked is that similar strictures attach to "symbol," whose role in religious thought depended upon the dominant philosophical idealism of nineteenth-century modernity. As Percy Gardner says, "A symbol is a visible or audible sign or emblem of some thought, emotion, or experience, interpreting what can be really grasped only by the mind and imagination" (ERE XII:139). There is no doubt that the act of baptism is at one level a symbol; so is the word "Halt!" a symbol; the question for us in either case is what use is being made of the symbol, by whom, and with what *force*.

In the prophetic and baptist heritage baptism is not merely a symbol but a **sign,** for it is the nature of signs not only to betoken but to do something, to convey something. I put a sign on my office door: "Students are welcome." It employs some symbols, namely letters and words, in order to *do* something, in this case, to *welcome* the students who read it. Speech-act theory, articulated by J. L. Austin (1911–60), uses this insight to present a theory of communicative action. When an eligible bride or groom, speaking in the context of a wedding ceremony, says "I do," she or he is not just symbolizing marriage, not just thinking about it, but (in Austin's laconic phrase) *indulging* in it. To say those words, in that setting, and with consequent behavior understood, is not to describe or symbolize marrying; it is to *marry*. Similarly, to *warn* (a stranger to leave the premises), to *promise* (a child a walk in the park), to *declare* (your foreign purchases to the customs agent) is in none of these cases mere reportage of inner thoughts, mere symbolizing, but is respectively warning, promising, declaring—acts in the world that have consequences for all concerned. This may come out vividly if the stranger was walking over your flimsy septic tank, or if the promise is callously broken, or if the customs declaration was dishonest and you are caught. Austin called those speech acts not disqualified in issuance by certain well-known defects "happy" speech acts; thus a "happy" warning, in this technical sense, simply means one issued by a speaker deliberately sounding an alarm (not by just any speaker blabbing the words), and one issued in light of a real future danger (and not just any event), and one that the hearer can and does recognize as a warning (see further McClendon and Smith, 1994 chap. 3).

That baptism is such an acted sign, part verbal speech act ("I baptize you . . ."), part associated ceremony (the actual overwhelming with water), seems clear enough. What complicates the case is that like all the prophetic and remembering signs, baptism is not just the act of a candidate and a human administrator, but is an act of God: "Baptized into union with him, you have all put on Christ like a garment" (Gal. 3:27). Yet in the 'happy' case, human action and divine action converge in baptism and indeed are one. Here we meet again, from Chapter Four, the concept of double agency: the authentic prophet speaks *God's* word not just her or his own; in the Lord's supper, the deacons feed the flock, and *eo ipso* Christ feeds the flock. In baptism the agency is actually triple: God's action, the candidate's, and the church's. While the verb is usually active, "Go, baptize them," or passive, "Be baptized," one well-known convert is instructed to "get himself baptized" (Acts 22:16, middle voice in Greek), the grammar emphasizing the convert's self-involvement in the act.

Against this 'effectual sign' understanding of baptism, it may be truly objected that some do in fact enter the eschatological community without baptism: there is no sure evidence that the very first disciple-baptizers were themselves baptized, and in any case there are Quakers and the Salvation Army, who practice no baptism. More puzzling, there are multitudes of 'infant-baptized' folk, many (but not evidently most) of whom show evidence of being faithful disciples. The answer is that such data indeed count against magical sacramental theories of baptismal salvation, but not against baptism as an effectual salvific sign. Though a gracious host stands at the door to welcome the guests, some may attend the party without receiving that welcome; perhaps they were in the house before the party began (cf. the first disciples); perhaps they mistakenly made another entrance (cf. the infant-baptized believer). Neither sort obviates the front-door welcome. A good host will not too severely censure those who missed, but will extend the postponed welcome whenever they will receive it. This analogy foreshadows the treatment of special cases here.

ii. The standard case.—First, though, we should attend to the standard case. (For what follows, cf. McClendon, 1967.) So far, we have found a current, contextual *approach* to baptism: it is a triply enacted sign, a deed in which *God* and *candidate* and (through its designated minister) *church* all act to effect a turn in one life-story (the candidate's) on the basis of Jesus' crucified and risen life. Baptism brings those two lives together in the ongoing 'life-story' of the people of God. Where Christians in other times thought in contexts of ancient mystery or medieval sacrament or modern symbol, our task is to provide an understanding of baptism that can function in our own (postmodern) world. This brings us again to the narrative context of baptism.

Two disparate New Testament models appear (an insight I owe to Tom Turner). The first is the story of Saul become Paul. He had resisted the Jesus movement, fought against it outwardly even while inwardly his life displayed "boundless devotion" to the sacred traditions (Gal. 1:14). When Jesus appeared to him, it was to commission Paul to "proclaim him among the Gentiles"—a project previously offensive to him as to many Jews and Christians as well. So unlikely was this reversal that it required a 'providential sign,' a vision, to bring the Syrian community to receive Paul as a candidate (Acts 9:10-19). Through the centuries many have followed the Apostle to the Gentiles in his radical reversal. These come to Jesus, as apparently he did

> Through many a conflict, many a doubt,
> Fightings within, and fears without . . .

Such converts can readily link their own story to Paul's; for them, "this is that."

The second model is the story of

> a young man, adamant in his commitment, who walks the road . . .
> fulfilling the destiny he has chosen—even sacrificing affection and
> fellowship when the others are unready to follow him—into a new
> fellowship. (Hammarskjøld, 1965:69)

This "young man" was Jesus of Nazareth, whose baptism was not a reversal, but a fulfillment: "it is right for us to do all that God requires" (Matt. 3:15). Through the centuries, I believe, many more have found it possible to come in faith to baptism's waters as Jesus did, not converted *from* flagrant opposition to him, but turning *with* him toward a life of full faithfulness. Both stories are conversion stories, turning stories; in both stories baptism is a commissioning, metaphorically an 'ordination' to service, and although these two have different pasts, their stories converge—at the cross.

The guiding principle to be observed here is this: because baptism is a sign of *salvation*, a sign of the new in Christ (Chapter Three), none who in good faith seeks this sign is to be turned away. "Salvation full and free" implies baptism free—and full. None is to be denied whom Christ accepts, and none of these is to be denied *baptism itself*. The ancient formula, "Who can forbid water?" (Acts 10:47; cf. 8:36) was rhetorically correct: slowly but surely the church has learned that it must not deny this water to Gentiles, but also not to barbarians, or Jews, or females, or slaves, "for you are all one person in Christ Jesus" (Gal. 3:28). Certainly, then, no intelligence barrier exists; our mentally retarded may be received along with our geniuses. But when in ancient times Christians of good intention also 'included' infants as candidates, and added the understanding that baptism is absolutely unrepeatable, they ironically denied this inclusive principle: for now neither story, Jesus' or Paul's, was applicable; instead there was an infant rite! "Whosoever will" became "whosoever is not already presumed baptized." Thus the privilege of Christian initiation was effectively revoked, this time not for Gentiles or barbarians or women or slaves, but for the child of many a Christian home. By this rule such a one is told she may not ever ask for baptism; nor is she permitted to remember her baptism; whatever else she may do in faith, she may not stand with a faith of her own in the baptismal waters and hear the glad words, "Upon the profession of your faith I baptize you, my sister, in the name of the Father, and of Jesus God's Child, and of the Spirit of God."

In this regard, baptism certainly differs from Jewish circumcision, which is performed only upon males, and typically upon infants. Nonetheless, some have seen a parallel. The best discussion is in Beasley-Murray (1962:334-43 et pass.).

iii. The present conflict.—What followed is a tale often told. The diminution of baptism coincided with the dissolving of Christian faith into culture, the Constantinian compromise. Though from time to time over the centuries individuals and groups rebelled (often at their life's risk), baptism for most became a birth-ceremony, or a safe-conduct badge for the dying, and lost its status as the commissioning of disciples setting out on their faith journey. The ideal alternatives to the conversion-models related above seem to be principally two: infants baptized soon after birth are to be brought by subsequent education to a confirmation that will signal conversion and be the fruit of the earlier baptism; or infants, baptized, confirmed, and given communion in one infant rite are already made "full participants" in the church. In both these alternative models faith is present—the church's or the sponsors' or the parents' vicarious faith. All that is wanting is the infant's faith. When some churches have later received such folk as candidates for "real" baptism—for their own conversion-baptism—they have been accused of repeating the unrepeatable, while they in turn have regarded the paedobaptists as having no baptism at all. Where in all this is the "one baptism" of Ephesians 4:5?

One approach to this "ecumenical dilemma" (Küng, ed., 1967) recalls certain spiritualists (e.g. Caspar Schwenkfeld) of the sixteenth century, and certain evangelists of the nineteenth and twentieth (Dwight L. Moody?) who emphasized inner conversion and insisted that baptism did not matter. The signs, on their view, were adiaphora, things that are not essential and can be done in many ways—or omitted. While this view seemed to solve the dilemma, it sat loose to the command of the risen Christ (e.g., Matt. 28:19f), and comported poorly with the baptist vision. World Council of Churches ecumenism (1948–) took another path. Christian unity via agreed doctrines or common ministerial orders ("Faith and Order") proving too elusive a near-term goal, the third, New Delhi Assembly (1961) of this mainline Protestant (and Orthodox) Council sought a new unity formula: the unity of "all in each place who are baptized into Jesus Christ and confess him as Lord and Saviour" (Fey, ed., 1970:43). The difficulty with this formula was that baptism meant many things to many Council members (to say nothing of non-members). To remedy this, the Faith and Order Commission of the Council produced a series of study documents on baptism, referring them to its constituent communions and further revising them (biblio. in Thurian, ed., 1983). The exhilarating sense of unity produced by this process overlooked one crippling flaw: unity was achieved by passing over the convictions of those considerable Christian communities not a part of the process.

For example, a widely circulated (and much praised) Faith and Order document, *Baptism, Eucharist, and Ministry* (1982), correctly treats baptism as an effectual sign (p. 2), but fails to mention that sign and thing signified may come unglued—a point which not only baptists but that strong sacramental theologian, Paul, was not hesitant to make (1 Cor. 10:1-6). It correctly links baptism and faith, but fails to say whose faith (p. 3). It reasonably predicts that when responsive believers are baptized, "A personal confession of faith will be an integral part of the baptismal service," but it immediately adds that "when an infant is baptized, the personal response *will be offered* at a later moment in life" (p. 4, emphasis added)—a prediction mocked by abundant counter-evidence. These are some of the severe internal tensions in a document hailed as providing "convergence," but at least at one point it displays no ambivalence: churches that might be *interpreted* as repeating baptism ("anabaptists"?) are simply scolded (¶13, also p. 5). Perhaps the trouble is that the document lacks a basis deeper than compromise among its framers.

Christian compromise is often desirable. Yet what if in fact this remembering sign is one place where "a classical structural disjunction is built into the meaning of the gospel," a place where the gospel itself will either stand or fall? (J. H. Yoder, "Introduction" to Strege, ed., 1986)

iv. An ecumenical solution.—If Protestants (and Orthodox) have not solved the dilemma, can Catholics and baptists help? Recent practical and theological developments among these offer fresh insights. No less a Protestant than Karl Barth has led the theological attack on paedobaptism (Barth, 1943; and again CD IV/4). For Roman Catholics, followed by other Catholic churches, the developments are *practical:* liberated to do so by the "Constitution on the Sacred Liturgy" of Vatican II (Abbott, ed., 1966), Catholic liturgists set out to recover the ancient church practice of Christian initiation. Briefly, they discovered that what developed in later Catholicism into three separate rites, baptism, confirmation, and (first) communion, was earlier one unified initiation process. In ancient times, applicants were admitted not as communicants but as 'catechumens' for a period of intense doctrinal and spiritual training prior to baptism. Baptism itself was not automatic, but was for those believed qualified; it was by immersion; and was accompanied by exorcisms, ritual bodily anointing, and prayers. This was followed by the eucharist and thus full admission to the ranks of the faithful (*Made, Not Born*, 1976:pass.). While infant baptism for most remains so far standard, albeit anomalous, in this Catholic renewal, the rich spiritual catechetical process in participating parishes, instituted yearly at Lent and climaxing at Easter, is so powerful that one wonders how long the now contextually outmoded infant rite can survive—*lex orandi, lex credendi?*

For the various sorts of baptists, whose assorted recoveries of elements of this ancient practice in earlier centuries have been too little celebrated, the new developments are theological. There is a new vocabulary in which to make clear the radical message of conversion-baptism. First, there is a fresh understanding of the way in which conversion-baptism cuts against **social control** of candidates; from John the Baptizer to Onesimus, from the author of Galatians to the Anabaptists, from John Smyth to the Africans who endured American slavery, baptism has been a "Yes" to the liberating God of the future and a "No" to dehumanizing institutions (e.g., Raboteau, 1978:98f). It helps to remember that in defiance of the fateful law that accompanied infant baptism (repeatable within Christendom only on pain of death), the revolutionary rite was a "No" to that social stranglehold. In all these cases baptism declared liberty to the captives.

This may be clarified by the close parallel between the conversion-baptism of early English Baptists and the rejection of all "outward" rites by the followers of George Fox, a parallel underlined by the close associations between Quakers and General Baptists. The Society of Friends rejected both baptism and eucharist, not because of 'mysticism,' but because these rites denied the immediacy of grace and interposed social control between the believer and God (Ahlstrom, 1972:176f). This Friends' policy cannot fairly be understood as a rejection of all signs (they powerfully continued prophetic preaching), but it denied a church-controlled rite they believed routinized beyond recovery. Some in our day may object that conversion-baptism has been similarly corrupted. Children are herded into baptistries in "evangelistic" harvests that bear little relation to either evangelism or conversion (see Timothy George in Strege, ed., 1986:47-51). Perhaps in our culture responsible baptism can hardly occur earlier than adolescence, when children find themselves again able to say "No" to parents, or even adulthood, when they can say "No" to their peers as well. For baptism's "Yes" to God and faith and church is hardly meaningful unless a "No" is psychologically possible. This point is made by Andrea Lee's moving story of the daughter of a black Baptist congregation, continually constrained by members of "First African" to present herself for baptism, but firmly protected by her pastor parents from that pressure, so that in the end it is a sign of the faith that she is never baptized. This protection was "the peculiar gift of freedom my father . . . had granted me" (Lee, 1983). At times baptists may likewise have to become Friends to the children of the church!

Finally, however, baptism cannot be a function of the age of the candidate alone. In the eloquent words of Aidan Kavanagh, OSB:

> Stop asking at what age [baptism] should be administered; the question is when and under what conditions we should initiate a Christian. . . . Stop asking how the church might better serve the world; the question is how the church might better serve the imperative of the gospel, and consequently aid this world in discovering itself made new in the church itself. (*Made, Not Born*, 1976:5)

This leads to the second new understanding, concerning the relation between the Christian community and its environment—in H. R. Niebuhr's phrase, the relation between *"Christ and culture"* (H. Niebuhr, 1951; cf. Scriven, 1988; my *Ethics*, pp. 23f; Yoder, Yeager, and Stassen,

1994). Are church and wider society to be merely opposed to one another ("Christ against culture"), or nearly identical with one another ("the Christ of culture"), or in some third relation? In a sympathetic review of Niebuhr's options, Geoffrey Wainwright argues for the transformative stance ("Christ the transformer of culture"), for it includes the strengths of the two sides without their weaknesses. Here existing human life and culture is not despised though it needs to be transformed. Wainwright, a Methodist theologian and liturgical expert, goes on to say that the "primary liturgical model of the transformist view is the sacrament of (believer's) baptism, which offers no easy integration of church and society" (Wainwright, 1980:388-94). John Yoder regards this cultural independence of the church as the most profound level in the sixteenth-century discussions of ("paedo" versus "re") baptism: what the radicals denied, and the self-styled orthodox affirmed, was that Europe had become a "Christian" enclave where no rejection of culture was needed. If the orthodox no longer believe this, the discussion must of course change (Yoder, 1989:205f).

The third 'new' understanding—a new term for an old way of under-standing—is loosely called primitivism, and in this book, **the baptist vision.**

It is not enough here to appeal to primitive baptismal practice (cf. the Aland-Jeremias debate, cited in Wainwright, 1980:n. 182). For example, whether the New Testament's household baptisms (1 Cor. 1:16; Acts 11:14, 16:15, 18:8?) included baptism of infants too young to respond in faith demands answers to at least two prior questions: First, do the New Testament's *concepts* of baptism even apply to non-agents, to those who cannot ask for themselves? (Beasley-Murray, 1962:314-20). If baptism was *metanoia*-baptism, for whom was it pro-vided? And second, is the mere *behavior* of such primitive churches normative (if so, why do we not baptize for the dead—1 Cor. 15:29?)? If not, there is yet a way to make the primitive appeal: this is by the "this is that" of the prophetic or baptist vision.

By the baptist vision, our task is not mere replication of primitive Christian behavior, but acting in our own context with an understanding of what we do formed by our identity with Jesus' first disciples. By this test, infant baptism may seem to be not the *metanoia*-baptism of Jesus and Paul but nearer the immersion of those Ephesian disciples who lacked both trust in Jesus and the Spirit's infilling, so that they needed baptizing again in order to *repair* this lack (Acts 19:1-7). The concept of baptismal repair will engage us soon, but now we see the point of application of the baptism of Jesus, and that of Paul, invoked above: as baptismal candidates we wait, blind with Paul, in the house of Judas in a street called Straight (Acts 9:11); in baptism we stand ready with Jesus our Joshua, our peaceful conqueror. On Jordan's stormy banks we stand

> And cast a wishful eye
> To Canaan's fair and happy land,
> Where our possessions lie.

Baptism is a paradigm test of the baptist vision. As such, it must fulfill that vision in the candidates it accepts and in the theological intent it displays. If our practice of baptism is by these standards faulty, perhaps it is not our understanding of baptism so much as our far more important understanding of all else that needs to change.

This brings us back to the ecumenical task. If infant baptism with its constricting "once only" rule is to be with us for a season, how should *unruly* baptists respond? There can be for them no doubt of the authenticity of the salvation that follows many a mistaken baptism, or of the "genuine partnership" of other churches than their own. Yet in the rest of Christian life, we do not hesitate to repeat a sign when a fresh beginning is required, or to repair what is lacking in our rites. Marriage is one example; welcome to guests is another. The appropriate remedy for an impaired baptism is not its utter denial ("this is no baptism"), but its *repair:* we may 'repeat' a wedding, an ordination, or a baptism, furnishing what had earlier been lacking (for example, this time a church for the wedding, collegial acknowledgment for the ordination, or the candidate's confession in baptism), and by this repetitive act *regularize the original one* rather than deny its (impaired) existence. Moreover, a wedding ten years late will not deny the existence of offspring but may incorporate them into the ceremony; baptismal repair can likewise acknowledge the earlier rite and the genuine faith that has appeared. While a baptism too late is almost as strange as one too early, brought together they may just fill the bill. In any case, let the guiding principle still be a welcome to each and every seeker, so that "whosoever will" may come.

"Look, here is water: what is to prevent my being baptized?"

(Acts 8:36)

The "once only" rule arose largely as a result of Augustine's struggle with the Donatists. By insisting that former Donatists who had been reclaimed (often by coercion) into the Catholic fold need not—indeed must not—be rebaptized, Augustine pointed out that it was God, and not the one administering baptism, upon whom the grace of baptism depends. Yet those who would charge that baptists violate this rule when they perform this remembering sign upon those previously baptized as infants forget a crucial difference: while for Augustine the issue was the character of the baptiz*er*, at stake in the current discussion is the integrity of the one baptiz*ed* and so of the sign itself.

b. Prophetic preaching.—In the thought and practice of many Christian churches, preaching is an optional rather than obligatory part of Christian worship. While a few public speakers can charm or arouse or inspire an audience, most cannot, and these churches arrange matters so that worship is independent of a sermon's failure or success. But for another sort of church—notably those constituting my community of reference—worship is first of all preaching and singing, and there is a great deal of both. Surprisingly, the quality of preaching appears to one ecumenical visitor not greatly better or worse in one sort than in the other! In both, preachers are plagued by inadequate preparation, hindered by inferior training, and not seldom defeated by a lack of those large human sympathies that are intrinsic to the task. Of course there are exceptions. Perhaps every Christian has sometime heard some sermon preached that called as deep calls unto deep, that declared the whole counsel of God, that found us where we were and brought us within sight of the land of promise. But most of the time, for most, it is not so.

Perhaps the difficulty has lain in the varied expectations laid upon preacher and sermon. In past ages the preacher has served many functions—town crier, entertainer, community psychologist and moralist, chaplain to the *Obrigkeit*. In Europe emerging from pagan tribalism, the church was a socializing institution and the preacher its voice. To preach "the faith" was a many-sided task. A like phenomenon appeared in frontier America, as in Catholic and Protestant churches the preacher wove the web of manners, morals, and beliefs that brought isolated farm and ranch folk together in new communities. But the twentieth century saw the closing of that frontier, and new modes of education, travel, and communication (e.g., television) met popular needs without the mediation of any preacher. Perhaps in the 'two-thirds world' of the Southern and Eastern hemispheres, the preacher remains an *ex officio* medicine man, political pundit, and moral guide. For most in the West, it is not so, and what is expected of the Christian preacher seems unclear. What is preaching, now?

Such questions deeply stirred such mid-twentieth-century theologians as Rudolf Bultmann, Paul Tillich, and Karl Barth. With others, they hammered out among them a new "theology of proclamation" or preaching. Consider Barth's version, as expounded in *Church Dogmatics*. Just as Jesus Christ, "this pure event," is God's revealed Word, and the Bible is "the written Word of God," the sermon is from time to time "the event of real proclamation," the word of God preached, whereby the church becomes the church (CD I/1, §4). Such proclamation becomes a "word-event," a happening that changes things. In its own medium it is of a piece with the incarnation of Jesus Christ. When this word is spoken, God speaks. With such a strong sense of the power of proclamation, Barth with other mid-century theologians came close to the sign-act theory of preaching that this chapter explores. All the more must some difficulties that appeared in their work be noted.

One question is this: What does it say, this preached word of God? The answer they gave was constricted by their theory of "non-propositional revelation"—the belief that the word of God was never identical with any exact verbal assertion. And in their approximations to the unsayable, they differed considerably from one another. Was the proclamation, "The whole world is redeemed in the event of Jesus Christ," or was it "You must decide (for God)"? or was it "God accepts us unconditionally; accept this acceptance"? (cf. Pitt-Watson, 1976:chap. 1) Still another version was that of Will Campbell in the 1950s: "We're all sinners, but God loves us anyway" (cf. *Ethics*, p. 238). If this was the content of "the preached word," it certainly gave heart to estranged, violence-torn, guilty mid-century listeners. There was a consequent renaissance of preaching to match the renaissance of theology in those days. Yet the theory seemed to deny to the preacher much that had occupied preaching in other ages, from the prophets on—what Paul in Acts calls "disclosing to you the whole purpose *[pasan tēn boulēn]* of God" (cf. Acts 20:27), offering not only forgiveness but life guidance, not only victory proclamations but orienting narratives suited to the needs of the scattered forces under the rule of Christ.

What is preaching? "It is proclamation, not just moralizing. It is Good News, not just good advice; it is gospel, not just law" (Pitt-Watson, 1986:12). Yet the previous paragraphs imply that sermons are subject to contextual demands even in those generations that believe themselves driven back upon the pure event, the pure word, of God. So far, they were right: in prophetic preaching, it is not the preacher's word that matters; what matters is that here God speaks. Yet contextual demands cannot be avoided, and those demands can both stimulate and limit the preacher. It is the business of practical theology (or of what Schleiermacher in the *Brief Outline* called "statistics"—1830) to discover and apply those demands afresh in each new season. Is there then no pole star, no constant such as baptism and eucharist provide? Can we name no objective *content* incapable of perversion? Baptismal immersion points mutely but inflexibly to Christ dead and rising again; the eucharistic bread and wine signify body incorporated and blood spilled.

These are fixed points; we can abuse them but we cannot efface them. Yet in "preaching the Bible," some sermons become mere Ancient Near East lectures; in "preaching the gospel," mere theologizing; in "preaching Christ," mere sentiment.

What can make preaching positive, make it good news, save it from becoming a parody of itself? It is finally a question of higher authority, and of preacher and hearers as servants of that authority (Forsyth, 1907). Where that authority is granted its right, authentic prophetic preaching occurs, even where the preacher is less than eloquent, the hearers less than mature, the setting less than suitable: a street, a living room, an almost abandoned downtown church. What, then, is the preacher's authority to preach and the listener's to listen? Chapter Eleven will address that question, but we can foreshadow its answer: The only final authority for children of God is their divine Parent; the only final authority for sinners is the grace of the Redeemer; the only final authority for a living fellowship is the Spirit that empowers it. This holy authority, one authority, is gracefully threefold (cf. 2 Cor. 13:14).

Let us anticipate that coming chapter. The Redeemer's own authority addresses preacher and people in the book, the library, that is Scripture. The New Testament centers in Christ risen; the Old looks forward to him and gains its claim upon Gentile Christians through him. The preacher who preaches the book with authority preaches with the authority of Jesus Christ. This means that the preacher's appeal to his or her hearers is no other than the appeal that Christ makes. Consider a case: the sermon subject is treatment of enemies. The preacher's text is Matthew 5:44: "Love your enemies." Shall she say, "On the authority of Scripture, love your enemies; the Bible says it; that settles it"? Or is it more than that? The preacher's authority is not "the Bible said it" (though she must be clear that it does), nor even "Jesus said it" (that, too). She must find her way, finally, to say and to say with authority, simply "Love your enemies." Only thus will she preach not as an authority *on* the Bible, or an authority *in* the church (though she may be both), but as a 'criterial authority,' one who as "a woman in Christ" (cf. 2 Cor. 12:2) participates in Jesus Christ so that Christ speaks his word, his Word, in her today (Farmer, 1942:83-92). Doubtless she will exegete, illustrate, apply, and all the rest. But her authority is more than her homiletical skill with the Bible; it is that which is authority even for the Bible; it is the Bible's own authority. That authority is God incarnate and risen; God the Redeemer.

How does anyone come to be in such a place of authority? That brings us to the preacher's life-story, to his or her individual experience with God. This is the sense in which the preacher's call to preach is patient of investigation by criteria open to the fellowship, and to the preacher, too

(Barth, 1963:33ff). It may be true, as ancient theologians argued, that sacraments work of themselves, *ex opere operato*, independent of the virtue of their ministers. Clearly, though, in the acted sign of prophetic preaching, the perceived character of the preacher is part of the constitutive matter of the sign: Phillips Brooks' definition of preaching, "the communication of truth through personality," however one-sided, makes that point. To return to our illustration, if our preacher knows that God is love because she knows that when she was herself God's enemy, she was forgiven, then her authority is immediate and personal; she knows *from God* that God loves his enemies and so we must love ours as well (Forsyth, 1907:chap. 2).

Where does the listener's authority come in? Is it a question of hierarchy, of the preacher of grace towering authoritatively over the objects of grace? No, for preacher and sermon are still dependent upon the authority of the Holy Spirit to make inward application of the preached word to hearers' lives. This is true of converted hearers; it is also true of the unconverted. Together listeners under the authority of the Spirit acknowledge the spoken word, and they do well together to give some signal of that acknowledgment (see §3 below). Only in this acknowledgment has the sign been an effectual sign; only God who is Spirit can apply God's truth to hearers' lives and practices. Forsyth spoke of the preacher as "himself a sacrament"; in our terms, the preacher's own life must *be* a providential sign if the sermon is to become a remembering sign of the gospel of God. Yet that cannot exalt preacher over listeners, for in them, too, God's Spirit must be at work, making of their lives as well providential signs of the reign at hand. In our illustration, the sermon on love of enemies hits home exactly when and as God's Spirit inwardly applies its truth to each listener, convicts, converts, consecrates, so that God's reign draws near once more.

Not all 'preaching' is prophetic sign; not all who speak are called to preach; not every assembly gathers "in the name" of Jesus to listen. Yet these things happen, and when they do there is a remembering sign from God.

c. Lord's supper.—The power of the acted sign Christians call Lord's supper (or eucharist, or covenant meal, or holy communion) lies especially in its nearness to the person of Christ: Our beliefs about him theologically shape the meal that we call by his name. Chapter Six showed that changing christological models afford us fresh ways of explaining who Jesus is. 'Narrative Christology' permits us to speak not of two substances but of two true narratives, the divine story and the human one, converging in this one crucified and risen life. A further test of the fruitfulness of that model is the help it gives for understanding the covenant meal. Here, too, stories significantly converge.

The treatment of the Lord's supper in *Ethics* hinted at this plurality of narratives at work and offered a condensed summary of the themes. The meal is about *forgiveness* ("blood shed for forgiveness of sins"); it is a meal about *solidarity* with Christ and with one another ("my body"); it is a *thanksgiving meal* ("giving thanks, he broke it"); it is a future-regarding or *eschatological* meal ("until he comes"). There the task was especially to lift up solidarity, showing how the Lord's supper played its part in building and maintaining Christian community. Here that account can be expanded via the other themes.

i. Solidarity.—If we had to ask of baptism how it could identify or admit to Christ's company, must we not ask how a meal can reunite? Much has been made of Jesus' striking saying: "this is my body" (1 Cor. 11:24 par.). Medieval theologians, committed to a metaphysic of substance, explained this saying in those metaphysical terms; more recent Catholic thought has produced a less foreign theory of "transsignification"—things that before the meal had "signified" only bread or wine now acquire "in a personal revelation of God" a new significance in use in the meal, now signify the body and blood of Jesus in their inner meaning and power (Powers, 1967). This seems correct, as far as it goes, but it appears to explain either too little or too much: too little, if it accounts for a local presence of the risen Lord in the elements on the table but not in the lives of those at the table to share; too much if it is the functional claim that the use we make of things is that which in some further sense they "are," so that if I use the screwdriver as a hammer, then it is no longer really a screwdriver.

Austin M. Farrer, recalling the truism that food is life, wrote that if in ancient times a Jew "blessed his food—that is, if he said grace for it—and added, before eating it, 'This is my body,' his friends would not have been altogether surprised. . . . It was his body, of course—his body to be; not actually his body, as anyone could see; he would need to digest it first. . . . Bread that is blessed is to be eaten; it is to be the eater's body. God has given it for that purpose." The Jewish custom was not only to give thanks for one's own bread, but to give thanks for the company's bread as well, and by breaking the loaf and passing it around, to enable each to share thanks and food alike. Paul reminded the Corinthians of a truth already old in Jesus' day: "Because there is one loaf, we, though many, are one body; for it is one loaf of which we all partake" (1 Cor. 10:17). If that is all, though, why did Jesus not say "This is the body of us all"? Because they were not equals. He was their Master. Just as, if people went to the temple, the food they ate was God's altar-food, which God graciously gave back to them to eat, so Jesus, sitting at table, was Master of the food and it was properly his, yet he gave it to them so that the food for his body became theirs. Thereby they had communion with him who would soon hang on a cross (Farrer, 1960:146ff; cf. Farrer, 1968).

At church we set bread and wine upon the table. Whose is it? Ours, but if we present it to the risen Lord, whom we trust to be there, is it not rather his? And if he returns it to us each in words first used long ago, "This is my body; this is for you" (cf. 1 Cor. 11:24) is it not rightfully his bread, his body, that we then receive? On this view, Christ does not lie slaughtered before us on the table to be eaten by hungry Christian cannibals; rather Christ risen is present in our eucharist to commune with us, to give us bread that is his, and so (by rights) his own body. When we have received it we can say with certain travelers to Emmaus, "He sat down with us at table, he took bread and said the blessing; he broke the bread, and offered it—to us." Afterward, perhaps we can tell "how he made himself known to us in the breaking of bread" (Luke 24:30-35). Such union with Jesus is re-membering, it is reconstitution, being made part of the whole. In it we are re-united, we are re-membered one to another as his members. Thus as in baptism there is here not only *reference* to God's great historic sign; here again is a (re-membering) sign from God in its own right.

ii. The forgiveness of sins.—There is a connection between the eucharist and the forgiveness of sins. Since the theme of forgiveness has already occupied us (*Ethics*, Seven, and above, Chapter Three), here we can be brief. Max Thurian tells how the Council of Trent, reacting to Protestant heresy, placed its seal of approval on a use of the mass that had developed in the Middle Ages: one could be a good Christian without personally participating in the mass more than once a year; the mass, then, was a propitiatory sacrifice, to be offered "for the living and the dead, for sins, penalties, satisfactions, and other things needful" (Thurian, 1960:10; Trent, *Sessio* XXII, ix.iii). From this conciliar authorization startling theories developed, and the multiplication of masses, against which the Reformers had protested in the first place, continued. Research in the nineteenth century and Vatican Council II in the twentieth enabled Catholic theologians to regain their bearings: now communion once again became important; the ancient patterns were recovered; the mass or eucharist became once again (at least for these experts) a *celebration* of the once-for-all sacrificial achievement of Christ, his victory over sin and death.

Despite this reversal of field, Roman Catholic theologians clung to the claim that the mass was itself a sacrifice (Rahner, 1965:278f), an insistence that involved them in somewhat tortuous language, since they wanted to deny what their Baroque predecessors had affirmed—that every mass was a *new* sacrifice. If however we turn our attention, not to this internal dispute but to the wider meaning of the term, we may say that their stubborn insistence had it right: Originally animal sacrifices had been festal barbecues of altar-roasted animals, and the Passover was (and is) a home dining table ceremony. In other words, insisting that the Lord's supper is a sacrifice is correct if by sacrifice we mean a ritual meal that is shared between deity and worshipers—perhaps the original sense of the term (G. Anderson, ABD V:870-86). There is even a newness in it—our new (or renewed) sacrificial commitment to make up what is left over of Christ's sufferings (cf. Col. 1:24)—to be part of God's own costly mission to humanity.

Another sort of connection between the Lord's supper and forgiveness of sin appeared in Reformation England. In 1549 and again in 1552, Thomas Cranmer set out to provide a liturgy for the reforming national church. There can be no doubt of Cranmer's deep religious feeling, or of his capacity to turn those feelings into powerful religious language—language matched only by the King James Bible. Yet at least in the "Lordes Supper or Holye Communion" of 1552, Cranmer was apparently so overcome by awe at "these holy misteries" that he set a tone of sinful unworthiness that dominates the whole. Before the service was done, Cranmer's 1552 communicant might have confessed or bewailed his or her sins in as many as ten distinct ritual acts (*First and Second Prayer Books of King Edward VI*, 1910). The point is worth remembering because of the influence this had upon subsequent Puritan (including English Baptist) eucharistic understanding. While Baroque Catholics might find themselves forbidden to celebrate in an action reserved to a priest who made a sacrifice for sins, the Baroque Protestant who followed Cranmer's line could hardly celebrate for bewailing. And all this in an act whose point (according to our earliest sources) was Jesus' pledge that his *forgiveness* was for all!

In light of its meaning, appropriate forms of the supper will provide appropriate acts of renewal of the covenant ties that bind us not only to the Lord but to our covenanting sisters and brothers. The task is to steer between the extreme of treating the eucharist (or mass) as if it were in itself sin's objective remedy, and the extreme of demanding of those who approach the table a purity of heart and intention that is likely best found in the dull of spirit. Neither a talisman nor a trial by ordeal, the Lord's table is a memorial of Christ who took sinners into his fellowship, but whose touch *transformed* them each and all. It is a role best unfolded by the four Evangelists, who (each in a distinctive way) display sinful disciples at table with their faithful Master.

iii. Thanksgiving.—Liturgical renewal has devoted considerable effort to investigating "memorial" and "memory" in the Old and New Testaments (Thurian, 1960–61). *Zakar, anamnesis,* and their cognates mean first not an internal, psychological 'remembering,' but a more objective "act to memorialize." This scholarly awareness was perhaps resisted by non-Catholics as part of their opposition to the (medieval and later) sense of "sacrifice" in Catholic thought. But then what did Paul's and Luke's Jesus mean in saying "Do this as an *anamnesis* of me"? (1 Cor. 11:24, 25; Luke 22:19 in some texts) Most clearly, that the meal of gratitude ("when he had given *thanks,* he broke it") was to be repeated and that its repetition was unfailingly to be a memorial. Not a memorial of his death alone, and not of his death and resurrection, though these are central, but a meal "in memory of *me,*" that is, of Jesus himself, and thus of the longer story that frames his life: the divine-human story of creation, and the election of Israel, and its existence as a people, and the birth of Messiah Jesus, his life and ministry, and the great signs from God that have followed.

How can a meal be a story? What does it mean to eat and drink "as a memorial"? Perhaps for Americans today the annual Thanksgiving Day with its associated dinner is the model nearest to hand. When the family gathers, it gathers *as a family*—church Thanksgiving Day meals are no effective substitute, benevolent though they may be. The family gathers, and it is family memories that are evoked. Yet there is a wider backdrop—of early American memories, of "the first Thanksgiving feast," of European settlers and Original Americans for once meeting in amity, of the goodness of a God who provided that feast and provides this one. Yet if we are Jews, another sort of "thanksgiving" feast serves as a model—the Passover meal. This was a celebration of the Exodus, the great sign by which God delivered the people from Egyptian slavery, and its accompaniments brought the reality to life again—the roast lamb, the bitter herbs, the ritual cups of memory, the *haggadah* or recital of the first Passover story. Perhaps we can see why New Testament writers were careful (by whatever assorted calendars they reckoned Passover) to give their meal a Passover setting (1 Cor. 5:7f; Mark 14:12 par.): that known ritual helped explain what the new thanksgiving meant. It also makes clear what it did not. For the disciples were to be drawn from no single national stock; their meal was intended not to exclude but to include (even Judas?); and the community into which they were being drawn was not their own brave creation (as with Americans) or even their covenantal arrangement with God (as with Jews), but an act of pure grace that saved them when they were lost, forgave them when they were sinners, set them at table when they had earned no place there. This thanksgiving meal is inseparable from *awed gratitude* (McClendon and Smith, 1994:63, 70-74).

iv. End-time banquet.—German exegete Hans Lietzmann once argued (1926) that the common meals of the early Christians celebrated the risen Christ, but until Paul wrote 1 Corinthians did not refer to his death. The theory had difficulties, but one aspect of it endures: the resultant New Testament rite did powerfully focus on the cross. When primitive Christians met to remember, they met to remember their Master facing his life's crisis. But it is not accidental, I think, that the passion account is also tightly interwoven, in all the Gospels, with Jesus' teaching about last things (thus Mark 13, the "little apocalypse," is immediately followed by Mark 14 with its account of the Last Supper). What this means is that the final crisis, the last judgment, and the last supper are all of a piece for Christian thought. The supper looks back—that is its association with Passover and the past. The supper looks forward, and in Mark that is its strong, new emphasis. Not only is "this that," but even more important, "then is now": God's future is immediately, presently relevant to this community. If Jesus' preaching was proclamation of the inbreaking of God's reign *now* (Mark 1:15), Jesus' supper was a kingdom meal already, this "blessed assurance" a "foretaste of glory divine."

Here difficulties arise for some whose picture of God's future is altogether placid. For the supper was not placid. In this regard baptism and supper are alike. An interesting project, not carried through here, would be to see how Jesus in the Gospels promises the disciples a "cup" that he identifies also as a "baptism." The cup, like the immersion, seems in Gospel language to be the suffering he and they will suffer at the hands of the powers (cf. Myers, 1988:362). So the remembering sign is an anticipatory sign as well, but the anticipation is of crisis, judgment. That is not the only eschatological picture; I have shown above that there are others (Chapter Two), and one of them is of a heaven with every tear wiped away, every dark shadow lightened by the light from the Lamb. But it remains true that the future to which the Lamb summons us is a feast with suffering, and that the final Marriage supper of the Lamb will seat at table many a scarred veteran of the Lamb's warfare. As it will be then, so must it be now; together these feasters dip their own garments in the Lamb's precious blood (Rev. 7:14; 19:9).

* * * * *

The meal tells again an old story that came true; it reenacts the naked truth about the church's (and each member's) story here and now:

The story then had deep roots in the soil of primal theophagous sacrifice— communion with the mysterious Deity, roots in a people hurrying to leave Egypt and follow a God whose name they must learn as they journeyed, roots of memory deep in the earth of Israel, where promised harvests matured, where prophets cried out, where sin would (someday) be blotted out.

The story now has those very roots, the chthonic awareness of blood sacrifice, the travelers' readiness to follow a God on the move, the thanksgiving pause to celebrate the grace and mercy of JHWH in the land of our sojourn.

The story then displayed the wary comradeship of men and women in peril at the hands of principalities and powers; they suspected treachery in their messmates (Judas?) and feared their own disloyalty ("Lord, is it I?"); they knew the certainty of established oppression. Jesus demanded trust and warned of betrayal; he pledged to them and to God his own life's blood.

The story now is of women and men who know Jesus' faithfulness and utter loss and surprising final triumph, but who, knowing him, still fear treachery in their midst, still doubt themselves betimes, still need Jesus' pledge written in his life's blood.

The story then was colored by hope—the wild apocalyptic hope of disciples confused by the times, the firm kingdom hope in Jesus, who in a dark hour grasped the cup of the future and with it God's inbreaking reign.

The story now is of disciples often perplexed about God's future, but infused with the virtue of hope; sometimes hopeless when they contemplate the obvious, but full of hope when they see *signs of God's coming Rule*—of which this meal is one.

§3. The Essential Shape of Christian Worship

The preceding sections offered a theory of worship and a brief account of the remembering signs that for Christians constitute its (God-given) language. There can be no one inflexible pattern of Christian worship, suitable for all places and times, in which these elements must appear. The Catholic mass has known endless variations east and west, while Protestant and baptist patterns may be more varied still. Yet some imperatives speak. The first part of this chapter (§1) showed authentic worship as divinely enabled response to the great historic signs by which God is creating of all peoples a new people. This offers clues about the when and how and where of worship, and these are followed up here under the headings of **time, structure,** and **space.**

a. Its time.—Recall the fourth commandment, "Remember (that is, keep, observe) the Sabbath" (Exod. 20:8; Deut. 5:12). The sense of *zakor* (*shamor* in one text) recurs in the New Testament commands to make a memorial of the Lord's supper. Keeping time by a calendar that could predict moonlit nights and seasons of seedtime and harvest was already essential to ancient peoples: Commandment Four did not invent calendric timekeeping (weeks, months, years) but presumed it and gave instructions for its more profound employment. One day in seven is liberated from toil, set apart to the Lord, a *memorial* of freedom from Egyptian slavery, the completion of God's creative work (Deut. 5:15; Gen. 2:2f). The seventh will be a day of awe, of wonder, interrupting work and thereby giving it a holy rhythm. Commandment One ("no other gods") freed Hebrews *from* slave labor (the Pharaoh was not to be their god); Commandment Four freed them *for* the privilege of doing their own work in their own homeland, while setting a limit to work lest it become itself a new oppressor. Israelites need not be self-enslaved by their toil, for they would pause and "remember." They had a *remembering* sign.

Thus the Redeemer God enjoined a rhythm of work and wonder, a rest note at the beginning of each new measure of earth's music, a reminder of its end inserted joyfully into the middle of creation (cf. *Ethics,* Six §2). How Christians maintained this rhythm while shifting its pivot to an 'eighth' day cannot long occupy us here. If it could, we would see that the shift was neither sudden nor total, and that it congealed only in connection with a tragic parting of the ways between gentile Christians and post-70 rabbinic Judaism. It is noteworthy that the modern Christian bodies that have challenged that shift, for example Seventh Day Baptists and Seventh Day Adventists, have been sharers of the baptist vision. It must surely be a liberating vision that permits such re-examination of old orthopraxies and testing of ancient prejudices. In what follows, we must probe still deeper, examining the actual contents of the Lord's day, asking whether those contents are themselves liberating.

One way to understand the larger rhythm of the "Christian year" is that it is no more than an agreed teaching device; as a church moves from Advent to Christmas to Epiphany to Lent to Good Friday and Easter, and finally to Pentecost, it *educates,* teaching disciples the story of their Lord from birth to ascension to the Spirit-baptism of followers. In that case, though, the other half-year may reverse that education with its pagan (or at best, civil) rhythms: In the U.S.A., Memorial Day (*dulce et decorum est pro patria mori*) and Independence Day, *Vacation* Bible School, Labor Day (whose Monday 'rest' evacuates one more Lord's day of holiness for many), a national Thanksgiving Weekend devoted to sport and to the onset of the pagan Christmas shopping period. Had not earlier baptists who altogether rejected all this some insight? For them, every Sunday was Easter; every Sunday was Pentecost. Nothing more was needed of the calendar. Thus they renounced what they felt they could not redeem, perhaps not reckoning that the omnivorous *weekend* of the industrial West would soon swallow up even their minimal rhythm of time.

Yet those radicals were right to retain the weekly rhythm of work and wonder, and wrong only to despair of any more extended Christian patterns in time. Massey Shepherd (quiet revolutionary, my friend of beloved memory) construed Christian worship as a reinterpretation of the whole of time. He saw the Christian year divided into two halves, with 'Pentecost' (meaning the entire fifty days that embrace the resurrection, ascension, and Spirit outpouring of the Lord) at the center, joining the two halves. The first half moves from the first advent of Christ to this pentecostal climax; the second half, appropriating the first, "moves forward to [prefigure] its perfect consummation in the final Advent"—and we are back to Advent again. In both halves, secular history is transformed, because Christians, in keeping this biblically based rhythm, realize here and now the new aeon that with Jesus has broken into earth's diurnal time (Shepherd, 1965:99f).

Massey Shepherd's interpretation brings us to the heart of time and worship. Mircea Eliade discovered that most of the world's religions celebrate a golden past, a mythic origin *"in illo tempore,"* to which mythic past time they return in worship. One may mistakenly suppose that Christianity envisions just such an escape from the present into the past, a return to biblical or past Christian events and circumstances, an archaizing of the faith community. *But that is nearer to fundamentalism than to the prophetic or baptist vision.* For biblical religion appears as an exception to Eliade's general rule (so Eliade, 1949:chap. 4). When Simon Peter on Pentecost said "this is that" (Acts 2:16 KJV), he did not mean that the disciples in Jerusalem had unaccountably traveled backward to Joel's day. He meant that Joel's vision, though revealed (and fully relevant) long before, was a key or frame for *interpreting* the present situation of the disciples. The first Christians did not dwell *in illo tempore*. Rather, as Shepherd insists, their worship looked forward; it was a foretaste of the coming glory of the Lord. True, over long periods of time Christian worship missed its mark by seeking a nostalgic *return* to real or mythical past time. But true biblical worship is never nostalgic and never mythical; its feet are firmly planted in the here and now of today, and its movement is forward, on to the beckoning end. The church

remembers only in order to re-member, and its re-membering, its reconstitution of Christ's body in the gathering, is focused on a future coming
that is already in part realized. Thus those who worship "redeem the
time" (*exagorazomenoi ton kairon*, Eph. 5:16).

b. Its structure.—Those here called baptists are a diverse people. No
single form of worship—no Latin mass, no Book of Common Prayer—
regulates their worship and no traditional model from Anabaptists or
Puritans or revivalists constitutes their norm. That none does may
constitute a strength, suggesting adaptability and sensitivity, or a weakness, implying crass indifference to truth and beauty. In either case, if
we are to discuss here the structure of worship, we need some model, if
only one to criticize. So I will sketch a composite model, the main Lord's
day worship of (fictional) Koinonia Church, a placeholder until better
models are better known, a 'model' in no grander sense than its ordi-
nariness. If Koinonia's practices contravene someone's actual present
practice—that is just a part of the doctrinal task we are about.

The service begins with a preparatory gathering of worshipers well
before the time set (cf. 'devotion' in black Baptist worship). As the
structure of Koinonia's service typifies the whole course of the Christian
life, this **preparation** corresponds to the formation some are currently
undergoing preparatory to baptism. (How shall we stand "on Jordan's
stormy banks" if we are not ready to be taken across? How are we to
meet Jesus anew on this Lord's day if we do not prepare?) So there is
preparatory singing, and prayers of preparation, and brief instruction
concerning the task and theme of the service to follow. Soon all is as
ready as can be. This day's worship is full-orbed, beginning (as does
Christian life itself) with a **baptism.** Here is an open baptistry, shimmer-
ing with water; here are the candidates, wearing baptismal white; now
there is an appeal to God who is Spirit; now Scripture's great words of
invitation and welcome are spoken and sung by the congregation that
has learned them, and now the administrator puts for the final time the
biblical question, "Is anyone prepared to forbid water?" (cf. Acts 10:47),
which the church answers with the consent it has prepared. Praying, the
candidates are baptized; praying hands are laid upon each; and the new
members of the body are led away to dress and make ready for what
follows. (When there is no baptism, Koinonia retains at this place in its
service tokens of its baptisms past and future: song and prayer and
Scripture summons that extend the invitation: "whosoever will.")

Meanwhile the congregation proceeds to the **ministry of the word,**
with its focal sign, *prophetic preaching.* Koinonia Church currently has
two or three who are gifted and trained to preach, and it prepares itself

to receive the prophetic sign by listening to Scripture read aloud, invariably from both Old Testament and New. (To omit the former is Marcionite and anti-Jewish; to omit the latter anachronistic; to omit both is simply pagan.) Members read from one of the best vernacular translations, word-for-word as it stands written (*gegraptai*); thus the church respects serious biblical scholarship. Typically sermons take one of two basic stances: Either *missionary*, addressed to unbelief (and thus in structural terms recalling the sign of baptism that preceded), or *educative*, addressed to faith in search of understanding (and thus structurally foreshadowing the Lord's supper to follow). In either case the sermon's aim is both formative and transformative. It seeks to form unbelief so that it yearns for belief; or it seeks to form existing faith so that it may be transformed anew. For believers need transformations all along the journey,

> Changed from glory into glory,
> Till in heaven we take our place . . .
> (Charles Wesley)

In Koinonia Church **offertory** has developed to include several significant elements: one is the evangelistic invitation to discipleship dramatically foreshadowed in the opening baptismal liturgy. Offertory includes also the making of gifts and the presentation of opportunities for giving—a team is forming to donate needed carpentry, another will establish a prison witness, a class is to train new Bible teachers. Here, too, is the liturgical place to acknowledge **providential signs,** God's gifts to members, designated significant by their place here in the church's prayer and praise (1 Cor. 14:35). Offertory at Koinonia risks chaos and discord, but after some mishaps, ways have been found to channel its variety, via hymns and Scripture sentences and apt, brief prayers, into the flow of the whole service, "for God is not a God of disorder but of peace." Offertory leads to the Lord's table by ending in a prayer that pledges the covenant anew and offers all to Christ Jesus.

At stated times, Koinonia Church proceeds to another room to share the **Lord's table;** on those occasions moving there is part of the liturgy, and that procession comes not now but at the beginning of offertory, so that the events just related would take place in the chosen "upper room." (The same sort of procession was required after baptisms before the church acquired its present baptistry, and that, too, was a debonair parade.) Today everything happens in one space, so members simply gather now about the centrally located, white-cloth-covered table.

"Members" implies some practical distinction here; Koinonia Church chooses to make it simply in terms of participants' intentions: a brief explanation indicates that for those who here renew their baptismal pledges, this is "the Lord's supper"; for any others, it is simply "an *agape* feast" (a familiar term, since the church regularly provides such a meal, especially inviting the hungry in its neighborhood to share).

How can a large congregation gather at one table? No answer suits all cases; somehow the symbolic configuration of disciples at table must emphasize a theological point: one loaf divided, one table shared, one disciple band dining with their Lord as host. As before, prayers, Scripture sentences, songs sung by all (the choir is here dispersed among the congregants), and the servant mode of those who preside underline the divine and human narratives that converge in this sign: Here God feeds the priestly people; here they memorialize their living Lord; here the Spirit transforms a simple rite into a moment in end-time.

> And thus that dark betrayal night
> With the last advent we unite,
> By one blest chain of loving rite,
> Until he come.
>
> (George Rawson)

Koinonia Church (fictional but not false) is far from perfect. What assembly is not? Nevertheless, what can we learn here? They have come to expect a weekly eucharist: this was a change in line with their "early church" studies and their Anabaptist heritage (cf. Yoder, ed., 1973:chap. 2). If they had not, they would be wise nonetheless to exhibit some token of the supper at the conclusion of each offertory time, perhaps by presentation of all the gifts (save bread and wine) at the table, with a closing prayer that gives thanks for Jesus, who is confessedly present in any case. What this congregation does, though, is effectual. Note the main feature: Ministry in worship is returned to the members. All Koinonia members say the ritual words drawn from Scripture (lined out to them until learned); any member here can with training be designated for any role in the liturgy; members discover that just as there is rehearsal for this sign-shaped worship, it is itself rehearsal for the wider worship that is the practice of Christian life (cf. *Ethics*, Eight).

* * * * *

Christians want to be Christian, but they need to learn how. We need a language of liturgy that can become the language of living, just as we need a Christian 'year' and 'week' that can redeem the times. God's language—the sign-language of baptism and sermon and supper—speaks clear and true: God washes; God forms; God feeds. Thereby it becomes a counterlanguage to the language of the principalities and powers (Wilder, 1982), a grammar and vocabulary by which we can speak, act, think, in kingdom ways. In this sense, worship fulfills though it does not exhaust the church's task of **education:** As sharers in the church's worship we take our place as students in the school of Christ. Insofar as worship is not mere symbolizing of something else somewhere else, but (as I have argued above) is itself an action, here is learning by doing. The Apostle Paul made the point long ago: "baptized into . . . him, you have all *put on* Christ like a garment" (Gal. 3:27); "when we bless the cup of blessing, is it not a means of *sharing* in the blood of Christ?" (1 Cor. 10:16). We want to be Christian; happily, in accepting this rule, this dominion, we are formed and transformed to be embodiers of the faith, sharers of the new in Christ.

Further, we want to be witnesses, and a properly **evangelistic** liturgy such as that of (fictional but authentic) Koinonia Church forms our speech into words of life. We say words at church with which we can witness at home or work. We want to render **service** to those in need, and indeed must do so if our Judge and King is to recognize us on judgment day (Matt. 25:31ff): authentic worship teaches us to wash one another's feet in all humility and thus shapes us to serve a sick neighbor whose elemental needs (a bedpan, clean sheets, a bowl of broth) require just such humility. We want to be friends, to share **fellowship** with those of kindred mind; worship changes our minds so that together we learn to "let the same mind be in you [all] that was in Christ Jesus" (Phil. 2:5 NRSV). Then our worship is our life in microcosm. For we are commissioned as disciples (Matt. 28:19f) to

> [1] *baptize them in the name of the Father and the Son and the Holy Spirit*
> [our liturgy, like our discipleship, begins in **baptism**],
> [2] *and teach them to observe all that I have commanded you*
> [the very task of the ministry of the **word**].
> [Since 3] *I will be with you always, to the end of time*
> [the promise that is renewed at the Lord's **table**].

c. Its space.—An architect turned divinity student wrote her theological honors treatise on church architecture. Architects like to illustrate what they write. On the cover she drew a picture that summed up the church builder's task. I anticipated a bold postmodern structure, or perhaps one of the classic buildings of the past, maybe a Christopher Wren church uniquely fitted to its site. To my surprise, the picture was not a building at all. It showed a baptism. The city church had no baptistry, and had placed in the churchyard a movable plastic pool of the sort one finds in suburban backyards. It was filled with water, and a small table stood nearby. Around the pool the people gathered; in it, the baptism began. That was the scene. The architect-theologian thus elegantly made her point: space for worship is not defined by buildings of this or that style, or by buildings at all; it is defined by the gathered people and by the signs enacted in their midst (Linley, 1990).

Yet so close has been the connection between the gathered community and its building that historically the very names have been exchanged: "Ecclesiastical architecture" takes its name from Greek *ekklēsia,* the same root that gave us the word for "church" in Latin and the Romance languages; while the Greek word for a church building, *kyriakon* (sc. *oikon*), "Lord's (house)," became German *Kirche,* Scots "kirk," and English "church." Hence our English word bears both meanings (we meet in a church and we are a church), the genetic link being the idea of a *gathering* community, an assembly, that is at once an organic living society and a textured web of bodies in a particular space over a stretch of time—a fellowship of the Spirit. That student had it right.

The upshot is to give unique yet never ultimate importance to the architectural task. In earliest Christianity there was no separate church meeting place. This fact echoed the beginnings of Israel's worship, which had centered either upon scattered commemorative shrines in the countryside (cf. biblical "Ebenezer") or upon the "tent of meeting," until Solomon's fabled temple rose to take their place. It was not the temple, however, but the synagogue, a kind of gathering begun during Babylonian exile and continued after the return, that furnished the immediate antecedent of Christian assemblies. Although Acts pictures the post-Pentecost community as "one and all [keeping] up their daily attendance at the *temple,* and breaking bread in their *homes . . .*" (2:46, emphasized), this is a selective account of beginnings, and must be set alongside the countryside and lakeshore meetings with the risen Lord in the Gospels, and the references to housechurches in the epistles and the later chapters of Acts. Before Constantine, churches in the Empire could not overtly own property, so even if a building was used exclusively by the community (as perhaps was the case with the archaeological find at Dura-Europos, dated A.D. 231) its nominal owner might be a single member. When in the fourth century, buildings began to be constructed legally as churches, they reflected the developing new theology as well. Now church officers were ranked with magistrates; they were rulers of the Christian domain; what more natural than to exercise their office in buildings like those of their civil counterparts. Thus the Roman *basilica* (from the Greek root *basil,* "king") became the new Christian basilica. At one end an 'apse,' a semicircular projection with raised floor, provided a place for clergy and altar as earlier it had perhaps sheltered an imperial image; the 'narthex,' a porch or vestibule, gave entry at the other; between these ends ran the main long rectangle, what came to be called the 'nave,' not so much a place for seated listeners (there were no fixed seats) as an imposing corridor, forming a pathway to the altar. And this is the floor plan that has survived, with some modifications, for fifteen centuries. Upon it, different elevations have been raised; there were Romanesque and Gothic and Baroque and Modern variations. It is one or another of these basilica-plan erections that still "looks like a church" to millions today.

The problem this basilica fixation presents is not one of architecture but of theology. Good architects are more than willing to translate the church at worship (e.g., the churchyard baptismal gathering described above) into architectural enclosure. Yet until the church can say *and show* more clearly the shape of its worship, why it meets as a fellowship of the Spirit, even the ablest architect cannot adequately enclose its space.

One generally ignored model should be mentioned here—the Byzantine. This did not make the basilica its model. In the sixth century, architects in Constantinople found a way to support a round dome so that it seemed to float over a cube of space below. They repeated this technique with near-magical skill in building Hagia Sophia (532-37) and Ravenna's San Vitale (547). For the Orthodox, the symbolism was cosmic: the cube was earth, the dome heaven; so the worshiper who came to church left earth with its blue-domed sky to enter a new earth (the cube) beneath a new heaven (the dome) where God reigned supreme. Thus the architect captured in space what the liturgy declared true of time: the future is present; this is the house of God, the gate of heaven (cf. Pevsner, 1957:37-40; Micks, 1970). The distinct numinous quality of Byzantine architecture is in no way inimical to baptist worship, which as we saw above (§1) depends on the awesome reality of God's presence.

No healthy architecture can simply copy past achievement. What is required of today's meetinghouse and meeting room? This is not a question for the grand scale only: It arises for churches who meet in a garage or a dining room and those who inherit crumbling basilicas as well. Every assembly has some control over its setting, however decayed or spare. From what has been said here of the structure of worship, four signals radiate: (1) If conversion-baptism is a sign for us, the space for worship must be **accessible;** it must not be a 'sanctuary' from unpleasing visitors. The church must not occupy space that says to any visitor, "Keep out." Ground floor meetinghouses, easy traffic flow from street to assembly, facades that open to the stranger, the fearful, the lame, the alienated, these belong to the gospel house of prayer. (2) If prophetic preaching is a sign for us, the liturgical space must be one where people can see and hear one another. Although this is easier in smaller spaces, even the larger baptist congregation can have a **visible, audible** meeting. My engineer friend Charles K. Leeper tells me acoustical design can provide, *without* the noisome use of amplifiers, space in which a congregation of five hundred can see and hear one another. (3) If servants are not greater than their Master (John 13:16), and the Lord's table provides servant's fare, then church space is **servant's quarters,** not a princely palace. This does not entail rooms either garish or unkempt; even a garage can be comely, even a storefront swept and garnished. A balance must be struck here: Lavish use of costly materials strikes the wrong note, but so does pinchpenny construction; "there is that withholdeth more than is meet" (Prov. 11:24 KJV) in church building, too, and tight-fisted builders waste more than those who plan (and spend) well. (4) Finally, we return to the theme of divine presence. "How awesome is this place! This is none other than the house of God; it is the gateway to heaven," exclaimed Jacob. He was in no building, but had camped at a lonely wayside shrine, where in his sleep he had dreamed a dream (Gen. 28:11-17). If in our meetinghouse of prayer we sense the awesome presence of the holy One, is it not a place where great dreams can be dreamed? Such **numinous space** may call to mind the wonder of San Vitale, or the simplest chapel in the woods, or no building that ever was. It may be that in these matters evangelical Christianity is still in its early childhood—our great plans not yet drawn or built. Whether or not that is so, we are to remember the limitations of any building. Solomon at the dedication of the temple asks:

> But can God indeed dwell on earth? Heaven itself, the highest heaven, cannot contain you; how much less this house that I have built! (1 Kings 8:27)

We are brought again to the wider sense in which the living Christ is the new temple, all the cosmos his sphere, all our lives the liturgy in which we offer in him "our reasonable worship."

* * * * *

Worship was chosen as a focus for understanding Christian community partly because lines lead from it to every part of Christian teaching: We cannot say what Christian worship must be without invoking God's salvific dominion over all to the end of time, without meeting at the center Jesus crucified and risen, without encountering the throbbing fellowship of the Spirit. To ask what the church must teach about worship to be the church is implicitly to inquire into all this. The task of this chapter has been to develop an account of worship, particularly of its remembering signs, and to glimpse its actual shape in such a way that our teaching about worship will cohere with all we teach. Yet something is lacking yet. I think it is this: when the church worships, it necessarily turns inward, finding its Lord but also itself. That centripetal movement is ordained for us and is "meet and right." Yet that movement if taken alone misrepresents church and kingdom. Besides the turn in, there is a turn out; besides liturgy, mission. That other, *centrifugal* movement is ordained for the church as well. Indeed, that has been represented here. Worship has been displayed as mission-oriented, outreaching, inclusive. Yet more must be said if we are to have a faithful view of the fellowship of the Spirit, and so we turn now to a concluding chapter on Holy Spirit and mission.

CHAPTER TEN

Holy Spirit and Mission

Explaining the Spirit is a difficult task—difficult, and not, as some say, merely neglected. It is not easy, though, to say whether the difficulty lies mainly in the struggle between rival interpretations (for example, Pentecostal versus 'orthodox' views), or is a difficulty more deeply embedded in the obscurity of the subject itself. Is 'Spirit' difficult because ecstatics such as Montanists and Pentecostals have over the centuries sought to wrest the understanding of the Holy Spirit away from more traditional Catholics and Protestants and vice versa, or because the very concept of the inner life of God in radical intimacy with our inner lives is perplexing and elusive? (cf. Hendry, 1956:11) In either case, the task here is to find out what is true and solid without falling into dense jargon or irrational appeals to 'mystery,' or on the other side taking up partial views that explain this vital doctrine ever so clearly, but do so at the expense of the full truth of the matter.

The theme of mission or evangelism, on the other hand, is a familiar one in Christian discourse. Without missionaries, there would be no Christian faith on earth. In the economy of the gospel, faith depends on hearing the glad tidings, which depends upon someone's being sent, whether from near or far—whether the 'beautiful footsteps' of the evangelist must walk a long distance or only as far as from a neighbor's house (cf. Rom. 10:14f). Here the surprise is that systematic theologians have rarely listed mission among the essential theological doctrines, leaving it aside as only a study of effective methods. (Thus this volume

417

displays some originality in treating *mission* as an essential part of doctrinal theology.) Certainly the question, whether and how those who have not followed Jesus' way are offered redemption in God's kingdom, or (to put it another way) whether outside the church there is salvation, has always concerned Christian doctrine and practice. Here, rather than relating the Spirit only to the inner life of the Trinity, or only to the spiritual development of each disciple (themes already explored in Chapters Seven and Three respectively), I hope to show that it is exactly by taking up the doctrine of God's Spirit in its relation to mission that we gain clarity about both questions, about our task (mission) and about God's holy nearness (Spirit).

If fellowship is the true genius of authentic Christian community (Chapter Eight), what reason have we to be hopeful even about our own churches? Is not one feature of all human existence on this planet, religious or other, the persistent enmity that not only divides human communities from one another but rends them within? And has the church been any different in this regard? Have not church folk rather persistently been part of the old quarrels between peoples and races and classes and sexes, been party to them, even been provokers of them? One has only to think of the history of warfare in modern times to recall the churches' sponsorship and chaplaincy of almost every war fought—usually on both sides! The same is true even where division has not issued in armed conflict, but only in setting group against group in the economic and cultural and ideological orders. In face of these facts, it may seem fatuous to consider the 'people of God,' the 'church universal,' as anything other than a divisive (and much divided) class of religious adherents. These facts cast into deep doubt the image presented here of church as a *redemptive* community (Chapter Eight). The faithful response is to concede the truth, so far as it is true, and to go on to recognize that the church is a redemptive community only when and as its mission is determined by God the Spirit: God's Holy Spirit alone creates the church as a uniting and redemptive community. By the Spirit and only by the Spirit is there born a divine fellowship that overcomes all division between creature and creature as well as between creature and Creator, for as we will see here, fellowship and ecstasy are the Spirit's ultimate gifts. These gifts were the dual themes of the first Christian Pentecost (Acts 2). Pentecost showed that one new human race, redeemed and reconciled to God and thereby joined into one, was the mission goal of the Holy Spirit.

This declaration is the thesis of the present chapter. We will begin (**§1**) with the challenging modern discovery of the many **'world religions'**— a discovery that has led to rethinking Christian mission. This will lead in turn (§2) to a mission-centered restatement of the **doctrine of the Spirit.** Finally, (§3) the very meaning of church will itself require further refinement in this chapter insofar as the church is disclosed as the locus of the Spirit's missionary action, **the place where ecstasy and fellowship converge.** By using the freshly clarified concept of *sign* (Chapter Nine), we can see the church not merely as a source of conflict, though sometimes it is that, but as a recurring historic sign of the realm where God rules, the dominion or reign of God. In other words, in this chapter we are to see what the church of Jesus Christ must teach about Holy Spirit and mission if that church is itself to be a community of the Spirit.

§1. The Mandate of Mission

What a section headed "the mandate of mission" must say will seem obvious to many Christian readers: *Every Christian is commissioned, like Jesus at his baptism, to be a missionary. This is made explicit in the Great Commission (e.g., in Matt. 28:19f. [cf. Mark 16:15ff]; Acts 1:8), a marching order that by the baptist vision applies to every disciple now as it did then. To be missionaries is to proclaim in our words and by our lives that Jesus is the Christ, the Savior of the world, so that 'all nations' are summoned to a like discipleship. Though the task is difficult and costly, those who obey it are promised power from on high: they will be equipped by God's Spirit to give their witness and to bear its cost.* What more need be said?

Properly interpreted, these words certainly do express the theme of this chapter. Yet if we are to be good teachers of doctrine we cannot simply make such assertions and expect agreement, or even comprehension, even from otherwise open-minded Christians today. For everyone now knows some disquieting counter-facts. The dignity of all peoples, their right to 'their own religions,' the long association of Christian missions with Western colonialism, the urgency of other needs of the world's peoples (for political autonomy, for physical sustenance, for freedom from oppression), and the rival claims of non-Christian religions have made the preceding description of the Christian mission suspect. Catholic theologian Hans Küng, no dogmatist, and himself a friend to much that this book advocates, sums up the doubter's case: In the countries (India, China) where significant "world religions" already existed, four hundred years of Christian mission have made only an imperceptible difference (a few years ago Küng found only .5 percent of Chinese, at most 2 percent of Indians reported as Christian). Hinduism, Buddhism, Confucianism, Taoism, and Islam have each deflected Christian evangelization in their respective areas. (Indeed, the Christian mission has sometimes stimulated counter-revivals of these ancient religions.) And (Catholic) Christianity, Küng says, has at last acknowledged these facts by teaching that there is salvation outside the Catholic and outside every church: all people "of goodwill" can attain salvation *in their own religions;* following Karl Rahner, these may be called "anonymous Christians" (Küng, 1976:89-100). If there is salvation in the world's religions, is that not enough? Why missions?

a. A fresh analysis of religion and religions.—We must add at once that Küng does not go on to reject the Christian world mission. In fact he rather scorns the imperialism implied in Rahner's phrase "anonymous Christians"; it is a mistake to treat all religions alike. Christianity, if no longer the exclusive way of salvation, must nonetheless be considered the bearer of a unique role *among* the religions. For Küng, this role is to minister to people in all religions, to be a "critical catalyst and crystallization point" in terms of which a great and mutually beneficial dialogue of religions can occur. This dialogue will require Christians to ask afresh, "What is really Christian?" even while they pursue a world mission, not of conversion, but of mutual understanding (Küng, 1976:100-116).

Yet recent thinking in the human and social sciences has provided a fresh analysis of religion and religions that may require a different conclusion. Rather than Küng's picture of "world religions in dialogue," this thinking, as we are shortly to see, makes way for the classic interpretation of the Great Commission. To see it in proper perspective, it will be helpful to provide a preliminary summary of historical thought about religion and religions. (A fuller discussion of Christianity among the religions is to appear in *Volume III.*)

An early Christian view attributed belief in the pagan gods to demonic influence (e.g., Tertullian, *Apol.,* xxiii). In effect, early writers explained the many religions as Satan's work. This may seem extreme, but it had the merit of exculpating pagan devotees—they had only been deceived by a demon; their gods were in reality demons. Nor is this ancient view merely forgotten: demythologized, it passed into the outlook of the eighteenth-century European Enlightenment, which taught that all religions are rooted in primitive error and confusion (Hume, 1777a:ii). Christianity was false, along with all the rest. Some Enlightenment philosophers offered a further twist: At least deism is true, and insofar as the several religions express the doctrines of deism (that God created the world, established the immutable laws of its operation, and will be its final judge) philosophy endorsed these religions. Alongside these Enlightened theories we may conveniently place the twentieth-century view of Karl Barth, Dietrich Bonhoeffer, and their followers: All religion, including Christianity *as a religion*, is to be identified with the story of the tower of Babel, a human attempt to climb godward; as such all religion is guilty of arrogant pride, and is condemned by the gospel. Not in the religions, said this approach, not even in Christianity as a religion, but only in the gospel has God spoken a truly humane and saving word.

This twentieth-century view, however, was not derived directly from the Enlightenment, but appeared in reaction to an intervening theory, the romantic glorification of religion that typified the nineteenth century. For the romantics, religion as such is a human good. Historical religions all point to and partake of the same 'reality'; they are alternate variations on a theme, complementary paintings of a single landscape. On this romantic view religion is not demonic falsehood but human aspiration. So the religions are not to be discarded as false, though they may certainly be ranked in order of value or comprehensiveness or 'finality.' Most advocates of the romantic view, being Christian, unsurprisingly named Christianity the 'final' religion (thereby pinning the best-of-class ribbon on their own chests). The chief advocates of this view were Schleiermacher and Hegel (preceded by Lessing and Kant); liberal theologians from their time to the present are their successors. Along the way, historicist understanding further relativized all religious claims—a key figure here was Ernst Troeltsch.

There is now a third view. While it contains some elements of the other two, it adds a new standpoint. On this third view a religion is a set of powerful *practices* that embody the life-forming convictions of its practitioners. There *is* no 'essence' of religion; religions are neither with the romantics all more or less true nor with the demonics all more or less evil. It follows that generalizations about religion are generally mistaken, since religions differ in kind, and only concrete, sympathetic historical and empirical study can tell us about any particular religion. We may call this the *practical theory* of religion, not in the sense that the theory itself is practical or effective (though it may turn out to be so), but in the sense that its concern is the life-shaping (as I will say, the convictional) *practices* religions embody. So religions are not to be identified with their abstracted teachings, far less with their 'errors.' Perhaps some who have employed this practical theory in previous centuries have been skilled missionaries, but we owe its present form to anthropologists and sociologists (e.g., Geertz, 1966, 1968; Bellah, 1968) and to theologian George Lindbeck, who dubs it the "cultural-linguistic" theory of religion (1984:chap. 2).

The practical theory has surprising theological consequences. To the extent that we use it, we are free to reject the numbing anti-mission dogma that "all religions are the same" as well as the inflammatory thesis that "all religions reflect human (or demonic) wickedness." Instead, this theory invites us again and again to look and see, and it is mainly work within its paradigm that has permitted the remarkable advances in the study of religions that have characterized the twentieth century (summarized, e.g., in Hutchison, 1991).

Moreover, the practical theory provides a clearer view of the nature and limits of Christian doctrine as well, a matter of crucial import for mission theory. As an example, consider once more the Christian doctrine of salvation. By the practical theory of religion, any doctrine discloses its meaning only within the practices and convictions of the community that embraces it. So what Christians call "salvation" is *not simply another word for* what Hindus call deliverance *(moksha)*, or simply another word for what Buddhists call release *(nirvana)*. This is so because the contents of religion are not typical experiences to which the religions just happen to have given different names. "Salvation" in Christian terms is not just any experience of success or religious attainment, but is having a share in the liberation and healing associated with the rule of God Jesus proclaimed (Part I). Salvation is exactly the 'success' that comes when in faith one shares the practices and convictions of that new rule, and to intelligent outsiders, that may seem more like failure than success! Salvation must mean exactly this (and not, for example, adopting one or another outlook or worldview) because, by the practical theory, the doctrines and language of a community are necessarily understood *in terms of its practices*. Christian practices include taking the way of the cross; they also include living one's life in the presence of the one Christians learn to identify as Jesus the risen Christ (see Chapters Five and Six), and Christian convictions include the conviction that this Risen One is fully divine (Chapter Seven). To talk of the salvation of non-Christians (or of misnamed 'Christians') apart from taking that cross, apart from living in that presence, apart from acknowledging that divinity is not as some have supposed to give salvation a *wider* meaning; it is rather to empty it of its real meaning. Talk of Christian salvation without Christian practices and Christian convictions is like talk of a fire that consumes no oxygen and releases no heat, like talk of a society that has no members and remembers no history. We simply have no way to conceive such 'fires' or envision such 'societies.' So when the Christian doctrine of mission indicates the need of *all* for salvation, it does not intend a vague need for all to be 'better,' though no doubt all of us do need to be better in some sense. Salvation for all means in part that the good news of God's Rule and the promise of new life in Christ are announced without any exclusive limits; kingdom membership is open; to be human qualifies one to become a subscriber to this good news. But to be the actual, glad recipient of salvation (cf. Acts 17:11f) is infinitely more; it is to be or to become a member under the reign of Christ, and (at least prospectively) to be a member of a human community that shares kingdom practices and convictions, in other words, a member of the church. Thus *extra ecclesiam nulla salus* ("outside church, no salvation") is true, not in Cyprian's Catholic-party sense, but in the sense that *the very meaning* of the word "salvation" (or *salus*) in Christian use turns upon the shared life Christians take up when they come to Christ.

Two further remarks need to be related here: First, similar points can be made about the "judgment" and "condemnation" and "damnation" that are so prominent a part of Jesus' teaching but tend to embarrass armchair Christians. On the practical theory of religion, the meaning and application of such terms as these is determined in relation to the community of practice in which they appear. It follows that they have no clear application *outside* the bounds of that community: Those who stand in risk of Jesus' hell (see e.g., Matt. 5:22; Mark 9:43-47; Luke 12:5, etc.) are not some unknown pagans, but are nominally God's own people; they are people within hearing of Jesus' gospel. Here we can correct an often repeated but needless doctrinal mistake. The plight of non-Christians (see 1 Thess. 1:9f; 2 Thess. 1:8-12) is quite adequately and profoundly expressed by saying that they need Jesus; this means, though, that the coming of the gospel brings with it both great opportunity and great risk (see further Chapters Two and Three).

Second, since as the sociologists are quick to assure us the practical theory is a second-order theory, about religion in general, it is not as such a part of any religion's doctrine. Thus there can be no corresponding objection to applying it to other communities than the Christian one; it is as true of other religious communities as it is of Christianity that their languages and doctrines are to be understood only within their own contexts of conviction and practice. If we are not all anonymous Christians, we need not be taken to be anonymous Buddhists, either. So Christians are in no position to claim, in nineteenth-century terms, that their religion is better than or subsumes all other religions. The doctrinal lesson follows: if the practical theory of religion be accepted (and there are compelling theoretical reasons to accept it), the existence of other religions constitutes no theoretical obstacle to Christian obedience to the Great Commission, which teaches a missionary existence for disciples based not on 'superiority' but on obedience. One of the necessary practices of the Christian community (in a strict, philosophical sense of "necessary") is the practice of evangelism or mission. Not only are Christians free to obey the great Commission, they are in fact obliged by the content of Christian faith itself to do so. It is their own salvation, and not in the first place their neighbors', that is at stake in the task. For how can they be Jesus' people if they ignore his mandate? This is entirely too important a point to allow for any lack of clarity. The practical theory of religions frees us to see that mission is one of the integral practices of the religion we call Christian, that without it Christianity *dis*-integrates, that is, loses its integrity. In short, to be Christian is to be on mission. Hence, the final motivation for mission need not rest in the unanswerable question of the status before God of those to whom we are sent, but rather on the far more immediate question of our own status as Christ's disciples. This means that we had better turn our attention to the question, What constitutes faithful obedience to this mission?

b. The missionary Spirit of the gospel.—Many Christians today live as though the following account were true: "Once Christian missions were truly important, even essential. When our ancestors adopted the faith they were benighted heathens who stood in great need of missionaries. Now, however, the gospel is spread worldwide; all who freely wish to believe may do so, and those who do not believe are either bad folk who deserve no help or good folk who rightly adhere to their own religions. In these other religions they find salvation. Anyway, the missions of modern times have become agents of Western colonialism and should be terminated with colonialism. Times change; the age of mission is ended." Perhaps it is well that this tacit account is usually left unspoken, for it is full of glaring errors and inconsistencies. Consider a few facts: First, the world in which the gospel first appeared was not lacking in powerful, rival religions; not least, there were the mystery cults of the first century. Second, Christianity has indeed now grown to global size, but powerful forces still block access to the gospel for those in many cultures, including American culture. Third, nothing in Christian ethics or Christian doctrine justifies the division of the world into 'good folk' and 'bad folk'; Jesus' announcement to some scribes that he came to call not the virtuous, but sinners, is nothing if not ironic (see Mark 2:17 par.). And fourth, if we reject (along with the 'demonic') the 'romantic' theory of religion described above, there is no good reason to abandon to assorted other religions the missionary task that the risen Lord entrusted to his own followers (Matt. 28:18-20 par.). This ongoing task is the discipling *(mathēteusate)* of all nations, that is, all peoples, all cultures, all human life. Admittedly, Christian missions have often been perverted or subverted to other ends including economic and nationalistic ones;

more often, though, missionaries have challenged and been opposed by state and corporate tyrannies that interfered with the coming rule. For a single example among many, Ann and Adoniram Judson, arriving as missionaries in Calcutta, found their stay in India forbidden, not by an oriental rajah, but by that powerful Western European corporate interest, the British East India Company (C. Anderson, 1956:95ff; cf. Dodwell, ed., 1963:pass.).

The true story of the gospel mission to the nations properly begins with Paul the Apostle. There has been much discussion of Paul's missionary method, some of it naive, but if we confine ourselves to the letters most surely from Paul's hand, we can say with certainty that he traveled from place to place within the Roman-Hellenistic world and on its borders, establishing upon the authority of Jesus Messiah redemptive communities (*ekklēsiai*, literally, gathered assemblies) that were racially, culturally, and gender inclusive, communities whose members lived as conscious participants in a new age rushing to its climax, a new world made theirs by the Spirit of God. God was the God of Israel, the providential God of Jew and Gentile, whose ancient saving love was now at the end of the times disclosed in a Servant (*pais*, child) whom he had raised from the dead "according to the Spirit of holiness"—that is, in line with that Spirit who is by nature true God. This was at once Paul's method and his message—the two are inseparable—and it led him not only to preach the gospel at Rome the imperial capital (as it were, *en passant*) but also to press on beyond the cultural world of Jews and Hellenes to evangelize the distant 'barbarians' (Rom. 1:14; 15:24).

Early in the twentieth century the missionary theorist Roland Allen published a provocative and influential volume, *Missionary Methods, St. Paul's or Ours?* (1912), that compared Paul's style of church planting with that of modern mission agencies. Only one feature of this comparison or contrast, but that a central one, need engage us here. Allen contended that Paul, having (1) proclaimed the good news of Jesus Messiah and the resurrection, (2) brought his converts "into personal contact with the divine source of life," (3) opened to them a way of reading the Scripture, and (4) shown them baptism and the Lord's supper, was characteristically ready to move on at once to another field. Utterly lacking, in the intensive but brief training Paul provided, were the administrative controls, the property arrangements, the financial purse strings, and above all the continual supervisory ministry that later mission boards have deemed indispensable (Allen, 1912:Part 3).

Now Roland Allen's thesis, and these undisputed facts about Paul's method, are fairly well known. My only point here is to ask how it is, Paul being both an intelligent and a Christianly convinced man, that he was willing to take such radical risks with his new converts? Knowing the temptations and distractions that had faced others and would face them, why did he dare leave his converts at Philippi and Thessalonica and Athens and Corinth to work out the shape of their Christian life— church order, ministry and ordination, doctrinal development, a common morality—on their own? Can the answer be that Paul believed they would not be alone? That in his absence as in his presence they would still confront the risen Christ? And that they would still belong to a fellowship bound together by the Spirit of God, guiding them into exactly that confrontation? We must pursue this question.

   c. The doctrine of the open door.—New Testament scholarship tells us that Paul the Missionary believed that the world was coming to an end. In fact, the world as he knew it did pass away, though it did not end as he expected. Instead, the ancient world was superseded by another, and that by still another, until today we in the West live in an age twice removed from his. If we view the matter in terms of the mission he began, Christian history after Paul has displayed a stubborn complexity. On the one hand enlarged awareness of the inhabited world has been accompanied by an enlarged mission vision. Where for Paul, Spain was at the world's edge, Christianity today is a global faith. The Bible (or portions of it) have been translated into more than the poetic "thousand tongues"; works of mercy in Jesus' name are performed from Phnom Penh to Calcutta to Addis Ababa, from city slums to remote fastnesses, on a scale that Paul could not have envisioned, and the righteousness of the kingdom gives nerve to the long struggle for justice from Gdansk to Buenos Aires, from Moscow to Cape Town to Washington, D.C. Yet all these gains are qualified by severe losses. Though the early gospel spread both West and East, the Christian lands of the East were overrun by the sword of Islam after the seventh century, and thereafter vast regions were closed to the gospel. Though the message penetrated pagan Europe and the Americas, regions where simple animisms and polytheisms had previously prevailed, the past four hundred years have yielded much smaller fruit in the mission fields of India and China (Korea may be an important exception), dominated as they are by what van Leeuwen (1964) has called "ontocratic" civilizations. While Christian membership has steadily grown, the non-Christian population of the world has grown even faster—in part, we should add, because of Christian ministries of medicine, sanitation, and peacemaking. Moreover, the gains claimed by Christianity East and West have often been achieved by conquest and edict and have been perpetuated by cultlike adherence to traditional rites, so that these traditional 'Christian' lands seem more nearly inoculated against faith in Jesus Christ than infected with it. In the West, on the other hand, the development of culture has entered a secular phase that makes biblical faith an affront to many, with the consequence that in the nations where it long flourished, Christianity seems now to be shrinking, even dying. Empty churches in many Western countries signal this loss of faith.

The response to these obstacles and setbacks has been a flurry of conflicting advice from mission theorists and leaders. For example, a World Congress of Evangelicals held in Lausanne, Switzerland, in 1974, subscribed a Covenant which noted that two-thirds of the human race was as yet not evangelized and which confessed that this constituted "a standing rebuke to us and to the whole church" (Lausanne Covenant, 1974, art. 9, in Douglas, ed., 1975:6). Personal evangelism was lifted up. The slogan of that Congress was "reaching the unreached." Yet a little earlier a World Mission Conference convened by the World Council of Churches in Bangkok, Thailand, had instead emphasized the relation of salvation to the many areas of life. For Bangkok, 1973, salvation was holistic. It was expressed in the struggle for economic justice and human dignity; it was "salvation of the soul and the body, of the individual and society, mankind and 'the groaning creation' (Rom. 8:19)." Salvation was "the peace of the people in Vietnam, independence in Angola, justice and reconciliation in Northern Ireland . . ." (*Bangkok*, 1974:88-90). Thus Bangkok implied that it is those Christians who work together for certain political and social ends (they and they alone?) who are properly engaged in evangelism.

Presented in this way, the two standpoints seem utterly contradictory. Salvation is one thing to Bangkok, to Lausanne another, perhaps to Rome another still. But should we pit them against one another thus? Emilio Castro (1927–), the Argentinian Methodist General Secretary of the World Council of Churches, could construe these and other views as parts of a single whole. Of course, as Bangkok had said, Christ's salvation is for the whole human reality, in all its social, economic, political, and religious dimensions, overcoming all divisions and ending all injustice and oppression. What Bible reader could suppose less? And of course, as Lausanne had said, salvation is ineffectual except as it touches each life with the life in Christ: "the gospel needs to be shared." For Castro the debate came down to a tension between a call to evoke faith in the unreached (Lausanne) and a complementary call to faithfulness on the part of the mission church itself (Bangkok). Both are necessary; neither is dispensable. (An attentive reading of Lausanne, we might add, shows it far from indifferent to social concern.) What remained was a question of strategy: is the world church to give priority to "reaching the unreached," or to "the struggle for justice for the poor"? Castro's answer was that "faith" and "faithfulness" cannot be rival methods, but only alternative entry points for the gospel. One situation (say in Belfast?) may demand one of these entries; another (say in Seoul?) the other. There are situations where an authentic gospel can be heard only when preceded by such signs of God's rule as costly peacemaking; there are other situations whose immediate demand is church growth that may itself constitute such a sign (cf. Castro, 1985:chap. 2; cf. Stromberg, ed., 1985). This analysis is close to the approach attempted in this chapter. To display it further, however, we must introduce still another New Testament theme, that of the open door.

The New Testament presents the Holy Spirit as the power by which in an often antagonistic world, gospel work is accomplished. Yet this kind of power is not some sort of religious magic, simply at the command of the human actors, the missionaries. Rather the missionaries are themselves commanded and constrained by the presiding and superintending Spirit.

> Thus the Spirit showed the church how to proceed in proclaiming the gospel and how not to. Philip was sent to the Ethiopian treasurer ([Acts] 8:29), Peter, against his own wishes, to the Gentile Cornelius (10:19; 11:12), Paul and Barnabas on their first missionary journey (13:2,4). . . . And whether it was a physical illness . . . or whether it was a dream (16:9) that stopped him, Paul is prevented by the Spirit from doing missionary work where he really wanted to. (Schweizer, 1980:76)

It is worth noting, Eduard Schweizer adds, that in these passages the Spirit is not sharply distinguished from God and Jesus. It is God who opened a door of faith to the Gentiles (Acts 16:27), but it is the Lord (i.e., the Risen One) who will perhaps permit Paul to remain over winter in Corinth (1 Cor. 16:7), while it is the Spirit who diverts the missionaries from Phrygia (Acts 16:6). There is some distinction, to be sure: Paul (and Luke) seem usually to name "God" when providential circumstances are recognized, but "the Lord Jesus" when authoritative commands are issued, and "the Spirit" when the missionaries' heartfelt awareness of either of these is being emphasized—distinctions that gave rise to later trinitarian reflection (citations in Schweizer, 1980).

How, then, does God who is Spirit work? Running through the New Testament is the image of a door. It can represent access of the missionaries to their task (2 Cor. 2:2). Yet the door that admits the missionaries opens for new believers as well (Acts 14:27), giving them access to the realm the missionaries proclaim. The door image is consummate in

Revelation 3:8, where the "open door which no one can shut" means God-given access to eschatological glory—the door to the great banquet feast of heaven (J. Jeremias, TDNT III:178). What guidance does this image of the open door offer today's missionary strategist? At the least it implies sensitivity to the changing and varied circumstances of earth's peoples. Latin American Liberation theologians are sometimes mistakenly understood to have narrowed the teaching of the gospel to just one remedy, political and economic liberation, addressed to just one sin, oppression. Is it not more accurate to see Liberation Theology as an instance of theological sensitivity to an era of rapid social change in which the peoples of Latin America are more fully entering the culture and economy of the modern West? In such a setting, with its often painful human stress and demand, a church can be of little missionary worth if it fails to recognize the 'open door' created by liberating economic forces and new political convictions—can become useless or worse if it fails to recognize and ally itself with these (Castro, 1985:2-7). For Europe a very different door stands ajar. There a profound problem for evangelization had been created by the old Constantinian fabric that so long enmeshed the church with the standing political order of Rome and its successors. Arend Th. van Leeuwen argued (1964) that secularization is the tearing of that fabric, and as such is the necessary deliverance of the gospel itself, re-establishing the pluralism or cultural diversity which the old regime had suppressed. While secularization's immediate effect is to make Christian faith difficult for many, the freedom from religiosity that it provides may ultimately open the way for a fresh hearing of the gospel on what today seems burnt-over ground.

Still a third instance is the North American situation. Here the open door is not the cry of the people in a time of rapid social change, nor is it the release of church and state from an unholy alliance. North America's distinctive defect might best be described as spiritual barrenness—barrenness in a land of pop entertainment, preoccupation with careers and success, and repeated dismal failures in human relations. As William Dyrness puts it, "We are people who cannot manage relationships, often cannot even understand the social dimension of life" (1989:164). And the painful truth is that these emptinesses invade Christian homes as well: we American Christians are in many cases lonely, or divided from those we loved, or gripped by an insatiable need for distraction from our own thoughts. In these circumstances the "wide door with plenty of opposition" (1 Cor. 16:9) is the invitation to establish for these lonely ones saving clusters of community, bound by webs of koinonic love, bound by "the koinonia (fellowship) of the Holy Spirit" (2 Cor. 13:14).

Other regions—and other epochs—will find other closed and open doors: in China, Africa, India, the Pacific Islands, the Islamic and Marxist lands. In none of them are disciples themselves required to make a way for the gospel to enter. Instead, their task in each is to find and faithfully to follow the way of the providential God, in obedience to Christ the commander, in the strength of the indwelling Spirit. Yet to do so effectively requires an acute sense of the Spirit's way and will. To a more exact investigation of that way and will, and thus of the character of God who is Holy Spirit, we now turn.

§2. The Holy Spirit of Mission

The present chapter states afresh the governing concern of this volume. "What must the church teach?" could be construed as merely a quest for internal consistency in Christian teaching. So construed, our task would be to set forth the church's own 'grammar'—the grammar of faith (Lindbeck, 1984:chap. 6). That is a worthy goal, but it is not enough. For theological doctrine must display the church's mission in and to the world. Our task is not only to clarify the grammar of faith but to furnish a tongue-tied world with language adequate to Christ's presence in its midst, and this may require a dialogue of religions and worldviews, not as the ultimate end of mission, but as its necessary prerequisite. By bringing the "nations" of the Great Commission of Matthew 28 within the scope of the question "What must the church teach?" this chapter declares that the answer to that question cannot be found merely by refining Christian utterance, but must go on to provide the nations (including each disciple's own nation) with a language in which all can declare the truth of God. So the task of mission is no narrow proselytism; it must rather be an evangelism concerned with the course of world history, with the gospel encounter with culture, with the shape of life on this planet (cf. Hauerwas, 1985). Evangelism's task is the gifting with speech of nations that use another speech; it is the superseding of every nation's speech by a truer speech in a language more adequate to human destiny under God. Who is sufficient for these things (cf. 2 Cor. 2:16)? It is exactly this question that drives us to inquire about God who is Holy Spirit.

For the concept of God as Spirit, as utterly holy Spirit, is among the boldest human thought confronts. Already (Chapter Seven) we have seen the harvest of some millennia of postbiblical reflection on the Spirit. That the Spirit is truly and fully divine, distinctly hypostatic or 'personal,' eternal and not a creature, divinely free and holy, all this in ways defined with some precision—these results of theological reflection have been embodied in Catholic and Protestant creeds and confessions and have often been acknowledged by baptists, where they employed such confessional machinery, as well. What we have now to recall is that an equally exalted role is already claimed for God's Spirit in the pages of the two Testaments, though there the language is narrative-formed, doxological, and 'spiritual,' rather than the later ecclesiastical or philosophical styles. The Scriptures' Spirit rages over primeval chaos, hurls power into holy prophets, furnishes intricate skill for sacred temple laborers, bears fruit in the matrix of a maiden's body, descends upon Messiah Jesus to initiate his mission, hovers grieving over recalcitrant Jerusalem, burns a way into a praying mission fellowship, drowns disciples in divine power, leads missionaries into far lands. The Spirit is sought, comes upon men and women, empowers, guides, graces, shapes lives, watches over destinies exactly as God does each of these things. For the Spirit of God *is* God; God is *Holy* Spirit, and this is said as truly (and more convincingly) in Scripture than it is in any creed. The Spirit's concern is as wide as the *shalom* of God's promise; the Spirit indwells the *plērōma* of human destiny; the Spirit draws God and man together into the *basileia* of divine love. Thus the wide mandate of gospel mission widely mirrors the mind of the Spirit. Yet the breadth of the Spirit's workings raises an urgent matter of spiritual guidance: Among all possibilities for us, how are we to know the Spirit's exact will (God's will) for present kingdom tasks?

a. The Spirit of Pentecost.—The question drives us to Pentecost, one among God's mighty historic signs (Chapter Four). On the way from Creation to Consummation, alongside Exodus and Sinai, beyond Calvary and Easter, stands this 'Fiftieth Day' monument to divine purpose. Here the mighty force present in Jesus and his Way is released to waiting disciples and thereby to nations waiting unawares. At Pentecost, via the Spirit, the historic involvement of the Risen One with the wide world begins.

Certainly eventful Pentecost cannot be interpreted apart from its antecedents, apart from Israel's story, from Jesus and his ministry, from the cross, the resurrection, the command to witness in all nations, apart from the prayerful gathering and waiting in Jerusalem. Pentecost came as a climax and incorporation of all that had gone before. Nor can it be understood apart from its consequences: the preaching of a gospel focused upon Jesus the crucified and risen hope of Israel, followed in turn by the conversion and baptism of many, the formation of a living community, and the missionary inclusion of both Jews and non-Jews, events that occupy the remainder of the Acts narrative. It is in this context that we must examine the sign of that day of destiny, with its cluster of miraculous events. The details of the Spirit's inrushing presence—coming upon all together, the sound as of a hurricane, the filling of "all the house," the tongues *as* of fire (the language here becomes fittingly apophatic), the distribution to "each," the speaking in "other tongues," the hearing in "other tongues"—all these illuminate the central fact: Now God's own Spirit occupies, masters, equips each resurrection witness for her or his assigned task of witness to Messiah Jesus as each witness finds his or her proper place in God's long history of salvation.

The immediate outcome of the event (as also of its parallel in John 20:19-23) is that each witness is henceforth fully enabled by God's own indwelling power. Witnesses will not be alone. And Pentecost's import is not confined to those first set alight by the flames. All subsequent disciples are heirs of this sign. It was not necessary that the Ten Commandments be issued afresh to each young Israelite: by the prophetic vision *all* had escaped Egyptian slavery, by it *all* had crossed the Reed Sea, by it *each* had been addressed by the "thou shalt" and the "thou shalt not" of JHWH at Sinai (see Deut. 5:3). Likewise Pentecost declares every Spirit-filled disciple, through all future time, equally endued, equally empowered. Already on that first day the pentecostal Spirit's orbit was widened to embrace three thousand who "received" Simon Peter's word and were in obedience baptized (2:38-41), though nothing is said about further tongues as of flame. That these others did nevertheless share the authority of the gift is evidenced by the sequel—their fellowship and worship, the wonders and signs in their midst, their generosity and their growth (Acts 2:42-47). As it was for them, so by the baptist vision is it for disciples today: Pentecost is here, waiting to be claimed as they claimed it.

i. Character of the Spirit.—What do we learn in this and related passages about the character of God's Holy Spirit? The answer can be summed up in three terms: the Spirit *is missionary;* the Spirit *provides for each disciple;* the Spirit *guides the gathered church.* Not, as for Hegel the philosopher, the development of nations and cultures, sciences and arts, politics and war, but the self-impartation of the very God: that is the divine mission. It is expressed in the call of Abraham ("in you all the families of the earth shall be blessed"—Gen. 12:3 NRSV), in the covenant at Sinai ("be a kingdom of priests"—Exod. 19:6), in the summons of Jesus ("Come to me, all who are weary and whose load is heavy"; "I am in my

Father, and you in me and I in you"—Matt. 11:28; John 14:20). That mission toward ecstasy—the multiplicity of earth's peoples not conformed one to another, but at one with one another in the oneness of God—is shown at Pentecost to express the character of God's Holy Spirit. The Spirit is a *missionary*, as Jesus is a missionary, as Torah's *Adonai* is a missionary God.

Second, in this self-giving, self-imparting role (what Scripture calls the "glory" of God), the Spirit accepts *partners*. It is not the case that only a select few disciples are to be missionaries who therefore receive (as a kind of pay bonus for overseas duty?) special assistance from God's Spirit. Rather the mission is God's own, and all the redeemed are recruited for the task. Witnessing disciples are not supported merely by a providential Father (as so many children needing God's love), nor merely by the example and friendship of an earthly and risen Lord Jesus (as in the story the Gospels tell); they are supported as well, even more immediately, by the present Spirit of Jesus Christ, who enables and guides and completes God's task—completes it in them. This ecstasy is for each, and it is for now.

A third defining feature of intimate pentecostal empowerment and guidance is that it comes to *gathered* disciples: "They were all with one accord in one place." God's action is not confined to gathered congregations. There are also history's crashing judgments; there is also the prophet's mantic word; supremely, there is that one life who is Life itself. But when the world mission of Jesus is launched, the disciples' community is chosen as the ship's company of the Spirit, and Christian community life (thus empowered) takes on a crucial role in history. Something new has appeared on earth: from the womb of messiahship there comes forth the congregation (*ekklēsia*); there the Holy Spirit claims a lasting home on earth. From Pentecost forward, spiritual *congregations* will take up the mission: Jerusalem's church will struggle with church order and ethnicity and the economics of discipleship, and from it disciples "filled with the Spirit" will spread the news. Antioch's assembly will hear the Spirit's bidding and will send out the first mission to the Gentiles. Ephesus' church will experience the inseparability of true discipleship from life in the Spirit, and with other congregations will find in its midst elders equipped for leadership and oversight (*episkopoi*, Acts 20:28). Tyre's assembly will "through the Spirit" warn Paul of danger ahead; and Paul the Missionary, himself Spirit-guided, will turn at last to Rome's congregation for assistance in reaching the end of the earth. The gathered community, for all its frailty and fallibility, will become the Spirit's agency for the world mission of the gospel. But before following this theme out we must address some disturbing questions about the Spirit's work that have divided many Christians.

ii. Pentecostals and Pentecost.—We cannot expect to settle Pentecost's meaning for today without reference to the vast, and impressively mission-oriented, Pentecostal Christian bodies that have sprung into being all over the world in the century now ending. These locate the Acts of the Apostles at the very center of the New Testament canon, while applying to it the idea (which seems a version of the baptist vision) that the Spirit-baptism of Acts is not merely remembered but *replicated* in today's churches. Although Pentecostal teaching takes myriad forms, it typically proclaims a further crisis of personal faith, one that must come after and be distinct from the first crisis of repentance, new birth, and baptism, awaiting every Christian. This second crisis is the baptism of the Holy Spirit, understood as a conscious experience evidenced by specific spiritual gifts, especially by the gift of tongues. Pentecostal worship and community life take form around this distinctive conviction. Along with other Christian bodies, many older baptist denominations (e.g., Mennonites, Baptists, Brethren, Disciples) have been reluctant to hear this Pentecostal witness to the Spirit. (They might do well to recall that their own witness was greeted with general derision when it first appeared.) In contrast consider the estimate of Scottish missionary bishop Lesslie Newbigin, whose little book *The Household of God* (1954) first put many on the track of the baptist vision itself. Newbigin regards the Pentecostals, along with the sixteenth-century Anabaptists, as the very paradigms of that "third force" in Christianity that is neither Protestant nor Catholic and that is in these pages called 'baptist.' And long before our century, that prototypical baptist, Roger Williams, wrote that "trying what a friend, yea what an (esteemed) enemy presents" has ever proved a special means by which differing disciples can come to Christ's truth (1652a:29). Shall Pentecostals' witness, then, remain untried, unheard?

To be sure, it is easy to misjudge the significance of this many-sided movement. What is the meaning of the modern Pentecostal revival, and how should we read its message of tongues and prophecy, healings and miracles, ecstasy and inclusiveness? An easy answer, indeed far too easy, is that this is simply fundamentalism. A much more insightful answer is presented by Swiss theologian Walter J. Hollenweger (1927–), whose work opposes fundamentalism, but whose comprehensive and sympathetic yet self-critical writings on Pentecostalism provide competent scholarly access to it. Here we cannot repeat Hollenweger's rich analysis of Spirit-baptism, speaking in tongues, miracles, and other phenomena, or trace with him and others the complexities of Pentecostal history (besides Hollenweger, 1972, see Dayton, 1987; Lederle, 1988; Burgess, McGee, and Alexander, 1988; Spittler, 1991). It must suffice to relate his sociological and finally theological assessment of the movement, adding our own assessment to his.

Sociologically, Hollenweger finds that the Pentecostal movement provides help and hope for those who realize that they exist on society's fringes. Pentecostal Christianity gives a voice to the voiceless. Thus its distinctive function "is to restore the power of expression to people without identity and powers of speech, and to heal them from the terror of the loss of speech" (1972:459). He finds Pentecostal communities epitomized in the hymns, often in narrative form, that express for the alienated their personal friendship with Jesus. Congregational meetings function also as group therapy for congregants alienated and defeated by life. At weekly, or often daily, meetings, the oppressed believers can pray; here a powerless woman can become a prophet or a preacher. While such compensatory patterns characterize first- and second-generation Pentecostals, at a later stage the movement becomes overtly world-changing; now social action succeeds emotional compensation as the focus of ministry. The highly visible Spirit-gifted phenomena persist through these changes, even when they come to play a more muted role. In sum, the central Pentecostal point "lies in the experience of being taken into a fellowship which involves a change in one's whole way of life, and which develops a scheme of values . . . controlled by [the Pentecostal worship services]" (1972:491). Now this sociological analysis closely coheres with the ecclesiological and cultural understanding already advanced in the present work: a gathering community, a redeemed and redemptive fellowship, these are the essentials of church itself (see e.g., *Ethics*, Eight, as well as Chapter Eight above).

Yet what of the central claims about the gifts of the Spirit? One must recall that Pentecostals and Charismatics form as such no unified movement. They stem from Methodists and American holiness denominations, from black Baptists, from European Reformed and Lutheran bodies, from Catholics and Anglicans, and from still others in the Western world alone (Dayton, 1987:pass.), while Charismatics have appeared in almost every Christian denomination in modern times. Besides the divisions stemming from these multiple origins, the movement has also split over the works of grace: are there three stages, conversion, entire sanctification, Spirit-baptism, or only two, conversion and Spirit-baptism? It has also divided over the concept of the Trinity: are there three divine persons, or is "Jesus only" the true God, as "oneness" Pentecostal bodies hold (cf. Piepkorn, 1977–79:vol. 3)? To these confessional differences one must add that more sophisticated Pentecostals (such as Hollenweger himself) have been trained in the critical use of the Bible, whereas most Pentecostal leaders so far have been fundamentalist in their approach to Scripture, rejecting the results of modern biblical science. Because of such internal contradictions, no simple theological account can sum up Pentecostal self-understanding (see, however, Pearlman, 1948; Nelson, 1948; Duffield and Van Cleave, 1983; Pruitt, 1981; J. R. Williams, 1988–90).

Interpretation comes to its crux, however, in the question of the baptism of the Spirit (Hollenweger, 1972:chap. 24). Pentecostals base their doctrine here upon the Gospel of Luke and especially upon Acts. According to Eduard Schweizer (TDNT VI:396-455), they read correctly: Luke does say that Christians must pray for and receive the Spirit in a distinct experience of grace later than their first conversion. Is Luke's theology, then, in sharp contrast to Paul's, in which every believer has the Spirit, and the extraordinary and ordinary gifts of the Spirit are not to be ranked above one another in value (cf. Romans 12 and 1 Corinthians 12)? If so, Pentecostal practice is based upon Luke's theology, traditional church practice upon Paul's. Still, Hollenweger reasons, we need not choose between the two or attempt to harmonize them, provided both Paul and Luke spoke relative to the context in which each wrote: Paul wrote to young mission churches and sought to temper excessive Spirit claims, Luke to churches that had lost their missionary zeal, urging them to seek an added gift—the Spirit of mission. Thus today's Pentecostal movement, if distinguished from a dogmatic fundamentalism that sometimes dogs it, can speak to churches (and individuals) in contexts that parallel that of the churches addressed by Luke. As Hollenweger says, "There are many people for whom the Lucan testimony is more comprehensible and therefore more appropriate than that of Paul" (1972:341). Yet I cannot rest content here; my concern is that such a contextual resolution leaves aside the urgent central thesis of most Pentecostals—the present applicability of their message to *all* Christians.

b. Signs of Holy Spirit.—This issue constitutes a genuine test case for the present book, since it displays a rift within the wider baptist ecclesial type. Is it theologically possible, under the assumptions that have so far guided us, to bridge the gap between Pentecostals and other baptists? Walter Hollenweger has set an important precedent by his sympathetic yet critical interpretation of the movement. This invites further reflection. So let us begin with a review of some of the major themes of Acts.

It is certainly correct that Luke's two-volume narrative (Luke and Acts) unites mission and the Spirit: where the Spirit is, there mission will flourish. Yet it is also true that Luke unites the Spirit with the rite of baptism, and with repentance toward and faith in the crucified and risen Lord Jesus. The Lucan narratives of normative discipleship in fact link all four themes: (1) hearing the gospel of Jesus Christ so as to repent and trust, (2) accepting baptism in Jesus' name, (3) receiving the Holy Spirit's overwhelming, infilling gift, and (4) a consequent life of witness in accord with the Spirit's saving mission. Again and again, as the gospel makes its way, Acts presents these four motifs together. This is true in the context of the original disciples at Pentecost (Acts 2:1-36), of the (Jewish) converts that very day (2:37–7:60), of the Samaritan converts (8:4-24, though in the Samaritan case, witness is highlighted only in the negative image of Simon Sorcerer's venality), biographically true of Saul or Paul himself (9:1-30), true of the first Gentile converts (10:1-48), true once more in the context of former adherents of John the Baptizer (19:1-6). The contexts vary, but the four themes cohere. It is the chronological order of the four that varies from context to context. The Samaritans receive the Spirit (by the laying on of hands) *after* their baptism (19:5f); Paul receives the Spirit (by the laying on of hands) *before* his baptism (9:17f); the converts at Pentecost are promised the Spirit *upon* their baptism, without mention of the imposition of hands (2:38). Again, the converts at Ephesus give witness by speaking in tongues and prophecy *after* their baptism, while the Gentile converts at Joppa give witness by these same signs "while Peter was still speaking," that is, *before* their baptism, so that (as Peter argues) it would be inappropriate not to baptize them (10:44-47). If there is any logic here other than that of a wooden chronological fidelity to past events, it is that Luke in each case places last the element best suited to his immediate narrative point: usually he makes the overall theme of Acts—the new Christians taking up the Spirit-empowered life of witness—the consummatory element. Sometimes, though, the point he must emphasize for the narrative's sake is the Spirit's inclusion of new categories of converts, overcoming missionary reluctance (e.g., Acts 10:47), and then that overlooked element comes emphatically last.

Thus the wider significance of Pentecostals for today's theology cannot merely be the rather patronizing insight that these, too, are God's children. Of course they are, but a theology that sees only that would be as backward as those apostles who reluctantly concluded that Gentiles could after all be disciples of Christ! Rather I believe that what the Spirit is saying by means of the Pentecostal revival is that *all God's children must be pentecostal*—since all share the Spirit, since all are called to be missionaries, since all require fellowship in the Spirit. The highly visible ecstasy-and-fellowship of Pentecostals is the Spirit's fresh signal that **ecstasy and**

fellowship are the distinguishing marks of the Spirit of God—the gifts of God who is Spirit and who in coming to us brings us into intimate relation with the Spirit and with one another (cf. Edwards, 1741). This does not mean that all of us must adopt each element of Pentecostal doctrinal teaching. By logic we cannot, for as we have seen, the concrete details vary crucially among Pentecostals themselves. This volume has already distinctly addressed the problems of the *ordo salutis* and the theology of Christian growth or spirituality (Chapter Three), while *Ethics* (especially Eight) sought to address the related topic of the relation of the church to its cultural context. The inescapable and necessary message of Pentecostals is undiminished by these judgments; to repeat, it is that the reality of present enjoyment in the Christian life, of Spirit-given full salvation now (albeit only a rich foretaste of eternal salvation) is fully claimed and rightly shared by all who bow the knee to Jesus Christ as Lord.

What, then, of those ordinary and extraordinary gifts or fruits of the Spirit, gifts or fruits not unlike those so carefully listed by (not Luke, but) Paul in Romans 12, 1 Corinthians 12, Galatians 5, and elsewhere? Already we have seen in Chapter Four that modern science and rational thought do not disprove a world in which events beyond the scope or ken of our everyday experience occur. We saw there as well that biblical religion has no stake in the marvelous for its own sake, so that the authentic works of biblical faith are best understood not as secular marvels, so-called 'miracles,' but as *signs* of the kingdom, evidencing God's presence and action for the coming Rule. There we distinguished three major classes of sign, *historic signs* (of which Exodus, Calvary, Easter, and Pentecost are prime examples), *remembering (anamnesis) signs* (of which the Sabbath, baptism, Lord's supper, and preaching are chief instances), and *providential signs*. These last are particular disclosures given to particular men and women or communities, indicating the relevance of the good news to the course of their own lives in particular circumstances. It is in this third category that we can class the Pentecostal phenomena in our times, giving a voice to the voiceless, strength to the weak of body and weak of soul, and guidance to them and to the entire people of God for a renewal of mission in a world weary of its own injustice and alienation and insignificance. Of course these signs can be abused and misused. In particular, God's signs can be tarnished and cast aside by believers who fail to listen and fail to obey—remember Simon Sorcerer (Acts 8:9-24). But the possibility of abuse implies the reality of right use. The signs vouchsafed the Pentecostals assure them that they are not left out by the Spirit of God. Yet these very signs are meant for the other disciples as well, declaring the Spirit's concern for all the churches. Ultimately they are signs for the whole world, as through Pentecostals and many, many others, the Spirit witnesses to Jesus Christ, thus glorifying God the Father.

§3. The End of Mission

Since evangelism is intrinsic to Christian mission, the teaching church must be aware of its potential—and alert to its perversions. A tragi-comic logic defeats many attempts to realize the Christian mission through the practice of evangelism. When the church's defining character becomes growth, its highest goal the making of converts, then church may be perceived as of little worth in itself: the church exists only as an extrinsic instrument, a means to something that it is not. Then the church preaches a grace it cannot honestly confess because it does not itself embody that grace. Put a little differently, if the goal is to win others who will win others who will win others, an infinite regress of mere recruitment has taken the place of any real (or realistic) understanding of the point of evangelism. Recruited to what? Certainly this misunderstanding is not the only way churches can misconstrue their task: one thinks of the church that is an ethnic enclave or the church that is a gang of chums or the church that is a fan club for some 'charismatic' leader or the church that is a circle for those of like taste. These entities may be flavored with a soupçon of religion. Yet the admixture simply marks them as perversions of church. Although these and still other perversions are serious, the perversion associated with evangelism is potentially the more demonic, becomes demonic just to the degree that in a crass way it succeeds. Members are added; the institution grows; but in this phony evangelism, the gospel is choked out by that growth. Thus the primary task in this section is to investigate the *point* of Christian mission: When is the news the church announces indeed *eu-angellion*, **good** news? What does it mean to feed (and not merely to bait or entrap) the sheep of Christ's flock (John 21:17; 20:21)? What food does the Spirit provide for those truly evangelized? What is the goal or end of mission? There is a common or single answer to these questions.

a. The Spirit and the end of creation.—The European version of the Christian tradition from Augustine of Hippo (*Conf.* 13:34) through John Calvin (*Inst.* 2.12.5; 3.22.2) has struggled over the question whether redemption from sin was God's ultimate goal in creating the world. If it was, the reasoning goes, God's goal must be contingent on the surd fact of human sinning—God's great purpose must finally be at the beck and call of human perversity, since God's is after all only a remedial goal. Or on the other hand, if redemption from sin was not God's great goal, what was? After Calvin many scholastic Protestants followed his lead by debating, in language Calvin himself had not used, whether the decree to elect some to salvation and others to damnation was "supralapsarian" or "infralapsarian," that is, whether God's logically prior choice was to save some and damn others, with the decree to create the world and permit the lapse or fall being logically subsequent to that electing decree (the supralapsarian view), or whether creation and the permission of the lapse was God's primary decree, with the decree to elect some to damnation and others to salvation logically subsequent to that (the infralapsarian view). On both sides an agreed belief was an iron divine determinism with a willingness to extend it to the eternal double predestination of some to hell and others to heaven. The present work (guided in part by such latter-day Calvinists as Barth) has taken a different path with regard to the doctrine of election (see Chapter Four) and in particular with regard to the terrible "decree" of divine damnation. Yet we will see that a genuinely Christian insight appeared within the supralapsarian-infralapsarian debate of the seventeenth century (showing itself in different ways on the two sides). This genuine insight reflects, even in the arcane vocabulary of their debate, the inner depth of God's redemptive purpose toward the creature, and it received qualified endorsement from Karl Barth, who wrote that the "primal and basic purpose of [a God who in his love is sovereign] is to impart and reveal Himself—and with Himself His glory" (CD III/2 §33, p. 140).

i. The 'glory' of God.—Here for many the moral difficulty will lie in the word "glory"—for we feel it ill becomes a God of love to be concerned with self-glorification. Yet the truth is that the biblical term "glory," when used of God, has a very different, nearly an opposite sense to the one that evokes the objection. In a strict biblical sense "God's glory" means God's character or divinity *emanating to the creature,* so that human beings, as they are "glorified" (cf. Rom. 8:30), come to share God's own character; *they become godlike.* This is the exact sense in which Jonathan Edwards (another sort of Calvinist) used the term in *The End for Which God Created the World* (1765*a*). That end, Edwards said, was precisely God's glory. To grasp his meaning we must relate that work to Edwards' companion 'dissertation,' *The Nature of True Virtue* (1765*b*), written at about the same time. There he argues that genuine human goodness consists exactly in a (godlike) "consent to being," that is, in the affirmation of and delight in God and all that is God's. Taken together, the two dissertations give the picture of a creative (and not merely a redemptive) plan, one that begins as God undertakes to give himself away and that reaches its goal as human selves answer God's gift with consenting, self-giving love toward one another and supremely toward God's own holy being. On this Edwardsean view, the supralapsarians were right to believe that God's intent to bring creatures into fellowship with God was prior to, was higher than the subsidiary intent to overcome the obstacle thrown up by human sin. And the infralapsarians were right in insisting that God's first decree was creative, not simply remedial. Creation, since it is creation in Christ (John 1:1-3), already purposes the good that Christians celebrate in the Redeemer.

Over the centuries this broad, Edwardsean view of the matter has had Christian support outside the Augustinian-Calvinist tradition, for example in the Eastern church. There it has been held that even if no sin had occurred, God's love would have led to the incarnation of Jesus Christ in the world (Ware, 1964:230). In this case God's profound goal was not redemption (which was viewed as a contingent means to a greater end) but sanctification, here understood as the taking up of human life into the divine holiness itself (H. Richardson, 1967:chap. 5). If we understand the Holy Spirit to be God effectively present to sanctify or make holy the creature, this second view is here of great interest.

How does this long and perhaps abstruse theological debate bear on our present question about the end of *mission?* At least for Edwards it did have a bearing: He served a frontier mission (Stockbridge) while writing the two essays just mentioned, and was at the same time involved in the contemporary (and all-important) New England controversy about revival and evangelism, a controversy that foreshadowed much subsequent American religious history. If God's ultimate end in creation was self-impartation, and if God is a holy God, Edwards reasoned, then evangelism, since it enabled that self-impartation, could not be separated from holy living. Evangelistic revival, holy living, and God's ultimate glory were as inseparable as the holy Trinity; they were ingredient to one another, and critics of revival as such would have to be opponents of holy living as well—and thus critics of God's ultimate glory (on this, see *Ethics*, Four). Edwards thus provides a way of relating the two foci of this chapter: the Christian world mission with its call to audacious and costly tasks, and the gift of the Spirit whose intimate presence grants ecstasy in God and fellowship with others. Is such intimacy with God, and with one another in God, indeed the end of mission, the end for which God created us along with all that is?

ii. The fellowship of the Spirit.—Both ecstasy and fellowship were certainly on Paul's mind when he set out to write the admonitory letter we call 1 Corinthians. As Paul saw it, ecstasy, the spiritual enjoyment held high by one party, had disrupted fellowship, the brotherly and sisterly love within the Christian community of his mission church at Corinth. In such a circumstance it might have seemed wise for Paul simply to decry the troubling practices and beliefs of the ecstatic party— a move that would surely have pleased the noncharismatics. Yet on Paul's own view to do so would have been to defeat the wisdom of the gospel itself, "God's hidden wisdom, his secret purpose framed from the very beginning to bring us to our destined glory" (1 Cor. 2:7). What was this hidden wisdom? Paul believed it was knowledge imparted to mature disciples by the Spirit in thought and language that transcended natural understanding and natural discourse. But how could he even raise this topic of transcendent 'wisdom' without playing into the hand of the pretentious Corinthian ecstatics?

To understand Paul's solution, we need to grasp his overall strategy in dealing with the Corinthian Christians. In general, his plan was to argue that Christ—indeed, Christ crucified—*is* the wisdom of God (1 Cor. 1:30). Yet for Paul any such claim required a basis in Scripture, and it is clear from the text of 1 Corinthians that the supporting passage he had in mind *here* was our Second Isaiah, with its Suffering Servant. There 'the cross' stands alongside another Isaiah theme, that of divine self-disclosure: As Paul wrote, "Scripture [i.e. Second Isaiah] speaks of 'things beyond our seeing, things beyond our hearing, things beyond our imagining, all prepared by God for those who love him'" (1 Cor. 2:9; cf. Isa. 64:4; 52:15; also cf. H. W. Robinson, 1955:chap. 2). It was plain to Paul that what Isaiah had predicted about ecstasy had come true in the messianic gift of the Spirit (1 Cor. 2:10*a*). Yet the Spirit's gift could not be given full expression in everyday terms, for the gift brought the mind of the human creature *(anthropos)* into intimate relation with the thought of God, a relation that the Spirit, being God's own, was unsurpassably qualified to explore and disclose. Here, then, Paul's readers would find the true ecstasy, reflecting the true intimacy, one that his Corinthian readers might not yet be in position to grasp, since spiritual things are spiritually discerned (1 Cor. 2:14). So he did not refuse the challenge offered by the 'spirituality' of his proto-gnostic Corinthian opponents; rather he raised the stake. True spirituality, he argued, is even more profound than their ecstasy could indicate, and at the same time (witness the Isaiah chapters) true spirituality disclosed Christ crucified, a concept abhorrent to proto-Gnostics. Christ crucified, the very thing the ecstatic party wanted to transcend, was the exact content of that Spirit-given wisdom. God as Spirit is a go-between God (John V. Taylor) whose nearness to human believers brings God in Christ into immediate relation with costly human life.

This states, or rather it half-states, the end of mission, the bringing of the divine self and human selves into an unspeakable, ecstatic intimacy. It is for this that Paul was a missionary. It is for this union that all else, all creation, exists. This is the 'glory' God intends. Yet now the other half of the statement follows: the same Spirit that brings us near God brings us near one another as well. The key term here is *koinōnia*, a common Hellenistic Greek word for the marital and other close human relations, therefore best translated "participation" or "sharing together," or even "congress" (in English a word that also has both political and sexual connotations), though "fellowship" is the customary translation. The strong sense of *koinōnia* throughout the New Testament is participation *with* someone *in* some common engagement—thus Paul will commend the participation *(koinōnias)* of the Corinthian church *with* other Macedonian churches *in* an offering for Jerusalem's poor saints (2 Cor. 9:13), and on another front he will warn them against any sharing *(koinōnous) with* Gentiles *in* sacrifices made to demons (1 Cor. 10:20). On this pattern, "The fellowship *[koinōnia]* of the Holy Spirit" (as presented, e.g., in 2 Cor. 13:14) is participation *in* nearness to God *with* others in whom the same Spirit works. Thus the term neatly designates the characteristic work of the Spirit, drawing believers Godward (i.e., Christward) and in the same act drawing them into fellowship or congress with one another. And since that work, that achievement, is the goal of the entire divine mission—the goal of creation, of the cross, of the consummation—the Spirit's work is no theological footnote or religious rickrack; rather the Holy Spirit, seen by eyes focused on mission, expresses Divinity's own ultimacy, God's inner nature, laid open to reverent and awe-struck human gaze.

b. The unity God promises.—With this expression of the end (i.e., goal or target) of the Spirit's mission to the world, we come toward the close of this treatment of doctrine, which began with the Christian doctrine of last things. There it was shown that the biblical pictures of end-time, of resurrection, judgment, hell, heaven, and Christ's comings, are not mere mythic fancies from a childlike human past, but are lively guides to the world-future. With a doctrine of the Spirit's mission sketched, we are now in position to say more clearly how this is so.

The end of creation, the end of redemption, the end of the mission of God who is Spirit—these three converge. The Spirit of God is utterly *holy* Spirit, and the end of the Spirit's mission is holiness for the whole, the sanctification of the world, the wholeness or unity of all creation. The rule of God is dynamic, a vector of divine purpose for all created being, guiding it to salvific ends. Jesus Christ is the *huios tou anthropou*, the Truly Human One whose story is God's own story; in his resurrection this son of man is fittingly designated Son of God, the one who has fulfilled God's earthly story fully and finally. Thus creation and redemption and mission are one divine process that issues in the convergence or unity of all things. Yet "convergence," "unity," and even that "wholeness" that is holiness are suspiciously vague terms in theological books: they are little more than pious gestures unless we can ground them each in a true story that makes their meaning clear. This volume has sought to indicate the applicable narrative frame—story of Israel, story of Jesus, story of the church—that can rescue such terms as "unity" and "wholeness" from vagueness, show them concrete and real in human history and life. There is little use in trying in a few paragraphs to repeat nine chapters. Nevertheless, it may be helpful at the end to pick out some clues that will help the reader to distinguish the sort of unity or convergence or holy wholeness at which preceding pages have aimed.

i. The quest for unity in religion, politics, economics.—Does the world mission of the Holy Spirit as it is construed here aim at concrete unity, unity that can be realized by Christians and others today? Is that its product, its gift? The world we know is torn by racial, national, economic, ethnic, sexual, cultural, and (not least) religious strife. Where is the driving force, the machinery that can stitch up earth's torn fabric? This is certainly a realistic, politically relevant question. The attempt to answer it has set armies marching, diplomats debating, populations migrating, yet without any final resolution. What sort of unity can there be on our planet that may declare God's wider intentions? No religious or military or economic or cultural movement has so far provided more than a fleeting glimpse of world unity.

What about **religious** unity? By far the largest religious movement in the world today is Christian. Figures compiled by the Lausanne Statistical Task Force put the 1991 world population at about 5.4 billion souls. Of these, the same source reports 1.8 billion were (at least) nominal Christians, fewer than a billion (again nominal) Muslims, somewhat fewer Hindus, while others, Buddhists, Sikhs, Jews, were well down the scale in size (Barrett, 1991). Starting with the missionary projects described in the book of Acts, the Christian world mission has displayed signal achievements: the Nestorian thrust to China as early as the seventh century, the even earlier Catholic mission in Europe and North Africa, the prodigious Roman Catholic exploits in the Far East from the sixteenth century onward and in the Americas from about the same time, the late but intense Protestant missions of the eighteenth and nineteenth centuries, all together yielding the results just quoted. Yet each of these projects displayed internal flaws or limits that checked its progress. Nestorians and Catholics accepted and exploited military alliances that spread Christianity by the sword of the flesh not the sword of the Spirit; the Protestant revolt of the sixteenth century defeated the Catholic dream even of Europe's Christian unity; the rise of secular thought on Christian soil from the Renaissance and Enlightenment onward eroded Christianity in the Protestant and later in the Catholic heartlands; the Protestant mission advances in the nineteenth century were not sustained in face of military, economic, and moral challenges to *Western* dominance in the world. Finally, a motley range of largely indigenous missionary efforts, usually uncoordinated, and which in generic terms appear baptist, grew periodically on the fringes of the better organized, better managed Catholic and Protestant organizations, examples being the house churches of Maoist China and the diverse spontaneous black churches of the African continent. Though this third range was from Catholic and Protestant standpoints on the fringe, it was not insignificant. The Barrett reports cited above indicate that it currently constitutes the largest non–Roman Catholic Christian population in the world. Yet on the surface the baptist movements provide little **unity,** inasmuch as they are divided into thousands of individual church bodies with no overarching ecclesial structure.

Only one other religious movement has had realistic pretensions to world unification—Islam. Enjoying signal successes in the Near East, Africa, South Asia, and Southeast Asia, Islam's attempts were closely tied from early on to military conquest, and (having taken the sword) were halted by the sword in Europe (though the outcome there was doubtful for centuries) and in Asia (where the opponent was the Mongol Empire under Genghis Khan); happily, more recent Muslim missions have been less dependent on political support. Hinduism has for the most part been limited to the Indian subcontinent. Judaism has spread worldwide but has for millennia limited the scope of its outreach. Buddhism has spread extensively for a still longer time in the East (Southeast Asia, India, China, and Japan), but has remained an exotic in the West.

Another vision of world unity has been **political-military.** From the Mongol Empire of the Middle Ages to the British Empire of the nineteenth and the American and Soviet domination of much of the twentieth century, various sovereignties have attempted the old dream of political mastery of the known world. In the estimate of Arnold Toynbee, these have been inescapably tied to the civilizations that gave rise to them, and as these civilizations declined (our own Western civilization currently shows such signs of declension) the military-political empires they nourished have declined as well (Toynbee, 1947). One idealistic twentieth-century dream of unity, expressed in the old League of Nations (1919–46) and its current successor, the United Nations, has so far proved little more than a diplomatic forum.

More impressive in recent times than conquest and parley was the economic-ideological-political movement of worldwide *Communism,* sponsored by the work of nineteenth-century theorist Karl Marx, and incarnated in two great twentieth-century empires, the Soviet and the Chinese. There is a tendency in the West at century's end to discount the power and appeal of this massive world-system in light of the collapse of Marxist governments in Eastern Europe and the Soviet Union, ignoring the protean Chinese phenomenon, yet its dialectical rationale, its piercing insights into social conditions, and its power to command the allegiance of vast numbers should not too quickly be counted out. The reaction of critical-minded literate Westerners to Communism was already epitomized in the brilliant essays by Arthur Koestler and others in *The God That Failed* (1949), but the movement remains a powerful force for one sort of world unity on its own class-oriented terms.

Mention of such criticism brings us to an alternative cultural-economic vision of unity; this can best be named **secularity,** insofar as it embraces no religious vision, is wedded to no single system of government (such as democracy or monarchy), and commits itself to no creedal statements (cf. N. Smart, 1981). Modern secularization has had two phases or moments: the secularization of the West, a movement that can best be described as the self-corrective rejection, in 'Christian' lands, of a *Corpus Christianum* that had forged church and state (earlier, church and empire) into an oppressive culture foreign to the spirit of the gospel. Seen in this revolutionary way, secularization is continuous with the prophetic movement in Israel and with the gospel itself, crying out against all idolatry, in particular against the idolatry that proclaims "the temple of the Lord, the temple of the Lord, the temple of the Lord are these" (Jeremiah) and the idolatry that debates whether God is to be worshiped "in this mountain" or "in Jerusalem" (cf. John 4:20). This Western secular iconoclasm has proved in the short run costly to Christian adherence, but it can be seen in the long run as the cleansing wind of the Spirit of God. The second moment of secularization occurs in non-Western lands where the power of Western technological civilization impinges upon 'ontocratic' traditional cultures (including the Muslim one) in the East. The first reaction of Easterners to secularization may be to clutch the dangerous trinkets of Western power (computers, chemical plants, weaponry) while otherwise maintaining timeless Eastern ways, but this foolishly underestimates the power of secularity. The longer result of its progress in the East is foreshadowed in such population centers as Singapore and Hong Kong, where industrial civilization makes older life patterns increasingly anachronistic, and a vast hunger, not unlike the restless emptiness of the secularized West, appears.

As an aside, we may note a particular mistake of Christian theory, that of *identifying* secularity with the gospel, memorialized in a study called *Rethinking Missions* (1932) which concluded evangelism on mission fields should be entirely replaced by Western medical technology and education. Here secularity *is* the gospel. No one should underestimate such benefits as scientific medicine, or discount the erosive power of the secularity that currently girdles the world. Yet there are limits to its beneficence, while the individualism it entails seems unlimited. A more balanced appraisal of secularity appears in the work of Arend Theodoor van Leeuwen, mentioned in Section §1 above. He suggests that secularity, by destroying ontocracies East *and* West, serves as a kind of John the Baptist, clearing obstacles and making a roadway along which eventually the gospel can travel (1964). Secularity cannot itself be the world-uniting force because its content is so largely negative; it can clear the way, but it cannot constitute the required unity (cf. Matt. 12:43-45).

ii. Sexual unity and 'syzygic' unity.—If religious, military, economic, or cultural modes will not unify even that portion of the cosmos exposed to our gaze, what will? Our answer will be found in the themes of intimacy, ecstasy, and fellowship staked out above. The Russian philosopher Vladimir Sergeyevich Solovyov wrote (in Schmemann, ed., 1965:73-134) that among the life forms known to us only the human species is capable of realizing the whole truth about the goal of existence, since only our species possesses a general consciousness capable of conceiving the whole spatio-temporal continuum. Snails cannot do this; neither can even clever monkeys. The trouble with this human capacity is that, although it must be exercised by individuals, the individual man or woman is "an isolated particle," and human egoism typically exalts this particle—himself or herself—into the whole. Such egoism necessarily hinders knowledge of the whole truth, and our only experience of a power that overcomes this barrier is the experience of true love. Love forces egoism to sacrifice itself to the beloved other, leading (at least in such a case) to an unforced and real unity (p. 108).

Now among the kinds of human love only sexual love *(erōs)* fulfills this description; Solovyov has arguments to show that other sorts of love, mystical love, parental love, sympathetic fellowship, all fall short for one reason or another. The beloved 'other' that can liberate our individuality from the blinders of egoism must correspond to the whole of our individuality: the other must be as real, as concrete, and as objective as we ourselves are, and at the same time *must differ from us in every way* so as to be really 'other.' Now this just describes the characteristic object of sexual love; sexual union strives for a total fusion of self with the alternate other.

Here, however, a complication appears. In practice sexual love never lives up to this billing. "Sooner or later the ecstatic element of love disappears." Does this mean that the erotic dream of total self-giving is only illusory? In answering No, Solovyov appeals to the long human evolutionary experience: Once art, science, civil society, the control of nature's forces seemed each to be only illusory, only farfetched dreams, but these have one-by-one been realized. Epochs have been required for the development of brains adequate to these other human projects. Now the task is the realization of the truly human, and this cannot be merely masculine or merely feminine, but will be the realization of the image of God (Gen. 1:27) in a union of pure love, not mere physical joining, in the material world.

Then how is such true union formed? Solovyov cites Scripture, Ephesians alongside Genesis: "God created human beings in his own image; in the image of God he created them; male and female he created them," and "there is hidden here a great truth, which I take to refer to Christ and to the church. But it applies also to each one of you. . . ." (Gen. 1:27; cf. 2:24; Eph. 5:32f). The "image of God," Solovyov declares, is just this unity, this reunion, of the two essential aspects of human nature, the male and the female. Like every analogy, this one is limited and imperfect (even the exemplary husband is certainly no god, the exemplary wife no redeemed creation!); rather in their union the human being (male and female) receives power *from God* to realize its divine purpose. In the dynamic of love's creativity, love's object (be it female or male) is seen in the ecstatic moment according to God's creative intent—seen fleetingly in his or her ultimacy. For Solovyov's Russian Orthodox way of thinking, this means that in imagination and moment by moment we sense a reality that is actual "in another, higher realm of being"—sense it, as the Disciples' Prayer has it, "on earth as it *is* in heaven" (p. 126).

And so the fleeting vision points beyond itself to faith in God and God's relation to the creation. Taking a leap, Solovyov declares that only together with *all other being* can the individual man or woman be saved, that is, be regenerated and preserved forever in his or her individuality, since only in that wide union does the fullness of God's purpose for each of us come to fruition. In short, conjugal or sexual love cannot realize what it fleetingly glimpses short of the transformation of its environment—a transformation that is (to revert to our own terminology) the end of the Spirit's mission. Just as one is married to a spouse and (ideally) finds in her or him an "other" who is "all," and for whom sacrifice is altogether appropriate, every social organism must be for its members an "other" and an "all" that, as Christians know, can be supported only by sacrifice, by taking up a cross. Only by such sacrifice can we complete the organism, even as it completes us. Here is a vision of wholeness that speaks to a more inclusive whole than the religious, political, and other alternatives canvassed above. Solovyov coins a term for this relation between each and all: it is "syzygic"—from Greek *syzygia*, sexual congress, conjunction. "Syzygy" speaks of full unity achieved without the cancellation of the individual. No participant is absorbed (as totalitarian systems attempt) into the whole, yet none flourishes in isolation (as Western individualism supposes), but each interacts in love. What Solovyov intends by "universal syzygy" is in fact no other than the unity of the Holy Spirit of God (Eph. 3:1-13).

Yet for this ideal unity to be realized, it must enter and rule "the kingdom of matter and death" by rising *within* each individual human being. Syzygic unity is not externally achieved by self-serving Don Juans, or externally imposed by a dictator God; it is not secured by any majority vote however clamorous: the mission of the Spirit achieves syzygic unity precisely by confronting each living human being with the reality of life in the risen Christ, displaying the way of his cross, accepting the uniqueness of each, and inviting from each a response that can be made only by the power of the Spirit of love. We are brought back to the claim with which this chapter began: Syzygic unity is a unity not of bland sameness but of fellowship, realized by the mission of the Spirit to each and all.

c. The church of the Spirit.—As a pilot entering a harbor takes the bearings of markers on the waiting shore and by them finds his current position and corrects his course, we have now to correct the course of this chapter. The church is still the church, the sign of God's rule, undertaking its ceaseless tasks of work and worship, word and witness ordered toward its last end. The great historic signs still reveal God's way for his people. The church of the Spirit is a church that knows these historic signs and shapes its life in accordance with them. In such a church the remembering signs speak. They point to the historic signs and restore their focal place in the church's life. Withal there appear providential signs, more or less startling, more or less visible, given to this or that solitary biblical traveler or company of travelers as redirection for crucial, contemporary gospel tasks. These remain.

Can a church that is itself a sign of the kingdom of justice and holiness, a church that is guided by these historic and remembering and providential signs so defined—can such a church be the church of the Spirit, aimed not at sectarian narrowness or dogmatic rigidity or organizational evolvement but at syzygy or wholeness, at the *apokatastasis*, the restitution of all things (Acts 3:21), the holy oneness that is the Spirit's aim and goal and gift? Three concluding lines of evidence bear on that question, and with them my argument must rest.

The first line of evidence is historical. The case to prove is the historic intention of the church itself. The *Catholic type* of church has indeed made this claim its stock in trade, and has appropriated to itself the very word that by its meaning belongs to all, the term "catholic." Nor has the *Protestant* ecclesial *type* failed to make such a claim; in recent times it has borrowed from antiquity the term "ecumenical," pertaining to the whole world. These claims of an aim toward wholeness are surely made in good faith. The case for Christianity will be complete, though, only if that vast, amorphous ecclesial type, the baptist, confirms this aim. Careful study suggests that in fact the *baptist type* does so (cf. McClendon and Yoder, 1990). Consider now only the evidence provided by the mission scope of each ecclesial type. Here the baptist claim is secure. While the largest Christian aggregates are catholic, statistics suggest that those here denominated "baptist," if construed to include the phenomenal growth of pentecostal movements and the unaligned congregations of Africa and Asia, are next in order of size (Barrett, 1991). In any case, such growth is ingredient to the baptist movement itself. Historian Franklin Littell, in his classic *Anabaptist View of the Church* (1952:109), made the case in a brilliant chapter titled "The Great Commission": no texts better typify sixteenth-century Anabaptist testimony than citations of the Great Commission (e.g., Matt. 28:19f) or passages such as Psalm 24:

> Die erde ist des HERREN vnd was drinnen ist
> Der erboden vnd was drauff wonet.
>   (Wittenberg Bible, 1534)

While other Christians left mission to a few specialists or to a past age, the radicals came "*to make the Commission binding upon all church members.* . . . The promise to go where sent was part of the ceremony of admission to the True Church" (Littell, 1952:112).

Yet a movement might be 'missionary,' even 'evangelistic,' yet so closed in spirit as only to propagandize its own closed view. Our second line of evidence must indicate that these "churches of the Great Commission" remain open to change as the Spirit leads—not merely tolerant of differing views or of some internal diversity, but willing to be restored and remade by the gospel itself. In the twentieth century good evidence of this lies in the Pentecostal and Charismatic churches. Though a scandal to some, these have broken down racial barriers, put women in highest leadership places, and revised the practices of piety via spiritual gifts. That these are intrinsic developments of this baptist ecclesial type can be seen from the baptist vision. John Robinson of Leyden declared in his sermon of dismissal to the pilgrims to America that they must be prepared to learn and to change, for "The Lord had more truth and light yet to break forth out of his holy word" (cited in George, 1982:91f). That utterance fixed the element of continuity, namely, Scripture and its Christ, while declaring the biblical word to be an agent of change that must itself change, releasing afresh the mighty, transforming power of God.

To argue for the catholicity of intent of the baptist movement, or to see that movement adjust its sails to Spirit winds, may even yet not persuade those whose sense of this style of Christian life has been warped by its visible excesses and defects, may not persuade those caught in alien crosscurrents. Yet there is a third line of evidence available even to these. This is the practice of worship in these communities, and it is accessible to any who will train their ear to its inner music. To these one can argue, "You have ears, so hear what the Spirit says to the churches" (Rev. 2:11ff). A tiny fragment of this evidence, in the form of a story, must here represent all the rest.

The story is from the Armenian American writer, William Saroyan; its name is "On the Train" (1966). The setting is America in wartime in the mid–twentieth century; a troop of draftees is being transported toward the front. Two young soldiers talk. One is a product of small-town, apple-pie America; the other is a city waif, an orphan. As the train rushes along, they talk about what they will do if they survive the war. The small-town youth, in a burst of generosity, confides his hope that the other will come home with him after the war, meet and marry his sister, settle down; they will be neighbors, friends for life. Saroyan's "Ithaca" here functions as a symbolic Promised Land. But will they live to fulfill those promises? Other soldiers talk; there are bawdy songs about girls and what they are good for. Then there is a silence, and one soldier asks for "a *real* song." An accordion appears, and someone names a song. This turns out to be "Leaning on the Everlasting Arms." The accordion plays, and two of the soldiers sing, one with a good voice, the other strong but unmusical. Soon the music draws everyone in.

> What a fellowship, what a joy divine,
> Leaning on the everlasting arms;
> What a blessedness, what a peace is mine,
> Leaning on the everlasting arms.

Saroyan's choice of songs in this story is remarkable. Neither very old nor very widely used, "Leaning on the Everlasting Arms" belongs to songbooks and congregations of baptist folk, to plain folk generally. The story presents the fears of such as these, fear of the future, fear of war, of alienation, of death. Against war, there is for soldiers the hope of lucky survival; against alienation, sometimes there are friends. Against death, there is nothing. Nothing but the Good News. Most striking for us is the song's text: it announces itself as a song about

> . . . a fellowship . . . a joy divine.

Now by our present account, these two are the very ends of the Spirit's mission—they are the creative goal of the great suffering divine holy Creator God. In the song, "joy divine" is what we have called ecstasy; "fellowship" is our *koinōnia*, our congress one with another in Jesus. Together these make up the intimacy that wipes away every tear, and gathers every lost sheep home.

> Leaning, leaning, safe and secure from all alarms;
> Leaning, leaning, leaning on the everlasting arms.

As Saroyan says, "By this time, everybody was singing."

RETROSPECT

I cannot pretend that Seth and Dinah were anything else but Methodists—not indeed of that modern type which reads quarterly reviews and attends in chapels with pillared porticoes; but of a very old-fashioned kind. They believed in present miracles, in instantaneous conversions, in revelations by dreams and visions; they drew lots, and sought for Divine guidance by opening the Bible at hazard; having a literal way of interpreting the Scriptures, which is not at all sanctioned by approved commentators; and it is impossible for me to represent their diction as correct, or their instruction as liberal. Still—if I have read religious history aright—faith, hope, and charity have not always been found in a direct ratio with a sensibility to the three concords; and it is possible, thank Heaven! to have very erroneous theories and very sublime feelings. The raw bacon which clumsy Molly spares from her own scanty store, that she may carry it to her neighbour's child to "stop the fits," may be a piteously inefficacious remedy; but the generous stirring of a neighbourly kindness that prompted the deed has a beneficent radiation that is not lost.

George Eliot, *Adam Bede*

This is not a call for the total abandonment of formal theological language. However, it does suggest a positioning within our systematic theology the narrative language and signs of the overwhelming majority of people who do not comprise the formal leadership in the academy, church, and society. If we do not, we run the negative risk of narrowing systematic theology to a conversation within a narrow stratum of formally educated elites. However, if we do, we run the positive risk of democratizing and empowering systematic theology so that the servants working at rich Christian banquets can correlate their stories with that of Jesus on par with the faith stories of the rich Christians. And then, perhaps, the question will not be how does authority relate to diversity, but how does authority deepen a community of equals.

Dwight Hopkins

Who gave you this authority?   Matthew 21:23

An Essay on Authority

For more than two centuries now, theologians have been filled with disquiet about their own discipline. Theology has seemed in urgent need of legitimation. In part this theological unease might have reflected only theology's need to pick out its identity in a world of increasing intellectual diversity. In the late eighteenth century, Benjamin Franklin could still be at once the American ambassador to Paris, an experimenter in the forefront of natural science, and the founder of a philosophical society. Nor did Franklin hesitate to offer theological judgments whenever he pleased. Three generations later, such self-confident mastery of many disciplines was no longer possible in America. Thus the brilliant Henry Adams, great-grandson of Franklin's contemporary John Adams, could sincerely say at the end of the nineteenth century, a few years after completing his formal education, that he was utterly unable to comprehend the modern world in which he lived: its multiplicity, complexity, and technological cast offered no purchase for a comprehensive grasp (Adams, 1906). During the same century it became apparent that a college education alone was no longer acceptable as preparation for ministers, and in America professional divinity schools or theological seminaries were established to undertake what had thus become an essentially parochial task. So far there has been no reversing of this two-centuries-long movement toward diversity and specialization: theology is no longer simply a part of a well-rounded intellectual formation but is left to those whose taste and training admit them to its mystic circle (cf. Farley, 1982).

In theology's case, however, the need to explain itself has not been merely a question of specialization, for the question was whether there was any real body of *theological* knowledge in which to specialize. Claude Welch, historian of nineteenth-century theology, writes that by the middle of that century the very possibility of theology had become a main topic of theological inquiry itself (Welch, 1972–85, I:57ff). Might not alternate disciplines (such as history or sociology) provide whatever explanation of religion was needed, allowing theology like medieval alchemy quietly to disappear? (V. Harvey, 1989) If this disappearance was to be forestalled, the century found that it required more and more preliminary footwork to say why; any serious work of theology came to have elaborate prolegomena 'establishing' the legitimacy of its task. Conscious of this trend and determined to reverse it, Karl Barth early in the twentieth century sought to abandon the task of digging a foundation somehow deeper, more assured than theology proper. His *Church Dogmatics* would have no external prolegomenon, but would move immediately to the task of explicating the Word of God (CD I/1 §§1-5). His critics, however, pointed out that Barth's thousand-page opening focus upon "revelation" (a theme of no such prominence in Scripture itself) became willy-nilly another kind of prolegomenon, by means of which Barth like all the rest sought to establish a theoretical foundation before he could speak directly of God or creation or reconciliation or redemption, the topics of the succeeding volumes. Thus his dogmatics was an exception that only proved the rule.

Neither the strategy of Barth nor that of his prolegomena-writing predecessors has been followed here. The present volume offers an introductory chapter ("What Is Doctrine?") more to be compared with the explanations an age of specialization must offer about any study ("what is biophysics?" "what is civil law?") than with the apologetic or self-justifying introductions of nineteenth-century theologies. The preceding volume *(Ethics)* set out, not to lay such a foundation, but to engage in theological ethics as an integral part of the theological task itself. However, not too much originality should be claimed for the present work. Its stance reflects a wider conceptual shift from a strictly modern understanding in which all knowledge is supposed to rest upon some universally available foundations, to an understanding some have labeled postmodern (see e.g., Murphy and McClendon, 1989), in which claims to knowledge are less breathtaking or absolute, but are more integrally tied to the actual tasks at hand. If such a shift is indeed taking place, the stance of the present work will in time seem less strange. At present, however, not everyone agrees. For example, the respected work of David Tracy continues within the old 'modern' paradigm. Among Tracy's chapter headings one finds telltale titles such as "The Crisis of the Christian Theologian," and "The Search for Adequate Criteria" (1975). So we are in a time of conflict between modern and postmodern procedures, that is, between those that assume the continuing dominance of the thought-forms that typify the previous two hundred years, and those that do not. The inclusion of this chapter on authority constitutes a recognition of the present state of conflict. A recognition, but not a change of strategies, and not even a full joining of the issue between modern and postmodern ways of proceeding. (Such a discussion must await *Volume III*.) Yet it is a recognition, since, as readers will see, were it not for the ongoing debate between foundationalists and non-foundationalists (i.e., moderns and postmoderns), the following material on authority for Christians might just as well have been distributed among the preceding doctrinal chapters.

For among Christian doctrines there is no "doctrine of authority" as such; the church must speak with authority, but need not single out "authority" as one of her teachings. (In like manner, the church must speak clearly, but need not single out "clarity" as a doctrinal topic.) Those who have turned here in the hope of discovering the underlying premises on which everything else in the volume is founded are themselves on the wrong track; those premises are integral to the preceding chapters, and are to be found throughout them; they cannot simply be gathered up here. Certain to be disappointed are those who seek here the older sort of apologetic that posited Scripture (or church tradition) as a propositional foundation on which everything else must rest. That old argument typically comprised three steps: (1) to prove the existence of a God on the basis of supposed foundational truths; (2) to reason that since God exists, a divine self-revelation is to be expected; (3) to find in the Bible (Protestant version) or in their Church (Catholic version) the contents of this expected revelation, contents that thereby constitute the matter of theology. However materially correct this apologetic may have been about God or Scripture or church doctrine, its argument is no longer persuasive. To set it aside is not to question the value of apologetics as such (as a part of evangelism and Christian nurture it has its own role), nor is it to reject the proximate authority of Scripture and church. Authority as it is used here is not an appeal to unbelief on grounds it already accepts to recognize the truth of Christian faith; rather, "authority" is here first of all a name for the Godhood of God. This chapter aims to help those who recognize that Godhood to locate the subsidiary authorities by which God's authority takes hold.

In many spheres of intellectual work, and particularly in the sciences, authority appears no longer to have a place. The appearance may be misleading (one still encounters, for instance, the 'authority' of scientific paradigms), but even in spheres such as law and politics, where authority has acknowledged work to do, there are difficulties about its proper use. Political authority, for example, is unfavorably (and perhaps unfairly) associated with absolute monarchy, authoritarianism, and dictatorship; on the other hand the absence of all authority is widely understood to portend anarchy and chaos. Political thought in the West has therefore struggled for a long time to find a concept of authority not open to serious abuse: one commonly proposed test of legitimate authority has been the consent of the governed. It was the work of Thomas Hobbes and John Locke to express this consent in mythic form in their political writings. By this test, authority rests upon self-government by each; that is, it comes to autonomy as the only real authority. If I do (or did) not consent, there is no authority over me; I alone am ultimate authority. On the other hand, in parts of the world where this liberal test has not been invoked, it has sometimes been hard to distinguish rightful authority from sheer power. Apparently might makes right. Faced with so clumsy a view of political authority, many have supposed (sometimes, it must be admitted, under Christian influence) that rightful political authority lay in the extension to earthly rulers of heaven's own authority; thus kings in the West like Oriental emperors were said to reign by divine right. This solution has the unfortunate consequence of putting believers on the side of every oppressive and authoritarian regime that comes along, thereby calling into question the logic (or exegesis) that produced the theory. In sum, it is not only for the Christian religion, and not only in religion, that authority has been problematic (cf. Simon, 1958; Sennett, 1978; Stout, 1981).

To some extent authority's problematic nature can be cleared by a well-known distinction between "authority in" and "authority on." Because the Dean is an authority *in* the College, she may choose the recipient of the next sabbatical leave. On the other hand a historian who has studied the College archives has become an authority *on* the same college; he can tell us the name of the first President, and when the Department of Psychology was added. (Of course, these sorts of authority may both reside in one person.) Behind these two stands a third, which (with James M. Smith) I call here "criterial authority." By it, native speakers of Russian, for example, are in position to tell us when one does and does not use a certain Russian expression, and they do this neither in virtue of holding a special office nor because they possess special training as Russian grammarians or linguists, but simply on the basis of their (authoritative) native fluency. To speak Russian is the *criterion* for knowing *how* to speak Russian. All three of these sorts of authority, and the dependence of the former two upon the third, will concern us in what follows.

Christians can hardly find authority as such problematic; indeed, reservations about other authorities arise partly because we know that God is God. God *is* the authority. For us the problem about authority shifts from its locus to its mode: How is God's authority enacted in the world? It is vital to keep in mind that this is not the same as asking how an absolute (or infinite) God can have relations with (present, finite) human life: that is an artificial problem generated by a God-concept removed from that of Christian faith (Chapter Seven, above).

It is fitting that in one of his benedictions Paul invoked the love of God, the grace of the Lord Jesus Christ, the fellowship of the Spirit (cf. 2 Cor. 13:14). Each fresh term discloses the dynamic nature of God who (1) reaches out in love, (2) gives grace, (3) evokes fellowship. **Love** is God's *interactive authority* at work: God's creative loving evokes the creature's love which (thus evoked) knows that it touches ultimacy. **Grace** is God's *redemptive authority:* God in Christ is God acting with ultimate grace, so that if Scripture is the Book of Christ it provides its faithful reader with access to that very grace. **Fellowship** is God's *unitive authority;* God evoking fellowship is God as Spirit, and those worshiping in that fellowship find their fellowship with God and one another to be in spirit and in truth. This chapter must acknowledge God's dynamic trine authority while carefully distinguishing it from the human responses it calls forth: it must distinguish God's love from human experience of love, distinguish God's voice in Scripture from the genuine human voice of Scripture, distinguish God's communion with the creature from the creaturely fellowship thus evoked. Nevertheless and all the more, on the human side of these pairs, each item possesses its own finite authority for Christian faith: the authority of evangelical *experience,* of holy *Scripture,* of salvific *community.* Though related to the ultimate, these authorities are in each case proximate, not themselves ultimate, not themselves God. Moreover, they are not on a flat par with one another, nor are they fragments to be played off (as some Anglicans have played off another triad—Scripture, tradition, and reason) against one another. To say, then, how our proximate authorities are related to God's ultimate authority, to one another, and to other, putative authorities for Christian faith and life is our present goal.

Methodists and other children of the Wesleyan movement will object that I have neglected the fourth leg of the so-called Wesleyan quadrilateral, "reason." Yet reason is omitted here not because I favor unreason or madness, but because reason or rationality is not properly understood as an authority or the authority; it is neither an authority in or on religion, nor a criterial authority for students of religion; rather it is a name for the thought processes by which we seek to maintain order in any sphere of conversation. To think is to reason, but to list thinking among one's authorities reflects either a category mistake (a misunderstanding of how the term is used) or a covert appeal to authorities one prefers to leave unnamed. When in the seventeenth and eighteenth centuries European Christians began to claim that their Christianity (and it alone?) was "reasonable," they were signaling that although the dominant assumptions of the day increasingly discounted Christianity, they were making a (covert) claim to line Christianity up with those dominant assumptions, however unchristian they might be. Might they not better have taken a cue from old Erasmus, who, saddened by the sixteenth century's wars, lusts, greed, and perversity carried on in the name of high reason, wrote a satirical book, *In Praise of Folly*, to characterize his standpoint over against the gods of his age? (see Erasmus, 1965)

§1. The Love of God

The phrase "love of God" is ambiguous. It may mean the love with which God *loves;* or it may mean the love with which God *is loved* by others. The former is God's own; yet the latter is not exclusively ours, but is God's gift to the creature: "we love because he loved us first" (1 John 4:19). Here we will take this answering, human love to stand for the wide range of affect and active experience that comprises human response to God. Such experience has a narrative form; by it we are formed within a story where we know ourselves loved "because he loved us first." But does this response, potentially my own response, make a rightful claim to authority? On its face, this seems puzzling in a way that the authority of a book (the Bible) or of a community (the church) does not. What can it mean to say that my love, or even living out a story of love, is 'authoritative'?

Puzzling or not, the move has been attempted; indeed "experience" became the bedrock of the theology that held sway, at least among non-Catholic Christians, at the beginning of the twentieth century. Where other attempted footings had not held, this one promised to endure. To be sure, theologians construed Christian (or religious) experience in a variety of ways. For the young Schleiermacher, it had been the epistemically primitive *awareness (Gefühl)* of the whole, or the All, an awareness differently colored in different religious traditions but definitively the same in each (1799:Speech 2). According to the Ritschlian Wilhelm Herrmann, believers could expect the "inner life" of Jesus, gleaned from a reading of the Gospels, to exert upon their own "inner lives" a profound *influence* that they would recognize as the very influence of God upon them (1903). In the thought of American philosopher-psychologist William James, experience was again the prime clue to religious truth, but for James this meant that *religious biographies* were to be consulted to discover the varied and irreplaceable deliverances of his assorted saints (1902). In this, James was followed by Baptists Edgar Young Mullins (1905, 1908, 1917) and Douglas Clyde Macintosh (1919). Nor was the claim of experience limited to theologians: a turn through the pages of Ira D. Sankey's *Sacred Songs and Solos* reveals the role of experiential testimony in the popular revivalism of the nineteenth century: there Peter Bilhorn's "Sweet Peace, the Gift of God's Love" took its place alongside John Newton's earlier "Amazing Grace" and Charles Wesley's still earlier hymn:

> Oh, the rapturous height
> Of that holy delight
> Which I felt in the life-giving blood
> Of my Saviour possessed,
> I was perfectly blessed
> As if filled with the fullness of God.

No English-speaking theologian of the modern period took evangelical experience more seriously than British Congregationalist Peter Taylor Forsyth (1848–1921)—and none wrestled more strenuously to subdue it, to get beyond it, employing the skills of his age. For Forsyth saw more clearly than most of his contemporaries that while experience is essential, it cannot of itself be foundational for Christians. Entering a scene dominated by theologians on the plane of Herrmann, Forsyth accepted the centrality of experience, but denied its priority. He made his argument by analyzing the content of normative evangelical experience—perhaps his personal experience, since he rarely cites any other save that witnessed in Scripture. He found this evangelical experience real enough, but it necessarily pointed away from itself. It was an experience of the love of God, but deeper than love in God's nature was holiness, which embraced even love and entailed it. By holiness, Forsyth understood a claim laid upon one's life such that one knew oneself both condemned of sin and forgiven. God's holiness was a claim that transformed the life that it claimed into one that could only confess itself so condemned, so claimed, so forgiven. If that is the content of experience, then experience has nothing of its own of which to boast, nothing save the authority of the Holy One that it meets in Christ Jesus (see e.g., Forsyth, 1913).

Forsyth found no broader context by which to comprehend this profound insight, no larger frame in which to interpret it, but would repeat it over and over, in slightly varying formulae, throughout his mature life (see e.g. 1897, 1907, 1909, 1911). Perhaps he knew too well that if he attempted more he would not be understood. The difficulty he faced for his contemporaries, and sought earnestly to overcome, was twofold: either they would treasure the evangelical experience, idolize it, and fail to see—what Forsyth so clearly saw—that it was there only to point beyond itself to God its author and source; or in skepticism his contemporaries would disdain the experience because they believed its referent was illusory: it was only their own experience, nothing more. Seeing these very puzzles a generation later, Karl Barth sought to meet them by providing a ninefold test for authentic faith-experience, and then arguing strenuously that such experience was never the "possibility" of religious human beings, but only a divine "possibility," as it were on loan from God (CD I/1, §6). Yet Forsyth, overlooked by his famous successor, had already hammered out just such an answer to the twofold problem. On his analysis, experience is of many sorts. Only that experience that points away from itself and toward a holy and loving God as its author and final authority deserves the claim made for it as (proximate) authority. Forsyth devoted energy to characterizing more fully the *sort* of evangelical experience that bore that self-renouncing character. But (and here is the wider frame he should have produced, but did not) to qualify experience in this way is to presuppose a formative community of interpretation (church) with its own definite history (Bible and its tradition); thereby the entire triad we are investigating here (experience, Bible, community) could have been invoked. Apart from that triad, Christian experience could not exercise even proximate authority.

With this triad we may contrast the theological method of Schleiermacher. For him, the primary reference of theology was *to the experience itself*, and theological statements (including those of Scripture as well as those of the *Glaubenslehre*) are always and necessarily secondary. Experience alone was authority, and even the grace of God only an inference from that (Schleiermacher, CF §3; Welch, 1972–85, I:chap. 3).

Today we might approach the task of Forsyth and the early Barth in a somewhat different way. We might see "experience" as a narrative word. To refer to human experience is to refer, either explicitly or implicitly, to an ongoing story. This sense is suggested both by the word's etymology ("experience," like "experiment," refers to an ongoing trial or test) and by common usage: in Christian circles *to relate one's experience means* not to divulge a timeless intuition, but *to tell the story of one's journey in faith*. This brings us from a fresh direction across territory earlier explored in these volumes. Once our question was how this narrative could be authoritative for Christian convictions and thus for theological ethics. We answered that it must be, because theological ethics "is the discovery, understanding, and creative transformation of a shared and lived story, one whose focus is Jesus of Nazareth and the kingdom he proclaims—a story that on its moral side requires such discovery, such understanding, such transformation to be true to itself" (Ethics, pp. 331f). Now we can make the same connection from the standpoint of doctrine: We participate in this ongoing biblical story, being formed and informed by it (thus narrative generates character), discovering the world of the Bible to be our own real world (thus narrative provides a setting), and finding its great signs and lesser signs significant as episodes not only of the great story it tells but also of our own stories therein contained (thus narrative issues in event). It is a story in which, though we supposed ourselves to be seekers, we found we were in reality the sought; not the hounds, but the hares (cf. Ethics, pp. 352f). As we live through this story, whose condensed plot is "God so loved the world" (John 3:16), it displays an authority that is none other than the bi-directional love of God: "this is how we know that we dwell in him and he dwells in us" (1 John 4:13).

Once we recognize its narrative quality, the primal authority claimed for Christian experience readily falls into place (cf. McClendon, 1990:158-60). It can neither be idolized as though itself God, nor be dissolved into human subjectivity. Schleiermacher implied this narrative quality when he indicated that we have no access to primal religious awareness as such, but only to that awareness qualified according to the tradition of some particular religion (1799:Speech 5; CF §10). Herrmann implied it when he spoke of the impact of the inner life of Jesus upon our own lives (though Herrmann almost completely separated one element of that life, its character, from the elements of setting and event that make a story whole, 1903:§9). James and his followers recognized it when they turned to the lives of the saints as their primary data. For Forsyth and early Barth this time-bound quality of experience seems sometimes obscured, though it came into its own for Forsyth in his account of his own journey into saving faith (cf. 1907:192-98), and for Barth in his later writings (cf. CD IV/3/2 §71.4, "The Christian as Witness"). In these narrative terms, experience will live as long as the gospel itself lives (cf. Matt. 26:13), but to represent religious experience as an independent authority in its own right (the foundationalist move) is logically and conceptually confused, since evangelical experience can bear such weight only in a context that shapes and interprets it. As Chapter Three has stressed, saving experience presupposes a community of interpretation or discernment. Thus it is that community (§3 below), but first its biblical norm (§2), that we must now address.

§2. The Grace of the Lord Jesus Christ

It is Jesus Christ who is the center of Christian faith (Chapter Six). Authority as Christians know it will be found in that center if it is found anywhere. Nor is it an absentee Christ who exercises this authority. Christological understanding begins with the present Christ—one who confronts Christians in their spiritual *worship* and their kingdom *work*, in their common *witness* and in Scripture's holy *word*. The authority of worship, work, and witness is redistributed in this chapter under the headings of experience (§1) and the fellowship of the Spirit (§3); here we are to examine the vexed question of the way Christ's authority makes its claim in the written and proclaimed word of Scripture. How shall we understand this (proximate) authority?

It is by no mere formalism, though, that Scripture is here subsumed under the grace of Christ. The Bible is the book of Jesus Christ, a book that is about him, a book that finds its interpretive key in him, a book that points as witness to him. Among the elements in our reading strategy, this centering has strongly shaped the baptist vision as well as the wider Christian movement. To locate Scripture's center in Christ may startle us if we include the Hebrew, Aramaic, and (eventually) Greek writings Christians recognize as the Old Testament: Were its parts not composed for an earlier people and had they not a different purpose and focus? This objection correctly identifies the Old Testament's first addressees, yet when "purpose" and "focus" are mentioned, it seems clear that under cover of the factual claim a quite different reading strategy is implied, one that either overlooks the eschatological vector of Hebrew Scripture or reads it differently than Christians will (cf. Childs, 1979). For the people of the New Testament, the Old is directed toward it and fulfilled in it. "You study the [Hebrew] scriptures," says Jesus to his challengers in John's Gospel, and "their testimony points to me" (5:39). To treat the New Testament as Scripture—as writings having their own biblical authority—already excludes reading it as mere midrash or embroidered comment upon the earlier Scripture. The New is fulfillment, not simply enlargement, of the Old. If both are indeed Scripture, we are obliged by the New to read the two Testaments in an ascending order of authority: While "it was said to those of ancient times . . . I say to you . . ." (Matt. 5:21f NRSV). Since these familiar principles have been at work in the preceding chapters, they can hardly require *illustration* here. What we must do is to focus their importance in defining a loyalty to Scripture that will not compete with loyalty to Jesus Christ.

We have the concept of Christian Scripture in its two volumes or Testaments. This does not mean, as the bare word "scripture" might suggest, only something written, a book or text. We have rather a text, a Book, that centers on that person in whom final authority rests, and by doing this acquires a delegated or proximate authority. This text is the chosen, written witness to Jesus Christ and to God in Christ. We might have had something else, a mantra or charm whose power lay magically in itself, or a law book or code whose authority lay in courts and legislatures that generated it and on occasion revised it, or a classic or epic whose significance lay in its reflecting the underlying ethos of a place or a people of the past and thereby speaking to all people. To be sure, the Bible does have some of the qualities of a mantra, of a code, of a classic. But that is not where its authority lies. Rather the Bible is for us the word of God written; it is that text in which the One who lays claim to our lives by the act of his life makes that claim afresh in acts of speech; it is for us God speaking; it is the word of God. Such a claim made by a book upon a people is radical and unsettling—an authority subversive of all sorts of competing, other, human authorities. Not surprisingly, then, Christian history itself is replete with schemes that— though not consciously so intended—serve to limit or control this radically unsettling Book. Three such schemes—(a) use of historical-critical exegesis in a way that keeps Scripture at a 'suitably' remote distance, (b) use of tradition so as to monopolize the interpretation of Scripture, and (c) use of inerrancy theories so as to confine the thrust of Scripture— these schemes are potent enough to require separate notice here.

a. The challenge of criticism.—The new historicism of the seventeenth and eighteenth centuries combined with curious new theories about the meaning of a text—any text, but particularly any text of Scripture—to produce a situation unique in Christian history. It was discovered that the Bible had a setting, so that it was not only a book that told a story, but a book that *had* a story, a history, of its own. This awareness, nonexistent or of little significance before the Enlightenment, seemed to the new historicism to have enormous consequences. The Bible came to be regarded as a set of texts whose point lay not in themselves, not, we might say, in their own meaning, but in the history that lay dimly, tantalizingly out of sight behind them. And as Hans Frei pointed out so compellingly, liberal *and* conservative exegetes of the seventeenth to nineteenth centuries unanimously accepted this curious shift in the value of Scripture; on both sides it ceased to possess intrinsic value; they disagreed only about the relative availability and precise content of the *history* for which the Bible's text had become, strictly speaking, merely evidence (Frei, 1974). For both sides, biblical study became historical study, with the only scholarly alternative being 'literary' study, which in the era we are considering meant attention to almost anything about the Bible save its authoritative claim upon its readers. The best because most crucial illustration of this shift in understanding was the creation in this period of "the Jesus of history." For according to both liberals and conservatives that Jesus was a historian's construct, something other than the mere Christ of the Gospels. For neither side was Christ any longer present *in* the Book; the authority about which they quarreled was exactly historian's authority; they themselves would become "authorities on" Jesus, and Scripture was for both a sheaf of data by means of which they could attain this authoritative position. In consequence, each side destroyed the (proximate) authority of *Scripture* as God's word to us. Of course, this was not what each then professed or even intended; it was nonetheless what each did.

Historical critical scholarship has come, and we can no more return to the mental attitude of the prior era than we can abolish the European discovery of America and think ourselves into pre-Columbian understandings. Hans Frei's broad cultural comment on the historical-critical displacement of biblical narrative should certainly not be taken as disparagement of the real gains of that scholarship in both its chief camps. What is at issue is not the growth of knowledge *about* the Bible and its peoples. Archaeology, comparative linguistics, culture history, comparative literature, semantics and syntactics, hermeneutics and the field-encompassing field of history have contributed irreversibly to the intelligibility of the Bible, its parts and the whole (see e.g. Davidson and Leaney, 1970). In many fields, biblical scholars have set the pace for other historians. There is a drive to truth and truthfulness in Christianity that has enabled, even required, such investigation, and all are indebted to it. Especially is this scholarship the creature of Protestantism. Ernst Käsemann has argued that the historical-critical method is inseparable from Protestantism, is indeed its very genius (1969:1-65; cf. Briggs, 1973:21-24). In distinction from this, we could say that Catholicism had sponsored the apologetic method of biblical interpretation, in which beliefs already grounded in the Church's magisterium were defended by selected texts. Whether, to complement these, there is a distinctive baptist reading strategy is a recurrent topic of these volumes (see e.g. *Ethics,* One). Yet these three modes of Bible reading are not, at least from our viewpoint, mutually exclusive. The immediate point to note is the *value* of the historical-critical reading method—a value to which this book is constantly indebted.

To overcome this modern remoteness of Scripture, the other chief element of our reading strategy is required. Throughout the biblical pages, alongside the centrality of Christ but in no competition with it, there appears a pattern by which Scripture reads Scripture. This is a method employed by prophet and evangelist and apostle alike for laying present claim to biblical words whose setting plainly lies in the past. In brief, the setting may change, and yet the old word be seen true and applicable, may come true as never before. Consider Deuteronomy 6. When a Hebrew child asks, "Why keep these laws?" the parent is to answer, "We were Pharaoh's slaves in Egypt, and the LORD brought us out" (v. 21). Now on its face this answer is false. Neither the child nor the parent will have been in Egypt, not on anybody's dating of Deuteronomy. Yet the parent is to say to the inquiring child, "*We* were slaves." And the whole force of Scripture's truth rests upon just such a vision, just such a sense that **this is that:** You, now, in the Deuteronomist's own generation—you are the generation of slaves freed by the Unnameable One. Personal gratitude evokes your obedience to this law. *You* were in Egypt. The story you are living out now *is* the story related in the text. History is real, *history matters*, exactly because in God's mysterious way the past is present. So the church of the New Testament is the church now; time, though not abolished, is in this manner transcended, and the church that reclaims its past stands today before the great final Judge as well. "This is that" and "then is now." Here is a mystical vision, mysterious exactly because it does not deny the facts of history but acknowledges them. Our study of the original setting does not cancel the vision but enhances its claim upon us. Christ-centered, this vision has formed baptist life from before Anabaptist times to the present. Thus I have here called it the baptist vision (cf. *Ethics,* One, and Chapter One above).

The preceding paragraph is a reprise, but now we are in better position to test its adequacy, using the Gospel accounts of the resurrection of Christ (cf. Chapter Six) as our test case. Historical critics tell us that the Gospels as we have them are *Ostergeschichte;* all are written in resurrection light. So far, criticism is correct. But authorities *on* these very Gospels may be tricked by their task into leaving Jesus in the past. If they do so, they may pray, not to a risen and present Lord, but only to a 'God' remote from the historically troubling question of who this risen One really is. Alternatively, the theological conservative *in* the church may acknowledge Christ in two natures as one of three Persons, a mighty dogmatic claim but one that leaves the biblical question unresolved— what have these critically read Scripture pages to do with that claim? Enter now the baptist vision. It tells us that this is that, that the story then *is* the story now; that the *Jesus* Christ who then rose, truly rose and appeared to the disciples in the breaking of bread is present now and does appear to us in our kingdom work and our spiritual worship, in our witness—*and in this very word.* It tells us the Gospel resurrection narratives both witness to what happened then and stake a claim on what happens now. It tells us his risen presence then coheres with his risen presence now; it is its determinative forerunner; it is its cause. It tells us his presence is the very matrix of the intelligibility of this word and of our world. It is under the hermeneutic guidance of this vision that authentic scriptural authority appears.

Or apply this reading strategy to the notoriously difficult Sermon on the Mount (Matthew 5–7; cf. Luke 6:17-49). Its apparent demands on the reader are so powerful that a little library of exegetical works has appeared in order to manage them. Not forgetting the real difficulties these well-meant efforts confront—difficulties of source, authorship, composition, redaction, language, ethical theory, readership, application, and more—let us now pick up the exposition of the Sermon on the Mount by the Southern agrarian radical (and skilled New Testament translator) Clarence Jordan (cf. McClendon, 1990, chap. 5). The educated reader may at first be disappointed, even angered, by Jordan's book (1970). Where in these pages can one recognize the distance between the Jesus of history and Matthew's Jesus? Or between Matthew's Pharisees and actual first-century Pharisaism? All such distinctions seem to vanish. The Pharisees have become as it were cunning Baptists and tricky Methodists, figuring ways to feign conformity to a law of God they secretly believe they can evade. Jesus appears in Jordan's translation of the Sermon not as a remote figure but as a present radical companion who sees through his contemporaries' (Baptist-Methodist) cunning and self-deceit and shows them what they must do to be rid of it: in sex, not calculated legality but wholehearted fidelity; in promise-making and keeping, not what is convenient or conventional or safe, but keeping one's word; in race relations, not contemptuous pride, but action springing from respect and love. To sort out, in this exposition, what is scientific exegesis (which Jordan undoubtedly employed), what is traditional, and what is canny application to 1950s Georgia, U.S.A. (or to the present-day reader), is difficult if not impossible.

Here a flurry of objections must arise. Clarence Jordan was admittedly a skilled Graecist, but was he not a scholar far less at home with New Testament history (McClendon, 1990:98f)? More generally, then, is not the obliteration of the lines between first-century Palestine and twentieth-century Sumter County, Georgia, excessive even for Jordan's purposes? These, however, are questions of skill and art. More generally, we may ask what controls exist to prevent such a method, in less skillful or less honest hands than Jordan's, from running riot—what to prevent a saying of Jesus from inciting self-mutilation (Mark 9:43-47), or prevent Genesis 10–11 from underwriting Apartheid? Not every such question can be addressed here, but at least two points must be kept firmly in mind: first, that the baptist vision does not abolish historical-critical study or a traditional heritage in its demand for application to *today;* but second, that no method is nullified merely because it can be abused. What we seek is not a foolproof reading strategy but a Christ-centered one; not a path from which none can possibly stray, but a trail plain enough to be followed by those who want to follow Jesus. Whatever his weaknesses, Jordan was on such a trail.

The reading strategy Clarence Jordan employed can be followed today if we have in place both the baptist vision ("this is that") and its necessary companion element: the centrality of Jesus in Christian Scripture. Fidelity to both may be indicated by pursuing the earlier example. The memory enshrined in Deuteronomy 6, "We were slaves" (v. 21), is a story that on its face seems to exclude most present-day readers. As the text recalls the story, it was Jews whom God liberated from Egypt, and non-Jews who were the oppressors. Liberal non-Jews may ground their ownership of the story upon their own comprehensive humanity: "I know exactly what slavery (or in parallel cases, exactly what being an oppressed woman, or exactly what Third World existence) is like." But they are not readers of the text. At worst they speak as condescending sentimentalists and at best they are victims of the delusion of their own limitless inclusiveness. In fact, their exegesis flatly contradicts Deuteronomy 6, for in that typical story non-Jews were indeed the oppressors who met their deserts in the Reed Sea. Awareness of this may yield the obverse of liberal sentimentality, namely liberal guilt: "We deserve whatever we suffer at the hands of the oppressed!" In contrast to this bathos, Jesus a Jew has come and has indeed endured oppression, some of it at the hands of his fellow Jews. He has thereby opened the door of liberty to Jew and non-Jew alike, a door not of sentiment but of faith (cf. Eph. 2:8, 12ff). If Jesus thus provides the key to the Christian reading of Deuteronomy, then it is he, the fulfiller of the law that Deuteronomy celebrates, the issue of the story that Deuteronomy recalls, the redeemer from the bondage to the principalities and powers that Deuteronomy discloses—it is only he who permits this non-Jewish reader (among others) to hear "We were slaves" as including himself. But if I thus find my identity through him, then my share in the cross is not a reward for my sentiment or an invitation to bathe in guilt, but is the gracious gift obtained once for all in my stead by Christ Jesus. So it is only in him that I can read "We were slaves," and reading know the authority, the divine, proximate authority, of God's Deuteronomic word.

b. The challenge of tradition.—My goal here is to ask whether tradition must monopolize the voice of God in Scripture. No one should deny that traditional biblical interpretation has proved inadequate to protect the Reformed Church in South Africa from the follies of Apartheid, inadequate to protect the medieval Catholic Church from the cruelty of the Inquisition—inadequate to protect American Christians from their twentieth-century military adventures (cf. *Ethics*, p. 314). We cannot correct all the excesses Christians have carried out under traditional cover, but we must ask if we ourselves are helpless prisoners of our traditional ways of reading the Bible. In the original Christian sense, "tradition" (Greek, *paradosis*) is what is delivered or handed on of Christian teaching. Thus Paul writes to the Corinthians, "First and foremost, I handed on to you the tradition *[paredōka]* I had received: that Christ died for our sins, in accordance with the scriptures" (1 Cor. 15:3). In this sense, tradition is not only transmitted to today's believers by the written Scripture (in this case, Paul's first Corinthian letter); it also necessarily preceded it. (Jesus wrote no book.) Such tradition undergirds and does not rival the Bible. On the other hand, there are church traditions, practices hallowed by repeated use in one church or another—such matters as the ringing of bells, the use of certain familiar words or hymns, the hour (or day?) of worship, the ceremony for (or practice of?) the ordination of ministers, the conduct of weddings and funerals, the art and architecture of Christian faith, and a multitude of other matters (Congar, 1966:pass.). Such church traditions vary from place to place and within denominations as well as among them, and though it is vital for each generation to ask whether any of its traditions contradict the gospel of Christ, it seems that the mere existence of tradition as such raises no challenge to the authority of Scripture. If there are exceptions, they fall into the class to be mentioned next.

During the Middle Ages in Europe many Catholic Christians had no firm grasp upon the unique authority of Scripture, a book most of them never read or held in their own hands. Thus it is not surprising that many members of the Council of Trent (1545–63) believed that the truths necessary to salvation were conveyed partly by Scripture and partly by unwritten tradition kept alive orally (and visually, in art and architecture) within the church. Neither Scripture nor unwritten tradition, they believed, was complete in itself. And that understanding continued to characterize post-Tridentine Catholic teaching. However, recent scholarship has disclosed that the term that best expressed the view just described (Latin, *partim . . . partim*) was deliberately *avoided* by Trent in its 1546 Decree on Scripture (Congar, 1966:165f), so that Vatican II, in the Constitution *Dei Verbum*, once again deliberately avoided that dubious view (Abbott, ed., 1966:115 n. 15). In other words, while the Catholic Church's polemical teaching long fostered the theme of two (partial) sources of revelation, namely Scripture and tradition, its official teaching had instead heeded the scholarship (and the evangelical conviction of many Catholics) that pointed to the sufficiency of the witness of Scripture, recognizing that already in primitive times apostolic *paradosis* undergirded and was thus no rival to the Bible. Yet if official Catholicism declines to make "unwritten tradition" a supplement and in some sense a rival to Scripture, it makes still less sense for baptists to do so. Unquestionably in every church, indeed in every human community, there is a strong tendency, as visible among Unitarians as it is among Anglo-Catholics, to hold fast to the ways of the recent past. The theological task is to recognize and honor this conservative tendency (without it, human life together would hardly be possible, since we could never in any circumstance know what to expect of others) while forever guarding against its fertile and poisonous excesses. Catholics have some urgent tasks of their own in regard to these excesses, but so do baptists. Yet these ongoing self-disciplinary tasks relating to church traditions hardly touch the central question of authority.

The term "tradition" has received still other meanings in Christian history. It can mean the entire complex of doctrines, practices, patterns of life and liturgy that constitute a religion or a segment of one. So understood, Christian tradition is not an authority on or in Christianity, it simply *is* Christianity. Or, with the Edinburgh Faith and Order Conference (1937) "tradition" can mean "the living stream of the Church's life," now not so much the *content* of Christianity as the process ("traditioning") by which that content is conveyed to the next generation—a process that includes teaching Scripture, understanding the past, promoting Christian education, preaching the very gospel itself (R. Hanson, 1963; Fey, ed., 1970:159-61). In these uses, the term meant more and more, and there was less and less point in contrasting it with any rival authority—or in treating it as an authority. It expanded to the horizons and there dissolved, save as this or that particular sense (such as those described in the preceding paragraphs) was once again precipitated out.

If, as Catholic and baptist Christians may now agree, Scripture and tradition (now in the sense of 1 Corinthians 15) are not two sources of authority but properly only one, both communities have a key to the role of creeds and confessions of faith as well. These can have no status as *additional* or supplementary authorities. Creeds and confessions cannot be invoked as witness to a truth that Scripture omits. But they may briefly witness to the truth that is more fully witnessed in Scripture. And indeed, according to their authors, that was the point of the early creeds; their makers always understood them as guides to the reading of Scripture, not as supplements to it. This is true of the Rule of Faith that Irenaeus summarizes (*Adv. haer.* x), true of the so-called Apostles' Creed that was in historical fact the baptismal confession developed within the Christian church at Rome, and true of the several creeds and conciliar declarations (notably the Nicene and Chalcedonian) adopted in the East.

While originally these creeds had functions as diverse as the confuting of Gnosticism, the guiding of converts, and the settling of interchurch controversies, all were understood to indicate the central teachings of Scripture itself. And the same is broadly true of those confessions of faith adopted by various Protestant bodies, and of the baptist confessions and covenants gathered up in collections such as those of Lumpkin (1969) and Loewen (1985), as well as of more detailed guidebooks such as the various Books of Discipline, Order, Common Prayer, and the like adopted as norms by many Christian bodies.

What Christian authority, then, have these utterances? They are not Scripture; indeed, many of them explicitly, and all implicitly, subordinate themselves to Scripture even while they offer interpretations of it. Are they tradition? It seems accurate to say, first, that they reflect with more or less faithfulness what some body of Christians at some time and place believed that in faith that body must declare. As such, they constitute *monuments* of tradition (a term I borrow from Latin theology— see Congar, 1966:288). They are cairns, trail-marks that indicate where the people of God have been on their journey through time. In this sense they tell us how Scripture has been (then and there) read, and invite us to read it that way if we can. Such invitations are often worthy ones, though the nearer we are in circumstances as well as in spirit to the adopters, the more helpful their monument may be in guiding our own attempts to read Scripture as the book of Jesus Christ, and to read it (by the baptist vision) as God's word to the present. Yet with the invitation to tradition should come a warning, which is, in the language of one of the confessions, that these articles of faith "are not intended to add anything to the simple conditions of salvation revealed in the New Testament . . . [or intended] as complete statements of our faith having any quality of finality or infallibility . . . [since they are] only guides in interpretation, *having no authority over the conscience*" ("The Baptist Faith and Message," 1963—Lumpkin, 1969:392, emphasis added). This means that, as distinguished both from churchly traditions such as the ringing of bells, and from the Pauline *paradosis* which is God's deliverance handed on, these monuments of tradition are simply hermeneutical aids, and like every reading strategy must remain subordinate to the scriptural texts we hope to read (partly) by their help.

Does this caveat therefore apply also to the authority of the two (traditional) elements of reading strategy invoked here: the centrality of Jesus Christ, and the "this is that" of the baptist vision? In consistency, it must. What are the consequences? Note first that our two elements are not on an equal footing with one another. The first (the centrality of Jesus) does not spring from the authority of the Bible, but explains how biblical authority arose for us in the first place: the Bible is Scripture for us because Jesus Christ makes it so. The second ("this is that" and "then is now") is an element characteristic of the Bible: it is Scripture's own way of reading itself, and thus becomes its way of engaging us in the story it tells. Yet on deeper reflection, it is not clear how we can have the first *as a principle of biblical interpretation* without having the second as well. For what can it mean to say that we read Scripture with Christ as center unless we acknowledge that the Jesus Christ we find there is the one who claims to be *our* Lord, here, now—which is to say, that this (our present situation as readers) is found to be that (the story Scripture tells, centered upon Jesus Christ). Thus it seems equally difficult to contemplate giving up, on Scripture's authority, either element in our strategy. Without the first, followers of Jesus Christ are not entitled to Scripture. And without the second, there is no "we" who are followers, no engagement of the reader with that authority, and thus again no effective authority *for us* in Scripture. These, then, are presuppositional convictions that are as central as Christ's salvation itself; they are the content of salvation applied to its narrative text.

And yet there ought to be here some doubt: Have we now argued ourselves into infallible hermeneutical convictions about the Bible? In an earlier work, James Smith and I invoked what we called the *principle of fallibility,* a principle that in a pluralistic world every convinced person or community would do well to embrace along with any other convictions held. This principle may take extreme forms, from the absurd to the trivial. Between these extremes there is, we thought, a coherent form of the principle of fallibility: Theoretically speaking, "Even one's most cherished and tenaciously held convictions might be false and are in principle always subject to rejection, reformulation, improvement, or reformation" (McClendon and Smith, 1975:118). While the two elements of Christian conviction I have laid out here are so nearly formal that it may not be possible flatly to reject them both without rejecting Christian faith itself, it certainly makes sense to say that their "reformulation, improvement, or reformation" is a lively possibility. At any rate, some readers of this book will probably think so! One should only be prepared to say why the reformulation is indeed an improvement. To speak of fallibility, however, raises the question of infallibility. Our reading strategy may be less than perfect, and so fallible, but have we in the Bible a book that is itself infallible or (in a more current term) inerrant? To that question, and to the third sort of challenge to Scripture's authority that we must set alongside critical historicism and church tradition, we therefore turn.

c. The challenge of inerrancy.—Theological discussion of Scripture has attended to various aspects of the subject, sometimes to Scripture's ultimate source, sometimes to the method by which these writings were produced (theories of inspiration), sometimes to the Bible's purpose or point, but sometimes to the special character of the written text itself. Here I wish to focus on the last of these, the character of the actual words of Scripture as this character affects the authority of the Bible. In the modern era theories of the infallibility or inerrancy of the text have limited the authority of Scripture in ways these theories' authors perhaps did not intend. It has been pointed out earlier that shifts in human consciousness evoke corresponding shifts in theological awareness; for example, the termination of the modern period brings current risks and challenges to Christian thought. Here, however, we must recall not the end of the modern period but its beginning. For it was in the time of Descartes (1596–1650) and John Locke (1632–1704) that some saw, in the demand for extrinsic foundations to support Christian belief, a need for a new theory to undergird Christians' acceptance of their own Bible. The baptists were not the first to sense this need, but eventually many conceded it and subscribed to the novel inerrancy theories that were being produced (Bush and Nettles, 1980).

Walter Klaassen, author of *Anabaptism: Neither Catholic nor Protestant* (1981*b*), has surveyed the understanding of the Bible in some typical documents of the sixteenth-century baptists. Although like Protestants these premoderns rejected the authority of the papacy, Anabaptists differed significantly from the Protestants of their day as well. Thus (1) they took Scripture's role to be the provision of broad models for Christian teaching and church order (cf. the baptist vision); (2) in finding these models they decisively subordinated the Old Testament to the New (cf. our Christocentric thesis); and (3) they sharply distinguished, though in different degrees, the outer word from the inner, or the letter from the spirit. Emphasizing the spirit, Bernard Rothmann (c. 1495–c. 1535) wrote that "an interpretation is reliable if it leads to behaviour that conforms to Christ. If such behaviour is not there, Scripture has not been understood" (Klaassen, ed., 1981*a*:chap. 7). And a similar emphasis on obedience to Scripture as a rule (or pattern) for life characterized the early English and American Baptists. Thus the earliest Baptist confession in America, that of Thomas Goold's Charlestown, Massachusetts, congregation (1665), characterized the Bible as "the rule of this knowlidge faith & obedience *Concerning the worship & service of God* & all other Christian duties" (in Smith, Handy, and Loetscher, 1960:I, 168, emphasis added). It was *practice*, then, that was the point of biblical authority.

Meantime, in seventeenth-century modernity a shift was underway in Lutheran and Reformed thinking. This shift was picked up as early as the Second London Confession of the Particular Baptists (1677, see Lumpkin, 1969:248-52; and cf. Wm. Estep in R. James, ed., 1987:chap. 11). The new view came to an overt climax in such documents as the Mennonite Church's confession of 1921 called "Christian Fundamentals": "We believe in the plenary and verbal inspiration of the Bible as the Word of God; that it is authentic in its matter, authoritative in its counsels, inerrant in the original writings, and the only infallible rule of faith and practice" (Loewen, 1985:71). In this final phrase, the old baptist concepts of "rule" and "practice" survive, but they are put last, preceded by the terminology of the newly dominant inerrancy theory. In this and similar documents of the modern period (1600–1900) the Bible became less a book of types than a book of information; it was no longer so much a criterial authority *of* shared practices as an informative authority *on* faith and practice.

Did this shift entail a limitation of biblical authority? The answer seemed to some to depend upon whether the "inerrant" information that the Bible furnished was confined to matters of religion (as E. Y. Mullins in 1925 persuaded Southern Baptists to affirm), or was extended to every field of human knowledge—history, music, architecture, physics, geology, and all the rest. Eventually, though, intelligent inerrancy theorists saw trouble wherever they turned (Marsden, 1987). Any Bible reader who followed the plain wording of the theory could find literally thousands of inconsistencies, verbal contradictions, and other conundrums throughout the book Christians were told to accept as inerrant. Such a reader would find many Bible texts that remained gloriously free from rationalist efforts at harmonization; if in the name of inerrancy the reader then attempted to smooth out the inconsistencies, severe cognitive dissonance could follow. Was the tribe of Levi to be included in the census commanded by God (so Num. 3:14-16) or excluded from it (so Num. 1:47-49; 2:33)? Did the flood (Genesis 7) cover the entire earth, including the tallest mountains "under the whole heaven"? Did Moses write the Pentateuch, including the past-tense account of his own death, in Deuteronomy 34? (for these and many other anomalies cf. Lindholm, 1986; more caustically, Lane Fox, 1992). To meet these problems such patriarchs of inerrancy theory as A. A. Hodge and B. B. Warfield (1881) had long since provided a way of escape: under specified limitations, apparent biblical errors were by their definition not errors at all. In a list I adapt from Fisher Humphreys (in R. James, ed., 1987:chap. 4), these qualifications ultimately came to include (1) that the theory applied only to the original manuscripts no longer available—a restriction that permitted textual criticism; (2) that it applied only to what the writers intentionally taught (taught as Scripture?), not to all they said; (3) that it applied only to the resultant (original) text, not to its human authors themselves; (4) that it made room for progressive revelation—thus later parts of Scripture "clarified" earlier parts; (5) that the theory taught that biblical language is phenomenal not scientific (e.g., "the sun rose"); (6) that biblical language included poetry and tropes as well as literal language; (7) that the writers employed imprecise or inexact expressions; (8) that their use of quotation was likewise acceptably inexact; (9) that Scripture's genres included "songs, prayers, laws, proverbs, apocalypses," and so on; (10) surprisingly, that some "apparent" errors were not covered by the preceding cases (these are simply anomalies for inerrancy theory); (11) and last, that the word "inerrancy" itself need not be adopted in expressing the theory.

In a word, ingenious inerrancy theorists managed to withdraw all the bizarre factual claims their theory seemed to require. Yet this did not mean, *pace* Humphreys, that the theory thus qualified made no difference. Their theory might die the death of eleven (or a thousand) qualifications, yet the unspoken presupposition of modern foundationalist inerrancy theorists, that the Bible is exclusively an authority *on* history, and so not a *criterial* authority displaying the typical believers' faith, far less an authority *in* the life of shared faith, remained. The Bible by this theory had become either a book limited to the severely qualified information it afforded (and was thus not an unlimited Word of God), or alternatively, its writ of inerrancy *was* unqualified—and skepticism stood at the gate once more. The root trouble in either case was that Bible readers were diverted from the role of the Bible as that is reflected in the baptist vision; the theory, qualified or unqualified, thus set unseen but harsh limits upon Scripture itself.

Still, it may be asked if inerrancy theorists did not have a point? Was their sort of modernity not right to shield the Bible against another modern limit, that reflected in the exaltation of religious experience and the reductive historicizing of Scripture? However flawed their theory, did it not rightly resist treatment of the Bible as a merely human product? Do not "infallible" and "inerrant" point to the majesty of the Book, to its exalted quality? The problem addressed here may without irreverence be compared with the problem of the person of Christ in Christian thought. Christologists have struggled to affirm now the fully divine, now the truly human nature of the Son of God. Though sometimes difficulties may seem eased by affirming only the divine, or only the human, yet long Christian reflection exposes each of these as false ways to think about Jesus Christ. Similarly, if inerrantists in a skeptical age sought to make of the Bible a fully divine book, they inadvertently diminished its human element, even while others made the contrary error. Some theologians have therefore proposed a two-natures model of Scripture to match historic two-natures Christology (cf. Charles Talbert in R. James, 1987:chap. 3). In line with Chapter Six above, I would substitute for "two natures" a narrative model as more appropriate both to the character of Scripture and to Scripture's Christ. **By this model the story the Bible tells is God's own story, told in the way God pleases to tell it.** Scripture is God's Book, God's word to us. At the same time, the story the Bible tells is our own story, a fully human story, human in its breadth and depth; human, too, in its foibles and failings. So the wonder, the miracle of Scripture is this: These two stories give us not two interwoven books, one human, one divine, which we can divide at will, but one indivisible Book, one Bible. God speaks not only in the grand moments but also in the foibles and failings of the telling of the human story; the exalted passages are not only divine but are still fully and truly human; the two stories, God's and our own, are fully present in each part of the one collection we call the Bible. We have seen that historical criticism and acceptance of traditional readings each risks dangerous limitations of the Bible, yet these limitations can be avoided. In contrast, it remains to be seen if inerrancy theory can find a way to overcome the limits it imposes—so far, it seems not to have done so, while the narrative approach provided here offers a promising alternative.

This brings us to the question of which books properly compose the Bible. Many Christian writers have spoken of the "canon" of Scripture as if that were a superimposed authority, a kind of superscripture defining Scripture, and this has led some to say that it is finally the church that by creating the canon or list of biblical books defines or creates Scripture itself. It seems truer to say that making such canons or lists of sacred books would have been an unfaithful act had these very books not already possessed scriptural attributes—such attributes as being at once God's own story and a truly human story, as centering upon Jesus Christ, as evoking in their readers the prophetic or baptist vision—so that churches, by their recognition of these attributes, thereby revealed themselves as real churches. In this sense their act of recognizing Scripture authenticated the church as church even while it acknowledged Scripture as Scripture (cf. Ramm, 1957). Canonicity (inclusion on somebody's list) is not for us merely the outcome of an act performed once for all by some church or council; the canon reports these monumental acts, but equally, if the list thus produced is correct, it foreshadows an act that must be repeated whenever a church, Spirit-guided, uses any part of the Scriptures *as* Scripture. In this sense, the canon is not merely "open in principle," as many have said, but open in fact. In a similar way, the coherence of these books in *one* collection displays their reciprocity: they quote one another, presume one another. Given time for the task, we could expect any Spirit-led church today, confronted with these scriptural books on a shelf alongside other books, to make just about the same selection that our spiritual ancestors did. The claim that the books of Scripture are canonical, when it finds its way into confessions of faith, typically acknowledges each of these features, saying in effect, "We commend *all* these books as Scripture; if you would read the Bible, read *all* these." (Thus those who speak of a canon within the canon, a shorter list of 'really important' texts, seem to contradict the very idea of the canonical claim.) Finally, it is worth noting that the baptists of the sixteenth century generally preferred using the Catholic rather than the (shorter) Protestant canon, and in light of the understanding of Scripture advanced here, it is at least worth asking whether they were not on the whole right to do so. It is a topic on which the churches, once freed from the artificial constrictions of criticism, tradition, and inerrancy listed above, can helpfully converse.

§3. The Fellowship of the Spirit

So far, I have been trying to say how ultimate authority grasps Jesus' followers if, as I have claimed, authority can finally belong to God alone. Two of three possible loci of authority have shown themselves to be proximate, not absolute. Religious experience cannot be an authority on its own; rather it partakes of the authority to which it submits, the authority of the holy God. Scripture is no free-standing authority, but comes to be authoritative just as it represents the present Christ in a reading practice that accepts Scripture's story as its own. So we come to our third locus, church, and we will see that its authority arises only as it functions as the fellowship of the Spirit. Thus the church, too, is a proximate not an ultimate authority. Yet it is not an authority that experiential, biblical faith can do without. For evangelical experience and authoritative Scripture both require assessment, discernment, judgment. Which experience is evangelical? What writing is Scripture, and how is it to be read? If these judgments should be muddled, how can God's authority be discerned? What if we mistake the experience? What if we misread the Book? A well-known answer invokes the inner witness of the Spirit, guiding experiential judgment, directing biblical interpretation (Calvin, *Inst.* I, 7, 4). But how does that inner witness operate? That is our question now.

Bernard Cooke, in a classic twentieth-century book on ministry, has pointed out that the Christian church through the centuries has recognized the need for the sure discernment of God's authority by its acknowledgment of prophets, gifted leaders, apostles, pastors, teachers, theologians, and others. To the extent that these make judgments recognized to be discerning, authority is exercised. Warnings of the riskiness of judgment (e.g., Matt. 7:1) and against mere private judgment (Rom. 14:10) must be balanced against the inevitability that in a living community someone, somehow, shall indeed judge. Thus the prophet judges the community, but the community also judges whether the prophet is true or false; each thereby exercises some judgmental authority over the other (Cooke, 1976:405ff). If we were to argue that in the final analysis the private judgment of each must have the last word, we would leave no place for authentic community life and would deny as well the very ground just gained, namely the real, objective authority of experience and Scripture as these mediate to us the final authority of God. Correspondingly, we affirm that God is not only Ultimate Love (or Father) and Compelling Presence (or Son); God is also Cohesive Spirit, the Holy Spirit that creates holy fellowship. By that creation, the entire community of faith, like the voice of evangelical experience and the written word of Scripture, becomes a bearer of proximate authority. For if we agree that no authority is final save that of God, then each human authority, including that of the solitary believer with his or her conscience, must find its place on a great moving circle, a Ferris wheel of discernment, interpretation, obedience, and action that has no top chair, no priestly summit—not 'the clergy,' not the solitary 'believer-priest' with his or her Bible, not 'the whole church in council,' since each of these is secured to and depends on others in the wheel, and since each in turn must swing beneath the discerning judgment of God.

In the present Section we look beyond the word to three other forms of Christ's presence, the *worship* of the community, its share in kingdom *work*, and the Christian *witness* that reaches out beyond its own circle to the wide world. In these, as well as in the objective written word of God already considered, divine authority shows itself. Objectively, this means that in each of these four a Presence, recognizable as the risen Christ (Chapter Six), awaits us. But it means also that the disciples' judgment active in all these operations, their shared discernment, is a gift, a mode of God's presence as Holy Spirit.

Such discernment is not a special revelation or disclosure that forecloses the thinking minds of those who share it. Discernment is rather an ongoing *practice*, as we can learn in the New Testament from such passages as Matthew 18 and 1 Corinthians 5 and 12–14. As these first disciples practiced it, discernment meant taking seriously the concern of God's Spirit for their own response to Jesus' summons, "follow me." Thus discernment in worship meant and means that a community of God's people find ways of praying together that permit them to be addressed by as well as to address their Lord. Discernment in kingdom work meant and means a communal undertaking in which God's people in a certain place meet and consider their next steps in the common life, bringing their shared journey under mutual study in the light of all the Scripture and all experience, committing it to ultimate authority in earnest prayer, and shaping the common judgment of all concerned (Yoder, 1967). Discernment in witness meant and means that evangelism is no haphazard enterprise, but is the deliberate task of the entire fellowship in which kingdom claims are declared and kingdom harvest reaped. And, to repeat, discernment in the written and proclaimed word (§2 above) meant and means that writer and readers alike are corporately engaged in placing Jesus Christ at the center of Scripture in such a way that the prophetic vision becomes the present vision of the community.

In all these matters the strength of congregational polity lies not in a mechanical democracy of yes or no votes taken upon some leadership ukase or majority report; it lies rather in the mutual trust of brothers and sisters who can and will assemble; it lies in a diversity of gifts, of which leadership is one while discernment of spirits is another; it lies in listening to concerned outsiders; it lies in obedience to the Spirit. And the strength of connectional polity lies in the extension of these very elements of trust, diversity, openness, obedience to the wider people-hood of which each congregation is but a part. What justifies any polity is not its effectiveness, for on occasion any may crumble, nor its convenience, for any may cause trouble: it is justified by the Spirit that indwells such communities of concern.

In these tasks there is rationale for a church polity. Others may have good reasons for supporting some kind of local polity—its pragmatic effectiveness, its agreement with the principle of subsidiarity, its historic precedence, its grassroots appeal—and all these have some weight (cf. Hopewell, 1987). A deeper reason, however, is found in the nature of authority itself. It must be evident that in congregational life we find each of the sorts of authority listed at the beginning of this chapter. In some degree there will be "authorities on" each Christian concern: authorities on Bible and doctrine and evangelism and the needs of neighbors near and far; these are the theologians and historians and experts of many sorts who (in person or by their writing) exercise some legitimate proximate authority over the common life. It is at this level that the theologian working at her or his word processor must acknowledge that she or he exercises some power, and must be prayerful and circumspect in its exercise. Again, "authorities in" the congregation, pastors and deacons and church callers and teachers and office secretaries and visiting church worthies exercise their servant offices, and (insofar as these reflect the servanthood of the Lord Jesus) constitute a second kind of legitimate proximate authority. Like theologians, and even more powerfully in most baptist contexts, these must recognize the power they exercise and the need for restraint in its exercise. Yet in every gathering of the people, still a third kind of authority can be found. This is what is called above 'criterial' authority, the authority for faith and life that is possessed by members of the Christian body just because they *are* members. Now criterial authority is of necessity social and communal; members' authority therefore differs from that of the solitary expert and that of the designated leader; it comes into its own only as the community communes, only as it walks and talks together and finds its own voice by listening to its constituent voices. This authority, like the other two, is only proximate: it gains its seat in the Ferris wheel of authority not from the native powers of those who share it, but from their ongoing communion with the (non-transferable) authority of God. God in the community is God the Holy Spirit; only by the Spirit's presence is the criterial authority of the community the fellowship of the Spirit. To the degree that 'authorities on' and 'authorities in' the community have a proximate authority of their own, they do so in dependence upon this third, criterial authority; they themselves are but its extension into the realms of community self-knowledge ('authorities on') and community action ('authorities in').

Now this understanding of communal authority is not likely to sit well with those who dream of building the church of God as another earthly empire, or who seek in legal and authoritarian terms the "reunion of the Church." For *in practice* discernment takes hold of divine authority in ways incurably diverse. Practical experience shows that communities of discernment from New Testament times onward have held not one but a variety of conceptual schemes and doctrines and understandings of work and worship and witness and word, a variety the preceding chapters have sought to respect. Yet this variety is evidence not just of the inevitable failures in discernment, though these occur, but also of the "manifold wisdom of God." For according to Ephesians God provides his people with remarkable diversity as well as with unity in Christ. This diversity may for a time actually inhibit the sharing of the "mystery," yet it only points to the "riches" of the Father's glory and to the need to pray for his Spirit so that we can *"with* all the saints" grasp the full measure of the Spirit's indwelling, Christ's love, God's fullness (Eph. 3:9–5:1).

* * * * *

In summary, when full authority is assigned to God alone, the result is the subordination of every human locus of authority. The *disciple* whose soul is competent, the *book* whose word is divine, the *church* whose fellowship is spiritual can make their claims only as *proximate* authorities, each beneath the sovereign authority of God. And as God is one, these varied proximate authorities rightly hold sway only as they draw together, the book giving light to the soul's experience, the fellowship interpreting the book in its ancient and present setting, the redeemed soul together with other redeemed souls constituting the structured fellowship. Paul Harrison, author of a milestone sociological study of American Baptists, remarks that *few* Baptists "have seen that authority rests with none of these alone but with all together" (1959:218). I boldly venture a somewhat different judgment: Every baptist at least dimly knows that these three belong together and do converge. Our tacit knowledge may come to speech only with difficulty; some may never speak the truth they know; we may in our journey lift up now only this authority, now only that; but the interactive presence of all is just what constitutes the priesthood of believers (cf. 1 Pet. 2:5, 9; Rev. 1:6) that we are.

Lest this seem a mere partisan claim on behalf of one sort of Christian self-understanding, we do well to see its link with another recurrent New Testament theme, nonviolence. Sixteenth-century baptists were divided on the issue of violence, as later generations have been as well (Stayer, 1976). But from Schleitheim to Martin Luther King, among Friends and Brethren and here and there even Southern Baptists, there has been a persistent peace witness that would not harm or destroy though required to do so by the claim of the state or even by the iron 'law' of self-preservation. There is a strong congruence between this way of nonviolence and the pattern of authority expressed in our triad: the experience of discipleship, the witness of Scripture, the discernment of congregations. It should be remembered, for example, that "the ban" was practiced by a people who refused to enforce their authority with sword and rack—or to require the state to do so for them. They believed that if they failed to *persuade* others to walk with them, the only Christian response was to say a reluctant good-bye: they could not enforce their sense of what was best for all by harming or destroying. Seen in that light, the ban is only the visible backbone of the gentle constraint of the Spirit in a community that knows it must neglect none of these proximate authorities if it would submit to the ultimate authority of God.

§4. Reprise: Roger Williams on Authority

It seems fitting to close this essay-chapter with a reflection on the life of Roger Williams (1603?–1683), whose thought has exercised a powerful if silent presence in the preceding sections. Among the Baptists, who celebrate their (genuine) connection with seventeenth-century Puritans, the name of Roger Williams has in recent decades loomed large. An immigrant to New from Old England, Williams was deeply involved in the Puritan revolution in church and state that reshaped Christian thinking on both sides of the Atlantic. His idealized statue justly occupies the only space the City of Geneva assigned to an American in its massive monument to the Reformation. Pious, biblical, learned, convinced, and withal charming, Roger Williams has seemed the granite exemplar of a certain sort of Puritan Baptist self-image. Yet there has been no corresponding interest in Williams among the self-conscious heirs of the Continental radical reformation: thus, though a host of other non-Mennonites are included, no entry on Williams appears in *The Mennonite Encyclopedia* or its 1990 Supplement (ME). I hope to indicate here, however, that both sorts of baptists have been significantly mistaken about him. For Roger Williams, if ever a Baptist, was properly one for only a few months at most. After that he was understood to be what was called in his day a Seeker—not a formal sect, but a designation for those who found no settled church their own in that turbulent century. As such, Williams deliberately though courteously rejected Baptists along with Papists, Anglican Protestants, Presbyterians, Independents, Boston Puritans, and any others he knew. Using the category developed here, however, we can call him a baptist, and a baptist of unusual present interest (cf. John Garrett, 1970:chap. 10). For what this Seeker sought above all else was a proper and sufficient *authority* in state and church.

The known external facts of Williams' life are few, and may be simply told (Miller, ed., 1953; Winslow, 1957; Moore, 1963; Morgan, 1967; Williams, 1988:intro.; Gaustad, 1991): born (we think) in 1603, the year Elizabeth died and James became England's king, the boy grew up in his merchant father's home in the heart of old London. Singled out by the great jurist Sir Edward Coke, he was sent to Charterhouse school and then to Cambridge, where Puritan thinking was at the flood. In 1629, graduated and ordained in the Church of England, he became chaplain in the Puritan manor house of the Masham family; there he met and married one of the "maydes" or ladies-in-waiting, Mary Barnard. That same year, a Puritan company was formed to settle Massachusetts Bay in New England, there to reconstitute the English church on new congregational lines. While William Laud maneuvered to purge Old England of Puritans (1630), Roger and Mary Williams set sail from Bristol to join the new experiment in church and state.

Yet here the story takes a strange turn. Offered clerical office in new Boston's First Church, Roger Williams declined. He moved to Salem, then Plymouth, then Salem again; these English settlements found him winsome and able, but he emerged severely at odds with Boston's clergy and magistrates, the more so as his thought developed. The tension lay in questions of *authority:* whether, as Williams feared, New England's churches were still "unseparated" from the Old English Church (and hence still "corrupt"); whether, as he knew too well, the King's Patent based English property claims not on purchase from the Original American residents, but instead on "Christian" voyages of discovery—as if Europe or England were God's own country, entitled to possess all the rest of the world. The tension lay also in Boston's persistent mingling of the authority of church and town—the very confusion Williams had come to New England to escape (Williams, 1988:12-29). And finally, the tension lay in Roger Williams' reading of the book of Revelation, in correspondences he found there between the high and the mighty of New England's state and church and their counterparts the "ten kings which have received no kingdom as yet" but who aspired to beastly power over the faithful (Rev. 17:12). Over against these clerical and magisterial gentry, Williams was coming to see himself associated with those who "carry on the mystery and glory of Christianity in the meanest and lowest of earthen vessels," so that it is against the Lamb's "declared will and course, that his servants should expect many Christian great or noble persons, many Christian mighty men either for wealth or valour, many Christian magistrates" (1652c:224f). Williams' New England enemies would see the conflict otherwise, and their scornful judgment would mightily affect his own future.

In January 1636, less than five years after his hopeful arrival in Massachusetts, Roger Williams had to flee Massachusetts under an Act of Banishment. In territory unclaimed by the English he purchased the site of future Providence, Rhode Island, from Narragansett Indians he knew. (The story is that on arrival by canoe he hailed these acquaintances in a mixture of English and Narragansett: "What cheare, Netop?" that is, "Hello, friend.") He was joined there by traveling companions, by his wife and their two children, and eventually by a growing horde of the dispossessed from other colonial settlements, notably by Anne Hutchinson and her group. Jews took opportunity to settle in Rhode Island as early as 1658. The colony that came into being was marked (in distinction from all the others) by what Williams called "soul-liberty," the freedom of each settler to worship only as his or her conscience dictated.

During these years from his 1636 arrival until his death in 1683, Williams was fully occupied, supporting his family by farming and trading with the Indians, writing *A Key into the Language of America* (1643), serving long terms as governor of the colony, and making two extended visits (1643–44, 1651–54) to old England to secure for the new colony charters that would incorporate its avowed freedoms, and betimes occupying himself with Bible study, preaching, and (pre)evangelism among the Original Americans who lived near his new home. Yet the conflicts with Boston from 1630–36 and the writings they stirred him to produce were so crucial to all that he thought and later wrote that we can fairly focus here upon them. His chief critic and opponent in these years was John Cotton (1584–1652), Boston cleric, who as Williams fled into the deep cold of the American wilderness was moved to write a letter to explain to the heretic why his treatment was perfectly just (Williams, 1988:31-52). An exchange of letters (considerably slowed by wilderness mail service) followed, issuing ultimately in Williams' great reply, *The Bloudy Tenent [Teaching] of Persecution for Cause of Conscience Discussed* . . . (1644b) and its sequels (Polishook, 1967). In these writings, Williams staked out a view of Scripture and authority in church and in civil society that constitutes a vast monument for those who hold religious liberty dear.

As LeRoy Moore (1963) and others have decisively shown, Williams' basis for soul liberty was not the Enlightenment view of human dignity and rights that influenced American thinking in the Revolution and (later) was to express itself in the Universal Declaration of Human Rights of the United Nations (1946). Nor was Williams' thought based on any skeptical diffidence concerning God's self-disclosure in Jesus Christ. What must eternally halt government, be it old Roman or new American or any other, from attempting to control the faith and worship of its subjects is that God has once and for all settled divine kingship upon Christ Jesus, whose disciples are forbidden to constrain anyone save by gospel preaching and gentle love. "The kingly power of the Lord Jesus troubles all the kings and rulers of the world" (1644b:346f). This being the case, there is no longer (though once, in Israel, there truly was) a civil sovereignty divinely ordered; all governments, East or West, European or Original American, are now alike limited—by Christ's sole kingship—to the task of seeking the civil good of their subjects; to that and nothing more.

Williams supported this position by several lines of argument. Perhaps most powerful for moderns was his vivid use of metaphor. Thus he offered his fellow colonists a "true picture" of the ship of state on its clamorous voyage: "there goes many a ship to sea," he wrote, "with many a hundred souls in one ship, whose weal and woe is common." This being so, though those embarked together be "Papists and Protestants, Jews, or Turks," it is the ship commander's task both to require each member of the company to fulfill his or her role in the ship as needed—passengers to pay their fare, seamen to perform their service—but to force none to "come to the ship's prayers or worship" or to prevent their own particular prayers or worship (Williams, 1988:423f). In other words, the ship of state is no church; its governors are to be selected not by divine right (or by their 'right' theology), but simply on the basis of their skill in handling complex and often divisive civil affairs. As argued in the "powerful practices" section of the previous volume of this work (*Ethics*, Six), only its developing skills and the goods to be achieved thereby can justify the practices of statecraft by any people anywhere.

Authority in church was another matter. This, Williams believed, should stem from the apostolic (or "converting") ministry, the missionary imperative to found a true church. But long ago, in the age of Constantine, that apostolic commission had been aborted, and "Papists," along with Protestants who traced their succession through Papists, were now only pretenders (1652*b*:160). Until the True Church appeared (and Williams believed that its reappearance would require Christ's personal return) there could be no authentic mission enterprise: witnesses such as he could only prepare sinful American hearts for a coming day. As divine authority in state was forever canceled, and divine authority in church was now postponed, biblical disciples were left the choice between the counterfeit Christ (Rome and the Protestants, with their hireling, tax-supported ministries) on the one hand, and on the other a covert, patient waiting upon Christ. Williams chose the latter. Nevertheless, even in the distressing present time,

> there have been and are many excellent prophets and witnesses of Christ Jesus, who never entred (as they say) into the ministry, to wit, lawyers, physitians, souldiers, tradesmen, and others . . . who by God's Holy Spirit . . . have attained and much improved, an excellent spirit of knowledge and utterance in the holy things of Jesus Christ. (1652*b*:166)

In these lay-witnesses (and was Roger Williams, providentially, not now one of them?) lay the hope of faithful Christianity until the Lord should come.

One might say that in the spirit of his times Williams took an exceedingly high view of church—so high that the true church could not be found on earth. He came to believe that Baptists (with their understanding of baptism and membership) were nearer to it than the others, yet with all the rest they, too, lacked a suitable apostolic ministry. Other sorts fell still farther short. Since Roger Williams' day, the baptists (as Chapter Ten has shown) have participated with many others in a modern missionary movement in which uncounted millions have bowed the knee to Christ's Lordship, a development that provides a validation of apostolic (i.e., missionary) authority such as Williams in his day did not foresee. Meanwhile, the theory of ecclesiastical successionism has enjoyed revision in the recognition that apostolic ministry is more nearly tested by its functioning than by historical connections or their lack (e.g., Cooke, 1976:513-20). And perhaps both Catholics and baptists have better learned how to read the rich symbolism of the book of Revelation (see Chapter Two above).

Yet Roger Williams' idea of authority still speaks a needed word to us. Two guidelines shaped all he wrote: (1) his skillful *use of typology* and (2) the *centrality of Christ* in theology. The former is what he called the "golden rule," by which he meant, not Jesus' summary of the law (Matt. 7:12; Luke 6:31), but the vivid "golden *mece* wand" or measuring rod mentioned in Revelation 11:1 and 21:15 (cf. Ezek. 40:3ff). This golden measuring stick required evaluating churches and Christians by the "first pattern" of the New Testament. For a single example, conversions are conversions only if they correspond to the New Testament pattern: (1) answering a free preaching of the gospel, (2) consisting in a turning of the "whole man" from Satan to God, and (3) comprising both a new, disciplined way of life and an authentic way of worship (Williams, 1645:39f). In other words, Williams' "mece wand" was no other than our baptist vision, and by making it normative he was so far a genuine baptist. Yet he realized that typology had its perils: in the hands of a John Cotton it could turn Old Testament types into constricted Puritan models for church and state—a persecuting, violent state protecting a compromised church. Against such a result, Williams set his other principle, Christ's centrality. All the "types" of the Old Testament, its kingdom and its priesthood in particular, were fulfilled in Jesus,

> Who disdained not to enter this world in a stable, amongs beasts, as
> unworthy the society of men: who past through this world with the esteeme

*of a mad man, a deceiver, a conjuror, a traytor against Caesar, and
destitute of an house wherein to rest his head: who made choice of his first
and greatest embassadours out of fisher-men, tent-makers, &c. and at last
chose to depart on the stage of a pianfull shamefull gibbet.* (1644a:317)

Therefore no claim to found Puritan or any other government on the
precedent of Israel as depicted in the Old Testament was valid; all its
typological force had been fulfilled in Jesus Christ. *From Jesus onward,*
government interference in anyone's faith, be that faith false or true,
constituted disobedience to Jesus himself; if undertaken for supposed
biblical reasons, it was self-refuted.

* * * * *

"By what authority are you acting like this? Who gave you this
authority?" This question, posed by the keepers of the most sacred
precinct in old Israel, we are told, to Jesus called the Christ (Matt. 21:23),
must arise again with special force within the sympathetic reader of this
volume, as it certainly does in its author. This volume has contravened
authority in many ways. It works within a part-spectrum of Christian
community that has been mightily ignored by the most famous theologians, and often scorned by the powers that be in church and society
alike. Perhaps that fact alone should have constrained its writer to follow
the familiar trails as much as possible, or should have sent readers to
seek out a different book. Yet this has not been the case. Instead, these
authorities, too, have in many places in the preceding pages been either
silently ignored or openly controverted. However, as this last chapter
has shown, the concept of authority is not dead, not transcended. Modernity itself found new ways to employ the appeal to authority, but not
how to do without it. There are still authorities on, still those whose labor
and skill yield knowledge others must seek. There are still authorities
in, still those who by the consent of the governed or by some other right
carry on the public life of our communities, including our ecclesial
communities, even though none of those authorities has any higher role
than do church maintenance persons or office secretaries or Sunday
morning greeters. And there is the inescapable criterial authority of
those who show by their practice what Christian living or Christian
teaching is. It may disturb us to find that the argument of this chapter
can be summarized in just this way: The authorities that under God we
know are the love of God *enjoyed*, the grace of Christ *written*, the fellowship of the Spirit *gathered*. These remain proximate, imperfect, and for
the time being. We have in them no eternal authority: "My knowledge

now is partial; *then* it will be whole" (1 Cor. 13:12). We have in them no flawless or inerrant authority; to pretend that we do is not to defend but to weaken the authority of God.

Yet to recognize their proximate character is a defeat only for those who despise Paul's apostolic patience. For the rest, it is a great gain. To be proximate is to be "next to." The love story in which we engage God's love is proximate because it is an answer to the unspeakable love of God. The book, the Book, in which we learn about Jesus the Christ is proximate because it is uniquely his book, relays his gospel, declares and imparts his grace. The community that gathers in his name, the fellowship of the Spirit, is proximate because the Spirit is God's Spirit, the name is Jesus' name, the gathering is at the call and under the eyes of God. The proximate adjoins the absolute; that is its wonder, its mission, its end. It is enough. There is more to say about all these things, but it must wait for another volume—or wait until that which is perfect is come.

> At present we see only puzzling reflections in a mirror,
>   but one day we shall see face to face.
> My knowledge now is partial;
>   then it will be whole, like God's knowledge of me.
>
> (1 Cor. 13:12)

Bibliography

ABBOTT, Edwin Abbott (pseudonym, A Square)
1884   *Flatland: A Romance of Many Dimensions.* London: Seeley.
ABBOTT, Walter M., ed.
1966   *The Documents of Vatican II.* New York: Guild.
ABRAHAM, William J., and Steven W. HOLTZER, eds.
1987   *The Rationality of Religious Belief: Essays in Honour of Basil Mitchell.* Oxford: Clarendon.
ADAMS, Henry
1906 (1983) *Henry Adams: Novels, Mont Saint Michel, The Education.* New York: Viking, Library of America.
AHLSTROM, Sydney E.
1967   (Ed.) *Theology in America: The Major Protestant Voices from Puritanism to Neo-Orthodoxy.* Indianapolis: Bobbs-Merrill.
1972   *A Religious History of the American People.* New Haven: Yale University Press.
ALBRIGHT, William Foxwell
1957   *From the Stone Age to Christianity: Monotheism and the Historical Process.* 2nd ed. Garden City: Doubleday.
ALLEN, Diogenes
1981   *The Traces of God in a Frequently Hostile World.* Cambridge: Cowley.
1985   *Philosophy for Understanding Theology.* Atlanta: John Knox.
ALLEN, Roland
1912 (1960) *Missionary Methods, St. Paul's or Ours?* London: World Dominion.
ALLISON, Dale C., Jr.
1985   *The End of the Ages Has Come: An Early Interpretation of the Passion and Resurrection of Jesus.* Philadelphia: Fortress.
ALSTON, William P.
1989   *Divine Nature and Human Language: Essays in Philosophical Theology.* Ithaca: Cornell University Press.

ALTHAUS, Paul
  1948   *Die Letzten Dinge: Lehrbuch der Eschatologie.* Gütersloh: Gerd Mohr.
AMMERMAN, Nancy Tatom
  1990   *Baptist Battles: Social Change and Religious Conflict in the Southern Baptist Convention.* New Brunswick: Rutgers University Press.
ANDERSON, Bernhard W., ed.
  1984   *Creation in the Old Testament.* Philadelphia: Fortress.
ANDERSON, Courtney
  1956   *To the Golden Shore: The Life of Adoniram Judson.* Boston: Little, Brown.
APPLEYARD, Brian
  1993   *Understanding the Present: Science and the Soul of Modern Man.* Garden City: Doubleday.
AQUINAS, Thomas
  1954   *Nature and Grace: Selections from the Summa Theologica.* Trans. and ed. A. M. Fairweather. Library of Christian Classics. Vol. 11. Philadelphia: Westminster.
  1964–76   *Summa Theologiae: Latin Text and English Translation.* 60 vols. New York: Blackfriars with McGraw-Hill.
  1989   *Summa Theologiae: A Concise Translation.* Trans. and ed. Timothy McDermott. Westminster, Md.: Christian Classics.
ARMOUR, Rollin Stely
  1966   *Anabaptist Baptism: A Representative Study.* Scottdale: Herald.
AUERBACH, Erich
  1953   *Mimesis: The Representation of Reality in Western Literature.* Trans. W. Trask. Garden City: Doubleday.
AULÉN, Gustaf
  1931   *Christus Victor: An Historical Study of the Three Main Types of the Idea of Atonement.* Trans. A. G. Herbert. New York: Macmillan.
AYER, Alfred Jules
  1936   *Language, Truth, and Logic.* New York: Dover.

BAILLIE, Donald M.
  1948   *God Was in Christ: An Essay on Incarnation and Atonement.* New York: Scribner's.
Baltimore Catechism No. 1
  1930   Ed. E. M. Deck. Buffalo: Rauch & Stoeckl.
BANCHOFF, Thomas F.
  1990   *Beyond the Third Dimension: Geometry, Computer Graphics, and Higher Dimensions.* New York: Scientific American Library.
Bangkok Assembly 1973
  1974   Geneva: World Council of Churches.
BANKS, Robert
  1987   "'Walking' as a Metaphor of the Christian Life." In *Perspectives on Language and Text,* ed. E. W. Conrad and E. G. Newing. Winona Lake: Eisenbrauns.
  1994   *Paul's Idea of Community: The Early House Churches in Their Cultural Setting.* Grand Rapids: Eerdmans.
Baptism, Eucharist and Ministry
  1982   Geneva: World Council of Churches.

BARBOUR, Ian G.
1971   *Issues in Science and Religion.* San Francisco: Harper & Row.
BARNES, William Wright
1954   *The Southern Baptist Convention 1845–1953:* Nashville: Broadman.
BARR, James
1989   "Literality." *Faith and Philosophy* 6 (October):412-28.
BARRETT, David B.
1991   "Annual Statistical Table on Global Mission: 1991." *International Bulletin of Missionary Research* (January).
BARROW, John D., and Frank J. TIPLER
1988   *The Anthropic Cosmological Principle.* Oxford: University Press.
BARTH, Karl
1921 (1933)   *The Epistle to the Romans.* Trans. E. C. Hoskyns. 2nd ed. Oxford: University Press.
1931 (1958)   *Anselm: Fides Quaerens Intellectum.* Trans. I. W. Robertson from the 2nd ed. Richmond: John Knox.
1943 (1948)   *The Teaching of the Church Regarding Baptism.* Trans. E. A. Payne. London: S.C.M.
1949   *Dogmatics in Outline.* Trans. G. T. Thomson. London: S.C.M.
1963   *The Preaching of the Gospel.* Ed. B. E. Hooke. Philadelphia: Westminster.
1972   *Protestant Theology in the Nineteenth Century: Its Background and History.* London: S.C.M. (digested edition 1959).
BARTH, Markus
1974   *Ephesians.* Anchor Bible, vols. 34 and 34A. Garden City: Doubleday.
BARTLEY, William W., III
1985   *Wittgenstein.* (2nd ed.) New York: Open Court.
BARTSCH, Hans Werner, ed.
1961   *Kerygma and Myth: A Theological Debate.* Rev. ed. Trans. R. H. Fuller. New York: Harper & Row.
BASDEN, Paul, and David S. DOCKERY, eds.
1991   *The People of God: Essays on the Believers' Church.* Nashville: Broadman.
BEASLEY-MURRAY, George R.
1962   *Baptism in the New Testament.* London: Macmillan.
1986   *Jesus and the Kingdom of God.* Grand Rapids: Eerdmans.
BELLAH, Robert
1968   "Religion, Sociology of Religion." *International Encyclopedia of the Social Sciences,* ed. D. L. Sills. New York: Macmillan and Free.
BENDER, Ross Thomas
1971   *The People of God.* Scottdale: Herald.
BERKHOF, Hendrikus
1986   *Christian Faith: An Introduction to the Study of the Faith.* Rev. ed. Trans. S. Woudstra. Grand Rapids: Eerdmans.
1989   *Two Hundred Years of Theology: Report of a Personal Journey.* Trans. J. Vriend. Grand Rapids: Eerdmans.
BETTENSON, Henry, ed.
1947   *Documents of the Christian Church.* New York: Oxford.

BETZ, Hans Dieter
 1979   *A Commentary on Paul's Letter to the Galatians.* Hermeneia Commentaries. Philadelphia: Fortress.
BLENKINSOPP, Joseph
 1983   *A History of Prophecy in Israel: From the Settlement in the Land to the Hellenistic Period.* Philadelphia: Westminster.
BLOCH, Ernst
 1986   *The Principle of Hope.* Trans. Neville Plaice, Stephen Plaice, and Paul Knight. 3 vols. Cambridge: M.I.T. Press.
BLOOM, Harold
 1992   *The American Religion: The Emergence of the Post-Christian Nation.* New York: Simon & Schuster.
BLOOM, Harold, and David ROSENBERG
 1990   *The Book of J.* Translated from the Hebrew by Rosenberg. Interpreted by Bloom. New York: Grove Weidenfeld.
BOFF, Clodovis
 1981   "The Nature of Basic Christian Communities." *Concilium* 144 (April).
BOFF, Leonardo
 1981   "Ecclesiogenesis: Ecclesial Basic Communities Re-invent the Church." *Mid-Stream* 20:431-88.
BONHOEFFER, Dietrich
 1964   *The Communion of Saints: A Dogmatic Inquiry into the Sociology of the Church.* New York: Harper & Row.
 1978   *Christ the Center.* Trans. E. H. Robertson. New York: Harper & Row.
BORSCH, Frederick H.
 1967   *The Son of Man in Myth and History.* London: Philadelphia: Westminster.
 1983   *Power in Weakness: New Hearing for Gospel Stories of Healing and Discipleship.* Philadelphia: Fortress.
BOUYER, Louis
 1956   *Life and Liturgy.* London: Sheed & Ward.
BOWDEN, Henry Warner
 1977   *Dictionary of American Religious Biography.* Westport: Greenwood.
BRIGGS, R. C.
 1973   *Interpreting the New Testament Today.* Nashville: Abingdon.
BRIGHT, John
 1953   *The Kingdom of God: The Biblical Concept and Its Meaning for the Church.* Nashville: Abingdon.
BRILIOTH, Yngve
 1961   *Eucharistic Faith and Practice, Evangelical and Catholic.* Trans. A. G. Hebert. London: S.P.C.K.
BROWN, Peter
 1969   *Augustine of Hippo: A Biography.* Berkeley: University of California Press.
 1982   *Society and the Holy in Late Antiquity.* Berkeley: University of California Press.

BROWN, Raymond E.
1973   *The Virginal Conception and Bodily Resurrection of Jesus*. New York: Missionary Society of St. Paul the Apostle.
1979   *The Birth of the Messiah: A Commentary on the Infancy Narratives in Matthew and Luke*. Garden City: Doubleday.
1986   *The Gospel According to John (i-xii)*. 2nd ed. The Anchor Bible. Vol. 29. Garden City: Doubleday.
BUBER, Martin
1946   *Moses*. Oxford: East and West Library.
1967   *Kingship of God*. Trans. R. Scheimann. 3rd ed. New York: Harper & Row.
BUCKLEY, Michael J.
1987   *At the Origins of Modern Atheism*. New Haven: Yale University Press.
BULTMANN, Rudolf
1951   *Theology of the New Testament*. Trans. Kendrick Grobel. Scribner Studies in Contemporary Theology. New York: Scribner's.
1958   *Jesus Christ and Mythology*. New York: Scribner's.
1960   *Existence and Faith*. Ed. S. M. Ogden. New York: World.
1971   *The Gospel of John: A Commentary*. Trans. G. R. Beasley-Murray. Philadelphia: Westminster.
BUNYAN, John
1678   *The Pilgrim's Progress and Grace Abounding*. Ed. J. Thorpe. Boston: Houghton Mifflin, 1969.
BURGESS, Stanley M., Gary B. McGee, and Patrick H. Alexander, eds.
1988   *Dictionary of the Pentecostal and Charismatic Movements*. Grand Rapids: Zondervan.
BURRELL, David B.
1982   "Does Process Theology Rest on a Mistake?" *Theological Studies* 43:125-35.
1986   *Knowing the Unknowable God: Ibn-Sina, Maimonides, Aquinas*. Notre Dame: University Press.
BUSH, L. Russ, and Tom J. NETTLES
1980   *Baptists and the Bible*. Chicago: Moody.
BUSHNELL, Horace
1849   *God in Christ*. Hartford: Brown & Parsons.
1866   *The Vicarious Sacrifice, Grounded in Principles of Universal Obligation*. New York: Scribner.
1874   *Forgiveness and Law, Grounded in Principles Interpreted by Human Analogies*. New York: Scribner, Armstrong.
1965   *Horace Bushnell*. Ed. H. Shelton Smith. Library of Protestant Thought. New York: Oxford.

CAIRD, George B.
1980   *The Language and Imagery of the Bible*. Philadelphia: Westminster.
CAIRNS, David S.
1928   *The Faith That Rebels: A Re-examination of the Miracles of Jesus*. (6th ed., 1954) London: S.C.M.

CARTWRIGHT, Michael G.
1992   "The Pathos and Promise of American Methodist Ecclesiology." *Asbury Theological Journal* 47 (Spring):5-25.

CASTRO, Emilio
1985   *Sent Free: Mission and Unity in the Perspective of the Kingdom.* Geneva: World Council of Churches.

CHADWICK, Owen
1975   *The Secularization of the European Mind in the Nineteenth Century.* Cambridge: University Press.

CHARLES, R. H.
1920   *A Critical and Exegetical Commentary on the Revelation of St. John.* 2 vols. ICC. Edinburgh: T. & T. Clark.

CHARLESWORTH, James H., ed.
1983–85   *The Old Testament Pseudepigrapha.* 2 vols. Garden City: Doubleday.

CHESNUT, Roberta
1978   "The Two Prosope in Nestorius' Bazaar of Heracleides," *Journal of Theological Studies* 29 (October): 392-409.

CHILDS, Brevard S.
1974   *The Book of Exodus: A Critical, Theological Commentary.* The Old Testament Library. Louisville: Westminster.
1979   *Introduction to the Old Testament as Scripture.* Philadelphia: Fortress.

CLEBSCH, William A.
1973   *American Religious Thought: A History.* Chicago: University of Chicago Press.

COBB, John B., Jr.
1965   *A Christian Natural Theology: Based on the Thought of Alfred North Whitehead.* Philadelphia: Westminster.
1967   *The Structure of Christian Existence.* Philadelphia: Westminster.
1975   *Christ in a Pluralistic Age.* Philadelphia: Westminster.
1982   *Beyond Dialogue: Toward a Mutual Transformation of Christianity and Buddhism.* Philadelphia: Fortress.

CONGAR, Yves M.-J.
1966   *Tradition and Traditions: A Historical and Theological Essay.* Trans. M. Naseby and T. Rainborough. New York: Macmillan.

CONNER, Walter Thomas
1936   *Revelation and God: An Introduction to Christian Doctrine.* Nashville: Broadman.
1945   *The Gospel of Redemption.* Nashville: Broadman.

COOKE, Bernard
1976   *Ministry to Word and Sacraments: History and Theology.* Philadelphia: Fortress.

COPLESTON, Frederick
1985   *A History of Philosophy.* Book One, comprising vols. 1, 2, 3. Garden City: Doubleday.

COUSAR, Charles B.
1990   *A Theology of the Cross: The Death of Jesus in the Pauline Epistles.* Minneapolis: Fortress.

CULLMANN, Oscar
1950   *Christ and Time: The Primitive Christian Conception of Time and History.* Trans. F. V. Filson. London: S.C.M.
CUPITT, Don
1980   *Taking Leave of God.* London: S.C.M.

DAVIDSON, Robert, and A. R. C. LEANEY
1970   *Biblical Criticism.* Baltimore: Penguin.
DAVIES, Alan, ed.
1979   *Antisemitism and the Origins of Christianity.* New York: Paulist.
DAYTON, Donald W.
1987   *The Theological Roots of Pentecostalism.* Grand Rapids: Zondervan.
DE TOCQUEVILLE, Alexis
1835   *Democracy in America.* 2 vols. Rev. ed. Ed. Francis Bowen and Phillips Bradley. New York: Vintage, 1954–56.
DENCK, Hans
1975   *Selected Writings of Hans Denck, Edited and Translated from the Text established by Walter Fellmann.* Ed. and trans. E. J. Furcha and F. L. Battles. Pittsburgh: Pickwick.
DIX, Dom Gregory
1945   *The Shape of the Liturgy.* Westminster, England: Dacre.
DODD, C. H.
1935   *The Parables of the Kingdom.* London: Nisbet.
1936   *The Apostolic Preaching and Its Developments.* London: Hodder & Stoughton. (new edition reset 1944)
DODWELL, H. H., ed.
1963   *The Cambridge History of India.* Vol. 5. New Delhi: S. Chand.
DOLAN, Jay P.
1978   *Catholic Revivalism.* Notre Dame: University Press.
DONAHUE, John R.
1988   *The Gospel in Parable: Metaphor, Narrative, and Theology in the Synoptic Gospels.* Philadelphia: Fortress.
DOUGLAS, J. D., ed.
1975   *Let the Earth Hear His Voice: International Congress on World Evangelization, Lausanne.* Minneapolis: World Wide.
DRIVER, John
1986   *Understanding the Atonement for the Mission of the Church.* Scottdale: Herald.
DUFFIELD, Guy P., and Nathaniel M. VAN CLEAVE
1983   *Foundations of Pentecostal Theology.* Los Angeles: L.I.F.E. Bible College.
DULLES, Avery
1974   *Models of the Church.* Garden City: Doubleday.
1977   *The Resilient Church: The Necessity and Limits of Adaptation.* Garden City: Doubleday.
1985   *The Catholicity of the Church.* Oxford: Clarendon.
DUNN, James D. G.
1991   *The Partings of the Ways: Between Christianity and Judaism and Their Significance for the Character of Christianity.* Philadelphia: Trinity Press International.

DYRNESS, William
1989   *How Does America Hear the Gospel?* Grand Rapids: Eerdmans.

EDWARDS, Jonathan
1741   *The Distinguishing Marks of a Work of the Spirit of God.* In Edwards, 1972.
1746 (1959) *A Treatise Concerning Religious Affections.* Ed. J. E. Smith. The Works of Jonathan Edwards. Vol. 2. New Haven: Yale University Press.
1754 (1957) *Freedom of the Will.* Ed. Paul Ramsey. The Works of Jonathan Edwards. Vol. 1. New Haven: Yale University Press.
1758 (1970) *Original Sin.* Ed. C. A. Holbrook. The Works of Jonathan Edwards. Vol. 3. New Haven: Yale University Press.
1765a   *The End for Which God Created the World.* In Edwards, 1989.
1765b   *The Nature of True Virtue.* In Edwards, 1989.
1972   *The Great Awakening.* Ed. C. C. Goen. The Works of Jonathan Edwards. Vol. 4. New Haven: Yale University Press.
1989   *Ethical Writings.* Ed. Paul Ramsey. The Works of Jonathan Edwards. Vol. 8. New Haven: Yale University Press.
ELIADE, Mircea
1949 (1954) *Cosmos and History: The Myth of the Eternal Return.* Trans. W. R. Trask. Princeton: University Press.
ELIOT, George
1859 (1992) *Adam Bede.* Everyman's Library. New York: Alfred A. Knopf.
ELLER, David, ed.
1990   *Servants of the Word: Ministry in the Believers Churches.* Elgin: Brethren.
ELLIS, William E.
1985   *A Man of Books and a Man of the People: E. Y. Mullins and the Crisis of Moderate Southern Baptist Leadership.* Macon: Mercer University Press.
ELLSBERG, Daniel
1972   *Papers on the War.* New York: Pocket Books.
ELLUL, Jacques
1967 (1948) *The Presence of the Kingdom.* Int. William Stringfellow. New York: Seabury.
EMERSON, Ralph Waldo
1983   *Emerson.* Ed. J. Porte. New York: Viking, Library of America.
ERASMUS
1965   *Essential Works of Erasmus.* Ed. W. T. H. Jackson. New York: Bantam.
ERICKSON, Millard J.
1990   *Christian Theology.* 3 vols. in 1. Grand Rapids: Baker.

FANT, Clyde E.
1975   *Worldly Preaching.* Contains Bonhoeffer's Lectures on Preaching, pp. 123-80. Nashville: Thomas Nelson.

FARLEY, Edward
    1982   *Ecclesial Reflection: An Anatomy of Theological Method.* Philadel-
                phia: Fortress.
FARMER, Herbert H.
    1938   *The Healing Cross: Further Studies in the Christian Interpretation of
                Life.* London: Nisbet.
    1942   *The Servant of the Word.* New York: Scribner's.
    1963 (1935) *The World and God: A Study of Prayer, Providence, and Miracle in
                Christian Experience.* London: Collins.
FARRER, Austin M.
    1960   *A Faith of Our Own.* Cleveland: World.
    1966   *God Is Not Dead.* New York: Morehouse-Barlow.
    1968   "The Eucharist in I Corinthians." In *Eucharistic Theology Then
                and Now.* R. E. Clements et al. London: S.P.C.K.
FERRÉ, Frederick
    1988   *Philosophy of Technology.* Englewood Cliffs: Prentice-Hall.
FEUERBACH, Ludwig
    1841 (1957) *The Essence of Christianity.* Trans. George Eliot. New York: Har-
                per & Row.
FEY, Harold E., ed.
    1970   *The Ecumenical Advance: A History of the Ecumenical Movement
                Volume Two, 1948–1968.* London: S.P.C.K.
FIDDES, Paul S.
    1988   *The Creative Suffering of God.* Oxford: Clarendon.
FINGER, Thomas N.
    1985–89   *Christian Theology: An Eschatological Approach.* 2 vols. Scottdale:
                Herald.
FINNEY, Charles Grandison
    1835 (1960) *Lectures on Revivals of Religion.* Ed. William G. McLoughlin.
                Cambridge: Harvard University Press.
The First and Second Prayer Books of King Edward VI.
    1910   Introduced by D. Harrison. London: Dent.
FISH, Stanley
    1980   *Is There a Text in This Class? The Authority of Interpretative Com-
                munities.* Cambridge: Harvard University Press.
FISHBURN, Janet Forsythe
    1981   *The Fatherhood of God and the Victorian Family: The Social Gospel
                in America.* Philadelphia: Fortress.
FLANNERY, Edward H.
    1965   *The Anguish of the Jews: Twenty-three Centuries of Anti-Semitism.*
                New York: Macmillan.
FLEW, Antony, and Alasdair MACINTYRE, eds.
    1955   *New Essays in Philosophical Theology.* London: S.C.M.
FORSYTH, Peter Taylor
    1897   *The Holy Father and the Living Christ.* London: Hodder &
                Stoughton.
    1907   *Positive Preaching and the Modern Mind.* London: Independent.
    1909   *The Person and Place of Jesus Christ.* London: Independent.
    1911   "Revelation Old and New." Repr. in *Revelation Old and New*
                (London: Independent, 1962).

1913   *The Principle of Authority in Relation to Certainty, Sanctity, and Society.* London: Independent.
FRAKES, Margaret
1952   "Theology Is Her Province." *Christian Century* 69:39 (September 24):1088-91.
FRANKS, Robert S.
1962   *The Work of Christ: A Historical Study of Christian Doctrine.* London: Nelson.
FREI, Hans W.
1974   *The Eclipse of Biblical Narrative: A Study in Eighteenth and Nineteenth Century Hermeneutics.* New Haven: Yale University Press.
1975   qThe Identity of Jesus Christ, the Hermeneutical Bases of Dogmatic Theology. Philadelphia: Fortress.
1986   "The 'Literal Reading' of Biblical Narrative in the Christian Tradition: Does It Stretch or Will It Break?" In *The Bible and the Narrative Tradition,* ed. F. McConnell, pp. 36-77. New York: Oxford.
FREUD, Sigmund
1913 (1950)   *Totem and Taboo: Some Points of Agreement Between the Mental Lives of Savages and Neurotics.* Ed. and trans. James Strachey. New York: Norton.
FUCHS, Joseph
1963-67   *Theologia Moralis Generalis.* 2 vols. Rome: Gregorian University Press.
1966   "Sin and Conversion." *Theology Digest* 14 (Winter):292-301.
FULLER, Reginald H.
1965   *The Foundations of New Testament Christology.* New York: Scribner's.
The Fundamentals: A Testimony to the Truth.
1910-15   12 vols. Chicago: Testimony Publishing Co. Reissued in 4 vols. Ed. Reuben Torrey, 1917.

GALILEA, Segundo
1981   *Following Jesus.* Trans. Helen Phillips. Maryknoll: Orbis.
GALLIE, W. B.
1964   *Philosophy and the Historical Understanding.* New York: Schocken.
GARRETT, James Leo
1969   (Ed.) *The Concept of the Believers' Church: Addresses from the 1967 Louisville Conference.* Scottdale: Herald.
1990-   *Systematic Theology: Biblical, Historical, and Evangelical.* Vol. 1. Grand Rapids: Eerdmans.
GARRETT, John
1970   *Roger Williams, Witness Beyond Christendom: 1603-1683.* London: Macmillan.
GARRIGOU-LAGRANGE, Reginald
1943   *The One God: A Commentary on the First Part of St. Thomas' Theological Summa.* Trans. Dom Bede Rose. St. Louis: Herder.

GAUSTAD, Edwin S.
1991   *Liberty of Conscience: Roger Williams in America*. Grand Rapids:
            Eerdmans.
GEERTZ, Clifford
1966   "Religion as a Cultural System." In *Anthropological Approaches
            to the Study of Religion*, ed. M. Banton. London: Tavistock.
1968   "Religion, Anthropological Study." In *International Encyclope-
            dia of the Social Sciences*, ed. D. L. Sills. New York: Macmillan
            and Free.
GEORGE, Timothy
1982   *John Robinson and the English Separatist Tradition*. Macon: Mercer
            University Press.
GEORGE, Timothy, and David S. DOCKERY, eds.
1990   *Baptist Theologians*. Nashville: Broadman.
GILKEY, Langdon
1964   *How the Church Can Minister to the World Without Losing Itself*.
            New York: Harper & Row.
1969   *Naming the Whirlwind: The Renewal of God-language*. Indianapo-
            lis: Bobbs-Merrill.
GILL, Athol
1989   *Life on the Road: The Gospel Basis for a Messianic Lifestyle*. Home-
            bush West, NSW, Australia: Lancer Books, Anzea.
GIRARD, René
1977   *Violence and the Sacred*. Trans. P. Gregory. Baltimore: Johns
            Hopkins University Press.
1986   *The Scapegoat*. Trans. Y. Freccero. Baltimore: Johns Hopkins
            University Press.
1987   *Things Hidden Since the Foundation of the World*. Trans. S. Bann
            and M. Metteer. Stanford: University Press.
GOERTZ, Hans-Jürgen, ed.
1982   *Profiles of Radical Reformers: Biographical Sketches from Thomas
            Muentzer to Paracelsus*. English ed. W. Klaassen. Scottdale:
            Herald.
GORE, Rick
1983   "The Once and Future Universe." *National Geographic* 163
            (June):704-49.
GOTTWALD, Norman K.
1979   *The Tribes of Yahweh: A Sociology of the Religion of Liberated Israel,
            1250–1050 B.C.* Maryknoll: Orbis.
GRANT, Robert M., and David TRACY
1984   *A Short History of the Interpretation of the Bible*. 2nd ed. Minnea-
            polis: Augsburg-Fortress.
GREEN, Joel
1991   *The Way of the Cross: Following Jesus in the Gospel of Mark*.
            Nashville: Discipleship Resources.
GREENSLADE, S. L., ed. and trans.
1956   *Early Latin Theology: Selections from Tertullian, Cyprian, Ambrose,
            and Jerome*. The Library of Christian Classics. Vol. 5. Philadel-
            phia: Westminster.

GREGG, Robert C., and Dennis E. GROH
1981   Early Arianism: A View of Salvation. Philadelphia: Fortress.
GREGORY, Frederick
1992   Nature Lost? Natural Science and the German Theological Traditions
            of the Nineteenth Century. Cambridge, Mass.: Harvard Univer-
            sity Press.
GRENZ, Stanley J., and Roger E. OLSON
1992   Twentieth Century Theology: God and the World in a Transitional
            Age. Downers Grove: InterVarsity.
GRIFFIN, David Ray
1976   God, Power, and Evil: A Process Theodicy. Philadelphia: West-
            minster.
1988   The Reenchantment of Science: Postmodern Proposals. Albany: State
            University of New York Press.
GRILLMEIER, Aloys
1975   Christ in Christian Tradition. Volume One: From the Apostolic Age
            to Chalcedon (451). 2nd ed. trans. John Bowden. Atlanta: John
            Knox.
GRIMSRUD, Ted
1987   Triumph of the Lamb: A Self-study Guide to the Book of Revelation.
            Scottdale: Herald.
GROTIUS, Hugo
1614 (1889) A Defense of the Catholic Faith Concerning the Satisfaction of Christ,
            Against Faustus Socinus. Andover: W. F. Draper.
GUELICH, Robert
1982   The Sermon on the Mount. Dallas: Word.
GUNTON, Colin E.
1989   The Actuality of Atonement: A Study of Metaphor, Rationality, and
            the Christian Tradition. Grand Rapids: Eerdmans.
GUSTAFSON, James M.
1961   Treasure in Earthen Vessels: The Church as a Human Community.
            New York: Harper.
GUTIÉRREZ, Gustavo
1973   A Theology of Liberation: History, Politics, and Salvation. Trans.
            and ed. C. Inda and J. Eagleson. Maryknoll: Orbis.

HALLIE, Philip
1979   Lest Innocent Blood Be Shed: The Story of the Village of Le Chambon
            and How Goodness Happened There. New York: Harper & Row.
HAMERTON-KELLY, Robert
1979   God the Father: Theology and Patriarchy in the Teaching of Jesus.
            Philadelphia: Fortress.
HAMMARSKJØLD, Dag
1965   Markings. Trans. W. H. Auden and L. Sjöberg. New York:
            Knopf.
HANDY, Robert T., ed.
1966   The Social Gospel in America: Gladden, Ely, Rauschenbusch. New
            York: Oxford University Press.
HANSON, Paul D.
1975   The Dawn of Apocalyptic. Philadelphia: Fortress.

HANSON, Richard P. C.
1963   *Tradition in the Early Church*. Philadelphia: Westminster.
HARDER, Leland, ed.
1985   *The Sources of Swiss Anabaptism*. Scottdale: Herald.
HARKNESS, Georgia Elma
1964   *Our Christian Hope*. Nashville: Abingdon.
HARNACK, Adolf
1896 (1961)   *History of Dogma* (7 vol. in 4). Trans. Neil Buchanan. New York:
                Dover.
1900 (1957)   *What Is Christianity?* Trans. T. B. Saunders. New York: Harper
                & Row.
HARRISON, Paul M.
1959   *Authority and Power in the Free Church Tradition: A Social Case
                Study of the American Baptist Convention*. Princeton: University
                Press.
HARTSHORNE, Charles
1941   *Man's Vision of God and the Logic of Theism*. New York: Willet,
                Clark.
1967   *A Natural Theology for Our Time*. LaSalle: Open Court.
HARVEY, Van A.
1989   "On the Intellectual Marginality of American Theology." In
                Religion and Twentieth-century Intellectual Life, ed. M. J. Lacey.
                Cambridge: University Press.
HAUERWAS, Stanley
1985   *Against the Nations: War and Survival in a Liberal Society*. Minnea-
                polis: Winston.
1988   *Christian Existence Today: Essays on Church, World, and Living in
                Between*. Durham: Labyrinth.
1991   *After Christendom*. Nashville: Abingdon.
HAUGHTON, Rosemary
1980   *The Transformation of Man: A Study of Conversion and Community*.
                Springfield: Templegate.
1981   *The Passionate God*. New York: Paulist.
HEBBLETHWAITE, Brian, and Edward HENDERSON, eds.
1990   *Divine Action: Studies Inspired by the Philosophical Theology of
                Austin Farrer*. Edinburgh: T. & T. Clark.
HEGEL, Georg W. F.
1821 (1979)   *The Christian Religion: Lectures on the Philosophy of Religion, Part
                III*. Ed. and trans. P. C. Hodgson. Missoula: Scholars.
HEIM, Karl
1953   *The Transformation of the Scientific World View*. Vol. 2. London:
                S.C.M.
HENDRY, George S.
1956   *The Holy Spirit in Christian Theology*. Philadelphia: Westminster.
1980   *Theology of Nature*. Philadelphia: Westminster.
HERRMANN, Wilhelm
1903 (1971)   *The Communion of the Christian with God*. Ed. R. Voelkel. Phila-
                delphia: Westminster.
HICK, John
1977   (Ed.) *The Myth of God Incarnate*. London: S.C.M.

1978   *Evil and the God of Love*. Rev. ed. San Francisco: Harper & Row.
HICKS, Frederick C. N.
1930   *The Fullness of Sacrifice: An Essay in Reconciliation*. London: Macmillan.
HODGE, A. A., and B. B. WARFIELD
1881   "Inspiration." *Presbyterian Review* 2 (April):225-60.
1979   *Inspiration*. Ed. Roger R. Nicole. (repr. of 1881 article) Grand Rapids: Baker.
HODGSON, Leonard
1943   *The Doctrine of the Trinity*. Welwyn, Herts: James Nisbet & Co.
HOLLENWEGER, Walter J.
1972   *The Pentecostals: The Charismatic Movement in the Churches*. Trans. R. A. Wilson. Minneapolis: Augsburg.
HOLMER, Paul L.
1978   *The Grammar of Faith*. San Francisco: Harper & Row.
HOPEWELL, James F.
1987   *Congregation*. Ed. Barbara G. Wheeler. Philadelphia: Fortress.
HUBERT, Henri, and Marcel MAUSS
1898 (1964)   *Sacrifice: Its Nature and Function*. Trans. W. D. Halls. Chicago: University of Chicago Press.
HUBMAIER, Balthasar
1989   *Balthasar Hubmaier, Theologian of Anabaptism*. Trans. and ed. H. Wayne Pipkin and John H. Yoder. Scottdale: Herald.
HUME, David
1777a (1956)   *The Natural History of Religion*. Ed. H. E. Root. London: Adam & Charles Black.
1777b (1975)   *Enquiries: Concerning Human Understanding and Concerning the Principles of Morals*. Ed. L. A. Selby-Bigge. 3rd ed. rev. P. H. Nidditch. Oxford: Clarendon.
1779 (1948)   *Dialogues Concerning Natural Religion*. Ed. H. D. Aiken. New York: Hafner.
HUMPHREYS, Fisher
1982   "Father, Son, and Holy Spirit." *The Theological Educator* 12 (Spring):78-96.
HUT, Hans
1526-27   *Of the Mystery of Baptism*. Trans. in Gordon Rupp, *Patterns of Reformation*, Appendix. Philadelphia: Fortress, 1969.
HUTCHISON, John A.
1991   *Paths of Faith*. 4th ed. New York: McGraw-Hill.

JAMES, Robison B., ed.
1987   *The Unfettered Word: Southern Baptists Confront the Authority-Inerrancy Question*. Waco: Word.
JAMES, William
1902 (1987)   *The Varieties of Religious Experience: A Study in Human Nature. Writings 1902–1910*. New York: Viking, Library of America.
JENSON, Robert W.
1982   *The Triune Identity: God According to the Gospel*. Philadelphia: Fortress.

JOHNSON, Paul
1987   *A History of the Jews.* New York: Harper & Row.
JONAS, Hans
1963   *The Gnostic Religion: The Message of the Alien God and the Begin-
                nings of Christianity.* 2nd ed. Boston: Beacon.
JORDAN, Clarence
1970   *The Sermon on the Mount.* Valley Forge: Judson.
JUNGMANN, Josef A.
1959   *The Early Liturgy; to the Time of Gregory the Great.* Trans. F. A.
                Brunner. Notre Dame: University Press.

KÄHLER, Martin
1896 (1964)   *The So-called Historical Jesus and the Historic, Biblical Christ.* Trans.
                C. E. Braaten. Philadelphia: Fortress.
KÄSEMANN, Ernst
1969   *New Testament Questions of Today.* Trans. W. J. Montague. Phila-
                delphia: Fortress.
KASPER, Walter
1984   *The God of Jesus Christ.* Trans. Matthew J. O'Connell. New York:
                Crossroads.
KAUFMAN, Gordon D.
1968   *Systematic Theology: A Historicist Perspective.* New York: Scrib-
                ner's.
1993   *In Face of Mystery: A Constructive Theology.* Cambridge: Harvard
                University Press.
KEE, Howard Clark
1977   *Community of the New Age: Studies in Mark's Gospel.* Philadel-
                phia: Westminster.
KEEL, Othmar
1985   *The Symbolism of the Biblical World: Ancient Near Eastern Iconog-
                raphy and the Book of Psalms.* New York: Crossroad.
KELLER, Rosemary Skinner
1992   *Georgia Harkness: For Such a Time as This.* Nashville: Abingdon.
KELLY, J. N. D.
1960   *Early Christian Doctrines.* 2nd ed. New York: Harper.
KENNEDY, George A.
1984   *New Testament Interpretation Through Rhetorical Criticism.*
                Chapel Hill: University of North Carolina Press.
KENNEDY, Paul
1989   *The Rise and Fall of Great Powers: Economic Change and Military
                Conflict from 1500–2000.* New York: Random House.
KERMODE, Frank
1979   *The Genesis of Secrecy: On the Interpretation of Narrative.* Cam-
                bridge: Harvard University Press.
KIERKEGAARD, Søren
1844 (1985)   *Philosophical Fragments.* Trans. H. V. and E. H. Hong.
                Kierkegaard's Writings, vol. 7. Princeton: University Press.
1850 (1967)   *Training in Christianity.* Trans. W. Lowrie. Princeton: University
                Press.

KIMEL, Alvin F., ed.
1992   *Speaking the Christian God: The Holy Trinity and the Challenge of Feminism*. Grand Rapids: Eerdmans.
KING, Martin Luther, Jr.
1986   *A Testament of Hope: The Essential Writings of Martin Luther King, Jr*. Ed. James M. Washington. San Francisco: Harper & Row.
KIRK, G. S.
1970   *Myth: Its Meaning and Function in Ancient and Other Cultures*. Berkeley: University of California Press.
KLAASSEN, Walter
1981a   (Ed.) *Anabaptism in Outline: Selected Primary Sources*. Kitchener: Herald.
1981b   *Anabaptism: Neither Catholic Nor Protestant*. Rev. ed. Waterloo: Conrad.
KOESTER, Helmut
1990   *Ancient Christian Gospels: Their History and Development*. Philadelphia: Trinity Press International.
KOESTLER, Arthur, et al.
1949   *The God That Failed*. Ed. R. Crossman. New York: Harper.
KRAUS, C. Norman
1990   *Jesus Christ Our Lord: Christology from a Disciple's Perspective*. Rev. ed. Scottdale: Herald.
1991   *God Our Savior: Theology in a Christological Mode*. Scottdale: Herald.
1992   "Interpreting the Atonement in the Anabaptist-Mennonite Tradition." *Mennonite Quarterly Review* 66 (July):291-311.
KÜNG, Hans
1967   (Ed.) *The Sacraments: An Ecumenical Dilemma*. Concilium. New York: Paulist.
1976   *On Being a Christian*. Trans. E. Quinn. Garden City: Doubleday.
1981   *Justification: The Doctrine of Karl Barth and a Catholic Reflection*. 2nd ed. Philadelphia: Westminster.

LAMPE, G. W. H., and K. J. WOOLLCOMBE
1957   *Essays on Typology*. London: S.C.M.
LANE FOX, Robin
1987   *Pagans and Christians*. New York: Knopf.
1992   *The Unauthorized Version: Truth and Fiction in the Bible*. New York: Knopf.
LASH, Nicholas
1986   *Theology on the Way to Emmaus*. London: S.C.M.
1988   *Easter in Ordinary: Reflections on Human Experience and the Knowledge of God*. Charlottesville: University Press of Virginia.
LEDERLE, Henny I.
1988   *Treasures Old and New: Interpretations of "Spirit Baptism" in the Charismatic Renewal Movement*. Peabody: Hendrickson.
LEE, Andrea
1983   "New African." *New Yorker* April 25, 46-53.

LEVENSON, Jon D.
1985   *Sinai and Zion: An Entry into the Jewish Bible.* Minneapolis: Winston.
1988   *Creation and the Persistence of Evil: The Jewish Drama of Divine Omnipotence.* San Francisco: Harper & Row.

LIETZMANN, Hans
1926   *Messe und Herrenmahl.* Bonn: A. Marcus und E. Weber's Verlag. (Eng. Trans. Leiden: E. Brill, 1953)

LINDBECK, George A.
1984   *The Nature of Doctrine: Religion and Theology in a Postliberal Age.* Philadelphia: Westminster.

LINDHOLM, Joseph
1986   *The Inerrantist's Checklist.* Berkeley: Joseph Lindholm, P.O. Box 7779, Berkeley, CA 94707. photocopied.

LINLEY, Eliza
1990   "Holy People, Holy Space: Housing the Church in a Time of Change." (Graduate Theological Union Library, Berkeley).

LITTELL, Franklin H.
1952   *The Anabaptist View of the Church.* Boston: Starr King. Revised as *The Origins of Sectarian Protestantism,* New York: Macmillan, 1964.

LOEWEN, Howard John
1985   *One Lord, One Church, One Hope, and One God: Mennonite Confessions of Faith in North America, An Introduction.* Elkhart: Institute of Mennonite Studies.

LOISY, Alfred
1902 (1976) *The Gospel and the Church.* Trans. C. Home. Philadelphia: Fortress.

LONGENECKER, Richard N.
1990   *Galatians.* Dallas: Word.

LOOFS, Friedrich
1927–28   "Das Altkirchliche Zeugnis Gegen die Herrschende Auffasung der Kenosisstelle (Phil. 2,5-11)." *Theologische Studien und Kritiken* 100:1-102.

LUMPKIN, William L.
1969   2nd rev. ed. *Baptist Confessions of Faith.* Philadelphia: Judson.

LUTHER, Martin
1961   *Martin Luther.* Ed. John Dillenberger. Garden City: Doubleday.
1966   *A Compend of Luther's Theology.* Ed. Hugh T. Kerr, Jr. Philadelphia: Westminster.

McCLENDON, James Wm., Jr.
1966a   "Some Reflections on the Future of Trinitarianism." *Review and Expositor* (Spring):149-56.
1966b   "Baptism as Performative Sign." *Theology Today* 23 (October):403-16.
1967   "Why Baptists Do Not Baptize Infants." In Küng, ed., 1967:7-15.
1969   "Can There Be Talk About God-and-the-World?" *Harvard Theological Review* 62 (January):33-49.
1971a   "Biography as Theology." *Cross Currents* 21 (Fall):415ff.

1971*b*   "Martin Luther King: Politician or American Church Father?"
             Journal of Ecumenical Studies 8 (Winter):115ff.
1990   *Biography as Theology: How Life Stories Can Remake Today's The-
             ology.* Philadelphia: Trinity Press International. (First ed., 1974).
1991*a*   "Balthasar Hubmaier, Catholic Anabaptist." *Mennonite Quar-
             terly Review* LXV (January):20-33.
1991*b*   "In the Light of Last Things: A Theology for the Believers
             Church." *Perspectives in Religious Studies* 18 (Spring).
1991*c*   "Philippians 2:5-11." *Review and Expositor* 88 (Fall):439-44.
1994   "Toward a Conversionist Spirituality." In *Ties That Bind: Life
             Together in the Baptist Vision*, ed. Gary Furr and Curtis Freeman.
             Macon: Smith and Helwys.

McCLENDON, James Wm., Jr., and James M. SMITH
1994   *Convictions: Defusing Religious Relativism*, Trinity Press (Revi-
             sion of *Understanding Religious Convictions.* Notre Dame: Uni-
             versity Press, 1975)

McCLENDON, James Wm., Jr., and John Howard YODER
1990   "Christian Identity in Ecumenical Perspective." *Journal of Ecu-
             menical Studies* 27 (Summer).

McFAGUE, Sallie
1982   *Metaphorical Theology: Models of God in Religious Language.* Phila-
             delphia: Fortress.
1987   *Models of God: Theology for an Ecological, Nuclear Age.* Philadel-
             phia: Fortress.

McGINN, Bernard, trans. and ed.
1979   *Apocalyptic Spirituality: Treatises and Letters of . . . Joachim of Fiore.*
             New York: Paulist.

MacGREGOR, Geddes
1975   *He Who Lets Us Be: A Theology of Love.* New York: Seabury.

MacINTOSH, Douglas Clyde
1919   *Theology as an Empirical Science.* New York: Macmillan (Arno
             Press repr. 1980).

MacINTYRE, Alasdair
1966   *A Short History of Ethics.* New York: Macmillan.
1984   *After Virtue: A Study in Moral Theory.* 2nd ed. Notre Dame:
             University Press.
1988   *Whose Justice? Which Rationality?* Notre Dame: University Press.
1990   *Three Rival Versions of Moral Enquiry: Encyclopaedia, Genealogy,
             and Tradition.* Gifford Lectures. Notre Dame: University Press.

McINTYRE, John
1954   *St. Anselm and His Critics: A Re-interpretation of the Cur Deus
             Homo.* Edinburgh: Oliver and Boyd.
1966   *The Shape of Christology.* Philadelphia: Westminster.

MacKAY, John A.
1964   *Ecumenics: The Science of the Church Universal.* Englewood Cliffs:
             Prentice-Hall.

McKENZIE, John L.
1968   *Second Isaiah: Introduction, Translation, and Notes.* The Anchor
             Bible. Vol. 20. New York: Doubleday.

McKNIGHT, Edgar V.
1985 *The Bible and the Reader: An Introduction to Literary Criticism.* Philadelphia: Fortress.
1988 *Postmodern Use of the Bible: The Emergence of Reader-oriented Criticism.* Nashville: Abingdon.
McWILLIAMS, Warren
1985 *The Passion of God: Divine Suffering in Contemporary Protestant Theology.* Macon: Mercer University Press.
Made, Not Born: New Perspectives on Christian Initiation and the Catechumenate
1976 Aidan Kavanagh, et al. Murphy Center. Notre Dame: University Press.
MALCOLM, Norman
1984 *Ludwig Wittgenstein: A Memoir* (2nd ed.). New York: Oxford.
MARSDEN, George M.
1980 *Fundamentalism and American Culture: The Shaping of Twentieth-century Evangelicalism: 1870–1925.* Oxford: University Press.
1987 Reforming Fundamentalism: Fuller Seminary and the New Evangelicalism. Grand Rapids: Eerdmans.
MARSHALL, Bruce, ed.
1990 *Theology and Dialogue: Essays in Conversation with George Lindbeck.* Notre Dame: University Press.
Martyrs Mirror, Being the Bloody Theater or Martyrs Mirror of the Defenseless Christians . . .
1660 (1979) Ed. Thieleman J. van Braght. Trans. J. F. Sohm. Scottdale: Herald.
MATHIS, Terry Richard
1985 *Against John Hick: An Examination of His Philosophy of Religion.* Lanham: University Press of America.
MBITI, John S.
1969 *African Religions and Philosophy.* London: Heinemann.
MEAD, Sidney E.
1963 *The Lively Experiment: The Shaping of Christianity in America.* New York: Harper & Row.
1975 *The Nation with the Soul of a Church.* New York: Harper & Row.
MEAD, Walter Russell
1987 *Mortal Splendor: The American Empire in Transition.* Boston: Houghton Mifflin.
MEIER, John P.
1991 *A Marginal Jew: Rethinking the Historical Jesus. Volume One: The Roots of the Problem and the Person.* Garden City: Doubleday.
MELVILLE, Herman
1851 (1983) *Moby-Dick,* ed. G. Thomas Tanselle. In *Redburn, White-Jacket, Moby-Dick.* New York: Viking, Library of America.
METZ, Johann Baptist
1981 *The Emergent Church: The Future of Christianity in a Postbourgeois World.* Trans. P. Mann. New York: Crossroad.
MICKS, Marianne H.
1970 *The Future Present: The Phenomenon of Christian Worship.* New York: Seabury.

MIDGLEY, Mary
    1978   *Beast and Man: The Roots of Human Nature.* Ithaca: Cornell University Press.
MILLER, Perry
    1953   (Ed. and introd.) *Roger Williams: His Contribution to the American Tradition.* New York: Bobbs-Merrill.
    1965   *The Life of the Mind in America from the Revolution to the Civil War.* Books 1-3. New York: Harcourt, Brace & World.
MINEAR, Paul S.
    1946   *Eyes of Faith: A Study in the Biblical Point of View.* Philadelphia: Westminster.
    1960   *Images of the Church in the New Testament.* Philadelphia: Westminster.
MINUS, Paul M.
    1988   *Walter Rauschenbusch, American Reformer.* New York: Macmillan.
MOBERLY, Robert Campbell
    1917   *Atonement and Personality.* London: John Murray.
MOFFATT, James
    1924   *A Critical and Exegetical Commentary on the Epistle to the Hebrews.* ICC. Edinburgh: T. & T. Clark.
MOLTMANN, Jürgen
    1967   *Theology of Hope: On the Ground and the Implications of a Christian Eschatology.* Trans. J. W. Leitch. New York: Harper & Row.
    1981   *The Trinity and the Kingdom: The Doctrine of God.* New York: Harper & Row.
    1991   *God in Creation.* Gifford Lectures. Trans. M. Kohl. San Francisco: Harper & Row.
MONK, Ray
    1990   *Ludwig Wittgenstein: The Duty of Genius.* New York: Free.
MOODY, Dale
    1981   *The Word of Truth: A Summary of Christian Doctrine Based on Biblical Revelation.* Grand Rapids: Eerdmans.
MOORE, LeRoy
    1963   "Roger Williams and the Historians." *Church History* 32:432-51.
MORGAN, Edmund S.
    1967   *Roger Williams: The Church and the State.* New York: Harcourt, Brace, and World.
MOULTON, James Hope, and George MILLIGAN
    1949   *The Vocabulary of the Greek Testament.* London: Hodder & Stoughton.
MOUW, Richard J.
    1990   *The God Who Commands.* Notre Dame: University Press.
MOZLEY, John Kenneth
    1926   *The Divine Impassibility: A Survey of Christian Thought.* Cambridge: University Press.
MULLER, Richard A.
    1985   *Dictionary of Latin and Greek Theological Terms: Drawn Principally from Protestant Scholastic Theology.* Grand Rapids: Baker.

MULLINS, Edgar Young
 1905 *Why Is Christianity True?* Philadelphia: American Baptist Publication Society.
 1908 *The Axioms of Religion.* Philadelphia: American Baptist Publication Society.
 1917 *The Christian Religion in Its Doctrinal Expression.* Philadelphia: Judson.
 1924 *Christianity at the Cross Roads.* Nashville: Sunday School Board of the S.B.C.
MUNCK, Johannes
 1967 *Christ and Israel: An Interpretation of Romans 9–11.* Trans. I. Nixon. Philadelphia: Fortress.
MURPHY, Nancey
 1990 *Theology in the Age of Scientific Reasoning.* Ithaca: Cornell University Press.
MURPHY, Nancey, and James Wm. McCLENDON, Jr.
 1989 "Distinguishing Modern and Postmodern Theologies." *Modern Theology* 5 (April).
MYERS, Ched
 1988 *Binding the Strong Man: A Political Reading of Mark's Story of Jesus.* Maryknoll: Orbis.

NELSON, Peter Christopher
 1948 *Bible Doctrines.* Springfield, Mo.: Gospel Publishing House.
NEUSCH, Marcel
 1982 *The Sources of Modern Atheism: One Hundred Years of Debate Over God.* Trans. from the French. New York: Paulist.
NEUSNER, Jacob
 1985 (Ed. and trans.) *Genesis Rabbah: The Judaic Commentary to the Book of Genesis, a New American Translation.* Vol. 2, Genesis 8:15 to 28:9. Atlanta: Scholars.
 1987 *What Is Midrash?* Philadelphia: Fortress.
NEWBIGIN, Lesslie
 1954 *The Household of God: Lectures on the Nature of the Church.* New York: Friendship.
NEWMAN, John Henry
 1864 (1956) *Apologia Pro Vita Sua.* Ed. A. Dwight Culler. Boston: Houghton Mifflin.
NEWMAN, Stewart A.
 1964 *W. T. Conner: Theologian of the Southwest.* Nashville: Broadman.
NIEBUHR, H. Richard
 1937 *The Kingdom of God in America.* New York: Harper & Row.
 1941 *The Meaning of Revelation.* New York: Macmillan.
 1951 (1956) *Christ and Culture.* New York: Harper & Row.
 1989 *Faith on Earth.* Ed. R. R. Niebuhr. New Haven: Yale University Press.
NIEBUHR, Reinhold
 1941–43 *The Nature and Destiny of Man: A Christian Interpretation. Volume I, Human Nature; Volume II, Human Destiny.* Gifford Lectures. New York: Scribner's.

NIEBUHR, Richard R.
1957   *Resurrection and Historical Reason*. New York: Scribner's.
NIETZSCHE, Friedrich
1885 (1966) *Thus Spoke Zarathustra*. Trans. W. Kaufmann. New York: Viking.
1901 (1968) *The Will to Power*. Trans. W. Kaufmann. New York: Random House.
NOCK, Arthur Darby
1961   *Conversion: The Old and the New in Religion from Alexander the Great to Augustine of Hippo*. London: Oxford.
NORRIS, Richard A., Jr.
1980   *The Christological Controversy*. Philadelphia: Fortress Press.
NYGREN, Anders
1952   *Commentary on Romans*. Trans. C. C. Rasmussen. London: S.C.M.

OGDEN, Schubert M.
1966   *The Reality of God and Other Essays*. New York: Harper & Row.
OTTO, Rudolf
1923   *The Idea of the Holy: An Inquiry into the Non-rational Factor in the Idea of the Divine and Its Relation to the Rational*. Trans. J. W. Harvey. London: Oxford.

PACKULL, Werner O.
1977   *Mysticism and the Early South German-Austrian Anabaptist Movement 1525–1531*. Scottdale: Herald.
PANNENBERG, Wolfhart
1968   *Jesus: God and Man*. Trans. L. L. Wilkins and D. A. Priebe. Philadelphia: Westminster.
The Papal Encyclicals.
1981   Ed. C. Carlen. Salem: McGrath.
PASSMORE, John
1968   *A Hundred Years of Philosophy*. 2nd ed. London: Penguin.
PAUL, Robert
1960   *The Atonement and the Sacraments: The Relation of the Atonement to the Sacraments of Baptism and the Lord's Supper*. Nashville: Abingdon.
PEACOCKE, A. R.
1979   *Creation and the World of Science*. Oxford: Clarendon.
1981   (Ed.) *The Sciences and Theology in the Twentieth Century*. Notre Dame: University Press.
PEARLMAN, Myer
1948   *Knowing the Doctrines of the Bible*. Springfield, Mo.: Gospel Publishing House.
PETERS, Ted, ed.
1989   *Cosmos as Creation: Theology and Science in Consonance*. Nashville: Abingdon.
PETERSON, Erik
1951   "Der Monotheismus Als Politische Problem." In *Theologische Traktate*. Munich: Kösel-Verlag.

PETTIT, Norman
  1989   *The Heart Prepared: Grace and Conversion in Puritan Spiritual Life.*
                2nd ed. Middletown: Wesleyan University Press.
PEVSNER, Nikolaus
  1957   *An Outline of European Architecture.* 5th ed. London: Penguin.
PIEPKORN, Arthur
  1977–79   *Profiles in Belief: The Religious Bodies of the United States and
                Canada.* 4 vols. in 3. New York: Harper & Row.
PIPKIN, Wayne H., ed.
  1989   *Seek Peace and Pursue It, Psalm 34:14: Proceedings from the 1988
                International Baptist Peace Conference, Sjovik, Sweden, August 3-7,
                1988.* Memphis: Baptist Peace Fellowship of North America.
PITT-WATSON, Ian
  1976   *Preaching: A Kind of Folly.* Philadelphia: Westminster.
  1986   *A Primer for Preachers.* Grand Rapids: Baker.
PLACHER, William
  1989   *Unapologetic Theology: A Christian Voice in a Pluralistic Conversa-
                tion.* Louisville: Westminster/John Knox.
PLANTINGA, Alvin
  1967   *God and Other Minds: A Study of the Rational Justification of Belief
                in God.* Ithaca: Cornell University Press.
POLISHOOK, Irwin H., ed.
  1967   *Roger Williams, John Cotton, and Religious Freedom: A Controversy
                in New and Old England: Selections.* Englewood Cliffs: Prentice-
                Hall.
POLKINGHORNE, John
  1989   *Science and Providence: God's Interaction with the World.* Boston:
                Shambala.
  1991   *Reason and Reality: The Relationship Between Science and Theology.*
                Philadelphia: Trinity Press International.
POWERS, Joseph M.
  1967   *Eucharistic Theology.* New York: Herder & Herder.
PRITCHARD, James B., ed.
  1969   *Ancient Near Eastern Texts Relating to the Old Testament.* 3rd ed.
                Princeton: University Press.
PRUITT, Raymond M.
  1981   *Fundamentals of the Faith.* Cleveland, Tenn.: White Wing Pub-
                lishing House.

RABOTEAU, Albert J.
  1978   *Slave Religion.* New York: Oxford.
RAHNER, Karl
  1967   (Ed.) *The Teaching of the Catholic Church as Contained in Her
                Documents.* Trans. J. Neuner and H. Roos. Staten Island: Mer-
                cier.
  1978   *Foundations of Christian Faith: An Introduction to the Idea of Chris-
                tianity.* Trans. W. V. Dych. New York: Seabury.
RAHNER, Karl, and H. VORGRIMLER
  1965   *Theological Dictionary.* Ed. C. Ernst. Trans. R. Strachan. New
                York: Herder & Herder.

RAMM, Bernard
  1957   *The Pattern of Authority*. Grand Rapids: Eerdmans.
RAUSCHENBUSCH, Walter
  1907 (1967)   *Christianity and the Social Crisis*. New York: Macmillan.
  1917   *A Theology for the Social Gospel*. New York: Macmillan (Abingdon, 1945).
  1968   *The Righteousness of the Kingdom*. Nashville: Abingdon.
REDEKOP, Calvin
  1989   *Mennonite Society*. Baltimore: Johns Hopkins University Press.
Rethinking Missions.
  1932   In *Layman's Foreign Missions Inquiry*. 7 vols. New York: Harper.
RICHARDSON, Herbert W.
  1967   *Toward an American Theology*. New York: Harper & Row.
The Rites of the Catholic Church as Revised by Decree of the Second Vatican Council and Published by Authority of Pope Paul VI.
  1976   2 vols. New York: Pueblo.
RITSCHL, Albrecht
  1888 (1966)   *The Christian Doctrine of Justification and Reconciliation*. Vol. 3, *The Positive Development of the Doctrine*. Trans. H. R. Mackintosh and A. B. Macaulay. Clifton: Reference Book Publishers.
ROBERTS, J. Deotis
  1971   *Liberation and Reconciliation: A Black Theology*. Philadelphia: Westminster.
  1974   *A Black Political Theology*. Philadelphia: Westminster.
ROBERTSON SMITH, William
  1889 (1969)   *Lectures on the Religion of the Semites: The Fundamental Institutions*. 3rd ed. New York: KTAV.
ROBINSON, H. Wheeler
  1928   *The Christian Experience of the Holy Spirit*. London: Nisbet.
  1955   *The Cross in the Old Testament*. London: S.C.M.
ROUSE, Ruth, and Stephen Charles NEILL
  1967   *A History of the Ecumenical Movement 1517–1948: A History of the Ecumenical Movement, Volume One*. 2nd ed. London: S.P.C.K.
RUETHER, Rosemary Radford
  1974a   (Ed.) *Religion and Sexism: Images of Woman in the Jewish and Christian Traditions*. New York: Simon & Schuster.
  1974b   *Faith and Fratricide*. New York: Seabury.
  1982   *Disputed Questions: On Being a Christian*. Nashville: Abingdon.
  1983   *Sexism and God-talk*. Boston: Beacon.
RUSSELL, Robert J., Nancey MURPHY, and C. J. ISHAM, eds.
  1993   *Quantum Cosmology and the Laws of Nature: Scientific Perspectives on Divine Action*. Castel Gondolfo, Italy: Vatican Observatory.
RUSSELL, Robert J., William R. STOEGER, and George V. COYNE, eds.
  1988   *Physics, Philosophy, and Theology: A Common Quest for Understanding*. Vatican City State: Vatican Observatory.

SAIVING GOLDSTEIN, Valerie
  1960   "The Human Situation: A Feminine View." *Journal of Religion* 40 (100-112).

SANDERS, E. P.
1992   *Judaism: Practice and Belief, 63 BCE–66 CE.* Philadelphia: Trinity
            Press International.
SANKEY, Ira D., comp.
n.d.   *Sacred Songs and Solos.* London: Marshall, Morgan, & Scott.
SANTMIRE, H. Paul
1985   *The Travail of Nature: The Ambiguous Ecological Promise of Chris-
            tian Theology.* Philadelphia: Fortress.
SAROYAN, William
1966   *The Human Comedy.* New York: Dell.
SCHAFF, Philip
1877   *The Creeds of Christendom, with a History and Critical Notes.* 3 vols.
            New York: Harper.
SCHINDLER, A., ed.
1978   *Monotheismus als Politisches Problem? Erik Peterson und die Kritik
            der Politischen Theologie.* Gütersloh: Gerd Mohn.
SCHLEIERMACHER, Friedrich
1799 (1958) *On Religion: Speeches to Its Cultured Despisers.* Trans. J. Oman.
            New York: Harper & Row.
1830 (1966) *Brief Outline on the Study of Theology.* Trans. T. N. Tice. Atlanta:
            John Knox.
1981   *On the Glaubenslehre: Two Letters to Dr. Lücke.* Trans. J. Duke and
            F. Fiorenza. Chico: Scholars.
SCHMEMANN, Alexander, ed.
1965   *Ultimate Questions: An Anthology of Modern Russian Religious
            Thought.* New York: Holt, Rinehart and Winston.
SCHREITER, Robert J.
1985   *Constructing Local Theologies.* Maryknoll: Orbis.
SCHULDINER, Michael
1991   *Gifts and Works: The Post-conversion Paradigm and Spiritual Con-
            troversy in Seventeenth-century Massachusetts.* Macon: Mercer
            University Press.
SCHÜSSLER FIORENZA, Elisabeth
1984   *In Memory of Her.* New York: Crossroad.
SCHWEITZER, Albert
1906 (1968) *The Quest of the Historical Jesus.* Trans. W. B. D. Montgomery.
            New York: Macmillan.
SCHWEIZER, Eduard
1980   *The Holy Spirit.* Trans. from the German. Philadelphia: Fortress.
SCRIVEN, Charles
1988   *The Transformation of Culture: Christian Social Ethics after H.
            Richard Niebuhr.* Scottdale: Herald.
SEGUNDO, Juan Luis
1979   *Liberation of Theology.* Trans. J. Drury. Maryknoll: Orbis.
SENNETT, Richard
1978   *The Fall of Public Man: On the Social Psychology of Capitalism.* New
            York: Random House.
SHEPHERD, Massey H., Jr.
1960   *The Paschal Liturgy and the Apocalypse.* London: Lutterworth.
1965   *Liturgy and Education.* New York: Seabury.

SICHERMAN, Barbara, and Carol Hurd GREEN
 1980   *Notable American Women, the Modern Period: A Biographical Dictionary.* Cambridge: Harvard University Press.
SIMON, Ulrich
 1958   *Heaven in the Christian Tradition.* London: Rockliff.
SIMON, Yves R.
 1962   .   *A General Theory of Authority.* Notre Dame: University Press.
SMART, Ninian
 1981   *Beyond Ideology: Religion and the Future of Western Civilization.* Gifford Lectures. San Francisco: Harper & Row.
SMITH, H. Shelton, Robert HANDY, and Lefferts A. LOETSCHER
 1960   *American Christianity: An Historical Interpretation with Representative Documents.* 2 vols. New York: Scribner's.
SMITH, Huston
 1988   "Has Process Theology Dismantled Classical Theism?" *Theology Digest* 35 (Winter):303-18.
SMITH, Kenneth L., and Ira G. ZEPP, Jr.
 1974   *Search for the Beloved Community: The Thinking of Martin Luther King, Jr.* Valley Forge: Judson.
SMITH, Theophus
 1994   *Conjuring Culture: Biblical Formations of Black America.* New York: Oxford.
SMITH, Theophus H., and Mark I. WALLACE
 1994   *Curing Violence: Religion and the Thought of René Girard.* Sonoma: Polebridge.
SNAITH, Norman H.
 1944   *The Distinctive Ideas of the Old Testament.* London: Epworth.
SOSKICE, Janet Martin
 1985   *Metaphor and Religious Language.* Oxford: Clarendon.
SPITTLER, Russell P.
 1991   "Theological Style Among Pentecostals and Charismatics." In *Doing Theology in Today's World: Essays in Honor of Kenneth Kantzer,* ed. J. Woodbridge and T. E. McComiskey. Grand Rapids: Zondervan.
STAYER, James M.
 1976   *Anabaptists and the Sword.* 2nd ed. Lawrence, Kansas: Coronado Press.
STAYER, James M., Werner O. PACKULL, and Klaus DEPPERMANN
 1975   "From Monogenesis to Polygenesis: The Historical Discussion of Anabaptist Origins." *Mennonite Quarterly Review* 49 (April):83-121.
STEUER, Axel D., and James Wm. McCLENDON, Jr., eds.
 1981   *Is God GOD?* Nashville: Abingdon.
STOUT, Jeffrey
 1981   *The Flight from Authority: Religion, Morality, and the Quest for Autonomy.* Notre Dame: University Press.
STRAUSS, David Friedrich
 1846 (1972)   *The Life of Jesus Critically Examined.* Ed. P. C. Hodgson. Trans. George Eliot. Philadelphia: Fortress.

STREGE, Merle D., ed.
1986   *Baptism and Church: A Believers' Church Vision.* Papers of 7th
                Believers' Church Conference, 1984. Grand Rapids: Sagamore
                Books.
STROMBERG, Jean, ed.
1985   *Mission and Evangelism: An Ecumenical Affirmation.* Geneva:
                World Council of Churches.
STRONG, Augustus Hopkins
1907   *Systematic Theology: A Compendium and Commonplace-book.* 3
                vols. in 1. Philadelphia: Judson.
SYKES, Stephen
1984   *The Identity of Christianity: Theologians and the Essence of Christi-
                anity from Schleiermacher to Barth.* Philadelphia: Fortress.

TALBERT, Charles H.
1992   "The Church and Inclusive Language for God?" *Perspectives in
                Religious Studies* 19 (Winter):421-39.
TANNEHILL, Robert C.
1986–90   *The Narrative Unity of Luke-Acts: A Literary Interpretation.* 2 vols.
                Philadelphia: Fortress.
TENNANT, Frederick Robert
1908   *The Origin and Propagation of Sin.* Hulsean Lectures. Cambridge:
                University Press.
TESELLE, Eugene
1975   *Christ in Context: Divine Purpose and Human Possibility.* Philadel-
                phia: Fortress.
THIEMANN, Ronald F.
1985   *Revelation and Theology: The Gospel as Narrated Promise.* Notre
                Dame: University Press.
THOMPSON, Marianne Meye
1988   *The Humanity of Jesus in the Fourth Gospel.* Philadelphia: Fortress.
THURIAN, Max
1960–61   *The Eucharistic Memorial.* 2 parts. Trans. J. G. Davies. London:
                Lutterworth.
1983   (Ed.) *Ecumenical Perspectives on Baptism, Eucharist, and Ministry.*
                Geneva: World Council of Churches.
TILLEY, Terrence W.
1991   *The Evils of Theodicy.* Washington: Georgetown University Press.
1994   "The Institutional Element in Religious Experience." *Modern
                Theology* 10:2 (April).
TILLICH, Paul
1951–63   *Systematic Theology.* Chicago: University of Chicago Press.
1957   *The Protestant Era.* Chicago: University of Chicago Press.
TOULMIN, Stephen E.
1970   "Contemporary Scientific Mythology." In *Metaphysical Beliefs,*
                ed. A. MacIntyre. New York: Schocken.
TOYNBEE, Arnold J.
1947   *A Study of History.* An Abridgement of Volumes 1-6. New York:
                Oxford.

TRACY, David
1975   *Blessed Rage for Order: The New Pluralism in Theology.* New York: Seabury.
TRAVIS, Stephen H.
1980   *Christian Hope and the Future.* Downers Grove: InterVarsity.
TRIBLE, Phyllis
1978   *God and the Rhetoric of Sexuality.* Philadelphia: Fortress.
TROCMÉ, André
1973   *Jesus and the Nonviolent Revolution.* Trans. M. H. Shank and M. E. Miller. Scottdale: Herald.
TROELTSCH, Ernst
1911 (1960) *The Social Teaching of the Christian Churches.* 2 vols. Trans. O. Wyon. New York: Harper & Row.
1977   *Writings on Theology and Religion.* Ed. R. Morgan and M. Pye. Atlanta: John Knox.
TUCHMAN, Barbara W.
1978   *A Distant Mirror: The Calamitous Fourteenth Century.* New York: Knopf.

UNDERHILL, Evelyn
1937   *Worship.* New York: Harper.
1961   *Mysticism: A Study in the Nature and Development of Man's Spiritual Consciousness.* New York: Dutton.

VAN BUREN, Paul M.
1963   *The Secular Meaning of the Gospel.* New York: Macmillan.
1980   *Discerning the Way: A Theology of the Jewish Christian Reality.* Vol. 1. New York: Seabury.
1983   *A Christian Theology of the People Israel: A Theology of the Jewish-Christian Reality.* Vol. 2. New York: Seabury.
1988   *Christ in Context: A Theology of the Jewish-Christian Reality.* Vol. 3. San Francisco: Harper & Row.
VAN DUSEN, Henry P.
1952   "Will Lund Be Ecumenical?" *Christian Century* 69 (July 23):848-51.
VAN LEEUWEN, Arend Th.
1964   *Christianity in World History: The Meeting of the Faiths of East and West.* Trans. H. H. Hoskins. New York: Scribner's.
VAN TIL, Henry R.
1959   *The Calvinist Concept of Culture.* Grand Rapids: Baker.
VAN TILL, Howard J., ed.
1990   *Portraits of Creation: Biblical and Scientific Perspectives on the World's Formation.* Grand Rapids: Eerdmans.
VON HÜGEL, Friedrich
1923   *The Mystical Element in Religion as Studied in Saint Catherine of Genoa and Her Friends.* 2nd ed. Vol. 1. London: Dent.
VON RAD, Gerhard
1972   *Genesis: A Commentary.* Rev. ed. trans. J. H. Marks from 9th German ed. Philadelphia: Westminster.
VON WAHLDE, Urban
1982   "The Johannine 'Jews'." *New Testament Studies* 28:33-60.

WAINWRIGHT, Geoffrey
    1980   *Doxology: The Praise of God in Worship, Doctrine, and Life: A Systematic Theology.* New York: Oxford.

WARE, Timothy
    1964   *The Orthodox Church.* Baltimore: Penguin.

WATTS, Alan W.
    1970   *Nature, Man, and Woman.* New York: Vintage.

WEAVER, J. Denny
    1984   "Perspectives on a Mennonite Theology." *Conrad Grebel Review* 2 (Fall):189-210.
    1990   "Atonement for the Nonconstantinian Church." *Modern Theology* 6 (July):307-23.

WEISS, Johannes
    1892 (1971)   *Jesus' Proclamation of the Kingdom of God.* Ed. R. H. Hiers and D. L. Holland. Philadelphia: Fortress.

WELCH, Claude
    1952   *In This Name: The Doctrine of the Trinity in Contemporary Theology.* New York: Scribner's.
    1965   (ed. and trans.) *God and Incarnation in Mid-Nineteenth Century German Theology: Thomasius, Dorner, Biedermann.* New York: Oxford University.
    1972–85   *Protestant Thought in the Nineteenth Century, Volume I, 1799–1870, Volume II, 1870–1914.* New Haven: Yale University Press.

WENGER, J. C.
    1954   *Introduction to Theology: A Brief Introduction to the Doctrinal Content of Scripture Written in the Anabaptist-Mennonite Tradition.* Scottdale: Herald.

WERNER, Martin
    1941 (1954)   *The Formation of Christian Dogma.* Trans. S. G. F. Brandon. New York: Harper.

WESTERMANN, Claus
    1968   *Blessing in the Bible and the Life of the Church.* Trans. Keith R. Crim. Overtures to Biblical Theology. Philadelphia: Fortress.

WHITE, Lynn, Jr.
    1967   "The Historical Roots of Our Ecologic Crisis." *Science* 155:1203-7.

WHITEHEAD, Alfred North
    1978   *Process and Reality: An Essay in Cosmology.* Corrected Edition. Ed. David Ray Griffin and Donald W. Sherburne. New York: Free.

WICKER, Brian
    1975   *The Story-shaped World: Fiction and Metaphysics: Some Variations on a Theme.* Notre Dame: University Press.

WILDER, Amos N.
    1971   *Early Christian Rhetoric: The Language of the Gospel.* Cambridge: Harvard University Press.
    1982   *Jesus' Parables and the War of Myths: Essays on Imagination in the Scriptures.* Philadelphia: Fortress.

WILKEN, Robert Louis
    1984   *The Christians as the Romans Saw Them*. New Haven: Yale University Press.
WILLIAMS, Daniel Day
    1968   *The Spirit and the Forms of Love*. New York: Harper & Row.
WILLIAMS, George Huntston
    1962   *The Radical Reformation*. Philadelphia: Westminster.
WILLIAMS, J. Rodman
    1988–90   *Renewal Theology*. 2 vols. Grand Rapids: Zondervan.
WILLIAMS, Norman Powell
    1927   *The Ideas of the Fall and of Original Sin: A Historical and Critical Study*. Bampton Lectures. London: Longmans, Green.
WILLIAMS, Roger
    1643   *A Key into the Language of America*. In Williams, 1963: Vol. 1.
    1644a   *Mr. Cotton's Letter . . . Examined and Answered*. London. In Williams, 1963: Vol. 1.
    1644b   *The Bloody Tenent, or Persecution, for Cause of Conscience*. In Williams, 1963: Vol. 3.
    1645   *Christenings Make Not Christians, or a Brief Discourse Concerning That Name Heathen Commonly Given to the Indians*. In Williams, 1963: Vol. 7.
    1652a   *The Examiner Defended*. London: James Cottrel. In Williams, 1963: Vol. 7.
    1652b   *The Hireling Ministry None of Christ's*. London. In Williams, 1963: Vol. 7.
    1652c   *The Examiner—Defended in a Fair and Sober Answer . . .* London: James Cottrel. In Williams, 1963: Vol. 7.
    1963   *The Complete Writings of Roger Williams*. 7 vols. New York: Russell and Russell.
    1988   *The Correspondence of Roger Williams*. Ed. Glenn W. LaFantasie. 2 vols. London: Brown University Press.
WILMORE, Gayraud
    1982   *Last Things First*. Philadelphia: Westminster.
WILMORE, Gayraud S., and James H. CONE, eds.
    1979   *Black Theology: A Documentary History, 1966–1979*. Maryknoll: Orbis.
WILSON, Peter J.
    1980   *Man the Promising Primate*. New Haven: Yale University Press.
WINGREN, Gustaf
    1960   *The Living Word: A Theological Study of Preaching and the Church*. Trans. V. C. Pogue. Philadelphia: Fortress.
    1961   *Creation and Law*. Trans. R. Mackenzie. Edinburgh: Oliver & Boyd.
    1979   *Creation and Gospel: The New Situation in European Theology*. New York: Edwin Mellen.
WINSLOW, Ola E.
    1957   *Master Roger Williams: A Biography*. New York: Macmillan.
WITTGENSTEIN, Ludwig
    1953   *Philosophical Investigations*. Trans. G. E. M. Anscombe. New York: Macmillan.

1967   *L. Wittgenstein: Lectures and Conversations on Aesthetics, Psychology, and Religious Belief.* Ed. B. Cyril. Berkeley: University of California Press.

WOLFSON, Harry Austryn
1970   *The Philosophy of the Church Fathers, Volume 1.* 3rd rev. ed. Cambridge: Harvard University Press.

WOLTERSTORFF, Nicholas
1984   *Reason Within the Bounds of Religion.* 2nd ed. Grand Rapids: Eerdmans.

WOOD, Ralph C.
1988   *The Comedy of Redemption: Christian Faith and Comic Vision in Four American Novelists.* Notre Dame: University Press.

WOOLLEY, Davis C., ed.
1971   *Encyclopedia of Southern Baptists.* Nashville: Broadman.

WRIGHT, G. Ernest
1962   *God Who Acts: Biblical Theology as Recital.* London: S.C.M.

YODER, John Howard
1967   "The Hermeneutics of the Anabaptists." *Mennonite Quarterly Review* 41 (October):291-308.
1968   *Täufertum und Reformation in Gespräch.* Basle Dissertation. Zurich: EVZ Verlag.
1972   The Politics of Jesus. Grand Rapids: Eerdmans. (Second edition 1993.)
1973   (Ed.) *The Legacy of Michael Sattler.* Scottdale: Herald.
1984   *The Priestly Kingdom: Social Ethics as Gospel.* Notre Dame: University Press.
1985a   *He Came Preaching Peace.* Scottdale: Herald.
1985b   "Reformed versus Anabaptist Social Strategies: An Inadequate Typology." *TSF Bulletin* 8 (May-June):2-7.
1987   The Fullness of Christ. Elgin: Brethren.
1988   "To Serve Our God and to Rule the World." *Annual of the Society of Christian Ethics*:3-14.
1989   "Adjusting to the Changing Shape of the Debate on Infant Baptism." In *Oecumennisme*, ed. A. Lambo. Amsterdam: Algemene Doopsgezinde Sociëteit.

YODER, John Howard, Diane M. YEAGER, and Glen STASSEN
1995   *Authentic Transformation; A New Vision of Christ and Culture.* Nashville: Abingdon Press (forthcoming).

YOLTON, John W., et al.,
1991   *The Blackwell Companion to the Enlightenment.* Oxford: Blackwell.

Index of Names
and Topics

Biblical Index

533

Printed in the United States
68048LVS00004B/7-27

9 780687 110216